PROFESSIONAL INDEMNITY INSURANCE

SECOND EDITION

PROFESSIONAL INDEMNITY INSURANCE

SECOND EDITION

MARK CANNON, QC
BRENDAN McGURK

OXFORD

UNIVERSITY PRESS

Great Clarendon Street, Oxford, OX2 6DP,
United Kingdom

Oxford University Press is a department of the University of Oxford.
It furthers the University's objective of excellence in research, scholarship,
and education by publishing worldwide. Oxford is a registered trade mark of
Oxford University Press in the UK and in certain other countries

© Mark Cannon and Brendan McGurk 2016

The moral rights of the authors have been asserted

First Edition published in 2010
Second Edition published in 2016

Impression: 1

Published in the United States of America by Oxford University Press
198 Madison Avenue, New York, NY 10016, United States of America

British Library Cataloguing in Publication Data
Data available

Library of Congress Control Number: 2015960858

ISBN 978–0–19–872518–3

Printed and bound by
CPI Group (UK) Ltd, Croydon, CR0 4YY

PREFACE

The interval between the first and second editions of this book has been somewhat longer than intended. For this we are to blame. But, as things have worked out, the delay has been a blessing, albeit very well disguised at times. In February 2015 Parliament passed the Insurance Act 2015, extending the long overdue reform of English insurance law beyond insurance for consumers. The main provisions of this Act will come into force in August 2016. We have been able to anticipate these developments, in particular in the contexts of the provision of information to insurers before a contract of insurance is made and of warranties given by the insured.

Changes since the first edition are not limited to the Insurance Act 2015. As well as the Third Parties (Rights Against Insurers) Act 2010 (enacted during the interval between proof reading and printing of the first edition), we have taken account of six years of decisions, both in England and Wales and elsewhere. We have also tried to take account of helpful comments about the first edition from friends and colleagues.

We have endeavoured to state the law as at 31 July 2015. While we have cited some Commonwealth and United States authorities, as before, this book aims to set out the law of England and Wales. As in the first edition we have commented on the current terms required of their members by the Solicitors Regulation Authority, the Institute of Chartered Accountants in England and Wales, and the Royal Institution of Chartered Surveyors. These terms are referred to as 'the SRA Minimum Terms and Conditions of Professional Indemnity Insurance', 'the ICAEW Minimum Approved Policy Wording', and 'the RICS Policy Wording', respectively. We have added a commentary on the policy wording for architects in use by the RIBA Insurance Agency, referred to as 'the RIBA Architects Premier Policy Wording'.

We have been assisted and encouraged throughout by our publishers. This time they were (in the order in which they became involved) Faye Judges, Laura Williamson, Eleanor Reedy, Emma Taylor, Alex Johnson, and Gayathri Viswanathan. Behind them throughout stood Rachel Mullaly, the senior commissioning editor whose patience in the face of our repeated inability to produce text on time was (almost) inexhaustible and greatly appreciated. Thanks are also due to those who provided helpful and supporting comments on the proposal for a second edition.

Finally, we would like to thank our families, friends, colleagues, and clerks, who have had to see less of us and do more for us during the lengthy gestation of this edition.

Mark Cannon
Brendan McGurk
October 2015

CONTENTS—SUMMARY

CONTENTS

TABLE OF CASES

the art of the standard. In: 2007 *Ahal ...*
and theoretical ... of ... classical ... Jones, Dean ... 217, 225-237.
... c. (1989) ... of ... world ... and ... Chy-Rivers ...
theory ... of the ... bound ... with ... 971 pp. 91-131 ...

... ... of ... ...

TABLE OF STATUES

TABLE OF SECONDARY LEGISLATION

LIST OF ABBREVIATIONS

FOS	Financial Ombudsman Scheme
ICAEW	The Institute of Chartered Accountants in England and Wales
ICOBS	*Insurance: Conduct of Business Sourcebook*
LAUTRO	Life Assurance and Unit Trust Regulatory Organisation
MIPRU	Financial Services Authority's MIPRU Prudential Sourcebook for Mortgage and Home Finance Firms, and Insurance Intermediaries
RIBA	Royal Institute of British Architects
RICS	Royal Institution of Chartered Surveyors
RPB	recognized professional body
SIB	Securities and Investments Board
SIF	Solicitors Indemnity Fund
SRA	Solicitors Regulation Authority
SROs	self-regulatory organizations

1

INTRODUCTION

A. Professions and Professional Indemnity Insurance

This book is not concerned with attempts to define or even describe 'the profes-   **1.01**
sions'. It is concerned with professional indemnity insurance, which is not affected
by the status, training, ethics, or regulation of those who are insured, but with
their liabilities to third party claimants. The liabilities which are insured arise from
the provision of specialist advice or of services which require a degree of expertise.
Whether or not those who provide such advice or services are to be regarded as
members of a profession, their potential liability is sufficiently akin to that of members of what are undoubtedly professions as to fall within the same class of liability
insurance. For the purposes of this book all those who obtain such insurance are
regarded as professionals.

Nor is this book concerned with seeking to define what is meant in law by 'insur-   **1.02**
ance'. It proceeds upon the basis that the elements identified by Channell J in
Prudential Insurance Company v Inland Revenue Commissioners[1] as being what is
needed for there to be a contract of insurance will be present in a contract of professional indemnity insurance. Those three elements are: (i) the contract must provide
that, in return for something (usually the payment of a premium) the insured will

---

[1] [1904] 2 KB 658. See also *Gould v Curtis* [1913] 3 KB 84 and *The Medical Defence Union Ltd v The Department of Trade* [1980] Ch 82.

become entitled to something (usually the payment of money) on the occurrence of some event; (ii) the event must involve some element of uncertainty; and (iii) the insured must have an insurable interest in the subject-matter of the contract.

1.03 The past fifty years have witnessed substantial growth in the numbers of professionals and in the range of professional activity. Increasing prosperity has resulted in more private individuals owning houses, which, in turn, need to be designed, built, extended, renovated, bought, mortgaged, sold, insured, and passed on to later generations. Increasing prosperity means that more people have savings to invest, whether directly or through a pension fund. Increasing economic activity means that there are more or larger businesses which require legal and financial advice, insurance, buildings, infrastructure, and so on. Advances in technology present new challenges to existing specialisms, such as engineering, and create new areas of expertise, such as IT consultancy.

1.04 An increase in the amount of professional activity inevitably brings with it an increase in the number of claims by clients and others against professionals. It is therefore not surprising to find that the increasing role and importance of professionals in society, not least insofar as they provide services to consumers rather than to fellow professionals or commercial organizations, have led to the introduction of requirements, both statutory and professional, that members of a given profession should hold a specified level of professional indemnity insurance.[2]

1.05 The reason for the introduction of these requirements has been not so much to protect the professionals who were insured, but to ensure that their clients and others who might have claims against them would be able to recover up to a certain level. For example, in *Swain v The Law Society*,[3] when considering the scheme for professional indemnity insurance introduced by the Law Society pursuant to powers given to it by s 37 of the Solicitors' Act 1974, Lord Brightman, with whom all members of the House agreed, said:[4]

> In exercising its power under section 37 The Law Society is performing a public duty, a duty which is designed to benefit, not only solicitor-principals and their staff, but also solicitors' clients. The scheme is not only for the protection of the premium paying solicitor against the financial consequences of his own mistakes, the mistakes of his partners and the mistakes of his staff, but also, and far more importantly, to secure that the solicitor is financially able to compensate his client. Indeed, I think it is clear that the principal purpose of section 37 was to confer on The Law Society the power to safeguard the lay public and not professional practitioners, since the latter can look after themselves. This is underlined by the position of section 37, which is one of a group of three sections, the other two of which are plainly enacted in the interests of the lay public. So, there is no doubt at all in my mind that the power given to The Law Society by section 37 is a power to

---

[2] See paras 1.12–1.31.
[3] [1983] 1 AC 598.
[4] Ibid at 618.

be exercised not only in the interests of the solicitors' profession but also, and more importantly, in the interests of those members of the public who resort to solicitors for legal advice.[5]

So, to the extent that professionals are required to obtain professional indemnity **1.06** insurance so as to be able to satisfy the claims of clients and others to whom they cause loss and damage while acting in their professions, the intended beneficiaries of the insurance include those clients and other claimants, even though they will not be parties to the contract of insurance with insurers. There is nothing unique or unusual about this—for example, employer's liability insurance is compulsory and intended to ensure that those injured at work by reason of any breach of duty can recover damages, and motorists are required to insure against causing death or personal injury whilst driving to ensure that those whom they injure or the dependents of those they kill will be compensated.

Before the enactment of the Consumer Insurance (Disclosure and Representations **1.07** Act 2012[6] the English law of insurance was not well suited to provide protection for consumers. For example, insurers could avoid cover for inadvertent, non-negligent failure to disclose a fact which was, unknown to the insured, material to the risk, even though had the fact been disclosed insurers would still have underwritten the risk, but at a slightly greater premium.[7] Insurers were entitled to include a term by which the insured warranted that every answer on a proposal form was accurate so that, if there was a relatively minor inaccuracy, the policy was deemed to have been void from the start. The non-disclosure or breach of warranty need have had no connection whatsoever with any loss suffered by the insured for which he was seeking an indemnity.[8]

As Rix LJ observed in *R (on the application of Heather Moor and Edgecomb) v* **1.08** *Financial Services Ombudsman*, a case concerning a decision by the Financial Ombudsman Scheme (FOS):[9]

> It is a feature of our commercial law, robust, pragmatic and internationally respected as it may be, that it grew up in an age of commerce between

---

[5] See also the speech of Lord Diplock at 610. Similar views have been expressed by Evans J in *Macmillan v AW Knott Becker Scott Ltd* [1990] 1 Lloyd's Rep 98, by Peter Gibson LJ in *Cox v Bankside Members Agency Ltd* [1995] 2 Lloyd's Rep 437, by Vinelott J in *The Mortgage Corporation v The Solicitors Indemnity Fund Ltd* [1998] PNLR 73, by Lightman J in *Bristol & West Building Society v Bhadresa* [1999] Lloyd's Rep IR 138, by Thomas J in *Kumar v AGF Insurance Ltd* [1999] 1 WLR 1747, by Kirby J in *McCann v Switzerland Insurance Australia Ltd* [2000] HCA 65; (2000) 203 CLR 579, at [76], and by Sir Andrew Morritt C in *Quinn Direct Insurance Ltd v Law Society* [2010] EWCA Civ 805; [2011] 1 WLR 308, at [26].

[6] This Act effected significant reform of insurance law where the insured is 'an individual who enters into the contract wholly or mainly for purposes unrelated to the individual's trade, business or profession' (s 1(a)). It is hard to conceive of circumstances in which it would apply to professional indemnity insurance.

[7] See Chapter 5.

[8] See Chapter 8.

[9] [2008] EWCA Civ 642; [2008] Bus LR 1486, at [87].

merchants, when what we now think of as financial consumer contracts must have been relatively few in number, limited in their scope, and entered into by a small range of professional, mercantile and land-owning people. I speak of contracts outside ordinary sale of goods. Nowadays, however, huge numbers of consumers have pensions, make investments, and enter into insurance contracts of all kinds. Our insurance law, for instance, has been based on a statute, the Marine Insurance Act 1906, designed for marine insurance but given a dominant status over insurance contracts in general, which encapsulates the common law of over a century ago. For some years the insurance ombudsman (now within the FOS scheme) has been developing a new common law of insurance for consumer contracts, without which the courts would have been constrained to find, or alternatively to reject, solutions to problems from which they have been in the main shielded.

1.09   While the 'the new common law of insurance' described by Rix LJ adjusted the balance of rights as between insurers and insured who are consumers, the insured under contracts of professional indemnity insurance are not themselves consumers, but professional firms, sometimes of considerable substance. The 'old common law' continues to apply to them. However, developments of that law in recent decades, not least in the area of composite insurance,[10] and the introduction of terms which exclude or cut down insurers' rights to deny cover,[11] if not going so far as to produce a 'new common law of insurance', considerably modified the old common law.

1.10   The old common law of insurance has been further reformed by the Insurance Act 2015. This Act received Royal Assent on 12 February 2015 and the reforms are due to come into force in August 2016. Among other things, it reforms the law as to the insured's duty of disclosure when seeking to obtain insurance,[12] warranties[13] and fraudulent claims.[14] The interval between the Royal Assent and the coming into force of the main provisions is to allow time for these reforms to be taken into account. At the time of writing that process is at a relatively early stage.

1.11   The non-statutory modification of the old common law has gone hand in hand with a tendency to increase the scope of the potential liabilities against which the insured is covered, although this inevitably varies both from profession to profession and, in some cases, within a single profession. Whether imposed by or under statute or by way of professional standard and codes of conduct, requirements that a professional maintain a given level of professional indemnity insurance sometimes include requirements that that insurance be in accordance with certain minimum terms, not limited to the level of cover.[15] Members of a given profession may

---

[10] See paras 1.32–1.45.
[11] See, eg, paras 5.73–5.113.
[12] See Chapters 5 and 6.
[13] See paras.7.91–7.99.
[14] See paras.11.63–11.64.
[15] See, eg, paras 1.13, 1.27, and 1.29.

also be required to insure with a particular insurer or from one or more members of a specified panel of insurers.

B. Professional Obligations to Obtain Insurance

Not every professional will be required to obtain a minimum level of professional **1.12** indemnity insurance, but many are. The obligation to do so can be made by or under statute or by way of rules of professional conduct. A number of examples are given below.

Accountants

The ICAEW's requirements as to the professional indemnity insurance which **1.13** its members must maintain are set out in its Professional Indemnity Insurance Regulations and Guidance.[16] Regulations 3.1(a) and (b) require firms to take reasonable steps to meet claims arising from being in public practice and, in particular, to arrange 'qualifying insurance' which meets the limits set out in regulations 3.2 to 3.5.

'Qualifying insurance', defined in regulation 1.6 as insurance which is underwrit- **1.14** ten by 'participating insurers', includes retroactive cover for liabilities arising from work carried out in the previous six years (except for claims or potential claims known about at the time the insurance was first taken out) and which is underwritten on the ICAEW Minimum Approved Policy Wording.

The usual minimum limit of indemnity is £1.5 million for any one claim or in **1.15** total, but for firms with gross fee income of less than £600,000, the minimum level of indemnity for any one claim and in total must be equal to two-and-a-half times the firm's gross fee income, with a minimum of £100,000.[17] The minimum limit of indemnity can include an aggregate excess provided that that excess is no more than £30,000 multiplied by the number of principals (ie no more than £30,000 per principal).[18] There are specific limits of indemnity for work falling within the Probate Regulations of the ICAEW's Probate Regulations and insurance mediation as defined in the Designated Professional Body Handbook of the ICAEW.[19]

---

[16] http://www.icaew.com/en/members/regulations-standards-and-guidance/practice-management/professional-indemnity-insurance-regulations-guidance-current

[17] Regulations 3.2 and 3.3.

[18] Regulation 3.7. If a firm has 50 or more principals, the minimum limit of indemnity is reduced to zero and such a firm is not obliged to obtain qualifying insurance. It can make its own insurance arrangements, but must still comply with regulation 3.1(a) and all other regulations except for regulation 3.1(b).

[19] Clauses C1. a) and b).

Architects

1.16 Standard 8 of the Architects Code[20]—Standards of Conduct and Practice issued by the Architects Registration Board—provides that architects should not undertake professional work without adequate and appropriate professional indemnity insurance cover. Standard 8(1) provides that architects are 'expected to maintain a minimum level of cover, including run-off cover, in accordance with the Board's guidance'. The Architects Registration Board recommends and expects that architects will maintain professional indemnity cover of at least £250,000 per claim.[21]

Barristers

1.17 Barristers are now regulated by the Bar Standards Board and are subject to the requirements of the Bar Standards Board Handbook which replaced the Code of Conduct of the Bar of England and Wales on 6 January 2014.[22] Rule rC76 requires barristers to have insurance which is adequate, taking into account the nature of their practice, and which covers all legal services supplied to the public. Rule rC77 states that when an individual is acting as a self-employed barrister, he or she must be a member of the Bar Mutual Indemnity Fund which has standard terms.[23] The amount of minimum cover which a barrister must have varies according to the amount of premium payable, which is related to gross fee income in the preceding year and each barrister's areas of practice. The lowest minimum level of cover is £500,000 and the highest is £2,500,000. Rule rC78 of the Code of Conduct requires members of the Bar Mutual Indemnity Fund to pay the appropriate premium required by the Bar Mutual Indemnity Fund.

1.18 In November 2014 the Bar Standards Board was approved as a regulator of entities as well as of natural persons under the Legal Services Act 2007. In March 2015 the Bar Standards Board published new minimum terms of the professional indemnity insurance it requires the entities it regulates to have in place pursuant to rC76.2 of the Code of Conduct. The BSB Minimum Terms of Entity Cover came into effect on 1 April 2015.[24] The limit of indemnity is required to be the Limit of Cover and defence costs without limit of amount.[25] The insurance must provide

---

[20] http://www.arb.org.uk/code-of-conduct-2010
[21] http://www.arb.org.uk/pii-guidance/Index
[22] https://www.barstandardsboard.org.uk/media/1663630/bsb_handbook_complete.pdf
[23] There are two exceptions. The first is for pupils who are covered by their pupil supervisors' insurance. The second is for those called to the Bar pursuant to rQ94 (which applies to Registered European Lawyers). The latter must either be insured with the Bar Mutual Indemnity Fund or have professional indemnity insurance in relation to their work in England and Wales on terms required by the Bar Standards Board with a copy of the certificate of insurance being provided to the Bar Standards Board.
[24] https://www.barstandardsboard.org.uk/media/1657322/bar_standards_board_-_minimum_terms_of_entity_cover_-_spring_2015.pdf
[25] Ibid, clause 2.

cover of at least £500,000 for each claim (although there can be a deductible payable by the insured).

Engineers

There are a number of professional bodies for engineers. By way of example, the **1.19** Institution of Civil Engineers has a Code of Professional Conduct for its members.[26] Rule 1 of that Code of Conduct requires all members to discharge their professional duties with integrity. Among the examples given of the ways in which members can fulfil this rule is:

> Members who do not carry appropriate insurance, either personally or through their employers must advise their clients of the position before accepting the engagement. Members must take all reasonable steps to ensure that their prospective clients understand the extent to which they are covered by appropriate insurance.

Insolvency practitioners

Members of the Insolvency Practitioners Association are required to take out and **1.20** maintain professional indemnity insurance in accordance with the Insolvency Practitioners Regulations 2005 and the Association's Professional Indemnity Insurance Regulations. Paragraph 2A of Schedule 2 to the Insolvency Practitioners Regulations 2005 provides that where an insolvency practitioner is appointed to act in respect of an insolvent there must be in force (a) a bond in a form approved by the Secretary of State which complies with paragraph 3 of the Regulations or (b) where the insolvency practitioner is already established in another EEA state and is already covered in that state by professional liability insurance or a guarantee, professional liability insurance or a guarantee which complies with paragraph 8A of the Regulations. Regulation 2 of the Association's Professional Indemnity Insurance Regulations[27] provides that it is compulsory for a member who holds one or more insolvency appointments to have professional indemnity insurance to at least the minimum level required by the Regulations. The minimum level is specified in Regulation 3, as whichever is the greater of £250,000 and two-and-a half times the member's gross fee income. Where a number of members practise together in partnership or association with each other, the limit of a single policy insuring all of them is calculated by aggregating their gross fee incomes. In the case of a professional indemnity policy covering a number of individual members practising in partnership or by association, the required minimum cover under the policy need not exceed £1,500,000. The insurers must be authorized by the

---

[26] https://www.ice.org.uk/ICEDevelopmentWebPortal/media/Documents/About%20Us/ice-code-of-professional-conduct.pdf

[27] http://www.insolvency-practitioners.org.uk/uploads/files/documents/9%20%20 Professional%20Indemnity%20Insurance%20Regulations_Sept0_8A4.pdf

Department for Business, Innovation and Skills and the terms must comply with the ICAEW Minimum Approved Policy Wording.

Insurance intermediaries

1.21 Insurance brokers and other insurance intermediaries are regulated by the Financial Conduct Authority under the Financial Services and Markets Act 2000. Authorized insurance intermediaries must comply with the Financial Conduct Authority's MIPRU Prudential Sourcebook for Mortgage and Home Finance Firms, and Insurance Intermediaries (MIPRU).

1.22 MIPRU 3.2 requires insurance intermediaries to take out and maintain professional indemnity insurance with insurers authorized in specified states. That insurance must provide cover which meets specified minimum terms. In particular, it must provide cover of at least €1,120,200 for each claim and the higher of either €1,680,300 or 10 per cent of annual income up to £30 million in the aggregate. The excess can be no more than the higher of £2,500 or 1.5 per cent of annual income for a firm which does not hold client money or other client assets or the higher of £5,000 or 3 per cent of annual income for a firm which does. There must also be 'appropriate cover' for defence costs.

Medical practitioners

1.23 Medical practitioners, dentists, osteopaths, and chiropractors are all required to have the benefit of professional indemnity insurance or other protection against claims. In the case of medical practitioners, s 44C of the Medical Act 1983 requires medical practitioners to have in force an 'an indemnity arrangement which provides appropriate cover for practising as such.' An 'indemnity arrangement' can be a policy of insurance, an arrangement made for the purposes of indemnifying a person, or a combination of the two. This enables medical practitioners to be indemnified by the National Health Service as well as or as an alternative to professional indemnity insurance.

1.24 Paragraph 63 of the Good Medical Practice (2013), issued by the General Medical Council provides:

> You must make sure you have adequate insurance or indemnity cover so that your patients will not be disadvantaged if they make a claim about the clinical care you have provided in the UK.

Paragraph 5 of the Good Medical Practice (2013) states that the words 'you must' indicate 'an overriding duty or principle'.

1.25 The General Dental Council has issued 'Standards for the Dental Team' which replaced 'Standards for Dental Professionals' from 30 September 2013. Standard 1.8 requires that dental practitioners must have appropriate arrangements in place and provides:

1.8.1 You must have appropriate insurance or indemnity in place to make sure your patients can claim any compensation to which they may be entitled (See our website for further guidance on what types of insurance or indemnity the GDC considers to be appropriate).

1.8.2 You should ensure that you keep to the terms and conditions of your insurance or indemnity and contact the provider as soon as possible when a claim is made. A delay in contacting the provider could disadvantage patients and may affect the level of help you receive from the provider.

This can be done by membership of a dental indemnity organization (eg Dental Protection Ltd or the Dental Defence League), by professional indemnity insurance, or by indemnity from the National Health Service.

Osteopaths must obtain professional indemnity insurance (and other forms **1.26** of cover) in accordance with the General Osteopathic Council (Professional Indemnity Insurance) Rules 1998, made pursuant to s 37 of the Osteopaths Act 1993. The obligation to insure is imposed by Rule 3(1). The minimum amount of insurance cover to be obtained by an Osteopath in respect of the prescribed risks is specified in Rule 6 to be £2,500,000 in the aggregate.

In the case of chiropractors, the General Chiropractic Council (Professional **1.27** Indemnity Insurance) Rules 1999 made pursuant to s 37 of the Chiropractors Act 1994 require chiropractors to secure and maintain insurance against potential liabilities. Cover must be of at least £3 million in the aggregate.[28]

Solicitors

The requirements in respect of professional indemnity insurance for solicitors in **1.28** England and Wales are found in the current edition of the Solicitors' Indemnity Insurance Rules.[29] At the time of writing, the current edition is 2013.[30] These Rules are made by the Solicitors Regulation Authority Board under ss 31, 37, 79, and 80 of the Solicitors Act 1974 and s 9 of the Administration of Justice Act 1985, and paragraph 19 of Schedule 11 to the Legal Services Act 2007, with the approval of the Legal Services Board under paragraph 19 of Schedule 4 to the Legal Services Act 2007.

The Rules require solicitors to take out and maintain qualifying professional **1.29** indemnity insurance with one or more participating insurers with effect from 30 April 2015. Rule 4.1 requires that the insurance be in accordance with the SRA Minimum Terms and Conditions of Professional Indemnity Insurance. Where the

---

[28] See Schedule 1 to the 1999 Rules.

[29] For a discussion of the requirement that solicitors obtain specified professional indemnity insurance under the then current rules see *Qualifying Insurers Subscribing to the ARP v Ross* [2004] EWHC 1181 (Ch); [2004] UKCLR 1483, and *Quinn Direct Insurance Ltd v Law Society* [2010] EWCA Civ 805; [2011] 1 WLR 308.

[30] Version 14 came into force on 30 April 2015.

solicitor practices through a 'Relevant Recognised Body',[31] the limit of cover must be at least £3 million for any one claim and, in all other cases, at least £2 million.

Surveyors and valuers

1.30 Rule 9 of the Rules of Conduct for Firms promulgated by the Royal Institution of Chartered Surveyors requires a firm to ensure that all previous and current professional work is covered by 'adequate and appropriate' professional indemnity insurance which meets the standards set by the regulatory board.[32]

1.31 Rule 9 is supplemented by a 'Policy Sheet', which advises that the professional indemnity insurance should be written with a limit on an 'each and every claim' basis (ie with no aggregate limit), that the RICS Policy Wording should be used (or some more comprehensive wording), and that cover should be at a variable minimum level, depending upon the firm's turnover in the preceding year. For firms with a turnover of £100,000 or less, the minimum level should be £250,000. For firms with a turnover between £100,001 and £200,000 it should be £500,000. For firms with a turnover of over £200,000 the minimum level of cover should be £1,000,000. For a limit of indemnity up to £500,000, the maximum excess will be the greater of 2.5 per cent of the sum insured or £10,000.

C. Composite Insurance

1.32 A key feature of professional indemnity insurance is that, where more than one person is insured under the same policy, the insurance is likely to be composite rather than joint. Although the difference between composite and joint insurance has been recognized for some time, it is an area in which the law has been clarified and developed in recent years, not least in the context of professional indemnity insurance.[33]

The *General Accident* case

1.33 The distinction between composite insurance and joint insurance was authoritatively stated by Sir Wilfrid Greene MR in *General Accident Fire and Life Assurance Co Ltd v Midland Bank Ltd*.[34] The case concerned fire insurance. There was a standard clause in the policy providing that:

> If the claim be in any respect fraudulent or if any fraudulent means or devices be used by the insured or anyone acting on his behalf to obtain any benefit under this policy or if any destruction or damage be occasioned by the wilful act or with the connivance of the insured all benefit under this policy shall be forfeited.

---

[31] The definition of 'Relevant Recognised Body' is to be found in the SRA Handbook Glossary. It includes a limited liability partnership.

[32] The current version came into force on 1 January 2012.

[33] *FNCB Ltd (formerly First National Commercial Bank plc) v Barnet Devanney (Harrow) Ltd* [1999] Lloyd's Rep IR 459, at 467–8.

[34] [1940] 2 KB 388.

The building which was insured was leased by P. The named insured were P, S (the freeholder and guarantor of P's debts to M), and M (P's bank). M had a floating charge over P's assets, including its interest in the building and the contents of the building. A fire occurred, damaging the building and the contents. P made a fraudulently exaggerated claim. Before the fraud was discovered, insurers sent cheques to each of the insured. S and M endorsed their cheques to P, which then paid them into its account with M. On discovering P's fraud, insurers invoked the clause set out above and sought to recover the amount of each cheque from S and M.

The claim failed at trial and the Court of Appeal affirmed the decision of the trial **1.34** judge. In doing so Sir Wilfrid Greene MR, with whom the other members of the Court of Appeal agreed, said:[35]

> That there can be a joint insurance by persons having a joint interest is, of course, manifest. If A and B are joint owners of property—and I use that phrase in the strict sense—an undertaking to indemnify them jointly is a true contract of indemnity in respect of a joint loss which they have jointly suffered. Again, there can be no objection to combining in one insurance a number of persons having different interests in the subject-matter of the insurance, but I find myself unable to see how an insurance of that character can be called a joint insurance. In such a case the interest of each of the insured is different. The amount of his loss, if the subject-matter of the insurance is destroyed or damaged, depends on the nature of his interest, and the covenant of indemnity which the policy gives must, in such a case, necessarily operate as a covenant to indemnify in respect of each individual different loss which the various persons named may suffer. In such a case there is no joint element at all.[36]

On the facts there had been no joint loss so there could not be joint insurance. **1.35** The policy was better described as a composite policy, being a convenient way of insuring the separate interests of a number of persons with different interests in the subject-matter of the insurance. Sir Wilfrid Greene MR was reinforced in his conclusion by a reference to the insured in an endorsement to the policy 'for their respective rights and interests'. The only insured who had suffered a loss as a result of the fire was P so only P had a claim under the insurance. Only P had been entitled to receive payment from the insurers and only P was obliged to repay it.

Identifying composite insurance

In *General Accident Fire and Life Assurance Co Ltd v Midland Bank Ltd*[37] Sir Wilfrid **1.36** Greene MR identified two considerations which went to whether a policy of insurance with a number of insured was joint insurance or composite insurance. The

---

[35] Ibid at 404–5.

[36] In *State of the Netherlands v Youell and Hayward* [1997] 2 Lloyd's Rep 440, at 447–8 Rix J described Sir Wilfrid Greene's judgment in the *General Accident* case as 'the classic statement of the difference between a joint and a composite insurance' which, although obiter, has 'been regarded as authoritative for more than 50 years'.

[37] [1940] 2 KB 388.

first was the 'true meaning and effect' of the contract of insurance. The second was whether joint insurance could exist on the facts.[38]

1.37 On the question of construction, while in the *General Accident* case the express reference to the 'respective rights and interests' of the insured had indicated that the policy was composite, rather than joint,[39] there is no need for such clear wording. The question of construction is linked to the consequences of a single policy providing composite rather than joint cover. If it appears that the parties intended such consequences, then on its true construction the policy will be composite.[40] This will be the case even if the policy describes the insured as 'joint policyholders'. While the parties' use of such words will be a relevant factor, it is not decisive.[41]

1.38 The second consideration identified by Sir Wilfrid Greene MR also informs the question of construction. The fact that the various insureds had different interests renders it hard, if not impossible, to construe the policy as providing joint insurance. Only if there is joint ownership of property[42] or an identity of interest will there be joint insurance. So, for example, in *New Hampshire Insurance Co v MGN Ltd*,[43] one issue was whether fidelity insurance policies over a number of years provided cover on a joint or composite basis. The insured was defined in the first two years as:

> Pergamon Holdings Limited &/Or Pergamon Group Plc &/Or Pergamon Media Trust Plc &/Or Hollis plc &/Or Maxwell Communications Corporation plc &/Or Mirror Holdings Ltd &/Or Subsidiary Companies &/Or Associated Companies &/Or Companies for whom they have instructions to insure.

In the third and fourth years the insured was defined as 'The Maxwell Group of companies', with a number of companies from the group specifically identified. Upholding the decision of Potter J that the policies provided composite insurance, the Court of Appeal said:[44]

> The companies that formed the Maxwell group had separate interests to insure, and not a joint interest in the same property. That must have been known to the insurers, in the light of the companies' disparate businesses and seeing that one of them was Mirror Group Newspapers. It is not clear why they adopted a different definition of the insured for year 3 and year 4. But that definition was still capable of referring to the companies rather than the group as parties to the insurance contract (as they

---

[38] Ibid at 404. See also *New Hampshire Insurance Co v MGN Ltd* [1997] LRLR 24, at 41 per Potter J.

[39] [1940] 2 KB 388, at 406.

[40] *Arab Bank Plc v Zurich Insurance Co* [1999] 1 Lloyd's Rep 262, at 272–6.

[41] *Parker v The National Farmers Union Mutual Insurance Society Ltd* [2012] EWHC 2156 (Comm); [2013] Lloyd's Rep IR 253, at [165] per Teare J.

[42] *Central Bank of India Ltd v Guardian Assurance Co Ltd* (1936) 54 Ll L Rep 247, at 260, per Lord Maugham giving the Opinion of the Privy Council. This was followed by the New South Wales Court of Appeal in *Lombard Australia Ltd v N.R.M.A. Insurance Ltd* [1969] 1 Lloyd's Rep 575. See also *Parker v The National Farmers Union Mutual Insurance Society Ltd* [2012] EWHC 2156 (Comm); [2013] Lloyd's Rep IR 253, at [165]–[167] per Teare J.

[43] [1997] LRLR 24.

[44] Ibid at 57.

must have been), and also as the owners of separate interests which were to be covered by insurance separately. That in our judgment was the intention of the parties, and the effect of the policies.

In the same way in *Cox v Bankside Members Agency Ltd*[45] Phillips J said of errors **1.39**
and omissions insurance of groups of companies of Lloyd's members' and managing agents:[46]

> A group cover against E & O liability of the kind I have to consider is not a joint policy. It is a policy which provides cover to each of the assured severally. In contradistinction to the position of co-insurers, the co-assured are not exposed in relation to the same interest and the same perils. Rights to claim under the cover will almost inevitably arise sequentially.

In the context of professional indemnity insurance policies which insure more than **1.40**
one person, the varying interests of the different persons within the definition of
'insured' will usually have the consequence that the cover provided is composite
rather than joint.[47] The very fact that the various named insured are insured for different interests indicates what the intention of the parties was (Sir Wilfrid Greene
MR's first consideration). It also goes to his second consideration: joint insurance
could not exist on the facts.

The consequences of composite insurance

In *General Accident Fire and Life Assurance Co Ltd v Midland Bank Ltd*,[48] having **1.41**
found the policy provided composite cover rather than joint cover and having
noted that the policy referred to the 'respective rights and interests' of the insured,
Sir Wilfrid Greene MR said:[49]

> It seems to me that, wherever the phrase 'the insured' appeared in the printed
> part of this document, it would be wrong to treat that as meaning, as a matter
> of construction, all the three persons named in the endorsement. The printed
> words 'insured' must be construed and qualified by the words 'for their respective rights and interests' and those printed words must be given a construction which will fit in with the essential nature of the contract which is being
> undertaken.

This approach is not limited to policies which expressly refer to each insured's
'respective rights and interests'.[50] It applies to all composite insurance and indicates that under a composite policy, subject to issues of attribution or agency, each
insured is to be treated as having his own separate interest.

---

[45] [1995] 2 Lloyd's Rep 437.
[46] Ibid at 443. See also Saville LJ at 466.
[47] See, for example, *McAleenan v AIG (Europe) Ltd* [2010] IEHC 128 (Finlay Geoghegan J): an
insurance policy which insured a sole principal and an employed solicitor was a composite policy.
[48] [1940] 2 KB 388.
[49] Ibid at 408.
[50] *Arab Bank Plc v Zurich Insurance Co* [1999] 1 Lloyd's Rep 262, at 273.

1.42 So, it is well-established that under a composite policy one insured is not precluded from claiming for a loss which was caused by the wilful misconduct of another insured.[51] As Viscount Cave explained in *P Samuel and Company Ltd v Dumas*, a case of composite insurance of shipowner and mortgagee:[52]

> It may well be that, when two persons are jointly insured and their interests are inseparably connected so that a loss or gain necessarily affects them both, the misconduct of one is sufficient to contaminate the whole insurance ... But in this case there is no difficulty in separating the interest of the mortgagee from that of the owner; and if the mortgagee should recover on the policy, the owner will not be advantaged, as the insurers will be subrogated as against him to the rights of the mortgagee.[53]

1.43 However, not only is each insured to be treated as separately insured once the policy is made, but, subject to issues of agency and attribution, each is to be treated as having entered a separate contract of insurance so that, for example, if insurers have rights to avoid against one insured for non-disclosure or misrepresentation,[54] that will not entitle them to avoid against other insureds.[55] This can extend to cases of deliberate non-disclosure or misrepresentation.[56]

1.44 In *Arab Bank Plc v Zurich Insurance Co*,[57] having referred to earlier authority, including the decision of the Court of Appeal in *New Hampshire Insurance Co v MGN Ltd*,[58] Rix J summarized the position as follows:[59]

> It seems to me that the Court of Appeal were saying that in the typical case of a composite policy where there are several assureds with separate interests, the single policy is indeed a bundle of separate contracts. That is the prima facie position under a composite policy, without any need for a meticulous examination, for instance, to see whether separate premiums have been agreed for the various interests. Indeed, one can well understand that on a practical level it would be unrealistic to expect the separate interests to be divided out and severally assessed.

1.45 The existence of separate, independent interests under composite insurance is an important safeguard for professionals and for their clients and other potential third party claimants.

---

[51] *Parker v The National Farmers Union Mutual Insurance Society Ltd* [2012] EWHC 2156 (Comm); [2013] Lloyd's Rep IR 253.

[52] [1924] AC 431, at 445–6.

[53] See also *General Accident Fire and Life Assurance Co Ltd v Midland Bank Ltd* [1940] 2 KB 388 and *State of Netherlands v Youell* [1997] 2 Lloyd's Rep 440.

[54] As to which see Chapters 5 and 6.

[55] *Panzera v Simcoe & Erie Insurance Co* (1990) 74 DLR (4th) 197; *New Hampshire Insurance Co v MGN Ltd* [1997] LRLR 24. See also *Woolcott v Sun Alliance and London Insurance Ltd* [1978] 1 WLR 493.

[56] *Arab Bank Plc v Zurich Insurance Co* [1999] 1 Lloyd's Rep 262, at 273. See also *Kumar v AGF Insurance Ltd* [1999] 1 WLR 1747 and *McAleenan v AIG (Europe) Ltd* [2010] IEHC 128.

[57] [1999] 1 Lloyd's Rep 262.

[58] [1997] LRLR 24.

[59] [1999] 1 Lloyd's Rep 262, at 277.

2

THE BASIS OF COVER

A. The Temporal Trigger

Policies of professional indemnity insurance will usually indemnify the insured **2.01** against sums which he is legally liable to pay to third party claimants in respect of specified types of liability, together with any liability for the third party claimants' costs and the costs of defending and settling the claims within the perimeters of cover specified in the particular policy. Those perimeters include the period of cover. For the policy to attach, some agreed event or 'trigger' has to occur within the specified period. In a policy of insurance of property against fire, the event will be a fire which damages the insured property: the trigger is the very event against which the insured is to be indemnified. In policies of liability insurance the choice is less obvious.

As is explained below, the ascertainment of the insured's liability to the third party **2.02** claimant is an essential precondition to the ability to recover an indemnity from liability insurers.[1] That ascertainment is the trigger of liability to indemnify, but is not

---

[1] See paras 9.106–9.132. In cases where cover includes the cost of defending claims by third parties which potentially fall within the cover provided, the right to an indemnity for defence costs arises when a claim is brought.

a practical candidate for the event which must occur during the policy period. Given the nature of the legal process, by the time that legal liability is ascertained the risk of loss will usually be all too apparent and the opportunity to obtain insurance against that liability on commercial terms will have been lost. The insured would usually know of his potential liability at the time he was seeking insurance for a particular year and so be obliged to disclose that potential liability as part of his obligation to disclose material facts so that insurers would either exclude that liability from cover or require an exorbitant premium to allow for it. It follows that it would be a 'disaster' for the insured if the insurance only covered liabilities which were ascertained during the policy period.[2] So some other trigger for the cover is needed.

2.03 There are two broad types of trigger in liability policies: (1) events occurring or occurrences;[3] and (2) claims made. In broad terms, under the former, the insurer is liable to indemnify against liability in respect of any specified occurrence which happens during the policy period, whenever the claim is made. Under the latter, the focus is on when the claim is made against the insured, rather than when the events which give rise to the claim occurred.[4] Professional indemnity insurance is now almost always written on a 'claims made' basis.[5] This is for good reason.

---

[2] *Robert Irving & Burns (a firm) v Stone* [1998] Lloyd's Rep IR 258, at 261 per Staughton LJ.

[3] There are various possible triggers in occurrence-based policies. In *Durham v BAI (Run Off Ltd (In Scheme of Arrangement) (Employers' Liability 'Trigger' Litigation)* [2008] EWHC 2692 (QB); [2009] 2 All ER 26, at [60] Burton J identified four such triggers in the context of employers' liability insurance: (i) occurrence or event—date of breach of duty; (ii) causation/exposure; (iii) occurrence of loss/damage ('injury in fact'); and (iv) manifestation/diagnosis/notice.

[4] *Reid Crowther & Partners Ltd v Simcoe & Erie General Insurance Co* (1993) 99 DLR (4th) 741 (Supreme Court of Canada) per McLachlin J at 746.

[5] *Friends Provident Life and Pensions Ltd v Sirius International Insurance Corporation* [2004] EWHC 1999 (Comm); [2005] Lloyd's Rep IR 135, 142, at [13] per Moore-Bick J: 'It is now almost invariable for liability underwriters in general, and professional negligence underwriters in particular, to issue policies that provide cover on what is known as a "claims made" basis, that is, which provide the insured with an indemnity against losses arising from claims made against him, as opposed to events occurring, during the policy period.'

In *Robert Irving & Burns (a firm) v Stone* [2003] [1998] Lloyd's Rep IR 258, at 260, Staughton LJ said that his experience was that the claims made method was 'commonly, if not universally, adopted nowadays in professional indemnity cases'. In *HLB Kidsons v Lloyd's Underwriters* [2007] EWHC 1951 (Comm); [2008] Lloyd's Rep IR 237 at [17] Gloster J said that the practice of writing professional indemnity insurance on a 'claims made' basis developed in the mid-1980s in response to the problems encountered under occurrence based policies. We suggest that the practice developed rather earlier: see, for example, *National Employers Mutual General Insurance Association Ltd v Haydon* [1980] 2 Lloyd's Rep 149, which concerned successive policies of professional indemnity insurance for solicitors underwritten between 1971 and 1976 on a 'claims made' basis. And the policy insuring the solicitors in *Simon, Haynes, Barlas & Ireland v Beer* (1945) 78 LI L Rep 337 was a 'claims made' policy. 'Claims made and notified' policies are also found and these are discussed in paras 2.47–2.49.

In *Maxwell v Price (Halford, Third Party)* [1960] 2 Lloyd's Rep 155 a firm of solicitors in Australia was insured on a 'claims made' basis in the 1950s.

In the United States 'claims made' policies were in use in the first half of the twentieth century, but only came into widespread use from about 1970 there and, apparently, somewhat later in Canada: *Reid Crowther & Partners Ltd v Simcoe & Erie General Insurance Co* (1993) 99 DLR (4th) 741 (Supreme Court of Canada) per McLachlin J at 747.

It has been said that occurrence policies were developed to provide cover against loss caused by identifiable events such as collision, fire, and war.[6] In such cases the insurer will know during or shortly after the policy period what his exposure is. Occurrence-based triggers are less satisfactory, where the full extent of exposure will not be known for some time after the end of the policy period. Insurers will be faced with a long tail and have to do their best to estimate their future exposure, bearing in mind not only the risk of future claims of which they do not know, but also the risk of changes in law and scientific knowledge which could create new or expanded heads of legal liability or means of proving loss.[7] This can result in insurers requiring higher premiums to reflect the greater risk created by the higher degree of uncertainty, or they may even withdraw from that particular market.

The attraction of a trigger based upon when claims are made against the insured is **2.04** therefore obvious. Insurers can assess the risk of future claims from recent experience and will know during (or shortly after) the policy period what third party claims have attached in that period. Greater certainty should mean lower premiums.[8]

B. The Consequences of a 'Claims Made' Trigger

The need to maintain insurance

The 'claims made trigger' does not provide a perfect solution, not least for the insured **2.05** and third party claimants. There will only be cover for a claim if insurance has been taken out for the period in which that claim is made. So, if he wishes to be insured against liability for his past acts or omissions, the insured will need to maintain insurance on a 'claims made' basis for many years, or make some other arrangement which provides him with cover should claims emerge from the woodwork.[9] Given the scope for stale claims to emerge and the possibility that the further policies may

---

[6] *Pacific Employers Insurance Co v Superior Court*, 221 Cal App 3d 1348, 270 Cal Rptr 779, at 1357 and 783, quoted in *Stuart v Hutchins* (1998) 164 DLR (4th) 67, at 73 (Ontario Court of Appeal) and *Slater v Lawyers' Mutual Insurance Company*, 278 Cal Rptr 479 (Cal App 2 Dist 1991).

[7] *Reid Crowther & Partners Ltd v Simcoe & Erie General Insurance Co* (1993) 99 DLR (4th) 741 (Supreme Court of Canada) at 747–8, where McLachlin J also noted that problems could occur when the insured had insured with successive insurers and there was then a dispute as to which policy should respond.

See also *Friends Provident Life and Pensions Ltd v Sirius International Insurance Corporation* [2004] EWHC 1999 (Comm); [2005] Lloyd's Rep IR 135, 142, at [13]; *Jesuit Fathers of Upper Canada v Guardian Insurance Company of Canada* (2006) 267 DLR (4th) 1 (Supreme Court of Canada) at [24]; *Robert Irving & Burns (a firm) v Stone* [1998] Lloyd's Rep IR 258, at 260; *FAI General Insurance Company Ltd v Perry* (1993) 30 NSWLR 89 (New South Wales Court of Appeal) at 96–7 and the authorities cited in the preceding footnote.

[8] *HLB Kidsons v Lloyd's Underwriters* [2007] EWHC 1951 (Comm); [2008] Lloyd's Rep IR 237 at [18]–[20]. See also *Safeco Title Insurance Company v Gannon* 774 P 2d 30 at 35 and *FAI Insurance Ltd v Australian Hospital Care Pty Ltd* [2001] HCA 38, (2001) 204 CLR 641 at [66] per Kirby J.

[9] *FAI Insurance Ltd v Australian Hospital Care Pty Ltd* [2001] HCA 38, (2001) 204 CLR 641 at [66] per Kirby J. In *Graham v Continental Casualty Company* Ill App 409 NE 3s 896 (1980)

only be available on exorbitant terms, this is no light burden. Moreover, the original insured may not continue to practise in the same form or at all over the relevant period. Partnerships change, dissolve, and merge. Practices are incorporated, either as limited liability partnerships or companies. Individuals retire from practice. Thus, insurance policies in later years need to provide cover not only in respect of claims against the current practice, but also against earlier practices.[10]

The need to be able to notify circumstances

2.06 A policy which only provided coverage in respect of claims made during its currency would provide imperfect protection to the insured and so, also, the insured's clients and other third party claimants.[11] The problem is illustrated by the case of *Jesuit Fathers of Upper Canada v Guardian Insurance Company of Canada*.[12] In that case insurers undertook:

> To pay on behalf of the Insured all sums which the Insured shall become legally obligated to pay as damages, because of injury arising out of the rendering of, or failure to render professional services in the practice of the Insured's profession, provided however, that coverage as provided herein shall apply only to claims which are first made against the Insured during the policy period as stated in the Declarations.

During the policy period the insured received a letter from a lawyer informing it of a potential claim. The insured instigated an investigation which revealed potential claims by others who were not represented by the lawyer who had written the letter. The insured advised insurers of these other potential claimants during the currency of the policy, but the other third party claimants only made claims after the policy period. Having received notice of these claims, insurers refused to renew and the insurance obtained from other insurers excluded cover for those potential claims. The Supreme Court of Canada upheld the insurers' denial of cover for those claims.

2.07 The policy in the *Jesuit Fathers* case contained a term requiring the insured to give insurers notice of any 'accident or occurrence' to which the insurance applied,[13]

---

architects had allowed their 'claims made' insurance to lapse and were not able to claim under earlier policies.

[10] See paras 9.01–9.24.

[11] For the interest of clients and other third party claimants see paras 1.05–1.06.

[12] (2006) 267 DLR (4th) 1 (Supreme Court of Canada). See also *QBE Insurance Ltd v Attorney General* [2005] NZCA 193, where the insured was required to give notice as soon as practicable of, among other things, 'knowledge of circumstances which could give rise to a claim against it', but the policy did not provide for an extension of cover in respect of any claim subsequently brought arising out of circumstances so notified. The New Zealand Court of Appeal declined to imply such a provision.

[13] *'Notice of Accident or Occurrence*. When an accident or occurrence takes place or upon the Insured becoming aware of any alleged injury to which this insurance applies, written notice of such accident, occurrence or injury shall be given by or on behalf of the Insured to the Insurer or any of its authorized agents as soon as practicable. Such notice shall contain particulars sufficient to identify

but there was no provision extending cover under the current policy to any claim subsequently made in relation to any accident or occurrence so notified. As Rix J observed in *J Rothschild Assurance plc v Collyear*,[14] a 'claims made' policy could hardly work on any basis other than that the insured should be both entitled and obliged to notify his current insurers of circumstances which might give rise to future claims and that any claims brought after the expiry of the policy period which arose from the circumstances which had been so notified should be deemed to have been brought during the policy period. In the absence of such a term— which it is now usual practice to include—an insured would be bound to disclose the circumstances when seeking insurance for the next and later years, but would find it impossible to obtain cover for any claim arising from those circumstances, at least at a commercially acceptable rate.[15]

So in the *Rothschild* case, the insured had cover against claims first made against **2.08** them during the period of insurance. Condition 2 of the policy provided:

> THE ASSUREDS shall as a CONDITION PRECEDENT to their right to be indemnified under this Policy give to the Underwriters notice as soon as possible during the period of this Policy as set forth in the Schedule:-
> (a) of any circumstances of which THE ASSURED shall become aware which may give rise to a claim or loss against them or any of them;
> (b) of the receipt of any notice from any person whether written or oral of an intention to make a claim against any of them;
> Such notice having been given to the Underwriters THE ASSURED shall give to the Underwriters as soon as possible full details in writing of the circumstances which may give rise to a claim or loss against them or any of them. Any claim or loss to which that circumstance has given rise which is subsequently made after the expiration of the period specified in the First Schedule shall be deemed for the purpose of this policy to have been made during the subsistence thereof.

The underlying claims concerned the alleged mis-selling of pensions. This had **2.09** been the subject of review by the insured's regulator under the Financial Services

---

the Insured and reasonably obtainable information respecting the time, place and circumstances of the accident, occurrence or injury, the names and addresses of the injured and of available witnesses and particulars of the damaged property.'

[14] [1999] Lloyd's Rep IR 6, at 22. The view expressed by Rix J was endorsed by Moore-Bick J in *Friends Provident Life and Pensions Ltd v Sirius International Insurance Corporation* [2004] EWHC 1999 (Comm); [2005] Lloyd's Rep IR 135, at 142, and their views were endorsed by Gloster J in *HLB Kidsons v Lloyd's Underwriters* [2007] EWHC 1951 (Comm); [2008] Lloyd's Rep IR 237, at [21]. See also *Thorman v New Hampshire Insurance Co (UK) Ltd* [1988] 1 Lloyd's Rep 7, at 9–10 per Sir John Donaldson MR, *Tioxide Europe Ltd v CGU International Insurance Plc* [2004] EWHC 2116 (Comm); [2005] Lloyd's Rep IR 114, at [56] per Langley J and *HLB Kidsons v Lloyd's Underwriters* [2008] EWCA Civ 1206; [2009] 1 Lloyd's Rep 8, at [4] and [114] per Rix LJ, and at [131] and [132] per Toulson LJ.

[15] *Friends Provident Life and Pensions Ltd v Sirius International Insurance Corporation* [2004] EWHC 1999 (Comm); [2005] Lloyd's Rep IR 135, at 142. See also *Kumar v AGF Insurance Ltd* [1999] 1 WLR 1747, at 1751–2, *FAI General Insurance Ltd v Australian Hospital Care Pty Ltd* [1999] QCA 243; 10 ANZIC 61.445 per Derrington J at [24]–[25] and *Immerzeel v Santam Ltd* [2007] Lloyd's Rep IR 106, at [18].

Act 1986. That review had identified the possibility of mis-selling, but the insured did not know which particular pensions might have been mis-sold. The insured purported to give notice of circumstances under general condition 2 in respect of some 2,500 pension transfer policies. Holding that the notification was effective, Rix J observed:

> [Counsel for the insurers] submitted that the notification was connected with [the insured's] difficulties in obtaining cover for the future year, and in this connection he pointed out that there was no evidence from those who were involved in the renewal and the decision to notify. It seemed to me that this submission rebounded on him, for in the course of it he was prepared to infer that the new insurers wished to exclude cover for claims arising out of [the regulator's] review or to load premium rates, and to concede that at any rate exclusion would be relevant to the objective risk which might justify notification under the existing policies. It seemed to me that in the light of the inference which [counsel for the insurers] was himself prepared to make, which is likely to have been correct, it would be obvious that there was objective justification for [the insured's] notice.[16]

2.10 There is, of course, no single term used in every professional indemnity policy which has the same or similar effect as condition 2 in the *Rothschild* case. Some are considered below.[17] However, if they are to be effective they need to enable the insured to give notice of anything which he would be obliged to disclose when seeking insurance for the following period.[18] Such clauses provide an important extension to the cover provided and change the essential basis of the policies in which they are found from an exclusively 'claims made' cover into something different.[19]

Claims which were, should, and/or could have been notified earlier

2.11 The obligation and right to notify are linked to a further consequence of the use of a 'claims made' trigger. If the insured gives notice of circumstances to insurer A and then a claim arising from those circumstances is made during a later period when he is insured on a 'claims made' basis with insurer B, it might be thought that both insurer A and insurer B would be liable to indemnify the insured in respect of that claim. In practice, however, insurer B will not be on risk on these facts because he will have excluded cover for the claim.

2.12 The example given in the preceding paragraph might be thought to give rise to a problem of double insurance, particularly if one or both policies contained

---

[16] [1999] Lloyd's Rep IR 6, at 23. A general practice did arise of excluding cover in respect of claims under the pensions review: see *Standard Life Assurance Ltd v Oak Dedicated Ltd* [2008] EWHC 222 (Comm), [2008] Lloyd's Rep IR 552 at [24].

[17] See paras 2.121–2.151.

[18] See paras 5.05–5.64.

[19] *HLB Kidsons v Lloyd's Underwriters* [2008] EWCA Civ 1206; [2009] 1 Lloyd's Rep 8, at [114] per Rix LJ. In *Friends Provident Life and Pensions Ltd v Sirius International Insurance Corporation* [2005] EWCA Civ 601; [2005] 2 Lloyd's Rep 517 at [11] Mance LJ described the primary role of such a clause as a 'trigger for the extension of cover'.

provisions avoiding, excluding, or limiting cover in the event of double insurance.[20] However, the correct analysis is (or will usually be) that there is no double insurance: only insurer A is ever on risk. This is established by the decision of the Court of Appeal in *National Employers Mutual General Insurance Association Ltd v Haydon*.[21] The Court's decision was based on the construction of the policies before it, but equivalent terms are usually found in professional indemnity policies.[22]

In the *National Employers Mutual* case, the insured firm of solicitors had been **2.13** insured with the plaintiff ('NEM') by a series of annual policies from 25 March 1971 to 24 March 1976. They were insured by the defendant ('Lloyd's') from 25 March 1976. Both the NEM and Lloyd's policies provided cover on a 'claims made' basis. The NEM policies excluded cover in respect of any claim 'for which the Insured is or would be but for the existence of this Policy entitled to indemnity under any other Policy except in respect of any excess beyond the amount payable by such other Policy'. The NEM policies also contained a provision requiring the insured to give notice of 'any occurrence which may subsequently give rise to a claim against him' and providing that cover would extend to any claim subsequently made arising out of any occurrence which was notified.[23] The Lloyd's policy contained a general exclusion 'in respect of any circumstance or occurrence which has been notified under any other insurance attaching prior to the inception of this Certificate'. The insured gave NEM notice of an occurrence on 24 March 1976, the last day of cover. A claim in respect of that occurrence was brought against the insured during the period of the Lloyd's policy. NEM indemnified the insured and then sought a contribution from Lloyd's, claiming that there was double insurance and that, following *Weddell v Road Transport and General Fire Insurance Co Ltd*,[24] both exclusions clauses should be ignored and the insurers should share the loss on the basis of the equitable principle of contribution.[25]

While approving the reasoning in *Weddell v Road Transport and General Fire* **2.14** *Insurance Co Ltd*, the Court of Appeal held that it did not apply to the policies before it. The general exclusion of the Lloyd's policy was different from the

---

[20] See chapter 24 of *MacGillivray on Insurance Law* (12th edn, Sweet & Maxwell, 2014).

[21] [1980] 2 Lloyd's Rep 149.

[22] *Immerzeel v Santam Ltd* [2007] Lloyd's Rep IR 106, at [22]. In the case of solicitors in England and Wales the SRA Minimum Terms and Conditions of Professional Indemnity Insurance prohibit any term which reduces or excludes the liability of the insurer by reason of (i) the existence or availability of any other insurance other than as provided by the Solicitors Indemnity Fund or under a professional indemnity insurance contract for a period earlier than the period of insurance or (ii) where the insured enters a policy which replaces existing extended cover.

[23] 'If during the subsistence of this Policy the Insured shall become aware of any occurrence which may subsequently give rise to a claim against him he shall give written notice to the Association of such occurrence immediately. Such notice having been given any such claim which may subsequently be made against the Insured arising out of that occurrence shall for the purposes of this Policy be deemed to have been made during the subsistence hereof.'

[24] [1932] 2 KB 563.

[25] See *MacGillivray* (see n 20 under para 2.12), [24-021].

exclusion in the NEM policies. It did not exclude cover if there was other insurance. It excluded cover unconditionally. Lloyd's had never been on risk in relation to the underlying claim. This must be correct. Clauses which require and entitle an insured to notify insurers of circumstances which might give rise to future claims provide (or should provide) an extension of cover in respect of any claims which are subsequently made. They define the risk being insured. Cover is also defined by exclusion clauses such as that in the Lloyd's policy. Lloyd's was not excluding liability in the event of double insurance. Rather, they were excluding from the risk they insured, any claims made against the insured arising from any circumstance or occurrence which had been notified under earlier policies.

2.15   In the *National Employers Mutual* case, the Court of Appeal also held, not without some doubt, that the effect of the term in the NEM policies deeming claims which were subsequently made arising out of a notified occurrence to have been made during the policy year was that, for the purposes of the NEM policy, the claim had been made during that period and so was not to be treated as having been made during the period of cover under the Lloyd's policy.

2.16   A different result was reached by the Supreme Court of Appeal of South Africa on the unusual facts of *Immerzeel v Santam Ltd*.[26] The insured engineers had a succession of policies with the same insurers. During one policy period they gave notice of circumstances which might possibly give rise to a claim. They were obliged to do so under the terms of the policy which also provided that, if a claim were subsequently made against them arising from a notified circumstance, it would be deemed to have been made during the period when it was notified. A claim was made eighteen months later, during the currency of a later policy. The later policy had more extensive cover and the insured claimed under that policy on the basis that the claim had only first been made against them during its currency.[27] There was no exclusion of cover in the later policy in respect of claims arising from circumstances notified under earlier policies. In the circumstances, it was held that the insured were entitled to cover under the earlier policy (having given notice of circumstances) and under the later cover (when the claim was actually first made).

2.17   It is, however, usual to find a term which, as a minimum, excludes from cover claims which arise from circumstances notified under earlier policies. The extent to which claims arising from circumstances known to the insured in earlier periods are excluded varies. The exclusion can be of matters disclosed on the proposal form, or of claims arising from circumstances notified under earlier policies, or of claims arising from circumstances which were or should have been notified under earlier policies. Some wordings are considered below.[28]

---

[26] [2007] Lloyd's Rep IR 106.
[27] See paras 2.19–2.38.
[28] See paras 2.121–2.151.

Insurers will usually wish to exclude from cover claims which arise from circum- **2.18** stances disclosed on the proposal form.[29] Although there has been some suggestion that such a term creates a gap in cover,[30] an exclusion of cover for claims and circumstances disclosed on the proposal form should not deprive the insured of cover: he can give notice under the current policy of both claims and circumstances and will be covered accordingly.[31]

C. Making a Claim

How a claim is made

Under a 'claims made' insurance policy the basic insuring clause will provide **2.19** an indemnity against liability for claims first made against the insured during the period of insurance. Some policies define 'claim'; others do not. But whether 'claim' is defined or not, it is a claim made against the insured which is required to trigger cover.

Meaning of 'claim'

'Claim' means 'a demand for something as due; an assertion of a right to some- **2.20** thing'.[32] It can also mean 'right of claiming; right or title (to something or to have, be, or do something; also on, upon the person, etc, that the thing is claimed from)'.[33]

---

[29] *HLB Kidsons v Lloyd's Underwriters* [2008] EWCA Civ 1206; [2009] 1 Lloyd's Rep 8, at [131] per Toulson LJ.

[30] *Reid Crowther & Partners Ltd v Simcoe & Erie General Insurance Co* (1993) 99 DLR (4th) 741 at 749 per McLachlin J and *Jesuit Fathers of Upper Canada v Guardian Insurance Company of Canada* (2006) 267 DLR (4th) 1, per LeBel J at [25]. In both cases it may be that the Court had in mind policies which did not provide an extension of cover in respect of claims arising from circumstances notified during the policy period.

[31] *Kumar v AGF Insurance Ltd* [1999] 1 WLR 1747, at 1752 per Thomas J and *HLB Kidsons v Lloyd's Underwriters* [2008] EWCA Civ 1206; [2009] 1 Lloyd's Rep 8, at [131]–[133] per Toulson LJ.

[32] *The Shorter Oxford English Dictionary*, applied in *West Wake Price & Co v Ching* [1957] 1 WLR 45, at 55 per Devlin J, in *Thorman v New Hampshire Insurance Co* [1988] 1 Lloyd's Rep 7, at 15 per Stocker LJ and in *Immerzeel v Santam Ltd* [2007] Lloyd's Rep IR 106, at [12] per Streicher JA. In *Thorman v New Hampshire Insurance Co* [1988] 1 Lloyd's Rep 7 at 11, Sir John Donaldson MR agreed with the trial judge, Steyn J, that 'a claim within the meaning of the policy was the assertion by a third party against the insured of a right to some relief because of the breach by the insured of the duty referred to in section 1 of the policy, i.e. professional negligence'. (See also (1) *Walton v National Employers Insurance Association* [1973] 2 NSWLR 73 per Bowen JA at 82: 'the word "claim" is here used in its primary sense of a demand for something as due, an assertion of a right to something. It imports the assertion, demand or challenge of something as a right'; and (2) *Safeco Title Insurance Company v Gannon* 774 P 2d 30 (1989) at 33: 'the plain, ordinary meaning of claim is a demand for compensation'.)

[33] *West Wake Price & Co v Ching* [1957] 1 WLR 45, at 55 per Devlin J. McNair J set out the two different meanings of 'claim' in *Australia & New Zealand Bank Ltd v Colonial & Eagle Wharves Ltd* [1960] 2 Lloyd's Rep 241, at 255: 'As it seems to me, both in the language of insurance and in common

The former, primary meaning requires communication to the person against whom the claim is asserted. The latter is the right to claim and does not involve communication to the person against whom the right lies. Given the requirement that the claim be made against the insured, 'claim' in the insuring clause of a professional indemnity contract will bear its primary meaning.

2.21   It does not follow that 'claim' will bear that meaning in other clauses. Moreover, it is not unusual to find 'claim' being used in two different ways in the same policy: a claim by the insured under the policy and a claim by a third party against the insured.[34] The relevant claim for the purposes of a 'claims made' insuring clause is the claim by a third party against the insured and not by the insured against insurers under the insurance policy.[35]

2.22   The definition of 'Claim' used in the SRA Minimum Terms and Conditions of Professional Indemnity Insurance well conveys what is required. That definition provides, in part, that 'Claim':

> means a demand for, or an assertion of a right to, civil compensation or civil damages or an intimation of an intention to seek such compensation or damages.[36]

As that definition shows, in the context of a 'claims made' trigger, 'claim' carries with it the idea of communication to the person against whom the demand or assertion is directed. It is not merely the right to claim which a third party has, it is the assertion of that right in a communication to the insured. So it was held in *American Insurance Co v Fairchild Industries Inc*[37] that the ordinary meaning of 'claim' is 'an assertion by a third party that in the opinion of that party the insured may be liable to it for damages [which are] within the risks covered by the policy'.

---

parlance "claim" may mean either the right to make a claim as in the expression "A. has a claim on B.", or it may mean his assertion of a right as in the expression "A. has made a claim on B."'

[34] See, for example, *Haydon v Lo & Lo (a firm)* [1997] 1 WLR 198. See also *Australia & New Zealand Bank Ltd v Colonial & Eagle Wharves Ltd* [1960] 2 Lloyd's Rep 241, where McNair J said at 255 immediately after the passage set out in the preceding footnote: 'Furthermore, in the context of this insurance (which in effect provides the [insured] with a qualified indemnity against claims made against them by their customers) it may mean either a claim against the [insured] by the [third party claimant] in either of the two senses indicated, or a claim by the [insured] on the insurers in either of those two senses.'

In *Standard Life Assurance Ltd v Oak Dedicated Ltd* [2008] EWHC 222 (Comm), [2008] Lloyd's Rep IR 552 Tomlinson J said at [97]: 'The word "claim" is a word frequently used by insurance market professionals but not always to mean precisely the same thing. The word takes its meaning and its colour from its context.'

[35] Some policies require the notification to insurers by the insured of a claim made against the insured within the period of insurance as an additional trigger: see paras 2.47–2.49.

[36] See also the definition of 'Claim' in the ICAEW Minimum Approved Policy Wording: '"CLAIM" shall mean any written or oral demand for compensation or damages from, or the assertion of a right against, any Insured …'

[37] 56 F 3d 435 (2d Cir, 1995) at 439. Applied in *Andy Warhol Foundation for the Visual Arts Inc v Hughes* 189 F 3d 208 1999 (United States Court of Appeals for the Second Circuit).

'Claims made'

In *Robert Irving & Burns v Stone*[38] Staughton LJ said: **2.23**

> To my mind, in the ordinary meaning of the English language, the words 'claims made' indicate that there has been a communication by the client to the [insured] of some discontent which will, or may, result in a remedy expected from the [insured]. There must, I say, be a communication. That seems to me the ordinary meaning of the word 'claim'. That is a view which I have in common with the majority in *St Paul Fire & Marine Insurance Company v Guardian Insurance Company of Canada* (1983) 1 DLR (4th) 342 at page 357, where Thorson JA said:
>
> > 'It follows in my opinion that the words claims made in the Guardian policy ought to be construed in accordance with the ordinary plain meaning of those words, which, simply stated, denote a claim that is made by being notified to or otherwise brought to the attention of the person against whom it is asserted.'

So, if proceedings are issued but not served or otherwise communicated to the insured, no claim has been made for the purposes of the insuring clause.[39] The claim must be communicated to the insured by or on behalf of the third party claimant. As Cardamone CJ said in *Andy Warhol Foundation for the Visual Arts Inc v Hughes*:[40]

> ... one necessary ingredient distilled from a survey of the decisional law is that a party that has a claim must itself assert it: a concept perfectly capsulized in Longfellow's 'Why don't you speak for yourself, John?' Henry W. Longfellow, *The Courtship of Miles Standish* ...

The need for the claim to be asserted by the third party also means that an assertion **2.24** or demand by A will not encompass a claim by B, even if B's claim is closely related to A's claim. So, in *Jesuit Fathers of Upper Canada v Guardian Insurance Company of Canada*[41] the insured received a letter from a lawyer acting for one claimant, asserting a claim for damages for physical and sexual abuse during the currency of the policy. Other claimants made claims after the policy period. Those claims were also for physical and sexual abuse at the same school. The insured argued that there was one 'claim' in respect of events at the school and that this claim had been

---

[38] [1998] Lloyd's Rep IR 258, at 261.

[39] *Robert Irving & Burns v Stone* [1998] Lloyd's Rep IR 258. At 261–3 Staughton LJ explained the earlier decision of the Court of Appeal in *Thorman v New Hampshire Insurance Co (UK) Ltd* [1988] 1 Lloyd's Rep 7, discussed in paras 2.40–2.46. In the *Thorman* case, a writ had also been issued, but not served, during one period of insurance. However, during that period the insured had received a letter of claim and a notice of arbitration. As Staughton LJ observed at 263: 'The truth of the matter is that nobody was really considering whether in point of time the issue of the writ on its own counted as a claim or not.'

In the *Thorman* case at 12 Sir John Donaldson MR had considered the possibility that the issue of a writ might not itself constitute a claim, but could be 'an occurrence which may be likely to give rise to a claim'.

See also *St Paul Fire & Marine Insurance Company v Guardian Insurance Company of Canada* (1983) 1 DLR (4th) 342, *Slater v Lawyers' Mutual Insurance Company* 278 Cal Rptr 479 (Cal App 2 Dist 1991) and *J Rothschild Assurance Plc v Collyear* [1999] Lloyd's Rep IR 6, at 25–6. And in *Watts v Vickers* (1916) 86 LJKB 177 the Court of Appeal held that a claim for compensation under the Workers Compensation Act 1906 was not made until it was communicated.

[40] 189 F 3d 208 1999 (United States Court of Appeals for the Second Circuit), at 210. See also *QBE Insurance Ltd v Attorney General* [2005] NZCA 193, at [26].

[41] (2006) 367 DLR (4th) 1.

made during the policy period. The Supreme Court of Canada rejected this argument because the further claimants had not themselves made any claim against the insured during the relevant period.[42]

Form in which claim is made

2.25 There is no need for the claim to be made in any particular way. A letter before action, pre-action protocol letter, or the service of proceedings or notice to arbitrate would clearly involve the making of a claim. But there is no need for such formality.[43] As McLachlin J explained in *Reid Crowther & Partners Ltd v Simcoe & Erie General Insurance Co*:[44]

> What is required, unless the policy expressly so stipulates, is a *form* of demand or assertion of liability, not a *formal* demand or assertion of liability. Under a policy such as the one in this appeal, which contains no express requirement of a formal demand or indeed any demand at all, what constitutes a claim 'made' is a question to be resolved on the facts of the case. There is no magic formula. One must look to the reality of what the third party was communicating to the insured by words and conduct. If the message was clear, the fact that the third party through politeness refrained from stating its demand or intention to hold the insured liable in categorical legal terms should not preclude a finding that a claim has been made. Where the reasonable insured in all the circumstances would conclude that a third party was making a claim against him or her in the sense that if satisfactory payment or other form of reparation were not made the third party would sue, then it may be said that a claim has been made, even though a formal statement of liability and/or demand has not been tendered. (emphasis in original)

However, mere requests for information or expressions of dissatisfaction which do not convey a demand for compensation are not claims.[45]

2.26 In the *Reid Crowther* case, the insured were engineers. In 1974 they had contracted with a water board to provide engineering services for the construction of a sewage collection and water distribution system. Their work involved design, supervision, and certification of the works, which were completed in 1976. Various problems arose and in 1978 the insured accepted that the installation was defective and acknowledged that its supervision of the contractor had been

---

[42] See also *Andy Warhol Foundation for the Visual Arts Inc v Hughes* 189 F 3d 208 1999 (United States Court of Appeals for the Second Circuit): claim for breach of copyright to a photograph of Jacqueline Kennedy; in 1994 a lawyer acting for the photographer sent the insured a letter alleging breach. When negotiations failed, proceedings were issued in 1996 in the name of both the photographer and the publishers of *Life* magazine, who were co-owners of the copyright; it was at this stage that the insured gave notice to its insurers. It was held that the insured was not in breach of a condition precedent requiring notification of claims as soon as practicable in relation to the magazine's claim, which had not been made before December 1996.

[43] In *Katz Drug Company v Commercial Standard Insurance Company* 647 SW 2d 831 (Mo App 1983) the insured was obliged to give insurers notice 'if claim is made or suit is brought against' him. It was held that 'claim' did not mean legal proceedings, so that insurers were on risk where a claim was made in some other way.

[44] (1993) 99 DLR (4th) 741, at 756–7.

[45] Ibid at 755.

inadequate. Remedial works were carried out at the insured's expense and an indemnity was obtained from insurers. During the course of works to expand the system in September 1981 further antecedent damage was discovered. The client's foreman showed the insured the damage, commenting that it was typical of the work done by the contractor and approved by the insured. A few days later the damage was videotaped by the client and the insured was again told that the client was dissatisfied with the condition of the works and the job which had been done. In the circumstances, which included the earlier claim and admission, it was clear that the client was holding the insured responsible for the newly discovered damage. The Supreme Court of Canada held that a claim had been made.

While there is no need for formality, there is a need for what is communicated to amount to a demand for something as due or to an assertion of a right.[46] A communication which falls short of that may well be a circumstance which might give rise to a claim and so be notifiable under the policy,[47] but it will not be a claim. For example, in *M J Gleeson Group Plc v AXA Corporate Solutions Assurance SA*[48] the insured has received a letter informing it that a building it had constructed was suffering from certain problems. A report identifying various shortcomings was enclosed. The insured was asked to confirm that the building was safe and then for its comments on the report and proposals for rectifying the apparent deficiencies. This was not a claim for the purposes of the policy. It did not assert a right to relief. Rather it was a communication of 'circumstances which might lead to a claim'.[49]   **2.27**

---

[46] See para 2.20. Or, if the policy defines 'claim', what is communicated must fall within that definition.

[47] See paras 2.50–2.120.

[48] [2013] Lloyd's Rep IR 677, HH Judge Raynor QC, sitting as a Judge of the High Court (contractor's all risks and public liability insurance).

[49] See also *Junemill Ltd (in liquidation) v FAI General Insurance Company Ltd* [1997] QCA 261; [1999] 2 Qd R 136, where the insured firm of valuers received a letter from solicitors acting for a lender alleging that the insured had provided negligent valuations and threatening legal proceedings if losses were sustained. Shortly afterwards the lender's solicitors wrote to the insured's brokers asking them to acknowledge receipt of that letter and to confirm that it would operate as a sufficient notification of a claim. It was held that, in context, the second letter was a claim, so that it was not necessary to decide whether the first letter, which had not alleged any loss, had already made a claim.

By way of contrast, in *Hellyer v Amp General Insurance Ltd* [2002] NSWSC 866, 12 ANZIC 61.544 the insured were scuba diving instructors. A woman who had been on one of their courses with her boyfriend telephoned the insured to inform them that she and her boyfriend had both suffered from the 'bends' after the course. She suggested that the insured contact others who had been on the same course. Smart AJ held that this did not constitute a claim, although it did amount to a circumstance which might subsequently give rise to a claim, as to which see para 2.86.

In *Livesay v Hawkins* [2012] QSC 112; (2012) 17 ANZ Insurance Cases 61–933 it was held that a claim had been made when tenants of a residence managed by the insured wrote complaining that one of them had suffered personal injuries when a fixture fell on her and saying that the insured 'will be held liable for any personal injury claims arising from damage caused to tenants due to poor living conditions'. This was a 'form of demand or assertion of liability'. The same conclusion was reached in (1) *Trisura Guarantee Insurance Company Ltd v The Belmont Financial Group Inc* (2008) 269 NSR (2d) 143 (taken together a number of letters contained allegations of misrepresentation by the insured, a suggested cause of action and express warnings that the insured would be sued: see the judgment of Fichaud JA, with whom the other members of the Nova Scotia Court of Appeal agreed,

2.28   It is not uncommon for a claimant or his lawyers to write to an insured putting them on notice of an intention to make a claim in the future and asking the insured to notify his insurers accordingly. The question arises whether notice of an intention to make a claim has the effect of making that claim. In *Thorman v New Hampshire Insurance Co (UK) Ltd*[50] the insured was required, as a condition precedent to the right to be indemnified, to give immediate notice in writing:

(a) of any claim made against them,

(b) of the receipt of notice from any person of an intention to make a claim against them.

Communication of a firm intention to make a claim might be thought to involve 'a communication by the client to the [insured] of some discontent which will, or may, result in a remedy expected from the [insured]'[51] and so the making of a claim. However, given the distinction in the policy between the making of a claim and the giving of notice of an intention to make a claim, cover was available under the policy when the threatened claim was eventually made not under the primary 'claims made' insuring clause, but by reason of the notification to the insurers of the intention to make a claim and by the operation of the usual clause deeming any claim subsequently made which arose from an occurrence notified during the period of insurance to have been made during the period of insurance.[52]

2.29   The distinction between the making of a claim and notification of an intention to make a claim is to be found in current policies, including the ICAEW Minimum Approved Policy Wording.[53] There are also policy wordings which define 'claim' so as to include notice of an intention to make a claim.[54] In any particular case the answer to the question whether notification of an intention to make a claim

---

at [35]) and in (2) *Travelers Guarantee Company of Canada v Hants Realty Ltd* 2014 NSCA 69 (the third party wrote that the insured should cover the cost of remedying the problem).

[50]   [1988] 1 Lloyd's Rep 7.

[51]   *Robert Irving & Burns v Stone* [1998] Lloyd's Rep IR 258, per Staughton LJ at 261.

[52]   [1988] 1 Lloyd's Rep 7, per Sir John Donaldson MR at 9–10.

[53]   Cf General Condition 3 in the policy considered in *HLB Kidsons v Lloyd's Underwriters* [2008] EWCA Civ 1206; [2009] 1 Lloyd's Rep 8 (set out at [100]). The distinction between the making of a claim and notice of an intention to make a claim can be found elsewhere too. For example, in *J Rothschild Assurance plc v Collyear* [1999] Lloyd's Rep IR 6 cover attached under the primary insuring clause in respect of 'any claim or claims first made against [the insured] during the period of insurance'. As well as the usual term requiring notification of circumstances which might give rise to a claim, the insured were also obliged to give insurers notice of 'the receipt of any notice from any person whether written or oral of an intention to make a claim against any of them'. Thus, on this policy wording, notice of an intention to make a claim was not to be taken to involve the making of the claim. A similar distinction can be found in the policy wordings in *Total Graphics Ltd v AGF Insurance Ltd* [1997] 1 Lloyd's Rep 599 and *Immerzeel v Santam Ltd* [2007] Lloyd's Rep IR 106.

[54]   For example, in the policy considered in *Fisher v Guardian Insurance Co of Canada* (1995) 123 DLR (4th) 336, 'claim' was defined as: 'any notice received by the Insured from a person or entity advising that it is the intention of such person or entity to hold the Insured responsible for an act, omission or personal injury covered under this policy'. See also the definition of 'claim' in the RICS Policy Wording set out in para 2.35.

involves making a claim will depend on the precise language used and the other relevant circumstances. If the notification does not involve the making of a claim, then the insured will generally need to give notice to insurers of circumstances which might give rise to a claim.[55] An insured who does notify his current insurers will usually be insured whether a claim has been made or not.[56]

Intervention by statutory regulators

Some professions, including, but not limited to, those in the financial services area, **2.30** are subject to regulation under statute and to regulators established by statute. Such regulators may require insured firms to take action, which results in payments by way of compensation to former clients in ways which do not involve the making of a claim in the conventional sense. For example, in 1994, the Securities and Investments Board ('SIB'), the regulator under the Financial Services Act 1986, issued 'guidance' which required regulated firms to investigate whether they had been guilty of mis-selling pensions so as to cause loss to investors and, if they had, to consider what redress to offer.[57] This was adopted by the Personal Investment Authority, a self-regulating organization under the Financial Services Act 1986, which required its members to carry out a review of past business. Under that review investors might simply complete a questionnaire sent to them by their former advisor and then receive and accept an offer of redress which was not made in response to any 'demand for something as due' or any 'assertion of a right to something'. The advisors claimed to be indemnified in respect of sums paid by way of redress under their professional indemnity insurance.

Not surprisingly, given the amounts at stake, insurers took the position that no **2.31** claim had been made in such circumstances. The issue was decided in *J Rothschild Assurance Plc v Collyear*.[58] Having set out the review process and considered particular cases, Rix J held that investors made claims by taking part in the review process and/or in accepting the offers of compensation.[59]

---

[55] As to which, see paras 2.50–2.120.

[56] In *Safeco Title Insurance Company v Gannon* 774 P 2d 30 (1989) it was held that no 'claim' had been made against the insured during the policy period for the purposes of a policy which, like most claims made policies, distinguished between 'claims' and 'facts and circumstances leading to claims'. The insured had learnt of the third party claimant's potential loss during the policy period and was advised by the third party claimant to 'see his attorney'. These were facts and circumstances which subsequently gave rise to the claim, but not the claim itself. See further *Reid Crowther & Partners Ltd v Simcoe & Erie General Insurance Co* (1993) 99 DLR (4th) 741 (Supreme Court of Canada) per McLachlin J at 756 and *QBE Insurance Ltd v Attorney General* [2005] NZCA 193, at [23], where *Safeco Title Insurance Company v Gannon* was followed.

[57] This guidance formed the subject of the decision of the Divisional Court in *R v Securities and Investment Board, ex parte Independent Financial Advisers Association* [1995] 2 BCLC 76. For the implications of this guidance for professional indemnity cover, see paras 11.36–11.37.

[58] [1999] Lloyd's Rep IR 6.

[59] Ibid at 28. See also *CGU Insurance Ltd v AMP Financial Planning Pty Ltd* [2007] HCA 36; (2007) 237 ALR 420, where the insured licensed security dealers proposed a protocol to respond to clients' claims which would result in compensation being paid without recourse to legal proceedings. This was done, in part, to preserve relations with the insured's regulator, the Australian Securities

Claims made to ombudsmen

2.32   The Financial Ombudsman Service set up pursuant to Part XVI of, and Sched 17 to, the Financial Services and Markets Act 2000 gives disgruntled clients of firms regulated under that Act an alternative means of redress up to specified limits of recovery. The clients do not make their complaint to the regulated firm, but to the Financial Services Ombudsman, who then investigates the claim and makes an award. A similar scheme is provided for by Part 9 of the Legal Services Act 2007. Although clients will usually have to have sought redress through the firm's own complaints procedures before complaining to the ombudsman (and so will have made a claim),[60] it is possible that the first time a claim is made is by the reference to an ombudsman. The question therefore arises whether the claim is first made when the client complains to the ombudsman or when the ombudsman contacts the firm. Although making a complaint to the ombudsman is not the same as issuing legal proceedings, the authorities considered above suggest that the answer is that the claim is made when the ombudsman informs the insured of the complaint. The ICAEW Minimum Approved Policy Wording provides within the definition of 'claim' that it is 'deemed to include any complaint or reference to the Ombudsman'[61] and that 'Claimant' includes 'a complainant to the Ombudsman'. This is a sensible reaction to the introduction of ombudsmen schemes.[62]

Specific contractual definitions of 'claim'

2.33   Thus far we have considered what is involved in a 'claims made' trigger where there is no definition of 'claim' in the contract of insurance. Given the various ways in which the word 'claim' is used in policies of indemnity insurance, it is not surprising that not all contractual definitions are directed towards the question as to what is a 'claim' for the purposes of the 'claims made' trigger.

2.34   For example, in *Standard Life Assurance Ltd v Oak Dedicated Ltd*[63] the definition of 'claim' was as follows:

---

and Investments Commission. The protocol fell outside the definition of 'Claim' in the policy, which was: 'Any originating process (in a legal proceeding or arbitration), cross claim or counter claim or third party or similar notice claiming compensation against and served on an Insured.'

[60]   Section 126 of the Legal Services Act 2007 provides that, subject to possible exceptions, complainants must have first used the respondent's complaints procedures in order to come within the jurisdiction of the ombudsman.

[61]   'Ombudsman' is defined as 'any ombudsman to whose jurisdiction the Insured is subject by virtue of contract or law'.

[62]   The RICS Policy Wording includes cover for awards by an ombudsman 'under any recognised scheme'. Reflecting the succession of complaints bodies to which solicitors have been and are subject, the SRA Minimum Terms and Conditions of Professional Indemnity Insurance provide cover for amounts paid or payable in accordance with the recommendation of the Legal Services Ombudsman, the Office of Legal Complaints (including the scheme administered by that Officer under Part 6 of the Legal Services Act 2007) or any other regulatory authority (save in relation to determinations that require the insured to refund fees).

[63]   [2008] EWHC 222 (Comm); [2008] Lloyd's Rep IR 552.

'Claim' shall mean each Claim or series of Claims (whether by one or more than one Claimant) arising from or in connection with or attributable to any one act, error, omission or originating cause or source or dishonesty of any one person or group of persons acting together and any such series of Claims shall be deemed to be one Claim for all purposes under this Policy.

This and similar definitions are directed towards the limit of indemnity and aggregation,[64] rather than the question as to what is or is not a claim for the purposes of the 'claims made' trigger.[65] The effect of this definition is that claims first made after the policy period which arise 'from or in connection with or attributable to any one act, error, omission or originating cause or source or dishonesty of any one person or group of persons acting together' are deemed to have been made at the same time (and to be the same claim) as a single claim falling within those terms which was made during the policy period, at least for the purposes of the current policy.

However, not all definitions go to what is or is not to be treated as a 'claim' for **2.35** the purpose of policy limits and aggregation. The RICS Policy Wording defines 'claim' as:

4.1 any demand for damages or compensation from, or the assertion of a right against, the INSURED

4.2 any notice of intention, whether orally or in writing, to commence legal proceedings against the INSURED

4.3 any communication with the INSURED in whatsoever form invoking any Pre-Action Protocols as may be issued and approved from time to time.

This is clearly intended to be a wide definition and it is consistent with the authorities considered above concerning policies in which there is no definition of 'claim'.

There was no definition of 'claim' in *Peacock v Roberts; Guardian Insurance Co of* **2.36** *Canada, Third Party*[66] but the insuring clause extended beyond the making of claims because the cover was provided 'only if the original claim or suit for damages is brought within the Period of Insurance'. The insured was a dentist. A writ

---

[64] The insurance in *Standard Life Assurance Ltd v Oak Dedicated Ltd* was 'Financial institutions Claims Made Comprehensive Insurance'. The wording of the aggregation clause in *J Rothschild Assurance plc v Collyear* [1999] Lloyd's Rep IR 6, where the insured were also financial services advisers, was not dissimilar to the definition of 'claim' in *Standard Life*: 'All claims resulting from the same act, error or omission or a series of acts, errors or omissions arising out of the same cause or the same acts, errors or omissions of one person or persons acting together or in which such person or persons is/are concerned or implicated are deemed to be one claim for all purposes of this Policy.'

[65] See also *Countrywide Assured Group plc v DJ Marshall* [2003] Lloyd's Rep IR 195, which contained the following definitions: '"ANY CLAIM" and "ANY LOSS" shall mean one occurrence or all occurrences of a series consequent upon or attributable to one source or original cause. This definition shall also mean the discovery of the dishonesty of any person(s) and shall constitute one occurrence or original cause.' Again, the focus is on policy limits and aggregation, rather than the making of claims. Neither an 'occurrence' nor 'the discovery of the dishonesty of any person' would be 'made' against the insured.

[66] (1990) 67 DLR (4th) 641.

was issued during the policy period but only served outside it. The insured gave no notice during the policy period. The British Columbia Court of Appeal held that no claim had been made during the policy period.[67] However, they held that a suit had been brought and so insurers were on risk for the claim.[68] If they were wrong as to the meaning of the insuring clause, it was at least ambiguous and should be construed *contra proferentem*.[69]

2.37 The definition of 'claim' in *Travelers Casualty and Surety Co of Canada v Sun Life Assurance Co of Canada (UK) Ltd*[70] was extensive. 'Claim' meant:

(i) a demand for monetary or non-monetary relief;
(ii) a civil proceeding;
(iii) a criminal proceeding;
(iv) arbitration;
(v) a judicial or formal administrative or regulatory proceeding commenced by the filing of a notice of charges, formal investigative order or similar document, or a review of all or part of its business, whether fully completed or not, prescribed by a financial service regulatory authority, or Self Regulatory Organisation in accordance with its regulations, rules, standards of practice or specifications against any Insured for a Wrongful Act, including any appeal therefrom.

The insuring clause provided cover for loss resulting from any 'claim first made during the policy period'. In the case of 'a judicial or formal administrative or regulatory proceeding commenced by the filing of a notice of charges' the claim would be made by the filing of the notice of charges, not by communication of the notice of charges to the insured. This would appear to leave open the question whether, under this definition, a claim by way of civil proceeding is first made by the issue of proceedings or by the service of them on the insured.[71]

2.38 Where the contract of insurance contains a definition of 'claim', a claim will only be made if it falls within that definition. For example, in *Smart v AAI Ltd*[72] 'claim'

---

[67] Following *St. Paul Fire and Marine Insurance v Guardian Insurance* (1982) 132 D.L.R. (3d) 60, affirmed (1983) 1 DLR (4th) 342.

[68] It may be, however, that the better view was that a suit was only brought when proceedings were served. Under the policy, the insured was required to give notice of claim or suit in these terms: 'If claim is made or suit is brought against the Insured, the Insured shall immediately forward to the Insurer every demand, notice, summons or other process received by the Insured or by the Insured's representative.' This appears to link the bringing of a suit to the receipt by the insured of the 'summons or other process'.

[69] See paras 7.70–7.75.

[70] [2006] EWHC 2716 (Comm); [2007] Lloyd's Rep IR 619.

[71] In *Slater v Lawyers' Mutual Insurance Company* 278 Cal Reptr 479 (Cal App 2 Dist 1991), the need for proceedings to be served was made clear. 'Claim' was defined as 'a demand, including service of suit or institution of arbitration proceedings, for money against the insured'. And the policy in *CGU Insurance Ltd v AMP Financial Planning Pty Ltd* [2007] HCA 36; (2007) 237 ALR 420 defined 'claim' as: 'Any originating process (in a legal proceeding or arbitration), cross claim or counter claim or third party or similar notice claiming compensation against *and served on an Insured*.' (emphasis added)

[72] [2015] NSWSC 392.

was defined in a contract of professional indemnity insurance as 'a demand by a third party upon the Insured for compensation however conveyed'. A request by lenders/investors for return of their money was not a demand for compensation and so did not amount to the making of a claim so as to trigger cover under the contract.

What is encompassed within a claim

When a claim is made against an insured, two issues can arise. The first is whether **2.39** the claim is to be treated as one claim or as more than one claim for the purposes of the limits of cover and any aggregation clause in the policy. That is addressed in **Chapter 10**.[73] The second is what is included within the scope of the claim which has been made. While this will not be an issue in the vast majority of cases, it does arise from time to time, for example when it later emerges, either by way of particularization or by amendment, that the claim(s) against the insured is (or are) wider than was understood when the claim was originally made. If the insurers who were on risk when the claim was first made were no longer on risk when the particularization or amendment occurs, does the claim as particularized or amended form part of the original claim or is it to be treated as a new claim?

The question as to what was encompassed within the original claim fell to be **2.40** decided in *Thorman v New Hampshire Insurance Co (UK) Ltd*.[74] The insured were architects. They were insured by New Hampshire Insurance (UK) Ltd ('NHIC') by a series of annual policies, the last of which expired on 30 September 1983. From 1 October 1983 they were insured by Home Insurance Co ('HIC'). During the late 1970s a former client complained of the quality of some brickwork at a housing development. The insured considered that the party mainly responsible was the engineer and remedial works were carried out 'without prejudice' largely at the expense of the engineer and without insurers making any payment. In May 1982 solicitors acting for the former client wrote to the insured informing them that they had been consulted by the insured's former client 'about the problems that have arisen in connection with this development' and that they would be issuing a protective writ. In June 1982 the solicitors issued a generally endorsed writ and sent another letter to the insured giving notice of arbitration which stated:

> As you know serious problems have arisen in this development, inter alia, with regard to cracking and defective brickwork, for which we hold you responsible.

The insured forwarded these letters to NHIC, commenting that unless 'new aspects' (ie matters other than brickwork) were being raised against them, they did not believe that a valid claim could be made against them. NHIC appointed solicitors who sought clarification of the allegations against the insured. Clarification

---

[73] See paras 10.18–10.80.
[74] [1988] 1 Lloyd's Rep 7.

was not forthcoming before 1 October 1983 when HIC came on risk. The writ was served in December 1983, but it was only when the Statement of Claim was served in January 1984 that it became apparent that the former client's complaints extended beyond brickwork. HIC maintained that the entire claim was covered by NHIC. NHIC maintained that it was only liable to indemnify the insured in respect of liability for defective brickwork.

2.41 The Court of Appeal held that the answer was to be found in how the former client's claim had been formulated and not in how it had been understood by the insured. Both the generally endorsed writ and the notice of arbitration were wide enough to encompass all the claims eventually particularized. The words 'inter alia' in the letter sent in June 1982 showed that the claim was not limited to brickwork. This must be right: otherwise the extent of cover would depend upon the subjective understanding of the insured rather than upon the actual claims made against the insured. Where a generally endorsed claim form or notice of arbitration or other form of complaint is communicated to the insured by a claimant, all claims which are subsequently particularized will have been made by that communication.

2.42 In his judgment at first instance in the *Thorman* case, Steyn J had expressed the view that, if a building owner claimed to have suffered loss because of defects to the floors and roof of the building and the insured notified his insurers, there would be one claim. If, however, the building owner subsequently added a new and unrelated assertion of damage to windows, Steyn J considered that that would be a separate claim. Sir John Donaldson MR agreed that the initial claim in relation to the floors and roof would be one claim, but expressed reservations as to whether the later claim would be a new claim. He gave some examples of what might or might not be a single 'claim':[75]

> An architect has separate contracts with separate building owners. The architect makes the same negligent mistake in relation to each. The claims have a factor in common, namely the same negligent mistake, and to this extent are related, but clearly they are separate claims. Bringing the claims a little closer together, let us suppose that the architect has a single contract in relation to two separate houses to be built on quite separate sites in different parts of the country. If one claim is in respect of a failure to specify windows of the requisite quality and the other is in respect of failure to supervise the laying of the foundations, I think that once again the claims would be separate. But it would be otherwise if the complaint was the same in relation to both houses. Then take the present example of a single contract for professional services in relation to a number of houses in a single development. A single complaint that they suffered from a wide range of unrelated defects and a demand for compensation would, I think, be regarded as a single claim. But if the defects manifested themselves seriatim and each gave rise to a separate complaint, what then? They might be regarded as separate claims. Alternatively, later complaints could be regarded as enlargements of the original claim that the architect had been professionally negligent in his execution of his contract. It would, I think, very much depend upon the facts.

---

[75] Ibid at 11–12.

These examples are not easy to relate to the issue before the Court of Appeal in the **2.43** *Thorman* case, which was whether all the matters particularized in the Statement of Claim served in January 1984 fell within the 'claim' which had been made in 1982. They appear to concern the separate question as to whether more than one claim is being made in a single complaint for the purposes of the limit of cover and aggregation.

So, in the first example given, there are two separate claimants, each owning a **2.44** different building. Unless they made their claims in the same document, it is hard to see how it could be thought that only one claim had been made against the insured.[76] The example of the same defect in different houses in different parts of the country ignores the crucial issue as to when the claim in respect of each house is first made against the insured. If the claimant complains of one house in one policy year and of another in the following year, two separate claims have been made. If the complaints in respect of both houses are made in succession in the same year, there might well be an issue as to whether they should be treated as a single claim for the purposes of policy limits and aggregation, but the claims would have been made separately. On the other hand, if the complaints about the same defect in both houses are made at the same time in the same document, then there might well be only one claim both in terms of whether more than one claim had been made and for the purposes of aggregation and policy limits.

The example of different defects in different houses is also unhelpful in relation **2.45** to the issue in the *Thorman* case. If a claim had been made in one policy year in respect of one house and the claim in respect of the other house was made in a later year, then obviously the claim in respect of the other house would not fall within the scope of the first claim. If, however, a widely framed letter of claim had been sent which was wrongly understood to relate to only one house, but it transpired that the complaints put in summary form in the letter extended to both houses, the claims in respect of both would have been made by the letter of claim.

Sir John Donaldson MR was, however, plainly right to conclude that the question **2.46** whether a complaint which is added on to an existing claim is a new claim or falls within the scope of the claim which has already been notified will depend upon the particular facts.[77] In this context it is important to bear in mind that 'claim' does not

---

[76] Nor could it be suggested that, if one building owner made his claim by, say a letter of claim, the claim of the other building owner had also been made by that letter: see paras 2.23–2.24.

[77] In *Wright Engineers Ltd v United States Fire Insurance Company* (1983) 48 BCLR 37 (Supreme Court of British Columbia); (1986) 19 CCLI 74 (British Columbia Court of Appeal) the insured engineers were responsible for the design of the PVC lining of tanks at a copper processing plant. They failed to specify that copper wire should run longitudinally along the joints so that it had been difficult to test the adequacy of the welds. In 1977 the welding was found to be inadequate, requiring remedial works. A claim was made against the insured and settled in 1981. When the PVC was rolled back in 1979 it was found to be brittle and the insured's clients claimed that this was the

mean 'cause of action'.[78] So, if the claimant amends to add a new cause of action which, if made good, would entitle him to the same compensation as that already claimed, there will not be a new claim for the purposes of the 'claims made' trigger.[79] In the same way, an amendment to add further particulars of loss and damage would not involve the making of a new claim. If, however, the amendment involves the addition not only of new grounds for entitlement to compensation but also new, distinct loss, then it is likely to constitute a new claim, separate from that already made. It follows that the example given by Steyn J in the *Thorman* case was right on the assumed facts.

D. Claims Made and Notified

2.47 Some professional indemnity policies contain a double trigger. Not only must the claim be made against the insured during the period of cover, but the insured must give insurers notice of the claim within the period of cover as well (or, in some cases, within a specified number of days after the end of the period of cover).[80] Such policies were relatively rare in the United Kingdom,[81] and were found more frequently in other common law jurisdictions.[82] Notice of claims by or shortly

---

result of a design error by the insured: the material selected was not resistant to acid and kerosene. It was held that this was a separate claim. Although both were matters of design, there were different breaches causing different losses. And there had been separate claims by the insured's clients.

In the same way in *Elstrom, Smith & Co v Kansa General Insurance Co* (1988) 29 BCLR (2d) 41 (Supreme Court of British Columbia) claims that the insured accountant/receiver manager had negligently failed to protect property, added by way of amendment to existing proceedings alleging that the insured had negligently failed to give advice to reduce income tax liability, were not the same as the original claim.

But in *Reid Crowther & Partners Ltd v Simcoe & Erie General Insurance Co* (1993) 99 DLR (4th) 741 (for the facts see para 2.26) the further sums sought against the insured were part of the original claim. They represented further losses caused by the same negligent act.

[78] *West Wake Price & Co v Ching* [1957] 1 WLR 45, at 55 and 57 per Devlin J and *Haydon v Lo & Lo (a firm)* [1997] 1 WLR 198 at 204–5 per Lord Lloyd giving the Opinion of the Privy Council. Cf *Thorman v New Hampshire Insurance Co* [1988] 1 Lloyd's Rep 7 at 15–16, where Stocker LJ derived little assistance from cases concerned with whether there were one or more causes of action.

[79] Cf *McCarthy v St Paul International Insurance Co Ltd* [2007] FCAFC 28, per Allsopp J at [76]–[77], where it was held that there was a single claim by each claimant, even thought that claim was put in a number of different ways.

[80] The requirement that notice of a claim be given during the period of the policy is to be distinguished from obligations to give notice of the claim 'immediately' or 'as soon as practicable' and suchlike, even if compliance with such obligations is stated to be a condition precedent to cover. Depending upon the facts, an insured may comply with such obligations by giving notice outside the policy period: see paras 2.116–2.120 and 11.03–11.11.

[81] An example is the policy considered in *MDIS Ltd v Swinbank* [1999] Lloyd's Rep IR 516 (computer consultants): 'The underwriters will indemnify the Assured to the extent and in the manner detailed herein against any claim for which the Assured may become legally liable, first made against the Assured and notified to the Underwriters during the period of this Certificate arising out of professional conduct of the Assured's business as stated in the Schedule ...'

[82] Eg the policies in *Clasper v Duns* [2007] NZHC 1000 (accountants; New Zealand); *FAI General Insurance Company Ltd v Perry* (1993) 30 NSWLR 89 (accountants; Australia); *Junemill Ltd (in liquidation) v FAI General Insurance Company Ltd* [1997] QCA 261; [1999] 2 Qd R 136

after the end of the policy period is of obvious benefit to insurers,[83] and so it is not surprising that claims made and notified policies are now more common in the United Kingdom.[84]

In a 'claims made and notified' policy, both the claim and the notice of it have to **2.48** be within the specified period(s) in order to cause the risk to attach to the policy. The obligation to give notice of the claim is an essential part of the trigger of cover. It is therefore of a different nature from a term which requires the insured to give notice in an occurrence-based policy, where an obligation to give insurers notice does not define the cover, but merely serves to protect insurers' interests.[85] It follows that the obligation to give notice during the policy period will be strictly enforced.[86] As Kirby J said in *FAI Insurance Ltd v Australian Hospital Care Pty Ltd*:[87]

> The centrality of notification provisions under claims made type policies has been emphasised by decisions in the United States. Thus in *Federal Deposit Insurance*

(valuers; Australia); *Nettle v Mathieson Group Pty Ltd* [2007] NSWCA 98 (engineers; Australia); *Suncorp Metway Insurance Ltd v Landridge Pty Ltd* [2005] VSCA 223 (real estate agents; Australia); *Zhang v Minox Securities Pty Ltd* [2008] NSWSC 689 (financial planning and insurance broking; Australia). Such policies are common in the United States: see the authorities in n 85 of this chapter.

[83] See para 2.04.

[84] The RICS Policy Wording requires the insured to give written notice to insurers of claims as soon as reasonably practicable and provides that this must be done 'in any event … within 10 working days after the expiry of the POLICY PERIOD'. And under the ICAEW Minimum Approved Policy Wording the insured is obliged to give insurers written notice of a claim 'as soon as reasonably practicable and in any event not later than 7 days after the end of the Period of Insurance'. The RIBA Architects Premier Policy requires the insured to give notice in writing during the period of insurance of any claim or the receipt of notice from any person of an intention to make a claim. Compliance with this obligation is a condition precedent to the right to be indemnified. In all three cases the obligation to notify insurers of claims is not part of the insuring clause and so these are not 'claims made and reported' policies.

[85] *Slater v Lawyers' Mutual Insurance Company* 278 Cal Reptr 479 (1991), citing *Pacific Employers Ins Co v Superior Court* 270 Cal Reptr 779 and *Gulf Ins Co v Dolon, Fertig and Curtis* 433 So 2d 512.

[86] *Stuart v Hutchins* (1998) 164 DLR (4th) 67, where the Ontario Court of Appeal declined to grant relief under s 129 of the Insurance Act, RSO 1990, c 18, which provides: 'Where there has been imperfect compliance with a statutory condition as to the proof of loss to be given by the insured or other matter or thing required to be done or omitted by the Insured with respect to the loss and a consequent forfeiture or avoidance of the insurance in whole or in part and the court considers it inequitable that the insurance should be forfeited or avoided on that ground, the court may relieve against the forfeiture or avoidance on such terms as it considers just.'
The period of insurance in that case expired on 31 December 1993. The claim was made against the insured on 7 December 1993, but notice of it was only given to insurers on 28 January 1994. The Court distinguished between 'imperfect compliance with a term of the policy' and 'non-compliance with a condition precedent to coverage', referring to the decision of the Supreme Court of Canada in *Falk Bros Industries Ltd v Elance Steel Fabricating Co* (1989) 62 DLR (4th) 236.
See also (1) *Graham v Continental Casualty Company* 409 NE 3d 896 (1980), at 392, where the Appellate Court of Illinois held that the requirement that notice be given to insurers during the policy period or within 60 days of its expiration was not an exclusion of cover, but 'relates directly to the coverage afforded under the policy' and (2) *Brelih v The St Paul Companies Inc* 20006 CanLII 10748 (ON SC) where Lax J held that the giving of notice was a condition precedent to cover under a 'claims made and reported' policy.

[87] [2001] HCA 38; (2001) 204 CLR 641, at [67].

Corporation v Barham [1993] USCA5 1692; 995 F 2d 600 at 604 n 9 (1993) the United States Court of Appeals commented:

'Because notice of a claim or potential claim defines coverage under a claims-made policy, we think that the notice provisions of such a policy should be strictly construed. See *Driskill v El Jamie Marine, Inc* 1988 WL 93606 (E D La Sept 7, 1988) ("In occurrence policies, the notice requirement is merely to 'aid the insurance carrier in investigating, setting, and defending claims,' but in claims-made policies, the notice requirement is as important as the requirement that the claim be asserted during the policy period. It is the transmittal of notice of the claim that invokes coverage.")'

2.49 Some policy wordings provide that notice of a claim can be given within a specified number of days after the end of the policy period.[88] This avoids the problem which might otherwise arise when a claim is first made against an insured at the very end of the policy period and the insured is unable to give notice to insurers as required. In the absence of such a provision, the problem has to be confronted. It was considered by the Ontario Court of Appeal in *Stuart v Hutchins*,[89] although in that case the claim was made over three weeks before the end of the policy period, so there had been ample time to give notice during the policy period. Nevertheless, the Court addressed the question of what would happen if a claim were first made on the last day of cover. Insurers had submitted that they would always grant a brief period of grace. The Court considered that it was not a question of grace from insurers:

> where circumstances beyond the control of the insured render it physically impossible for the insured to comply with the notice provision, general principles

---

[88] Eg in *Pioneer Road Services Ltd v QBE Insurance Ltd* [2002] NSWSC 137, 12 ANZIC 61.520 the insuring clause provided an indemnity against 'legal liability for any Claim for compensation first made against the Insured during the Period of Cover and which is notified to [insurers] during the Period of Cover'. Another clause recorded that insurers agreed that: 'the Insured may notify a Claim (in accordance with Condition 5.1 Reporting and Notice) either during the Period of Cover or within twenty-eight (28) days after its expiry, PROVIDED ALWAYS THAT such Claim was made against the Insured during the Period of Cover'.

And in *QBE Insurance Ltd v Attorney-General* [2005] NZCA 193, the insurance was against liability for: 'all sums which the Insured shall become legally liable to pay as damages ... as a result of any claim or claims made against the Insured and reported to the Insurers during the period of insurance specified in this Section (for any claim or claims first made against the Insured within ten (10) days of the expiry of the Period of Insurance specified, the Insurers will allow an additional ten (10) day notification period after expiry of the Period of Insurance specified) ...'

In *Aussie Tax Pty Ltd v Markel Capital Ltd* [2008] VSC 592, the policy allowed notice of a claim to be given 'within 30 days after the Period of Insurance provided that a replacement policy commencing from the expiry of the Period of Insurance is effected within the Scheme'.

Finally, in *Graham v Continental Casualty Company* 409 NE 3d 896 (1980), the policy provided that: 'The insurance afforded by this policy applies to errors, omissions or negligent acts which occur on or after the date stated in item 6 of the declarations (the effective date of the first policy issued and continuously renewed by the Company) provided that claim therefore is first made against the insured during this policy period or within 60 days after the expiration of this policy period.'

[89] (1998) 164 DLR (4th) 67.

of contract interpretation would come to the insured's aid … Specifically, I think it would be open to the court to construe the notice provision as containing an implied term that non-compliance due to physical impossibility would not be fatal to coverage but that the insured be given a reasonable opportunity to comply.[90]

There is obvious sense in this. However, it does involve the addition of a gloss to the otherwise unqualified words of the insuring clause requiring both the claim and notice of it to occur during the policy period.[91]

E. Notifying Circumstances and Occurrences

As has been explained, it is essential for the proper working of a 'claims made' pol-   **2.50**
icy that the insured should be entitled (as well as obliged)[92] to notify insurers in the current period of insurance of matters which he would be obliged to disclose when seeking insurance for the following period and that any claim subsequently arising from such matters should be deemed to have first been made during the current policy period. This provides an important extension to the cover provided.[93] Given that the purpose of notification clauses is to avoid the insured being deprived of cover (or only being able to obtain cover at prohibitive cost) in respect of claims which arise from matters which he is obliged to disclose, such provisions should entitle the insured to give notice of anything which he is obliged to disclose as part of his duty of good faith and so to be fully covered in relation to claims which fall within the cover from year to year. However, when construing policy terms which set the threshold as to what can (and should) be notified, the courts should not

---

[90] Ibid at [27].

[91] See further *Reid Crowther & Partners Ltd v Simcoe & Erie General Insurance Co* (1993) 99 DLR (4th) 741 at 749–50 per McLachlin J: 'Another type of restriction of coverage in "claims-made" and hybrid policies is found in what are referred to as "claims made and reported" policies. Coverage under such policies applies only to claims which are both made of the insured *and reported to the insurer* during the policy period. This type of policy creates obvious problems for insureds regarding claims discovered and/or made by third parties just before the expiry of their coverage. In his article 'Professional Liability Insurance: The Claims Made and Reported Trap' (1991), 19 *W St UL Rev* 165, Lee Roy Pierce, Jr. writes at p. 171:

"Claims made and reported policies are less expensive because it is statistically prob-able that a certain number of insureds will find it impossible or impracticable to timely report their claims. Thus, premium costs to the group are reduced because it is statisti-cally probable that many insureds (who actually encounter the insured loss) will forfeit coverage."

In Pierce's view, this situation is antithetical to the purpose of purchasing liability insurance, which is for the insured to trade a contingent loss (uncertainty) for a certain loss (the premium paid to the insurer).' (emphasis in original)

It appears that McLachlin J did not see an easy solution to the problem.

[92] Some, but not all, of the professional indemnity policies considered by the Australian Courts in recent years did not require notification, but merely permitted it.

[93] See paras 2.06–2.10.

strain in favour of the insured. This is because, as with aggregation clauses,[94] such terms can work in favour of either party. In the case of notification clauses, there may well be another clause which excludes from cover matters which should have been notified in earlier periods, so that a finding that the threshold for notification was low will work to the potential detriment of the insured. As will be shown, a pragmatic approach has been suggested.[95]

2.51 Notification provisions are also intended to work for the benefit of insurers. Prompt notification to insurers enables them to investigate potential claims at an early stage, perhaps before evidence is lost or memories fade, and to take such steps as might be available and appropriate to reduce the potential loss.[96] That is why there is usually both an obligation and an entitlement to notify.

The threshold for notification

2.52 The scope of the requirement and entitlement to notify matters which fall short of claims which have been made will depend upon the terms of the particular policy. There are three elements to most clauses: (i) what has to be or may be notified; (ii) the degree of probability of a future claim; and (iii) the extent to which the insured must or should be aware of the relevant matters. The proper protection of the interests of the insured under policies of professional indemnity insurance (and of their clients and other potential claimants) will usually be achieved by a term requiring and enabling the notification of circumstances which may give rise to a claim of which the insured is aware. However, not all policies contain terms to that effect.

2.53 When considering the various policy wordings, it is worth bearing in mind what Rix LJ said in *HLB Kidsons v Lloyd's Underwriters*:[97]

> It is not an easy matter to construct a policy on a 'claims made' basis which allows for an extension to cover future claims to mitigate the difficulty for an assured who learns during the policy year of circumstances which may give rise to a claim in the future after that year's expiry.

---

[94] Cf *Lloyds TSB General Insurance Holdings Ltd v Lloyds Bank Group Insurance Co Ltd* [2003] UKHL 48; [2003] 4 All ER 43, at [30] per Lord Hobhouse. See further para 10.19.

[95] Paras 2.83–2.84.

[96] See, for example, *Pioneer Concrete (UK) Ltd v National Employers Mutual General Insurance Association Ltd* [1985] 2 Au BR395 at 400 per Bingham J, *Moore v Canadian Lawyers Insurance Association* (1993) 105 DLR (4th) 258, at 264–5 per Hallett JA, giving the judgment of the Nova Scotia Supreme Court, Appeal Division, *Alfred McAlpine plc v BAI (Run off) Ltd* [1998] 2 Lloyd's Rep 694, at page 698 per Colman J, *J Rothschild Assurance plc v Collyear* [1999] Lloyd's Rep IR 6, at 22 per Rix J, *Bankers Insurance Co Ltd v South and Gardner* [2003] EWHC 380 (QB); [2004] Lloyd's Rep IR 1, at 7 per Buckley J, *Friends Provident Life and Pensions Ltd v Sirius International Insurance Corporation* [2004] EWHC 1799 (Comm); [2005] Lloyd's Rep IR 135, at [20] per Moore-Bick J, and *HLB Kidsons v Lloyd's Underwriters* [2007] EWHC 1951 (Comm); [2008] Lloyd's Rep IR 237, at [22] per Gloster J.

[97] [2008] EWCA Civ 1206; [2009] 1 Lloyd's Rep 8 at [121].

Occurrences

Some policies only require and enable notification of 'occurrences'.[98] For example,   **2.54**
in *National Employers Mutual General Insurance Association Ltd v Haydon*[99] the
policies in issue contained this term:

> If during the subsistence of this Policy the Insured shall become aware of any occur-
> rence which may subsequently give rise to a claim against him he shall give written
> notice to the Association of such occurrence immediately. Such notice having been
> given any such claim which may subsequently be made against the Insured arising
> out of that occurrence shall for the purposes of this Policy be deemed to have been
> made during the subsistence hereof.[100]

The difficulty with such a term is that an 'occurrence' is an event rather than a state
of affairs. Something has to have happened which has the potential to give rise to
a claim. Although insurers benefit from prompt notification, they have an obvious interest in denying the validity of a notification of a serious possible loss. An
insured may be aware of a state of affairs which could give rise to a claim against
him, but be unable to identify an 'occurrence' which could form the basis of an
effective notification. So the fact that a patient has a particular disease or condition
is not itself an occurrence. But the fact that the patient contracted that disease or
developed that condition while in the insured's hospital can be an occurrence even
if the mechanism by which the disease was contracted or the condition developed
is not known. Something has happened with the potential to give rise to a claim.[101]

Save perhaps for policies insuring medical practitioners,[102] notification clauses   **2.55**
limited to occurrences are better suited to classes of liability insurance other than

---

[98] The professional indemnity policies of the insured lawyers in *McNish & McNish v American
Home Assurance Co* (1989) 68 OR (2d) 365 and *Royal Trust Corp of Canada v American Home
Assurance Co* (1992) 90 DLR (4th) 582 required the assured to give notice to insurers of any 'happening which may give rise to a claim'. 'Happening' is equivalent to 'occurrence' in that it requires
there to be some event.
[99] [1980] 2 Lloyd's Rep 149: for the facts see para 2.13. See also *Forney v Dominion Insurance Co
Ltd* [1969] 1 WLR 928.
[100] In *St Paul Fire & Marine Insurance Company v Guardian Insurance Company of Canada* (1983)
1 DLR (4th) 342 one of the policies, which dated from 1971, entitled the insured to give notice of a
'specific occurrence'. The policies before the Court of Appeal in *Thorman v New Hampshire* [1988]
1 Lloyd's Rep 7 limited notification to 'any occurrence which may be likely to give rise to a claim'.
More recently, in *Stuart v Hutchins* (1998) 164 DLR (4th) 67, the policy entitled, but did not require,
the insured listing brokers (a form of estate agent) to give notice of 'any occurrence which may reasonably be expected to give rise to a claim against the Insured for a Wrongful Act which first occurs
during or prior to the Policy Period' of which they became aware.
[101] *FAI General Insurance Ltd v Australian Hospital Care Pty Ltd* [1999] QCA 243: for the wording of the notification clause see n 102 in this chapter. The point did not arise on the appeal to the
High Court of Australia: [2001] HCA 38; (2001) 204 CLR 641.
[102] Cf (1) *Peacock v Roberts; Guardian Insurance Co of Canada, Third Party* (1990) 67 DLR (4th)
641, where the insured was a dentist and the clause required him to give notice of 'an accident or
occurrence which may reasonably be expected to give rise to a claim hereunder', and (2) *FAI General
Insurance Ltd v Australian Hospital Care Pty Ltd* [2001] HCA 38, (2001) 204 CLR 641 on appeal
from [1999] QCA 243, where the insured operated a number of hospitals and the clause required it
to give notice 'of any occurrence which may subsequently give rise to a claim against him or them

professional indemnity insurance. In the commercial and industrial contractors combined liability policy before the Court of Appeal in *Layher v Lowe*,[103] the insured was obliged to give 'immediate notice in writing, with full particulars, of the happening of any occurrence likely to give rise to a claim'. And in *Jacobs v Coster (t/a Newington Commercials Service Station) and Avon Insurance (Third Party)*[104] the insurance was a combined all risks policy insuring a service station. The insured was obliged and entitled to give notice of any 'event [which] gives rise or is likely to give rise to a claim'. The circumstances which would give rise to a claim under such policies are likely to be events (typically accidents) so that the insured is adequately protected by the limitation of what is to be notified to occurrences.[105]

Circumstances

2.56 Nowadays policies of professional indemnity insurance usually require and enable the insured to give notice of circumstances. For example, the SRA Minimum Terms and Conditions of Professional Indemnity Insurance require professional indemnity insurance of solicitors in England and Wales to provide cover in respect of claims made against the insured during or after the period of insurance and arising from 'Circumstances' first notified to insurers during the period of insurance. 'Circumstances' are widely defined as 'an incident, occurrence, fact, matter, act or omission which may give rise to a Claim in respect of civil liability'. The RICS Policy Wording is substantially the same. These definitions reflect the broad scope of 'circumstances', which encompass but are far wider than 'occurrences'.

2.57 The ICAEW Minimum Approved Policy Wording requires and entitles the insured to give notice of 'any circumstance which may give rise to a loss or Claim' without defining 'circumstance'. Many policies of professional indemnity are in like terms. Where there is no definition of 'circumstances', the courts are likely to find that anything which would fall within the duty of disclosure on renewal constitutes a 'circumstance' for the purposes of the notification provision.

2.58 Thus in *J Rothschild Assurance plc v Collyear*[106] Rix J had to decide whether valid notice had been given of 'any circumstances of which THE ASSURED shall become aware which may give rise to a claim or loss against them or any of them'. The 'circumstances' in that case were that the insured's regulator under

---

for breach of professional duty, whether by way of act, error or omission' of which it became aware during the subsistence of the policy.

[103] [2000] Lloyd's Rep IR 510.
[104] [2000] Lloyd's Rep IR 506.
[105] For the difference between an 'accident' and an 'occurrence' see *Forney v Dominion Insurance Co Ltd* [1969] 1 WLR 928, at 934, referring to *South Staffordshire Tramways Co Ltd v Sickness and Accident Assurance Association* [1891] 1 QB 402 and *Allen v London Guarantee and Accident Co Ltd* (1912) 28 TLR 254.
[106] [1999] Lloyd's Rep IR 6.

the Financial Services Act 1986 had commissioned a report from a firm of accountants into the possible mis-selling of pensions. That review, which was not of the insured's files or specifically directed at the insured, found that only nine per cent of the files inspected were compliant with the regulator's conduct of business rules. Not all breaches of the conduct of business rules would have caused loss, but those that had done so were actionable by clients. The regulator wrote to the insured and other firms informing them of the review and stating that 'there is a problem which needs to be tackled'. The insured's solicitors wrote to insurers notifying them of the review and of the letter from the regulator. They enclosed a schedule of clients who might have claims against the insured. These circumstances were held to be sufficient for the purposes of notification, despite the fact that they did not include the intimation of any complaint by a client of the insured and no specific potential claimants were identified.

Notice of intention to make a claim

While some professional indemnity policies include notice by a third party of an **2.59** intention to make a claim within the contractual definition of 'claim',[107] others treat such notice as something of which the insured is obliged and entitled to give insurers notice. This will usually be in addition to an obligation and right to give notice of occurrences or circumstances.[108]

There may be an extension of cover both in respect of claims made which arise out **2.60** of notified circumstances or occurrences and in respect of claims made pursuant to an intention to make a claim of which notice has been given. If there is, then the result will be overlapping provisions, because notice by a third party of an intention to make a claim will certainly be a circumstance with the potential to give rise to a claim and will also almost certainly be an occurrence with that potential too. However, it may be that the requirement to give notice of receipt of notice from a third party of an intention to make a claim against the insured is solely for the benefit of insurers and carries with it no extension of cover under the policy. In the latter case, the only extension of cover is in respect of claims arising from circumstances or occurrences of which notice is given.

---

[107] See paras 2.28–2.29.

[108] Thus in *Murphy and Allen v Swinbank* [1999] NSWSC 934 the professional indemnity policy of a firm of solicitors contained the following term: 'The Assured shall give notice in writing to the Insurers as soon as is practicable of any claim the subject of the Insuring Clauses hereof made during the Period of Insurance against the Assured or of the receipt of notice from any person of any intention to make a claim against the Assured. The Assured shall also give notice in writing as soon as practicable to the Insurers of any circumstances of which the Assured is or shall become aware during the Period of Insurance which may give rise to a claim. If notice is given to the Insurers under this paragraph any claim subsequently made (whether before or after the expiration of the Period of Insurance) pursuant to such an intention to claim or arising from circumstances so notified shall be deemed to have been made at the date when such notice was given.'

2.61 The purpose and effect of an obligation to give notice of receipt of notice from a third party of an intention to make a claim are not always easy to ascertain. In *J Rothschild Assurance plc v Collyear*[109] the policy provided that:

> THE ASSUREDS shall as a CONDITION PRECEDENT to their right to be indemnified under this Policy give to the Underwriters notice as soon as possible during the period of this Policy as set forth in the Schedule:
> (a) of any circumstances of which THE ASSURED shall become aware which may give rise to a claim or loss against them or any of them;
> (b) of the receipt of any notice from any person whether written or oral of an intention to make a claim against any of them;
> Such notice having been given to the Underwriters THE ASSURED shall give to the Underwriters as soon as possible full details in writing of the circumstances which may give rise to a claim or loss against them or any of them. Any claim or loss to which that circumstance has given rise which is subsequently made after the expiration of the period specified in the First Schedule shall be deemed for the purpose of this policy to have been made during the subsistence thereof.

On one view the provision deeming any claim subsequently made to have been made during the policy period appears to be limited to claims or losses arising from notified circumstances (ie sub-clause (a)). On that view there is no provision extending cover for claims subsequently made which are made outside the policy period, after notice had been given of the intention to make such claims and notice given under sub-clause (b). Sub-clause (b) is therefore solely for the protection of insurers. However, the alternative, better view is that the provision extending cover does apply to notifications under sub-clause (b), even though its wording appears to follow that of sub-clause (a) and does not follow that of sub-clause (b). The words 'Such notice' refer to notice under either sub-clause (a) or (b).[110]

2.62 The policy in *HLB Kidsons v Lloyd's Underwriters*[111] also contained potentially overlapping obligations on the insured to give notice of circumstances which might give rise to a claim and to give notice of an intention to make a claim against the insured. General Condition 4 of the policy required and entitled the insured to give notice of circumstances which might give rise to a claim.[112] It was preceded by General Condition 3, which required the insured, as a condition precedent to

---

[109] [1999] Lloyd's Rep IR 6. The policy in *Hamptons Residential Ltd v Field* [1998] 2 Lloyd's Rep 248 and the primary layer policy in *Friends Provident Life and Pensions Ltd v Sirius International Insurance Corporation* [2004] EWHC 1799 (Comm); [2005] Lloyd's Rep IR 135; [2005] EWCA Civ 601; [2005] 2 Lloyd's Rep 517 contained similar provisions.

[110] In *Hamptons Residential Ltd v Field* [1998] 2 Lloyd's Rep 248, the equivalent provision had an additional sub-clause (c) requiring notice to be given: 'of the discovery (or reasonable cause for suspicion) of dishonesty or fraud on the part of a past or present partner director or employee of the Firm(s) whether giving rise to a claim or loss under this Policy or not'.

The decision of the Court of Appeal concerned the scope of a notice given under sub-clause (c) and proceeded upon the basis that the deeming provision applied to notifications under that sub-clause as well as under sub-clause (a).

[111] [2008] EWCA Civ 1206; [2009] 1 Lloyd's Rep 8.

[112] The relevant provision, General Condition 4, is set out in para 2.67.

cover, to give insurers notice in writing as soon as possible of, among other things, 'the receipt of notice from any party of an intention to make a claim against them'. General Condition 6 then provided:

> Any claim first notified to the Assured prior to the expiry of the date of this policy will be deemed to be dealt with under this policy provided it is properly notified to Underwriters within 15 calendar days of the expiry date.

Toulson LJ considered that General Condition 6 applied to the receipt of notice of an intention to make a claim and that it extended neither to claims actually made against the insured (which also had to be notified under General Condition 3) nor to General Condition 4.[113] This gives the words 'claims first notified' in General Condition 6 their natural meaning (because the claim is only notified, not made). On the other hand, the result is that a claim which was not made during the policy period, but of which notice was given by the third party during the policy period, is treated differently from claims made outside the policy period which arise from circumstances of which the insured became aware during the policy period. Only the former fall within General Condition 6. It is hard to see why the parties would have intended such a result.

Rix LJ interpreted General Condition 6 differently.[114] He considered that it **2.63** applied to claims first made against the insured during the policy period and had the result that claims which were not notified in accordance with General Condition 3 (ie 'as soon as possible') still fell to be dealt with as a matter of indemnification under the policy as long as insurers were notified within fifteen days of the end of the policy period. On this reading the requirement that the insured give notice to insurers of the receipt by the insured of notice from any party of an intention to make a claim against the insured in General Condition 3 is solely for the protection of insurers: the only extension of cover is under General Condition 4.

Potential to give rise to a claim

The occurrences or circumstances have to have the potential to give rise to a claim. **2.64** In some cases it will be easy to see which occurrences or circumstances have the required potential, but in others it may be more difficult. The issue was addressed by the Court of Appeal in *HLB Kidsons v Lloyd's Underwriters*.[115]

The insured in the *HLB Kidsons* case were accountants. Part of their prac- **2.65** tice involved advising on tax avoidance products. This was done through an insured company ('S@FI'). An employee of the insured ('T') became concerned about S@FI's products in two respects. T's first concern was that S@FI was not

---

[113] [2008] EWCA Civ 1206; [2009] 1 Lloyd's Rep 8 at [154].
[114] Ibid at [123].
[115] [2008] EWCA Civ 1206; [2009] 1 Lloyd's Rep 8. The decision at first instance—[2007] EWHC 1951 (Comm); [2008] Lloyd's Rep IR 237—was upheld save in one respect.

implementing its tax avoidance schemes correctly when strict compliance with the required procedure was necessary for them to be effective. This concern focused on a particular product. T's second concern was wider. T thought that some of the schemes would not work even if correctly implemented. In August 2001 T expressed his concerns in a number of strongly worded memoranda, which he sent to the insured's national executive committee and to the board of S@FI. T's first concern had some support from a Scottish tax QC.

2.66 The insured decided to set up a review and to notify insurers. They did so by sending a letter which was addressed to someone on the underwriting side of their brokers (as opposed to the claims side). The letter rehearsed what S@FI did and that its products had been validated by the opinion of one (and in some cases two) counsel. It explained that T had 'expressed the view that the Inland Revenue, if minded, could be critical of some procedures followed in certain cases' and concluded:

> The Board has taken the view that this might be regarded as material information for insurers. There is no sign of a claim arising at the present time but the Board feels that it is appropriate in the circumstances to advise what is happening and to take your instructions.

2.67 There followed a number of presentations to various insurers with varying consequences. This aspect of the *HLB Kidsons* case is addressed below.[116] In due course, a number of claims alleging that S@FI's products were flawed were made against the insured. The insured claimed that they had given notice as required by the following clause (General Condition 4):

> The Assured shall give to the Underwriters notice in writing as soon as practicable of any circumstance of which they shall become aware during the period specified in the Schedule which may give rise to a loss or claim against them. Such notice having been given any loss or claim to which that circumstance has given rise which is subsequently made after the expiration of the period specified in the Schedule shall be deemed for the purpose of this Insurance to have been made during the subsistence hereof.

One issue which arose was the identification of the circumstances which would require and entitle the insured to give notice. Were the circumstances the expression of concern by T? Or were they the underlying substance of his concerns?

2.68 When considering this point Rix LJ referred to the following example given by Sir John Donaldson MR in *Thorman v New Hampshire Insurance Co (UK) Ltd*, where the insured were architects:[117]

> A typical example would be a belated realization, based upon a study of professional journals, that perhaps he had specified inadequate foundations for a building which he had designed and which had already been erected.

---

[116] See paras 2.93–2.96, 2.98, and 2.108.
[117] [1988] 1 Lloyd's Rep 7 at 10.

Rix LJ expressed doubt that an insured's own concern, without more, that he had made a mistake, could be a relevant circumstance and pointed to the reference by Sir John Donaldson MR to a 'study of professional journals'.[118]

It should be noted, however, that the notification clause in the *Thorman* case only **2.69** provided for notice to be given of occurrences so that there had to be some identifiable event of which notice could be given. It is submitted that if the architect in the example given had realized his error without recourse to professional literature, he would have been entitled and obliged to give notice under a 'circumstances' clause, if not under an 'occurrences' clause. This result would be consistent with the purpose of such clauses, which is to enable the insured to be covered for claims arising from matters which would have to be disclosed when obtaining insurance for later periods.[119]

As for the question whether it was the expression of T's concerns or the underly- **2.70** ing substance of them which constituted the relevant circumstances in the *HLB Kidsons* case, it is suggested that the answer is to be found in the requirement that the circumstances should have the potential to give rise to a claim against the insured which would fall within the insuring clause. In the *HLB Kidsons* case, the reason why the insured was sued by former clients was not because T had expressed concerns to the insured's national executive committee or to the board of S@FI, but because there was some substance in those concerns. Had T been a client or a lawyer acting for a client, then the fact that he was expressing such concerns would have been a circumstance because the potential for a claim would have been clear. But given that T was neither a potential claimant nor acting for a potential claimant, expressions of concern by him could not of themselves be circumstances which could give rise to a claim. It was the substance of T's concerns which constituted a 'circumstance of which they [had] become aware during the period specified in the Schedule which may give rise to a loss or claim'.[120]

The need for the occurrence or circumstances to have the potential to give rise to a **2.71** claim was emphasized by the Queensland Court of Appeal in *FAI General Insurance*

---

[118] [2008] EWCA Civ 1206; [2009] 1 Lloyd's Rep 8 at [72]–[74].

[119] See paras 2.10 and 2.50. In *Gardner v Lemma Europe Insurance Company (In Liquidation)* [2014] EWHC 3674 (Ch) HH Judge David Cooke, sitting as a Judge of the High Court suggested at [28] that:

> 'A solicitor may become aware of some default on his own part even if a client is not aware of it or where a client who is aware of it has not given any indication that he is dissatisfied let alone he is seeking or intending to make a claim. He may nevertheless notify those circumstances in order to ensure that he has cover.'

[120] See the approach of Toulson LJ as to how the insured could have responded to T's concerns in the *HLB Kidsons* case [2008] EWCA Civ 1206; [2009] 1 Lloyd's Rep 8 at [143], where he set out three possible assessments of the *substance* of T's concerns.

Ltd v Australian Hospital Care Pty Ltd.[121] In that case, the insured operated a number of hospitals. During the policy period the insured became aware that a patient had contracted septicaemia while at one of its hospitals and had instructed solicitors to investigate the cause. Condition 3 of the policy provided that the insured was entitled, but not obliged, to give notice of 'any occurrence which may subsequently give rise to a claim against him for breach of professional duty' of which the insured became aware during the policy period. The Queensland Court of Appeal held that the insured had the requisite knowledge. Derrington J, with whose reasons on the issue Pincus JA agreed, said at [10]:

> It is also correct that in order to come within the terms of condition 3, the insured had to be aware of more than the mere circumstances forming the occurrence; it had to be aware of the possibility of a claim against itself for malpractice associated with those circumstances.

The facts of which the insured was aware had the necessary potential to give rise to a claim.

2.72 The potential claim must be against the insured. This is illustrated by the decision of the Federal Court of Australia in *HIH Casualty & General Insurance Australia Ltd v Della Vedova.*[122] The insured was a firm of accountants. In 1992 the insured was instructed by a client to prepare a cash flow forecast for a delicatessen business based upon information provided by the client. The cash flow projection was provided to a prospective licensee of the business who entered a license to operate it. In 1993 the insured received a number of letters from solicitors instructed by the licensee querying the accuracy of the claims made in the cash flow forecast and asking for details of the underlying assumptions and the supporting material upon which the forecast had been based. The last of these communications showed that the licensee had commenced proceedings against the licensor, but not against the insured. A claim was made against the insured early in 1994, shortly after the inception of a new policy. Insurers relied upon an exclusion of cover for loss arising out of any circumstance or occurrence of which the insured was aware at the commencement of the period of insurance. The argument was rejected: on the material of which the insured was aware, there was no indication of any intention to make a claim against the insured, as opposed to the insured's client, the licensor.[123]

---

[121] [1999] QCA 243. The issue of whether, on the facts, the insured was aware of an occurrence which might subsequently give rise to a claim against it did not arise on the appeal to the High Court of Australia: [2001] HCA 38; (2001) 204 CLR 641.

[122] [1999] FCA 456, 10 ANZIC 61.431.

[123] The same conclusion was reached in *Sayle v Jevco Insurance Co Ltd* (1984) 58 BCLR 122 (Supreme Court of British Columbia, McLachlin J). The insured real estate agent was joined to two sets of proceedings relating to the deposit for a sale transaction which had turned sour. The insured was advised by his lawyers that he was only involved as a stakeholder and this was confirmed by a court order. At the relevant time there had been no suggestion that the insured might be liable.

There is no need for the insured to have any view as to the merits of the potential **2.73**
claim or, indeed, for the potential claim to have any particular merit. It is the
potential for a claim to be made, not for it to succeed, which matters.[124]

Degree of probability of a claim

Some notification clauses in professional indemnity policies permit (and require) **2.74**
the insured to give notice of circumstances which 'may' or 'might' give rise to a
claim.[125] Others require a claim to be 'likely'.[126]

A claim will only be 'likely' if there is at least a 50 per cent chance that it will be **2.75**
made.[127] This is a high threshold and might well prevent an insured from giving
an effective notification under his current policy of a potential claim which he is
obliged to disclose when seeking insurance for the following period.

---

[124] *FAI General Insurance Ltd v Australian Hospital Care Pty Ltd* [1999] QCA 243, per Derrington
J at [10]. This was expressly stated in the term considered by Anthony Butcher QC, sitting as a deputy Official Referee in *BNP Mortgages v Page & Wells and Sun Alliance*, 16 September 1994, unre-
ported, set out in *HLB Kidsons v Lloyd's Underwriters* [2007] EWHC 1951 (Comm); [2008] Lloyd's
Rep IR 237, at [63], which was as follows: 'The Insured shall give written notice to the company
(regardless of the Insured's contribution) as soon as possible after becoming aware of circumstances
which might reasonably be expected to produce a claim *irrespective of the Insured's views as to the
validity of the claim* or on receiving information of a claim for which there may be liability under this
Insurance. Any claim arising from such circumstances shall be deemed to have been made in the
period of insurance in which such notice has been given.' (emphasis added)
[125] Eg (1) the SRA Minimum Terms and Conditions of Professional Indemnity
Insurance: 'Circumstances' defined as 'an incident, occurrence, fact, matter, act or omission
which may give rise to a Claim in respect of civil liability'; (2) ICAEW Minimum Approved Policy
Wording: 'If during the Period of Insurance the Insured becomes aware of any circumstance which
may give rise to a Claim ...'; (3) the RICS Policy Wording: 'CIRCUMSTANCES' defined as 'an
incident, occurrence, fact, matter, act or omission that might give rise to a CLAIM'.
[126] Eg (1) *Moore v Canadian Lawyers Insurance Association* (1993) 105 DLR (4th) 258 (Nova
Scotia Supreme Court, Appeal Division), where the professional indemnity policy of the insured
lawyers provided that the insured 'as soon as practicable after learning of a claim or of a circumstance which would likely give rise to a claim hereunder, shall give notice.'; (2) *Sinclair Horder
O'Malley & Co v National Insurance Co of New Zealand Ltd* [1995] LRLR 347; [1995] 2 NZLR 257
(New Zealand Court of Appeal): where the insured lawyers were required to 'give to the Company
immediate notice in writing of any circumstance, of which they shall become aware during the
subsistence hereof, which is likely to give rise to a claim against them'. The RIBA Architects Premier
Policy Wording requires and permits the insured to notify 'any circumstance or event which is likely
to give rise to a claim'.
[127] *Layher v Lowe* [2000] Lloyd's Rep IR 510 (CA), followed in *Jacobs v Coster (t/a Newington
Commercial Service Station) and Avon Insurance (Third Party)* [2000] Lloyd's Rep IR 506 (CA) and
in *Maccaferri Ltd v Zurich Insurance Plc* [2015] EWHC 1708; [2015] Lloyd's Rep IR 598. None of
these cases concerned professional indemnity insurance. In *Laker Vent Engineering Ltd v Templeton
Insurance Ltd* [2009] EWCA Civ 62; [2009] Lloyd's Rep IR 704, the parties agreed that 'likely'
meant 'probable' or 'more likely than not'.
In *Sinclair Horder O'Malley & Co v National Insurance Co of New Zealand Ltd* [1995] LRLR 347;
[1995] 2 NZLR 257, which did concern professional indemnity insurance, McKay J held that the
word 'likely' in the notification clause set out in the preceding footnote 'in this context, having
regard to the purpose of the condition, means such as raises a real risk of a claim being made against
[the insured], or such that a claim could well be made'. That is a very purposive construction. See
also *Bass Brewers v Independent Insurance Co* [2002] SLT 512, where an obligation in a property
insurance policy that the insured report 'any occurrence likely to give rise to a claim' was held to

2.76   The threshold is much lower where all that is required is that a claim may or might be made. In such cases, as Rix J said in *J Rothschild Assurance plc v Collyear*,[128] 'the test of materiality for notice is a weak one'. There is, however, a need for more than just some fanciful or speculative chance of a claim.[129] This follows from the need for there to be an occurrence or circumstance known to the insured which has the potential to give rise to a claim. Moreover, it would be contrary to the interests of both the insured and insurers if it were otherwise. It would be contrary to the interests of the insured, because of the potential impact of clauses excluding cover for claims arising from circumstances which could and should have been notified in earlier years.[130] And it would be contrary to the interests of insurers, who would receive notifications where there was no real prospect of a claim, for example when an insured sought to give a notification in very wide terms at the end of the policy period.[131]

---

require reporting of an occurrence which was 'liable' to give rise to a claim rather than 'probable'. *Layher v Lowe* and *Jacobs v Coster (t/a Newington Commercial Service Station) and Avon Insurance (Third Party)* were not referred to.

   [128] [1999] Lloyd's Rep IR 6, at 22.

   [129] *CGU Insurance Ltd v Porthouse* [2008] HCA 30; (2008) 235 CLR 103, at [34] and [75]; 14 ANZIC 61.727.

   See also *Pech v Tilgals* (1994) 94 ATC 4206, at 4217 per Dunford J: an exclusion of cover with respect to claims arising from any circumstance or circumstances which may give rise to a claim of which the insured was aware before the policy period 'does not include a bare theoretical possibility of a claim'. And in *HLB Kidsons v Lloyd's Underwriters* [2007] EWHC 1951 (Comm); [2008] Lloyd's Rep IR 237, at [73], Gloster J held that the words 'circumstance which may give rise to a claim': 'requires that the circumstance should be one which, objectively evaluated, creates a reasonable and appreciable possibility that it will give rise to a loss or claim against the assured. It is necessary to emphasise, however, that a circumstance may give rise to a loss or claim when there is a possibility or perceived possibility that, at some stage in the future, it will do so. There need not be a certainty that it will do so; there need not be a probability or likelihood that it will do so. All that need exist is a state of affairs from which the prospects of a claim (whether good or bad) or loss emerging in the future are "real" as opposed to false, fanciful or imaginary.'

   [130] In *FAI General Insurance Co Ltd v McSweeney* [1998] FCA 1789 Lindgren J, considering the effect of question 13(b)(ii) on a proposal form which asked if the partners in the insured firm of accountants were aware of 'any claim or circumstance which may give rise to a claim' said: 'In my opinion, it is not desirable to attempt to define precisely the shade of meaning signified by the expression "may give rise to a claim". The appropriate connection between the known circumstances and the claim referred to in question 13(b)(ii) is, perhaps, best described by saying that circumstances "may give rise to a claim" if they would, as at the time of the proposing of the insurance, immediately suggest to a reasonable person in the proponent insured's position who reflected upon those known circumstances, that the bringing of a claim against the insured in respect of them was a "definite risk" or a "real possibility" or "on the cards". Perhaps the notion of the "springing to mind" of the making of a claim also appropriately expresses the shade of meaning intended.'

   This passage in the judgment of Lindgren J was approved by Mallon J in *Attorney-General v Aon New Zealand Ltd* [2008] NZHC 479 at [66], although Mallon J held that 'providing there is a real or definite risk of a claim, notice is required even if the claim is not probable'. Insofar as Lindgren J's interpretation suggests a somewhat higher threshold than that propounded by Rix J in the *Rothschild* case, it is suggested that the words 'might give rise to a claim' must mean the same whether they appear in the proposal form or in a term of the policy, and that the approach of Rix J is to be preferred.

   [131] *HLB Kidsons v Lloyd's Underwriters* [2008] EWCA Civ 1206; [2009] 1 Lloyd's Rep 8 at [139] per Toulson LJ.

Some professional indemnity policies require and permit the insured to give notice **2.77** of circumstances which 'might reasonably be expected' to give rise to a claim.[132] This is a lower threshold than 'likely'.[133] It might be thought to be a higher threshold than that in clauses which require and permit the notification of circumstance which 'may' give rise to a claim. However, it might equally be thought that this wording merely gives effect to the objective element in determining whether a claim may arise from circumstances known to an insured.[134] In this regard it is noteworthy that some policies exclude claims arising from circumstances known to the insured before the policy period which the insured either knew or should reasonably have known might give rise to a claim.[135]

Awareness and understanding of the insured

Example It is convenient to address the issue as to what awareness and under- **2.78** standing an insured has to have in order to be able and obliged to notify in the context of typical policy wording. A suitable example is to be found in the ICAEW Minimum Approved Policy Wording:

> If during the Period of Insurance the Insured becomes aware of any circumstance which may give rise to a Claim …

On one reading of this clause it is sufficient that the insured becomes aware of the **2.79** circumstance during the period of insurance and not of the potential of that circumstance to give rise to a claim. That would, however, be an incorrect construction of the clause. The insured has to be aware not only of the circumstance but also of those aspects or qualities of the circumstance which cause it to have the potential to give rise to a claim. So, for example, it is not enough that an insured engineer knows that he has designed a bridge which has been built. He has to be aware of some further fact which indicates that there is reason to believe that he may face a claim in respect of his design.

It will be a question of fact whether the insured was aware of both the circumstance **2.80** and those qualities or aspects of it which cause it to have the potential to give rise to a claim. Either the insured is aware of something or he is not. However, the insured may or may not appreciate the significance of the circumstance of which

---

[132] Eg *Kajima UK Engineering Ltd v The Underwriting Insurance Company Ltd* [2008] EWHC 83 (TCC); [2008] Lloyd's Rep IR 391: 'The Insured shall give written notice to the Underwriters as soon as possible after becoming aware of circumstances which might reasonably be expected to produce a claim or on receiving information of a claim for which there may be liability under this insurance. Any claim arising from such circumstances shall be deemed to have been made in the Period of Insurance in which such notice has been given.'

[133] Ibid at [99](a) per Akenhead J.

[134] See paras 2.83–2.85.

[135] Eg *MDIS Ltd v Swinbank* [1999] Lloyd's Rep IR 516, where the policy excluded cover in respect of 'any claim or circumstance known to the Assured prior to the inception of this Certificate and which the Assured at such time knew or should have reasonably assumed might result in a claim against the Assured'.

he is aware. Viewed objectively, that circumstance may have the potential to give rise to a claim, but the insured may not himself appreciate that it does. The assessment of the potential of the circumstance of which the insured is aware to give rise to a claim is objective. If, objectively, the insured should understand that the circumstance of which he is aware has the requisite potential to give rise to a claim, then, even though he does not in fact have that understanding, he is obliged to notify. Conversely, if the insured mistakenly believes that the circumstance has the requisite potential and purports to notify, the notification will not be effective.

2.81 **The insured's awareness**   An insured professional who has been negligent will not usually appreciate that he has been negligent at the time of his negligent act, but he will be aware of his own act. The act has the potential to give rise to a claim, but the insured is unaware of this because he is not aware that he has been (or might be said to have been) negligent. All he knows is that he has done something. If that knowledge were sufficient to trigger the obligation (and entitlement) to notify, it would result in non-compliance with it and prevent the proper operation of the notification provision, which is an essential element of a claims made policy. As Hallett JA said in *Moore v Canadian Lawyers Insurance Association*:[136]

> It is one thing for a lawyer to make a mistake and not be aware that it was a mistake nor aware of its consequences; but it is quite another to have it brought to his attention that he has made an obvious error that would likely lead to a claim if not remedied. In the former situation you would not say the lawyer had an obligation to report on the basis that a reasonably prudent solicitor would have known of the mistake and reported to the insurer; that would be absurd as it would negate the coverage in the very circumstances it was intended to apply. In the latter situation, however, the lawyer ought to meet the standard of a reasonably prudent solicitor in reporting; otherwise a solicitor who has breached a duty to his client that has damaging consequences could ignore with impunity the notice requirement by stating that he did not understand that his apparent breach of duty, of which he had been made aware, would likely give rise to a claim.[137]

---

[136] (1993) 105 DLR (4th) 258 at 261.

[137] See also (1) *Kallos v Saskatchewan Government Insurance* (1983) 4 DLR (4th) 34 at 39; (2) *Royal Trust Corp of Canada v American Home Assurance Co* (1992) 90 DLR (4th) 582 at 600; (3) *Travelers Casualty and Surety Co of Canada v Sun Life Assurance Co of Canada (UK) Ltd* [2006] EWHC 2716 (Comm); [2007] Lloyd's Rep IR 619 at [35] per Christopher Clarke J, applying the law of Ontario; (4) *FAI General Insurance Co Ltd v McSweeney* [1998] FCA 1789 per Lindgren J; and (5) *Permanent Trustee Australia Ltd v FAI General Insurance Co Ltd* [1998] NSWSC 1011; (1998) 153 ALR 529 at 567–8 per Hodgson CJ, construing a clause excluding cover for 'circumstances which may give rise to a claim which are known to the insured prior to the inception of this insurance': 'The policy gives insurance against liability for breach of duty, and is a claims-made policy. If any breach of duty by the insured has occurred and damage resulted, and if a claim is subsequently brought, then ipso facto there must *at the time of the occurrence* have been circumstances which might give rise to a claim; and it is likely that the insured would have known of these circumstances at the time, although not have known that they might give rise to a claim. In my opinion, the retroactive clause should be interpreted as applying only if the insured knows the circumstances *as circumstances which might give rise to a claim*, because otherwise the clause would have the unreasonable effect of excluding many or even most circumstances that were purportedly insured against.' (emphasis in original)

It follows that the insured must be aware of something which indicates the pos-   **2.82**
sibility of a claim against him, whether he appreciates the significance of what he
is aware or not.[138]

The insured's understanding of the significance of the matters of which he is   **2.83**
aware   The significance of the matters of which the insured is aware is assessed
objectively.[139] However, as Toulson LJ observed in *HLB Kidsons v Lloyd's*
Underwriters,[140] what is being assessed objectively is a matter of opinion as to the
likelihood of a future claim. While there will be only one possible answer in some
cases, there will be other cases in which a reasonable person in the position of the
insured might have held different views as to whether there was a real possibility of
a claim rather than a remote risk. If the insured has formed a reasonable view on the
basis of the matters of which he was aware it would be wrong to penalize him for failing to notify or to hold that his notification was ineffective. Toulson LJ concluded:

> In short, in my judgment the right general approach to a policy clause which
> entitles an insured to give notification of a circumstance which may give rise to a
> claim, and thereby cause the risk to attach to that policy, is to treat the right as sub-
> ject to an implicit requirement that the circumstance may reasonably be regarded
> in itself as a matter which may give rise to a claim. The right general approach to
> a policy clause which goes further and imposes a duty on the insured to give such
> a notification is to treat it as implicitly limited, not only by the requirement that
> the circumstance may reasonably be regarded as a matter which may give rise to a
> claim, but to a circumstance which either the insured notifies or which any reason-
> able person in his position would recognise as a matter which may give rise to a
> claim and therefore requiring notification to the insurer.[141]

Toulson LJ's analysis gives effect to one of the main purposes of notification clauses   **2.84**
in 'claims made' policies, which is to secure protection for the insured against

---

See also *HIH Casualty & General Insurance Australia Ltd v Della Vedova* [1999] FCA 456 at [38];
10 ANZIC 61.431.

[138] In *Maccaferri Ltd v Zurich Insurance Plc* [2015] EWHC 1708 (Comm); [2015] Lloyd's Rep IR
594, a product liability insurance case, insurers argued that a clause requiring the insured to give
notice of an occurrence which was likely to give to a claim 'as soon as possible' required the insured
to be proactive so as to be under a duty to inquire. Knowles J rejected this argument: the words
'as soon as possible' applied merely to the promptness with which notice was to be given once the
insured had the requisite awareness.

[139] *HLB Kidsons v Lloyd's Underwriters* [2008] EWCA Civ 1206; [2009] 1 Lloyd's Rep 8 at [72]
per Rix LJ. See also *Moore v Canadian Lawyers Insurance Association* (1993) 105 DLR (4th) 258 at
261–2, *FAI General Insurance Co Ltd v McSweeney* [1998] FCA 1789, and *Attorney-General v Aon*
New Zealand Ltd [2008] NZHC 479.

[140] [2008] EWCA Civ 1206; [2009] 1 Lloyd's Rep 8, at [137]–[142].

[141] Toulson LJ's approach was considered by the Court of Appeal in *Laker Vent Engineering Ltd*
v Templeton Insurance Ltd [2009] EWCA Civ 62; [2009] Lloyd's Rep IR 704. Aikens LJ observed
at [81] in the latter case, that Toulson LJ's approach, like that of the other members of the Court of
Appeal in the *HLB Kidsons* case, was objective. This objective approach was adopted by HH Judge
Mackie QC in *Loyaltrend Ltd v Creechurch Dedicated Ltd* [2010] EWHC (Comm); [2010] Lloyd's
Rep IR 466 when considering a notification of circumstances clause in a policy of business interruption insurance.

claims which have yet to be made but which, if and when made, will arise from circumstances of which the insured is already aware and bound to disclose when seeking insurance for any later period. An insured who has formed a reasonable view as to the likelihood of a future claim should not be penalized, whether he decides to notify or not. Moreover, the implicit requirement that the circumstance may reasonably be regarded in itself as a matter which may give rise to a claim both secures the other purpose (namely to enable insurers to take whatever steps they can to avoid or reduce any loss) and protects insurers from vague or insubstantial notifications by over-cautious insureds.[142]

2.85 The recognition that, objectively, there may be more than one reasonable assessment of the likelihood of a future claim is consistent with clauses found in some professional indemnity policies excluding cover for claims arising from circumstances which the insured knew or should reasonably have considered might give rise to a claim in the future.[143] Such exclusions should not apply unless the only reasonable assessment was that a claim was sufficiently likely as to require notification. An insured who forms a reasonable view should not be penalized under them or held to have breached any obligation to give notice under an earlier policy.

2.86 Nevertheless, the insured would be well advised to err on the side of caution in any genuinely doubtful case, particularly if the threshold for notification in his policy is low. Recognition of the possibility that, in some cases, it would be objectively reasonable either to notify or not to notify should not obscure the fact that in many cases there will be only one reasonable assessment. For example, in *Moore v Canadian Lawyers Insurance Association*[144] the insured was a lawyer who had drawn up a mortgage at the request of his senior partner to secure a loan to the partner and his wife in February 1988. The mortgaged property was owned by the partner's infant son and the insured failed to obtain the necessary

---

[142] For this approach to work, the insured who has formed a reasonable view as to whether circumstances should be notified should not be held to have been in breach of his duty of disclosure in relation to later policies: see para 5.40.

[143] Eg *MDIS Ltd v Swinbank* [1999] Lloyd's Rep IR 516 noted in n 135 under para 2.77.

In *Pech v Tilgals* (1994) 94 ATC 4206 the exclusion included claims: 'Arising from any circumstance or circumstances of which You shall become aware, prior to the commencement of insurance cover under this Policy 1 and which a reasonable Accountant in Your position would at any time prior to the commencement of cover have considered may give rise to a Claim or Claims.'

In *CGU Insurance Ltd v Porthouse* [2008] HCA 30; (2008) 235 CLR 103 there was no cover for 'known circumstances', which included: 'any fact, situation or occurrence which an Insured knew before this Policy began; or a reasonable person in the Insured's professional position would have thought before this Policy began, might result in someone making an allegation against an Insured in respect of a liability, that might be covered by this Policy.'

In *Aussie Tax Pty Ltd v Markel Capital Ltd* [2008] VSC 592 there was an exclusion in respect of: 'any civil liability or loss arising from ... any circumstance of which the Practitioner ... knew, or a reasonable person in the circumstances could be expected to know, prior to the Period of Insurance, to be circumstances likely to give rise to a claim ...'

[144] (1993) 105 DLR (4th) 258.

court authorization for the mortgage. In December 1988 the mortgagee's legal officer wrote to the insured querying the validity of the mortgage and stating that he was looking to the insured to resolve the issue. The insured hoped he could obtain retrospective approval and only notified in October 1990. By then the insured's senior partner was insolvent and refused to sign an affidavit in support of an application for retrospective authorization. The Nova Scotia Court of Appeal held that the insured had had the necessary knowledge in December 1988. There was no proper basis for thinking that the court would authorize the mortgage retrospectively because the money had not been borrowed for the infant's benefit. No prudent lawyer would have formed the view which the insured did.[145]

In the same way, in *CGU Insurance Ltd v Porthouse*[146] the insured barrister had **2.87** failed to commence proceedings on behalf of his client before a change in the law came into force which had the effect of reducing the damages which his client could recover. The defendant took the point and, while it did not succeed at first instance, at the time when the insured barrister completed the proposal form an appeal was pending and the barrister knew that it had a reasonable prospect of success. Objectively, a barrister in that position should have realized that there was a real possibility that a claim would be made against him and insurers were held to be entitled to rely upon an exclusion in respect of claims arising from circumstances known before the policy began.[147]

Where the insured did obtain legal advice or should have done so, this will be **2.88** relevant to the question as to whether he should have notified. The insured in *Attorney-General v Aon New Zealand Ltd*[148] was a ministry in the New Zealand government ('MAF'). In 1995 the ministry suspended the export of woodchips, confirming this by a regulation made in 1996. The third party claimant ('AJS') started judicial review proceedings in 1997 and they resulted in the setting aside of the regulation in 1999. At that stage MAF gave notice to its insurers. A claim for damages was subsequently made by AJS. In proceedings between MAF and its brokers the issue arose whether a notification should have been made in earlier years. The argument that notification should have been made in 1996 failed. At that stage MAF considered that a claim for judicial review might be made, but on grounds which, according to legal advice it received, would not provide a proper basis for a claim for damages, so that a claim for damages was no more than a remote possibility.

---

[145] See also *Hellyer v Amp General Insurance Ltd* [2002] NSWSC 866, 12 ANZIC 61.544 (for the facts see n 49 under para 2.27). Smart AJ held that the circumstances of which the insured were aware made a claim probable.

[146] [2008] HCA 30; (2008) 235 CLR 103.

[147] The relevant wording is set out in n 143 under para 2.85.

[148] [2008] NZHC 479. This was a claim against the brokers following earlier proceedings between the insured and insurers: *QBE Insurance Ltd v Attorney-General* [2005] NZCA 193.

2.89 However, when the judicial review proceedings were commenced in 1997 the basis of the challenge to the decision and regulation was different from that anticipated by MAF in 1996. The new basis of the challenge could lead to a claim for damages. Holding that MAF should have notified at this stage, Mallon J said:

> A reasonable person in the position of MAF would have sought advice on the prospects of this proceeding succeeding and therefore ought to have known that there was a reasonable possibility that it would succeed. MAF also knew that it was likely that AJS had suffered loss from the export ban. If the judicial review proceeding succeeded a reasonable person in the position of MAF ought to have known that there was a reasonable possibility that a damages claim would be brought.

2.90 In *J Rothschild Assurance plc v Collyear*,[149] Rix J expressed the view that it was legitimate to test a view as to what the future may bring against what eventually happened. In that case, the insured's view that it was aware of circumstances which might give rise to claims against it had proved to be all too correct. Given that it is unlikely, if not impossible, that a dispute as to whether the insured was aware of sufficient indications of a possible claim would come before a court if there had not subsequently been a claim, this approach will almost always favour the party who contends that there were sufficient indications. It is important to assess the risk of a claim on the basis of the insured's awareness at the time and not to apply hindsight.[150]

Making a notification

2.91 It is not enough that the insured has the awareness needed to make a notification. He has to make it. Effective notification is essential if the risk of subsequent claims is to attach to an insured's current policy and not to be excluded from cover under later policies.[151] Failure to make an effective and comprehensive notification can prejudice not only the insured but also the interests of third party claimants.

Method

2.92 Some policies will specify how notice of a claim or of a potential claim is to be given to insurers. Such provisions, and the potential consequences of failure to comply with them, are considered below in the context of notification of claims.[152]

2.93 Where the policy does not prescribe how a notification should be made, any communication (or, if written notice is required, any written communication) by the insured which conveys to insurers that a notification is being made will be effective.

---

[149] [1999] Lloyd's Rep IR 6, at 23, citing *Bank Line Ltd v Arthur Capel and Company* [1919] AC at 454, a case concerning frustration.

[150] *Attorney-General v Aon New Zealand Ltd* [2008] NZHC 479, at [72] per Mallon J.

[151] *HLB Kidsons v Lloyd's Underwriters* [2008] EWCA Civ 1206; [2009] 1 Lloyd's Rep 8, at [132] per Toulson LJ.

[152] See paras 11.03–11.19.

Thus in *Friends Provident Life and Pensions Ltd v Sirius International Insurance Corporation*[153] the insured wrote to insurers at its broker's address during renewal negotiations stating that it was unaware of any circumstances which were likely to give rise to a claim save for, among other things:

> Pension transfers and opt outs which are a matter of public record and relate to all pensions providers. Detailed investigation will be conducted into pensions related transactions in accordance with any SIB/LAUTRO guidelines and notification of any potential claims given to underwriters in the usual way.

This letter was addressed to the insurers who were considering whether to insure the insured for the next period, who included a number of primary insurers who were on risk for the current period. Moore-Bick J, whose judgment on this point was fully endorsed by the Court of Appeal, held that this was an effective notice to those of the current insurers to whom it was addressed.

2.94 The letter in the *Friends Provident* case was presented to the insurers' placing side rather than to the insurers' claims side. This will not always be effective to notify insurers.[154] So in *HLB Kidsons v Lloyd's Underwriters*[155] the insured drafted a letter to be put before insurers in the terms set out in para 2.66. That letter was put before insurers on the placing side and was not understood by them to be a notification of a circumstance which might give rise to a claim against the insured, not least because the letter stated that there was 'no sign of a claim arising at the present time'. This first notification was held to have been ineffective.

2.95 The distinction between the *Friends Provident* case and the *HLB Kidsons* case is a fine one and turns upon the precise wording of the two letters. However, the method of presentation to insurers was important too. In the *HLB Kidsons* case, the same letter was presented to insurers on a second occasion. This time the presentation was made to the claims side and the letter accompanied a 'claim circumstance notification bordereau'. The Court of Appeal held that this second notification was effective.[156] The letter did not purport to give notice of a claim, but to provide 'information of a circumstance which might give rise to a claim'. This was confirmed by the bordereau, which, while it could not go further than the letter itself, made it clear what was being done. Obviously, a communication to insurers' claims side will be more readily found, objectively, to have been a notification than will a communication to the underwriting side.

---

[153] [2004] EWHC 1999 (Comm); [2005] Lloyd's Rep IR 135; [2005] EWCA Civ 601; [2006] Lloyd's Rep IR 45.

[154] In *HLB Kidsons v Lloyd's Underwriters* [2008] EWCA Civ 1206; [2009] 1 Lloyd's Rep 8, Rix LJ referred to the decisions in the *Friends Provident* and *HLB Kidsons* cases on this point and observed that the *Friends Provident* case showed that 'the presentation of a notice of circumstances on the placing side might not necessarily be fatal to the effectiveness of such a notice'.

[155] [2007] EWHC 1951 (Comm); [2008] Lloyd's Rep IR 237. This point did not arise on the appeal.

[156] [2008] EWCA Civ 1206; [2009] 1 Lloyd's Rep 8, at [80]–[89].

2.96 Where there are a number of insurers, each with its own line or layer, notification to one will not be effective notification to the others unless the others have made the insurer to whom notification is made their agent for this purpose.[157]

2.97 In the same way, the insured must himself make the notification, whether personally or through an agent. In many cases where there are a number of separate persons insured under a single, composite policy, notification by one insured will be on behalf of all.[158] However, this will not always be the case. In *John Connell Holdings Pty Ltd v Mercantile Mutual Holdings Ltd*,[159] where two related companies with common directors had separate professional indemnity policies, notification by one company under its policy was not an effective notification by the other company under its policy.

Contents

2.98 The range of matters which can fall within a notification clause is extremely wide. The insured may not himself know the precise nature or scope of a complaint threatened against him. His obligation and right are to notify insurers of whatever the relevant matters are. If there is sufficient probability that those matters will give rise to a claim, then the notification should be effective.[160] So, in *Kajima UK Engineering Ltd v The Underwriting Company Ltd*,[161] when considering a

---

[157] *Friends Provident Life and Pensions Ltd v Sirius International Insurance Corporation* [2004] EWHC 1799 (Comm); [2005] Lloyd's Rep IR 135; [2005] EWCA Civ 601; [2006] Lloyd's Rep IR 45 (notice to primary insurers sufficient to extend cover under both primary and excess policies). *HLB Kidsons v Lloyd's Underwriters* [2008] EWCA Civ 1206; [2009] 1 Lloyd's Rep 8 (notification to some insurers not effective as against others).

[158] In the case of large partnerships or other organizations, there will usually be a designated partner who is authorized to receive information as to potential notifications from others and to make a notification if appropriate: *HLB Kidsons v Lloyd's Underwriters* [2007] EWHC 1951 (Comm); [2008] Lloyd's Rep IR 237, at [68]. Notification by such a designated person will usually be effective for all other insured. It is, however, possible for a notification to be made only on behalf of one of a number of insured, for example where that insured is the only potential defendant to any claim which might arise from the notified matters.

[159] [1999] QCA 429.

[160] *HLB Kidsons v Lloyd's Underwriters* [2008] EWCA Civ 1206; [2009] 1 Lloyd's Rep 8, at [86] per Rix LJ. The decision of the Court of Appeal in the *HLB Kidsons* case that the second notification was effective (see para 2.95) involved overturning the decision of Gloster J on that point: [2007] EWHC 1951 (Comm); [2008] Lloyd's Rep IR 237. Gloster J had held at [205](iii) that the second notification was ineffective because: 'there is no identification of any error, act or omission, or potentially negligent or otherwise wrongful conduct on the part of the assured; there is no identification of any victim or possible claimant; there is no mention of the possibility that any client of the firm or S@FI, or other individual, might suffer loss as a result of any identified error, act or omission, or potentially negligent or otherwise wrongful conduct on the part of the assured; there is no statement in the body or the heading of any of the letters that the assured is in fact by means of those letters notifying a circumstance which may give rise to a claim, unlike other letters sent by Kidsons in respect of other unrelated circumstances, and which were (and were at the time) accepted by Underwriters to constitute notifications under the policy ...'
The Court of Appeal did not accept that a notification needed to contain this degree of detail and specificity in order to be effective.

[161] [2008] EWHC 83 (TCC); [2008] Lloyd's Rep IR 391. The clause provided: 'The Insured shall give written notice to the Underwriters as soon as possible after becoming aware of circumstances

notification clause in a policy insuring a design and building contractor, Akenhead J said:[162]

> There is no restriction in [the clause] as to what circumstances might be notified. They may be specific or general. They may relate to damage, symptoms of damage, or actual, potential or perceived defects, liabilities or losses. It is not necessary that the notified circumstances will probably give rise to a claim; it is enough that they might reasonably be expected to do so. The circumstances might impinge upon a particular project although they arise on another. An example put to Counsel was the design and build contractor to whose notice it comes that a design engineer working for it on other projects has been extensively negligent on other projects. It might then be legitimate to notify the insurers in respect of the particular project to the effect that it has come to the insured's attention that a named individual's possible incompetence on other projects might well have been repeated on the particular project in question. It is impossible and unhelpful to produce a finite definition of circumstances which might reasonably be expected to produce a claim because, given the factual permutations and possibilities, the type of such circumstances may be almost infinite.

The example given by Akenhead J of a design engineer whose negligence on other **2.99** projects comes to the notice of a design and build contractor is instructive. It is not unheard of for insurers to exclude cover for claims arising from the conduct of specified individuals.[163] If a notification clause is to achieve one of its main purposes, it should enable an insured to give notice under his current policy of the potential for claims arising from the acts of a specific individual so long as there are some particular grounds to query that individual's competence. In the same way, Akenhead J considered that it should be possible to give notification of a 'hornet's nest' or 'can of worms'.[164] In such cases, the insured will not know precisely what claims might be made, but will be aware of matters which suggest that some claim or claims against him might be made. What matters is that the insured is aware of and gives notice of something which fits the description 'may subsequently give rise to a claim'.[165] A notification should not be held to be ineffective because there is scope for argument as to its precise width.[166]

It follows that in appropriate circumstances an insured should be able to give notice **2.100** of circumstances which might give rise to a large number of claims, even though

---

which might reasonably be expected to produce a claim or on receiving information of a claim for which there may be liability under this insurance. Any claim arising from such circumstances shall be deemed to have been made in the Period of Insurance in which such notice has been given.'

[162] Ibid at [99](a)–(b).

[163] Eg *TSB Bank plc v Robert Irving and Burns* [2000] 2 All BR 826, discussed in paras 12.43–12.48, where the professional indemnity insurance of a firm of surveyors and valuers excluded from cover claims in respect of work carried out by a named individual.

[164] [2008] EWHC 83 (TCC); [2008] Lloyd's Rep IR 391, at [99](c).

[165] *FAI General Insurance Ltd v Australian Hospital Care Pty Ltd* [1999] QCA 243, per Chesterman J at [14].

[166] *HLB Kidsons v Lloyd's Underwriters* [2008] EWCA Civ 1206; [2009] 1 Lloyd's Rep 8, at [87] per Rix LJ.

he is not able to provide specific details. The classic example of this is *J Rothschild Assurance plc v Collyear*,[167] where the circumstances indicated a sufficient possibility of claims against the insured by individuals to whom the insured had given advice about pensions.[168] The notification considered in *HLB Kidsons v Lloyd's Underwriters*[169] did not identify specific clients, but it was not disputed that, if and when claims were made about the potential errors in procedures which were notified, those claims would fall within the scope of the notification. These decisions were followed in *McManus v European Risk Insurance Co*.[170] In that case the insured had received claims about a number of files. Realizing that they appeared to share a number of features, the insured commissioned an investigation which identified thirty-two files as showing a consistent pattern of breaches. The insured made a notification in the widest possible terms. Insurers contended that the only circumstances which had been effectively notified under the policy were the thirty-two files. The Judge, Ms Vivien Rose, sitting as a Deputy Judge of the Chancery Division, held that insurers had taken too restrictive view of the scope of the notification. She noted that in the *Rothschild* and *HLB Kidsons* cases the notifications had not referred to specific transactions from which later clams arose. Nor had they identified specific defects. On the facts before her she held that insurers' position was 'misconceived and at odds with the case law'. It was possible that future claims relating to other transactions would arise from the circumstances which had been notified, although she declined to make a declaration which defined the class of future claims which would do so.[171]

2.101   The ability to make an effective notification without being able to provide insurers with specific details is important both because of the need to be able to give effective notice under the current policy of matters which would have to be disclosed when seeking insurance for the following period or periods and because, as discussed below,[172] notification clauses often require the insured to give notice of circumstances within a short time of becoming aware of them, whether immediately or as soon as practicable or within some other time frame. Compliance with such time limits may be a condition precedent to the right to an indemnity.[173] An insured who spends time investigating circumstances in order to be able to provide insurers with chapter and verse might find that he has lost the right to notify.[174] The insured should give prompt notice of the matters of which he is aware and

---

[167] [1999] Lloyd's Rep IR 6.
[168] See para 2.58.
[169] [2006] EWCA Civ 1206; [2009] 1 Lloyd's Rep 8. For the relevant facts see paras 2.65–2.67.
[170] [2013] EWHC 18 (Ch); [2013] Lloyd's Rep IR 533.
[171] Ibid at [43]–[45]. The decision not to make a declaration was upheld on appeal: *McManus v European Risk Insurance Co* [2013] EWCA Civ 169; [2014] Lloyd's Rep IR 171.
[172] Paras 2.116–2.120.
[173] See paras 7.100–7.106.
[174] *HLB Kidsons v Lloyd's Underwriters* [2008] EWCA Civ 1206; [2009] 1 Lloyd's Rep 8, at [87] per Rix LJ.

then, if necessary, make further notifications as and when he becomes aware of further matters.[175]

An insured may not know the nature or scope of potential claims against him. On **2.102** the facts of *Thorman v New Hampshire Insurance Co (UK) Ltd*[176] the insured firm was aware that a protective writ was being issued against it. The potential for a claim against the insured was obvious, but the insured did not know what claim or claims would eventually be made if and when the writ was served. All the insured could do (apart from informing insurers of its own belief as to the likely basis or scope of any claim) was to notify insurers that a protective writ had been issued.[177] In the same way, in *J Rothschild Assurance plc v Collyear*[178] a 'block' notification was held to be effective, invalidating the standard form objection to such notifications in the early and mid-1990s.[179]

The RICS Policy Wording requires the insured to give notice 'as soon as reason- **2.103** ably practicable' of any 'CIRCUMSTANCES' of which the insured first becomes aware during the policy period, together with specific particulars of the relevant circumstance 'where possible'.[180] If it is not possible to give all or even any of the specified particulars, a valid notice may still be given.

The RICS Policy Wording also contains a provision requiring the insured to pro- **2.104** vide 'such further information as INSURERS may reasonable require'. An equivalent provision is found in many, but not all, professional indemnity policies. For example, in *Friends Provident Life and Pensions Ltd v Sirius International Insurance Corporation*[181] the obligation in the primary policy to give notice of 'any circumstance of which the assured shall become aware and which may give rise to a claim or loss against them or any of them' was followed by the following provision:

> Such notice having been given to underwriters the assured shall give to underwriters as soon as possible full details in writing of the circumstances which may give rise to a claim or loss against them or any of them.[182]

---

[175] *Kajima UK Engineering Ltd v The Underwriting Insurance Company Ltd* [2008] EWHC 83 (TCC); [2008] Lloyd's Rep IR 391 at [99](e).

[176] [1988] 1 Lloyd's Rep 7. For the facts see para 2.40.

[177] Cf *FAI General Insurance Co Ltd v Australian Hospital Care Pty Ltd* [1999] QCA 243, per Derrington J at [10]–[11].

[178] [1999] Lloyd's Rep IR 6, at 22. For the relevant facts see para 2.58.

[179] *Alexander Forbes Europe Ltd v SBJ Ltd* [2002] EWHC 3121 (Comm); [2003] Lloyd's Rep IR 432, at 438.

[180] This provision is discussed further in para 2.142.

[181] [2004] EWHC 1799 (Comm); [2005] Lloyd's Rep IR 135; [2005] EWCA Civ 601; [2006] Lloyd's Rep IR 45.

[182] The same provision appeared in the policies considered in *Hamptons Residential Ltd v Field* [1997] 1 Lloyd's Rep 302 and [1998] 2 Lloyd's Rep 248, and *J Rothschild Assurance plc v Collyear* [1999] Lloyd's Rep IR 6. In *Total Graphics Ltd v AGF Insurance Ltd* [1997] 1 Lloyd's Rep 599, as well as requiring the insured to give notice of any circumstance which might subsequently give rise to a claim against him, the policy provided that the insured 'shall upon request, give to the Insurers such information and assistance as the Insurers may reasonably require'. A similar provision appeared in the solicitors' indemnity policy considered in *Schipp v Cameron* [1998] NSWSC 997.

And in *Moore v Canadian Lawyers Insurance Association*[183] an insured who had given notice of 'a circumstance which would likely give rise to a claim' to a nominated person was subject to this further obligation:

> The Insured shall furnish promptly thereafter to such person such information as the Insurer may reasonably require and is in the Insured's power to give ...

Such provisions enable the insured to give notice promptly and, where the insured does not know the specific details of the potential claim or claims, without providing such details, while enabling insurers to obtain such further details as the insured is able to provide.[184]

2.105　The insured must be aware of a matter with the requisite degree of potential to give rise to a claim in order to give an effective notice of it. It follows that a general, vague concern that there might be some future claim would not form the basis of an effective notification.[185] And an insured cannot inflate his awareness of a matter which indicates the potential for a particular claim into a more general notification of the risk of other claims.[186]

2.106　The insured may not wish to disclose to insurers the full potential for claims of which the insured is aware. The insured may take the view that the chances of future claims are low and that, while it would be prudent to make some form of notification to insurers, it would be in the insured's interests to avoid, if possible, informing insurers fully if this might result in higher premiums in future years or in difficulties in obtaining cover. This will rarely, if ever, be a sensible course to adopt. While the point was not decided in *HLB Kidsons v Lloyd's Underwriters*,[187] Toulson LJ indicated a willingness to accept that in an insurance policy which contained a notification clause it was 'impliedly incumbent on the insured to see that any such notification is a fair, if summary, presentation of what the insured knows' and that a notification which was deliberately misleading or economical

---

[183] (1993) 105 DLR (4th) 258.

[184] In *Jesuit Fathers of Upper Canada v Guardian Insurance Company of Canada* (2006) 267 DLR (4th) 1, the policy conditions included the following: '*Notice of Accident or Occurrence.* When an accident or occurrence takes place or upon the Insured becoming aware of any alleged injury to which this insurance applies, written notice of such accident, occurrence or injury shall be given by or on behalf of the Insured to the Insurer or any of its authorized agents as soon as practicable. Such notice shall contain particulars sufficient to identify the Insured and *reasonably obtainable information* respecting the time, place and circumstances of the accident, occurrence or injury, the names and addresses of the injured and of available witnesses and particulars of the damaged property.' (emphasis added).

[185] *Kajima UK Engineering Ltd v The Underwriting Insurance Company Ltd* [2008] EWHC 83 (TCC); [2008] Lloyd's Rep IR 391 at [99](d).

[186] *HLB Kidsons v Lloyd's Underwriters* [2008] EWCA Civ 1206; [2009] 1 Lloyd's Rep 8, at [139] per Toulson LJ: 'an insured at the end of a policy period may have an incentive to give a notification in the widest possible terms for which there may be no real justification. The insurer would be entitled to refuse to accept such a purported notification.'

[187] [2008] EWCA Civ 1206; [2009] 1 Lloyd's Rep 8.

with the truth should be invalid.[188] Were the point to be taken and argued, a court might well adopt this approach.

Scope

The scope of any notification depends upon what the words by which it was made **2.107** would have conveyed to a reasonable person in the position of the recipient. It is then a question of fact whether any claim subsequently made against the insured arises out of the subject matter of the notification.

So in the *HLB Kidsons* case the insured argued that the effective, second noti- **2.108** fication encompassed not only potential claims arising from possible errors in procedures implementing tax avoidance schemes, but also claims involving more fundamental concerns as to the soundness of the schemes themselves.[189] Rejecting this argument, Rix LJ held that a 'reasonable reader' of the insured's letter would have formed the view that the only concern which was being notified to insurers related to procedures and not to the schemes themselves.[190]

When making a notification the insured should be communicating the matters **2.109** of which it is aware and which have the requisite potential to give rise to a claim. These may be a combination of the specific and the general. The fact that specific matters are notified should not obscure the fact that a more general notification is also being made. This is illustrated by the decision of the Court of Appeal in *Hamptons Residential Ltd v Field*.[191] In that case the professional indemnity policy also included some fidelity cover.[192] In relation to that cover the insured firm of surveyors was required and entitled to give notice:

> of the discovery (or reasonable cause for suspicion) of dishonesty or fraud on the part of a past or present partner director or employee of the Firm(s) whether giving rise to a claim or loss under this Policy or not.

Having given such notice, the insured was obliged to provide insurers with full details of the circumstances which might give rise to a claim or loss against them as soon as possible. The insured discovered that one of its employees had been complicit in a fraud on a building society. It gave notice, providing details of the particular fraud, in a memorandum which was headed with the name of the defrauded building society. Some time later the insured became aware of a second

---

[188] Ibid at [147]. At [65] Rix LJ considered that the insured's subjective intention might be relevant, but did not decide the point. Sir Richard Buxton's dissenting judgment that the second notification was ineffective was based on the fact that the insured in the *HLB Kidsons* case had sought to avoid making a formal notification by their letter to insurers.

[189] See paras 2.65–2.67 for the facts.

[190] [2008] EWCA Civ 1206; [2009] 1 Lloyd's Rep 8, at [91]. See also the judgment of Toulson LJ at [144].

[191] [1998] 2 Lloyd's Rep 248.

[192] As to which see paras 8.61–8.62.

fraud on another lender committed by the same employee and informed the insurers of it. The insurers accepted liability to indemnify in relation to the first fraud, but not the second.

2.110 The Court of Appeal held that the memorandum of notification had operated on two levels. At one level it had been a general notification of the discovery of the fraud of the employee. This necessarily involved the risk that the fraudulent employee had been dishonest in respects of which the insured was not yet aware. Thus, on the general level, there was a notification which encompassed all future claims and losses resulting from that employee's dishonesty. The memorandum also included further details in relation to the one claim of which the insured was aware at the time, namely that by the named building society. In providing this specific information the insured was complying with its obligation to provide full details of the circumstances which might give rise to a claim or loss. This did not limit the scope of the more general notification.

2.111 The decision in the *Hamptons Residential* case did not involve any choice between a narrow and a broad interpretation of the notification, but the objective analysis of the memorandum in the light of the relevant provisions of the policy. In any given case, it is not a question of preferring a narrow or a broad interpretation, but of the objective interpretation of the words used in the context in which they were used.[193] That context includes the fact that the insured may himself be uncertain of the scope of the matters which he is notifying[194] and that a notification should not be ineffective merely because there is scope for argument as to its precise scope.[195] In this regard, it may be legitimate to have regard as to what matters the insured was aware of at the time of the notification. Clearly the insured could not notify matters of which he was not aware and it will usually be reasonable to assume that he was trying to notify insurers of those matters of which he was aware,[196] although consideration of what the insured was trying to notify may introduce an unwarranted degree of subjectivity.

2.112 If and when a claim is eventually made against the insured, it must arise from the notified matters, rather than being related to them. In other words 'there must be some causal, as opposed to some coincidental, link between the notified circumstances and the claim'.[197] Whether it does so is a matter of fact in each case. The

---

[193] *Kajima UK Engineering Ltd v The Underwriting Insurance Company Ltd* [2008] EWHC 83 (TCC); [2008] Lloyd's Rep IR 391 at [99](h).

[194] See para 2.102.

[195] *HLB Kidsons v Lloyd's Underwriters* [2008] EWCA Civ 1206; [2009] 1 Lloyd's Rep 8, at [87] per Rix LJ.

[196] *Kajima UK Engineering Ltd v The Underwriting Insurance Company Ltd* [2008] EWHC 83 (TCC); [2008] Lloyd's Rep IR 391, at [99](f) per Akenhead J.

[197] *Kajima UK Engineering Ltd v The Underwriting Insurance Company Ltd* [2008] EWHC 83 (TCC); [2008] Lloyd's Rep IR 391, at [99](h).

decision of the Court of Appeal of Queensland in *John Connell Holdings Pty Ltd v Mercantile Mutual Holdings Ltd*[198] provides a helpful illustration.

In the *John Connell* case, the relevant insured was a company of civil and structural **2.113** engineers ('JCH'). JCH was related to another company ('Conasoc'), which had designed a warehouse building and acted as consulting engineer during its construction. The warehouse suffered from movement, initially thought to be related to the movement of a pier. It was suggested that JCH had been remiss in interpreting the soils report. This was notified to insurers in May 1980. Proceedings were commenced against JCH by the owner of the warehouse in February 1983. The claim against JCH was misconceived, being for allegedly negligent design of the foundations of the warehouse, as it was Conasoc and not JCH which had produced the design. This claim, although misconceived, fell within the scope of the notification of May 1980.

In February 1989 the building owner reformulated its claim against JCH. **2.114** Abandoning its original claim, the owner now alleged that JCH had given it negligent advice when it purchased the building in May 1980. The negligent advice was that the movement of the pier was localized and could be easily remedied. Rejecting the insured's argument that this reformulated claim also fell within the scope of the notification of May 1980, de Jersey CJ, with whom McPherson JA agreed, adopted the following passage from the judgment at first instance:

> The claim articulated in 1989 against JCH does not, in my opinion, arise out of the occurrence notified in 1980. Designing inadequate foundations because of a negligent failure to appreciate the ground conditions is altogether different from a negligent failure to appreciate and advise that the foundations designed by someone else were inadequate. The occurrence was negligence in designing. The claim was negligence in not deducing that the design was flawed. The one does not arise out of the other. It is true that the occasion for the giving of the allegedly negligent advice would not have existed had there not been a problem with the foundations. But this is, in my view, an insufficient connection between the negligent design of the foundations and the negligent advice that the movement in the pier was not a serious problem. The policy provides cover against a claim for breach of professional duty by reason of negligence. When notification of an occurrence is given it is notification of such an occurrence that might give rise to a claim for breach of duty by reason of negligence. The duty with which the notified occurrence is concerned is quite different to the duty breach of which founded the claim. The duty to take care in designing foundations and the duty to advise whether an existing building is sound are wholly different in content, time of performance and identity

---

[198] [1999] QCA 429. The relevant term provided: 'If during the subsistence hereof the Insured shall become aware of any occurrence which may subsequently give rise to a claim against them for breach of professional duty as specified in the Schedule by reason of any negligent act, error or omission and shall during the subsistence hereof give written notice to the Company of such occurrence, then any such claim which may subsequently be made against the Insured arising out of that negligent act, error or omission shall for the purposes of this Policy be deemed to have been made during the subsistence hereof.'

of obligee. The difference in the description of the duties provides an indication that the claim did not arise out of the occurrence of which notice was given. The negligent advice does not 'spring from' carelessness in reading a soils report or designing foundations. It was not 'caused by' the negligent design. That alleged negligence did no more than give rise to the circumstances in which the advice was sought.[199]

2.115   Had JCH only been aware of no more than that there was a potential claim against it in relation to the movement of the warehouse and given notice accordingly, then the result might well have been different. But JCH was aware that the potential claim concerned alleged misinterpretation of the soils report (and so related to the design of the foundations), rather than to alleged failure to appreciate and advise upon the movement of the warehouse once it had been constructed.

Timing

2.116   There will usually be one or more provisions as to the time by which a notification must be made. At present, we are concerned with what the requirements are, rather than whether compliance with them is a condition precedent to obtaining an extension of cover in respect of claims arising from the matters notified.[200] Requirements fall into two categories: (1) requirements related to the time at which the insured first has the necessary awareness; and (2) requirements by reference to the period of cover. It is possible for both sorts of requirement to be present in the same policy.

2.117   There are a variety of terms in the first category. For example, the insured may be required to make a notification 'as soon as possible', 'as soon as practicable', or 'immediately'. Once he is aware of the relevant matters and either does appreciate or should appreciate that they have the requisite potential to give rise to a claim, the insured is obliged to notify insurers in accordance with the wording in his policy. There is some scope for argument as to what, in practice, is meant by 'as soon as possible', 'as soon as practicable', and 'immediately'. All such wordings impart a degree of urgency, 'immediately' more so than the others. Their practical requirements are considered further below in the context of the insured's requirement to give notice of claims.[201]

2.118   It will be a matter of the construction of the particular policy as a whole whether compliance with an obligation to give notice is a condition precedent or not.[202] This issue

---

[199] See also (1) *Kajima UK Engineering Ltd v The Underwriting Insurance Company Ltd* [2008] EWHC 83 (TCC); [2008] Lloyd's Rep IR 391, where the notification was held to be limited to some specific matters, rather than to wider concerns; and (2) *Gardner v Lemma Europe Company Ltd (In Liquidation)* [2014] EWHC 3674 (Ch), where, had a claim been made by one client (as to which see para 2.122), there would have been no cover in respect of the costs of defending disciplinary proceedings brought in relation to similar transactions where the insured solicitor had acted for different clients, because those proceedings did not arise from the first client's claim.

[200] As to which, see paras 7.100–7.106.

[201] See paras 11.13–11.16.

[202] *Cox v Bankside Members Agency Ltd* [1995] 2 Lloyd's Rep 437, at 453 per Phillips J, approving what is now para [20-037] of *MacGillivray* (see n 20).

is addressed in **Chapter 7**.[203] An English Court will not readily accede to a construction which would entitle the insured to make an effective notification so as to obtain an extension of cover at a time of the insured's choosing well after the end of the policy period.[204] However, an insured who first becomes aware of matters with the requisite potential to give rise to a claim at the end of the policy period may be able to make an effective notification after the policy period so long as he complies with a requirement as to timing which is not fixed by reference to the policy period.[205]

The second category of requirements as to the timing of notification is by reference **2.119** to the policy period. The term can require the notification to be made during the policy period itself[206] or within a specified number of days of the end of the policy period.[207]

---

[203] See paras 7.100–7.106.

[204] *HLB Kidsons v Lloyd's Underwriters* [2008] EWCA Civ 1206; [2009] 1 Lloyd's Rep 8, at [109], [120], and [121] per Rix LJ and [152] per Toulson LJ.

[205] Ibid at [125] per Rix LJ. At [157]–[160] Toulson LJ stated that he was attracted to an argument, which was not pressed, to the effect that the notification had to be made during the policy period. With respect, while many policies contain an express provision to that effect, it would be wrong to imply such a term, particularly where the express terms as to the timing of notification appear on their face to allow notification outside the policy period. In the *HLB Kidsons* case the requirement was to make a notification 'as soon as practicable'. That might well be after the end of the policy period.

In *Sinclair Horder O'Malley & Co v National Insurance Co of New Zealand Ltd* [1995] LRLR 347; [1995] 2 NZLR 257, the period of insurance ended at 4 pm on 31 March. The notification provision was as follows: 'The Insured shall give to the Company immediate notice in writing of any circumstance, of which they shall become aware during the subsistence hereof, which is likely to give rise to a claim against them. Such notice having been given, any claim, to which that circumstance has given rise, which may be made after the expiration of the period specified in the Schedule shall be deemed for the purpose of this Policy to have been made during the subsistence hereof.' The New Zealand Court of Appeal held that, so long as the notice was given immediately, it did not need to be given before the end of the policy period at 4 pm on 31 March.

[206] Eg the policies in *Cox v Bankside Members Agency Ltd* [1995] 2 Lloyd's Rep 437 (Lloyd's managing and members' agents; notice to be given during the period of insurance); *FAI Insurance Ltd v Australian Hospital Care Pty Ltd* [2001] HCA 38; (2001) 204 CLR 641 (insurance of hospital; notice to be given during the subsistence of the policy); *Friends Provident Life and Pensions Ltd v Sirius International Insurance Corporation* [2004] EWHC 1799 (Comm); [2005] Lloyd's Rep IR 135; [2005] EWCA Civ 601; [2006] Lloyd's Rep IR 45 (financial institution; condition precedent to right to indemnity that notice be given 'as soon as possible during the period of this policy'); *Hellyer v Amp General Insurance Ltd* [2002] NSWSC 866, 12 ANZIC 61.544 (scuba diving instructors' insurance; notice to be given during the subsistence of the policy); *John Connell Holdings Pty Ltd v Mercantile Mutual Holdings Ltd* [1999] QCA 429, 10 ANZIC 61.454 (engineers; notice to be given during the subsistence of the policy); *Junemill Ltd (in liquidation) v FAI General Insurance Company Ltd* [1997] QCA 261; [1999] 2 Qd R 136 (valuers; notice to be given during the subsistence of the policy); *Kajima UK Engineering Ltd v The Underwriting Insurance Company Ltd* [2008] EWHC 83 (TCC); [2008] Lloyd's Rep IR 391 (design and build contractor; any claim subsequently made deemed to be made in the period of insurance during which the notification was given); *McCarthy v St Paul International Insurance Co Ltd* [2007] FCAFC 28 (solicitors; notice during the period of insurance); *MDIS v Swinbank* [1999] Lloyd's Rep IR 516 (computer consultants; notice to be given 'as soon as practical during the period hereof'); and *Peacock v Roberts; Guardian Insurance Co of Canada, Third Party* (1990) 67 DLR (4th) 641 (dentists; notice during the policy period).

See also the RICS Policy Wording discussed in para 2.142.

[207] Eg *Clasper v Dunns* [2007] NZHC 1000 (accountants' insurance; notification either during the period of insurance or within 28 days of its expiry) and *Pioneer Road Services Pty Ltd v QBE*

2.120 Such requirements are likely to be strictly interpreted, and purported notifications made outside the specified period are unlikely to be effective. They define the cover provided rather than regulate how a notification of a potential claim which falls within cover is to be made.[208] Policies which require both the awareness of the matter which is to be notified and the notification to occur during the policy period give rise to a potential problem in cases in which the insured only becomes aware of the relevant matter at the very end of the policy period and is not able to make a notification before its expiry. This problem has already been addressed in the context of 'claims made and notified' policies.[209]

F. Particular Policies

SRA Minimum Terms and Conditions of Professional Indemnity Insurance

2.121 The SRA Minimum Terms and Conditions of Professional Indemnity Insurance have a conventional 'claims made' trigger: cover is provided for claims first made against the insured during the period of insurance. The definition of 'claim' includes 'a demand for, or an assertion of a right to, civil compensation or civil damages or an intimation of an intention to seek such compensation or damages'.

2.122 The second limb ('intimation of an intention') requires communication of an intention to seek to recover civil compensation or civil damages, and not merely of the possibility or even very strong probability of doing so. The possibility or probability of a claim is not a claim, although, obviously, it is a circumstance which might give rise to a claim. This distinction is illustrated by the decision of HH Judge David Cooke, sitting as a Judge of the High Court, in *Gardner v Lemma Europe Insurance Company Ltd (In Liquidation)*.[210] The insured solicitor had received a letter during the policy period from a firm of solicitors acting for former clients for whom he had acted on the purchase of a house. The letter demanded the clients' file and asked for the date on which completion occurred, concluding with a statement that if the information was not provided within forty-eight hours the solicitors might issue protective proceedings. In a later conversation with the other solicitors the

---

Insurance Ltd [2002] NSWSC 137 (design and consultancy services re road construction; notification either during the period of cover or within 28 days after its expiry); *QBE Insurance Ltd v Attorney-General* [NZCA] 193 (government department; notice during the period of insurance or within 21 days of the expiry date).

In *Aussie Tax Pty Ltd v Markel Capital Ltd* [2008] VSC 592, the insured accountants had to make a notification either during the period of insurance or within 30 days after it. In the latter case this was only possible if 'a replacement policy commencing from the expiry of the Period of Insurance is effected with the Scheme'.

[208] See the discussion of 'claims made and notified' policies in paras 2.47–2.49.
[209] See paras 2.47–2.49.
[210] [2014] EWHC 3674 (Ch).

insured was told that there was a suggestion that there was 'some negligence' and that 'there may be a claim for negligence'. The insured did not give any notice to his current insurers. The insured argued that the letter and conversation fell within the definition of 'Claim'. The argument failed. The letter was 'not an indication that they indicated to issue protective proceedings, still less that they intended to issue and pursue a substantive claim for negligence or any other civil wrong'. The later conversation suggested the possibility of a claim, but 'there was nothing said to [the insured] or written in that letter which indicated in any way that an intention had been formed by [the former clients] or their solicitors to pursue a civil action'.

The definition of 'Claim' also includes an obligation on an insured to remedy a **2.123** breach of the Solicitors' Accounts Rules 1998 (as amended from time to time) or any rules which replace them. Any such obligation is deemed to be a claim for the purposes of the insuring clause in the SRA Minimum Terms and Conditions of Professional Indemnity Insurance whether or not any person actually makes a demand for, or an assertion of a right to, civil compensation or civil damages. The purpose behind this clause is clear.[211] What is less clear is when a 'Claim' is made. Is it when the breach of the Solicitors' Accounts Rules 1998 took place (that being when the obligation to remedy arises), when the breach is discovered or when the clients ask for their money? The first fits the language of the definition, but conflicts with the rationale for 'claims made' policies, namely that insurers will know or be able to estimate their exposure during or shortly after the expiry of the policy.[212] The second would work well in practice, but is not obvious from the definition. The third would also work in practice and can be reconciled with the definition: there is a demand, but not for civil compensation or civil damages: the client simply asks to be paid his money. At present the point is not the subject of judicial decision.

The insured also has the right, but no obligation, to notify 'Circumstances' during **2.124** the policy period. As has been observed above, the definition of 'Circumstances' is wide.[213] However, solicitors (and barristers) may face a difficulty in notifying circumstances to their insurers. Apart from professional and legal duties of confidentiality, documents and information of and about clients are held by lawyers subject to legal privilege which, save in cases of fraud, only the client can waive. When a client makes a claim against his former lawyer he impliedly waives that privilege so that there is no obstacle to the lawyer providing full details to his insurers.[214] But a lawyer who becomes aware of circumstances which might give rise to a claim against him before the client has waived privilege is in a difficult position. He is entitled to notify his current insurers of those circumstances and will be obliged

---

[211] See para 9.49.
[212] See paras 2.02–2.04.
[213] See para 2.56.
[214] *Lillicrap v Nalder & Son (A Firm)* [1993] 1 WLR 94. This and other decisions on implied waiver of privilege are discussed in more detail in paras 5.49–5.53.

to disclose them when seeking cover for the next year. But he must preserve his client's privilege.

2.125 The issue arose in *Quinn Direct Insurance Ltd v Law Society*.[215] The Law Society had intervened in the insured firm of solicitors and held its files. The firm's insurers wanted to review those files in order to decide whether it was obliged to indemnify the insured. The Law Society refused access to the files. Insurers brought a claim for an order permitting them to inspect the files and take copies of documents. The application failed. Sir Andrew Morritt C, with whom the other members of the Court of Appeal agreed, gave a number of reasons for his decision. The first two are of particular relevance to professional indemnity insurance.

2.126 The first was that the Chancellor did not accept that an insured solicitor 'is either entitled or bound to disclose to his insurer, either on inception, renewal or notification, confidential and privileged documents or information of the client without the client's consent'. If the client would not waive his privilege, then the insured could inform the insurer.

2.127 The second was that the insured lawyer could not rely upon the client's failure to waive privilege to justify any failure to comply with his contractual and legal obligations of disclosure to his insurers. The Chancellor referred to *March Cabaret Club & Casino Ltd v London Assurance*,[216] where May J held that the privilege against self-incrimination does not excuse a failure by someone who has committed a criminal offence from disclosing it, if material, to his prospective insurers. The Chancellor concluded that:

> the privilege is that of his client and cannot be broken or waived without the client's consent. It may be that, if the client will not waive his privilege to enable proper disclosure to be made, the consequence of the resulting conflict of interest will be that the insurance is vitiated or the notification inadequate but that is the problem of the solicitor not the client: cf *Hilton v Barker Booth & Eastwood* [2005] 1 WLR 567. The solicitor's duty of disclosure cannot override the entitlement of the client.

2.128 There is some tension between the first ground (which suggests that an insured solicitor is not bound to disclose privileged documents and information to his insurers) and the second (which suggests that he is, but that that is the solicitor's problem). But there is no doubt as to the result: lawyers cannot pass privileged information to their insurers without their clients' consent. The difficulties which arise are real,[217] but may not be insuperable. First, solicitors are under a professional obligation to inform current clients if they discover any act or omission which could

---

[215] [2010] EWCA Civ 805; [2011] 1 WLR 308.

[216] [1975] 1 Lloyd's Rep 169, at 177.

[217] One reason why a declaration was not made as to the scope of the notification in *McManus v European Risk Insurance Co* [2013] EWHC 18 (Ch); [2013] Lloyd's Rep IR 533 (for the facts see para 2.100) was that much of the material relevant to the notified circumstances was subject to the clients' privilege.

give rise to a claim.[218] Second, solicitors can obtain their clients' informed consent in advance by appropriately worded letters of retainer. Third, it may be possible to make a notification which excludes privileged (and confidential) information, for example by omitting details which would identify the client.[219] If and when a claim is subsequently made, privilege will be waived and the full details can be provided.

Only certain specified exclusions are permitted. They include: **2.129**

> Any Claim in respect of which the Insured is entitled to be indemnified by the Solicitors Indemnity Fund (SIF) or under a professional indemnity insurance contract for a period earlier than the Period of Insurance, whether by reason of notification of circumstances or otherwise.

This is a narrow exclusion. Insurers cannot exclude cover for claims arising from circumstances of which the insured was aware before the policy period which might give rise to a claim and which could have been notified under earlier policies, but were not. This is highly favourable to the insured and to third party claimants.

However, that is not the end of the matter. Insurers are entitled to ask questions in **2.130** the proposal form as to claims or circumstances of which the insured is aware and the insured is under a duty to disclose material facts.[220] The policy may include a term requiring an insured who commits or condones (whether knowingly or recklessly) any non-disclosure or misrepresentation to reimburse insurers to the extent that it is just and equitable having regard to the prejudice caused to insurers by such non-disclosure or misrepresentation.[221]

The policy must also provide that insurers are not entitled to reduce or deny their **2.131** liability on any grounds whatsoever, including any breach of any term or condition of the policy, except to the extent that one of the specified exclusions operates. The specified exclusions do not include any requirement as to notifying claims or circumstances within any particular time of the claims being made or the insured becoming aware of notifiable circumstances so that no term can be included requiring the insured to give notice or make a notification, whether as a condition precedent to cover or otherwise.

The ICAEW Minimum Approved Policy Wording

Cover is provided for claims first made against the insured during the policy **2.132** period. 'Claim' is defined as:

> any written or oral demand for compensation or damages from, or the assertion of a right against, any Insured and shall be deemed to include any complaint or

---

[218] Outcome O(1.16) in the SRA Handbook 2011. This does not apply to former clients.
[219] See the guidance from the Law Society set out in n 100 under para 5.53.
[220] As to which see Chapter 5.
[221] As to which see paras 5.109–5.111 and 8.59.

reference to any Ombudsman which arises out of the conduct of Professional Business carried on by, or on behalf of, the Insured.

'Claimant' includes a complainant to any such ombudsman.

2.133 The insured is required to give notice in writing as soon as practicable and in any event within seven days after the end of the period of insurance of any claim made against him and of the receipt of notice from any party of an intention to make a claim against him. This obligation to notify within seven days after the end of the policy period is not part of the insuring clause and so does not form part of the trigger of cover. In relation to notices of intention to make a claim, the ICAEW Minimum Approved Policy Wording provides that 'Any Claim arising therefrom and/or in connection therewith shall be deemed to have been first made during the Period of Insurance'.

2.134 An extension of cover is given for claims arising from circumstances of which the insured becomes aware during the policy period, which may give rise to a claim and of which the insured gives notice in writing as soon as reasonably practicable and, in any event, during the policy period.[222] Any claim arising from circumstances which have been so notified is deemed to have been first made in the period of insurance.

2.135 Cover is excluded for any claim for any loss arising out of any circumstance which has been notified under any other policy before the commencement of cover under the current policy. There is no definition of circumstance.

2.136 There is no exclusion of cover in respect of circumstances which should have been notified, but were not. It follows that if a claim is first made during the period of insurance arising out of circumstances of which the insured was aware before the period of insurance might give rise to a claim, the claim will attach to the current policy if the insured failed to notify under an earlier policy.

2.137 Before agreeing to accept the risk, insurers are entitled to ask questions about the insured's awareness of circumstances which might give rise to a claim and the insured is obliged to disclose material facts.[223] Insurers' rights to avoid are limited to cases where the insured is unable to establish that non-disclosure or misrepresentation was free of any fraudulent conduct.[224]

2.138 However, if the non-disclosure or misrepresentation consists of or includes a failure to inform insurers of any circumstance of which the insured was aware which might give rise to a claim, then the indemnity is restricted to that to which the insured would have been entitled had the circumstance been properly notified. These terms are considered further in Chapter 5.[225]

---

[222] As to which see n 206 under para 2.119.
[223] As to which see Chapter 5.
[224] As to which see paras 5.92–5.99.
[225] See para 5.95.

The RICS Policy Wording

Cover is on a 'claims made' basis for claims first made against the insured during **2.139** the policy period. There is a wide definition of 'claim':

1 any demand for damages or compensation from, or assertion of a right against the INSURED
2 any notice of intention, whether orally or in writing, to commence legal proceedings against the INSURED
3 any communication with the INSURED in whatsoever form invoking any Pre-Action Protocols as may be issued and approved from time to time.

The insuring clause also provides an indemnity against claims 'arising out of **2.140** any CIRCUMSTANCE(S) which the INSURED shall first notify during the POLICY PERIOD'. 'CIRCUMSTANCE(S)' are defined as follows:

an incident, occurrence, fact, matter, act or omission that might give rise to a CLAIM.

As has been noted already, this is a wide definition.[226]

The insured is required to give insurers written notice of the receipt of any claim **2.141** during the policy period. This is to be done as soon as reasonably practicable and, in any event, within 10 working days after the expiry of the policy period. As with the ICAEW Minimum Approved Policy Wording, this obligation is not contained within the insuring clause and so the giving of notice in accordance with it is not part of the trigger of the right to an indemnity.

The insured is also required to give insurers written notice if he becomes aware dur- **2.142** ing the policy period of any circumstance(s) as soon as reasonably practicable. This must be done during the policy period, there being no extension such as that provided in respect of notification of claims. Such notice must, where possible, include the name of the potential claimant(s), the date of the incident, occurrence, fact, matter, act, or omission which has given rise to the circumstance(s), the name(s) of the individual(s) involved in the circumstance(s), the date of the insured's first awareness of them, and the estimated amount of any potential claim.

Notification of both claims and circumstances is deemed to have been made to **2.143** insurers if and when made to a named person. This term does not preclude notification being effected in some other way: it merely provides a certain means of making a notification.

The indemnity under the RICS Policy Wording extends to awards by adjudica- **2.144** tors under the Housing Grants, Construction and Regeneration Act 1996.[227] Adjudications under this Act are intended to provide a quick resolution of a dispute

---

[226] See para 2.56.
[227] See paras 11.12–11.15.

and so are conducted on a tight timetable. The RICS Policy Wording therefore requires notification to insurers within two working days of receipt of any notice of intention to adjudicate, notice of adjudication, referral notice, or any adjudication notice pursuant to contract. This is stated to be a condition precedent to cover.

2.145 There is an exclusion of cover in respect of any claim or circumstances of which the insured was or should have been aware before the inception of the policy.[228] However, this does not reduce the rights of the insured under the 'Special Institution Condition' or otherwise affect the application of the 'Special Institution Condition'. By the 'Special Institution Condition' insurers surrender their right to avoid the policy for non-disclosure or misrepresentation or by reason of untrue statements in the proposal form or other information provided to or warranted to insurers, but only if there was no intention to deceive or mislead insurers.

2.146 The 'Special Institution Condition' also provides that, where a claim is first made against the insured during the policy period which claim arises out of a circumstance which the insured had earlier knowledge and should have notified under an earlier policy, cover is limited to that which would have been available under the earlier policy.[229] The effect of this provision is to exclude from the scope of the exclusion clause (and so include within cover) claims first made during the policy period arising from circumstances which should have been notified under earlier policies.

2.147 However, the 'Special Institution Condition' does not enable the insured to make an effective notification of a circumstance which should have been notified in an earlier year. It only applies to claims.

The RIBA Architects Premier Policy Wording

2.148 The RIBA Architects Premier Policy Wording provides an indemnity on a 'claims made' basis. Insurers agree to indemnity the insured 'against any claim first made against them during the Period of Insurance in respect of civil liability together with claimant's costs, fees and expenses in accordance with any judgment, award or settlement'. There is no definition of 'claim', but to fall within the insuring clause the claim has to be for the consequence of specified legal wrongs or losses.

2.149 The insured is required to give insurers notice in writing of any claim or of the receipt from any person of notice of intention to make a claim 'as soon as possible

---

[228] The exclusion of cover in respect of a claim of which the insured was or should have been aware before the inception of cover is rather odd. Cover is only provided in respect of claims first made against the insured during the policy period. The definition of claim in the RICS Policy Wording appears to require some communication with the insured which will involve the making of the claim. It is therefore not clear how the exclusion clause could ever apply in practice, because a claim made before the policy period would not be covered in any event.

[229] See further para 5.95.

during the Period of Insurance'. This is expressed to be a condition precedent to the right to an indemnity, but is not part of the insuring clause.

It is also a condition precedent to the right to be indemnified that the insured **2.150** should give insurers full details in writing of any circumstance or event which is likely to give rise to a claim and that the insured should do so as soon as possible and during the period of insurance. If the insured does so, then, if the notified circumstance subsequently gives rise to a claim, that claim is deemed to have been made during the period of insurance.

Cover is excluded in respect of any claim or circumstance or event or later claim **2.151** arising out of any circumstances or events which have been notified by the insured to any previous insurer. But there is no exclusion in respect of claims which arise from circumstances which should have been notified under earlier policies, but were not. So there is cover for such claims, subject to the provisions as to non-disclosure and misrepresentation.[230]

---

[230] See paras 5.83–5.91.

3

THE INSURANCE BROKER

A. Introduction

Some contracts of professional indemnity insurance are negotiated and made **3.01** directly between the insured and insurers. For example, self-employed barristers in England and Wales arrange their primary insurance cover directly with their mutual insurer. However, most contracts are negotiated and made through intermediaries. The traditional intermediary is an insurance broker who acts for the insured. As such, he owes duties to his client, while at the same time acting as his client's agent in dealing with insurers. Insurance intermediaries may also be agents of insurers. Sometimes one broker will instruct another broker to carry out a task which he has undertaken for a client, so that there will be both a broker and a sub-broker involved. The Financial Service and Markets Act 2000 has added a further dimension, because insurance intermediaries are now generally subject to regulation under that Act.

This chapter first explains the various roles which insurance brokers and other **3.02** intermediaries undertake and for whom they act when undertaking those roles. It then addresses the duties which they owe to those on whose behalf they are acting, whether in contract, tort, or by way of statutory regulation. The final section analyses the role of insurance brokers as agent of the insured as it may affect the relationship between the insured and insurers.

B. The Role of the Insurance Broker

The traditional role of the insurance broker

3.03 Traditionally an insurance broker acts for the insured and is the insured's agent in arranging for the insured to obtain insurance. This can involve advising as to such matters as the risks or perils against which insurance should be sought, the amount of cover, the terms of cover, and the identity of insurers. The broker can also have a role in drawing up the policy terms and in reporting claims and notifying the insurers of circumstances or occurrences which have the potential to give rise to a claim.

3.04 Insurance cover of major financial institutions[1] or international partnerships[2] against professional liability will often involve an insurance broker in giving detailed advice to his client and in undertaking protracted negotiations with a number of insurers. Such cover would usually involve a number of different policies and, where some insurers require the reinsurance of part of the risk they are to underwrite, seeking to arrange such reinsurance.[3]

3.05 In other cases, the insurance broker's role may be much more limited in practice. The choice of insurer may be restricted by the insured's professional body, the terms of any policy may also be fixed in whole or in part, and the insured may require no more than the minimum cover which he is obliged to obtain.

3.06 Whatever the insurance broker does in this traditional role, the insured will usually be the insurance broker's client for the purposes of the policy of insurance.[4] This should include the handling of claims.[5]

---

[1] Eg *Lloyds TSB General Insurance Holdings Ltd v Lloyds Bank Group Insurance Co Ltd* [2003] UKHL 48; [2003] 4 All ER 43; *Standard Life Assurance Ltd v Oak Dedicated Ltd* [2008] EWHC 222 (Comm); [2008] Lloyd's Rep IR 552 and *Travelers Casualty and Surety Co of Canada v Sun Life Assurance Co of Canada (UK) Ltd* [2006] EWHC 2716 (Comm); [2007] Lloyd's Rep IR 619.

[2] Eg *Brit Syndicates Ltd v (1) Italaudit SPA (2) GTI* [2008] UKHL 18; [2008] 2 All ER 1140, where the insured were a number of related accountancy firms across the world.

[3] As in *Youell v Bland Welch & Co Ltd (The 'Superhulls Cover' Case) (No 2)* [1990] 2 Lloyd's Rep 431 and *Aneco Reinsurance Underwriting Ltd v Johnson & Higgins Ltd* [2001] UKHL 51; [2002] 1 Lloyd's Rep 157. See also *HIH Casualty and General Insurance Ltd v JLT Risk Solutions Limited* [2007] EWCA Civ 710; [2007] 2 Lloyd's Rep 278, where the position in which an insurance broker who adopts multiple roles is addressed.

[4] *Rozanes v Bowen* (1928) 32 LIL Rep 98, *McNealy v The Pennine Insurance Co Ltd* [1978] 2 Lloyd's Rep 18, *Arif v Excess Insurance Group* 1986 SC 317, *Winter v Irish Life Assurance Plc* [1995] 2 Lloyd's Rep 274, and *Searle v AR Hales & Co* [1996] LRLR 68. Where the insurance broker is also involved in obtaining reinsurance, the reinsured will also be his client for the purposes of the reinsurance.

[5] *Anglo-African Merchants Ltd. v Bayley* [1970] 1 QB 311, *North and South Trust Co v Berkeley* [1971] 1 WLR 470, and *Callaghan and Hedges v Thompson* [2000] Lloyd's Rep IR 125. See also *Alexander Forbes v SBJ* [2002] EWHC 3121 (Comm); [2003] Lloyd's Rep IR 432: see further paras 3.71–3.74.

Acting for insurers

Although they traditionally act on behalf of the insured, insurance brokers may **3.07** also act on behalf of insurers. For example, insurers can give brokers express or implied authority to bind insurances on their behalf, thereby rendering the broker agent of the insurer. The broker acts as the insured's coverholder.[6] Insurance brokers who have authority to bind temporary cover on behalf of insurers are the insurers' agents for the purpose of that temporary cover.[7]

Brokers and sub-brokers

A broker instructed by a client who is seeking insurance may in turn instruct a **3.08** further broker, the sub-broker.[8] The original broker is called the 'producing broker' and the sub-broker is called the 'placing broker'. If the producing broker wishes to seek insurance at Lloyd's, then, unless he is himself an approved Lloyd's broker, he will need to instruct a Lloyd's broker as placing broker. This is because only brokers approved by the Committee of Lloyd's can broke risks at Lloyd's.[9] Outside Lloyd's there is no such restriction, but a sub-broker may still be involved. Other reasons for seeking the service of a placing broker include greater specialist expertise and geography.

As is explained later,[10] there will usually be no direct contract between the insured **3.09** and a placing broker, although it is possible that the placing broker may owe the insured a duty of care in tort. The placing broker will be acting as agent of the producing broker and owe the producing broker a duty of care in both contract and in tort. The scope of that duty will depend on what the placing broker has agreed

---

[6] See, for example, *Woolcott v Excess Insurance Co Ltd (No 2)* [1979] 2 Lloyd's Rep 210 and *Excess Life Assurance Co Ltd v Firemen's Insurance Co of Newark, New Jersey* [1982] 2 Lloyd's Rep 599.
  Where an insurance broker is interposed between insurers and the coverholder he usually acts on behalf of the coverholder: *Empress Assurance Corp Ltd v CT Bowring & Co Ltd* (1905) 11 Com Cas 107 and *Glasgow Assurance Corp Ltd v William Symondson & Co* (1911) 16 Com Cas 109. On the particular facts in *Pryke v Gibbs Hartley Cooper Ltd* [1991] 1 Lloyd's Rep 602 the brokers had assumed responsibility towards insurers for a specific task and so owed them a duty of care in tort in respect of the execution of that task.
[7] *Stockton v Mason* [1978] 2 Lloyd's Rep 430. See also *Jimaco Clothing Pty Ltd v Norwich Winterthur Insurance (Aust) Ltd* (1985) 3 ANZIC 60.640.
[8] There may be a longer chain: in *Anglo-African Merchants Ltd v Bayley* [1970] 1 QB 311, for example, there were three insurance brokers involved.
[9] Lloyd's Act 1982, s 8(3). There are exceptions to the rule that only Lloyds' brokers can undertake business at Lloyds and these are set out at paras 27–9 of the Lloyd's Underwriting Byelaw (No 2) of 2003 (as amended). It is possible for a non-Lloyd's broker to enter the room at Lloyd's under an 'umbrella' agreement with a Lloyd's broker: see *Johns v Kelly* [1986] 1 Lloyd's Rep 468 at 470: an 'umbrella' agreement is: ' … an arrangement between a Lloyd's broker and a non Lloyd's broker whereby business is transacted at Lloyd's by the directors, partners or employees of the non Lloyd's broker, acting as if they were directors, partners or employees of the Lloyd's broker itself, using the Lloyd's broker's slips.'
[10] See paras 3.76–3.84.

to do. In *Dunlop Haywards (DHL) Ltd v Barbon Insurance Group Ltd*[11] Hamblen J said of the duties owed by a placing broker to the producing broker:[12]

> As to what the duty to exercise reasonable skill and care required, there are clearly differences in the relationship between a client and his insurance broker, and between the producing broker and the sub-broker he employs to place the cover. However, many of the background regulatory provisions relating to the professional standards to be expected of insurance brokers are also relevant to sub-brokers. Indeed it was accepted, with one qualification, that in most cases the duties which I have held will generally arise in a client/broker relationship[13] will also arise in a producing broker/placing broker relationship, with the difference that the client in such a case will ordinarily be the producing broker.

C. Duties Owed to the Insured

Contract

3.10 In the past it was not at all unusual for an insurance broker not to enter into any written contract with his client. The broker would simply take his client's instructions without more. Broking has traditionally shied away from reducing the services to be provided into a form of words, whether through letters of engagement or terms of business. No doubt this informality was at least in part a consequence of the fact that traditionally the insured did not pay the insurance broker a fee: the consideration for the insurance broker's service was the opportunity to earn commission by way of brokerage.

3.11 However, it is now becoming increasingly common for brokers and the insurance market more widely to send their professional clients letters of engagement or terms of business agreements.[14] This is particularly the case for larger clients with complex insuring requirements. The advantage of a written agreement should be clarity as to the extent of the insurance broker's duties.

3.12 Without a letter of engagement or standard terms of business agreements, the role of the broker and so the duties he will owe to the insured will be fleshed out by implied terms which themselves will arise out of industry practice, any previous course of dealing between the parties if there is a pre-existing relationship, and any judicial decisions setting out what is expected of a broker in similar circumstances.

---

[11] [2009] EWHC 2900 (Comm); [2010] Lloyd's Rep IR 149.
[12] Ibid at [241].
[13] Ibid at [168].
[14] ICOBS 4.1.2 requires certain information to be provided by an insurance broker to an insured before a policy is placed: see para 3.25. This will usually be done in writing.

Whether the contract is in writing, oral, or implied by conduct, it will be an implied **3.13** term of the contract between the insurance broker and the insured that the insurance broker will exercise reasonable skill and care.[15]

It is possible, but unusual, for an insurance broker to contract on terms which **3.14** create a strict obligation to achieve a particular result so that, even if the insurance broker exercises reasonable skill and care in trying to achieve that result, failure to do so will be a breach of contract.[16] However, it will usually require clear language to create a strict obligation.[17]

Duty of care in tort

It has long been established that, when acting for an insured, an insurance broker **3.15** owes him a duty of care in tort to exercise reasonable skill and care.[18] The existence of a concurrent duty was confirmed by the decision of the House of Lords in *Henderson v Merrett Syndicates Ltd*.[19]

The standard of skill and care

The contractual and tortious obligations to exercise reasonable skill and care **3.16** require of an insurance broker the standard of performance of a reasonably competent insurance broker in the circumstances.[20] This means that a broker is not usually under a strict obligation to achieve a particular result. The standard of care does, however, require proper professionalism, skill, and expertise.

Professional indemnity insurance is a specialist area of insurance and an insurance **3.17** broker who undertakes work in that area will be expected to do so with a degree of skill and care appropriate for that market. He is not required to have substantial experience of the particular market, but he must have enough experience and knowledge to be able to provide his client with a reasonable level of service in that market. In other words, while he is not required to be an expert, the insurance broker must know enough about the particular market to be able to know what needs to be done to protect and promote the insured's interests.[21]

---

[15] Such a term will be implied by law and, now, by s 13 of the Supply of Goods and Services Act 1982. The level of skill and care required of specialist brokers is addressed in para 3.17.

[16] The classic example is *Dickson & Co v Devitt* (1916) 86 LJKB 315, where the brokers were instructed to obtain insurance for '*Suwa Maru* and/or steamers', but only obtained cover for '*Suwa Maru*'.

[17] See, for example, *Midland Bank Plc v Cox McQueen* [1999] PNLR 593. But see also *Platform Funding Ltd v Bank of Scotland PLC* [2008] EWCA Civ 930; [2009] QB 426.

[18] The authorities are collected in para 16-011 of *Jackson & Powell on Professional Liability* (Sweet & Maxwell, 2012).

[19] [1995] 2 AC 145.

[20] See, for example, *Harvest Trucking Co Ltd v Davis* [1991] 2 Lloyd's Rep 638, at 643 per HH Judge Diamond QC, sitting as a High Court Judge.

[21] Cf *Sharp and Roarer Investments Ltd v Sphere Drake Plc: The Moonacre* [1992] 2 Lloyd's Rep 501 at 523, where A D Colman QC, sitting as a deputy judge of the High Court, said this of an

3.18 In the area of professional indemnity insurance the insured may himself have rele-vant knowledge and expertise. This may be because the insured is himself practis-ing in that area (for example, an insurance broker or an underwriting agent at Lloyd's) or in a related area (for example, a lawyer specializing in insurance law). It may also be because the insured has its own risk management department or dedi-cated partner or other principal.[22] In the context of the standards to be expected of solicitors, it has been held that:

> An inexperienced client will need and will be entitled to expect the solicitor to take a much broader view of the scope of his retainer and of his duties than will be the case with an experienced client.[23]

3.19 However, insurance brokers should not proceed upon the basis that experienced or sophisticated clients need no advice or can be relied upon, for example, to read and understand policy wordings themselves. So, in *Youell v Bland Welch & Co Ltd (No 2) (The 'Superhulls Cover' Case)*[24] the defendant insurance brokers argued that their reinsured clients should themselves have noticed a fatal flaw in the policy wording and that this broke the chain of causation between the brokers' negligence and the loss which resulted from the flawed drafting. Phillips J rejected that argu-ment, although he did reduce damages by twenty per cent to reflect the reinsured's contributory negligence.

3.20 No deduction at all was made for contributory negligence in *Standard Life Assurance Ltd v Oak Dedicated Ltd*.[25] In that case, insurance brokers had drafted a policy of professional indemnity insurance which failed to meet the needs of their client.[26] The client was a major financial services institution and insurer. The brokers argued that the client should have noticed the problem with the drafting. Tomlinson J rejected that argument firmly:

> Although an insurer, [the insured] is not in the business of providing professional indemnity insurance cover and in fact before taking out this cover in 1994 had no experience of it. From the beginning and throughout the history [the insured] was

---

insurance broker who was seeking insurance of a yacht: 'it is appropriate … to require that a non-specialist marine broker should bear no greater skill than that which would be expected from a reasonably skilled non-specialist broker. This is not the same thing as saying that the standard is that of a marine broker substantially inexperienced in the insurance of large yachts. It is rather the standard of a broker who has such general knowledge of the yacht insurance market and the cover available in it as to be able to advise his client on all matters on which a lay client would in the ordi-nary course of events predictably need advice, in particular in the course of the selection of cover and the completion of the proposal.'

[22] Under the ICOBS partners in firms taking out professional indemnity insurance are treated as 'commercial customers' rather than as 'consumers': see ICOBS 2.1.4G and para 3.23.

[23] *Carradine Properties Ltd v D J Freeman & Co* [1999] Lloyd's Rep PN 483, at 487 per Donaldson LJ. See also ICOBS 6.1.7G and para 3.23.

[24] [1990] 2 Lloyd's Rep 431. See also *National Insurance and Guarantee Corporation v Imperio Reinsurance Co (UK) Ltd* [1999] Lloyd's Rep IR 249.

[25] [2008] EWHC 222 (Comm); [2008] Lloyd's Rep IR 552 at [102].

[26] See para 3.48.

reassured by its brokers that the cover which had been placed met its requirements. It was specifically and repeatedly reassured that it had cover in respect of its liability for claims which in their nature were individually likely to be well under the policy excess but which together might exceed that figure where such claims were properly capable of aggregation because arising from a common cause or source.

This suggests that there is little scope for arguing that the insured in policies of professional indemnity insurance should themselves have a good understanding of matters such as policy wordings. The insured can be expected to have the understanding and intelligence of professional people, but, save in exceptional cases, not to be experts.

In *Dunlop Haywards (DHL) v Barbon Insurance Group Ltd*[27] Hamblen J would **3.21** have been inclined to find that an insured who had failed to read the policy wording at all had been at fault had it not been for the terms in which the producing broker referred him to the placing broker's report. These drew the insured's attention to a number of specific matters so as to suggest that there was no need for the insured to concern himself with the policy documents. In the circumstances no reduction was made to the award of damages for contributory negligence.[28]

Regulation: The Financial Services and Markets Act 2000

Since 14 January 2005 insurance intermediaries have been subject to regulation **3.22** under the Financial Services and Markets Act 2000[29] unless they are 'appointed representatives' of an 'authorized person' (ie someone who is regulated under the Act) who is 'responsible, to the same extent as if he had expressly permitted it, for anything done or omitted by the representative in carrying on the business for which he has accepted responsibility'.[30]

All regulated insurance intermediaries are required to comply with the rules con- **3.23** tained in the *Insurance: Conduct of Business Sourcebook* (ICOBS),[31] which forms

---

[27] [2009] EWHC 2900 (Comm); [2010] Lloyd's Rep IR 149. For the facts see para 3.49.
[28] Ibid at [218]–[224].
[29] Financial Services and Markets Act 2000 (Regulated Activities) Order 2001, SI 2001/544, as amended. Under this Order contracts of insurance are investments and an insurance broker is likely to carry out one or more of the following regulated activities in relation to them: (a) dealing in investments as agent (art 21); (b) arranging (bringing about) deals in investments (art 25(1)); (c) making arrangements with a view to transactions in investments (art 25(2)); (d) assisting in the administration and performance of a contract of insurance (art 39A); (e) advising on investments (art 53); (f) agreeing to carry on a regulated activity in (a) to (e) (art 64).
There are a number of exemptions but they are unlikely to apply to an insurance broker whose client is seeking professional indemnity insurance. The regulatory regime under the Financial Services and Markets Act 2000 is beyond the scope of this work: see Lomnicka and Powell, *Encyclopedia of Financial Services Law* (Sweet & Maxwell).
[30] Financial Services and Markets Act 2000, s 39(3).
[31] ICOBS was made under Part X, Chapter 1 of the Financial Services and Markets Act 2000 and came into operation on 6 January 2008. It is subject to change from time to time and can be found at http://www.fca.org.uk/handbook.

part of the Financial Conduct Authority's handbook. ICOBS contains some detailed rules as to the conduct of business which are considered below. There are also general principles requiring a regulated firm to act with integrity and to 'conduct its business with due skill, care and diligence'.[32] Where the insurance broker's client is seeking professional indemnity insurance, he is classified as a 'commercial customer' rather than as a 'consumer' for the purposes of ICOBS.[33] ICOBS recognizes that the level of advice which an insurance broker should be required to give to the insured about the policy depends, in part, upon the relevant circumstances.[34] And ICOBS does not apply to an insurance broker who is 'mediating' a 'contract of large risks', which includes professional indemnity insurance for a client who exceeds at least two of the following: (i) a balance sheet of €6.2 million, (ii) net turnover of €12.8 million, and (iii) an average number of employees during the year of 250.[35]

3.24 Apart from general principles and detailed provisions as to the conduct of business, ICOBS sets out standards on communications with clients[36] and financial promotions,[37] inducements, record-keeping, and the exclusion of liability.[38] ICOBS 3

---

[32] See ICOBS, PRIN 2.1, The Principles. In *Dunlop Haywards (DHL) Ltd v Barbon Insurance Group Ltd* [2009] EWHC 2900 (Comm); [2010] Lloyd's Rep IR 149 Hamblen J explained at [164]:

'The ICOB rules might be said to be a high target by which to set a standard in the present case given that its provisions were very new. However, the principles under which regulated entities were at that time required to operate were based on existing industry standards and best practice. The ICOB rules reinforce the FSA Principles by providing practical guidance on various issues, including ways of establishing a customer's demands and needs and of matching arranged insurances to those needs. The FSA Principles sit above the ICOB rules and the rules are to be read against the background of (and are clarified by) the FSA Principles.'

[33] ICOBS 2.1.4G.

[34] ICOBS 6.1.7G. The factors include: '(1) the knowledge, experience and ability of a typical customer for the policy; (2) the policy terms, including its main benefits, exclusions, limitations, conditions and its duration; (3) the policy's overall complexity; (4) whether the policy is bought in connection with other goods and services; ... and (6) whether the same information has been provided to the customer previously and, if so, when.'

[35] In *Dunlop Haywards (DHL) Ltd v Barbon Insurance Group Ltd* [2009] EWHC 2900 (Comm); [2010] Lloyd's Rep IR 149 Hamblen J said that while certain key ICOB rules would not apply to the contract with which he was concerned because it was a contract for large risks, 'nevertheless, the rules remain informative as to the conduct expected of a broker'. In particular he considered that the equivalents to (i) the current ICOB 5.2.2R (statement of demands and needs) (ii) the current ICOB 5.3.1R and 5.3.2G (suitability) and (iii) the current ICOB6.1.5R (provision of information to client) were of relevance in cases involving contracts for large risks.

[36] 'When a firm communicates information, including a financial promotion, to a customer or other policyholder, it must take reasonable steps to communicate it in a way that is clear, fair and not misleading.' (ICOBS 2.2.2R)

[37] '(1) Before a firm approves a financial promotion it must take reasonable steps to ensure that the financial promotion is clear, fair and not misleading.

(2) If, subsequently, a firm becomes aware that a financial promotion is not clear, fair and not misleading, it must withdraw its approval and notify any person that it knows to be relying on its approval as soon as reasonably practicable.' (ICOBS 2.2.3R)

[38] 'A firm must not seek to exclude or restrict, or rely on any exclusion or restriction of, any duty or liability it may have to a customer or other policyholder unless it is reasonable for it to do so and the duty or liability arises other than under the regulatory system.' (ICOBS 2.5.1R)

regulates distance marketing and e-commerce. ICOBS 4 sets out requirements in relation to the provision of information by the intermediary.

ICOBS 4.1.2R provides for the provision of information about the insurance bro- **3.25** ker to the client before the 'conclusion of an initial contract of insurance'. ICOBS 4.1.6(1)R requires an insurance broker to tell a client whether:

(a) it gives advice on the basis of a fair analysis of the market; or
(b) it is under a contractual obligation to conduct insurance mediation business exclusively with one or more insurance undertakings; or
(c) it is not under a contractual obligation to conduct insurance mediation business exclusively with one or more insurance undertakings and does not give advice on the basis of a fair analysis of the market.[39]

ICOBS 4.1.8G provides guidance to intermediaries on how to use panels to advise **3.26** on the basis of a fair analysis. ICOBS 4.1.9G sets out the requirements on communicating information to customers. ICOBS 4.3 and 4.4 set out the requirements on fee and commission disclosure to clients.

D. Discharging the Duties

As has been explained,[40] the extent to which an insurance broker does or should **3.27** advise as to matters such as scope of cover, terms of cover, and choice of insurer will depend upon the particular facts. The scope of the insurance broker's duties may also depend upon the express terms of his contract with the insured.[41] It follows that there is no single template of duties which applies every time an insurance broker acts for an insured in relation to professional indemnity insurance.[42]

However, general statements of an insurance broker's duties can be found in the **3.28** authorities. In *Standard Life Assurance Ltd v Oak Dedicated Ltd*,[43] Tomlinson J accepted expert evidence which supported the following 'uncontroversial propositions':

1) It is the duty of a broker to identify and advise the client about the type and scope of cover which the client needs and, in doing so, to match as precisely as possible the risk exposures which have been identified within the client's business with the coverage available.

---

[39] ICOBS 4.1.6(2)R applies in the case of (b) and (c): 'A firm that does not advise on the basis of a fair analysis of the market must inform its customer that he has the right to request the name of each insurance undertaking with which the firm may and does conduct business. A firm must comply with such a request.'
[40] Paragraphs 3.04–3.06.
[41] Paragraphs 3.10–3.14.
[42] As Hamblen J said in *Dunlop Haywards (DHL) Ltd v Barbon Insurance Group Ltd* [2009] EWHC 2900 (Comm); [2010] Lloyd's Rep IR 149 at [158]: 'What that core duty [to exercise reasonable skill and care] requires in the context of a particular client/broker relationship will depend on all the circumstances.'
[43] [2008] EWHC 222 (Comm); [2008] Lloyd's Rep IR 552 at [102].

2) Having identified what cover the client needs, it is the broker's duty to arrange insurance cover which clearly meets those requirements....

3) If the cover which is needed by the client is not available, the broker must take care to ensure that the precise nature of what is and is not covered is made entirely clear to the client.

4) In relation to the preparation of the policy, the broker must be careful to ensure that the policy language clearly encompasses the needs of the client.

5) The duties of the broker on the renewal of an existing policy are no different from on the initial placement, and at each renewal the broker must ensure that the cover arranged clearly meets the client's needs in the most appropriate manner.

3.29 This formulation was not exhaustive and was directed to the issues before Tomlinson J. In the same way, in *Youell v Bland Welch & Co Ltd (No 2) (The 'Superhulls Cover' Case)*[44] Phillips J accepted submissions that the insurance broker was subject to the following duties:

(i) He must ascertain his client's needs by instruction or otherwise.

(ii) He must use reasonable skill and care to procure the cover which his client has asked for, either expressly or by necessary implication.

(iii) If he cannot obtain what is required, he must report in what respects he has failed and seek his client's alternative instructions.

3.30 *Standard Chartered Life Assurance Ltd v Oak Dedicated Ltd* and *Youell v Bland Welch* concerned very substantial insurance cover. The formulations of the insurance broker's duties in them are very helpful and are of general application so long as it is borne in mind that in the case of more routine transactions proper discharge of the duties will be achieved without the scale of involvement which the brokers had in the *Standard Chartered* and *Youell* cases.

The duty to assess the insured's needs

3.31 The extent of an insurance broker's duty to assess his client's insurance needs will depend upon the particular facts.[45] For example, an insurance broker who receives clear instructions from a client to procure insurance against a particular risk will not usually be under a duty to advise the client as to the desirability of obtaining insurance against some other risk.[46] On the other hand, an insurance broker will

---

[44] [1990] 2 Lloyd's Rep 431 at 445. See also *Dunlop Haywards (DHL) Ltd v Barbon Insurance Group Ltd* [2009] EWHC 2900 (Comm); [2010] Lloyd's Rep IR 149 at [168] where Hamblen J set out a similar list.

[45] As HH Judge Diamond QC said in *Harvest Trucking Co Ltd v Davis (t/a Davis Insurance Services)* [1991] 2 Lloyd's Rep 638, at 641: 'The precise extent of the insurance intermediary's duties must depend in the last resort on the circumstances of the particular case, including the particular instructions which he has received from his client.' Relevant factors include the client's sophistication and understanding (*William Jackson & Sons Ltd v Oughtred & Harrison (Insurance) Ltd* [2002] Lloyd's Rep IR 230, at [29], property insurance) and how many times the insurance broker has met his client in the past (*Eurokey Recycling Ltd v Giles Insurance Brokers Ltd* [2014] EWHC 2989 (Comm); [2015] Lloyd's Rep IR 225, at [86(v)], business interruption insurance).

[46] *O'Brien v Hughes-Gibb & Co Ltd* [1995] LRLR 90 (bloodstock insurance; insured wanted cover against the risk of death of a horse, not theft; brokers not liable for failing to advise that cover

often advise (or be under a duty to advise) as to the level and scope of professional indemnity cover which his client should be seeking to obtain. And he may be duty bound to question an instruction, however clear, which appears to be contrary to the client's interests.[47]

In this regard, ICOBS 5.2.2R is relevant. It provides: **3.32**

(1) Prior to the conclusion of a contract, a firm must specify, in particular on the basis of information provided by the customer, the demands and the needs of that customer as well as the underlying reasons for any advice given to the customer on that policy.

(2) The details must be modulated according to the complexity of the policy proposed.

For the purposes of ICOBS 5.2.2R a client's demands and needs are different things. The insurance broker needs to take reasonable steps to identify both.[48] Having done so, the insurance broker must communicate the statement of those demands and needs in writing or other durable medium in clear and accurate manner comprehensible to the insured.[49] Where the insurance broker has not advised that the insured agree to a particular policy, a degree of flexibility is allowed.[50]

---

be obtained against theft). The position is different if the insured instructs the broker to obtain full coverage: *Fine's Flowers Ltd v General Accident Assurance Co of Canada* (1977) 81 DLR (3d) 139.

[47] *Dunlop Haywards (DHL) Ltd v Barbon Insurance Group Ltd* [2009] EWHC 2900 (Comm); [2010] Lloyd's Rep IR 149: Placing broker held negligent for failing to question an instruction from the producing broker which he should have appreciated would result in a 50 per cent reduction in the insured's cover for its most risky activity of property valuation for no apparent reason. Damages payable to the producing broker were reduced by 80 per cent to reflect the producing broker's contributory negligence.

[48] *Saville v Central Capital Ltd* [2014] EWCA Civ 337; [2014] CTLC 937, at [29] per Floyd LJ, with whom the other members of the Court of Appeal agreed. There are limits to the broker's duty to make enquires: he need only ask the questions which a reasonably competent insurance broker would be expected to ask in the circumstances: *Synergy Health (UK) Ltd v CGU Insurance Plc* [2011] EWHC 2583 (Comm); [2011] Lloyd's Rep IR 500, at [206] per Flaux J.

[49] ICOBS 5.2.3R. An oral communication is allowed where 'the customer requests it, or where immediate cover is necessary'.

[50] ICOBS 5.2.4G: 'The format of a statement of demands and needs is flexible. Examples of approaches that may be appropriate where a personal recommendation has not been given include:

(1) providing a demands and needs statement as part of an application form, so that the demands and needs statement is made dependent upon the customer providing personal information on the application form. For instance, the application form might include a statement along the lines of: "If you answer 'yes' to questions a, b and c your demands and needs are those of a pet owner who wishes and needs to ensure that the veterinary needs of your pet are met now and in the future";

(2) producing a demands and needs statement in product documentation that will be appropriate for anyone wishing to buy the product. For example, "This product meets the demands and needs of those who wish to ensure that the veterinary needs of their pet are met now and in the future";

(3) giving a customer a record of all his demands and needs that have been discussed; and

(4) providing a key features document.'

3.33   The insurance broker should also consider what, if any, further questions should be asked to identify the insured's needs.[51] For example, care may be needed to ensure that liability for earlier practices is covered: while the existence of earlier practices may be the subject of a question on the proposal form and while such liability may be covered without express mention of the earlier practice,[52] this is an area where problems can arise in practice.[53]

3.34   Having taken reasonable steps to identify his client's demands and needs, the insurance broker needs to assess how to meet them. In the context of a consumer claim under ICOB, that task was explained by Floyd LJ, with whom the other members of the Court of Appeal agreed, in *Saville v Central Capital Ltd*:[54]

> The intermediary, whose sole responsibility this is, must address his mind to the information and assess whether the cover he intends to recommend is suitable for those demands and needs. This involves an active comparison of the policy or policies it can offer with the demands and the needs of the customer.

ICOBS 5.3.1R provides that an insurance broker 'must take reasonable care to ensure the suitability of its advice for any customer who is entitled to rely upon its judgment'. This is also the effect of the duty of care in contract and tort. In discharging this duty the insurance broker will need to consider a number of factors.

3.35   Underinsurance is not at all uncommon, as the authorities concerning applications for costs under s 51 of the Senior Courts Act 1981 against insurers who have unsuccessfully defended claims in the names of their insured show.[55] When considering the level of cover to be sought, an insurance broker and the insured should have in mind not only the possible exposure in damages on a single claim, but also the possible impact of any aggregation clause on the limit of cover,[56] the need to allow for interest on any award of damages (which might be made years after the original loss and damage),[57] and whether the limit of cover is inclusive or exclusive of third

---

[51] There are limits, however. The insurance broker cannot be expected to anticipate unusual needs. So, for example, in *National Insurance and Guarantee Corporation v Imperio Reinsurance Co (UK) Ltd* [1999] Lloyd's Rep IR 249, Colman J held that insurance brokers had not been negligent for failing to appreciate that the insured wanted excess of loss cover to include loss of interest on the insured's own funds applied in the insured scheme.

[52] As in *Maxwell v Price (Halford, Third Party)* [1960] 2 Lloyd's Rep 155, discussed in para 9.03.

[53] In *TBI Pty Ltd v AON Financial Planning Ltd* [2004] VSC 40, (2004) 13 ANZIC 61.601 the defendant broker wrongly thought that professional indemnity cover obtained for one company also insured the claimant engineering company under a prior corporate entity clause. This belief was described at [57] by Ashley J as 'hopelessly ill-founded' and based, apparently, upon a misunderstanding of the substance of a sale of some of the claimant company's assets to the company which was insured. Ashley J held that there was no good reason for this misunderstanding in the first place, but that any uncertainty in the broker's mind as to the position could have been resolved by 'a simple question'. He found the brokers liable. On the question of insurance for earlier practices, see further paras 9.01–9.21.

[54] [2014] EWCA Civ 337; [2014] CTLC 97, at [30].

[55] See paras 13.03–13.38.

[56] See paras 10.18–10.84.

[57] Interest will usually be included in cover, but subject to the policy limits: see *Cox v Bankside Members Agency Ltd* [1995] 2 Lloyd's Rep 437, at 447–8 and 461.

party claimants' costs and defence costs.[58] To do this the broker will need information about the insured's work. That information may be required by insurers on the proposal form, but it is material not only to the risk which insurers are considering underwriting but also to the level of cover which the insured should be advised to seek to obtain.[59]

It may also be necessary to consider the types of liability against which indemnity **3.36** insurance is required. This will require an understanding of the insured's profession or business and of the types of liability to which that profession or business might give rise. For example, in *Encia Remediations Ltd v Canopius Managing Agents Ltd*[60] the cover was for environmental consultants' professional indemnity. The insured was a company engaged in civil and environmental engineering. There was an exclusion clause in respect of:

> Any claim arising from the provision of advice design or specification where the Insured contracts to manufacture construct erect install or supply materials or equipment unless defined in the Business as stated in the Schedule.

The insured had designed and carried out piling works and a claim was made against it. Cresswell J held that the design element was covered because of the description of the insured's business in the Schedule to the policy read with other information provided to insurers, including information provided by a related company which was separately insured. The decision was finely balanced and, had it gone the other way, there might well have been a question as to whether a broker who agreed to this exclusion had exercised reasonable skill and care, given the nature of the insured's business.

In order to discharge his duty, an insurance broker will also need to be aware of the **3.37** types of cover which are available in the insurance market.[61] As has been explained,

---

[58] See, for example, *Citibank NA v Excess Insurance Company Ltd* [1999] Lloyd's Rep IR 122.

[59] In *JW Bollom & Co Ltd v Byas Mosley & Co Ltd* [2000] Lloyd's Rep IR 136, a case concerning property insurance, Moore-Bick J found that the defendant insurance brokers had been in breach of duty in failing to appreciate and advise their clients that they were seriously underinsured. A different result was reached in *William Jackson & Sons Ltd v Oughtred Harrison (Insurance) Ltd* [2002] Lloyd's Rep IR 230, another case concerning property insurance. In that case, Morison J distinguished *JW Bollom & Co Ltd v Byas Mosley & Co Ltd* because, on the facts before him, the insured had a valuation from another professional and the insured was aware of the risk of underinsurance. The brokers were held to have been in breach of duty because of significant underinsurance in *Eurokey Recycling Ltd v Giles Insurance Brokers Ltd* [2014] EWHC 2989 (Comm); [2015] Lloyd's Rep IR 225 (business interruption insurance): Blair J held that, while the broker was not expected to calculate the business interruption sum required, he had to provide sufficient explanation to enable the client to do so. He observed that the level of client sophistication can vary enormously.

[60] [2007] EWHC 916 (Comm); [2008] Lloyd's Rep IR 79.

[61] ICOBS 5.3.3R: 'If an insurance intermediary informs a customer that it gives advice on the basis of a fair analysis, it must give that advice on the basis of an analysis of a sufficiently large number of contracts of insurance available on the market to enable it to make a recommendation, in accordance with professional criteria, regarding which contract of insurance would be adequate to meet the customer's needs.'

the scope of professional indemnity cover has expanded[62] and the broker needs to be aware of changes to policy wording which could benefit those for whom he is acting.[63] If an insurance broker is to 'match as precisely as possible the risk exposures which have been identified within the client's business with the coverage available',[64] he has to know what is available.

Arranging cover which meets the insured's needs

3.38 Having identified the insurance which is needed, it is the insurance broker's duty to exercise reasonable skill and care to obtain insurance which meets those needs. This involves a number of matters. First, insurance must be obtained, or, if it is not available, the client must be informed. Second, it must be obtained on appropriate terms. Third, it must be obtained in a way which does not leave the insured vulnerable to avoidance of cover for non-disclosure of material facts or misrepresentation or to automatic cancellation of cover for breach of warranty or to loss or reduction of cover because of the insurer's insolvency.

3.39 When a contract of professional indemnity insurance is underwritten by a single insurer the insurance broker will not need to identify and approach suitable lead underwriters whose judgment will carry weight with the following market. Moreover, the choice of insurers and the contract terms may be limited or prescribed by the insured's professional body.[65] Subject to such matters, the following passage from the judgment of Hobhouse J in *General Accident Fire & Life Assurance Corporation v Tanter, The 'Zephyr'*,[66] a marine insurance case, encapsulates what is required of an insurance broker:

> The broker's skill and expertise extends beyond merely giving his client advice and complying with his clients instructions. He must make use of his knowledge of the market and use appropriate skill. He must approach suitable leaders. He must agree with the leaders' realistic premium levels and terms of insurance. If he fails to do this he will fail to find sufficient following underwriters willing to subscribe to the risk and therefore fail to obtain for his client the cover he requires.

---

[62] See para 1.11.

[63] So in *QBE Insurance Ltd v Attorney-General* [2005] NZCA 193 the New Zealand Court of Appeal expressed the view that the availability of professional indemnity policies which contained a clause extending cover to claims arising out of circumstances of which notice had been given during the current policy year: 'must have been well known in New Zealand following the decision of this Court in *Sinclair Horder O'Malley & Co v National Insurance Co of New Zealand* [1995] 2 NZLR 257; [1995] LRLR 347 delivered on 12 April 1995. The effect of the absence of such a condition is not something which would be known to a broker only with the benefit of the hindsight of this case ... ' The brokers admitted liability in subsequent proceedings: *Aon New Zealand v Attorney-General* [2008] NZCA 524, 15 ANZIC 61.800 on appeal from *Attorney-General v Aon New Zealand Ltd* [2008] NZHC 479.

[64] *Standard Life Assurance Ltd v Oak Dedicated Ltd* [2008] EWHC 222 (Comm); [2008] Lloyd's Rep IR 552 at [102]: see para 3.28.

[65] See paras 1.11, 1.14, 1.17, and 1.29.

[66] [1984] 1 Lloyd's Rep 58 at 67.

Obtaining insurance

An insurance broker is not himself an insurer. He is obliged to exercise reasonable **3.40** skill, care, and diligence in seeking to obtain insurance which matches his client's needs, but will not be in breach of duty if it is unavailable. As Ashely J said in *TBI Pty Ltd v AON Financial Planning Ltd*:[67]

> By the retainer, I consider, the broker relevantly agreed to use its best endeavours, exercising all due care and skill, to obtain and maintain pertinent insurance policies. That is what would ordinarily be expected; and nothing in the facts of this matter suggests that here it was anything different. I agree, then, with the submission of counsel for the defendant that the retainer did not make it obligatory upon [the broker] to obtain the unobtainable.

If insurance is not available in whole or in part, the insurance broker must inform **3.41** his client.[68] He must also inform his client if he has failed to obtain insurance, when insurance could have been obtained.[69] And if an insurance broker purports to effect a contract of insurance, but no contract was in fact made, he will almost inevitably be in breach of duty.[70]

There are three respects in which a policy obtained by an insurance broker falls to **3.42** be tested. First, he must apply skill and care to obtaining a policy which provides the insured with the cover which he requires. Second, he should use skill and care to assess whether the terms of the policy do so clearly. Thirdly, he should exercise skill and care in the choice of insurer or insurers.

The terms of the policy

The first respect identified in the preceding paragraph requires the insurance bro- **3.43** ker to have a sufficient understanding of the cover which the insured requires, which has been addressed above.[71] The second requires the insurance broker to review the proposed wording with reasonable skill and care.

---

[67] [2004] VSC 40, (2004) 13 ANZIC 61.601 at [56]. In *Avonale Blouse Co Ltd v Williamson & Geo Town* (1948) 81 Ll L Rep 492 brokers were instructed to obtain an extension of cover to new premises. Insurers agreed an immediate extension for cover against fire, but required a survey before extending cover against burglary to the new premises. It was held that the brokers were not in breach of duty in failing to obtain temporary cover against burglary from other insurers. The brokers had informed the insured of the lack of burglary cover pending the survey and the insured was not particularly concerned. (See also *Smith v Cologan* (1788) 2 T R 188n, 100 ER 102.)

And in *Waterkeyn v Eagle Star & British Dominions Insurance Co Ltd* (1920) 5 Ll LR 42 brokers were held not to have been negligent in failing to obtain cover as wide as the insured wished, because they had obtained all that was reasonably available.

[68] *Eagle Star Insurance Co Ltd v National Westminster Finance Australia Ltd* (1985) 58 ALR 165, at 174; *Youell v Bland Welch & Co Ltd (No 2) (The 'Superhulls Cover' Case)* [1990] 2 Lloyd's Rep 431, at 445; *TBI Pty Ltd v AON Financial Planning Ltd* [2004] VSC 40, (2004) 13 ANZIC 61.601, at [58]; and *Standard Life Assurance Ltd v Oak Dedicated Ltd* [2008] EWHC 222 (Comm); [2008] Lloyd's Rep IR 552, at [102].

[69] *Marchand v Jackson* [2012] NZHC 2893; [2013] Lloyd's Rep IR 440.

[70] *Seavision Investment SA v Evennett, The 'Tiburon'* [1990] 2 Lloyd's Rep 418 and *Mander v Commercial Union Assurance Co Plc* [1998] Lloyd's Rep IR 93.

[71] See paras 3.31–3.37.

3.44   The broker's duties were put in these terms by Cooke J in *Talbot v Nausch Hogan & Murray Inc:*[72]

> A number of authorities make it clear that the duty of a broker is, so far as possible,[73] to obtain insurance coverage which clearly and indisputably meets its clients' requirements.

In *FNCB Ltd v Barnet Devanney (Harrow) Ltd* [1999] Lloyd's Rep IR 459 (CA) Morritt LJ at para 21 said this:

> '... it is not the function of an insurance broker to take a view on undetermined points of law. The protection to be afforded to the client should, if reasonably possible, be such that the client does not become involved in legal disputes at all. As in the case of a solicitor the insurance broker should protect his client from unnecessary risks including the risk of litigation.'

> Reference was then made to *Dixey & Sons v Parsons* (1964) 192 EG 197 which was, like *Levy v Spyers* (1856) 1 F & F 3, an action involving a negligent solicitor who had failed to secure the clients' position with consequent expense in argument and litigation. Whether or not the argument advanced by the broker or solicitor is ultimately found to be correct, the fact remains that, by not doing what a competent professional person would do to avoid such argument, cost and expense can be incurred. In those circumstances liability for loss and damage which flows from that negligence and is not too remote must be recoverable.

So, if the insurance does not provide the full cover which it could and should have done, the insurance broker will be in breach of duty.[74] But an insurance broker will not necessarily be in breach of duty because, when a loss occurs, an issue arises as to the meaning and effect of the terms of the policy. The exercise of reasonable skill and care will not necessarily identify or anticipate every point which is or may be taken when a claim is made under the policy.

3.45   In order to be able to obtain coverage which 'clearly and indisputably' meets his client's requirements, an insurance broker needs to have a reasonable understanding of the meaning and effect of policy terms. The authorities evidence an expectation that insurance brokers should have such an understanding. For example, in *Axa Reinsurance (UK) PLC v Field*,[75] when deciding the meaning and effect of an aggregation clause in a reinsurance treaty, Lord Mustill said:

> Although not much of it has penetrated beyond the practitioners of this arcane business, there is sufficient published literature to show that keen interest was

---

[72] [2005] EWHC 2359 (Comm); [2006] 2 Lloyds Rep 195, at 218. Applied in *Ramco Ltd v Weller Russell & Laws Insurance Brokers Ltd* [2008] EWHC (QB) 2202; [2009] Lloyd's Rep IR 27.

[73] This is not a strict duty. As Blair J put it in *Ground Gilbey Ltd v Jardine Lloyd Thompson UK Ltd* [2011] EWHC 124 (Comm); [2012] Lloyd's Rep IR 12 at [73]: 'In short, a broker owes his client a duty to take reasonable steps to obtain a policy which clearly meets his client's needs and is suitable for the client. An aspect of that is that the client should not be exposed to an unnecessary risk of legal disputes with the insurer'.

[74] Eg *Dickson & Co v Devitt* (1916) 86 LJKB 315, where cover was obtained for '*Suwa Maru*' but should have been obtained for '*Suwa Maru* and/or steamers'.

[75] [1996] 1 WLR 1026. This decision is discussed in para 10.36.

shown ... in the techniques of limits, layers and aggregations. I am wholly unwilling to start from an assumption that those who drew up these clauses were so indifferent to their meaning that whatever words were used the intention was in every case much the same.[76]

While in the context of reinsurance, both parties to the contract are themselves insurers, the 'practitioners' to whom Lord Mustill referred must have included insurance brokers.

An understanding of the meaning and effect of policy terms can require some **3.46** knowledge of the law, including the effect of earlier decisions. So in *MDIS v Swinbank*[77] the Court of Appeal had to determine the true meaning of an insuring clause in a policy of indemnity insurance for computer consultants. Reliance was placed on the earlier decision of Devlin J in *West Wake Price & Co v Ching*.[78] Following the approach to construction set out by Lord Hoffmann in *Investors Compensation Scheme Ltd v West Bromwich Building Society*,[79] Clarke LJ said that:

both the decision and the dicta in that case can in my judgment properly be treated as relevant to the construction of this clause since they have been well known amongst insurance lawyers and indeed brokers for many years and would be likely to have been in the back of the minds of those negotiating this contract.[80]

West Wake Price & Co v Ching is a leading case in the area of professional indemnity law. Insurance brokers who negotiate insurance contracts for their clients need to have it and similar cases in the backs of their minds, at least.[81]

An insurance broker who undertakes work in the area of professional indemnity **3.47** also needs to have a reasonable understanding as to how a 'claims made' policy is intended to work and of the terms which will be needed to ensure that it does so. For example, he will need to check that his client insured has an adequate right

---

[76] Ibid at 1035.

[77] [1999] Lloyd's Rep IR 516.

[78] [1957] 1 WLR 45.

[79] [1998] 1 WLR 896, at 912 and 913: 'interpretation is the ascertainment of the meaning which the document would convey to a reasonable person having all the background knowledge which would reasonably have been available to the parties in the situation in which they were at the time of the contract and the meaning of the document is what the parties using the relevant words against the relevant background would reasonably have been understood to mean.'

See further paras 7.02–7.04.

[80] [1999] Lloyd's Rep IR 516, at 522. Peter Gibson LJ agreed with Clarke LJ on this point at 527: 'I accept that cases such as *Goddard & Smith v Frew* [1939] 4 All ER 358 and *West Wake Price & Co v Ching* [1957] 1 WLR 45 would be so well-known to those operating in this field that they must have been in the minds of the draftsman and of those negotiating the contract.' See also *QBE Insurance Ltd v Attorney-General* [2005] NZCA 193 at [42] discussed in note 63 under para 3.35.

[81] In *Standard Life Assurance Ltd v Oak Dedicated Ltd* [2008] EWHC 222 (Comm); [2008] Lloyd's Rep IR 552 the background material included the relevant regulatory regime, namely that under the Financial Services Act 1986: at [16] per Tomlinson J. Again, an insurance broker should have an understanding of this in order to be able to represent his client's interests with proper skill.

to notify matters which have the potential to give rise to future claims during the period of the policy which the broker is seeking to obtain.[82]

3.48 The decision of Tomlinson J in *Standard Life Assurance Ltd v Oak Dedicated Ltd*[83] provides a striking example of an insurance broker who failed to obtain appropriate, clear wording for his client. The problem in that case was that the deductible or excess was '£25 million each and every claim and/or claimant including costs and expenses'. The words 'and/or claimant' had the effect of depriving the cover of much of its practical value, because the obvious, but not only, exposure of the insured to claims, was from the sale of retail financial products to consumers, none of whom would be likely to have a claim of anything like £25 million. However, having held that the excess applied to the claim of each claimant,[84] Tomlinson J had no difficulty in holding that the brokers, who had drafted the policy, had been negligent:[85]

> No reasonably competent broker could reasonably have come to the view that [the insured's] requirements were clearly met. The ability to aggregate claims by different claimants arising from a common cause or source was, as [the broker] knew, of critical importance to [the insured] in the context of the professional indemnity cover which it sought, the need for which had incidentally been identified by [the broker's] predecessors. The wording proffered by [the broker] in the slip to which it invited underwriters to subscribe contained the 'each and every claim and/or claimant' wording which has no recognised market meaning.... The inclusion in a description of an excess of the wording 'each and every claimant' gives rise to the obvious inference that what is sought to be achieved is the application of the excess separately to each individual claimant. In the event I have concluded that that is what was in fact achieved, although my conclusion as to [the broker's] breach of duty would have been precisely the same had I thought that either of the suggested constructions of the cover put forward by [the insured] and [the broker] was correct. Even in such circumstances, the wording used was insufficiently clear to achieve that result without exposing [the insured] to an unnecessary risk that insurers might contend to the contrary, as has in fact occurred and which has given rise to what can only properly be described as significant debate.

3.49 The insurance broker must apply his knowledge and expertise to the wording of the policy which he is obtaining for his client. This requires him not only to read the terms of the policy carefully in order to identify any respects in which it is not suitable, but also to see if there are any terms which he should bring to the insured's attention.[86] These could include unusual or onerous terms or terms which required

---

82 See paras 2.50–2.120. Cf *Park v Hammond* (1816) 6 Taunt 495, 128 ER 1127.
83 [2008] EWHC 222 (Comm); [2008] Lloyd's Rep IR 552.
84 As to which see paras 7.58–7.62.
85 [2008] EWHC 222 (Comm); [2008] Lloyd's Rep IR 552, at [104].
86 *Ground Gilbey Ltd v Jardine Lloyd Thompson UK Ltd* [2011] EWHC 124 (Comm); [2012] Lloyd's Rep IR 12, at [73] per Blair J. In cases in which insurance brokers have been held liable for agreeing to unsuitable terms, they have often also been held liable for failing to inform their clients of the unsuitable terms: see, for example, *Youell v Bland Welch & Co Ltd (No 2) (The 'Superhulls Cover' Case)* [1990] 2 Lloyd's Rep 431.

the insured to take some action. And in cases in which insurance brokers have been held liable for agreeing to unsuitable terms, they have often also been held liable for failing to inform the insured. For example, in *Dunlop Haywards (DHL) Ltd v Barbon Insurance Group Ltd*[87] excess layer professional indemnity insurance was obtained on terms which confined cover to 'liability arising from the Assured's Commercial Property Management activities only'. This rendered the policy unsuitable for the insured. Hamblen J held that the producing brokers had been in breach of duty in failing to read the report made by the placing brokers, the cover note and the policy properly so as to identify the provision which limited cover. They were also in breach of duty in failing to draw this term and the significance of the term to the insured's attention and for failing to arrange insurance which met or met clearly and unambiguously the insured's needs as requested by the insured.[88]

In the same way, if there is any material change in the terms of cover on renewal, the **3.50** insured should be informed.[89] The duty continues after the risk has been placed. As Longmore LJ explained in *HIH Casualty and General Insurance Ltd v JLT Risk Solutions Ltd*:[90]

> an insurance broker who, after placing the risk, becomes aware of information which has a material and potentially deleterious effect on the insurance cover which he has placed is under an obligation to act in his client's best interest by drawing it to the attention of his client and obtain his instructions in relation to it.

Where there will be one or more excess layers of insurance above the primary **3.51** policy, the insurance broker should take reasonable care to ensure that the policy wordings of the excess layers provide cover on materially the same terms as the primary policy.[91] Where the broker is instructed to obtain proportionate reinsurance, he should usually ensure that the wording of the reinsurance treaty describes the underlying risk in the same terms as the underlying insurance.[92]

---

[87] [2009] EWHC 2900 (Comm); [2010] Lloyd's Rep IR 149. See also *Strategic Property Holdings No 3 Pty Ltd v Austbrokers RWA Ltd* [2012] NSWSC 1570, where insurance brokers were found liable to a client for failing to advise the client that the effect of a sub-limit within the policy was that if the insured property, with a 'declared value' of $22 million, suffered 'accidental damage' cover would be limited to $200,000.

[88] Ibid at [170].

[89] *Dunlop Haywards (DHL) Ltd v Barbon Insurance Group Ltd* (ibid) was, in part, a renewal. See also *Attorney-General v Aon New Zealand Ltd* [2008] NZHC 479, discussed in n 63 under para 3.37.

[90] [2007] EWCA Civ 710; [2007] Lloyd's Rep IR 717, at [116]. See also *Ground Gilbey Ltd v Jardine Lloyd Thompson UK Ltd* [2011] EWHC 124 (Comm); [2012] Lloyd's Rep IR 12.

[91] See, for example, *Friends Provident Life and Pensions Ltd v Sirius International Insurance Corporation* [2004] EWHC 1799 (Comm); [2005] Lloyd's Rep IR 135, where Moore-Bick J said at [14]: 'Although a material difference between the scope of the primary and excess layers might not render the cover wholly unworkable, the insured would inevitably bear a greater part of the risk himself if the scope of the cover provided by the excess layer were more limited than that provided by the primary layer.'

[92] See, for example, *British Citizens Assurance Co v L Woolland & Co* (1921) 8 Ll L R 89 and *Youell v Bland Welch & Co Ltd (No 2) (The 'Superhulls Cover' Case)* [1990] 2 Lloyd's Rep 431 and *GE Reinsurance Corp v New Hampshire Insurance Co* [2003] EWHC 402; [2004] Lloyd's Rep IR 404.

Choice of insurer

3.52 Some professional bodies limit the choice of professional indemnity insurer for members of their profession, at least for the required primary level of cover.[93] Insurance companies in the United Kingdom (and European Union) are regulated and it might be thought that a broker would be entitled to place any risk with any of them. However, there may be particular reason to question the solvency of a given insurer, in which case the broker may well be obliged to place a risk elsewhere.[94]

3.53 In *Osman v J Ralph Moss*,[95] the insured unknowingly found himself without motor insurance at the time of a road traffic accident. The Court of Appeal held that he was entitled to recover not just his premium from his brokers, but also the fine incurred as a result of driving without insurance. Sachs LJ held that the defendant brokers:

> negligently recommended this Belvedere company which, together with another company, London & Midland Insurance Company Ltd., which underwrote its policies, was much under attack in the financial Press. That was something which was held at the trial must have been known to the brokers, though it was not known to the plaintiff ... Meanwhile the brokers, on whom lay the duty not only of advising their client, but also in the circumstances of protecting him, wrongfully and negligently failed either to inform him as to whether the proposal had been accepted, in which case he had been insured by a substantially worthless policy, or whether it had not been accepted, in which case he was wholly uninsured.

3.54 In *Lewis v Tressider Andrews Associates*,[96] the broker placed the risk with a new insurer despite the fact that he knew that the insurer might not be financially stable. It was held that an insurance broker is obliged to inform the insured of any information which he receives which indicates that the insurer may not remain financially sound, even if the broker is personally satisfied that no real problem exists.

3.55 The question of the potential liability of an insurance broker in relation to the choice of reinsurer arose in the Lloyd's litigation in the 1990s and was addressed

---

This would not be the case if the reinsurance were an excess of loss treaty for a layer of the whole account such as that considered in *Axa Reinsurance (UK) Ltd v Field* [1996] 1 WLR 1026.

[93] Paragraphs 1.11, 1.14, 1.17, and 1.29.

[94] The third party brokers in *Quintano v B W Rose Pty Ltd* [2008] NSWSC 793 faced a claim for negligently insuring their client with an unregistered overseas insurer which had gone into liquidation. They claimed unsuccessfully to be indemnified against that claim by their own professional indemnity insurers, who relied upon a clause excluding cover in respect of any claim: 'arising from:

    a)   the insolvency of any insurer or reinsurer; or

    b)   any breach of the Assured's duty to advise on the suitability (which expression shall, without prejudice to the generality of such term, including financial standing) of any insurer or reinsurer utilised;...'

[95] [1970] 1 Lloyd's Rep 313.

[96] [1987] 2 Qd R 533.

in *Berriman (Sir David) v Rose Thomson Young (Underwriting) Ltd.*[97] Morison J held that, as between insurers/reinsured and brokers, the former had the particular knowledge as to the risk which was sought to be ceded. The brokers presented a list of 'sound' potential reinsurers and it was for the specialist insurer/reinsured to produce an appropriate shortlist. He therefore held that a managing agent who placed reinsurance with an insurer about whom he had no information, but whom he considered to be 'very nice' was negligent.[98]

Today, most brokers, particularly the larger brokers, will run a security committee **3.56** which will continually review insurers for the purposes of being able to approve or recommend those insurers as suitable and sound to their clients.[99] If and to the extent that such reviews become part of accepted professional standards, failure to undertake them, either at all or with reasonable skill and care, could be a breach of the duty to exercise reasonable skill and care.

Solvency of the potential insurer or insurers is not, of course, the only factor which **3.57** should inform a broker's choice. The insurer's approach, so far as known, to taking coverage issues and to settling or fighting third party claims may well be relevant considerations.

Non-disclosure, misrepresentation, and breach of warranty

The insurance broker will represent his client insured in any negotiations with **3.58** insurers. Until the material provisions of the Insurance Act 2015 come into force, the insurance broker is himself subject to a duty to disclose material facts.[100] And the insured is also subject to a duty to disclose material facts and, should he make any misrepresentation to insurers, they might be entitled to avoid the policy.[101] When the material provisions of the Insurance Act 2015 come into force, the insured will be under a duty of fair presentation. This requires the insured to disclose every material circumstance which the insured knows or ought to know or, failing that, to give the insurer sufficient information to put a prudent insurer on notice that it needs to make further enquiries for the purpose of revealing those material circumstances. And this all has to be done in a manner which would be reasonably clear and accessible to a prudent insurer.[102]

The duty of the insurance broker in relation to these matters is threefold. First, he **3.59** has to give appropriate advice and assistance to his insured client to try to ensure

---

[97] [1996] LRLR 426.

[98] Ibid at 455–60.

[99] Eg in *Permanent Trustee Australia Ltd v FAI General Insurance Company Ltd* [2003] HCA 25; (2003) 214 CLR 514 the brokers had a security committee which instructed the brokers to reduce their business with a given insurer following a reduction of its rating by a rating agency.

[100] See paras 3.87–3.97.

[101] See Chapters 5 and 6.

[102] Insurance Act 2015, s 3. See paras 5.135–5.151. It is expected that this provision will come into force in August 2016.

that the client complies with his duties. Second, as the law is at the time of writing, he must himself disclose all material facts he knows[103] and exercise skill and care to avoid making any misrepresentation himself to insurers. Third, he must make and maintain a record of his fair presentation of the risk so that this can be proved if necessary.[104]

3.60 ICOBS 5.1.4G provides:

> A firm should bear in mind the restriction on rejecting claims for non-disclosure (ICOBS 8.1.1R (3)).[105] Ways of ensuring a customer knows what he must disclose include:
> (1) explaining to a commercial customer the duty to disclose all circumstances material to a policy, what needs to be disclosed, and the consequences of any failure to make such a disclosure; or
> (2) ensuring that the commercial customer is asked clear questions about any matter material to the insurance undertaking.[106]
> ... and
> (4) asking the customer clear and specific questions about the information relevant to the policy being arranged or varied.

It is part of an insurance broker's duty to explain the duty of disclosure to his insured clients, including commercial clients.

3.61 In this regard it is not sufficient for the insurance broker simply to tell the insured client what the duty of disclosure is. The insurance broker needs to take reasonable steps to ensure that the insured understands the kinds of facts which might be material and so which need to be disclosed. The insured may not appreciate which facts are material and the broker should be alert as to which facts are or may be material and take such steps as are consistent with the exercise of reasonable skill and care to obtain pertinent information from his insured client. Where there is a detailed proposal form, the broker might reasonably consider that completion of it will elicit all material facts, but even then there will be no guarantee that there are not other material facts known to the insured.

3.62 In *Jones v Environcom Ltd (No 2)*[107] David Steel J explained:[108]

> The rationale for the imposition of these duties on a broker is that it is an unusual obligation for a contracting party, and an area of the law which can have harsh

---

[103] The scope of this obligation is discussed in paras 3.87–3.97.

[104] *Mander v Commercial Union Assurance Co Ltd* [1998] Lloyd's Rep IR 93, at 148.

[105] This provides that a regulated insurer should 'not unreasonably reject a claim (including by terminating or avoiding a policy)'.

[106] 'Insurance undertaking' is defined in the Glossary to the FSA Handbook. Essentially an 'insurance undertaking' is an undertaking which carries on the business of effecting or carrying out contracts of insurance.

[107] [2010] EWHC 759 (Comm); [2010] Lloyd's Rep IR 676. See also *Marchand v Jackson* [2012] NZHC 2892; [2013] Lloyd's Rep IR 440.

[108] Ibid at [56]. See also *Involnert Management Inc v April Grange Ltd* [2015] EWHC 2225 (Comm); [2015] 2 Lloyd's Rep 289, at [317]–[322] per Leggatt J.

consequences, not least because any non-disclosure relied upon by the underwriter to avoid the policy may have no causative significance as regards the claim that will as a result not be paid. This makes it all the more important that the lay client is told of the paramount duty to disclose and what it involves.

Further, in case the client does not appreciate what may be material, (as will often be the situation) he needs to be advised to err on the side of caution so as to disclose anything that might impinge on the judgment of a competent underwriter in assessing the risk and be helped to unearth such matters.

In that case the insurance brokers had given their client a written explanation of the duty of disclosure, but David Steel J held that it was not adequate to discharge their duty.[109]

There are limits to the steps which an insurance broker can be expected to take, **3.63** particularly where the insured is a substantial firm or other body with numerous professional practitioners.[110] The broker cannot be expected to discuss the duty of disclosure with each principal, let alone more junior employees or former partners or employees. He has to be able to deal with a single partner or other principal who is responsible for the insured's professional indemnity insurance or with a risk management department. He will, it is submitted, be entitled to rely upon that individual or department to explain to others within the insured the duty of disclosure and what information might be required to be disclosed in order to comply with it.[111]

The completion of the proposal form should be a matter for the insured, although **3.64** it is not unknown for insurance brokers to take it upon themselves to do so. If an insurance broker does complete a proposal form, he will be obliged to exercise reasonable care and skill when doing so. As Megaw LJ said in *O'Connor v BDB Kirby & Co*:[112]

When the broker took it upon himself to fill in the proposal form, the duty upon him was to use such care as was reasonable in all the circumstances towards ensuring that the answers recorded to the questions in the proposal form accurately represented the answers given to the broker by the insured. But the duty was not a duty to ensure that every answer was correct ...

If the broker does complete the proposal form, he should make it clear to the insured that the insured is responsible for the accuracy and completeness of the form.

---

[109] Ibid at [57].

[110] Care must be taken in applying cases concerning consumers or private individuals such as *McNealy v The Pennine Insurance Co Ltd* [1978] 2 Lloyd's Rep 18 in the field of professional liability insurance. This is not to say that they have no application at all, but that the relative roles and sophistication of insured and broker will often be materially different.

[111] Cf *Fisher v Guardian Insurance Co of Canada* (1995) 123 DLR (4th) 336, at [59], discussed in paras 5.129–5.130.

[112] [1972] 1 QB 90, at 101.

3.65 In the leading case of *Arab Bank plc v Zurich Insurance Co*,[113] there was a warranty that the statements made in the proposal form were 'to the best of my/our knowledge true and complete'. The form had been completed by one of the insured, who was dishonest. Rix J held that there was no breach of a warranty by the other insured. This was because to the best of their knowledge the answers were true and complete.[114] However, a different result might have followed had the warranty been purely as to the truth of the statements.[115] It follows that an insurance broker acting for multiple insureds who will be obtaining a composite policy of insurance[116] should consider carefully the form of warranty, if any, which is made in respect of the answers on any proposal form.

3.66 While the consequences of material non-disclosure or misrepresentation are mitigated or excluded in many contemporary polices of professional indemnity insurance,[117] an insurance broker whose client is seeking professional indemnity insurance should still advise that client of his duty to disclose all material facts. If there is any doubt, the prudent course is to disclose.[118] The insured client may well still be prejudiced by any failure to disclose and will usually be able to notify any matters which he is obliged to disclose under his current policy.[119]

Duties on renewal

3.67 An insurance broker who has assessed his client's needs, given appropriate advice to the client as to his duty of disclosure, arranged cover which meets the client's needs and explained any unusual or material terms to his client will have discharged his duty in relation to the policy he has obtained. When the client instructs him to obtain insurance for the following period of insurance he cannot simply rely upon what he did and said when obtaining the current policy. The insurance broker has to review and repeat what he did then, albeit taking account of what he did and learnt on that occasion.

3.68 This follows from the decision of Christopher Clarke J in *Beazley Underwriting Ltd v The Travelers Companies Incorporated*.[120] The case concerned liability under a contract by which the defendant sold a group of insurance brokers to another insurance broker. Under that contract the defendant had provided an indemnity against loss arising out of any event or matter relating to the business of the group being sold which occurred before the sale. The indemnity was extended where there was a

---

[113] [1999] 1 Lloyd's Rep 262.
[114] See further paras 6.30–6.31.
[115] [1999] 1 Lloyd's Rep 262, at 283.
[116] As to which see paras 1.32–1.45.
[117] See paras 5.73–5.104.
[118] Cf *Aiken v Stewart Wrightson Members Agency Ltd* [1995] 1 WLR 1281, at 1313.
[119] For the potential prejudice see paras 5.95 and 5.109–5.113. For the right to notify under the current policy see para 2.18.
[120] [2011] EWHC 1520 (Comm); [2012] Lloyd's Rep IR 78.

'continuing series of related events, occurrences or matters which amount or would amount to an Indemnified Claim'. One of the insurance broking businesses being sold had obtained insurance for a client on unsuitable terms. It had done so over a number of years. After the sale further policies were taken out, incorporating the same unsuitable term. The problem came to light leading to a substantial claim. The purchaser claimed under the indemnity and the defendant paid a significant proportion of the loss. The claimant had insured the defendant against its liability under the indemnity.

The claim failed for a number of reasons. One reason was that the insurance bro- **3.69**
kers had been under a duty to assess the suitability of the policy on each occasion that they acted. They could not just rely upon what they had (or had not) done in earlier years. In rejecting the claim on this ground Christopher Clarke J observed that the insurance broker was paid the same fee on renewal as for the original place-ment. The present case was particularly strong because there was a material change in the other terms which greatly increased the significance of the unsuitable term. It followed that the defendant was not liable under the indemnity and so had no claim under the insurance.

While this decision was concerned with the duty to consider the suitability of the **3.70**
policy, the reasoning must apply to other aspects of the insurance broker's duty in relation to obtaining insurance. On renewal the due discharge of his duties may not require him to do everything that he had to do when first instructed.[121] For example, it may be that on appropriate facts an insurance broker can rely on advice he has given in earlier years or confine his questions as to his client's insurance needs to whether there has been any change. But he still has to have taken appropri-ate steps to discharge the full range of his duties.

Notification of claims and circumstances

The broker's role and duties do not end with the placement of the risk.[122] The broker **3.71**
remains the insured's agent for the purposes of making claims under the policy.[123] Of particular importance in the context of professional indemnity insurance is the

---

[121] See, for example, *Eurokey Recycling Ltd v Giles Insurance Brokers Ltd* [2014] EWHC 2989 (Comm); [2015] Lloyd's Rep IR 225 (claim against insurance brokers about business interruption insurance) per Blair J at [86(vii)]: 'Further, although as a matter of common sense a client may not need annual repetition of advice previously given and understood, this assumes that the responsible personnel remains the same. It also assumes that the giving of the advice can be properly demon-strated by documentation (or otherwise), and the onus is likely to be on the broker to show this.'

[122] For recent discussion of post-placement duties of insurance brokers see, eg, *Great North Eastern Railway v JLT Corporate Risks Ltd* [2006] EWHC 1478 (Comm); [2007] Lloyd's Rep IR 38 and *HIH Casualty and General Insurance Ltd v JLT Risk Solutions Limited* [2007] EWCA Civ 710; [2007] 2 Lloyd's Rep 278. The duty of the broker in *Lewis v Tressider Andrews Associates* [1987] 2 Qd R 533 discussed in para 3.54 was a continuing one.

[123] *Anglo-African Merchants Ltd. v Bayley* [1970] 1 QB 311, *North and South Trust Co v Berkeley* [1971] 1 WLR 470 and *Callaghan and Hedges v Thompson* [2000] Lloyd's Rep IR 125.

insurance broker's role in advising as to notification of claims and of matters which have the potential to give rise to future claims and of giving notice to insurers. The right to give notice of circumstances is an important extension of cover and is linked to the duty to disclose material facts.[124] The insured may be under strict time limits for notifying circumstances.[125]

3.72 The duty of a broker in relation to the notification of claims and circumstances was considered by David Mackie QC, sitting as a Deputy High Court Judge, in *Alexander Forbes Europe Ltd v SBJ Ltd*.[126] One company in a group of brokers had separate professional indemnity insurance because the insurers of the rest of the group would not insure firms which were regulated by FIMBRA under the Financial Services Act 1986. The same firm of insurance brokers ('SBJ') acted both on the main policy insuring all members in the group save for the FIMBRA member and on the policy insuring the FIMBRA member. In October 1994 one former client of this firm made a complaint about inappropriate advice concerning her pension. At the same time, a review of possible mis-selling of pensions was underway and the insured's compliance officer identified some 500 cases in which problems were expected to arise. Another company in the group wrote to SBJ with details of the specific claim and of the review of possible mis-selling. SBJ notified the insurers of the rest of the group rather than the insurers of the FIMBRA member and only realized their mistake after the end of the policy period. The correct insurers retrospectively accepted cover for the specific claim, but denied that there had been any valid notification of circumstances.[127]

3.73 The deputy judge found that SBJ had been negligent:[128]

> SBJ as a company was well aware of the existence of two separate policies and in 1994 had recently negotiated both of them. It received a letter from [the claims manager/ director of the insured], who himself did not know the details of the Group's cover. Brokers owe duties going beyond those of a post box. It was for the brokers to get a grip on the proposed notification, to appraise it and to ensure that the information was relayed to the right place in the correct form. As the expert put it they needed a strategy for handling claims.
>
> ...
>
> If I am wrong and the memorandum and letter did not of themselves, if passed on, constitute notification of circumstances it was the duty of SBJ to have a strategy in place ... that ensured that when such information was received from clients, the broker was alive to making such notifications accurately and promptly.

3.74 Thus the insurance broker should consider the significance of information relating to claims which he receives from the insured. It is not enough for him simply

---

[124] See paras 2.06–2.10.
[125] See paras 2.116–2.120.
[126] [2002] EWHC 3121 (Comm); [2003] Lloyd's Rep IR 432.
[127] As to which see *J Rothschild Assurance plc v Collyear* [1999] Lloyd's Rep IR 6, discussed in paras 2.07–2.09.
[128] [2002] EWHC 3121 (Comm); [2003] Lloyd's Rep IR 432, at 441.

to forward it to insurers without more. He should be alert to the possible need to notify circumstances and of the extent of any contractual obligation to do so promptly.[129] He should also ensure that, where appropriate, information is conveyed to insurers in a manner which is an effective notification under the policy.[130]

Duty upon insured becoming uninsured

If an insured's cover is or will be terminated for any reason, and the broker becomes **3.75** aware of this, the broker must notify the insured of the same as soon as possible.[131] In addition, a broker may, depending on the terms of his retainer, be under a continuing duty to appraise himself of whether the insured's cover remains in place. If cover lapses or is terminated, the broker will again come under a duty to inform the insured.

The contractual relationship between insured, placing broker, and sub-broker

If a sub-broker is engaged,[132] any misrepresentation or non-disclosure in placing **3.76** the insurance will entitle the insurer to avoid as against the insured. The question therefore is whether the sub-broker owes either contractual or tortious duties of care to the insured or just to the producing broker. The usual position in law is that there will be no contract between the insured and the sub-broker.[133]

This principle was considered in *Calico Printers Association Ltd v Barclays Bank* **3.77** *Ltd*,[134] where Wright J stated that:[135]

> [English law] has in general applied the rule that even where the sub-agent is properly employed, there is still no privity between him and the principal … The agent does not as a rule escape liability to the principal merely because employment of the sub-agent is contemplated. To create privity it must be established not only that the

---

[129] As to which see paras 11.03–11.15.

[130] As to which see paras 2.51–2.115.

[131] *London Borough of Bromley v Ellis* [1971] 1 Lloyd's Rep 97. This was a further ground upon which brokers were held liable in *Youell v Bland Welch (No 2)* [1990] 2 Lloyd's Rep 431, at 446, even though this required the broker to draw the insured's attention to the shortcomings in cover that it had obtained.

[132] The broker must have authority to delegate to a sub-broker. This is normally expressly provided for in the broker's retainer.

[133] Privity of contract does not arise between the insured and the sub-broker, even though the insured has authorized the broker to contract with the sub-broker. Two separate contracts arise: one between the insured and the broker and the other between the broker and the sub-broker. While the sub-broker will not be liable in contract directly to the insured, he may owe the insured a duty of care in tort and fall under fiduciary obligations and a duty to account: see Article 35(3) of *Bowstead & Reynolds on Agency* (20th edn, Sweet & Maxwell, 2014).

[134] (1930) 36 Com Cas 71.

[135] Ibid at 77–8.

principal contemplated that a sub-agent would perform part of the contract, but also that the principal authorised the agent to create privity of contract between the principal and the sub-agent, which is a ... matter requiring precise proof.[136]

3.78 If privity is established, the principal can sue the sub-broker for breach of its various obligations directly. If there is no privity, the broker will be liable to the insured for any failure by the sub-broker to exercise reasonable care and skill or any other breach of duty.[137]

Tortious liability of the broker/sub-broker

3.79 Whether a duty of care should be imposed on the sub-broker in tort depends upon the balance to be struck between two competing principles. On the one hand, the sub-broker is speaking for the insured at placement.[138] On the other, there is a contractual chain in place between insured and broker, and between broker and sub-broker, along which the insured will be able to seek redress from his broker and the broker from the sub-broker.[139] The sub-broker will not usually owe the insured a common law duty of care. The parties have chosen to arrange their relations by a chain of contracts and good reason is needed to impose on the parties a duty of care in tort which cuts across the contractual structure which they have chosen.[140]

3.80 However, liability for economic loss may now be imposed in the event of a negligent mis-statement where the maker of that statement assumed responsibility to another in respect of that statement. This principle has been extended to parties in a chain of contracts, so that it is clear that the existence of a contractual chain is not necessarily inconsistent with a finding that one party owed a duty of care to another party even though they were not directly linked in that chain.[141] The issue

---

[136] See too *Prentis Donegan & Partners Ltd v Leeds & Leeds Co Inc* [1998] 2 Lloyds Rep 326, at 332, where Rix J held that there would only be privity between insured and the sub-broker (there the placing broker) if the insured, the broker, and the sub-broker all intended that a direct contractual relationship should arise. Where one broker employed another, the normal situation was that there was privity of contract between the two brokers. The exception, ie where the principal knew and acknowledged that the agent had to delegate all of his responsibilities to a sub-agent, was a narrow one and it was for the defendants to show some special factors to raise an argument that the general rule made way for the exception. Such cases will be rare. So in *Pangood Ltd v Barclay Brown & Co Ltd* [1999] Lloyd's Rep IR 405, it was held that there was no evidence of any intent to create privity of contract between the insured and the Lloyd's broker, as their sub-agents, and hence there could be no question of any contractual obligation to exercise skill and care being owed by the sub-agents to the insured.

[137] A point confirmed by Phillips J in *Youell v Bland Welch & Co Ltd (No 2)* [1990] 2 Lloyd's Rep 431, at 445. See also *Tudor Jones II v Crowley Colosso Ltd* [1996] 2 Lloyd's Rep 619.

[138] See para 3.76.

[139] See *Henderson v Merrett Syndicates Ltd* [1995] 2 AC 145, at 195 per Lord Goff.

[140] The question of whether and when a sub-broker will owe a duty of care in tort to the insured was discussed by Leggatt J in *Involnert Management Inc v April Grange Ltd* [2015] EWHC 2225 (Comm); [2015] 2 Lloyd's Rep 289, at [283]–[292]. He emphasized the significance of direct contact (or the lack of direct contact) between the insured and the placing broker when considering whether the latter was to be taken to have assumed responsibility to the former.

[141] *Hedley Byrne & Co v Heller & Partners Ltd* [1964] AC 465; *Henderson v Merrett Syndicates Ltd* [1995] 2 AC 465.

arose in the contract of insurance brokers in *Pangood Ltd v Barclay Brown & Co Ltd.*[142] There the insured instructed brokers to insure its premises against fire. The brokers in turn instructed Lloyd's brokers, who placed the insurance at Lloyd's. A fire occurred at the insured's premises, but the insurers refused to indemnify, relying upon a defence of breach of warranty. The insured sued the brokers on the basis that they had failed to alert the insured to the requirements of the warranty. The brokers in turn brought proceedings against the Lloyd's brokers under the Civil Liability (Contribution) Act 1978 on the basis that the Lloyd's brokers were liable to the insured for the same loss. That claim was struck out.

The Court of Appeal held that, although it was possible for a sub-agent to owe a **3.81** duty of care in tort to an ultimate principal, in the present circumstances there had been no assumption of responsibility capable of giving rise to such a duty. Beldam LJ said:[143]

> Whether it is possible to infer an assumption of contractual obligation by a sub-agent depends upon the terms on which he has been instructed by the agent. In my view, an instruction by an insurance broker to a Lloyd's broker to obtain a quotation and subsequently to effect insurance in accordance with the terms of the quotation is an inadequate basis upon which to infer the assumption of direct responsibility by the Lloyd's broker to the broker's principal.[144]

That said, it is always necessary to consider the particular facts. A duty of care was **3.82** found, despite the existence of a contractual chain, on the basis of the sub-broker's assumption of responsibility in *BP Plc v AON Ltd (No 2)*.[145] The claimant company ('BP') and a number of co-insureds instructed US brokers ('Aon Texas') to obtain all risks open cover. To obtain cover under such insurance, declarations would have to be made to the appropriate insurers. Management of the open cover was transferred to sub-brokers in London ('Aon London'), who made declarations to lead insurers but not to the following market. It was held as a preliminary issue that for a declaration under the open cover to be valid, it had to be made to the specific insurer and not just to the lead insurer. BP made a claim against Aon London in negligence on the basis that it had assumed a responsibility to BP to make valid declarations under the open cover. Aon London denied liability on the basis that all its activities were carried out within the contractual framework between BP and Aon Texas.

Colman J stated that it was clear from the authorities that the key question was **3.83** whether the sub-agent's conduct, judged objectively, was such as to amount to the

---

[142] [1999] Lloyd's Rep IR 405.

[143] Ibid at 408.

[144] Beldam LJ did consider that any responsibility assumed by the Lloyd's brokers was confined to obtaining a quotation and communicating it accurately to the brokers on behalf of the insured, which they did. He held that there was no assumption of responsibility by the third party to bring the terms of the warranty to the attention of the plaintiff: ibid at 408.

[145] [2006] EWHC 424 (Comm); [2006] Lloyd's Rep IR 577.

assumption of a personal obligation as explicitly as if the sub-agent were personally contractually binding himself to provide the advice, the information, or the services.[146] The question on the facts, therefore, was whether there was an assumption of responsibility to BP by Aon London to make declarations under the open cover. Colman J held:[147]

> There was adopted such a close relationship between Aon London and BP involving repeated direct contact between them that the substance of Aon's representation to BP was that Aon London was to perform such a crucial function in the process of effecting valid cover that in spite of the initial undertaking of Aon Texas to effect cover, Aon London was *independently* to be responsible for obtaining that cover. For this purpose it is clearly not necessary that there should have been express words to the effect that BP would have a right of action against Aon London. It would be enough if BP were entitled to infer from what was said and done that Aon London was to provide its professional services with regard to declarations and that, independently of Aon Texas or any other Aon entity, it could be relied upon by BP as undertaking responsibility to provide those services in accordance with the proper professional standards of an insurance broker on the London and European markets including Lloyd's.

3.84   Nor was this finding displaced by the contractual framework that had been put in place between BP and Aon Texas. The only contract to which Aon London was a party was with Aon Texas and the only express term of that contract was as to the sharing of fees. The position was very different from a carefully constructed chain of contracts.[148]

E. Duties to Third Party Claimants

3.85   One of the principal purposes of professional indemnity insurance is to protect the clients of the professional insured.[149] However, absent perhaps, an express assumption of responsibility to the insured's clients, a broker who negligently places professional indemnity insurance on behalf of the professional insured will not be liable in negligence to the professional's clients who would otherwise have obtained protection from the insured's policy had it been properly placed.

3.86   This issue was considered in *Macmillan v A W Knott Becker Scott Ltd.*[150] AW Knott Becker Scott (KBS) carried on business as an insurance broker at Lloyd's but went into liquidation. It was alleged to have been negligent towards certain of its clients who were claimants in the proceedings. KBS could not meet these claims.

---

[146] Ibid at [167].
[147] Ibid at [181].
[148] Ibid at [221]–[223].
[149] See paras 1.05–1.06 and see paras 7.10–7.19 as to the limits of this purpose in the construction of professional indemnity policies.
[150] [1990] 1 Lloyd's Rep 98.

The claimants claimed under the errors and omissions insurance which KBS was required to have as an insurance broker. This insurance was placed on behalf of KBS by another Lloyd's broker, Nelson Hurst & Marsh Ltd (NHM). NHM had themselves been negligent and the cover had been avoided as a result. A preliminary issue arose as to whether NHM was liable for its negligent placement of KBS's cover, not only to its clients, KBS, but also to KBS's clients—the claimants. In the absence of any direct right of action by the claimants against NHM, any damages recovered from NHM by the liquidator of KBS would be paid to KBS's creditors as a body rather than to the claimants. Nevertheless, the claim failed. Evans J held:[151]

> Insurance brokers, I am sure, would accept professional instructions on the basis that their liability for financial or economic loss arising from negligence in the performance of those instructions was restricted to their clients. If asked about possible insolvency of the clients, they would assume that their liability was towards the liquidator and towards no-one else. They would not regard themselves as effectively guaranteeing that third party claimants, even those whose claims were intended to be covered by the liability insurance, would not suffer some eventual loss should liquidation intervene. Nor would they expect to receive separate and independent claims from each of the claimants as well as from the liquidator. There being no compelling reasons why direct recovery should be permitted, that contractual expectation in my view is justified.

F. The Broker's Duty of Disclosure

The current duty

Section 19 of the Marine Insurance Act 1906

3.87 The broker's duty to act in good faith when presenting the risk to insurers derives from the insured's duty of good faith, and thus requires the broker to avoid misrepresentation and to disclose all factors material to the risk. The broker's duty of disclosure is set out in s 19 of the Marine Insurance Act 1906, which provides:

> Subject to the provisions of the preceding section as to circumstances which need not be disclosed, where an insurance is effected for the insured by an agent, the agent must disclose to the insurer—
> (a) Every material circumstance which is known to himself, and an agent to insure is deemed to know every circumstance which in the ordinary course of business ought to be known by, or to have been communicated to, him; and
> (b) Every material circumstance which the insured is bound to disclose, unless it comes to his knowledge too late to communicate it to the agent.

3.88 This duty is owed by the broker personally, and not just as agent of the insured.[152] The duty is only placed upon a broker who effects or places the insurance ('an agent

---

[151] Ibid at 110–11.
[152] The position is identical for marine and non-marine insurance: *Pryke v Gibbs Hartley Cooper Ltd* [1991] 1 Lloyd's Rep 602.

to insure') or someone that the agent to insure in turn employs to place cover. It has been held that this duty does not apply to an intermediary further back in the chain who does not place the cover,[153] although this is controversial.[154]

3.89 The information which has to be disclosed is limited to information which the insurance broker has received as agent of the insured,[155] although there have been suggestions that the obligation extends to any information which the insurance broker has.[156] An insurance broker who is defrauding his client is not obliged to disclose that fact to insurers.[157]

3.90 The insured's own duty of disclosure is considered in **Chapter 5**. The nature of the broker's duty of disclosure pursuant to ss 18 and 19 of the Marine Insurance Act 1906 was expounded by Kerr LJ in *Container Transport International Inc v Oceanus Mutual Underwriting Association (Bermuda) Ltd*,[158] as follows:

> ... one way of formulating the test as to the duty of disclosure is to ask one-self: 'Having regard to all the circumstances known or deemed to be known to the insured and to his broker, and ignoring those which are expressly excepted from the duty of disclosure, was the presentation of the risk in summary form to the underwriter a fair and substantially accurate presentation of the risk proposed for insurance, so that a prudent insurer could form a proper judgment—either on the presentation alone or by asking questions if he was sufficiently put on enquiry and wanted to know further details—whether or not to accept the proposal, and if so on what terms?' This is not an onerous duty for brokers to discharge in practice.

Misrepresentation and non-disclosure: the lead underwriter

3.91 The broker may often provide a fuller presentation of the risk to a lead underwriter, who normally acts as such because of his particular experience or standing in that area of insurance. The following market may rely on his assessment of the risk and the level of premium he sets when deciding whether to describe to the same risk too.

3.92 In *General Accident Fire & Life Insurance Corporation Ltd v Tanter, The Zephyr*,[159] Mustill LJ doubted whether a misrepresentation made by the insured or his broker to the lead underwriter would constitute a misrepresentation to the following

---

[153] See *PCW Syndicates v PCW Reinsurers* [1996] 1 WLR 1136, at 1149H per Saville LJ, with whom Rose LJ agreed on this point.
[154] See, for example, *ERC Frankona Reinsurance v American National Insurance* [2005] EWHC 1381 (Comm); [2006] Lloyd's Rep IR 157, at [124] per Andrew Smith J. See also the report of the Law Commission and the Scottish Law Commission, Law Com No 353, Scot Law Com No 238, Insurance Contract Law: Business Disclosure; Warranties; Insurers' Remedies for Fraudulent Claims; and Late Payment, July 2014, para 9.13.
[155] See *PCW Syndicates v PCW Reinsurers* [1996] 1 WLR 1136, at 1147F per Staughton LJ
[156] *El Ajou v Dollar Land Holdings Plc* [1994] 2 All ER 685, at 702 per Hoffmann LJ and *Société Anonyme d'Intermediares Luxembourgeois (SAIL) v Farex Gie* [1995] LRLR 116, at 149 per Hoffmann LJ.
[157] *Group Josi Re (formerly Groupe Josi Reassurance SA) v Walbrook Insurance Co Ltd* [1996] 1 WLR 1152.
[158] [1984] 1 Lloyd's Rep 476.
[159] [1985] 2 Lloyd's Rep 529, at 539.

market, even where the lead writer informed all or part of the following market of the content of the representation in question. Mustill LJ did say that:[160]

> One can perhaps just accept that since the slip embodies all the individual con-tracts between underwriters and assured, a misrepresentation made to the leader upon whose judgment all other subscribers in some degree rely, might be regarded as infecting all the other contracts.

However, in *Aneco Reinsurance Underwriting Ltd v Johnson & Higgins Ltd*[161] **3.93** Cresswell J held that a broker, when representing the risk to the following market, made an implied representation that the risk had been fairly presented to the lead underwriter and that misrepresentation or non-disclosure *vis-a-vis* the lead under-writer entitled the following market to avoid the policy as well. This approach was endorsed in *Peter Malcolm Brotherton v Aseguradora Colseguros SA (No 3)*,[162] where Morison J found that:[163]

> the overwhelming evidence was that the following market wrote the risk partly on the basis that there had been a fair presentation to the lead underwriter. This is commercially sensible and, it would have thought, obvious. If [the lead underwrit-er's] participation was voidable because of non-disclosure then that was a material fact which should have been, but was not disclosed to the following market.

Morison J noted that the decision in *Aneco* was confined to its own facts but that a **3.94** similar conclusion had been reached in two other cases. He concluded by saying:[164]

> … on the evidence, the expectation of the market is clear: the line goes down on the basis that there has been no material misrepresentation to the lead underwriter; if the lead underwriter is entitled to avoid the policy, so must the following market be entitled.

The reasoning of Creswell J and Morison J is convincing. **3.95**

The consequences of failure to disclose

Insurers' remedy for non-disclosure in breach of the duty set out in s 19 of the **3.96** Marine Insurance Act 1906 is avoidance of the contract of insurance or such other remedy as he may have against the insured,[165] not a claim for damages against the insurance broker. If insurers can establish that the insurance broker owed them a duty of care in tort and that the effect of the non-disclosure was that the insurance broker made a negligent misrepresentation on which they relied to their detriment, they will have a remedy in damages in the tort of negligence. And if the necessary ingredients are made out, they could have a claim in the tort of deceit. But other-wise the remedy is against the insured, not the insurance broker.

---

[160] Ibid at 539.
[161] [1998] 1 Lloyd's Rep 565, at 596.
[162] [2003] EWHC 1741; [2003] Lloyd's Rep IR 762.
[163] Ibid at [44].
[164] Ibid at [44].
[165] Eg some contractual right against the insured in lieu of the right to avoid: see paras 5.109–5.113.

3.97 If insurers avoid or establish some other remedy against the insured by reason of non-disclosure by the insurance broker in breach of the duty set out in s 19, then, if the non-disclosure was negligent, the insurance broker will be liable to the insured.

The duty under the Insurance Act 2015

3.98 The Insurance Act 2015, which is expected to come into force in August 2016, reforms the law in this area significantly. There is no longer any separate duty of disclosure on the insurance broker. Rather the insurance broker's relevant knowledge is part of what the insured is taken to know and so, potentially, to be under a duty to disclose.

3.99 Under the Insurance Act 2015 the primary duty of the insured is to disclose every material circumstance which he knows or ought to know.[166] For this purpose an insured's knowledge includes what is known to one or more individuals who are 'responsible for the insured's insurance'.[167] A person is 'responsible for the insured's insurance' if 'the individual participates on behalf of the insured in the process of procuring the insured's insurance (whether the individual does so as the insured's employee or agent, as an employee of the insured's agent or in any other capacity)'.[168] So the knowledge of all intermediaries who are involved is included, and not just that of the insurance broker who places the risk.[169]

3.100 There is no restriction as to the capacity in which the insurance broker acquired relevant knowledge as such.[170] But the reference to 'individuals' is intended to limit the knowledge to that of the natural persons who are responsible for the broking, rather than the corporate knowledge of a large broking firm. And the insured is not taken to know confidential information which an insurance broker or an individual employed by an insurance broker has acquired as a result of a business relationship with a person who is not connected with the contract of insurance.[171] This should avoid an insurance broker facing a conflict of interest between his duty to disclose material information for one client and the duty of confidentiality which he owes another client in respect of that information.

3.101 As is the case under the current law, insurers have no remedy against the insurance broker for non-disclosure unless they can establish a cause of action in either negligence or deceit. Their remedy is against the insured. But, again as is the case under the current law, an insurance broker who negligently fails to disclose material information to insurers so as to cause his client loss will be liable to his client in damages.

---

[166] Section 3(4)(a) see further paras 5.138–5.140.
[167] Sections 4(2)(b) and (3)(b).
[168] Section 4(8)(b).
[169] In possible contrast to the position before the Insurance Act 2015 comes into force: see para 3.88.
[170] As to which see para 3.89.
[171] Section 4(4).

4

ENTERING THE CONTRACT

A. Application of the Law of Contract

Contracts of insurance, including contracts of professional indemnity insurance, **4.01** are contracts and the legal principles and authorities which apply to how they are made are to be found in the law of contract rather than specifically in the law of professional indemnity insurance, or even the law of insurance.[1]

The parties must be in agreement and their agreement must encompass the mate- **4.02** rial or essential terms. The parties' agreement must be objectively demonstrated by the making of an offer by one party and the acceptance of that offer by the other party or by other circumstances. There must also be an intention to create a contract and consideration. At all stages the test is objective: the parties are judged upon appearances rather than upon their subjective intentions and understanding.

These basic principles have to be applied to a wide variety of negotiations and cir- **4.03** cumstances. There is no single way in which contracts of professional indemnity insurance are made.

The negotiations leading to the formation of a contract of professional indem- **4.04** nity insurance may amount to little more than the quotation of a rate by insurers in response to a completed proposal form or they may involve a number of exchanges between the parties. The facts considered by the Court of Appeal in

---

[1] See chapters 2 and 3 of *Chitty on Contracts* (31st edn, Sweet & Maxwell, 2014).

Dunlop Haywards Ltd v Erinaceous Commercial Property Services Ltd [2] provide a helpful example of the latter.[3]

4.05 The insured were property consultants whose business included the management of commercial property, surveying, and valuations. They sought to obtain cover through their in-house broker ('HPC'), who in turn instructed a Lloyd's broker as sub-broker.[4] In April 2005, HPC sent a draft application for insurance to the Lloyd's broker. The application was eventually signed and dated and contained details of such matters as a breakdown of the insured's fee income by areas of work. The Lloyd's broker went into the market to obtain quotations.

4.06 The first underwriter to give a quotation gave a 'very rough indication', which was expressly subject to the position of the leading underwriter. The leading underwriter subsequently gave a quotation at the same figure. The rest of the market concurred and the Lloyd's broker reported back to HPC, who forwarded the quotation to the insured. The quotation was subject to the provision of further information by the insured. The insured instructed the brokers to accept the quotation before the information requested by insurers was provided to them. The brokers did so and insurers initialled a 'firm order noted' ('FON'). The only evidence before the Court of Appeal was that an FON was a binding contract, albeit, where the quotation was subject to matters which had not been resolved ('subjectivities'), it would only be conditionally binding until the subjectivities were satisfied. Cover incepted on this basis on 1 May 2005.

4.07 The further information requested by insurers was provided at the end of May, satisfying the subjectivities. At the same time, or about the same time, the brokers obtained insurers' signatures to the slip. Cover notes were sent by the Lloyd's broker to HPC in early June and policies were issued later in the same month.

B. The Offer

An offer capable of acceptance

4.08 An offer to enter a contract must be distinguished from a mere invitation to treat. It must evince a willingness to enter a contract on particular terms with the party to whom it is addressed upon that other party accepting it. As is discussed in more detail in the following chapter,[5] it is usual for the insured to complete a proposal form before a contract of professional insurance is made. The proposal form will be

---

[2] [2009] EWCA Civ 354; [2009] Lloyd's Rep IR 464. See also *Dunlop Haywards (DHL) Ltd v Barbon Insurance Group Ltd* [2009] EWHC 2900 (Comm); [2010] Lloyd's Rep IR 149.
[3] See also *Encia Remediations Ltd v Canopius Managing Agents Ltd* [2007] EWHC 916 (Comm); [2008] Lloyd's Rep IR 79, at [81]–[99] for a detailed history of the placing of a professional indemnity policy at Lloyd's and in the companies' market.
[4] As to which see paras 3.08–3.09.
[5] See paras 5.35–5.36.

produced by insurers and will ask questions material to the risk to be insured. It is most unlikely that any communication to or from insurers before they have seen a completed proposal form will be an offer.

A broker who approaches insurers seeking their agreement to a slip will usually be **4.09** making an offer on behalf of his client. However, if the broker is seeking to test the market and circulates a 'quotation slip', he will clearly only be seeking a quotation, not a binding contract.[6]

To be capable of acceptance so as to give rise to a contract, an offer must encompass **4.10** all the terms which are necessary for there to be a contract of insurance. These are the identity of the insured, the nature of the risk to be insured, the amount to be insured, the period of cover, and the premium.[7] But in the absence of express proposals as to these matters it may be possible to deduce what the parties intended. For example, in professional indemnity insurance the period of cover for a particular profession may usually be a year. It may be implicit in such cases that the proposed duration of the risk is a year. The same may follow from previous dealings between the particular insured and insurer.

In the case of an offer by insurers an offer will usually be conditional upon there **4.11** being no material change in the risk between the time at which the offer is made and its acceptance.[8] Since the insured's duty of disclosure or of fair presentation continues until the contract of insurance is made, the insured will be obliged to inform insurers of any material change.[9]

Terms of an offer

While there are certain necessary terms which must be included within an offer, **4.12** there is no need for every term of the proposed contract to be referred to expressly or to be the subject of specific negotiation or agreement. Insurers will usually have standard terms for particular types of insurance or, in the case of some professions, there will be specified terms for professional indemnity insurance. Even if not referred to in an offer, it may be inferred that an offer is being made on terms which incorporate such standard or specified terms. In such circumstances it does not matter that the insured has not seen those terms so long as they are insurers' usual terms.[10]

---

[6] *General Reinsurance Corporation v Forsakringsaktiebolaget Fennia Patria* [1983] QB 856 at 865–7 per Kerr LJ, with whom the other members of the Court of Appeal agreed.

[7] See, for example, *Assicurazioni Generali SPA v Arab Insurance Group (BSC)* [2002] EWCA Civ 1642; [2003] Lloyd's Rep IR 131 at [50]–[51] and [209], where it was held that no reinsurance contract was made until essential terms were agreed.

[8] See, for example, *Canning v Farquhar* (1886) 16 QBD 727, where the Court of Appeal held that an offer of life insurance was made on condition that there was no material change in health between offer and acceptance.

[9] See paras 5.65 and 5.68.

[10] *Rust v Abbey Life Assurance Co Ltd* [1979] 2 Lloyd's Rep 334, per Brandon LJ at 339, citing *Adie & Sons v The Insurances Corporation Ltd* (1898) 14 TLR 544 and *General Accident Insurance Corporation v Cronk* (1901) 17 TLR 233.

4.13 So, in *Rust v Abbey Life Assurance Co Ltd*[11] the insured claimed that she had never intended to enter a property bond investment which, in substance, was a form of life insurance. The terms of the proposed policy were not seen by the insured before she sent a cheque for the premium together with a completed application form. Brandon LJ addressed the issue in these terms:

> until the policy was received by the plaintiff, she had never seen the detailed terms contained in it. That being so, can it be said that there was ever an offer by the plaintiff capable of acceptance by the first defendants on those unseen terms? The view of the learned Deputy Judge was that the application form should be interpreted as an application for investment in property bonds on the terms of the first defendants' usual form of policy, the basic terms of such usual form of policy having been clearly and sufficiently explained to the plaintiff by the second defendant at his various meetings with her, and also made known to, and approved by, two independent advisers of the plaintiff, Mr. Abrahams and Mr. Roberts. It is clear that in ordinary insurance cases a policy may become a binding contract between an insured and insurers even though the insured has not seen or expressly assented to all the detailed terms of the policy, provided always that such terms are the usual terms of the insurers.

Brandon LJ, with whom the other members of the Court of Appeal agreed, held that the Deputy Judge's conclusion that the insured had made an offer on insurers' usual terms by sending in the cheque and application form was 'a correct and justifiable analysis in law'.[12] Offers are to be considered objectively, so that any subjective intent on the part of the offeror which is unknown to the offeree is to be disregarded.

4.14 If there is an express reference to insurers' standard terms then, unless and to the extent that they conflict with terms which are the subject of express agreement, it will be readily inferred that any offer was made on the basis that the contract would incorporate those terms. So, where insurers sent a fax to insurance brokers which included the words 'terrorism exclusion (wording to be agreed)' the contract of insurance was held to include an exclusion of cover for terrorism.[13]

4.15 Because the parties are judged by objective appearances rather than internal, subjective, intention and knowledge, it does not matter that the insured fails to notice or consider the effect of the reference to insurers' standard terms and conditions. What matters is that the insured has had sufficient, that is, reasonable, notice of them. This applies to any standard terms and conditions in any contract. So, in

---

[11] [1979] 2 Lloyd's Rep 334.

[12] Ibid at 349–50.

[13] *AXA Corporate Solutions SA v National Westminster Bank Plc* [2010] EWHC 1915 (Comm); [2011] Lloyd's Rep IR 438 (Hamblen J), a case concerning product and public liability insurance. It did not matter that the insurance brokers had not forwarded the fax to the insured. See also *Livesay v Hawkins* [2012] QSC 122 (Daubney J), where insurers had given a quotation which made it clear that any contract would be on the terms in a particular policy wording and the insured had previously contracted with insurers on the same terms. It was held that the contract incorporated that wording.

Circle Freight International Ltd (t/a Mogul Air) v Medeast Gulf Exports Ltd (t/a Gulf Export)[14] the Court of Appeal held that, in the context of a carriage of goods dispute, reasonable notice of the plaintiff freight forwarding agent's standard terms of trading had been given to the defendant exporter in that they had been incorporated on eleven previous invoices sent by the former to the latter. The fact that the defendant had neither noticed the reference to the terms nor read them made no difference, as he was aware that freight forwarders normally dealt on standard terms. Taylor LJ, with whom O'Connor and Bingham LJJ agreed, said:[15]

> ... it is not necessary to the incorporation of trading terms into a contract that they should be specifically set out provided that they are conditions in common form or usual terms in the relevant business. It is sufficient if adequate notice is given identifying and relying upon the conditions and they are available on request. Other considerations apply if the conditions or any of them are particularly onerous or unusual.

In *Wyndham Rather Ltd v Eagle, Star & British Dominions Insurance Co Ltd*[16] a slip **4.16** was issued insuring the contents of premises against burglary. The proposal form indicated that it was subject to the usual conditions of the company's policy. These conditions were not mentioned on the slip but the slip stated that it was subject to the proposal form. The Court of Appeal held that those conditions referred to on the proposal were incorporated into the slip.[17]

Considered objectively an offer may incorporate insurers' standard terms even **4.17** though no express reference is made to them. For example, in *General Accident Insurance Corporation v Cronk*[18] the insured submitted a proposal of accident insurance to insurers, who purported to accept the proposal by sending a policy which contained terms not mentioned in the proposal. The insured later argued that, as the terms of the policy did not correspond with those of the proposal, insurers had rejected the proposal. Rather, the insured contended, insurers had made a counter-offer to which the insured had not consented, so that no contract came into being. The Divisional Court rejected this argument and found that the proposal must be taken to have been submitted on the basis that any contract would include the ordinary form of policy issued by insurers. Therefore, the proposal did correspond with the terms of the policy sent and insurers had accepted the offer by sending their standard policy.[19]

---

[14] [1988] 2 Lloyd's Rep 427.
[15] Ibid at 433.
[16] (1925) 21 Ll L Rep 214.
[17] See also *Nsubuga v Commercial Union* [1998] 2 Lloyd's Rep 682, where insurers relied upon the following clause: 'If any claim be in any respect fraudulent or if any fraudulent means or devices are used by the Insured ... to obtain benefit under this Policy all benefit will be forfeited'. The proposal form signed by the insured had referred to insurers' standard terms, but not drawn attention to this particular term. Thomas J held that, given that the term was 'a very common type of clause to be found in all fire policies', there was no need for it to have been brought to the insured's specific attention.
[18] (1901) 17 TLR 233.
[19] See also *Rust v Abbey Life Assurance Co Ltd* [1979] 2 Lloyd's Rep 334.

4.18   In such cases the insured knows (or is taken objectively to know) that insurers will have standard terms which they will expect to be included in any policy. He is willing (or is taken objectively to be willing) to contract on those terms, on the assumption that they are terms which would be expected to be in a policy of the kind he is seeking. However, if a particular insurer's standard terms are unusual to the prejudice of the insured, the insured will not be taken to have offered to agree a policy which included such terms. Again, this is part of the general law of contract.

4.19   It is well established in the general law of contract that, if a party has unusual and onerous standard terms which are to be incorporated into the contract, they must be fairly brought to the other party's attention during the negotiations.[20] So in *Interfoto Picture Library Ltd v Stiletto Visual Programmes Ltd*[21] the defendant hired 47 transparencies from the plaintiff's photographic transparency lending library. They arrived with a delivery note which contained nine printed conditions. Condition 2 required return of the transparencies in fourteen days or the payment thereafter of £5 a day plus VAT for each transparency retained.

4.20   The Court of Appeal held that where a particularly onerous or unusual condition was sought to be incorporated in a contract, the party imposing it must show that that particular condition was brought fairly to the attention of the other party. Bingham LJ said:[22]

> The crucial question in the case is whether the plaintiffs can be said fairly and reasonably to have brought condition 2 to the notice of the defendants. The judge made no finding on the point, but I think that it is open to this court to draw an inference from the primary findings which he did make. In my opinion the plaintiffs did not do so. They delivered 47 transparencies, which was a number the defendants had not specifically asked for. Condition 2 contained a daily rate per transparency after the initial period of 14 days many times greater than was usual or (so far as the evidence shows) heard of. For these 47 transparencies there was to be a charge for each day of delay of £235 plus value added tax. The result would be that a venial period of delay, as here, would lead to an inordinate liability. The defendants are not to be relieved of that liability because they did not read the condition, although doubtless they did not; but in my judgment they are to be relieved

---

[20] *Thornton v Shoe Lane Parking Ltd* [1971] 2 QB 163, at 172–3, per McGaw LJ, citing *Parker v The South Eastern Railway Company* (1877) LR 2 CPD 416, at 424 per Mellish LJ and *Hood v Anchor Line (Henderson Brothers) Ltd* [1918] AC 837, at 846–7 per Lord Dunedin, who said: 'Accordingly it is in each case a question of circumstance whether the sort of restriction that is expressed in any writing (which, of course, includes printed matter) is a thing that is usual, and whether, being usual, it has been fairly brought before the notice of the accepting party.'

McGaw LJ distinguished between what is necessary to show that one party's standard conditions have been brought to the attention of the other party and what is necessary to show that a particular, unusual condition was brought to the other party's attention. In the latter case, it must be shown that the intention to include a term of that particular nature was fairly brought to the other party's attention.

[21] [1989] QB 433.

[22] Ibid at 445.

because the plaintiffs did not do what was necessary to draw this unreasonable and extortionate clause fairly to their attention.

In his judgment in the *Interfoto* case, Bingham LJ drew attention to the absence **4.21** of 'an overriding principle that in making and carrying out contracts parties should act in good faith'. However, as he observed, the common law has held that certain classes of contract, including contracts of insurance, are contracts of the utmost good faith.[23] In an insurance context, another way of considering the question of adequacy of notice of unusual terms may be the application of that doctrine so that the party who seeks to introduce an unusually onerous provision should disclose that term to the other party before the contract is made.[24]

In the final analysis, the answer to the question as to whether an offer was made on **4.22** the basis that the contract, if made, would include a particular term will depend upon the apparent intention of the party making the offer. Where a party has signed a document which expressly incorporates the other party's standard terms and contains an offer to contract on that basis, it will be harder for him to persuade a court that he did not intend the contract, if made, to incorporate those terms, even if he did not know what they were, unless the terms are exceptionally unusual and onerous. However, where the party merely knows (or is taken to know) that the other party will expect to include terms in the contract, because such contracts usually have such terms, he is less likely to be taken to have offered to contract on the basis of unusual and onerous terms which he would not reasonably be expected to have anticipated.

Termination of offer

An offeror may specify the time during which his offer is open for acceptance. In **4.23** the absence of such a stipulation offers are open for acceptance for a reasonable time. However, an offeror can always withdraw an offer unless and until it has been accepted. To do so, the offeror must communicate the withdrawal to the offeree before the latter accepts the offer.[25]

An offer will also be terminated if it is rejected.[26] Rejection of an offer must be **4.24** distinguished from a request for further information about the offer, although

---

[23] Ibid at 439.

[24] However there are practical difficulties with this. It will be insurers whose standard terms are in issue. The remedy available to the insured for non-disclosure by insurers is avoidance of the contract of insurance. That is not likely to be an attractive or practical option if the insured has a claim for an indemnity under the contract of insurance. And after the relevant provisions of the Insurance Act 2015 come into force, insurers will not be subject to an obligation to disclosure material circumstances to the insured (see paras 5.135–5.151).

[25] See, for example, *Byrne v Van Tienhoven* (1880) 5 CPD 344 and *Henthorn v Fraser* [1892] 2 Ch 27.

[26] See, for example, *OTM Ltd v Hydranautics* [1981] 2 Lloyd's Rep 211, at 214.

the difference may be slight. For example, a response to an offer to sell at a given price couched in terms of an offer to buy at a lower price will be a rejection,[27] but a response inquiring whether the seller is prepared to reduce the price may only be a request for information.[28]

C. The Acceptance

Correspondence with offer

4.25   For a contract of insurance to come into existence, the terms of the offer must be mirrored by the terms of the acceptance. If the purported acceptance does not mirror the terms of an offer, it will constitute a counter-offer which will in turn be capable of acceptance. A response may be an acceptance even if, at first sight, it appears to introduce new terms. For example, if an offer implicitly incorporated insurers' usual standard terms,[29] a response by insurers which includes those terms can be an acceptance, even though there has been no express mention of the terms before.

4.26   The terms in which the response to an offer is couched are to be construed objectively. If so construed the response shows an intention to accept the offer, there will be a contract. For example, in *Colonial Insurance Co of New Zealand v Adelaide Marine Insurance Co*[30] marine insurance was sought for a cargo of wheat 'at and from Timaru' (the port at which the cargo was to be loaded) to the destination. Insurers replied to the insured that 'in accordance with your written request' the insured was provisionally insured 'from Timaru'. When the vessel and cargo were lost in a gale while still at Timaru, the defendant insurers sought to avoid liability for the loss on the ground that there was no correspondence between the request for insurance and their response to it, because of the omission of the words 'at and'. The argument failed. Giving the opinion of the Privy Council, Sir Barnes Peacock said:[31]

> There could be no doubt entertained by the defendants as to the meaning of the words 'at and from' contained in the proposal, and their Lordships are of opinion that the answer shewed that their acceptance was intended to be in all respects in accordance and in conformity with the proposal, and that, notwithstanding they used only the word 'from' they intended to accept the proposal at and from, and consequently that there was a binding contract to that effect.

---

[27]   As occurred in *Hyde v Wrench* (1840) 3 Beav 334; 49 ER 132. The addition of any new term will involve a counter-offer, which will 'kill' the original offer: see *Butler Machine Tool Ltd v Ex-Cell-O Corporation (England) Ltd* [1979] 1 WLR 401, at 404 per Lord Denning MR and at 406 per Lawton LJ.

[28]   As in *Gibson v Manchester City Council* [1979] 1 WLR 294, at 302 per Lord Edmund-Davies.

[29]   As to which see paras 4.12–4.22.

[30]   (1886) 12 App Cas 128.

[31]   Ibid at 134.

Where, however, objective analysis of the response shows that it is not just an **4.27** acceptance of the offer, albeit not in identical language, but that it introduces some new term or qualifies some term of the offer, then the response is not an acceptance, but a counter-offer.[32]

In the London insurance market acceptance will usually occur when insurers **4.28** scratch a slip presented to them by the insurance brokers acting on behalf of the insured.[33] It is not unknown for insurers to scratch the slip but to add 'subjectivities', that is, to stipulate that cover is subject to one or more things. When this is done there are at least three possibilities. First, insurers' acceptance may be qualified and not binding unless and until the subjectivity is removed or waived. For a binding contract to come into place, insurers' further unqualified agreement will be needed. Second, there may be a conditional contract so that, once the subjectivity is satisfied, it will come into operation without more. Third, the insured is held covered for a limited period.[34]

The meaning and effect of the subjectivity in issue determine which of these pos- **4.29** sible analyses is correct in any given case.[35] But the conventional analysis is the first.[36] A qualified acceptance is not an acceptance which gives rise to a binding contract. So, when insurers scratched a slip for professional indemnity insurance, but did so subject to satisfactory reinsurance, proposal forms and completion of a millennium (Y2K) questionnaire, there was no contract.[37] Subjectivities of that type go beyond mere 'administrative requirements, or stipulations that are required to be satisfied during the course of the insurance'.[38]

A qualified acceptance does not give rise to a binding contract, but can be a counter- **4.30** offer which is capable of acceptance unless and until it is revoked. Where, however, the subjectivity is provision of a proposal form, the position is more difficult. In such a case insurers would expect to be able to reach a final decision as to whether

---

[32] See, for example, *Lark v Outhwaite* [1991] 2 Lloyd's Rep 132, at 139, where Hirst J applied the test set out by Kerr J in *Global Tankers Inc v Amercoat Europa NV* [1975] 1 Lloyd's Rep 666, at 671: 'The test is whether or not a reasonable person in the position of the recipient ... would regard this telex as introducing a new term into the bargain, and not as a clean acceptance of the offer.'

[33] See para 4.09.

[34] See the analysis of Christopher Clarke J in *Beazley Underwriting Ltd v The Travelers Companies Incorporated* [2011] EWHC 1520 (Comm); [2012] Lloyd's Rep IR 78, at [168].

[35] In *Involnert Management Inc v April Grange Ltd* [2015] EWHC 2225 (Comm); [2015] 2 Lloyd's Rep 289 the subjectivity on the declaration was 'subject to satisfactory proposal form ... within 7 days of inception'. Leggatt J held that the effect of these words as the insurers agreed to insure for 7 days unconditionally. They also agreed to insure after the first 7 days if the insured presented a satisfactory proposal form within the 7 day period.

[36] *Beazley Underwriting Ltd v The Travelers Companies Incorporated* [2011] EWHC 1520 (Comm); [2012] Lloyd's Rep IR 78 at [169].

[37] Ibid at [169]–[194]. See also *Société Anonyme d'Intermediaries Luxembourgeois (SAIL) v Farex Gie* [1995] LRLR 116, at page 121 per Evans J.

[38] Ibid at [175]. For an example of subjectivities which were matters of administration see *Bonner v Cox Dedicated Corporate Member Ltd* [2004] EWHC 2963 (Comm); [2005] Lloyd's Rep IR 569, at [93]–[94] per Morison J.

to accept the risk and, if so, on what terms, in the light of the information on the proposal form so that a scratch on those terms may not be an offer capable of acceptance.[39]

Method of acceptance

4.31 Acceptance is usually made by the use of language, but may be by conduct. For example, insurers may accept an offer by issuing the policy and the insured may accept an offer by tendering the premium.

4.32 It is not unusual for a number of different insurers to subscribe to a particular professional indemnity policy. Each will insure a stated percentage of the total risk for his own account alone. In the London market each insurer will accept separately, usually by scratching (ie stamping, dating, and initialling) a slip. In each case a contract is made when the slip is scratched and not when the risk is fully subscribed.[40] However, this is the general practice and it is not always followed.[41]

4.33 It sometimes happens that a slip is oversubscribed in that the total of the lines accepted by the various insurers exceeds 100 per cent. When that happens the custom is for the lines to be written down proportionately. Despite this possibility, a binding contract is made when each insurer scratches the slip and each insurer is bound, subject to the possibility that his line will be written down.[42]

Communication of acceptance

4.34 No contract can be concluded until the acceptance is brought to the attention of the offeror.[43] As the rule is for the benefit of the offeror, he can waive the rule that acceptance is ineffective until actually received. The offeror may even waive the requirement of communication altogether. Waiver may be inferred from market practice.[44]

---

[39] The difficulties which arise in such circumstances were considered by Christopher Clarke J in *Beazley Underwriting Ltd v The Travelers Companies Incorporated* [2011] EWHC 1520 (Comm); [2012] Lloyd's Rep IR 78, at [184].

[40] *Eagle Star Insurance Co Ltd v Spratt* [1971] 2 Lloyd's Rep 116, at 124 per Lord Denning MR; *General Reinsurance Corporation v Forsakringsaktiebolaget Fennia Patria* [1983] QB 856. See also *ERC Frankona Reinsurance v American National Insurance Co* [2005] EWHC 1381 (Comm); [2006] Lloyd's Rep IR 157, at [74]–[78], where Andrew Smith J held that the addition of the initials 'TBE' ('to be entered') after the scratch without more meant that the insurer did not have to hand his records in which to enter the contract. Had further words of qualification been added after 'TBE', the position might have been different.

[41] *Crane v Hannover Ruckversicheringsaktiengesellschaft* [2008] EWHC 3165 (Comm); [2010] Lloyd's Rep IR 93, at [112] per Walker J.

[42] *General Reinsurance Corporation v Forsakringsaktiebolaget Fennia Patria* [1983] QB 856.

[43] *Brinkibon Ltd v Stahag Stahl und Stahlwarenhandelsgesellschaft GmbH* [1983] 2 AC 34.

[44] See, for example, *General Accident Fire and Life Assurance Corporation v Tanter (The Zephyr)* [1984] 1 Lloyd's Rep 58, at 71–2 per Hobhouse J (reversed on other grounds: [1985] 2 Lloyd's Rep 529) and *Mander v Commercial Union Assurance Co Plc* [1998] Lloyd's Rep IR 93, at 104–5 per Rix J.

While acceptance should be communicated to the offeror, it is possible for accept- **4.35** ance to be shown by an absence of response or reaction, ie by silence. An alternative ground upon which a binding contract was found in *Rust v Abbey Life Assurance Co Ltd*[45] was the insured's silence. The insured had received the policy wording, which, on her case was an entirely different document from that which she was expecting, and did nothing about it for seven months. On the facts this was sufficient to constitute acceptance. However, such a finding will only be made in exceptional circumstances.[46] Usually silence will not constitute acceptance.[47]

So, in *New Hampshire Insurance Co v MGN Ltd*[48] in two years in succession one **4.36** insurer ('Chubb') who participated in a programme of fidelity insurance for a number of companies produced a form of policy wording which differed materially from the terms already agreed between the parties and recorded on the slips. In the first year a copy of the policy was sent via the brokers to the insured, who wrote on it 'checked and OK' and put it in a cupboard. In the second year the policy wording was given to the brokers. No response was made to Chubb in either year. Potter J held that the production of the policies constituted offers to vary the terms which had previously been agreed as recorded in the slips and that those offers had not been accepted by silence. He said:[49]

> As to those rules, [counsel for Chubb] accepts the position that communication of acceptance is in principle required and that, in the absence of evidence of custom or the existence of a previous course of dealing, silence as such cannot amount to acceptance. Nonetheless, he submits that in the particular circumstances of this case, receipt of an anticipated policy and its retention without demur amounted to acceptance by conduct of any variations from the slip contract.
>
> I do not accept that submission. Given [counsel for Chubb's] concession that silence or inactivity in the face of a counter offer is not in itself enough, it seems to me that he must demonstrate that Chubb fall within the ambit of one of the recognized formulations of exception to the rule which, in given circumstances, enable the Court to treat such silence or inactivity as a form of acceptance by conduct or as amounting to a form of representation by silence, which may give rise to some kind of estoppel. Such exceptions are usually (as it seems to me) predicated on some kind of duty to speak in the face of the likelihood that the offeror, in the absence of objection or demur from the offeree within a reasonable period, will act or forebear to act on the reasonable assumption that his offer has been accepted.

Potter J's judgment on this issue was upheld by the Court of Appeal.[50] In *New* **4.37** *Hampshire Insurance Co v MGN Ltd* the policies in question were part of a wider

---

[45] [1979] 2 Lloyd's Rep 334: for the other ground, see para 4.13.

[46] Per Lord Steyn in *Vitol SA v Norelf Ltd, The Santa Clara* [1996] AC 800, at 812. While approving *Rust v Abbey Life Assurance Co Ltd* [1979] 2 Lloyd's Rep 334, Lord Steyn said that it was only in exceptional cases that English law recognized acceptance by silence.

[47] *Brogden v The Metropolitan Railway Co* (1877) 2 App Cas 666, at 692 per Lord Blackburn.

[48] [1997] LRLR 24.

[49] Ibid at 34.

[50] Ibid at 52–5.

programme of insurance and all the other insurers had contracted on the terms which were to be found in the slips agreed between the insured and Chubb. It would therefore have been surprising if the insured had actually agreed that part of the programme should be on materially different terms. It may also be harder to find acceptance by silence in cases in which the parties had reached an agreement on one set of terms and a policy in different terms is then sent to the insured than in cases in which there is no prior agreement and the policy wording is sent as a counter-offer to an offer from the insured.[51]

4.38 In upholding Potter J's decision, Staughton LJ, observed:[52]

> The field of insurance may well be one where it is normal practice to make a pre-liminary contract, and then for one party (the insurers) to send detailed terms to the other, not expecting a reply unless the other regards them as unsatisfactory. This may be what happens in ordinary life with motor insurance or householder's comprehensive insurance. Often the necessary acceptance can be inferred when the insured, having received the proposed policy, pays the premium.

This applies to some, but not all, contracts of professional indemnity insurance.

D. Form of Contract

4.39 While there is no requirement in law for a contract of professional indemnity insurance to be in writing, in practice there will usually be one or more documents which either evidence or contain the terms of the contract. They include cover notes, FONs,[53] slips initialled by insurers, certificates of insurance, and full policy wordings.

4.40 As has been shown, it is possible for one of these documents to be replaced or supplemented by another.[54] Where that occurs, issues may arise as to whether later documents accurately reflect what was agreed in earlier documents and as to whether earlier documents may be used to ascertain the true meaning and effect of later documents. These issues are addressed in **Chapter 7**.[55]

---

[51] Ibid at 54; see also *MacGillivray*, para 2-025.

[52] Ibid at 54.

[53] See para 4.06. This is based upon the evidence before the Court of Appeal in *Dunlop Haywards Limited v Erinaceous Commercial Property Services Limited* [2009] EWCA Civ 354; [2009] Lloyd's Rep IR 464.

[54] Paragraphs 4.07 and 4.36.

[55] See paras 7.43–7.44.

5

THE DUTY OF FAIR PRESENTATION

A. Introduction: The Changing Law

At the time of writing, when the insured is not an individual who is entering the contract wholly or mainly for purposes unrelated to the individual's trade, business, or profession, the law requires the parties to a contract of insurance to show the utmost good faith to each other when making the contract. This requires each party to disclose to the other party material circumstances of which it knows or is deemed to know. Unless the contract provides otherwise, the remedy for failure to do so is avoidance of the contract of insurance. This is the common law as codified in the Marine Insurance Act 1906. **5.01**

Where the insured is an individual who is entering the contract wholly or mainly for purposes unrelated to the individual's trade, business, or profession, the common law duty of good faith no longer applies. Instead, the Consumer Insurance **5.02**

(Disclosure and Representations) Act 2012 imposes a new duty on the insured: a duty to take reasonable care not to make a misrepresentation to the insurer.[1] The Act also provides for a range of remedies in the case of 'qualifying' misrepresentations which are careless rather than deliberate or reckless.[2] The insured under contracts of professional indemnity insurance will be entering the contract wholly or mainly for the purposes of their profession. Therefore the Consumer Insurance (Disclosure and Representations) Act 2012 is not considered further.

5.03 When they come into force the relevant provisions of the Insurance Act 2015 will modify the duty of disclosure in contracts of professional indemnity insurance. The duty of utmost good faith will be replaced by a 'duty of fair presentation' with a range of remedies for breaches of that duty which are neither fraudulent nor reckless. At the time of writing the relevant provisions are due to come into force on 12 August 2016.

5.04 In this chapter the existing law is considered first. Then the relevant provisions of the Insurance Act 2015 are discussed.

B. The Duty of Good Faith in Outline

5.05 In common law all contracts of insurance are contracts of the utmost good faith.[3] The parties are expected to show the utmost good faith towards each other both when making and performing the contract.[4] When it comes to the making of a contract of insurance, each party is obliged to disclose to the other party material circumstances of which it knows or which it is deemed to know. The common law rule governing the insured's duty of disclosure is codified in s 18 of the Marine Insurance Act,[5] subsections (1) and (2) of which provide:

---

[1] Subsection 2(2) of the Consumer Insurance (Disclosure and Representations) Act 2012. Subsection 2(3) provides that a failure by the consumer to comply with the insurer's request to confirm or amend particulars previously given is capable of being a misrepresentation for the purposes of this Act (whether or not it could be apart from that subsection).

[2] 'Qualifying representations' are defined in s 4 of the Act. Section 5 specifies what is required for a qualifying representation to be 'deliberate or reckless' rather than 'careless'. The remedies are set out in Schedule 1 to the Act. In the case of careless qualifying representations, the remedy depends upon what insurers would have done had the insured complied with the duty to take reasonable care not to make a representation and so are not limited to avoidance of the contract of insurance.

[3] Section 17 of the Marine Insurance Act 1906 provides that a contract of insurance is 'based upon the utmost good faith' and may be avoided by either party if the utmost good faith is not observed by the other. (This is subject to amendment by s 14(3)(a) of the Insurance Act 2015 so as to delete the remedy of avoidance for non-observance.)

[4] *Manifest Shipping Co Ltd v Uni-Polaris Co Ltd, The Star Sea* [2001] UKHL 1; [2003] 1 AC 469. For the impact of the obligation of the utmost good faith on the construction of contracts of professional indemnity insurance, see paras 7.66–7.69. For the impact of the obligation on the making of and response to claims, see paras 11.56–11.62 and 12.52–12.55.

[5] Sections 17–20 of the Marine Insurance Act 1906 codified the common law of insurance and, subject to the Consumer Insurance (Disclosure and Representations) Act 2012 and the Insurance Act 2015, have general application beyond marine insurance: see, for example, *PCW Syndicates v*

Duties of the Assured

(1) Subject to the provisions of this section, the assured must disclose to the insurer, before the contract is concluded, every material circumstance which is known to the assured, and the assured is deemed to know every circumstance which, in the ordinary course of business, ought to be known by him. If the assured fails to make such disclosure, the insurer may avoid the contract.

(2) Every circumstance is material which would influence the judgment of a prudent insurer in fixing the premium, or determining whether he will take the risk.[6]

While the obligation to make disclosure applies to both parties, in practice it will **5.06** usually be the insured who has, or is deemed to have, knowledge of circumstances which have to be disclosed. This is because the insured will usually have much greater knowledge of the risk sought to be insured than will insurers. As Lord Mansfield said in *Carter v Boehm*:[7]

The special facts, upon which the contingent chance is to be computed, lie most commonly in the knowledge of the insured only: the under-writer trusts to his representation, and proceeds upon confidence that he does not keep any circumstance in his knowledge, to mislead the under-writer into a belief that the circumstance does not exist, and to induce him to estimate the risque, as if it did not exist.

The consequences of failure to comply with the duty of disclosure can be severe. **5.07** Non-disclosure by either party entitles the other to avoid the policy from the beginning even if the non-disclosure was unintentional, non-negligent, and unconnected with the circumstances which have given rise to a claim on the policy. The right to avoid can be excluded by contract[8] or waived.[9]

C. What Must be Disclosed

The insured's knowledge

The insured is obliged to disclose material circumstances of which he knows. In the **5.08** case of an insured who is a single, natural person, his knowledge of any particular material circumstance is a question of fact.[10]

PCW Reinsurers [1996] 1 WLR 1136, at 1140 and *HIH Casualty & General Insurance Ltd v Chase Manhattan Bank* [2003] UKHL 6; [2003] 2 Lloyd's Rep 61, at [42].

[6] Subsection (3) sets out what need not be disclosed and is considered in paras 5.54–5.64.

[7] (1766) 3 Burr 1905, at 1909; 97 ER 1162, at 1164. See also *Pan Atlantic Insurance Co Ltd v Pine Top Insurance Co Ltd* [1995] 1 AC 501, at 543 per Lord Mustill: 'the inequalities of knowledge between assured and underwriter have led to the creation of a special duty to make accurate disclosure of sufficient facts to restore the balance and remedy the injustice of holding the underwriter to a speculation which he had been unable fairly to assess'.

The insured will not always be better informed than insurers. See, for example, *HIH Casualty & General Insurance Ltd v Chase Manhattan Bank* [2003] UKHL 6; [2003] 2 Lloyd's Rep 61.

[8] See paras 5.73–5.106.

[9] See para 5.72.

[10] *PCW Syndicates v PCW Reinsurers* [1996] 1 WLR 1136, at 1141.

5.09 As is explained below,[11] the fact that most policies of professional indemnity insurance are composite[12] means that there can be a number of separate insureds and the question of whether there has been any non-disclosure of material circumstances may have to be considered in relation to each of them separately. In order to decide whether a particular insured has failed to comply with his duty of disclosure, the knowledge of that particular insured has to be considered.

Actual knowledge of bodies corporate

5.10 Where the insured is a body corporate (a limited liability company or limited liability partnership), it is necessary to establish which pieces of information known by which natural persons are to be treated as the knowledge of that body corporate.

5.11 There are two ways in which the knowledge of a natural person will be that of a body corporate. The first is where the natural person is the embodiment of the company so that his acts, omissions or knowledge are taken to be those of the company itself. This is usually referred to as attribution. The second is on the basis of agency: in some circumstances the acts or knowledge of an agent will be imputed to his principal. Neither attribution nor imputation of knowledge is the same as vicarious liability. Each has its own set of rules and it is important not to confuse them.[13]

5.12 In the context of the duty of disclosure, imputation of knowledge of a body corporate's agents to that body is effectively covered by the combination of: (i) the fact that the body corporate is deemed to know everything which in the ordinary course of business should be known by it;[14] and (ii) by the separate obligation, embodied in s 19 of the Marine Insurance Act 1906, on an agent employed to effect insurance to disclose not only what the insured knows but also material facts known by the agent, even if not known by the insured.[15] In the circumstances, there is little, if any, scope for imputing knowledge held by other agents.[16]

Attribution of knowledge

5.13 In relation to attribution, the 'primary' rules are to be found in the constitution of a body corporate, either as expressly stated in the constitution or as implied by law.[17] So, in the case of a limited liability company the articles of association will

---

[11] See paras 5.114–5.134.

[12] As to which see paras 1.32–1.45.

[13] *Man Nutzfahrzeuge AG v Freightliner Ltd* [2005] EWHC 2347 (Comm), at [154] per Moore-Bick LJ.

[14] Section 18(1) of the Marine Insurance Act 1906: see paras 5.15–5.22.

[15] As to which see paras 3.87–3.97.

[16] *PCW Syndicates v PCW Reinsurers* [1996] 1 WLR 1136, at 1142–3.

[17] *Meridian Global Asset Management Asia Ltd v Securities Commission* [1995] 2 AC 500, at 506.

be its constitution. These will usually provide that decisions by a majority of the shareholders will be decisions of the company for some purposes and decisions by a majority of the board of directors will be decisions of the company for other purposes.

These 'primary' rules cannot provide the answer in all circumstances: limited **5.14** liability companies do not act solely through resolutions of shareholders or directors, but through individual directors and other senior managers and employees. Generally, the rights and liabilities of a body corporate for the acts and omissions of its management and other employees will be determined by the usual principles of agency and vicarious liability. However, where, as with the duty of disclosure, questions of the knowledge (or other mental states) of the body corporate arise, these usual principles will not provide the answer. In relation to attribution of knowledge, it will usually be a question of identifying those natural persons who are the 'directing mind and will' of the body corporate.[18] In practice this will usually mean the body's high management and, if different, those employees responsible for arranging the insurance.[19] Where the insurance is composite,[20] as is often the case with professional indemnity insurance, the knowledge of one insured, even if he is responsible for arranging the insurance, may not be attributed to the other insureds. And it may be that the relevant rule of attribution is not the 'directing mind and will' test, but will be derived from the terms of the contract of insurance and other relevant documents such as the proposal form. This is discussed further below.[21]

Constructive knowledge

The insured's duty of disclosure extends to 'every circumstance which, in the ordi- **5.15** nary course of business, ought to be known by him'.[22] This is potentially very wide, but in practice the circumstances of which an insured is deemed to know are carefully circumscribed.

---

[18] See, for example, *Tesco Supermarkets Ltd v Nattrass* [1972] AC 153, per Lord Reid at 170. In *Meridian Global Asset Management Asia Ltd v Securities Commission* [1995] 2 AC 500, at 507, Lord Hoffmann explained that it was always necessary to construe the relevant rule or statutory provision in order to ascertain its purpose and how it was intended to apply to bodies corporate. This will identify the natural persons whose acts or state of mind are to be taken as those of the body corporate for the purposes of the rule or provision. It follows that 'the question is one of construction rather than metaphysics'. Usually, but not always, the answer will be that the natural person or persons who are the 'directing mind and will' of the company will be identified with the company (ibid at 511).

[19] *PCW Syndicates v PCW Reinsurers* [1996] 1 WLR 1136, at 1142. See also *Regina Fur Company Ltd v Bossum* [1957] 2 Lloyd's Rep 466, where Pearson J held that a director of the insured company had sufficient authority and involvement in the placing of all-risks insurance for his knowledge to be imputed to the company.

[20] As to which see paras 1.32–1.45.

[21] Paras 5.114–5.134. See also paras 8.45–8.54.

[22] Section 18(1) of the Marine Insurance Act 1906.

No duty to acquire knowledge

5.16 The insured's duty of disclosure does not require disclosure of every circumstance of which the insured could have learned had he chosen to make the necessary inquiries, nor even of every circumstance which the insured would have learned had he run his business in an efficient way.[23] The insured is not under any duty to make inquiries or investigations as to facts outside his knowledge in order to obtain information for insurers.[24] However, for this purpose the insured will be deemed to know matters to which he has deliberately turned a blind eye by failing to ask questions to which he did not want to know the answer.[25]

Agents to know

5.17 An insured will also be deemed to know information known to his agents if those agents are under a duty to pass on that information to him.[26] For example, in *London Marine Insurance Company Ltd v General Marine Underwriters' Association Ltd*[27] the reinsured was deemed to know of a partial loss of a ship which they insured. The loss was reported on a casualty slip received by the reinsured's underwriters, but the underwriters had simply placed the casualty slip in a drawer, rather than passing it on to the claims department, which should have passed the information on to the reinsurance department.[28]

Agents identified with their principals

5.18 An insured will also be deemed to know information known to an agent to whom he has so delegated or entrusted a matter or matters that, in respect of that matter or matters, the agent is in effect to be identified with his principal, the insured.[29] For example, in *Inversiones Manria SA v Sphere Drake Insurance Co Plc (the 'Dora')*[30] the insured yacht owners entrusted the management of their yacht

---

[23] *Australia & New Zealand Bank Ltd v Colonial & Eagle Wharves Ltd* [1960] 2 Lloyd's Rep 241, at 252 per McNair J, where, rejecting insurers' submissions that the board of the insured company should have made inquiries which a reasonable, prudent insured in its position would have done, said: 'To impose such an obligation upon the proposer is tantamount to holding that insurers only insure persons who conduct their business prudently, whereas it is a commonplace that one of the purposes of insurance is to cover yourself against your own negligence or the negligence of your servants.' See also *ERC Frankona Reinsurance v American National Insurance Co* [2005] EWHC 1381 (Comm); [2006] Lloyd's Rep IR 157, per Andrew Smith J at [120].

[24] *Simner v New India Insurance Co Ltd* [1995] LRLR 240, at 253.

[25] Ibid at 253 per HH Judge Diamond QC, sitting as a High Court Judge and *ERC Frankona Reinsurance v American National Insurance Co* [2005] EWHC 1381 (Comm); [2006] Lloyd's Rep IR 157, per Andrew Smith J at [120].

[26] *Australia & New Zealand Bank Ltd v Colonial & Eagle Wharves Ltd* [1960] 2 Lloyd's Rep 241, at 253–4; *Simner v New India Insurance Co Ltd* [1995] LRLR 240, at 254–5.

[27] [1921] 1 KB 104. The position of the reinsurers was different: see n 103 under para 5.57.

[28] In the same way, a shipowner who employs a ship's master and a manager on the basis that they will keep him informed of the condition of his ship is deemed to know what they should have reported to him: see, for example, *Proudfoot v Montefiore* (1867) LR 2 QB 511.

[29] *Simner v New India Insurance Co Ltd* [1995] LRLR 240, at 255, citing Lord Halsbury LC in *Blackburn Low v Vigors* (1887) 12 App Cas 531, at 537–8.

[30] [1989] 1 Lloyd's Rep 69.

to L. L's duties included both arranging insurance and choosing and employing a skipper. L employed M without making the usual checks as to whether M had a criminal record. Philips J held that the yacht owners, through L, were deemed to know of M's criminal record, which should have been disclosed to insurers.[31] However, where there is composite insurance,[32] those insureds who entrust the task of arranging the insurance to another insured may not be deemed to know what that individual knows.[33]

Inquiries of others and the proposal form

In the context of professional indemnity insurance, it will usually be the case that insurers require the completion of a proposal form. Where more than one person is to be insured, this will usually require the individual who completes the form to certify that he has made inquiries of others who are to be insured. If that individual has not made such inquiries but states that he has done so, then there will be a misrepresentation.[34] If he does make such inquiries, then he is obliged to inform insurers of any material circumstance which he has learned from them.

5.19

Agents defrauding their principals

An agent who has defrauded his principal or is defrauding his principal is most unlikely to volunteer this information to his principal. The agent's knowledge of his own fraud will not be imputed to his insured principal. This result can be explained on the wording of s 18(1) of the Marine Insurance Act 1906 because 'in the ordinary course of business' an agent does not voluntarily inform his principal of his own fraud.[35] It can also be explained by applying the *Hampshire Land* principle,[36] which is that 'knowledge of the agent will not be attributed to the principal when the knowledge relates to the agent's own breach of duty to his principal'.[37]

5.20

For the *Hampshire Land* principle to apply, the agent must have defrauded his principal, rather than a third party. The 'classic case' in which 'an individual's knowledge of fraud cannot and should not be attributed to a company ... is where the company is itself the target of an agent's or employee's dishonesty'.[38] However, where the principal is a 'secondary victim', in the sense that the principal is exposed

5.21

---

[31] Ibid at 95. L's involvement in the insuring of the yacht brought into play s 19 of the Marine Insurance Act 1906 so that L himself was obliged to disclose circumstances which he ought to have known in the ordinary course of business: see further paras 3.87–3.97.

[32] See paras 1.32–1.45.

[33] See paras 5.114–5.134.

[34] As to which see paras 6.19–6.31.

[35] *PCW Syndicates v PCW Reinsurers* [1996] 1 WLR 1136, at 1143.

[36] *Re Hampshire Land Company (No 2)* [1896] 2 Ch 743.

[37] Per Lord Philips in *Moore Stephens (a firm) v Stone & Rolls Ltd (in liquidation)* [2009] UKHL 39; [2009] 1 AC 1391, at [43].

[38] *Bank of India v Morris* [2005] EWCA 693; [2005] 2 BCLC 328, at [114] per Mummery LJ, giving the judgment of the Court of Appeal. The decision concerned the test for attribution under s 213(2) of the Insolvency Act 1986, which provides that persons who are 'knowingly parties' to the carrying on of an insolvent company's business with the intent to defraud creditors are liable to make such contributions to the company's assets as the court thinks proper.

to a claim as a result of the agent's dishonest conduct towards a third party, the relevant rule of attribution may result in the principal being liable to the third party. The agent is acting dishonestly in what he believes to be his principal's interests, rather than consciously acting counter to those interests.[39] In cases of composite insurance,[40] it may be sufficient that the principal is a 'secondary victim' for the knowledge of the dishonest agent not to be attributed to the principal.[41]

Bodies corporate

5.22   When considering whether a body corporate has constructive knowledge of a particular circumstance, the test is whether there are natural persons who ought in the ordinary course of business to know of the particular circumstance and, if there are, whether their deemed knowledge is to be attributed to the body corporate.[42]

D. Materiality: The Objective and Subjective Tests

5.23   The burden on proving breach of the duty of disclosure is on insurers. To do so, insurers have to establish that a circumstance of which the insured knew or is deemed to have known was not disclosed to them. They must also prove that the undisclosed circumstance was material and that they were induced to enter the insurance contract on the terms in which they did by the non-disclosure, that is, that, had they been aware of the undisclosed circumstance they would either not have insured the risk at all or would have done so on different terms.[43] The test for materiality is set out in s 18(2) of the Marine Insurance Act 1906, which provides that a circumstance is material if it 'would influence the judgment of a prudent insurer in fixing the premium, or determining whether he will take the risk'.

5.24   The effect of the need to prove both materiality and inducement is that insurers have to prove that they would have regarded the undisclosed information as material (a subjective test) and that a prudent insurer would have done so too (an objective test).

---

[39]   Ibid at [114]–[1124]. See also *McNicholas v Customs and Excise Commissioners* [2000] STC 533 (Dyson J), where the taxpayer company had attributed to it the dishonesty of an employee who had the dishonest state of mind of its employee attributed to it for the purposes of s 60(b) of the Value Added Tax 1994.

[40]   See paras 1.32–1.45.

[41]   See paras 5.132–5.133.

[42]   *Group Josi Re (formerly Groupe Josi Reassurance SA) v Walbrook Insurance Co Ltd* [1996] 1 WLR 1152, at 1169–70 per Saville LJ. The test for attribution is considered in paras 5.10–5.14 in general and in paras 5.114–5.134 in the context of composite insurance.

[43]   'The materiality of an individual fact must be considered in the light of those other facts which are, and those which are not, disclosed to underwriters. To consider whether there has been a fair presentation of the risk it is necessary to look at the whole picture presented to underwriters and to compare that with the picture as the assured or the assured's agent knew it to be.': per Philips J in *Inversiones Manria SA v Sphere Drake Insurance Co Plc (the 'Dora')* [1989] 1 Lloyd's Rep 69, at 89. This was followed by HH Judge Waksman QC in *Joseph Fielding Properties (Blackpool) Limited v Aviva Insurance Ltd* [2010] EWHC 2192 (QB); [2011] Lloyd's Rep IR 238, at [145].

The subjective test: inducement

The need to establish inducement was only finally established in 1994 by the deci-   **5.25**
sion of the House of Lords in *Pan Atlantic Insurance Co Ltd v Pine Top Insurance
Co Ltd*.[44] Lord Mustill explained that the requirement for inducement, 'in the
sense that it is used in the general law of contract' in relation to material misrepresentation, should be implied in the Marine Insurance Act 1906, both in relation
to misrepresentation[45] and non-disclosure. The requirement was also necessary
in cases of non-marine insurance,[46] including professional indemnity insurance.

In *Assicurazioni Generali v Arab Insurance Group (BSC)*,[47] Clarke LJ reviewed   **5.26**
authority[48] and summarized the principles relevant to inducement as follows:[49]

1. In order to be entitled to avoid a contract of insurance or reinsurance, an insurer or
   reinsurer must prove on the balance of probabilities that he was induced to enter
   into the contract by a material non-disclosure or by a material misrepresentation.
2. There is no presumption of law that an insurer or reinsurer is induced to enter
   in the contract by a material non-disclosure or misrepresentation.
3. The facts may, however, be such that it is to be inferred that the particular
   insurer or reinsurer was so induced even in the absence from evidence from him.
4. In order to prove inducement the insurer or reinsurer must show that the non-
   disclosure or misrepresentation was an effective cause of his entering into the
   contract on the terms on which he did. He must therefore show at least that, but
   for the relevant non-disclosure or misrepresentation, he would not have entered
   into the contract on those terms. On the other hand, he does not have to show
   that it was the sole effective cause of his doing so.

Insurers need not show that they would not have insured the risk at all. It is suffi-   **5.27**
cient that they would have done so on different terms.[50] It is also sufficient if proper
disclosure would have caused them to ask questions, the answers to which would
have caused them either not to insure the risk or to do so on different terms.[51] But
there must be some difference in the terms.[52]

---

[44] [1995] AC 501.

[45] As to which see para 6.14.

[46] [1995] AC 501, at 550–1. Lord Mustill's reasons are at 541–51.

[47] [2002] EWCA Civ 1642; [2003] Lloyd's Rep IR 131.

[48] In particular, the earlier decision of the Court of Appeal in *St Paul Fire & Marine Insurance Co
(UK) Ltd v McConnell Dowell Constructors Ltd* [1996] 1 All ER 96.

[49] [2002] EWCA Civ 1642; [2003] Lloyd's Rep IR 131, at [62].

[50] It is not necessary to prove precisely what the difference would have been, merely that there
would have been a difference. So in *New Hampshire Insurance Co v Oil Refineries Ltd* [2002] 2
Lloyd's Rep 462 it was sufficient that insurers had proved that they would have required a greater
premium, without proving the precise amount.

[51] *International Management Group (UK) Ltd v Simmonds* [2003] EWHC 177 (Comm); [2004]
Lloyd's Rep IR 247, at [150].

[52] *Assicurazioni Generali v Arab Insurance Group (BSC)* [2002] EWCA Civ 1642; [2003] Lloyd's
Rep IR 131, at [187] per Sir Christopher Staughton: 'A misrepresentation or non-disclosure which
did not make any difference, in the sense that the underwriter would have agreed to the same contract on the same terms if it had never been made, cannot be an inducement. Benjamin Franklin
once wrote that for want of a nail a shoe was lost; for want of a shoe the horse was lost; and for want

5.28 Evidence from the underwriter who accepted the risk is the best proof of inducement. In some cases, insurers will have clear internal rules for calculating an appropriate premium. The impact of the undisclosed circumstance may be clear from those rules. So in the motor insurance case of *Drake Insurance Plc v Provident Insurance Plc*,[53] insurers had an established approach to the effect on the level of premium of earlier accidents involving the insured. On that established approach, full disclosure of the circumstances of an accident in which the insured had been involved without any fault on his part would have made no difference to the terms on which insurers would have insured him.

5.29 Some professional indemnity insurers have clear internal rules as to what risks they will and will not accept and as to how the premium should be calculated. Where they do, those internal rules will probably be the best evidence as to whether the non-disclosure of a particular circumstance did or did not induce insurers to enter the contract on the terms on which they did.[54] Insurers' underwriting manual or other written guidelines may also provide strong evidence as to whether there was or was not inducement.

5.30 It is not always necessary for there to be evidence from the underwriter (or, where there are a number of insurers, from every underwriter). It has been suggested that in some cases, the significance of the undisclosed circumstance will be so obvious that such evidence is unnecessary.[55] In others, the evidence of co-insurers may suffice.[56] Given that the undisclosed circumstance must have been objectively material, it has been said that there is a rebuttable presumption that the particular insurer will have been induced to accept the risk on the terms on which he did by the failure to disclose it.[57] However, where witnesses could have been called to

---

of a horse the rider was lost (*Poor Richard's Almanac*). But in my view, causation cannot in law exist when even the "but for" test is not satisfied.' See also *Drake Insurance Plc v Provident Insurance Plc* [2003] EWCA Civ 1834; [2004] QB 601, where disclosure of the relevant circumstance would have led to a discussion which would have resulted in insurers learning of further information which would have resulted in insurance on the same terms.

[53] [2003] EWCA Civ 1834; [2004] QB 601. In *Hazel v Whitlam* [2004] EWCA Civ 1600; [2005] Lloyd's Rep IR 168, another motor insurance case, the broker could obtain a quotation from insurers by putting an electronic copy of the completed proposal form into a computer system provided by insurers.

[54] Cf *Mundi v Lincoln Assurance Ltd* [2005] EWHC 2678 (Ch); [2006] Lloyd's Rep IR 353, at 360: a life insurance case, insurers had a checklist they used when reinstating cover. That checklist was put in evidence and showed inducement.

[55] *St Paul Fire & Marine Insurance Co (UK) Ltd v McConnell Dowell Constructors Ltd* [1996] 1 All ER 96, at 112. See also *Mundi v Lincoln Assurance Ltd* [2005] EWHC 2678 (Ch); [2006] Lloyd's Rep IR 353, at 357.

[56] Ibid. See also *Aneco Reinsurance Underwriting Ltd (in liquidation) v Johnson & Higgins Ltd* [1998] 1 Lloyd's Rep 565, at 597.

[57] *Pan Atlantic Insurance Co Ltd v Pine Top Insurance Co Ltd* [1995] AC 501, at 530–51 per Lord Mustill. It has been suggested that presumption is weaker if the underwriter is shown to have been careless when writing the risk in issue and is displaced by the actual evidence of the underwriter: *Marc Rich & Co AG v Portman* [1996] 1 Lloyd's Rep 430, at 441–2. And it was doubted in *Insurance Corporation of the Channel Islands v Royal Hotel Ltd* [1998] Lloyd's Rep IR 151, at 158.

prove inducement and are not and no evidence is called on the point, inducement will not have been proved.[58]

The objective test: materiality

As stated in s 18(2) of the Marine Insurance Act 1906 a circumstance is material **5.31** if it 'would influence the judgment of a prudent insurer in fixing the premium, or determining whether he will take the risk'. The test is whether the judgment of the prudent insurer would have been influenced by knowledge of the undisclosed circumstance. It is not necessary that his judgment would have been influenced to the extent of declining to accept the risk or of requiring a greater premium.[59]

As Kerr LJ said in *Container Transport International Inc v Oceanus Mutual* **5.32** *Underwriting Association (Bermuda) Ltd*,[60] the insured's duty to disclose material circumstances means that the insurer is entitled:

> to the disclosure to him of every fact which would influence the judgment of a prudent insurer in fixing the premium or determining whether he will take the risk. The latter words … must comprise any terms, and not only the level of premium, which an insurer might require in the wording of the cover, e.g. warranties, franchises, deductibles, exceptions, etc. The word 'judgment'—to quote the Oxford English Dictionary to which we were referred—is used in the sense of 'the formation of an opinion'. To prove the materiality of an undisclosed circumstance, the insurer must satisfy the Court on a balance of probability—by evidence or from the nature of the undisclosed circumstance itself—that the judgment, in this sense, of a prudent insurer would have been influenced if the circumstance in question had been disclosed. The word 'influenced' means that the disclosure is one which would have had an impact on the formation of his opinion and on his decision-making process in relation to the matters covered by s. 18 (2).

Thus stated, the threshold for materiality is low. However, the duty of disclosure **5.33** does not require detailed, specific disclosure of every circumstance which could conceivably affect the judgment of a prudent insurer. What is required is:

> a fair and substantially accurate presentation of the risk proposed for insurance, so that a prudent insurer could form a proper judgment—either on the presentation alone or by asking questions if he was sufficiently put on enquiry and wanted to know further details—whether or not to accept the proposal, and, if so, on what terms.[61]

---

[58] *Laker Vent Engineering Ltd v Templeton Insurance Ltd* [2009] EWCA Civ 62; [2009] Lloyd's Rep IR 704 at [69]–[70].

[59] *Pan Atlantic Insurance Co Ltd v Pine Top Insurance Co Ltd* [1995] AC 501, at 530–41 per Lord Mustill, with whom Lords Goff and Slynn agreed.

[60] [1984] 1 Lloyd's Rep 476, at 492.

[61] Ibid at 496–7. As Lord Esher MR said in *Asfar v Blundell*, [1896] 1 QB 123, at 129: 'But it is not necessary to disclose minutely every material fact; assuming that there is a material fact which he is bound to disclose, the rule is satisfied if he discloses sufficient to call the attention of the underwriters in such a manner that they can see that if they require further information they should ask for it.'

While this should not be a difficult test to satisfy in practice,[62] it should be noted that the test of what the insured should disclose is framed in terms of the impact of the circumstance on the judgment of a prudent insurer, rather than on whether the insured should have appreciated that the circumstance would be material.

5.34 The question as to whether a fact is or is not material may be the subject of expert evidence from underwriters. But it is not always necessary. As Scrutton LJ stated in *Glicksman v Lancashire and General Assurance Co Ltd*:[63]

> [It was submitted] that you cannot find that a fact was material unless somebody gave evidence of the materiality. That is, in my view, and I agree with Mr Justice Roche, entirely contrary to the whole course of insurance litigation. It is so far contrary that it is frequently argued that you are not entitled to call other people to say what they think is material. That is a matter for the Court on the nature of the facts. I entirely agree with Mr Justice Roche that the nature of the facts may be such that you do not need anyone to come and say: 'This is material'.[64]

Complying with the duty of disclosure

Identifying material circumstances

5.35 Insurers will usually have given an indication as to what information they regard as material or potentially material by asking specific questions in the proposal form. While, as a matter of logic, the questions asked by a particular insurer cannot be decisive as to whether a circumstance would influence the judgment of the theoretical, prudent insurer,[65] the fact that insurers of a particular class of insurance ask about a particular matter will indicate that they regard it as material.[66]

5.36 A review of currently available proposal forms and those which appear in decided cases suggests that insurers usually want to know: (i) details of the firm or company to be insured, including information on subsidiaries and associated companies;[67] (ii) confirmation as to whether cover is required for predecessors in title or partners or principals for work undertaken outside the proposed insured; (iii) a list of partners and/or directors, their experience and qualifications, as well as details of other staff or any consultants; (iv) details of the insured's income or turnover in the preceding years and the estimated income for the forthcoming year (sometimes,

---

[62] Ibid at 497.

[63] [1925] 2 KB 593, at 609.

[64] This passage was cited and applied by Flaux J in *AC Ward Sons Ltd v Catlin (Five) Ltd* [2009] EWHC 3122 (Comm); [2010] Lloyd's Rep IR 695, at [218] and in *Synergy Health (UK) Ltd v CGU Insurance Plc* [2011] EWHC 2583 (Comm); [2011] Lloyd's Rep IR 500, at [152].

[65] *Mutual Life Insurance Company of New York v Ontario Metal Products Company Ltd* [1925] AC 344.

[66] *Glicksman v Lancashire and General Assurance Co Ltd* [1925] 2 KB 593, at 609 per Scrutton LJ.

[67] See, for example, the proposal form in *Johns v Kelly* [1986] 1 Lloyd's Rep 468, which required the insured (insurance brokers) to provide 'Names and addresses of all Subsidiary and/or Associated Companies and/or Branch Offices, including all those offices in which the Firm has a controlling interest'.

depending on the nature of the insured's business, broken down according to work down in geographical blocks); (v) a breakdown of business activity by type of work;[68] (vi) information about the type of clients (and/or projects) for whom the insured typically undertakes work; (vii) information about the use of sub-contractors and vetting of them; (viii) average fees/largest fees by type of work or client;[69] (ix) information about any disciplinary proceedings against any partner or officer; (x) details of previous professional indemnity insurance (including any refusal, cancellation, or withdrawal of insurance); (xi) information about any circumstances that may give rise to a loss or claim against the insured;[70] (xii) information about any previous claims made by the proposed insured; and (xiii) any other information that is material to the insurers' decision on whether to insure and if so at what premium.[71] Insurers will also want to know about any 'moral hazard', ie dishonest or fraudulent conduct.[72]

One of the most material circumstances will be the potential for future claims. **5.37** While the insured 'is deemed to know every circumstance which, in the ordinary

---

[68] For example, accountants' proposal forms may require a breakdown into: (i) audit work for different types of company; (ii) taxation; (iii) book keeping; (iv) computer consultancy; (v) insolvency/ liquidation; (vi) management consultancy; (vii) mergers and acquisitions, etc. Architects will typically be asked about how much work is (i) new build or restorative; (ii) town planning/feasibility work; (iii) abandoned works; (iv) quantity or other surveying; (iv) interior design; (v) drafting; (vi) project management; (vii) valuation. And in *Encia Remediations Ltd v Canopius Managing Agents Ltd* [2007] EWHC 916 (Comm); [2008] Lloyd's Rep IR 79, the insured engineers who were seeking environmental consultants professional indemnity insurance were asked to state their gross fees received in the last financial year for: (i) air pollution; (ii) noise pollution; (iii) water pollution; (iv) waste treatment/ disposal; (v) waste management; (vi) contaminated land, including removal of underground storage tanks; (vii) land fill reclamation and design; (viii) environmental assessments.

[69] In *Mabey & Johnson Ltd v Ecclesiastical Insurance Office* [2003] EWHC 1523 (Comm); [2004] Lloyd's Rep IR 10, the prospective insured was required to give details (a) 'on seven largest contracts commenced during the last five years where the Design and Consulting Department has been involved' and (b) 'of any major new operations being undertaken during the next twelve months'.

[70] In *Kumar v AGF Insurance Ltd* [1999] 1 WLR 1747, the proposal for the excess layer required details to be 'given of claims against the original practice in which partners of the proposing practice were involved'. The relevant section was entitled 'Claims and circumstances known but not yet reported to LIB' and provided: 'Please give details of all such claims and circumstances which may give rise to a claim'.

In *Arab Bank plc v Zurich Insurance Co* [1999] 1 Lloyd's Rep 262, question 14(a) asked: 'Is any Partner, Director, Principal, Consultant or employee, AFTER ENQUIRY, aware of any circumstances/incidents which might: (i) give rise to a claim against the Proposer or his predecessors in business or any of the present or former Partners, Directors, Principals? ... (ii) otherwise affect the consideration of this proposal for Professional Indemnity Insurance?'

In *J Rothschild Assurance Plc v Collyear* [1999] Lloyd's Rep IR 6, the proposal form asked: 'Is the Proposer or any of its Partners or Directors, or Officers, AFTER INQUIRY, aware of any circumstance which may give rise to a claim against the Proposer or its predecessors in business?'

[71] The effect of the last category is to reduce the scope for the insured to argue that insurers had waived the right to disclosure of any material circumstance which did not fall within the categories of information sought in the proposal form. As to waiver see paras 5.60–5.63.

[72] *Locker and Woolf Ltd v Western Australian Insurance Co* [1936] 1 KB 408, at 414; *Woolcott v Sun Alliance and London Insurance Ltd* [1978] 1 WLR 493, at 498; *Insurance Corporation of the Channel Islands v Royal Hotel Ltd* [1998] Lloyd's Rep IR 151, at 156–8. The phrase 'moral hazard' means 'circumstances, invariably involving dishonesty on the part of the assured, which give rise to

course of business, ought to be known by him',[73] he will not be deemed to be aware of his own earlier negligence or other inadvertent breach of duty. In the same way that an insured cannot be aware of his own negligence as a circumstance which might give rise to a claim,[74] he cannot be deemed to know that he has been negligent merely because, with the exercise of reasonable professional skill and care, he would have appreciated his error. The whole basis of a 'claims made' policy is that the insured may already have acted or failed to act in circumstances which might give rise to a claim. That is the risk against which he seeks to be insured. If insurers could successfully raise a defence of non-disclosure when a claim is made by the insured for an indemnity under the policy by reason of the insured's failure to disclose the circumstance which gives rise to the claim, then the insurance would be deprived of any substance.

5.38   In *Simon, Haynes, Barlas & Ireland v Beer*,[75] insurers of a firm of solicitors denied that they were liable to indemnify the insured firm on two alternative grounds: either the insured had been in breach of their duty of disclosure in failing to disclose their earlier negligence on renewal, or the insured had not been negligent, in which case they should not have made any payment in settlement of the third party's claim because they were not liable. Both arguments failed. Atkinson J found that there had been no negligence and no non-disclosure. In doing so he observed:[76]

> a man seeking such a policy as that in this case is, in effect, saying to the underwriters: 'I may have been guilty of negligence at some time during the past years. Claims may be made against me, and I want to seek indemnity from those possible claims. I can think of nothing in respect of which a claim can be made against me. I have no dissatisfied client, I have had no complaint and no reproach; but you never can tell.'

On the facts, at the time the contract of insurance was made, the former client had raised no complaint and had no proper basis for a complaint. In the circumstances, the insured was under no obligation to disclose the possibility of a claim by him.[77]

---

a concern that there will be dishonesty in the reporting and presentation of claims': *Sharon's Bakery (Europe) Ltd v AXA Insurance UK Plc* [2011] EWHC 210 (Comm); [2012] Lloyd's Rep IR 164, at [61] per Blair J. For disputed allegations of dishonesty, see *Brotherton v Asequradora Colsequros SA (No. 2)* [2003] EWCA Civ 705; [2003] Lloyd's Rep IR 746, *North Star Shipping Ltd v Sphere Drake Insurance plc* [2006] EWCA Civ 378; [2006] 2 Lloyd's Rep 183, and *Norwich Union Insurance Ltd v Meisells* [2006] EWHC 2811; [2007] Lloyd's Rep IR 69. In the context of professional indemnity insurance an allegation of dishonesty which is demonstrably unfounded will still be a material circumstance if it has the potential to give rise to a claim on the proposed policy.

[73]   Section 18(1) of the Marine Insurance Act 1906; see paras 5.15–5.22.

[74]   See paras 2.80–2.89.

[75]   (1945) 78 Ll L Rep 337.

[76]   Ibid at 349.

[77]   After an exhaustive statement and review of the facts, Atkinson J concluded at 366: 'There was [the client], I repeat, satisfied, and satisfied for months afterwards, knowing perfectly well every transaction that had been entered into and still regarding [the solicitor] as a man whom he could trust, and a man whom he was ready to trust with his affairs. That has a very important bearing on

The insured's knowledge of circumstances which might give rise to a claim for **5.39** the purposes of compliance with his duty of disclosure is linked to the right and obligation which he should have if a 'claims made' policy is to work to give notice of such circumstances under his current policy so that any claim eventually made arising out of those circumstances is deemed to have been made in the current policy.[78] It will usually, but not always, be the case that insurers will exclude from cover any claim which is disclosed when seeking insurance and any claim arising from circumstances disclosed at the same time. As Thomas J observed in *Kumar v AGF Insurance Ltd*:[79]

> The purpose of the declaration in the proposal form is to make it clear, that when matters that might give rise to a claim are known to the insured, they must be noted on to the proposal form so that they can be taken into account in assessing the premium for the policy and can be excluded under that policy. This is because, as is common under this form of claims made policy, when circumstances are notified and become known to the professional practice concerned, they can be notified under the current or existing policy and a claim that is subsequently made will fall within that existing policy. These are very common provisions.

So, the same considerations should apply to whether an insured has sufficient **5.40** knowledge of a possible future claim for the purposes of compliance with his duty of disclosure when seeking a new policy as apply to his right and obligation to give notice under his current policy. Those considerations have been addressed in **Chapter 2**.[80] As explained there, there will be circumstances in which an insured could reasonably form the view that he should notify under his current policy or that he should not.[81] The duty of disclosure is strict, in that it can be broken without negligence and it is no answer to a claim of non-disclosure that the insured formed a reasonable assessment. However, in any case where there was genuine scope for alternative views, it should be difficult for insurers to establish materiality and inducement. That said, where the potential claim, even if very unlikely, would be very substantial, an insured who reasonably considered the chances of it being made as so remote as not to merit notification or disclosure could find himself in difficulty, if a claim were made. The insured would be well advised to err on the side of caution in any genuinely doubtful case.

An insured who fails to appreciate the materiality of information will be in breach **5.41** of the duty of disclosure, even if others in similar positions did not do so either. This is illustrated by the case of *Johns v Kelly*.[82] The insured in that case was a firm

---

the matter when I come to ask myself whether there was anything which [the solicitor], even if he were the most honourable or most reasonable solicitor in Christendom, ought to have disclosed at that time. I think there was not.'

[78] See paras 2.06–2.10.
[79] [1999] 1 WLR 1747, at 1751.
[80] Paras 2.78–2.90.
[81] See para 2.83.
[82] [1986] 1 Lloyd's Rep 468.

of Lloyd's brokers ('RMB') which had entered into an umbrella agreement with another firm of insurance brokers ('CR') who were not Lloyd's brokers and so not entitled to place business directly with Lloyd's underwriters.[83] Under this agreement Mr Roberts of CR was employed by RMB on terms that CR indemnified RMB against the cost of doing so. CR also agreed to indemnify RMB against any liability in tort which RMB might have to CR's clients.

5.42 Under the umbrella agreement Mr Roberts was able to place business directly at Lloyd's and he did so. A claim was made against both CR and RMB in relation to a particular policy brokered by Mr Roberts. The claim was settled on terms which involved a payment by RMB, who sought to recover it from their professional indemnity insurers. Insurers raised defences, including failure to disclose the umbrella agreement.

5.43 RMB (and other Lloyd's brokers) had tended to suppose that they would not be liable for anything done by non-Lloyd's brokers under umbrella agreements and that, even if they were, the indemnity from CR (and other non-Lloyd's brokers) would cover any claim. They therefore believed that there was little risk to their own professional indemnity insurers. At the relevant time, Bingham J found that umbrella agreements were not disclosed by Lloyd's brokers to their professional indemnity insurers or were referred to 'in terms so general or oblique as to leave the underwriter in ignorance of what was being disclosed'.[84] But this general approach did not avail RMB.

5.44 Bingham J held that to an insurer who was being asked to give professional indemnity cover nothing would be more material than the identity of the proposed insured. The risk to be insured was of claims against the insured, so that the insured's competence, experience, and trustworthiness, the quality of his management and staffing, and the reputability of his clients affected the degree of risk. He also observed that the volume and nature of the insured's business were material, because some classes of business give rise to a higher incidence of claims than others. No great legal sophistication was needed in order to appreciate that under the law of agency a Lloyd's broker could be liable for the wrongs of a non-Lloyd's broker acting under an umbrella agreement. An insurer who was properly informed of an umbrella agreement would want to know about the non-Lloyd's broker and about what degree of control or supervision the Lloyd's broker exercised over his activities. The existence of an umbrella agreement was therefore material.[85]

5.45 While the question whether circumstances of which the insured knows are such as to require disclosure can involve an element of judgment, many other matters which require disclosure are matters of fact. Failure to disclose fully and accurately

---

[83] As to which, see para 3.08.
[84] [1986] 1 Lloyd's Rep 468, at 481.
[85] Ibid at 481–2.

facts such as claims actually made against the insured will almost inevitably constitute a breach of the duty of disclosure.[86]

Disclosing material circumstances

As has been explained, the duty of disclosure requires 'a fair and substantially accurate presentation of the risk proposed for insurance'.[87] This requires the insured to disclose material circumstances in terms which are sufficiently clear for insurers to understand what it is that is being disclosed and to be in a position to ask appropriate questions. **5.46**

Again, this is illustrated by the case of *Johns v Kelly*.[88] The insured had included Mr Roberts among the number of employees stated in the proposal form. The insured had included income from the umbrella agreement in the total income stated there. The insured had stated that it had no subsidiary or associated companies, but had disclosed in one year that CR had placed their Lloyd's account 'via our intermediary' and in a later year that the figure for income included net premium income to Lloyd's generated by another broker but placed through the insured. Bingham J held that this was insufficient to disclose the umbrella agreement to insurers. Increasing the number of employees and the total income to take account of the umbrella agreement was necessary if the answers in the proposal form were to be correct, but doing so did not put insurers on notice of the umbrella agreement itself. The references to CR were ambiguous and likely to be thought to refer to the receipt of income by way of a sub-agency (ie where a broker instructs a sub-broker), as opposed to an umbrella agreement.[89] **5.47**

In this context the crucial difference is between a fair presentation of the risk which would lead insurers to ask further questions and obtain further information on the one hand, and an unfair presentation of the risk during which insurers are not given sufficient information to alert them to the need to make further inquiries. In the former case, insurers may have waived the right to disclosure of the information which would have been elicited by the questions they should have asked.[90] In the latter, there has been non-disclosure and no waiver.[91] **5.48**

---

[86] However, where insurers only seek details of claims made within a specified period, they may have waived disclosure of claims made outside that period: see para 5.61.

[87] *Container Transport International Inc v Oceanus Mutual Underwriting Association (Bermuda) Ltd* [1984] 1 Lloyd's Rep 476, at 496–7.

[88] [1986] 1 Lloyds Rep 468. For the facts, see paras 5.41–5.42.

[89] Ibid at 482.

[90] As to waiver see paras 5.60–5.63.

[91] *Container Transport International Inc v Oceanus Mutual Underwriting Association (Bermuda) Ltd* [1984] 1 Lloyd's Rep 476, at 497 per Kerr LJ and at 511–12 per Parker LJ; applied in *Marc Rich & Co AG v Portman* [1996] 1 Lloyd's Rep 430, at 442–3 and [1997] 1 Lloyd's Rep 225, where Leggatt LJ said at 234: 'An insurer cannot waive a class of information that he does not know exists. That requires a fair presentation of the risk. It is obvious that a presentation cannot be fair if unusual facts are not disclosed. The insurer is entitled to assume the fairness of the presentation. Without it he cannot sensibly be said to refrain from asking questions. He must be on notice of the existence

Lawyers and Privilege

5.49   Lawyers may be faced with a particular problem when seeking to comply with the duty of disclosure of material facts. Documents and information about a client or former client are held by lawyers subject to the client's privilege. Unless the client waives privilege, the lawyer is not entitled to disclose the information.

5.50   Where a client makes a claim against his former lawyer he impliedly waives privilege in relation to all matters which are relevant to an issue in the claim.[92] The reason for this implied waiver is 'to prevent the unfairness which would arise if the plaintiff were entitled to exclude from the Court's consideration evidence relevant to a defence by relying upon the privilege arising from the solicitor's duty of confidence'.[93] Perhaps inevitably, the question of implied waiver has arisen for decision after the former client has brought proceedings in court against the lawyer. So, while referring to the unfairness of preventing the lawyer from deploying otherwise privileged and confidential material in defence of the claim against him, there is greater emphasis in the relevant authorities on the fact that the former client has chosen to bring his otherwise privileged and confidential relationship with his lawyer before the court and so into the public domain.[94]

5.51   If privilege is only impliedly waived by the issue of proceedings, then, unless there is an express waiver of privilege (for example by asking the insured lawyer to notify his professional indemnity insurers of the claim or potential claim[95]), an insured lawyer will not be entitled to disclose privileged and confidential information to his insurers. For example, a lawyer may have reason to anticipate a claim from a former client, but the former client may yet to have made any complaint. Or the former client may have sent a letter of claim, but not yet issued proceedings.

5.52   The fact that the law of privilege prevents a lawyer insured from disclosing a material fact does not relieve him of his duty to disclose that fact to potential insurers. Just as privilege against self-incrimination does not allow an insured to withhold

---

of information before he can be said to waive it.' See also *WISE (Underwriting Agency) Ltd v Grupo Nacional Provincial SA* [2004] EWCA Civ 962; [2004] 2 Lloyd's Rep 483.

[92]   *Lillicrap v Nalder & Son (A Firm)* [1993] 1 WLR 94; *Nederlandse Reassurantie Groep Holding NV v Bacon & Woodrow (No.1)* [1995] 1 All ER 976; and *Paragon Finance Plc (formerly National Home Loans Corp) v Freshfields (A Firm)* [1999] 1 WLR 1183.

[93]   *Nederlandse Reassurantie Groep Holding NV v Bacon & Woodrow (No 1)* [1995] 1 All ER 976, at 986c–d per Colman J. His statement of the principle upon which this implied waiver of privilege is based was approved by the Court of Appeal in *Paragon Finance Plc (formerly National Home Loans Corp) v Freshfields (A Firm)* [1999] 1 WLR 1183, at 1191F.

[94]   *Paragon Finance Plc (formerly National Home Loans Corp) v Freshfields (A Firm)* [1999] 1 WLR 1183, at 1188E–G and 1192G. See also *Lillicrap v Nalder & Son (A Firm)* [1993] 1 WLR 94, at 99A–C per Dillon LJ, with whom the other members of the Court of Appeal agreed.

[95]   Paragraph 5.3 of the Professional Negligence Pre-Action Protocol provides that a Preliminary Notice should ask the professional to whom it is addressed to notify his professional indemnity insurers, if any. And para 6.2(h) provides that Letter of Claim should ask the professional to whom it is addressed to forward it to his professional indemnity insurers. This could amount to a waiver of privilege.

from his insurers the fact that he has committed a criminal offence,[96] so a lawyer cannot justify his failure to disclose material information on the basis that he would be in breach of the obligation to maintain his former client's privilege in that information.[97]

The same difficulty can arise when an insured lawyer wants or is obliged to notify a **5.53** claim or circumstance to his professional indemnity insurers.[98] As in those circumstances, there are three possible solutions. The first is to inform the client or former client and obtain consent to disclose the potential claim to insurers.[99] The second is to disclose the relevant information in such a way as to retain the former client's privilege and confidentiality by omitting all details which would identify the particular client or transaction.[100] The third is to include a term in appropriately clear terms in the contract with the client by which the client consents to the provision of otherwise privileged and confidential information to the lawyer's professional indemnity insurers.

What need not be disclosed

It is not every material circumstance known to the insured which has to be disclosed **5.54** to insurers. Section 18(3) of the Marine Insurance Act 1906 lists four exceptions:

> In the absence of inquiry the following circumstances need not be disclosed, namely:
> (a) Any circumstance which diminishes the risk;
> (b) Any circumstance which is known or presumed to be known to the insurer. The insurer is presumed to know matters of common notoriety or knowledge, and matters which an insurer in the ordinary course of his business, as such, ought to know;
> (c) Any circumstance as to which information is waived by the insurer;
> (d) Any circumstance which it is superfluous to disclose by reason of any express or implied warranty.

---

[96] *March Cabaret Club & Casino Ltd v London Assurance* [1975] 1 Lloyd's Rep 169, at 177 per May J.

[97] *Quinn Direct Insurance Ltd v Law Society* [2010] EWCA Civ 805; [2011] 1 WLR 308, at [23]–[24] per Sir Andrew Morritt C, with whom the other members of the Court of Appeal agreed.

[98] See paras 2.124–2.128.

[99] Outcome O(1.16) in the SRA Handbook 2011 requires solicitors to inform current clients if they discover any act or omission which could give rise to a claim by their current clients against them. It does not apply to former clients.

[100] Guidance from the Law Society (http://www.lawsociety.org.uk/support-services/advice/practice-notes/professional-indemnity-insurance/) in the light of *Quinn Direct Insurance Ltd v Law Society* [2010] EWCA Civ 805; [2011] 1 WLR 308 explains:

> This potentially places you in a difficult position in terms of insurance as you are, of course, required to notify insurers of any circumstances that might lead to a claim being made against you. If a firm is notifying a circumstance rather than a claim, there will be no implied waiver of privilege and so the information it is able to provide the insurer could be very limited.

The position is the same in relation to the duty of disclosure.

To these can be added circumstances which insurers would wish to know, but which are not relevant to the risk to be insured.[101]

5.55 **Circumstances which diminish the risk**   A circumstance which reduces the risk will still be material in that it will influence the judgment of the prudent insurer. It will, of course, be in the insured's interest to disclose such circumstances, but it would be wrong to hold that he was in breach of the duty of disclosure should he fail to do so.

5.56 **Any circumstance which is known or presumed to be known to insurers**   In order to avail himself of this exception to the duty of disclosure, the insured must establish that insurers knew of the undisclosed circumstance or that they are presumed to have known of it.

5.57 Actual knowledge is a question of fact. However, it is not sufficient to show that insurers knew of the undisclosed circumstance at some point in time. What must be shown is that it was in insurers' minds at the time when the risk was accepted. So an insurer who was once aware of a material circumstance but reasonably does not link it to the risk he is being asked to accept will not be taken to have known of the material circumstance at the relevant time.[102] In the same way, an insurer is not to be taken to know information which he received at a time when it was of little, if any, importance to him and which he will therefore not have taken on board.[103]

5.58 In relation to deemed knowledge, insurers are taken to know about the practices and customs of any trade or profession which they insure. As Lord Mansfield said in *Noble v Kennoway*:[104]

> Every under-writer is presumed to be acquainted with the practice of the trade he insures ... If he does not know it, he ought to inform himself.

So insurers of commodity traders are taken to know that successful commodity traders must take advantage of market opportunities and be prepared to conduct their business in innovative ways.[105] In the same way, professional indemnity

---

[101] *Permanent Trustee Australia Ltd v FAI General Insurance Company Ltd* [2003] HCA 25; (2003) 214 CLR 514: no duty under s 21 of the Insurance Act 1984 (Cth) to disclose to an insurer when seeking an extension of a current policy pending obtaining a new policy a provisional decision not to seek to renew with that insurer.

[102] *Bates v Hewitt* (1867) LR 2 QB 595: insurance of ship which had been a Confederate warship in the American Civil War and so was liable to be seized by the US Navy; insurers had been aware of the earlier history of the 'Georgia', but did not identify it with the vessel of that name which they were asked to insure some months later.

[103] *London General Insurance Company v General Marine Underwriters' Association* [1921] 1 KB 104. Reinsurers received a casualty slip reporting loss of a vessel which they did not insure. Later on the same day they were asked to reinsure that vessel. The Court of Appeal held that reinsurers were not to be expected to have had in their minds the information from the casualty slip, which was of no interest to them at the time. (The position of the reinsured was different: see para 5.17.)

[104] (1780) 2 Dougl. 510, at 513, 99 ER 326, at 327.

[105] *Glencore International AG v Alpina Insurance Company Ltd* [2003] EWHC 2792 (Comm); [2004] 1 Lloyd's Rep 111, at 124–5.

insurers of financial advisers regulated under the Financial Services Act 1986 are taken to be familiar with or to have a working understanding of that regulatory regime.[106]

There are, however, limits to the knowledge which insurers are deemed to have. **5.59** The test is always whether there has been a fair presentation of the risk.[107] A presentation which assumes that insurers will have in mind information relevant to the risk which was in the public domain will not be fair if it requires exceptional feats of memory on their part.[108] But today information may be available in an electronic database or online and so be readily accessible. If it is market practice for insurers to search such potential sources of information, they may be treated as having knowledge of information which would have been revealed by having done so.[109]

Waiver of disclosure There are two obvious ways in which insurers may waive **5.60** disclosure of material circumstances. The first is by asking a specific, limited question in the proposal form which effectively excludes disclosure of material circumstances falling outside the scope of the question. The second is by failing to ask questions when presented with the risk.

In relation to waiver by asking questions on the proposal form, if, for example, **5.61** insurers ask about claims made against the insured over the preceding five years, they may well waive disclosure of claims made before then.

Thus, in *Roberts v Plaisted*[110] the insured operated a discotheque as part of his hotel **5.62** business. The proposal form asked a number of questions as to the use of the insured premises, which the insured answered accurately, stating that they were used as a hotel, whose facilities were not exclusively for the use of residents. One question asked whether part of the premises were used as a casino. No other questions were asked as to possible ancillary uses. It was held that, while the fact that part of the premises was used as a discotheque was material, insurers had waived disclosure of ancillary uses of parts of the premises other than as a casino. In any particular

---

[106] *J Rothschild Assurance plc v Collyear* [1999] Lloyd's Rep IR 6, at 28; *Standard Life Assurance Ltd v Oak Dedicated Ltd* [2008] EWHC 222 (Comm); [2008] Lloyd's Rep IR 552, at [16].

[107] *Kingscroft Insurance Company Ltd v Nissan Fire & Marine Insurance Company Ltd (No 2)* [1999] Lloyd's Rep IR 603, at 629–30 per Moore-Bick J.

[108] So marine insurers, who might be expected to read *Lloyd's List* are not expected to remember everything that they have read in it: *Morrison v Universal Marine Insurance Co* (1872) LR 8 Ex 40, at 54 per Bramwell B: 'But to hold that the underwriter is bound to carry in his head all that is contained in Lloyd's List relating to a ship in which he has no interest, rather than to hold the owner of the ship bound to disclose it, would be to put a difficult and needless burden on the underwriter, while the opposite view puts no difficulty at all in the way of the owner.'

[109] *Sea Glory Maritime Co v Al Sagr National Insurance Co (The 'MV Nancy')* [2013] EWHC 2116 (Comm); [2014] 1 Lloyd's Rep 14, at [170]–[175] per Blair J. See also *Hua Tyan Development Ltd v Zurich Insurance Co Ltd (The 'Ho Feng 7')* [2013] HKCA 414; [2014] Lloyd's Rep IR 14, at 16.13–16.21 per Hon Cheung JA, with whom the other members of the Court of Appeal, Hong Kong Special Administrative Region agreed.

[110] [1989] 2 Lloyd's Rep 341.

case the question of waiver will depend upon how a reasonable insured would have understood the effect of the proposal form: by asking a specific question, have insurers restricted their right to receive all other material information and consented to the omission of information beyond that sought by the question?[111]

5.63 Waiver by failing to ask questions on presentation of the risk is inextricably linked to the question whether there has been a fair presentation of the risk. This has been considered earlier.[112] Unless there has been a fair presentation of the risk, the issue as to whether insurers have waived disclosure of information by reason of having failed to ask questions does not arise.[113] If a fair presentation of the risk would put a reasonable insurer on inquiry, then an insurer who fails to make that inquiry will waive disclosure of material information which would have been disclosed as a result.[114]

5.64 **Disclosure superfluous because of warranty or condition**   If an insured gives a warranty as to a matter or if something is a condition of cover, then any breach of such warranty or condition will provide insurers will full protection.[115] There is therefore no need for the insured to disclose circumstances which are only material to matters covered by warranties and conditions.

E. Duration of the Duty to Disclose

5.65 The duty of disclosure arises when negotiations for a contract of insurance start and continues until those negotiations end in the making of a binding contract. It follows that any material circumstance of which the insured learns during negotiations and before a contract is made should be disclosed.[116]

---

[111] *Doheny v New India Assurance Co Ltd* [2004] EWCA Civ 1705; [2005] Lloyd's Rep IR 251, at [17]–[20] per Longmore LJ. See also *Synergy Health (UK) Ltd v CGU Insurance Plc* [2010] EWHC 2581 (Comm); [2011] Lloyd's Rep IR 500, at [167] per Flaux J. In the *Doheny* case it was held that, on its true construction, the proposal form did not have the limiting effect for which the insured contended, but, had it done, the Court of Appeal would have been inclined to find a waiver. In the *Synergy Health* case Flaux J rejected the insured's argument that, by requiring the insured to sign a declaration of material facts, insurers had waived a further disclosure of material facts beyond that express declaration. See also *R&R Developments Ltd v Axa Insurance UK plc* [2009] EWHC 2429 (Ch); [2010] Lloyd's Rep IR 521, at [40]–[43].

[112] Paras 5.46–5.48.

[113] *Synergy Health (UK) Ltd v CGU Insurance Plc* [2010] EWHC 2581 (Comm); [2011] Lloyd's Rep IR 500, at [172] per Flaux J.

[114] As Parker LJ explained in *Container Transport International Inc v Oceanus Mutual Underwriting Association (Bermuda) Ltd* [1984] 1 Lloyd's Rep 476, at 511–12: 'In order to establish waiver by implication from non-enquiry the insurer must be put on enquiry by the disclosure of facts which would raise in the mind of a reasonable insurer at least a suspicion that there were other circumstances which would or might vitiate the presentation made to him.'

[115] See paras 7.83–7.99 and 7.100–7.106.

[116] *Cory v Patton* (1874) LR 9 QB 577; *Lishman v Northern Maritime Insurance Company* (1875) LR 10 CP 179; *Hadenfayre Ltd v British National Insurance Ltd* [1984] 2 Lloyd's Rep 393, at 398; *Newbury International Ltd v Reliance National Insurance Co (UK) Ltd* [1994] 1 Lloyd's Rep 83, at 85; *New Hampshire Insurance Co Ltd v MGN Limited* [1997] LRLR 24, at 48.

The duty of disclosure also applies to the negotiation of any variation of the terms **5.66** of the contract of insurance which would have the result of making the contract more onerous for insurers. However, the duty is limited to disclosure of circumstances material to the proposed variation. As Blackburn J explained in *Lishman v The Northern Maritime Insurance Company*:[117]

> concealment of material facts known to the assured before effecting the insurance will avoid the policy, the principle being that with regard to insurance the utmost good faith must be observed. Suppose the policy were actually executed, and the parties agreed to add a memorandum afterwards, altering the terms: if the alteration were such as to make the contract more burdensome to the underwriters, and a fact known at that time to the assured were concealed which was material to the alteration, I should say the policy would be vitiated. But if the fact were quite immaterial to the alteration, and only material to the underwriter as being a fact which showed that he had made a bad bargain originally, and such as might tempt him, if it were possible, to get out of it, I should say that there would be no obligation to disclose it.[118]

However, where a contract of insurance is terminable by insurers, the insured is **5.67** not under a continuing duty of disclosure so as to enable insurers to decide whether to exercise their right to terminate the contract.[119] In *New Hampshire Insurance Co Ltd v MGN Limited*,[120] insurers argued that there was a continuing duty because there was a cancellation clause entitling them to cancel on 15 days' notice. This argument was rejected by Potter J, whose judgment was upheld by the Court of Appeal.[121] Potter J said:[122]

> Thus while I accept that the obligation of good faith as between insurer and insured is one which continues throughout the policy, in particular in relation to the making of claims, it does not in my view apply so as to trigger positive obligations of disclosure of matters affecting the risk during the currency of the cover except in relation to some requirement, event or situation provided for in the policy to which the duty of good faith attaches. I do not consider that a simple right of termination on notice constitutes such event or situation.

As Potter J explained, the duty of good faith continues throughout the perfor- **5.68** mance of a contract of insurance. However, it does not take the form of a duty of disclosure save in limited circumstances. In relation to the making of claims, for

---

[117] (1875) LR 10 CP 179, at 182.

[118] This passage from the judgment of Blackburn J was cited with approval by Lord Hobhouse in *Manifest Shipping Co Ltd v Uni-Polaris Co Ltd, The Star Sea* [2001] UKHL 1; [2003] 1 AC 469, at [54]. See also *Niger Co Ltd v Guardian Assurance Co Ltd* (1922) 13 Ll L Rep 75, particularly per Lord Buckmaster at 76–7 and *New Hampshire Insurance Co Ltd v MGN Limited* [1997] LRLR 24, at 48.

[119] *Niger Co Ltd v Guardian Assurance Co Ltd* (1921) 6 Ll L Rep 239, particularly per Bankes LJ at 245, and (1922) 13 Ll L Rep 75.

[120] [1997] LRLR 24.

[121] Ibid at 58–62.

[122] Ibid at 48.

example, it requires the insured to be honest, but no more than that.[123] The duty of good faith also informs the construction of the terms of insurance contracts[124] and has implications for the conduct of claims against the insured by third parties which fall within the cover.[125]

F. Consequences of Non-Disclosure

5.69 Any failure to comply with the duty of disclosure will render the contract voidable as against the party who is in breach. Avoidance is the remedy provided by the law and breach of the duty of disclosure does not sound in damages.[126]

5.70 Avoidance is at the election of insurers. If they elect to avoid, then the avoidance is *ab initio* rather than prospective. The contract of insurance is undone from the beginning. Save in cases of fraud, insurers must return the premium.[127]

5.71 Where there is composite insurance, as will often be the case in professional indemnity insurance,[128] it may be possible to avoid against one insured, but not against others. This is addressed below.[129]

5.72 The right to avoid can be lost by affirmation of the contract of insurance (usually referred to as waiver). This involves an informed choice by insurers to treat the contract as continuing. The decision has to be informed in that insurers must know enough of the relevant facts which give them the right to avoid, even if they do not know every detail. It also appears that, generally, insurers must know that they have the right to avoid. Affirmation requires insurers to make an unequivocal communication of their choice to the insured.[130]

---

[123] *Manifest Shipping Co Ltd v Uni-Polaris Co Ltd, The Star Sea* [2001] UKHL 1; [2003] 1 AC 469: see further paras 11.56–11.62.

[124] Paragraphs 7.66–7.69.

[125] Paragraphs 12.52–12.55.

[126] *Banque Keyser Ullmann SA v Skandia (UK) Insurance Ltd* [1990] 1 QB 665, at 774–81, affirmed at *Banque Financière de la Cité SA (formerly Banque Keyser Ullmann SA) v Westgate Insurance Co Ltd (formerly Hodge General & Mercantile Co Ltd)* [1991] 2 AC 249, at 280 and 281; approved in *Manifest Shipping Co Ltd v Uni-Polaris Co Ltd, The Star Sea* [2001] UKHL 1; [2003] 1 AC 469, at [46] and in *HIH Casualty & General Insurance Ltd v Chase Manhattan Bank* [2003] UKHL 6; [2003] 2 Lloyd's Rep 61, at [75]. See also s 17 of the Marine Insurance Act 1906, which provides that avoidance is the remedy for breach of the duty of the utmost good faith.

[127] For non-fraudulent non-disclosure see s 84(3)(a) of the Marine Insurance Act 1906. Where the non-disclosure was fraudulent the position is different. Eg *Rivaz* v *Gerussi Brothers & Co* (1880) 6 QBD 222, at 229–30 per Brett LJ: 'Here it was not only a concealment, but a fraudulent concealment, for the matter concealed was kept back from the knowledge of the underwriters in order that the assured might thereby derive an advantage. Being therefore fraudulent, it seems to me there should be no return of premium ...'

[128] Paragraphs 1.32–1.45.

[129] Paragraphs 5.114–5.134.

[130] *Insurance Corporation of the Channel Islands v Royal Hotel Ltd* [1998] Lloyd's Rep IR 151, at 161 per Mance J. See also *Kosmar Villa Holidays Plc v Trustees of Syndicate 1243* [2008] EWCA Civ 147; [2008] Lloyd's Rep IR 489 at [36]–[38] per Rix LJ.

G. Exclusion of the Right to Avoid

Innocent non-disclosure by an insured of a matter which is wholly unrelated to a **5.73** loss and disclosure of which would only have led insurers to seek a slightly higher premium or some relatively minor variation in terms will enable insurers to avoid cover. The perceived harshness of this result has led the legislatures in a number of Commonwealth countries to reform the law in this area. And Parliament has recently reformed the law of England and Wales.[131] It has been suggested that avoidance for non-disclosure should be confined to plain cases.[132] In the area of professional indemnity insurance, the consequences of the existing law for professionals and their clients are such that it has become commonplace for professional indemnity insurance policies to contain provisions excluding or restricting insurers' right to avoid for non-disclosure and misrepresentation.[133]

Insurers' option to affirm, but to exclude cover for a particular claim

A modest amendment of insurers' rights in the event of non-disclosure or misrepre- **5.74** sentation is a provision excluding from cover any claim which arises from circumstances which should have been disclosed, but were not, when the risk was accepted, but leaving cover otherwise in place. This avoids visiting the full consequences of non-disclosure on the insured who will be covered in respect of other claims. If such a provision is expressed as an alternative to avoidance at the option of insurers, the insured will still face the risk of avoidance even for innocent nondisclosure. However, insurers will not be faced with the stark choice between avoidance and affirmation so as to be on risk for a claim which should have been disclosed.

A term to that effect appeared in the policies considered in *Thorman v New* **5.75** *Hampshire Insurance Co (UK) Ltd*.[134] In that case, architects were insured by NHIC until 30 September 1983 and from 1 October 1983 with Home Insurance Co ('HIC'). Both policies were written in materially identical terms that were approved by RIBA. Condition 7 provided:

> It is hereby agreed by the Insured that in the event of the Company being at any time entitled to void this Policy ab initio by reason of any inaccurate or

---

[131] The Consumer Insurance (Disclosure and Representations) Act 2012 (discussed in para 5.02) and the Insurance Act 2015 (discussed in paras 5.135–5.166).

[132] *Kausar v Eagle Star Insurance Co Ltd* [2000] Lloyd's IR 154, at 157 per Staughton LJ: 'Avoidance for non-disclosure is a drastic remedy. It enables the insurer to disclaim liability after, and not before, he has discovered that the risk turns out to be a bad one; it leaves the insured without the protection which he thought he had contracted and paid for. Of course there are occasions where a dishonest insured meets his just deserts if his insurance is avoided; and the insurer is justly relieved of liability. I do not say that non-disclosure operates only in cases of dishonesty. But I do consider that there should be some restraint in the operation of the doctrine. Avoidance for honest non-disclosure should be confined to plain cases.'

[133] *HIH Casualty and General Insurance Ltd v New Hampshire Co* [2001] EWCA Civ 735; [2001] 2 Lloyd's Rep 161 per Rix LJ, at [205].

[134] [1988] 1 Lloyd's Rep 7.

misleading information given by the Insured to the Company in the proposal form the Company may at their election instead of voiding this Policy ab initio give notice in writing to the Insured that they regard this Policy as of full force and effect save that there shall be excluded from the indemnity afforded hereunder any claim which has arisen or which may arise and which is related to circumstances which ought to have been disclosed in the proposal form but which were not disclosed to the Company. This Policy shall then continue in full force and effect but shall be deemed to exclude as if the same had been specifically endorsed ab initio the particular claim or possible claim referred to in the said notice.

5.76 The HIC policy introduced further terms, including Special Provision 1:

INNOCENT MISREPRESENTATION AND NON-DISCLOSURE:

The Company will not exercise its rights to avoid this Policy where it is alleged that there has been non-disclosure or misrepresentation of facts or untrue statements in the proposal form, provided always that the Insured shall establish to the Company's satisfaction that such alleged non-disclosure, misrepresentation or untrue statement, was innocent and free of any fraudulent conduct or intent to deceive ...

Another Special Provision excluded from cover any liability arising out of circumstances disclosed in the proposal form.

5.77 It appears from the judgment of Sir John Donaldson MR[135] that at first instance Steyn J had held that, while Condition 7 preserved insurers' right to avoid *ab initio* for non-disclosure, Special Provision 1 deprived them of that right where the insured had acted honestly.

5.78 The decision of the Court of Appeal concerned which of two insurers who had insured the same firm of architects in different years was on risk for a particular claim.[136] Sir John Donaldson MR went on to give some guidance, obiter, as to the effect of the two clauses. He read Condition 7 and Special Provision 1 as working together as follows:[137]

As at present advised, I consider that the starting point is the position at common law, in the absence of both condition 7 and special provision 1. Innocent, but material, non-disclosure would give rise to a right to avoid the whole policy upon returning the premium. The insured would be uninsured not only in respect of the undisclosed potential liability, but in respect of *all* liabilities. If the non-disclosure came to light, and the policy was avoided, towards the end of the policy year, this would be a calamity for the insured, because it is most unlikely that there would be any way in which he could insure retrospectively. Condition 7 varies the common law by permitting, but not obliging, underwriters to waive the right of avoidance and to affirm the policy, but to do so subject to a deemed exclusion of liability for undisclosed actual or potential claims. Special provision 1 then requires underwriters to give the architect an opportunity of satisfying them that the non-disclosure

---

[135] Ibid at 13.
[136] See paras 2.40–2.46.
[137] [1988] 1 Lloyd's Rep 7, at 13.

was innocent and, if he can do so, further obliges underwriters to elect to affirm the policy, subject to the deemed exclusion. So construed no practical problem arises.

Sir John Donaldson MR prefaced this part of his judgment by explaining that **5.79** he was not in a position to give authoritative guidance on this point, on which the Court of Appeal had heard only brief argument. In the circumstances it would be right to treat what he said with some care. In particular, it may be that Sir John Donaldson MR's reading of the effect of Special Provision 1 was wrong. The right to avoid the policy for non-disclosure came not from Condition 7, but from the law. Special Provision 1 only applied where the insured could show that the non-disclosure was 'innocent and free of any fraudulent conduct or intent to deceive'. In such circumstances, insurers lost their right to avoid the policy and remained fully on risk. This would not be subject to an exception as provided by Condition 7, the application of which was not limited to 'innocent' non-disclosure.

Sir John Donaldson MR preferred his reading of the two conditions to that of **5.80** Steyn J because, on Steyn J's construction of them, an insured who innocently failed to disclose a potential claim would be covered if and when a claim was made, whereas an insured who did disclose the potential claim would not be. Sir John Donaldson said:

> This puts the non-disclosing insured in a better position than one who makes full disclosure. This cannot be right.

However, this could be said to ignore the fact that the disclosing insured would have been able to notify under his current policy. This was the answer given by Thomas J to the argument that it could not have been the parties' intention to reward non-disclosure in the later decision of *Kumar v AGF Insurance Ltd*.[138] In that case, condition 5 of the policy included a wider exclusion of the right to avoid than that contained in Special Provision 1 in the *Thorman* case.[139] There was also an express exclusion of cover in respect of claims arising from matters declared in the proposal form. The insured sought cover for a claim which arose out of circumstances which should have been disclosed, but had not been.

Insurers pointed to the express exclusion of cover for claims arising from mat- **5.81** ters declared in the proposal form. They argued that it would be remarkable if a claim arising from circumstances which should have been disclosed but had been concealed, was covered, whereas a claim which had been disclosed was not. That would be to reward non-disclosure and the parties could not have intended such a result. In this respect, the insurers' argument echoed the views of Sir John Donaldson MR in the *Thorman* case. Insurers contended that it was so obvious that cover was not intended for such concealed circumstances that it went without

---

[138] [1999] 1 WLR 1747.
[139] See para 5.76.

saying and a term should be implied on the well-known test set out in *Shirlaw v Southern Foundries (1926) Ltd.*[140] Thomas J rejected this argument:

> The purpose of the declaration in the proposal form is to make it clear, that when matters that might give rise to a claim are known to the insured, they must be noted on to the proposal form so that they can be taken into account in assessing the premium for the policy and can be excluded under that policy. This is because, as is common under this form of claims made policy, when circumstances are notified and become known to the professional practice concerned, they can be notified under the current or existing policy and a claim that is subsequently made will fall within that existing policy. These are very common provisions.

5.82 It is submitted that the decision of Thomas J is to be preferred, not least because it was part of the decision rather than obiter and because it was made after full argument.

Exclusion of right to avoid for innocent and non-fraudulent non-disclosure and misrepresentation

5.83 Special Provision 1 in the *Thorman* case[141] was typical of many found in professional indemnity policies which exclude insurers' right to avoid if the insured can show that the non-disclosure or misrepresentation was 'innocent' and not fraudulent. For example, the RIBA Architects Premier Policy Wording provides:

> Insurers will not exercise their right to avoid the Policy nor will Insurers reject a request for indemnity when it is alleged that there has been:
>
> Non-disclosure of facts; or
>
> Misrepresentation of facts; or
>
> Incorrect particulars of statements;
>
> …
>
> Provided also that the Insured shall establish to Insurers' satisfaction that such alleged nondisclosure, misrepresentation … was innocent and free of any fraudulent conduct or intent to deceive.

Similar wording, with a different proviso, appeared in the policies considered in *Arab Bank Plc v Zurich Insurance Co*[142] and in *Immerzeel v Santam Ltd.*[143]

---

[140] [1939] 2 KB 206.

[141] Set out in para 5.76.

[142] [1999] 1 Lloyd's Rep 262. The clause provided: 'The Company will not exercise its right to avoid this Certificate of Insurance where it is alleged that there has been non-disclosure or misrepresentation of facts or untrue statements in the proposal and in conjunction with any subsequent proposal forms provided always that the Insured shall establish to the Company's satisfaction that such alleged non-disclosure, mis-representation or untrue statement was innocent and free of any fraudulent conduct or intent to deceive.'

[143] [2007] Lloyd's Rep IR 106. The additional proviso is considered at 5.95. The rest of the clause provided: 'The Insurers will not avoid this Certificate on the grounds (a) of failure on the part of the Insured at any time to disclose to the Insurers facts material to the assessment of the risk.

The need for the insured to show that the non-disclosure, misrepresentation, or **5.84** untrue statement was 'innocent and free of any fraudulent conduct or intent to deceive' raises the question as to what is meant by 'innocent'. For the purposes of the duty to disclose material circumstances, it makes no difference whether non-disclosure was negligent or non-negligent. However, there is a difference between negligent and non-negligent misrepresentations, for example under the Misrepresentation Act 1967. Insofar as the insured has to satisfy insurers that any misrepresentation was 'innocent', the effect of the clause is clear: the insured must show that the misrepresentation was made without negligence. It might be thought to be surprising if the parties had intended that the right to avoid would only be excluded for misrepresentations which were neither fraudulent nor negligent, but that it would be excluded for non-disclosure which was only non-fraudulent.[144]

However, in *Arab Bank Plc v Zurich Insurance Co*[145] Rix J, considering such a **5.85** clause in the context of composite insurance,[146] held that its effect was that 'any insured who is personally innocent of an intent to deceive should be entitled to resist avoidance'.[147] And in *Switzerland Insurance (Australia) Ltd v Gooch*[148] the New Zealand Court of Appeal, while recognizing that there was an 'element of surplusage' if 'innocent' were given its natural meaning,[149] rejected the argument on behalf of insurers that it encompassed equitable fraud.[150]

The facts and decision in *Switzerland Insurance (Australia) Ltd v Gooch*[151] illustrate **5.86** the potential impact of this type of clause when it limits insurers' right to avoid to cases where the non-disclosure or misrepresentation is, in effect, deliberate or fraudulent. In that case the insured was a firm of solicitors. An existing claim against the insured firm of solicitors was covered by their previous insurers. They disclosed the fact that the claim had been made and been tried to their current

---

(b) that the Insured made an incorrect representation of a nature likely to have materially affected the assessment of the risk under this insurance. Provided that (a) the Insured proves that such alleged non-disclosure or misrepresentation was innocent and free from fraudulent conduct or intent on the part of the Insured.'

[144] *O'Connor v Bullimore Underwriting Agency Ltd* [2004] Scot CS 42, at [102] per Lord MacFadyen. See also *HIH Casualty & General Insurance Ltd v Chase Manhattan Bank* [2003] UKHL 6; [2003] 2 Lloyd's Rep 61 at [11]–[13], [58]–[67], [95], and [114]–[117] for an illuminating discussion of the question whether a very differently worded exclusion in an insurance policy encompassed negligence, including negligent non-disclosure.

[145] [1999] 1 Lloyd's Rep 262.

[146] As to which see paras 5.114–5.134.

[147] [1999] 1 Lloyd's Rep 262, at 274.

[148] [1996] 3 NZLR 525.

[149] Taken from the Oxford English Dictionary: 'Entirely free of responsibility for or involvement in any event while suffering circumstantially from it. Devoid of cunning or artifice ...'

[150] The differing interpretations of this provision were noted by Mr Kevin Prosser QC, sitting as a Deputy High Court Judge in *Dowling v Bennett Griffin (A Firm)* [2013] EWHC 1995 (Ch). On the facts before him the insured architect had deliberately not disclosed the fact that a claim had been made.

[151] [1996] 3 NZLR 525.

insurers. They did not disclose that in an oral judgment the trial judge had found the firm liable for considerable damages, had made an adverse finding as to the credibility of one of the partners and had criticized the firm's procedures concerning file notes and confirming advice. Instead they said, correctly, that a written judgment was awaited. The new insurers claimed that there had been non-disclosure of material facts and that the non-disclosure had not been 'innocent and free from any fraudulent conduct or intent to deceive'.

5.87 At trial the evidence showed that there had been non-disclosure of material facts namely the making of a substantial award of damages against the firm and the adverse findings as to credibility and the firm's procedures. But the trial judge held insurers' right to avoid was excluded by the clause. He accepted the firm's evidence that they did not think that the judgment in the earlier claim was material because it was covered by their earlier insurers and that they did not think that the judgment would result in higher premiums in future. The partner responsible was not a litigator and so was less alive to the nuances of the judgment. Insurers appealed, but the Court of Appeal of New Zealand was not prepared to reverse the judge's findings: it was open to the judge to find as he had done on the evidence before him.

5.88 Insurers succeeded in *McAleenan v AIG (Europe) Ltd*,[152] where the insured was a solicitor in the Republic of Ireland. The proposal form stated, wrongly, that she was a partner in the firm. The proposal form had been filled in by someone else, but the insured signed it without reading it. Finlay Geoghegan J held that she had therefore been reckless as to the truth of the statements in the proposal form and so the misrepresentation was not innocent and free of any fraudulent intent.[153]

5.89 As appears above, some versions of clauses excluding insurers' right to avoid a contract for non-disclosure or misrepresentation which is shown to be innocent and free of any fraudulent conduct or intent to deceive require the insured to satisfy insurers that the clause applies.[154] It is implicit in such provisions that insurers will provide the insured an opportunity to advance a case that any non-disclosure or misrepresentation fell within the scope of the exception.[155] This requires insurers to inform the insured that they are considering avoiding the contract for non-disclosure or misrepresentation, with sufficient detail to enable the insured to decide whether to seek to persuade insurers that any non-disclosure or misrepresentation fell within the exception. Once that is done, it is a matter for the insured whether to seek to do so.[156] It has been held, obiter, that

---

[152] [2010] IEHC 128.

[153] Ibid at [123]–[124].

[154] The clause considered in *McAleeman v AIG (Europe) Ltd* [2010] IEHC 128 put the burden on insurers to prove that the non-disclosure or misrepresentation was not innocent and free from fraudulent intent.

[155] *O'Connor v Bullimore Underwriting Agency Ltd* [2004] Scot CS 42, at [100].

[156] Ibid at [101].

if insurers fail to give the insured the required information and opportunity, the insured's remedy is to apply to the Court which can decide the question in place of insurers.[157]

If insurers reject the arguments and evidence put forward by the insured, the question arises whether and, if so, on what basis the insured can challenge a decision by insurers that they are not persuaded that the insured's 'nondisclosure, misrepresentation or untrue statement was innocent and free of any fraudulent conduct or intent to deceive'. If the purported effect of giving the decision-making power to insurers were to oust the jurisdiction of the Court entirely, it would be contrary to public policy and void.[158] Decisions concerning insurance policies show that, at lowest, insurers' decision could be challenged on the ground of fraud or abuse of power and, probably, on the ground that no reasonable insurer could have reached the decision which insurers did.[159] Insurers' decision would also be open to challenge if they had taken an incorrect view of the law,[160] including the correct test for dishonesty. **5.90**

In this context 'reasonableness' does not mean that the court can set aside a decision on the ground that, considered objectively, the reasonable conclusion to be reached on the basis of the material and arguments put before insurers by the insured was that the insured had shown that non-disclosure or misrepresentation was innocent and free of any fraudulent conduct or intent to deceive. Rather it means that insurers must have reached their decision rationally. This has two elements. The first is that the decision must be one which a reasonable insurer could have reached (or not be one which no reasonable insurer could have reached). The second is that, in reaching their decision, insurers must have taken into account the material which was relevant to their decision and not have failed to take account of extraneous considerations.[161] It is important not to overstate what is required of insurers in **5.91**

---

[157] Ibid at [103].

[158] *Czarnikow v Roth Schmit & Co* [1922] 2 KB 478; *Lee v The Showmen's Guild of Great Britain* [1952] 2 QB 329; *West of England Shipowners Mutual Insurance Association (Luxembourg) v Cristal Ltd (The 'Glacier Bay')* [1996] 1 Lloyd's Rep 370; *Brown v GIO Insurance Ltd* [1998] Lloyd's Rep IR 201.

[159] *West of England Shipowners Mutual Insurance Association (Luxembourg) v Cristal Ltd (The 'Glacier Bay')* [1996] 1 Lloyd's Rep 370, at 377 per Neill LJ; *Brown v GIO Insurance Ltd* [1998] Lloyd's Rep IR 201. But see *Napier v UNUM Ltd* [1996] 2 Lloyd's Rep 550 where Tuckey J held that a provision in a permanent health policy that insurers would pay benefits upon proof satisfactory to them did not require a court to decide whether a reasonable insurer would have accepted the evidence put forward by the insured, but to decide whether that evidence proved what had to be proved.

[160] Ibid.

[161] *Braganza v BP Shipping Ltd* [2015] UKSC 17; [2015] 1 WLR 161 (a case concerning a provision in a contract of employment which gave the employer or its insurers the power to decide whether the employee's death, accidental injury or illness resulted from the employee's wilful act, default or misconduct). See also *Socimer International Bank Ltd v Standard Bank London Ltd* [2008] EWCA Civ 116; [2008] 1 Lloyd's Rep 558, at [66] per Rix LJ, with whom the other members of the Court of Appeal agreed.

this context. As Mocatta J observed in *CVG Siderurgicia del Ornioco SA v London Steamship Owners' Mutual Insurance Association Ltd (The 'Vainquer José')*:[162]

> Where, as here, the success or failure of a claim depends upon the exercise of a discretion by a lay body, it would be a mistake to expect the same expert, professional and almost microscopic investigation of the problems, both factual and legal, that is demanded of a suit in a Court of law.

Exclusion of right to avoid for non-fraudulent non-disclosure and misrepresentation

5.92 A variant on the clause considered in the preceding paragraphs is to be found in a number of reported cases. For example, in *J Rothschild Assurance plc v Collyear*[163] Special Condition 1 provided:

> Underwriters will not exercise their right to avoid this Policy where it is alleged that there has been non-disclosure or misrepresentation of facts provided always that THE ASSURED shall establish to Underwriters' satisfaction that such alleged non-disclosure, misrepresentation or untrue statement, was free of any fraudulent intent.[164]

5.93 Clauses to similar effect are to be found in the ICAEW Minimum Approved Policy Wording and the RICS Policy Wording. The ICAEW Minimum Approved Policy Wording provides that:

> Insurers will not avoid this policy or claim to be discharged from any liability to provide any indemnity under this policy, on the grounds of any alleged non-disclosure or misrepresentation of facts or untrue statements in the proposal form or in any other information which may have been supplied by or on behalf of the Insured to Insurers, provided always that the Insured shall establish to Insurers' reasonable satisfaction that such alleged non-disclosure, misrepresentation or untrue statement was free of any fraudulent conduct or intent to deceive.

The RICS Policy Wording is:

> Where there has been non-disclosure or misrepresentation of facts or untrue statements in the proposal form or in any other information or statements provided to

---

[162] [1979] 1 Lloyd's Rep 557, at 577, column 1, cited with approval by Baroness Hale DPSC in *Braganze v BP Shipping Ltd* [2015] UKSC 17; [2015] 1 WLR 161, at [30]. Baroness Hale went on to explain that it would not matter if there were some slight misdirection, 'at least if it were clear that, had the legal position been properly appreciated, the decision would have been the same. It may very well be that the same high standards of decision-making ought not to be expected of most contractual decision-makers as are expected of the modern state'.

[163] [1999] Lloyd's Rep IR 6, at 22.

[164] In *HLB Kidsons v Lloyd's Underwriters* [2008] EWCA Civ 1206; [2009] 1 Lloyd's Rep 8 the exclusion, subject to provisos considered at para 5.95, was as follows: 'The underwriters will not exercise their right to avoid this insurance where it is alleged that there have been untrue statements or non-disclosure or misrepresentations of facts in the proposal form or in any other information which may have been supplied provided always that the assured shall establish to underwriters' satisfaction that such alleged untrue statements or non-disclosure or misrepresentation of facts was free of any fraudulent conduct or intent to deceive.'

or made to or warranted to INSURERS and there has been no intention to deceive or mislead INSURERS, INSURERS will not exercise their right to avoid this policy nor will INSURERS be discharged from any liability under this policy ...

The effect of all these provisions is to exclude the right to avoid for non-disclosure **5.94** and misrepresentation save where the insured is unable to show that he was not acting fraudulently.

One proviso often found to such provisions is, while the policy is not avoided, if the **5.95** insured should have notified under an earlier policy, the cover available under the current policy will be no greater than that which would have been available under the policy under which the insured should have given notice. Again, the clause in *J Rothschild Assurance plc v Collyear*[165] is typical:

> However, in any case of a claim first made against THE ASSURED during the period of this insurance where (1) they had previous knowledge of the circumstances which could give rise to a claim and (2) they should have notified the same under any preceding insurance, then, where the indemnity or cover under this Policy is greater or wider in scope than that to which THE ASSURED would have been entitled under such preceding insurances Underwriters shall only be liable to afford indemnity to such amount and extent as would have been afforded to THE ASSURED by such preceding insurance.

Similar provisions are to be found in the policy considered in *Arab Bank Plc v Zurich Insurance Co*[166] and *Immerzeel v Santam Ltd*,[167] the ICAEW Minimum Approved Policy Wording,[168] the RICS Policy Wording,[169] and RIBA Architects Premier Policy Wording.[170]

---

[165] [1999] Lloyd's Rep IR 6.

[166] [1999] 1 Lloyd's Rep 262. The earlier part of the clause is set out in n 142. The proviso was as follows: 'However in any case of a claim first made against the Insured during the period specified in the schedule where (I) they had previous knowledge of the circumstances which could give rise to such claim and (II) they should have notified the same under the terms of any preceding insurance, then, where the indemnity or cover under this Certificate is greater or wider in scope than that to which the Insured would have been entitled under such preceding insurances (whether with other insurers or not), the Company shall only be liable to afford indemnity to such amount and extent as would have been afforded to the Insured by such preceding insurance.'

[167] [2007] Lloyd's Rep IR 106. The earlier part of the clause is set out in n 143. The proviso was as follows: 'where the insured could have notified under any preceding insurance circumstances which could give rise to a claim any indemnity in respect thereof to which the Insured may be entitled under Section 1 shall not be greater or wider in scope than the indemnity to which the Insured would have been entitled under such preceding insurance.'

[168] The ICAEW Minimum Approved Policy Wording provides that where the insured notifies insurers of a circumstance and the insured knew of that circumstance before the period of insurance and should have notified it under any previous policy of insurance, the indemnity under the policy is limited to that which would have been available under the earliest previous policy under which the circumstance should have been notified. Unless 'circumstance' (which is not defined) includes a claim, this term will not apply to a claim made during the policy period arising out of a circumstance which should have been notified under an earlier policy.

[169] Which makes it clear that the insured's cover is restricted both by the amount of cover and its scope, which would have applied had he notified as he should have done.

[170] Which, like the RICS Policy Wording, restricts cover by both amount and scope to that to which the insured would have been entitled under the earlier policy, but also gives insurers a

5.96 One of the issues in *J Rothschild Assurance plc v Collyear*[171] was the relationship between the Special Conditions which excluded the right to avoid for non-fraudulent non-disclosure and misrepresentation and an exclusion of cover in relation to claims:

> Arising out of any circumstances or occurrence which has been notified under any other policy or certificate attaching prior to the inception of this Policy or which were known to THE ASSURED prior to the inception of this Policy.

5.97 The insured claimed to have made an effective notification of circumstances in January 1994 so that subsequent claims for pensions mis-selling were covered.[172] Insurers argued that, if the insured had made an effective notification in 1994, then the insured had had sufficient notice of the potential claims in February 1992 when LAUTRO, its regulator under the Financial Services Act 1986, published a bulletin relating to investors being given wrong advice to transfer out of occupational pension schemes and into personal pensions.

5.98 The insured had two answers. The first was that the LAUTRO bulletins had not been such, either in content or result, to constitute a circumstance or occurrence known to the insured. They had required the insured to undertake a review of its cases which had produced a nil return. That issue turned on the facts. The second was that the exclusion was inconsistent with Special Conditions 1 and 2. Rix J resolved the construction issue in favour of the insured, saying:[173]

> Special Condition 2 ... states that even 'where (1) [the assureds] had previous knowledge of the circumstances which could give rise to such a claim and (2) they should have notified' them under a preceding insurance, then underwriters 'shall only be liable to afford indemnity' to the extent and amount of the preceding insurance. It follows that under Special Condition 2, there will be cover to the extent of cover in the previous year. That is simply inconsistent with a view of Exclusion 2 that would simply deny cover in all cases of knowledge prior to inception of circumstances which have given rise to a claim. The whole logic of the Special Conditions is that underwriters can only avoid the policy for non-disclosure etc in the case of fraudulent intent (with the burden being on the assured to disprove such intent). It would run entirely counter to such logic if, irrespective of fraudulent intent, the underwriters could deny cover for non-disclosure etc of matters known before inception.[174]

5.99 The exclusion clause was not deprived of all effect. It would apply where the insured had been unable to show an absence of fraudulent intent, but insurers did not wish

---

discretion as to whether to restrict cover and, if there are a number of earlier policies, as to which limits should apply.

[171] [1999] Lloyd's Rep IR 6.

[172] For this aspect of the decision see para 2.58.

[173] [1999] Lloyd's Rep IR 6, at 24.

[174] This issue would not arise under the RICS Policy Wording because the exclusion in respect of previous claims or circumstances is stated expressly not to reduce the rights of the insured under the condition which limits insurers' rights to avoid the policy.

to avoid the entire policy. It enabled them to affirm the policy, but to exclude cover for the particular claim which should have been notified under an earlier policy.[175]

Complete exclusion of the right to avoid

Some professional indemnity policies seek to exclude insurers' right to avoid for non-disclosure and misrepresentation even where that non-disclosure or misrepresentation has been fraudulent. It is, of course, most unusual for a party to agree to exclude his remedies for fraud. Clear words will be needed to show such an intention.[176] Moreover, it is not possible in law to exclude liability for your own fraud. As to whether a principal can exclude liability for the fraud of is agents, the position is undecided.[177]   **5.100**

Clauses excluding insurers' right to avoid for fraudulent non-disclosure or misrepresentation are found in the professional indemnity insurance of solicitors. For example, in *Kumar v AGF Insurance Ltd*[178] clause 5 of the policy, entitled 'non-avoidance' provided in part: **5.101**

> Subject to paragraph 13, the insurers will not seek to avoid, repudiate or rescind this insurance upon any ground whatsoever, including in particular non disclosure or misrepresentation. However, in circumstances where before the inception or renewal of this insurance a principal has fraudulently failed to disclose and/or fraudulently misrepresented the circumstances which might give rise to a claim or claims, the insurer shall be entitled to seek reimbursement from their principal in respect of any loss arising from such claim or claims.

While on their own the words 'any ground whatsoever' might not be sufficiently clear to include fraud, it is clear from the second sentence that the parties intended to do so.[179]

In the *Kumar* case, a partner in a firm of solicitors signed a proposal form for a policy with the defendant insurers for a top-up layer of £1 million insurance cover for professional liability in excess of the firm's existing compulsory £1 million cover with the Solicitors Indemnity Fund. For the purposes of the case it was assumed that the partner who completed the proposal form had acted dishonestly so as to give rise to the claim against the firm in respect of which his partner was seeking an indemnity. The partner whose dishonesty had given rise to the claim had also completed the proposal form. It was assumed that in doing so he fraudulently failed to disclose his earlier dishonesty. The proposal form ended with a certificate   **5.102**

---

[175] [1999] Lloyd's Rep IR 6, at 25.

[176] *HIH Casualty & General Insurance Ltd v Chase Manhattan Bank* [2003] UKHL 6; [2003] 2 Lloyd's Rep 61, at [16], [68], and [97].

[177] Ibid. See also *Pearson (S) & Son Ltd v Dublin Corporation* [1907] AC 351, considered in the *HIH Casualty* case.

[178] [1999] 1 WLR 1747.

[179] *Arab Bank Plc v Zurich Insurance Co* [1999] 1 Lloyd's Rep 262, at 272.

that the relevant inquiries had been made, followed by a basis of contract clause.[180] Thomas J held that the 'innocent' partner was entitled to an indemnity, despite the fraudulent non-disclosure and misrepresentation of the partner who had completed the proposal form.[181] Far from considering that public policy precluded the 'innocent' partner from recovering an indemnity, Thomas J held that it was appropriate to approach the construction of the policy in question on the basis of the regulatory background and, in particular, the object of protecting the clients of solicitors.[182]

5.103 In *Fisher v Guardian Insurance Co of Canada*,[183] the insured were a firm of lawyers. One partner, who had misappropriated client money, had made a dishonest declaration to the firm's excess layer insurers. The policy included the following condition:

> **WAIVER OF EXCLUSIONS AND BREACH OF CONDITIONS**
> Whenever coverage under any provision of this Policy would be excluded, suspended or lost:
> (i) because of any dishonest, fraudulent, malicious or criminal act or omission by any Insured …
> the Insurer agrees that such insurance as would otherwise be afforded under this policy shall continue in effect, cover and be paid with respect to each and every Insured who did not commit or personally participate in, or acquiesce in such activity …

The Court of Appeal of British Columbia held that the 'innocent' partners were entitled to an indemnity despite the dishonest declaration made by their partner.[184]

5.104 The SRA Minimum Terms and Conditions of Professional Indemnity Insurance require the insurance policy to provide that the insurer 'is not entitled to avoid or repudiate the insurance on any grounds whatsoever including, without limitation, non-disclosure or misrepresentation, whether fraudulent or not'. However, they do permit an exclusion of liability of the insurer to indemnify any particular person to the extent that any liability to third parties and defence costs arise from dishonesty or a fraudulent act or omission condoned by that person.[185] Any other person who is insured must remain insured and the insurance must provide that no dishonesty, act, or omission will be imputed to a body corporate unless committed or condoned by either all the directors of a company or all the members of a limited liability partnership.

---

180 As to which see paras 7.86–7.87.
181 For the arguments on the construction of the policy raised by insurers see paras 5.80–5.81 and 5.106–5.107.
182 [1999] 1 WLR 1747, at 1752. See further paras 7.08–7.10.
183 (1995) 123 DLR (4th) 336.
184 See further paras 5.129–5.130.
185 This exclusion is considered further in paras 8.40–8.43.

Insurers' other remedies

Breach of warranty: discharge from liability

Proposal forms often contain statements to the effect that the answers provided in **5.105** them and any other information provided by the insured formed the basis of the contract. It follows that any answer on the proposal form is a warranty.[186] In *Bank of Nova Scotia v Hellenic Mutual War Risks Association (Bermuda) Ltd (The Good Luck)*,[187] the House of Lords held that breach of warranty has the effect of discharging insurers from liability from the date of breach. In contrast with the right to avoid for non-disclosure or misrepresentation, there is no need for any election or other action on the part of insurers, who can, however, waive by estoppel the breach of warranty.[188]

It follows that many cases of non-disclosure and misrepresentation will also involve **5.106** a breach of warranty. In *Kumar v AGF Insurance Ltd*,[189] insurers sought to take advantage of this, arguing that by the relevant clause, condition 5, they had undertaken not to 'seek to avoid, repudiate or rescind this insurance upon any ground whatsoever, including in particular non disclosure or misrepresentation'.[190] The assumed breach of warranty had the effect of discharging them from liability, without the need for them to seek to do anything. Noting that the decision of the House of Lords in *Bank of Nova Scotia v Hellenic Mutual War Risks Association (Bermuda) Ltd (The Good Luck)*[191] had set out the precise consequences of a breach of warranty more fully and clearly than had been done before, Thomas J said:[192]

> In my judgment, it is clear that what the parties were doing in 1990 was stating that in whatever way insurers sought to escape from liability, they were not entitled to do so. The words were and are, in my judgment, to be read as preventing underwriters escaping from liability either by repudiating, avoiding or rescinding the policy itself, or being discharged from liability under the insurance because of a breach of warranty.[193]

Where there is a complete exclusion of the right to avoid, the result will be to **5.107** deprive the 'basis of contract' statement in the proposal form of any effect, at least against insureds who have not acted fraudulently or dishonestly. That was the result of the decision in the *Kumar* case, but Thomas J had no difficulty in depriving the equivalent provision in that case of effect, observing that 'it is not uncommon to find surplusage in a policy of insurance'.[194]

---

[186] *Condogianis v Guardian Assurance Co Ltd* [1921] 2 AC 125. See further paras 7.86–7.87.
[187] [1992] 1 AC 233.
[188] See further para 7.90.
[189] [1999] 1 WLR 1747.
[190] For the full clause see para 5.101.
[191] [1992] 1 AC 233.
[192] [1999] 1 WLR 1747, at 1755.
[193] See also *McAleeman v AIG (Europe) Ltd* [2010] IEHC 128, at [92]–[94].
[194] [1999] 1 WLR 1747, at 1756.

5.108 The RICS Policy Wording addresses the point raised in the *Kumar* case, referring to 'untrue statements in the proposal form' and providing that insurers will not be entitled to exercise their right to avoid the policy, 'nor will INSURERS be discharged from any liability under this policy' by reason of any non-disclosure or misrepresentation of the facts or untrue statements in the proposal form.[195] The ICAEW Minimum Approved Policy Wording achieves the same result in that Insurers undertake not to 'claim to be discharged from any liability' under the policy by reason of 'untrue statements in the proposal form'. The RIBA Architects Premier Policy Wording is less clear. Insurers promise not to 'reject a request for indemnity', which may preclude them from raising a defence of breach of warranty save where the non-disclosure is not innocent and free from any fraudulent conduct and intent to deceive. The limitation of insurers' rights applies where it is alleged that there has been 'incorrect particulars or statements' and this could extend to statements in a proposal form which had the effect of warranties.[196]

Claims for damages

5.109 The making of negligent mis-statements, fraudulent statements, and breaches of warranty can all sound in damages as well as giving rise to a right to avoid or discharging insurers from liability. Exclusion of the right to avoid and provision that insurers will not be discharged from liability by breach of warranty will be of limited use to the insured if insurers can recover as damages the amount which they are obliged to pay by way of indemnity under the insurance contract.

5.110 The point was considered in *Kumar v AGF Insurance Ltd*.[197] The relevant condition in that case gave insurers an express right to seek reimbursement from any principal of the insured who had 'fraudulently failed to disclose and/or fraudulently misrepresented the circumstances which might give rise to a claim or claims' for any loss suffered from such claim of claims.[198] Thomas J held that a claim against a non-fraudulent partner in the insured was excluded by the inclusion of an express right of reimbursement against a fraudulent partner. If necessary, he would have implied a term to that effect.[199]

5.111 Thomas J acknowledged that in *Toomey v Eagle Star Insurance Co Ltd (No 2)*[200] Colman J had held that a clause in a run-off agreement by which insurers

---

[195] For the full wording see para 5.93. The clause in *Fisher v Guardian Insurance Co of Canada* (1995) 123 DLR (4th) 336 set out in para 5.103 also appears to extend to breach of warranty, in that it applies where 'coverage under any provision of this Policy would be excluded, suspended or *lost*' (emphasis added).

[196] See paras 6.27–6.31 and 7.83–7.90.

[197] [1999] 1 WLR 1747.

[198] For the full clause see para 5.101.

[199] [1999] 1 WLR 1747, at 1757.

[200] [1995] Lloyd's Rep 88.

reinsured a large part of their previous underwriting which provided that the contract was 'neither cancellable nor voidable by either party' did not exclude a remedy in damages for misrepresentation. Colman J reached this conclusion even though it 'would drive a coach and horses through the commercial purpose which the parties had in entering into this contract'.[201] In the *Kumar* case, Thomas J was able to express agreement with this decision on the facts and circumstances of that case, which were very different from those before him. Since then the approach of Colman J to the construction of the clause in the *Toomey* case has been subject to criticism at the highest level.[202] It is suggested that the *Toomey* case should not be applied to policies of professional indemnity insurance.

5.112 The RICS policy wording gives insurers a means of at least partial redress. It allows insurers to charge an additional premium if non-disclosure or misrepresentation has prejudiced their consideration of terms under the policy. This does not enable insurers to change the terms of the contract other than the amount of premium paying. A similar clause was considered in *Gardner v Lemma Europe Insurance Company Ltd (In Liquidation)*.[203] In that case a term in the policy of solicitors' indemnity insurance[204] before the Court provided:

> If, during a period of insurance, but for special condition 4.1, the insurer would have been entitled to avoid this policy on the grounds of any non-disclosure or misrepresentation by the insured of any material fact or matter, either prior to inception or prior to any variation of cover, the insurer shall have the right to adjust the premium payable from inception, or from any variation in cover, to that which in its absolute discretion it decides that it would have charged had the material facts or matters been disclosed or accurately represented.

5.113 The liquidator of the insurers argued that the insured had failed to disclose various matters which had led to claims being made. He argued that under this clause insurers would be entitled to adjust the premium by the total of their exposure in respect of those claims so as to have a defence of set-off to their liability to indemnify the insured. The argument failed. It was not certain that the premium would be adjusted so as to cover the full amount of the indemnity, not least because the full amount payable would not be known at the time.[205]

---

[201] Ibid at 319.

[202] *HIH Casualty & General Insurance Ltd v Chase Manhattan Bank* [2003] UKHL 6; [2003] 2 Lloyd's Rep 61, at [116] per Lord Scott.

[203] [2014] EWHC 3674 (Ch).

[204] The SRA Minimum Terms and Conditions of Professional Indemnity Insurance allow the parties to agree other terms as long as they do not conflict with those Minimum Terms. The term in question is not in those Minimum Terms.

[205] The SRA Minimum Terms and Conditions of Professional Indemnity Insurance require the contract to include a term providing that any sum payable to indemnify the insured against civil liability must be paid only to the third party claimant and that insurers are to have no right of set-off, including in relation to unpaid premiums. The argument advanced by the liquidator appears to have assumed that this provision would be overridden by insolvency law.

H. Non-disclosure and Composite Policies

5.114 The nature of composite insurance has been explained already.[206] In summary, save where there is only one natural person who is insured, professional indemnity policies will usually be composite policies rather than joint policies. Each individual insured is insured for his own interest. This is so even though there is only one proposal for the insurance and only one premium is paid. Subject to issues of agency and attribution, each insured is treated as having made a separate application for separate insurance. It follows that non-disclosure by one insured will not entitle insurers to avoid against another insured.

The usual position

5.115 The interaction between composite insurance and non-disclosure was considered by Caulfield J in *Woolcott v Sun Alliance and London Insurance Ltd*,[207] a case concerning property insurance. The insured mortgagor had insured his house against fire. His mortgagee was also an insured. The mortgagor had convictions for robbery which he did not disclose to insurers. The house burnt down. Insurers paid the mortgagee's claim, but alleged material non-disclosure against the mortgagor and refused to provide cover to him. The mortgagor argued that the insurance was joint, rather than several, relying on a reference in the mortgagee building society's rules to joint insurance. Caulfield J rejected the mortgagor's argument, applying the decision of the Court of Appeal in *General Accident Fire and Life Assurance Corporation Ltd v Midland Bank Ltd*.[208] The insurance was composite and insurers had been entitled to avoid as against the mortgagor, without doing so against the mortgagee.

5.116 The position in relation to non-disclosure was fully established by the decisions in *New Hampshire Insurance Co Ltd v MGN Limited*.[209] The case concerned a number of policies of fidelity insurance against loss resulting from the dishonest or fraudulent acts of employees. The insured were various companies in the Maxwell group. Both Potter J and the Court of Appeal held that the insurance was composite.[210]

5.117 Potter J then considered how non-disclosure, misrepresentation, or breach of the duty of utmost good faith by one insured affected the cover of other insureds under such a policy. Potter J recorded insurers' argument based upon the single presentation of the risks to insurers and the payment of a single premium by the insured and continued:[211]

---

206 See paras 1.32–1.45.
207 [1978] 1 WLR 493.
208 [1940] 2 KB 388: see paras 1.33–1.35.
209 [1997] LRLR 24.
210 See para 1.38.
211 [1997] LRLR 24, at 42.

The claimants, on the other hand, have argued that in these circumstances the principle to be applied is that, where an independent interest is separately insured, there can be no question of avoiding the policy for non-disclosure quoad that interest unless the person so insured was privy to the non-disclosure. Equally, save to the extent that the contrary may be expressly provided for, breach by one assured does not constitute breach by any other assured, in entitling insurers or Chubb to avoid against such other assured (cf *P Samuel & Co Ltd. v Dumas* [1924] AC 431 at pp. 445–446 and p. 469).

In my view, the claimants are correct in their statement of the principle prima facie applicable in the case of composite insurance. While it is common to speak in terms of avoiding a policy of insurance, the right to avoid for non-disclosure relates to the contract of insurance made with the individual assured, of which there were a number in this case.

The Court of Appeal agreed.[212]

The usual position strengthened: the *Arab Bank* case

Some professional indemnity policies provide that 'innocent' insured will be **5.118** indemnified against vicarious liability for the fraud and dishonesty of others.[213] Insurers may also expressly waive the right to avoid for non-disclosure or misrepresentation during the making of the contract of insurance.[214] In *Arab Bank plc v Zurich Insurance*,[215] Rix J had to determine how the decision on composite insurance and non-disclosure in *New Hampshire Insurance Co Ltd v MGN Limited*[216] was to be applied in that context. The insured was a limited liability company of valuers. Its managing director, Anthony Browne, completed the proposal form and he was assumed to have made a number of fraudulent valuations before doing so. On the assumed facts, it was taken that Mr Browne knew he had acted fraudulently and had deliberately not given details of his overvaluations in the proposal form.

That form included the following question: **5.119**

Is any Partner, Director, Principal, Consultant or employee, AFTER ENQUIRY, aware of any circumstances/incidents which might:
(i) give rise to a claim against the Proposer or his predecessors in business or any of the present or former Partners, Directors, Principals?
...
(iii) otherwise affect the consideration of this proposal for Professional Indemnity insurance?

Mr Browne's answers to these questions did not disclose his assumed fraudulent overvaluations. The proposal form concluded:

I/We warrant that the above statements made by me/us or on my/our behalf are to the best of my/our knowledge true and complete and I/we agree that this proposal shall be the basis of the contract between me/us and the Insurer.

---

[212] Ibid at 57–8.
[213] See para 8.34.
[214] See paras 5.73–5.104.
[215] [1999] 1 Lloyd's Rep 262.
[216] [1997] LRLR 24.

Mr Browne signed and dated the proposal over the words '(Partner, Director, Sole Proprietor)' and above the line 'on behalf of (insert the name of the business/ practice)', but he did not fill this in.

5.120 Part 1 of the policy was headed 'Professional Indemnity, Money, Documents and Infidelity', and Section 1 of Part 1 contained the terms on which professional indemnity insurance was provided. The insuring clause provided an indemnity against all sums which the insured 'shall become legally liable to pay as damages and/or compensation in respect of any Civil Liability whatsoever'. This would include liability for dishonesty. For the purposes of this section 'the insured' were defined as:

1. The Firm(s) named as THE INSURED in the General Schedule of this Certificate of Insurance ('The Firm(s)') and/or the predecessors in business of the Firm(s)
2. Those persons named under Question 4 of the VEAGIS proposal form and subsequent proposal form(s) as Partner, Director, Sole Proprietor and any other person or persons who may at any time become Partner or Director of the Firm(s)
3. Any former Partner, Director or Sole Proprietor of the Firm(s) including any retired former Partner or Director who is acting or has acted as Consultant to the Firm(s)
4. Any person who is or has been an employee or deemed to be under a contract of service with the Firm(s)
5. Executors, Administrators or Legal Representatives of any of the persons hereinbefore referred to under (2), (3) or (4) above in the event of such persons' death, incapacity, insolvency or bankruptcy
6. Any other firm(s) engaged in the Business subsequently notified by the Insured and accepted by the Company

PROVIDED that such definition of the term 'Insured' shall NOT be construed to mean that the Company shall indemnify any person knowingly committing, making or condoning any dishonest, fraudulent or malicious act or omission.

5.121 Section 2, sub-section B, dealt with Fidelity and provided as follows:

The Company under this Sub-section agrees, subject to the terms, exceptions, conditions and Geographical Limits specified herein or otherwise endorsed hereon, to indemnify the Insured up to the limit of liability specified hereinafter against loss of any money or any other property whatsoever belonging to the Insured or in his custody where they are legally liable for such loss (including Accountants fees incurred as a direct result of such loss) and which the Insured shall first discover during the Period of Insurance, or in the event of non-renewal, within 6 (six) calendar months after the expiration of the Period of Insurance that the Insured shall in the course of the Business have incurred or sustained in consequence of any dishonest or fraudulent act of any Partner, Director, Sole Proprietor, Consultant and/or Employee (past or present) of the Insured PROVIDED ALWAYS that no indemnity shall be provided under this Sub-section to any person knowingly committing, making or condoning such act and the sum payable under this Sub-section shall only be for the balance of liability in excess of the amount(s) (if any) recovered from any Partner, Director Sole Proprietor, Consultant and/or Employee (past or present) of the Insured.

The policy also included a clause excluding insurers' right to avoid the policy for **5.122**
non-disclosure or misrepresentation or untrue statements in the proposal form, provided that the insured established to insurers' satisfaction that the non-disclosure
or untrue statement was innocent and free of any fraudulent intent or intention
to deceive.[217] The policy went on to provide that, if insurers made any payment in
respect of a claim, insurers would not exercise any rights of subrogation against any
partner, director, or employee of the insured unless the claim was brought about
or contributed to by the dishonest, fraudulent, criminal, or malicious act of such
persons.

Among the issues to be determined on these assumed facts were whether insurers **5.123**
were entitled to rely upon the fraud and dishonesty of Mr Browne in avoiding the
policy for non-disclosure or misrepresentation or breach of warranty. Rix J identified three interlinked questions: the construction of the policy, the conceptual
analysis of a composite policy such as that before him, and attribution.

The specific question of construction was whether the policy responded in the case **5.124**
of the dishonesty of one insured in favour of another insured who was not complicit in that dishonesty. Having referred to the earlier decisions to the effect that,
in composite insurance, one insured is not prejudiced by the dishonesty of another,
Rix J observed:[218]

> In the present case, however, the policy goes much further than is normally done
> (at any rate outside the context of professional indemnity insurance) in emphasiz-
> ing that the dishonesty of one insured will not be held against another insured who
> is not complicit.

Rix J pointed to a number of sections in the policy that made this clear. First, **5.125**
the words 'any civil liability whatsoever' in the insuring clause, taken with the
excluding cover for 'any person knowingly committing, making or condoning any
dishonest, fraudulent or malicious act or omission' made it clear that liability for
dishonesty was covered. Second, the fidelity section was to similar effect. Third,
the subrogation clauses made it clear that insurers would indemnify in respect of
a claim involving dishonesty and then be subrogated to any rights an innocent
insured had against those who had been dishonest.[219] Rix J concluded:[220]

> Therefore, this policy is not merely a composite policy with the normal attributes
> of such, but has been specifically designed to provide cover to innocent insureds
> despite the guilt of their close associates and agents.

That left two questions. Neither General Condition 1 (on Fraud) nor the non- **5.126**
avoidance clause made it clear whether they operated for or against each insured

---

[217] As to which, see paras 5.83–5.91.
[218] [1999] 1 Lloyd's Rep 262, at 272.
[219] As to which, see paras 8.58–8.60.
[220] [1999] 1 Lloyd's Rep 262, at 272.

separately or whether dishonesty on the part of any insured, whether in making a claim or in non-disclosure at the time of making the contract, rendered the policy liable to forfeiture or avoidance once and for all. Rix J stated that although these questions of construction were closely bound up with the analysis of composite policies and rules of attribution, he would approach them initially as a matter of pure construction. Taking each in turn, General Condition 1 provided as follows:

> 1. Fraud
>
> If any claim under this Certificate of Insurance shall be in any respect fraudulent or if any fraudulent means or devices are used by the Insured to obtain any benefit under this Certificate of Insurance all benefit thereunder shall be forfeited.

5.127 On the question whether the fraud of one insured (here the managing director, Mr Browne) entailed the loss of any benefit of the policy for all other insureds, Rix J said:[221]

> It seems to me that the clue is to be found in the words 'or if any fraudulent means or devices are used by the Insured'. If one insured is innocent and another guilty, it seems to me that those words can only apply to the guilty insured. It is only the guilty insured who can be 'the insured' for such purposes, for where an insured is innocent, it cannot be said of him that 'fraudulent means or devices are used by the Insured'. If therefore the underwriters had intended to forfeit the policy against all insureds, the innocent as well as the guilty, then they should have drafted the clause at least in terms of 'if any fraudulent means or devices are used by *any* Insured'. (emphasis in the original)

5.128 That left the question as to the effect of one insured's fraud on other insureds' entitlement to rely on the non-avoidance clause.[222] Rix J held that:[223]

> in the context of this policy the term 'the insured' should again be regarded as applying to each of the insureds separately. Therefore any insured who is personally innocent of an intent to deceive should be entitled to resist avoidance.

5.129 In reaching his decision, Rix J relied upon the decision of the British Columbia Court of Appeal in *Fisher v Guardian Insurance Co of Canada*.[224] The policy in that case was a lawyers' errors and omissions insurance issued in response to a fraudulent application completed by a dishonest lawyer, A, in favour of himself and his former partners, B and C, who were entirely innocent of any fraud. A previous judgment had held the three partners liable to a third party, and the question was whether B and C were entitled to be indemnified under their professional indemnity policy. A had fraudulently stated in his application that he had no reason to anticipate claims against him. This was demonstrably untrue. Insurers argued that A's false declaration should be imputed to B and C. It also relied on an exclusion

---

[221] Ibid, at 273.
[222] It is set out in n 142 under para 5.83.
[223] [1999] 1 Lloyd's Rep 262, at 273.
[224] (1995) 123 DLR (4th) 336.

of any claim arising out of any act committed by 'the Insured' with actual dishonest intent. For their part, B and C relied on a term of the policy waiving insurers' rights.[225]

Finch, JA, who gave the judgment of the Court in the *Fisher* case, applied the reasoning of the Supreme Court of Canada in *Panzera v Simcoe & Erie Insurance Co*,[226] a case concerning the composite insurance obtained by mortgagor and mortgagee, held that insurers' waiver had superseded any doctrine of attribution by which the dishonesty of one insured was to be attributed to 'innocent' insureds, and observed that the insurer:[227]   **5.130**

> had the means to protect itself either in the way it chose to issue the coverage, or by the choice of language in the policy.
>
> It seems more realistic, in these circumstances, to resolve disputes over the rights of multiple insureds under the contract on the basis of the language the insurer chose to employ in the policy, than to impute wrongdoing to an innocent insured on the basis of a notional and wholly artificial 'agency'.
>
> Such an approach is also more in accord with the realities of modern law practice. Modern firms frequently comprise dozens, sometimes hundreds, of lawyers. Some are partners, some are employees. The members of the firm in both categories change from time to time, as partners and associates retire, new partners are created, and new associates are employed. The only practical means of insuring against liability, in these circumstances, is for one application to be made by a responsible member of the firm, acting on behalf of all the others. If insurers could deny coverage to the hundreds of Canadian lawyers insured in this way, because of the misrepresentation of the individual who filled out their application on their behalf, the consequences to the public and to the profession would be enormous, quite unanticipated, and entirely inconsistent with the practical realities faced by the legal profession and the insurance industry.

Having answered the question of construction, Rix J turned to the question of the conceptual analysis of the nature of composite insurance. He reviewed the authorities[228] and concluded that they supported the conclusion that the policy of composite insurance before him was a 'bundle of separate contracts' under which each person falling within the definition of 'insured' was separately insured and, if innocent, not affected by the dishonesty of another insured.[229]   **5.131**

The third question was whether the assumed dishonesty of Mr Browne was to be attributed to the company of which he was managing director and in whose name he had been acting when producing the assumed fraudulent valuations and of which he had been acting as the authorized agent in completing the proposal form. In relation to the making of the valuations, Rix J held that the relevant rule of attribution   **5.132**

---

225 The clause is set out in para 5.103.
226 (1990) 74 DLR (4th) 197.
227 (1995) 123 DLR (4th) 336, at [57]–[59].
228 See paras 1.32–1.45 and 5.115–5.117.
229 [1999] 1 Lloyd's Rep 262, at 276–8.

was to be found in the scheme of the policy which was that each insured should be treated separately in relation to dishonesty so that Mr Browne's assumed dishonesty was not to be attributed to the company, which was a separate insured.[230]

5.133 The same reasoning led to the conclusion that Mr Browne's assumed dishonesty when completing the proposal form was not to be attributed to the other, innocent insured. Were it otherwise, 'everything under this policy would depend on the fortuity whether the director (or partner) who was delegated to sign the proposal was the director or partner who, ex hypothesi, had guilty knowledge'.[231] This conclusion was also reached on the basis that an agent who was committing a breach of duty in circumstances in which the usual inference that an agent would communicate his knowledge to his principal.[232]

5.134 It is often the case in contracts of professional indemnity insurance, there is composite insurance on terms which show an intention that innocent insured will be indemnified against liability for the wrongful acts of a dishonest insured and that each insured will be treated as having a separate contract of insurance to which any provision excluding or restricting insurers' right to avoid for non-disclosure or misrepresentation will apply. The *Arab Bank* case shows how effect is to be given to that intention when insurers seek to raise allegations of non-disclosure or misrepresentation.

I. The Duty of Fair Presentation under the Insurance Act 2015

The duty of fair presentation

5.135 The Insurance Act 2015 received Royal Assent on 12 February 2015. The relevant provisions are due to come into force on 12 August 2016.[233] It will abolish any rule of law which permits a party to a contract of insurance to avoid the contract on the ground that the other party has not observed the utmost good faith.[234]

5.136 In relation to contracts of insurance which are not consumer insurance contracts as defined in the Consumer Insurance (Disclosure and Representations) Act 2012, the Insurance Act 2015 introduces a new duty of fair presentation. A consumer

---

[230] Ibid at 279. This aspect of the decision of Rix J is considered further in paras 8.51–8.53.

[231] Ibid at 279.

[232] Ibid at 280–3, applying the principle derived from *In re Hampshire Land Co* [1896] 2 Ch 743 (as to which see paras 5.20–5.21). This part of Rix J's decision was obiter and it involved acceptance that the innocent insured were 'secondary' victims of the fraud practised by Mr Browne on insurers.

[233] Section 23 (2).

[234] Section 14 (1). For a full, helpful discussion of the Insurance Act 2015 see the Law Commission Report, Insurance Contract Law: Business Disclosure; Warranties; Insurers' Remedies for Fraudulent Claims; and Late Payment: Law Com No 353. It is available online at http://www.lawcom.gov.uk/wp-content/uploads/2015/03/lc353_insurance-contract-law.pdf.

contract is a contract of insurance between a person who carries on the business of insurance and a person who is 'an individual who enters into the contract wholly or mainly for purposes unrelated to the individual's trade, business or profession'.[235] So the duty of fair presentation in the Insurance Act 2015 will apply to contracts of professional indemnity insurance. That duty arises both when the contracts are made and when they are varied.[236]

Unlike the common law duty of good faith, the duty of fair presentation only applies to the insured.[237] There are three limbs to the duty of fair presentation. **5.137**

The first limb requires the presentation to disclose every material circumstance known by the insured or which the insured ought to know or, failing that, disclosure which gives the insurer sufficient information to put a prudent insurer on notice that it needs to make further enquiries in order to reveal those material circumstances.[238] An insured who is an individual (ie a natural person) is only taken to know what he knows and what is known by one or more individuals who are responsible for the insured's insurance.[239] An insured who is not an individual is taken to know only what is known by one or more of the individuals who are part of the insured's senior management or responsible for the insured's insurance.[240] The duty does not extend to information known by an individual who is either an agent of the insured or an employee of an agent of the insured if that information is confidential and was acquired by that individual through a business relationship with a person who is not connected with the contract of insurance.[241] An insured ought to know information which would have been revealed by a reasonable search of the information available to the insured.[242] The information available to the insured includes information held within the insured's organization or by any other person (such as the insured's agent or a person for whom cover is provided by the contract of insurance).[243] **5.138**

A circumstance is material if 'it would influence the judgement of a prudent insurer in determining whether to take the risk and, if so, on what terms'.[244] **5.139**

---

[235] Consumer Insurance (Disclosure and Representations) Act 2012, s 1.
[236] Insurance Act 2015, s 2(2).
[237] Section 3(1).
[238] Section 3(3) and (4).
[239] Section 4(2).
[240] Section 4(3).
[241] Section 4(4). This is to prevent insurance brokers from being subject to a duty to disclose confidential information about client A when making a contract of insurance for client B. Section 4(5) provides that the persons connected with a contract of insurance are the insured and any other persons for whom cover is provided by the contract of insurance and, if the contract is of re-insurance of a contract of insurance, persons who are insured under the underlying contract of insurance.
[242] Section 4(6).
[243] Section 4(7).
[244] Section 7(3). Section 7(4) gives examples of material circumstances: '(a) special or unusual facts relating to the risk; (b) any particular concerns which led the insured to seek insurance cover for the risk; (c) anything which those concerned with the class of insurance and the field of activity in question would generally understand as being something that should be dealt with in a fair presentation of risks of the type in question'.

5.140   There are a number of exceptions to the first limb of the duty. Section 3(5) provides:

> In the absence of enquiry, subsection (4) does not require the insured to disclose a circumstance if—
> (a) it diminishes the risk,
> (b) the insurer knows it,[245]
> (c) the insurer ought to know it,[246]
> (d) the insurer is presumed to know it,[247] or
> (e) it is something as to which the insurer waives information.

5.141   The second limb of the duty is a duty to make the disclosure 'in a manner which would be reasonably clear and accessible to a prudent insurer'.[248]

5.142   The third limb is that the presentation must be one in which every material representation[249] as to a matter of fact is substantially correct[250] and every material representation as to a matter of expectation is made in good faith.[251]

5.143   Both the insured and insurers are taken to know things which they suspected and of which they would have had actual knowledge had they not deliberately refrained from asking about them.[252]

5.144   Section 6(2) makes it clear that the preceding provisions do not affect 'any rule of law' according to which, when an employee or agent has committed a fraud on his employer or principal, the knowledge on the part of the employee or agent of that fraud is not attributed to the employer or principal. So the *Hampshire Land* principle survives.[253]

5.145   The new statutory duty of fair presentation clearly owes much to the duty of utmost good faith and disclosure at common law, which has been described as requiring 'a fair and substantially accurate presentation of the risk proposed for

---

[245] For this purpose an insurer is only deemed to know something if 'it is known to one or more of the individuals who participate on behalf of the insurer in the decision whether to take the risk, and if so on what terms (whether the individual does so as the insurer's employee or agent, as an employee of the insurer's agent or in any other capacity)': s 5(1).

[246] For this purpose an insurer only ought to know something if either (i) an employee or agent of the insurer knows it and ought reasonably to have passed the relevant information to the individual or individuals who underwrite the risk or (ii) if the information is held by the insurer and is readily available to the individuals who underwrite the risk: s 5(2).

[247] An insurer is presumed to know things which are common knowledge or 'which an insurer offering insurance of the class in question to insureds in the field of activity in question would reasonably be expected to know in the ordinary course of business': s 5(3).

[248] Section 3(3)(b). This is intended to prevent insureds from sending large quantities of unsorted and unanalysed information to insurers (commonly known as 'data dumping').

[249] Section 7(3) provides that a representation is material if 'it would influence the judgement of a prudent insurer in determining whether to take the risk and, if so, on what terms'.

[250] Section 7(5) provides that a material representation is substantially correct 'if a prudent insurer would not consider the difference between what is represented and what is actually correct to be material'.

[251] Section 3(3)(c).

[252] Section 6(1).

[253] *Re Hampshire Land Company (No 2)* [1896] 2 Ch 743. See para 5.20.

insurance'.[254] The Law Commission, which produced a draft bill on which the Insurance Act 2015 is very substantially based, aimed to build on existing case law and incorporated much of the terminology of the Marine Insurance Act 1906 in order to preserve the benefit of existing case law.[255] But there are changes.

An important change is made by the provision that an insured can comply with the **5.146** duty of fair presentation by a presentation which 'gives the insurer sufficient information to put a prudent insurer on notice that it needs to make further enquiries for the purpose of revealing those material circumstances'.[256] While this is based upon the existing law,[257] it puts greater emphasis upon the role of an insurer in asking pertinent questions, rather than as a passive recipient of information from the insured.

The new provision as to what an insured knows or ought to know is also significant, not **5.147** least for large organizations.[258] Actual knowledge is limited to 'senior management'[259] and the individuals who participate in obtaining insurance. The insured is also deemed to know what would have been revealed by a 'reasonable search' (undefined).[260] Clearly there is scope for argument as to whether a given individual is or is not part of the insured's senior management and as to the scope of a 'reasonable search'.

The Act gives examples of material circumstances.[261] The first two are aimed at **5.148** knowledge of the insured which insurers will not know and which may fall outside the scope of the standard questions insurers ask. The third is 'anything which those concerned with the class of insurance and field of activity in question would generally understand as being something that should be dealt with in a fair presentation of risks of the type in question'. The Law Commission hope that insurers, brokers, and policyholders will work together to develop guidance and protocols as to what should be disclosed.[262] As noted above,[263] in the context of professional indemnity insurance, the questions asked on the proposal form should cover and help identify the key standard areas of material information.

When it comes to what insurers know or ought to know[264] the Act introduces an **5.149** element of certainty by identifying the individuals whose knowledge is to be taken

[254] *Container Transport International Inc v Oceanus Mutual Underwriting Association (Bermuda) Ltd* [1984] 1 Lloyd's Rep 476, at 496–7.
[255] Law Com No 353, paras 5.73 and 6.5.
[256] Section 3(4)(b).
[257] See para 5.48.
[258] See para 5.14.
[259] Defined in s 4(8)(c) as 'those individuals who play significant roles in the making of decisions about how the insured's activities are to be managed or organised'.
[260] This represents a change in the scope of what needs to be disclosed: see para 5.16. The new duty to carry out a reasonable search can be seen as a quid pro quo for the change in the remedy for non-compliance.
[261] Section 7(4): see note 244 under para 5.139.
[262] Law Com No 353, para 6.14.
[263] Paragraph 5.35.
[264] Paragraphs 5.56–5.59.

into account. But the relevant provisions lack the subtlety of the common law, which takes account of the possibility that an individual may 'know' something in that he was aware of it once, but that that piece of knowledge will not have sprung to mind at the time when he was asked to underwrite the risk.[265] It may be, however, that the relevant authorities in common law will continue to be relevant to the question of what constitutes 'knowledge'.

5.150 The provision that an insurer ought to know something which is known to his employee and agent 'and ought reasonably to have been passed to the underwriter' again turns on what is 'reasonable' in the circumstances. The provision that an insurer ought to know something 'if it was held by the insurer and was readily available to the underwriter' appears to be limited to data held by the insurer, rather than to information on external databases to which insurers have ready (and, in practice, frequent) access.[266]

5.151 While it will no doubt take time for the potential issues which arise under the new duty of fair presentation to be resolved, it may be that insurers will be slower to take points. This is because the remedy for breach of the duty under the Insurance Act 2015 is not limited to avoidance of the contract of insurance.

Remedies for breach of the duty of fair presentation

5.152 As in the common law, insurers will only have a remedy for breach of the insured's duty in relation to the provision of information when the contract of insurance is being made if the undisclosed information or misrepresentation was objectively material in that 'it would influence the judgement of a prudent insurer in determining whether to take the risk and, if so, on what terms'.[267] And, as in common law, insurers also have to show that either they would not have entered the contract of insurance or that they would have done so on different terms.[268]

5.153 The Insurance Act 2015 introduces a new scheme of remedies for breach of the duty of fair presentation. First it divides breaches into two classes: 'deliberate or reckless' breaches and those which are neither 'deliberate nor reckless'.[269] The burden lies on insurers to prove that a breach was deliberate or reckless.[270] To do so insurers must prove that the insured either knew that he was in breach of the duty of fair presentation or that he did not care whether he was in breach of that duty or not.[271]

---

[265] See para 5.57.

[266] As to which see *Sea Glory Maritime co v Al Sagr National Insurance Co (The 'MV Nancy')* [2013] EWHC 2116 (Comm); [2014] 1 Lloyd's Rep 14, at [170]–[175] per Blair J, discussed in para 5.59.

[267] Section 7(3). For the position at common law see paras 5.31–5.34 and para 6.14. The wording in s 7(3) echoes, but does not replicate, ss 18(2) and 20(2) of the Marine Insurance Act 1906.

[268] Section 8(1). For the position at common law see paras 5.25–5.30 and para 6.14.

[269] Section 8(4).

[270] Section 8(6).

[271] Section 8(5).

In the case of breaches which were deliberate or reckless, insurers may avoid the **5.154** contract of insurance and need not return any of the premiums paid.[272]

In the case of breaches which were neither deliberate nor reckless, the insurers' rem- **5.155** edy is linked to the causative effect of the breach. So insurers may only avoid the contract of insurance if they prove that, in the absence of the breach, they would not have entered the contract of insurance at all. If they do so, they must return the premiums paid.[273] This is, of course, a significant reduction in insurers' right to avoid.

In the same way, where, but for a non-deliberate and non-reckless breach, insurers **5.156** would have entered the contract of insurance on different terms, the contract is deemed to have been made on those different terms.[274] Those different terms might exclude cover for a claim or potential claim which should have been disclosed, but was not.[275] And where, but for such a breach, insurers would have charged a higher premium, insurers are entitled to reduce proportionately the amount they are obliged to pay on a claim.[276] The proportionate reduction is calculated by reducing the amount otherwise payable by a percentage reflecting the difference between the premium actually charged and the higher premium which would have been charged. So, to take a simple example, if the premium actually charged was £50 and the premium which would have been charged would have been £100, insurers need only pay 50% of the claim (£50 being 50% of £100). And where the premium which was actually charged was £90 and the higher premium would have been charged is £100, insurers need only pay 90% of the claim (£90 being 90% of £100).[277]

Contracting out of the Insurance Act 2015

It is open to insurers to include in non-consumer contracts of insurance[278] terms **5.157** which place a more onerous duty of disclosure on the insured than the statutory duty of fair presentation. However such a term will only be effective if the insurer has complied with the 'transparency requirements'.[279]

Those requirements are set out in s 17 of the Insurance Act 2015. They require **5.158** insurers to take sufficient steps to draw the term to the insured's attention before the contract is entered into or the variation to the contract is agreed. And the term must be clear and unambiguous as to its effect. In deciding whether these requirements have been met the characteristics of insured persons of the kind in question and the circumstances of the transaction are to be taken into account.

---

[272] Schedule 1, para 2.
[273] Schedule 1, para.4.
[274] Schedule 1, para 5.
[275] But see *Gardner v Lemma Europe Insurance Company Limited (In Liquidation)* [2014] EWHC 3674 (Ch) discussed in paras 5.112–5.113.
[276] Schedule 1, para 6.
[277] The mathematical formula is set out in para 6(2) of Schedule 1.
[278] For the difference between 'consumer' and 'non-consumer' contracts of insurance see para 5.02.
[279] Section 16(2).

5.159 The insured is not able to rely upon any failure to comply with those requirements if either he or his agent had actual knowledge of the relevant term when the contract was entered or variation agreed.[280] This includes actual knowledge on the part of an insurance broker acting for the insured.

The duty of fair presentation and professional indemnity insurance

5.160 As has been explained above, it is often the case in relation to contracts of professional indemnity insurance that insurers' right to avoid for non-disclosure or misrepresentation is limited or excluded completely (in the latter case only in relation to those insured who have not acted fraudulently or dishonestly). And, as has been shown, there is a range of ways in which that is done in policies commonly in use. While the Insurance Act 2015 has reformed the law in this area, particularly in relation to insurers' remedies, it does not go as far as do some contracts of professional indemnity insurance in restricting insurers' rights where there has been no fair presentation of the risk.

5.161 For those professions which have stipulated minimum terms of professional indemnity insurance[281] it is and will be a matter of negotiation between the relevant professional bodies and regulators on the one hand and the insurance market on the other as to what, if any, modification of the regime introduced by the Insurance Act 2015 there should be.

5.162 In cases of composite insurance[282] each insured is subject to the duty of fair presentation.[283] This can either be done by each insured separately (unlikely in reality) or through the main insured acting as their agent.[284] Breach of the duty by one insured will not affect the position of the other insureds. And when it comes to the question of whether a breach of the duty was deliberate or reckless, the position of each insured under a composite policy will fall to be decided separately.[285]

5.163 However, the express provision that an insured is deemed to know what is known by the individuals who are responsible for the insured's insurance[286] could mean that where the insured who is responsible for arranging composite professional indemnity insurance for himself and others is in breach of the duty of fair presentation by failing to disclose a material circumstance of which he knows, all the other insureds will be in breach of the duty too. No doubt they would not be guilty of a deliberate or reckless breach, but if the consequences were sufficiently serious

---

[280] Section 17(4).

[281] See paras 1.12–1.31.

[282] See paras 1.32–1.45 and 5.114–5.134.

[283] That is the view of the Law Commission: Law Com No 353, para 7.15(2).

[284] As to the question of attribution between principals and agent in such circumstances see paras 5.18–5.21.

[285] See paras 5.114–5.134.

[286] Sections 4(2)(b) and (c) of the Insurance Act 2015.

insurers could be entitled to avoid the contract of insurance with each of them or to vary the terms so as to exclude cover for a claim which arises from a circumstance which should have been disclosed to them, but was not. And an insured which is not a natural person is deemed to know all that each member of its senior management knows. That may be a wider, inappropriate rule of attribution of knowledge than that at common law.[287]

In this regard the express preservation of the *Hampshire Land* principle[288] is of limited assistance. It only applies so as to prevent the attribution of an agent's knowledge to his principal if the principal is properly characterized as the victim of the agent's fraud.[289] So where the individual insured who is responsible for arranging insurance both for himself and for other insureds under a composite policy innocently fails to disclose something which he knows, the *Hampshire Land* principle will not apply. In such circumstances under the present law the other insureds might be able to rely upon the fact that they would not know the fact in the ordinary course of business and so not be under a duty to disclose it to insurers.[290]   **5.164**

This all suggests that the existing restrictions on insurers' rights in the case of breach of the common law duty of utmost good faith will continue to be relevant under the Insurance Act 2015.   **5.165**

In some respects those restrictions may need to be changed if they are to fall into line with the new duty of fair presentation and new system of remedies. For example, it is not unusual to find a term in a policy of professional indemnity insurance requiring the insured to prove that any non-disclosure or misrepresentation was innocent and free of any fraudulent conduct or intent to deceive and to do so to insurers' satisfaction.[291] But under the Insurance Act 2015 the burden is on insurers to show that a breach of the duty of fair presentation was either deliberate or reckless[292] and a term reserving to insurers the power to decide the question might be said to put the insured in a worse position than under the Act so that insurers would need to satisfy the 'transparency requirements'.[293]   **5.166**

---

[287] See paras 5.132–5.134.

[288] *Re Hampshire Land Company (No 2)* [1896] 2 Ch 743. See paras 5.20 and 5.144.

[289] See paras 5.21 and 5.133. However, at common law the surer safeguard for an innocent insured is a clause excluding the right to avoid for innocent non-disclosure and misrepresentation.

[290] As to which see para 5.20, in the context of a dishonest agent. But it may well be that in the ordinary course of business one insured under a composite policy would not inform another insured of every material fact known to him without there being the slightest whiff of fraud or dishonesty.

[291] Paragraphs 5.83–5.88.

[292] Paragraph 5.153.

[293] Paragraphs 5.158–5.159.

6

MISREPRESENTATION

A. Introduction: The Changing Law

As has been explained in **Chapter 5**,[1] the law in this area has been and is the subject **6.01** of extensive statutory reform. The effect of that reform insofar as relevant to professional indemnity insurance will be felt from 12 August 2016 when the relevant provisions of the Insurance Act 2015 are to come into force. Their effect will be to bring the specific insurance law of misrepresentation within the ambit of a wider duty of fair presentation. This duty and the new range of remedies for breaches of it are discussed in **Chapter 5**.[2] This chapter addresses the position before the statutory reforms come into force.

B. Outline of Legal Principles

Misrepresentation in the general law

If, during the course of negotiations leading to the formation of a contract, whether **6.02** of insurance or otherwise, one party (the representor) makes a misrepresentation[3] to the other (the representee), then the representee will have a number of remedies, depending upon the nature of the misrepresentation.

---

[1] Paragraphs 5.01–5.04.
[2] Paragraphs 5.135–5.166.
[3] The question of what constitutes an actionable misrepresentation is addressed in paras 6.08–6.18.

6.03   A fraudulent misrepresentation is a statement which is false, made dishonestly, and relied upon by the representee. A representation will be dishonest if the representor made it knowing that it was false or not caring whether it was true or false, and with the intention that the representee should rely upon it.[4] The effect of a fraudulent misrepresentation is to render any contract entered into in reliance on it voidable at the election of the representee[5] and to entitle the representee to recover from the representor damages for loss suffered by reason of his reliance on the misrepresentation.[6]

6.04   A representee will also be entitled to remedies if a non-fraudulent misrepresentation is made. Where the representation was made carelessly, the representor may owe the representee a duty of care in tort, in which case, if the representee suffers loss, the representor will be liable in the tort of negligence.[7] Whether a duty of care is owed in tort or not, the representee will be entitled to recover damages for a negligent misrepresentation if they would have been recoverable in fraud under s 2(1) of the Misrepresentation Act 1967.[8]

6.05   A non-fraudulent and non-negligent misrepresentation, usually described as an innocent misrepresentation, will not of itself entitle the representee to recover damages. However, the representee may be able to rescind the contract and s 2(2) of the Misrepresentation Act 1967 gives the court a discretion to award damages in lieu of rescission. Rescission is an equitable remedy available to the representee, subject to equitable defences. It is now established that if the right to rescind has been lost, then the court has no discretion to award damages in lieu of rescission.[9]

The principles of misrepresentation as applied to insurance contracts

6.06   While the general principles of law set out above apply to contracts of insurance,[10] the law of insurance affords insurers to whom a misrepresentation has been made

---

[4]   *Derry v Peek* (1889) 14 App Cas 337.

[5]   There is no need for the representee to show that he would not have entered the contract but for the fraudulent misrepresentation. It is sufficient that it was something he had in mind when entering the contract: *Edgington v Fitzmaurice* (1885) 29 Ch D 459; *Re Leeds Bank* (1887) 56 LJ Ch 321.

[6]   *Doyle v Olby (Ironmongers) Ltd* [1969] 2 QB 158; *Smith New Court Securities Ltd v Citibank NA* [1997] AC 254.

[7]   *Hedley Byrne & Co Ltd v Heller & Partners Ltd* [1964] AC 465. A duty of care is not usually owed by the insured to insurers when completing the proposal form: *HIH Casualty and General Insurance Ltd v Chase Manhattan Bank* [2001] EWCA Civ 1250; [2001] 2 Lloyd's Rep 483.

[8]   *Royscot Trust Ltd v Rogerson* [1991] 2 QB 297. The decision in that case that damages should be calculated on the same basis as they are in cases of fraud has been criticized: see, for example, *Cheltenham Borough Council v Laird* [2009] EWHC 1253 (QB); [2009] IRLR 621, at [524] per Hamblen J and *Yam Seng Pte Ltd v International Trade Corp Ltd* [2013] EWHC 111 (QB); [2013] 1 Lloyd's Rep 526, at [206] per Leggatt J.

[9]   *Zanzibar v British Aerospace (Lancaster House) Ltd* [2000] 1 WLR 2333; *Floods of Queensferry Ltd v Shand Construction* [2000] BLR 81, and *Salt v Stratstone Specialist Ltd (trading as Stratstone Cadillac Newcastle)* [2015] EWCA Civ 745; [2015] CTLC 206.

[10]   *HIH Casualty and General Insurance Ltd v Chase Manhattan Bank* [2001] EWCA Civ 1250; [2001] 2 Lloyd's Rep 483.

a remedy to which they are likely to resort in practice rather than to those available in the general law of contract, save possibly in the case of fraud. In the case of contracts of insurance, including contracts of professional indemnity insurance, insurers' usual remedy in the event of misrepresentation by the insured is as codified in s 20 of the Marine Insurance Act 1906, which is entitled 'Representations pending negotiation of contract'[11] and subsection (1) of which provides:

> Every material representation made by the assured or his agent to the insurer during the negotiations for the contract, and before the contract is concluded, must be true. If it be untrue the insurer may avoid the contract.

A further particular feature of the law of insurance is that where a contract of insurance provides that a pre-contractual misrepresentation forms the basis of the contract, the party who makes that representation will be taken to have warranted its accuracy so that, if it is inaccurate, the other party is automatically discharged from liability under the contract of insurance.[12] Unlike the general law of contract, in order to establish a breach of warranty, insurers do not need to demonstrate the materiality of the representation or that they were thereby induced to provide cover. **6.07**

The requirements of actionable misrepresentation

Statements of fact and statements of expectation or belief

Section 20(3) of the Marine Insurance Act 1906 provides that: **6.08**

> [a] representation may be either a representation as to a matter of fact, or as to a matter of expectation or belief.

The state of person's mind is question of fact.[13] If a representation of fact is made, s 20(4) provides that it will be regarded in law to be true 'if it be substantially correct, that is to say, if the difference between what is represented and what is actually correct would not be considered material by a prudent insurer'.[14] This test of

---

[11] The principles set out in s 20 apply to non-marine as well as to marine insurance: *Pan Atlantic Insurance Co v Pine Top Insurance Co* [1995] 1 AC 503; *HIH Casualty & General Insurance Ltd v Chase Manhattan Bank* [2001] EWCA Civ 1250; [2001] 2 Lloyd's Rep 483; *Avon Insurance Plc v Swire Fraser Ltd* [2000] Lloyd's Rep IR 535. The 1906 Act deals only with the remedy available to the insurer. It does not provide a remedy for the insured where there has been a misrepresentation by the insurer. The insured, however, will be entitled to a remedy in the ordinary way under the general law.

[12] Warranties are considered at paras 7.83–7.90. For a recent decision on a 'basis of contract' warranty see *Genesis Housing Association v Liberty Syndicate Management Ltd* [2013] EWCA Civ 1173; [2014] Lloyd's Rep IR 318. This aspect of the law of insurance will change substantially on 12 August 2016 when the relevant provisions of the Insurance Act 2015 come into force.

[13] *Brown v Raphael* [1958] Ch 636. For a helpful summary of what constitutes an actionable representation see *Cassa di Risparmio della Repubblica di San Marino SpA v Barclays Bank Ltd* [2011] EWHC 484 (Comm); [2011] 1 CLC 701, at [215]–[224] per Hamblen J.

[14] This has the effect of merging the questions of truth and materiality. A representation will not be regarded as being false if it would not have influenced the judgment of the prudent insurer. For example, in *Re Universal Non-Tariff Fire Insurance Co.* (1875) LR 19 Eq 485, in the context of the description of a building in a fire insurance policy, Malins VC said: 'If the description of the

substantial truth applies beyond the context of marine insurance.[15] This is linked to the requirement that the misrepresentation be material.[16]

6.09 If a statement of expectation or belief is made, s 20(5) provides that it will be true 'if it be made in good faith'. Such representations may give rise to a further, implied representation that the representor has reasonable grounds for expectation or belief. In *Bank Leumi le Israel BM v British National Insurance Co Ltd*,[17] Saville J said:

> A statement as to a future state of affairs ... can and often does carry with it a representation that the person making the statement has an honest belief or expectation, based on reasonable grounds, that events will turn out to be as stated or forecast.

If the matters which are the subject of the representation are not equally well known to insured and insurer, it will usually be found that the insured has impliedly represented that he has reasonable grounds for making the statement.[18]

6.10 A representation as to a person's expectation or belief will not be true if the representor was not in a position to form a proper opinion as to the prospects of the future event or state of affairs.[19] A representation as to expectation and belief made without any basis will not be made in good faith.[20] An insured who knows or ought to know matters as a fact will make a misrepresentation if he seeks to obscure the position by couching a statement in terms of belief.[21]

6.11 The superior knowledge or means of knowledge of the representor is important when determining what, if any, implied representation accompanies a representation of expectation or belief.[22] If the facts are not equally well known to both insurer and insured, then a statement of opinion by the party who is more aware of the relevant circumstances will carry the implication that he has knowledge of facts such as to justify that opinion.[23] The court will look at the precise circumstances in which the expectation, belief, or opinion is stated. In particular, the

---

property be substantially correct and a more accurate answer would not have varied the premium, the error is not material.'

[15] *Yorke v Yorkshire Insurance Co Ltd* [1918] 1 KB 662; *Avon Insurance Plc v Swire Fraser Ltd* [2000] Lloyd's Rep IR 535.

[16] As to which, see para 6.14.

[17] [1988] 1 Lloyd's Rep 71 at 75. See also *Brown v Raphael* [1958] Ch 636 and *Howard Marine & Dredging Co Ltd v Ogden & Sons (Excavations) Ltd* [1978] QB 574.

[18] *Highlands Insurance Co v Continental Insurance Co* [1987] 1 Lloyd's Rep 109.

[19] *International Lottery Management Ltd v Dumas* [2002] Lloyd's Rep IR 237.

[20] *Economides v Commercial Union Assurance Co Plc* [1998] QB 587, where Simon Brown LJ, with whom Peter Gibson LJ agreed, said at 598D-E that the representor must 'have some basis for his statement of belief ... he could not simply make a blind guess: one cannot believe to be true that which one has not the least idea about'.

[21] *Ionides and Chapeaurouge v Pacific Fire & Marine Insurance Co* (1871) LR 6 QB 674.

[22] *Brown v Raphael* [1958] Ch 636 and *Howard Marine & Dredging Co Ltd v Ogden & Sons (Excavations) Ltd* [1978] QB 574.

[23] *Smith v Land and House Property Corp* (1885) 28 Ch D 7.

court will consider who is making the representation, the circumstances in which it was made, the likely experience and sophistication of the representor, and the likely knowledge of the representee.[24]

A representation which appears on first reading to be one of expectation in that **6.12** it concerns something which has yet to occur may, on closer consideration, carry with it a representation of fact, for example that something is already underway or has already happened. For example in *Synergy Health (UK) Ltd v CGU Insurance Plc*[25] the insured represented on 28 December that an alarm would be completed by the end of that month. Flaux J held that this was not just a representation of future intention. Given that there were only two working days left for the alarm to be completed the insured had represented, incorrectly, that work was underway and was about to be completed.[26]

In the field of professional indemnity insurance declarations in proposal forms are **6.13** often qualified with phrases to the effect that the answers provided by the insured are true to the best of the maker's knowledge and belief. It is likely that an insured who makes such a representation will be held to have impliedly represented that he had reasonable grounds upon which to make it.

Materiality and inducement

As with any breach of the duty of disclosure, the misrepresentation must be mate- **6.14** rial. Thus s 20(2) of the Marine Insurance Act 1906 provides that:

> [a] representation is material which would influence the judgment of a prudent insurer in fixing the premium, or determining whether he will take the risk.

The test of materiality in respect of misrepresentation is therefore the same objective test as that applicable to non-disclosure as set out in s 18(2) of the Marine Insurance Act 1906.[27] Moreover, as with non-disclosure, insurers will have to prove inducement. This requires them to prove that, had they known the truth, they would either have declined to insure or would only have insured on different terms.[28] As Clarke LJ explained in *Assicurazioni Generali v Arab Insurance Group (BSC)*:[29]

> In order to prove inducement the insurer or reinsurer must show that the nondisclosure or misrepresentation was an effective cause of his entering into the contract on the terms on which he did. He must therefore show at least that, but for the relevant non-disclosure or misrepresentation, he would not have entered into the contract on those terms. On the other hand, he does not have to show that it was the sole effective cause of his doing so.

---

[24] *Rendall v Combined Ins Co* [2005] EWHC 678 (Comm); [2006] Lloyd's Rep IR 732.
[25] [2011] EWHC 2583 (Comm); [2011] Lloyd's Rep IR 500.
[26] Ibid at [161].
[27] See paras 5.31–5.34.
[28] *Pan Atlantic Insurance Co Ltd v Pine Top Insurance Co Ltd* [1995] AC 501.
[29] [2002] EWCA Civ 1642; [2003] Lloyd's Rep IR 131, at [62].

It is therefore necessary both to prove that the misrepresentation was objectively material and that, subjectively, it had a material effect on the mind of the particular insurers. In many cases, insurers will have no difficulty in showing that a material misstatement induced them to accept the risk on the terms which they did. However, that is not inevitable.[30] One difficulty which can arise in relation to a representation as to an intention to act in a certain way in the future is that the representee will often rely upon what is represented as a promise to act in that way, rather than as a representation as to the representor's current state of mind.[31]

6.15 The duty not to make a misrepresentation as to the nature of the risk is an incident of the duty of the utmost good faith, the duty of disclosure being another, related incident of the same duty. These two incidents of the duty of good faith are not hermetically sealed. There may come a point at which non-disclosure, coupled with other positive words or conduct, may in addition amount to a misrepresentation.

6.16 As with the duty of disclosure, the obligation not to make a misrepresentation continues until the contract of insurance is made.[32] It follows that there is a duty to correct representations that, although true when made, have been falsified by events which have occurred up to the point at which the insurance incepts.[33] However, once the contract has been entered there is no duty to bring to insurers' attention the fact that a statement which was accurate when it was made has ceased to be accurate.

6.17 It is often the case that insurance is renewed over successive years with the same insurer. When this happens the question may arise whether an earlier representation which is not corrected or qualified is of continuing effect. Where there is an express representation that there has been no material change in circumstances since the previous negotiations the position is clear. But there may be a continuing representation without an express confirmation that nothing has changed. For example, in *Synergy Health (UK) Ltd v CGU Insurance Plc*[34] a representation made four months before renewal that completion of installation of an alarm would be completed within days was impliedly repeated on renewal.[35]

---

[30] See para 5.30 as to whether there is any presumption of inducement.
[31] *Clipper Maritime Ltd v Shirlstar Container Transport Ltd (The 'Anemone')* [1987] 1 Lloyd's Rep 546, at 557–8 per Staughton J.
[32] See paras 5.65–5.68.
[33] *With v O'Flanagan* [1936] Ch 575.
[34] [2011] EWHC 2583 (Comm); [2011] Lloyd's Rep IR 500.
[35] In so finding Flaux J did not follow *Dawson v Atty* (1806) 7 East 367; 103 ER 142. See also *Glencore International AG v Alpina Insurance Co Ltd* [2003] EWHC 2792 (Comm); [2004] Lloyd's Rep IR 111, at 131–2 per Moore-Bick J (by proposing that cover be renewed at the same premium the insured impliedly represented that an estimate given during the previous year's negotiations was substantially the same).

Misrepresentation by agents

As was previously noted, it is generally the case that the rights and liabilities of a body **6.18** corporate for the acts and omissions of its management and other employees will be determined by the principles of agency and vicarious liability.[36] When it comes to knowledge and other mental states, the tests are of attribution or imputation of knowledge.[37] Where the body corporate makes a representation through a natural person acting as its agent, the knowledge of that agent may be deemed to be that of the body corporate on the usual principles of agency. However, where the agent is acting in fraud of his principal, the agent's knowledge will not be imputed to the principal.[38]

C. Misrepresentation and the Proposal Form

Ambiguous questions and incomplete answers

Difficulties may arise in a number of ways where a positive representation is made **6.19** on the proposal form. The first is where a question posed in the proposal form is ambiguous. The court will always seek to put a fair and reasonable interpretation on the question. If that is how the insured understood the question, insurers will not be allowed to rely on their own ambiguity if on another interpretation, the answer given by the insured was inaccurate.[39] However, there is no presumption that the insured's interpretation of a question is correct or that the insured is entitled to the interpretation which is most favourable to him.[40]

The decision in *Doheny v New India Assurance Co Ltd*[41] illustrates this point. In that **6.20** case the insured were a husband and wife as well as a company of which they were directors. The issue was whether insurers were entitled to decline liability because of a failure to disclose the fact that the individual insured had been connected to companies which had become insolvent. The insured had taken out two insurance policies against the risk of material damage to property. At the end of the proposal forms there was a box headed 'Declaration' consisting of five specific declarations made 'to the best of my/our knowledge and belief'. The last declaration was that 'No director/partner in the business, or any Company in which any director/partner have had an interest, has been declared bankrupt, been the subject of bankruptcy proceedings or made any arrangement with creditors'. The insured had given a negative answer.

---

[36] See paras 5.17–5.18.
[37] See paras 5.10–5.14.
[38] See paras 5.20–5.21.
[39] *Condogianis v Guardian Assurance* [1921] 2 AC 125. See also *Joel v Law Union & Crown Insurance Co* [1908] 2 KB 863; *Golding v Royal Auxiliary Insurance Co* (1914) 30 TLR 350; *Sweeney v Kennedy* (1948) 82 Ll L Rep 294. See now *R&R Developments Ltd v Axa Insurance Plc* [2009] EWHC 2429 (Ch); [2010] Lloyd's Rep IR 521, and *Involnert Management Inc v Apple Grange Ltd* [2015] EWHC 2225 (Comm); [2015] 2 Lloyd's Rep 289, at [193] per Leggatt J.
[40] *Yorke v Yorkshire Insurance Co* [1919] 1 KB 662.
[41] [2004] EWCA Civ 1705; [2005] Lloyd's Rep IR 251.

6.21 The insured submitted that the declaration only applied to individuals, who could be declared bankrupt or be the subject of bankruptcy proceedings. They argued that it did not apply to companies, which could only be the subject of liquidation proceedings but could not, in strict legal terminology, be declared bankrupt or be the subject of bankruptcy proceedings. The Court of Appeal disagreed. While the declaration could have been better drafted, it was clear that it required details of corporate insolvency as well as of personal insolvency. It was held that a reasonable insured completing the proposal form would, if he or she had thought about it, have concluded that insurers were interested in the solvency not only of themselves but also of any corporate vehicle used by them. There had therefore been a misrepresentation (as well as non-disclosure) which entitled insurers to avoid.

6.22 The insured's interpretation of a question was reasonable in *Johns v Kelly*.[42] In that case, a non-Lloyd's broker ('CR') entered into an umbrella agreement with a firm of Lloyd's brokers ('RMB') pursuant to which RMB were to make available to CR all facilities to enable it to place insurance at Lloyd's. CR and RMB were then sued in relation to a risk that CR had placed. RMB paid certain sums in settlement and sought an indemnity from its professional indemnity insurers. Insurers refused to provide an indemnity on the basis of non-disclosure and misrepresentation by RMB, as insured.[43]

6.23 The misrepresentation was said to consist in RMB declaring on the proposal form that CR was not an 'associate company'. Question 2 (a) of the relevant proposal form was in these terms: 'Names and addresses of all Subsidiary and/or Associated Companies and/or Branch Offices, including all those offices in which the Firm has a controlling interest'. The answer 'Nil' was given. But in a subsequent covering letter to RMB's brokers, it was said on behalf of RMB that:

> I have answered question 2 (a) as *nil*, as I do not believe that the two companies with whom we have links are 'Associated' companies in the intended sense, or within the context of the present insurance.
>
> These two companies are in fact W. J. Shore & Co. Ltd. of Bristol, who we did in fact mention on the proposal form last year, and Campbell Roberts & Co. Ltd. of London. The first named have a 10% share in [RMB], but are a totally independent concern. [CR] have for the past few months placed their Lloyd's account via our intermediary but they likewise are an entirely independent concern. Neither our company nor theirs has any financial interest in the other. For this reason we do not come within the meaning of question 2 (a) and the other questions have been answered without reference to either company. Furthermore, each of them carries their own professional negligence cover.

6.24 Insurers contended that in answering 'Nil' to question 2 (a) in the proposal form, RMB made a misrepresentation, since on any view (it was said) CR was an associated company. Insurers argued that RMB's letter did not correct the misrepresentation, since it wrongly described CR as an entirely independent concern. Insurers

---

[42] [1986] 1 Lloyd's Rep 468, the full background to which was set out at paras 5.41–5.42.
[43] The non-disclosure point was considered at paras 5.43–5.47.

therefore submitted, in reliance on *Dawsons Ltd v Bonnin*,[44] that they were entitled to avoid the policy, irrespective of any question of materiality, since the truth of the proposal form had been warranted pursuant to the basis of contract clause such as to be a condition of the contract. RMB resisted insurers' contention on the ground that there had been no misrepresentation by them. Bingham J decided the misrepresentation question in the following terms:[45]

> To a lawyer the expression 'associated company' has a precise and defined meaning ... But question 2 is not a legal questionnaire directed by lawyers to lawyers but a commercial document passing between insurers and Lloyd's brokers as prospective assured. What meaning, in that context, is to be given to the question? Mr. Morris of RMB gave evidence and was asked about his understanding of the question. He understood an associate company of RMB to be one with which RMB was bound by cross shareholdings, trading as part of a group, and he thought this part of the question was directed to ascertaining whether RMB traded as one company in a group with inter-linked companies. This was in my opinion an entirely reasonable meaning to put on the words in the proposal form, particularly since the reference was to 'Subsidiary and/or Associated Companies', and it is the sort of meaning which (even without his evidence) I would expect an intelligent and reasonably informed but not legally qualified Lloyd's broker to put on them ... I conclude that the meaning which Mr. Morris gave to this question was the correct one, and his answer involved no misrepresentation of any kind.

6.25 If an insured construes an ambiguous question in one fashion for the purposes of answering one question, but construes it otherwise for the purpose of another answer, he may find that he cannot have it both ways and that at least one of his answers will be a misrepresentation.[46]

6.26 If the insured does not answer a question at all, that will constitute non-disclosure where the result is to fail to disclose material information. Similarly, where the proposer has answered a question in a proposal incompletely in order to avoid telling the full truth, that will amount not only to a non-disclosure but also a misrepresentation entitling insurers to avoid the policy.[47]

Declarations and basis clauses

6.27 This area of law will be reformed when the relevant provisions of the Insurance Act 2015 come into force on 12 August 2016.[48] What follows is a discussion of the law before then.

---

[44] [1922] 2 AC 413.

[45] [1986] 1 Lloyd's Rep 468, at 473.

[46] *Glicksman v Lancashire and General Assurance Co Ltd* [1925] 2 KB 593 and [1927] AC 139.

[47] *Roberts v Avon Insurance Co Ltd* [1956] 2 Lloyd's Rep 240, where Barry J said at 249: 'If the omission to deal with some part of an answer carries with it the irresistible inference that the proposer intends that part of the answer to be negative, then the answer cannot be said to be incomplete and the insurers are not, in my judgment, put upon their inquiry, nor are they precluded at a later stage from saying that the answer was inaccurate.' See also *HIH Casualty & General Insurance Co v Chase Manhattan Bank* [2001] EWCA Civ 1250; [2001] 2 Lloyd's Rep 483 and *Condigianis v Guardian Assurance* [1921] 2 AC 125.

[48] See paras 7.91–7.99.

6.28 Proposal forms will often contain declarations to be signed by the person completing the proposal. The declarations are usually in two forms. Either the insured is asked to state that the answers given by the insured are 'true' or that they are 'true to the best of his knowledge and belief'. The language of the declaration will have a bearing on the scope of the insured's obligation in the sense that:

(a) If the insured states that the answers set out are true he is representing that they are true.[49] If any answer turns out to be false then the insurer will be entitled to avoid, however innocent the insured was in so declaring. This, of course, will be subject to any argument as to the correct construction of any individual question on the proposal.

(b) If the insured states that the answers set out are 'true to the best of his knowledge', he is taken to have answered the questions in good faith if he has a genuine basis for answering as he did.[50]

6.29 Those declarations may in addition indicate that the answers in the proposal are to be the basis of the contract, such that any misrepresentation in the proposal will constitute a breach of warranty. The relationship between basis clauses which are qualified by the proposer's 'best knowledge and belief' and avoidance clauses has been considered in the professional indemnity context.[51] Given the qualification, the insured was in each case not warranting 'the truth' but rather that which was to their 'best knowledge and belief'. In *Kumar v AGF Insurance Ltd & Ors*,[52] it was held that the non-avoidance clause was drafted to mean that whatever way insurers sought to escape liability, they were not entitled to do so whether by avoiding the policy itself, or by being discharged from liability because of a breach of warranty. There was no need to consider whether this was a composite insurance. Nor could insurers seek to recover their loss against the innocent partner, as this was also precluded by the wording of the non-avoidance clause.

6.30 In *Arab Bank Plc v Zurich Insurance Co*,[53] it was held that the truth of the answers in the proposal was a condition of insurers' liability. Therefore, insurers would

---

[49] In *Fisher v Guardian Insurance Company of Canada* (1995) 123 DLR (4th) 336, the declaration on proposal form to a lawyer's professional indemnity policy contained the following declaration: 'I/We hereby declare that the above statements and particulars are true, and I/we have not suppressed or misstated any material facts, that at the present time I/we have no reason to anticipate any claims being brought against me/us for any negligent act, error or omission on the part of any member or employee of this insured or their predecessors in business, and agree that this declaration shall be the basis of the Insurance between me/us and the Insurer.' For discussion of this case, see paras 5.103 and 5.129–5.130.

[50] *Economides v Commercial Union Assurance Company Plc* [1998] QB 587. However, if the insured does know the true position but makes an honest mistake, his answer will not be true to the best of his knowledge and belief: *Genesis Housing Association v Liberty Syndicate Management Ltd* [2013] EWCA Civ 1173; [2014] Lloyd's Rep IR 318, at [69] per Jackson LJ, with whom the other members of the Court of Appeal agreed.

[51] *Kumar v AGF Insurance Ltd* [1999] 1 WLR 1747 and see paras 5.106–5.107, and para 7.79; *Arab Bank plc v Zurich Insurance* [1999] 1 Lloyd's Rep 262, and see paras 5.118–5.134.

[52] [1999] 1 WLR 1747.

[53] [1999] 1 Lloyd's Rep 262.

without more be discharged from liability under it as a result of any misrepresentation in the proposal form. In the *Arab Bank* case, the proposal form was signed by an individual (Mr Browne), who was assumed to have acted dishonestly and to have known that the answers he had given were false. It was also assumed that none of the other directors (bar one) was aware of Mr Browne's earlier dishonesty or his false statements in the proposal form. Therefore, so far as each of those directors was concerned, the statements in the proposal form were true to the best of his knowledge and belief. Rix J stated:[54]

> It seems to me, therefore that reliance on Mr. Browne's warranty goes no further than reliance on his misrepresentations and non-disclosures. It would have been otherwise if the warranty had been purely as to the truth of the statements. Then ignorance would have been no defence, and I am prepared to assume that the terms of the proposal, incorporated into the policy by means of the 'basis of the contract' provision, would have taken precedence over the other provisions of the policy, such as the insuring clause and general condition 2:[55] see *Yorkville Nominees Pty. Ltd. (in liquidation) v. Lissenden*.[56]

Thus it was of critical importance that the warranty was as to whether the answers **6.31** were true to the best of each insured's knowledge and belief. Had the warranty been that the answers were true the result would have been different. But this difference appeared to be deliberate and part of the overall scheme of the policy. Rix J explained that, given the 'best of knowledge and belief' qualification to the declaration, the warranty appeared to be designed to fit with, rather than to override, the provisions of the contract as a whole:[57]

> Thus general condition 2 refers in terms to the proposal when it states that Zurich will not exercise its right to avoid the insurance because of non-disclosure or misrepresentation of facts 'or untrue statements in the proposal', provided that the insured establishes that the untrue statements were 'innocent and free of any fraudulent conduct or intent to deceive'. The question was raised whether the language 'right to avoid' could properly fit with a breach of warranty, since such a breach automatically discharges an insurer from the time of breach (subject to his election to affirm) and does not operate, as does a misrepresentation or non-disclosure, by way of providing him with a right to avoid: see *The Good Luck*.[58] The fact remains that the presence of a reference to the proposal in general condition 2 indicates an intention that breach of warranty should be treated in the same way as misrepresentation and non-disclosure. Consistently with that, the language of avoidance reflects the (albeit erroneous) understanding of the law relating to warranties as it was at the time of the proposal and the policy and prior to the reversal of the Court of Appeal judgment in *The Good Luck* by the House of Lords in May, 1991.

---

[54] Ibid at 283.
[55] General Condition 2 containing the non-avoidance clause.
[56] [1986] HCA 6; (1986) 160 CLR 475.
[57] [1999] 1 Lloyd's Rep 262, at 283.
[58] [1992] 1 AC 233.

D. Waiver and Affirmation

6.32 At the time the contract is made insurers might appreciate that an answer is incomplete in that the insured has further information which he has not included or that there is an inconsistency between two or more statements made by the insured. However, insurers will only be taken to have waived such misrepresentations where it was clear on the face of the proposal that certain information was lacking or where further inquiry should otherwise be made. If the inconsistency is not obvious, then insurers will not be required to be astute to potential inconsistencies and will not be deemed to have waived any misrepresentation. If the inconsistency or blank or incomplete answer is clear and does call for further inquiry, then issue of a policy will constitute a waiver of the misrepresentation.[59] In either case, the test must be whether the incomplete answer puts insurers on inquiry. If it does, or ought to, but insurers agree to insure without further inquiry, it is likely that the insurers will be held to have waived their right to complete information. If it does not, then there will have been no waiver. Waiver by failing to ask questions on presentation of the risk is inextricably linked to the question whether there has been a fair presentation of the risk. This has been considered above.[60] In this context, it is important to bear in mind that the duty of disclosure and the duty not make a material misrepresentation are both incidents of the duty of the utmost good faith. Insurers are entitled to expect a fair presentation. So, for example, if they interpret an incomplete answer as to claims history on the proposal form in the light of limited information provided by the insured about previous claims, they will not be taken to have waited disclosure of the fuller claims history.[61]

6.33 Insurers may also lose the right to avoid a contract of insurance for misrepresentation by affirmation. This is considered in **Chapter 5**.[62]

E. Exclusion of the Right to Avoid

6.34 Non-avoidance clauses of various forms are common in professional indemnity policies. These provisions have been considered in **Chapter 5**.[63]

---

[59] See *Thomson v Weems* (1884) 9 App Cas 671; *Armenia Fire v Paul 91*, Pa. 520 (1879); *Roberts v Avon Insurance Co* [1956] 2 Lloyd's Rep 240.

[60] Paragraphs 5.46–5.48.

[61] *Stowers v GA Bonus plc* [2003] Lloyd's Rep IR 402.

[62] See para 5.72.

[63] See paras 5.73–5.113.

7

THE CONSTRUCTION
OF THE CONTRACT

A. The General Principles of Construction

The starting point for determining the meaning and effect of a contract is the words **7.01** of the contract itself. But those words have to be read in context, the context including the other words used and the circumstances in which the contract was made. For example, at the most basic level of the meaning of a word, 'avoid' has several meanings. When used in a contract of insurance it will usually bear a particular meaning, known to few who are not lawyers or involved in the insurance industry. In trying to ascertain what the parties meant by the words they used, the law puts their words into context. It does by an objective assessment of the words, facts and circumstances: a party's subjective understanding or intention are usually irrelevant and inadmissible. But the aim is to discover the parties' shared intention as it appears from their agreement.[1]

Like all other contracts, professional indemnity insurance contracts are to be con- **7.02** strued in accordance with the principles set out by Lord Hoffmann in his speech in *Investors Compensation Scheme Ltd v West Bromwich Building Society:*[2]

---

[1] As Lord Steyn said in *Sirius International Insurance Co v FAI General Insurance Ltd* [2004] UKHL 54; [2004] 1 WLR 3251, at [18]: 'The aim of the inquiry is not to probe the real intentions of the parties but to ascertain the contextual meaning of the relevant contractual language. The inquiry is objective: the question is what a reasonable person, circumstanced as the actual parties were, would have understood the parties to have meant by the use of specific language. The answer to that question is to be gathered from the text under consideration and its relevant contextual scene.'

[2] [1998] 1 WLR 896, at 912–13.

189

(1) Interpretation is the ascertainment of the meaning which the document would convey to a reasonable person having all the background knowledge which would reasonably have been available to the parties in the situation in which they were at the time of the contract.

(2) The background was famously referred to by Lord Wilberforce as the 'matrix of fact,' but this phrase is, if anything, an understated description of what the background may include. Subject to the requirement that it should have been reasonably available to the parties and to the exception to be mentioned next, it includes absolutely anything which would have affected the way in which the language of the document would have been understood by a reasonable man.

(3) The law excludes from the admissible background the previous negotiations of the parties and their declarations of subjective intent. They are admissible only in an action for rectification. The law makes this distinction for reasons of practical policy and, in this respect only, legal interpretation differs from the way we would interpret utterances in ordinary life. The boundaries of this exception are in some respects unclear. But this is not the occasion on which to explore them.

(4) The meaning which a document (or any other utterance) would convey to a reasonable man is not the same thing as the meaning of its words. The meaning of words is a matter of dictionaries and grammars; the meaning of the document is what the parties using those words against the relevant background would reasonably have been understood to mean. The background may not merely enable the reasonable man to choose between the possible meanings of words which are ambiguous but even (as occasionally happens in ordinary life) to conclude that the parties must, for whatever reason, have used the wrong words or syntax. (See *Mannai Investments Co Ltd v Eagle Star Life Assurance Co. Ltd.* [1997] AC 749.)

(5) The 'rule' that words should be given their 'natural and ordinary meaning' reflects the common sense proposition that we do not easily accept that people have made linguistic mistakes, particularly in formal documents. On the other hand, if one would nevertheless conclude from the background that something must have gone wrong with the language, the law does not require judges to attribute to the parties an intention which they plainly could not have had. Lord Diplock made this point more vigorously when he said in *The Antaios Compania Naviera SA v Salen Rederierna AB* [1985] 1 AC 191, 201:

> '… if detailed semantic and syntactical analysis of words in a commercial contract is going to lead to a conclusion that flouts business commonsense, it must be made to yield to business commonsense.'

To these five propositions a sixth must now be added:

> in every case in which it is said that some provision ought to be implied in an instrument, the question for the court is whether such a provision would spell out in express words what the instrument, read against the relevant background, would reasonably be understood to mean …[3]

---

[3] *Attorney-General of Belize v Belize Telecom Ltd* [2009] UKPC 10; [2009] 1 WLR 1988, at [21] per Lord Hoffmann. See also *Mediterranean Salvage & Towage Ltd v Seamar Trading & Commerce Inc* [2009] EWCA Civ 531; [2009] 2 Lloyd's Rep 639, at [8] per Lord Clarke MR.

While Lord Hoffmann emphasized the significance of the 'background knowledge' **7.03**
and its width, it is important not to overestimate the field of inquiry. When construing commercial documents, judges have always had their context in mind.[4] In
the years since the decision in *Investors Compensation Scheme Ltd v West Bromwich
Building Society*[5] they have continued to do so without, in most cases, unnecessary
evidence of uncertain admissibility as to their background.[6] The background or
context is always an essential element of the process of construction. It is not simply
a means of resolving an ambiguity in the wording of a contract. The context always
informs the meaning of the words used.[7]

Lord Hoffmann also underlined the objective nature of the inquiry by referring to **7.04**
the meaning which the document would convey to 'a reasonable person having all
the background knowledge which would reasonably have been available to the parties in the situation in which they were at the time of the contract'.[8] But while the
court ascertains the meaning which the document would convey to such a reader,
the object is to ascertain what the parties meant.[9]

What the parties intended by a particular clause in a contract is found by consid- **7.05**
ering the clause in the light of (i) the natural and ordinary meaning of the words
used, (ii) any other related provisions and the contract as a whole, (iii) the overall
purpose of the clause and the contract, (iv) the facts and circumstances which the
parties knew or assumed at the time they entered the contract and (v) commercial
common sense, (vi) but not in the light of the parties' subjective intentions.[10]

In many cases the parties' intention will be clear from the words they have chosen **7.06**
to use. The court does not seek to contrive a problem with the drafting so as to
enable it to depart from the natural meaning. But, the worse the drafting, the more
scope there is to do so.[11]

---

[4] Eg in *Hydarnes Steamship Co v Indemnity Mutual Marine Insurance Co* [1895] 1 QB 500 Lord
Esher MR said at 504: 'The instrument which we have to construe is a puzzle; but we must endeav-
our to construe it in a businesslike way, so as to give it a sensible application. In order to do so, we
must look at the facts which existed at the time when it was made.'

[5] [1998] 1 WLR 896.

[6] See, for example, *Static Control Components (Europe) Ltd v Egan* [2004] EWCA Civ 392;
[2004] 2 Lloyd's Rep 429, at [29] per Arden LJ.

[7] *Vector Gas Ltd v Bay of Plenty Energy Ltd* [2010] NZSC 5; [2010] 2 NZLR 444, at [22]–[23]
per Tipping J.

[8] Anything which the parties said or did after the contract was made is not admissible as evi-
dence as to the construction of the contract: *James Miller and Partners Ltd v Whitworth Street Estates
(Manchester) Ltd* [1970] AC 583 and *Schuler (L) AG v Wickham Machine Tool Sales Ltd* [1974]
AC 235.

[9] *Bank of Credit and Commerce International SA v Ali* [2001] UKHL 8; [2002] 1 AC 251, at [39]
per Lord Hoffmann and *Rainy Sky SA v Kookmin Bank* [2011] UKSC 50; [2011] 1 WLR 2900, at
[14] per Lord Clarke JSC, with whom the other members of the Supreme Court agreed.

[10] *Arnold v Britton* [2015] UKSC 36; [2015] 2 WLR 1593, at [15] per Lord Neuberger PSC, with
whom Lord Sumption, Lord Hughes, and Lord Hodge JJSC agreed.

[11] Ibid at [18] per Lord Neuberger PSC, with whom Lord Sumption, Lord Hughes and Lord
Hodge JJSC agreed.

7.07 While commercial common sense is something to which the court will have regard, it does so with some care. It can be of value when there are two competing constructions and one makes more sense commercially than the other.[12] But the court is, or should be, slow to rewrite what is, on its face, a bad bargain for one of the parties. Parties can enter what appear or transpire to be bad bargains, either because of a poor bargaining position, bad advice, or the impact of subsequent events. The court does not rewrite a contract to assist an imprudent party.[13]

B. The Construction of Contracts of Professional Indemnity Insurance

7.08 Contracts of professional indemnity insurance can consist of a series of terms, classed as 'General Conditions', 'General Exclusions', 'Special Conditions', 'Memoranda', etc, and be supplemented by one or more endorsements.[14] They may expressly incorporate the proposal form and any other information provided by the insured on placement. They may have evolved over time, accruing new terms from year to year without discarding original terms.[15] Lord Mustill said in *Touche Ross & Co v Baker*[16] that 'experience shows that insurance documents in the London market are rarely drawn with the precision of language needed for grammatical contrasts to be a reliable guide to intention'. Nor is it uncommon to find surplusage in contracts of insurance.[17] It is therefore not surprising that issues

---

[12] *Rainy Sky SA v Kookmin Bank* [2011] UKSC 50; [2011] 1 WLR 2900, at [15]–[30] per Lord Clark JSC, with whom the other members of the Supreme Court agreed. Longmore LJ, with whom Sir Robin Jacob agreed, adopted this approach in *Teal Assurance Co Ltd v WR Berkley Insurance (Europe) Ltd* [2011] EWCA Civ 1570; [2012] Lloyd's Rep IR 315, at [17]. In the same case the Supreme Court would have done so too, if necessary: [2013] UKSC 57; [2013] 4 All ER 643, at [31] per Lord Mance JSC, with whom the other members of the Supreme Court agreed.

[13] *Arnold v Britton* [2015] UKSC 36; [2015] 2 WLR 1593, at [19]–[21] per Lord Neuberger PSC, with whom Lord Sumption, Lord Hughes, and Lord Hodge JJSC agreed. See also (1) *Chartbrook Ltd v Persimmon Homes Ltd* [2009] UKHL 35; [2009] 1 AC 1101, at [20] per Lord Hoffmann, with whom the other members of the House of Lords agreed; (2) *Rathbone Brothers Plc v Novae Corporate Underwriting Ltd* [2014] EWCA Civ 1464; [2015] Lloyd's Rep IR 95, at [76] per Elias LJ, with whom Sharp LJ agreed; and (3) *Wood v Sureterm Direct Ltd* [2015] EWCA Civ 839, at [29]–[31] per Christopher Clarke LJ, with whom the other members of the Court of Appeal agreed. Relevant decisions in the context of professional indemnity insurance are considered in paras 7.49–7.65.

[14] In *HLB Kidsons v Lloyd's Underwriters* [2008] EWCA Civ 1206; [2009] 1 Lloyd's Rep 8, at [150] Toulson LJ observed: 'The root cause of the problems is that each policy is a patchwork of provisions, which have no doubt been largely drawn from other policies but do not all fit well together.'

[15] This appears to have happened in *Thorman v New Hampshire Insurance Co (UK) Ltd* [1988] 1 Lloyd's Rep 7, giving rise to the need to read an original term and a new term together: see paras 5.75–5.82.

[16] [1992] 2 Lloyd's Rep 207, at 213. In *The London Guarantie Company v Fearnley* (1880) 5 App Cas 911, a case concerning fidelity insurance, Lord Blackburn said at 917: 'the whole question is reduced to that of the construction of an ill-penned instrument: a matter on which opinions always may differ'.

[17] As Thomas J observed in *Kumar v AGF Insurance Ltd* [1999] 1 WLR 1747, at 1756. See also *Genesis Housing Association Ltd v Liberty Syndicate Management Ltd* [2013] EWCA Civ 1173; [2014] Lloyd's Rep IR 318, at [77] per Jackson LJ, with whom the other members of the Court of Appeal agreed.

frequently arise as to the true meaning and effect of contracts of professional indemnity insurance.

The relevant background

While there is no conceptual limit to what might form part of the relevant back- **7.09** ground to a contract, for a matter to be taken into account when construing a contract it must be something which a reasonable man would have regarded as relevant.[18] It follows that there can be no exhaustive statement of the relevant background. However, it is suggested that when construing contracts of professional indemnity insurance the following matters will often be relevant:

(1) The purpose for which professional indemnity insurance is obtained, ie to protect clients as much as to protect the insured
(2) The fact that professional indemnity insurance is written on a 'claims made' basis and an expectation as to how such policies should work
(3) The law
(4) The nature of the insured's business and the liabilities to which the insured is or may be exposed
(5) Earlier dealings between the parties and the development of the particular type of cover, ie the genesis of the particular policy.

Relevant background: the purpose of professional indemnity insurance

While evidence of specific requests as to the scope of cover is inadmissible, courts **7.10** have been prepared, indeed willing, to pray in aid the purpose for which professional indemnity insurance is obtained or required when construing policies. At least to the extent that it is required by law or professional regulation that purpose is not only, or even chiefly, to provide protection to the insured, but to ensure that clients of professionals and others who suffer loss as a result of breaches of legal duty by their professional advisers will be compensated, at least up to a minimum level.[19] As with all commercial contracts, regard is had to the object or purpose of the transaction.[20] This includes the background, or context in which the parties

---

[18] *Investors Compensation Scheme Ltd v West Bromwich Building Society* [1998] 1 WLR 896, at 912–13. See also *Chartbrook Ltd v Persimmon Homes Ltd* [2009] UKHL 35; [2009] 1 AC 1101 at [33]. The background material must have been known by or have been reasonably available to both parties to the contract: *Arnold v Britton* [2015] UKSC 36; [2015] 2 WLR 1593, at [21] per Lord Neuberger PSC, with whom Lord Sumption, Lord Hughes, and Lord Hodge JJSC agreed.

[19] See paras 1.05–1.06.

[20] See, for example, *Lake v Simmons* [1927] AC 487 per Viscount Sumner, cited by Gleeson CJ in *McCann v Switzerland Insurance Australia Ltd* [2000] HCA 65; (2000) CLR 579, at [22]. As Lord Wilberforce said in *Prenn v Simmonds* [1971] 1 WLR 1381, at 1385: 'the commercial, or business object, of the transaction, objectively ascertained, may be a surrounding fact'. See also *Gerling General Insurance Co v Canary Wharf Group Plc* [2005] EWHC 2234 (Comm); [2006] 1 Lloyd's Rep 68, at [49].

were contracting.[21] The purpose is to be deduced objectively and not from evidence from the parties as to what their intention was.[22]

7.11 A clear example of this is the decision of Thomas J in *Kumar v AGF Insurance Ltd*,[23] a case concerning top-up insurance of a firm of solicitors. The decision concerned the effect of a clause in the policy by which insurers undertook not to 'seek to avoid, repudiate or rescind this insurance upon any ground whatsoever, including in particular non disclosure or misrepresentation'. The partner who had completed the proposal form was assumed to have been guilty of fraud before doing so and of having dishonestly concealed his fraud when completing the proposal form. The other partner claimed to be entitled to an indemnity under the policy and insurers raised a number of defences on the terms of the policy. These are considered in **Chapter 5**.[24]

7.12 One argument raised by insurers was that, if the insured were right, then an insured who wrongly failed to disclose matters on a proposal form would be in a better position than an insured who complied with his duty and did so. In rejecting that argument, Thomas J said that an insured who disclosed a matter on a proposal form could also give notice of it under his current policy:[25]

> That means that the clients of the practice concerned are protected, as it is the overriding objective of the regulators of such professions that this is achieved. It is clear that in this form of professional indemnity policy, as in others, one must approach the construction against that regulatory background to which I have referred, in particular that protection must be provided to the clients of the solicitors ...

7.13 Insurers' second line of defence was based upon the construction of the clause in question. By it insurers undertook not to 'seek to avoid, repudiate or rescind this insurance upon any ground whatsoever, including in particular non disclosure or misrepresentation'. Insurers argued that there had been a breach of warranty, the effect of which was to discharge them from liability automatically. They argued that this was not within the scope of the clause. On a strict reading of the clause that was right. Rejecting insurers' second line of defence, Thomas J held that the clause had to be construed against the relevant background in accordance with

---

[21] *Reardon Smith Line Ltd v Hansen-Tangen (The Diana Prosperity)* [1976] 1 WLR 989 per Lord Wilberforce at 996: 'No contracts are made in a vacuum: there is always a setting in which they have to be placed. The nature of what is legitimate to have regard to is usually described as "the surrounding circumstances" but this phrase is imprecise: it can be illustrated but hardly defined. In a commercial contract it is certainly right that the court should know the commercial purpose of the contract and this in turn presupposes knowledge of the genesis of the transaction, the background, the context, the market in which the parties are operating.'

[22] *Reardon Smith Line Ltd v Hansen-Tangen (The Diana Prosperity)* [1976] 1 WLR 989 per Lord Wilberforce at 996: 'the parties cannot themselves give direct evidence of what their intention was ... Similarly, when one is speaking of aim, or object, or commercial purpose, one is speaking objectively of what reasonable persons would have in mind in the situation of the parties.'

[23] [1999] 1 WLR 1747.

[24] See paras 5.80–5.82 and 5.102–5.103.

[25] [1999] 1 WLR 1747, at 1752.

the decision of the House of Lords in *Investors Compensation Scheme Ltd v West Bromwich Building Society*.[26] He held:[27]

> The important background to this agreement is the Solicitors Indemnity Fund Rules, particularly rules 29 and 30, and the fact that the scheme of the insurance was meant to provide an indemnity to clients in circumstances where they had been caused loss by a solicitor.[28]

The same approach was adopted by Vinelott J in *The Mortgage Corporation v The* **7.14** *Solicitors Indemnity Fund Ltd*.[29] In that case, the insured solicitors had acted on a loan to one of their own partners. The loan should have been secured by a first charge on the partner's house. The solicitors failed to obtain this security because there was an existing first charge securing another loan. When things went wrong, the earlier loan was discharged in full from the proceeds of sale but most of the later loan remained unpaid. Insurers argued that the insured had suffered no loss because, had they complied with their instructions, they would have had to pay off the earlier loan: the proceeds of sale of the house could only be applied once to reduce their overall borrowings. If the insured had suffered no loss, there was no loss in respect of which they were entitled to an indemnity from their professional indemnity insurers ('SIF').

This argument failed. Vinelott J observed that if it were right, then the protection **7.15** provided to members of the public (including mortgage lenders) would be severely limited. If there was any doubt on the point, he was entitled to take into account the policy of s 37 of the Solicitors Act 1974 as explained by Lord Brightman in *Swain v The Law Society*.[30] Vinelott J said:[31]

> It is plainly important for the protection of the public and to ensure that the public continues to have confidence in the integrity and standing of solicitors that claims founded on the negligence of a solicitor should be met, and if the solicitor is unable to meet his liabilities following the bankruptcy order met by SIF.

However, the purpose for which professional indemnity is obtained and required **7.16** is only part of the relevant background and can only be a guide to construing

---

[26] [1998] 1 WLR 896.
[27] [1999] 1 WLR 1747, at 1754.
[28] Thomas J appears to have been referring to Rules 29 and 30 of the Solicitors' Indemnity Rules 1992, which set out respectively the Special Conditions and General Conditions on which the Solicitors Indemnity Fund would provide indemnity to solicitors. Rule 29.4 provided, in part: 'In respect of any loss arising from any claim or claims as described by Rule 26(1) arising out of any dishonest or fraudulent act or omission of any Member of the Practice or any Successor Practice the Fund shall nonetheless be available to afford indemnity in accordance with these Rules to the Practice or any Successor Practice and any Member thereof, other than and excluding in each case the particular Member concerned in such dishonesty or fraud ...'
[29] [1998] PNLR 73.
[30] [1983] 1 AC 598: see para 1.05.
[31] [1998] PNLR 73, at 80.

the words of the contract. It does not at all follow that professional indemnity insurance policies will always be construed so that insurers are liable.[32] The courts recognize the interest of insurers (and of other insureds) in holding the particular insured to his bargain as reflected in the terms of his policy. As LeBel J said when giving the judgment of the Supreme Court of Canada in *Jesuit Fathers of Upper Canada v Guardian Insurance Company of Canada*:[33]

> This Court has recognized the public purpose served by insurance. In particular, it can help ensure that the needs and expectations of third parties who are injured accidentally or through negligence are met by giving them access to a compensation fund. The appellant argues that, given this public purpose, the meaning of the word 'claim' should be interpreted broadly in order to recognize the reality of abuse claims made in the context of residential schools.
>
> ...
>
> Nevertheless, even with all these factors being considered, courts must remain mindful of the rules and principles governing insurance law. In the long run, a contextual but unprincipled approach would render a disservice not only to the industry, but also to insured and to victims. It would lead to further difficulties in obtaining coverage and compensation. Both parties to an insurance contract are entitled to expect that well-established principles will be reflected in the interpretation and application of that contract. In this respect, another form of public interest is also at stake. For these reasons, courts must pay close attention to the structure and actual wording of the policy, read as a whole.

The court refused to strain the meaning of 'claim' in favour of the insured.[34]

7.17 The words used in the contract will often indicate how and how far the parties have agreed that the particular contract of insurance will achieve the wide, general object. As Longmore LJ observed in *Bedfordshire Policy Authority v Constable*,[35] a case concerning public liability insurance, it was

> not unreasonable to start with the premise that a public liability policy will give an indemnity in respect of liability to the public at large. Of course that will depend on the precise terms of cover ... [36]

---

[32] For example, in *HLB Kidsons (a firm) v Lloyd's Underwriters* [2008] EWCA Civ 1206; [2009] 1 Lloyd's Rep 8 on appeal from [2007] EWHC 1951 (Comm); [2008] Lloyd's Rep IR 237, the insured argued that failure to give notice of circumstances which may give rise to a claim as soon as practicable was not fatal to a claim for indemnity under the policy. In support of that argument, they prayed in aid the policy behind professional indemnity set out by Lord Brightman in *Swain v The Law Society* [1983] 1 AC 598 (see the judgment of Gloster J at first instance at [28 (v)]). See further paras 7.23–7.25.

[33] (2006) 267 DLR (4th) 1, at [31] and [33].

[34] See para 2.06.

[35] [2008] EWCA Civ 64; [2009] Lloyd's Rep IR 607. The other members of the Court of Appeal agreed with Longmore LJ. See also *Impact Funding Solutions Ltd v Barrington Support Services Ltd (Formerly Lawyers at Work Ltd)* [2015] EWCA Civ 31; [2015] Lloyd's Rep IR 371, at [19], where Longmore LJ, with whom the other members of the Court of Appeal agreed, identified the 'essential purpose' of an exclusion clause in respect of trade and personal debts (as to which see para 9.78) in order to ascertain its scope.

[36] Ibid at [19].

There will be terms which clearly reflect some compromise between the overall aim **7.18** of ensuring that compensation is available to the insured's clients and the scope, and so the cost, of cover. For example, the effect of an aggregation clause may well be that, where an insured has caused losses to numerous clients, his total liability to them will exceed the amount insured because the various claims will be treated as one claim for the purposes of the limit of cover.[37] The effect of such a clause is to reduce the potential exposure of a primary insurer to multiple claims and so to reduce the cost of insurance. When interpreting such a clause little, if any, significance can be attached to the presumed purpose of professional indemnity insurance. The parties to the contract of insurance have agreed a term which may leave clients without compensation and the insured insolvent. The extent to which the parties have agreed that the general aim of ensuring that the insured's clients will receive compensation should be compromised is to be found in the words they have chosen.[38]

The parties' choice of words was decisive in *McCann v Switzerland Insurance* **7.19** *Australia Ltd*.[39] The issue in that case was whether the insured's liability had been 'brought about by' the dishonest or fraudulent act or omission of one partner. It if had been, then insurers could rely upon an exclusion clause. The partner had released client's funds into a fraudulent prime bank guarantee scheme. In doing so it was held that he had acted dishonestly, but his partners argued that the loss of the money was caused by the subsequent theft of the money by others and so had not been 'brought about' by the dishonest partner. Agreeing with the other members of the High Court of Australia, Kirby J said that it was relevant that the insurance in question was required by the Legal Professions Act 1987 (NSW)[40] and acknowledged that professional indemnity policies:[41]

> are required for important social purposes. These are not confined to protecting particular legal practitioners, such as the partners in this case. They are intended

---

[37] See Chapter 10.

[38] See also *Sawyer v Canadian Lawyers Insurance Association* 2015 ABQB 132 at [20] per Strekal J: 'It does appear that a consequence of the Law Society's decision to have ALIA provide a "claims made" rather than an "occurrence based" insurance policy is that there is a potential insurance coverage gap for some individuals who suffer a loss as a result of a lawyer's negligence. While lawyers are required to maintain insurance while they are practicing law, a client who suffers a loss as a result of a lawyer's negligence may be precluded from recovering on that loss from the lawyer's insurers if the lawyer was no longer practicing law (and thus no longer insured) at the time that the loss is discovered, or if the lawyer fails to report the loss or potential loss to the insurers while the policy is in effect, which is what happened in this case.'

Strekal J could not construe the policy before her so as to fill the gap in coverage.

[39] [2000] HCA 6; (2000) 203 CLR 579.

[40] Now replaced by Legal Profession Act 2004 (NSW).

[41] [2000] HCA 6; (2000) 203 CLR 579, at [76]. See also *Australian Breeders Co-operative Society Ltd v Jones* [1997] FCA 1405; (1997) 150 ALR 488, at 563 per Lee J: 'It is a matter of public concern that rules which govern the practise of a professional business such as that engaged in by Beattie McDonald be sufficient to require the practitioners to obtain insurance indemnifying them against liability arising out of the practise of their profession. Such insurance is a professional obligation to be undertaken to safeguard the interests of clients. Beattie McDonald met that obligation in applying for insurance under the Australian Accountants' Professional Indemnity Insurance Facility.'

to protect clients of legal practitioners where such practitioners would not be able otherwise to meet liability from their own resources. Such clients would then be dependent upon the existence and availability of insurance indemnity ... The relevant terms of the exclusion clause must be approached in light of these important social purposes. Whilst it is true that the exclusion clause appears in policies approved for a statutory purpose, an overly broad ambit should not be attributed to it, at least if doing so would undermine the objectives for which the insurance was required in the first place.

Nevertheless, Kirby J held that the exclusion clause applied: the liability had been brought about by the acts of the dishonest partner. He concluded that 'the context is not a sufficient reason to distort the meaning of the exclusion clause as derived from its language'.[42]

Relevant background: 'claims made' policies and how they are expected to work

7.20 In *Friends Provident Life and Pensions Ltd v Sirius International Insurance Corporation*,[43] Moore-Bick J and the Court of Appeal had to decide a number of issues concerning excess layer professional indemnity cover. Moore-Bick J held that the relevant background material included 'the general practice of the insurance market in relation to the underwriting of professional indemnity risks and the insuring of large risks by means of primary and excess layer policies'. Two particular aspects had been described in evidence, the first of which was of general application to professional indemnity insurance. It was:[44]

> ... the practice of the market in relation to liability insurance. It is now almost invariable for liability underwriters in general, and professional negligence underwriters in particular, to issue policies that provide cover on what is known as a 'claims made' basis, that is, which provide the insured with an indemnity against losses arising from claims made against him, as opposed to events occurring, during the policy period. This has an advantage for underwriters in that they are less exposed to unforeseen losses arising long after the period of cover has expired, but it poses a serious problem for any insured who becomes aware during the policy period of circumstances that may give rise to a claim in the future. When seeking insurance for the following year he would be bound to disclose the existence of any circumstances, but might well find it impossible to obtain insurance in respect of that potential loss at a commercially acceptable premium, if indeed at all. As a result the practice has grown up of including in 'claims made' policies a term extending cover to losses arising from circumstances that may give rise to a claim

---

Having regard to the foregoing, it is to be expected that any limitation of the indemnity provided by the policy will be expressed in words of clear meaning and will apply only to events for which the denial of insurance is appropriate.'

Lee J was dissenting, but this passage from his judgment was cited with approval by the Federal Court of Australia in *HIH Casualty & General Insurance Australia Ltd v Della Vedova* [1999] FCA 456, at [7].

  [42] [2000] HCA 6; (2000) 203 CLR 579, at [81]. See also the discussion at [74](2) by Kirby J.
  [43] [2004] EWHC 1799 (Comm); [2005] Lloyd's Rep IR 135; [2005] EWCA Civ 601; [2005] 2 Lloyd's Rep 517.
  [44] [2004] EWHC 1999 (Comm); [2005] Lloyd's Rep IR 135, at [13].

in the future provided that they have been notified to the underwriters during the period of cover. So significant are these factors that in *J Rothschild Assurance Plc* v *Collyear* [1999] 1 Lloyd's Rep IR 6, 22 Rix J expressed the view that a 'claims made' policy could hardly work on any other basis. Mr Hancock suggested that Rix J put the matter too high, but having regard to the current practices of the market I do not think that he did and I respectfully endorse his view.

In the same way, in *Robert Irving & Burns (a Firm)* v *Stone*[45] the issue before the **7.21** Court of Appeal was whether a claim was made under a policy insuring surveyors when proceedings were issued or when they were served. Rejecting insurers' argument that the claim was made when proceedings were issued, Staughton LJ said:[46]

> It seems to me that in construing this provision one should have regard to the requirement that an insured person, on renewal, disclose circumstances which are liable to expose him to loss in the future. If the surveyors knew nothing about the prospect of a claim there was nothing that they could disclose. Yet it is said that a claim had already been made against them. That seems to me to have everything the wrong way round.

The point was put slightly differently by McLachlin J when giving the judgment **7.22** of the Supreme Court of Canada in *Reid Crowther & Partners Ltd* v *Simcoe & Erie General Insurance Co*:[47]

> ... where the policy is ambiguous, the courts should consider the reasonable expectations of the parties ... The insured's reasonable expectation is, at a minimum, that the insurance plan will provide coverage for legitimate claims on an ongoing basis. The presumption must be that the intention of the parties is to provide and obtain coverage for all legitimate claims on an ongoing basis, whether through renewal with the same insurer or through securing new insurance with a different insurer. This presumption is consistent with the discovery principle discussed earlier in these reasons, in that the insurer is able to secure a means of certainty in calculating its risk without unfairly creating gaps in coverage.

This expectation as to how a 'claims made' policy should operate (and be intended **7.23** by the parties to operate) does not always work in favour of the insured, as the decision in *HLB Kidsons (a firm)* v *Lloyd's Underwriters*[48] shows. The insured argued that compliance with the requirement in the condition which required and entitled them to give notice of circumstances which might give rise to a claim 'as soon as practicable' was not a condition precedent to the right to give an effective notice.[49] The insured's case was that, so long as it became aware of the circumstances during the policy year, it did not matter when it gave notice of them to insurers. They drew attention to an anomaly which would arise if the requirement was a condition precedent. Finding for the insurers, Rix LJ said that the Court was faced with a

---

[45] [1998] Lloyd's Rep IR 258.
[46] Ibid at 261.
[47] (1993) 99 DLR (4th) 741, at 753.
[48] [2008] EWCA Civ 1206; [2009] 1 Lloyd's Rep 8.
[49] As to which, see paras 7.103–7.105.

choice between avoiding an anomaly and 'on the other hand turning a claims made policy on its head'. He explained:[50]

> if a late notice of circumstances was not destructive of the right to an indemnity for any loss or claim arising out of such circumstances, even though such loss or claim should emerge after the end of the policy year, then a claims made policy would become entirely open-ended: however much delayed a notice of circumstances may be, and however long after the end of the policy period the claim which arises out of such circumstances comes to be made, the policy extends to cover that claim.

7.24 Toulson LJ agreed. Describing the insured's argument as a 'hopeless contention', he said:[51]

> The notion that a risk may attach to the policy by reason of something known to the insured but not to the insurer, and which the insured may decide to disclose to the insurer after the expiry of the policy at any time of his own choosing, is so contrary to the way in which a professional indemnity policy would ordinarily be expected to work that it would need the clearest words to produce that effect.
>
> The natural assumption in the case of a claims made professional indemnity policy is that claims or risks of claims (where the insured becomes aware of a threatened or possible claim and gives notice of it to the insurer) may attach during the policy but not after it.

7.25 There is, however, a limit to the extent to which the court can impose its view of how a claims made policy should work onto a particular policy. For example, in the *HLB Kidsons* case Toulson LJ was attracted to the argument that notice of circumstances would have to be given during the policy period even though the relevant clause only stated that notification be given 'as soon as practicable'. Toulson LJ considered that 'the natural assumption in the case of a policy of this nature is that claims or risks of claims may attach during the policy period, but not retrospectively'.[52] The clause did require the insured to have first become aware of the circumstance during the policy period and so did provide that the relevant event had to happen within the policy year. However, as Rix LJ observed, it did not expressly require that notice be given within the policy period as well. A notice given as soon as practicable might be outside the policy period.[53] It is important not to impose an assumption as to the parties' intentions when that assumption is not borne out by the plain words which they have used, particularly if the result of giving those words their natural meaning is not commercially absurd.[54]

---

[50] [2008] EWCA Civ 1206; [2009] 1 Lloyd's Rep 8, at [108]. See also [121].

[51] Ibid at [152]–[153].

[52] [2008] EWCA Civ 1206; [2009] 1 Lloyd's Rep 8, at [158].

[53] Ibid at [125]. For the problems that can arise when notice must be given within the policy period, see paras 2.47–2.49 and 2.120.

[54] As to which see paras 7.49–7.65.

Relevant background: the law

The relevant material can include well-known authorities on professional indem- **7.26** nity law. So, in *MDIS Ltd v Swinbank*[55] insurers relied on the decision of Devlin J in *West Wake Price & Co v Ching*,[56] which concerned a 'similar but different clause', in support of their construction of the term in issue. Clarke LJ, with whom Judge LJ agreed, said:[57]

> [Counsel for the insured] submitted that this contract must be construed in accordance with its terms and not by reference to the terms of a different contract between different parties in different circumstances at a different time. I accept of course that we are construing this contract and not the contract in the *Ching* case. However, both the decision and the dicta in that case can in my judgment properly be treated as relevant to the construction of this clause since they have been well known amongst insurance lawyers and indeed brokers for many years and would be likely to have been in the back of the minds of those negotiating this contract.[58]

Clarke LJ considered the clause itself and then against the background of the decision in *West Wake Price & Co v Ching*, finding in favour of insurers' construction.

Peter Gibson LJ agreed with the result, but not the reasoning. He said:[59]   **7.27**

> I accept that cases such as *Goddard & Smith* v *Frew* [1939] 4 All ER 358 and *West Wake Price & Co* v *Ching* [1957] 1 WLR 45 would be so well-known to those operating in this field that they must have been in the minds of the draftsman and of those negotiating the contract. Yet the striking fact is that the language of the Operative Clause is quite different, and again this leads to the inference that the insertion of a condition in terms of 'any claim alleging' was deliberately intended to mean something other than 'all demands by reason of' (as in the *Frew* case) or 'any claim in respect of' (as in the *Ching* case).

It is certainly the case that a decision as to the meaning and effect of one con- **7.28** tractual provision is not an authority as to the meaning and effect of a differently worded clause.[60] The starting point has to be the words actually used by the parties and not the law reports. But professional indemnity policies are now usually the product of expert drafting, whether it be the specified minimum terms prescribed by some professional bodies[61] or the professional indemnity policies for financial

---

[55] [1999] Lloyd's Rep IR 516.
[56] [1957] 1 WLR 45.
[57] [1999] Lloyd's Rep IR 516, at 522.
[58] See also *Astrazeneca Insurance Co Ltd v XL Insurance (Bermuda) Ltd* [2013] EWHC 349 (Comm); [2013] Lloyd's Rep IR 290, at [55] per Flaux J.
[59] [1999] Lloyd's Rep IR 516, at 527.
[60] As Buckley LJ said in *In re an Arbitration between Coleman's Depositories Ltd and Life and Health Assurance Association* [1907] 2 KB 798, at 812: 'The question is one of construction, and upon such a question authorities are of little or no value. Authorities may determine principles of construction, but a decision upon one form of words is no authority upon the construction of another form of words.'
[61] Eg, the SRA Minimum Terms and Conditions of Professional Indemnity Insurance, the ICAEW Minimum Approved Policy Wording, and the RICS Policy Wording.

institutions regulated under the Financial Services Act 1986 developed in the late 1980s by specialist brokers with legal assistance.[62]

7.29 As Clarke LJ explained in *Sunport Shipping Ltd v Tryg-Baltica International (UK) Ltd*:[63]

> Where a contract has been professionally drawn … the draftsman is certain to have in mind decisions of the Courts on earlier editions of the clause. Such decisions are part of the context or background circumstances against which the particular contract falls to be construed. If the draftsman chooses to adopt the same words as previously construed by the Courts, it seems to me to be likely that, other things being equal, he intends that the words should continue to have the same meaning.[64]

7.30 Knowledge of the law reports was also assumed in *QBE Insurance Ltd v Attorney-General*.[65] In that case, the New Zealand Court of Appeal refused to imply a term into a 'claims made' policy extending cover to claims arising out of circumstances notified to the same insurer under earlier policies which did not have a clause deeming any claim arising out of such circumstances to have been made in those earlier years. The Court held that the availability of a term to that effect (no doubt at an extra premium):

> must have been well known in New Zealand as a result of the decision of this Court in *Sinclair Horder O'Malley & Co v. National Insurance Co of New Zealand* [1995] 2 NZLR 257. The effect of the absence of such a condition is not something that would be known to a broker only with the hindsight of this case …

7.31 And in *McCann v Switzerland Insurance Australia Ltd*,[66] a case concerning the professional indemnity insurance of solicitors, Kirby J said:[67]

> Where, especially in an insurance contract written for application in different jurisdictions, language has been used which enjoys a settled meaning, courts will ordinarily endeavour to adhere to such a meaning, particularly in a policy of a commercial character upon which the parties might have been expected to obtain expert advice from lawyers or insurance brokers.

7.32 This aspect of the 'background knowledge' involves the imputation to market professionals of knowledge of the law. The admissible material also includes market practice and understanding of a non-legal nature. For example, in the Australian case of *Towry Law Plc v Chubb Insurance Company of Europe SA*[68] the policy had

---

[62] *Standard Life Assurance Ltd v Oak Dedicated Ltd* [2008] EWHC 222 (Comm); [2008] Lloyd's Rep IR 552 (Tomlinson J) at [18].
[63] [2003] EWCA Civ 12; [2003] 1 Lloyd's Rep 138, at [28]. The other members of the Court of Appeal agreed with Clarke LJ.
[64] See also *The Annefield* [1970] P 169, at 183G–H per Lord Denning MR.
[65] [2005] NZCA 193.
[66] [2000] HCA 65; (2000) 203 CLR 579.
[67] Ibid at [74].
[68] [2008] NSWSC 1352; 15 ANZ Insurance Cases 61–790.

been insured in the London market. Evidence was admitted as to the London market's understanding of the words 'retroactive date'.

Relevant background: the nature of the insured's business

The proposal form will provide insurers with information about the insured's business or practice.[69] But insurers will be taken to have a wider understanding of the nature of the insured's business.[70] So, in *J Rothschild Assurance plc v Collyear*[71] one issue was whether the review of pension mis-selling put in train by the insured's regulator under the Financial Services Act 1986 involved the making of claims for the purposes of the insuring clause.[72] Holding that it did, Rix J said: **7.33**

> I think that the investors made claims on [the insured] by participating in the review process and/or in accepting the redress offered in the light of its terms. I am persuaded that any other answer would do insufficient justice to the context of the regulatory regime as a whole. If that regime made claiming easy, it was designed to do so, because that was the policy of the Act itself, because of regard for the complexities of the subject matter, for the sake of the good name of the industry, and because the alternative prospects of dealing with these matters in the courts was not to be contemplated. It seems to me that [the insured's] underwriters were familiar with the regulatory regime and cannot complain that they are being asked to underwrite risks of a different nature from those they entered upon.

More recently, in *Standard, Life Assurance Ltd v Oak Dedicated Ltd*[73] Tomlinson J included within the admissible factual background knowledge: **7.34**

> the nature of [the insured's] business, which was in any event comprehensively described in the proposal form, and the nature of the professional indemnity risks to which the parties could reasonably have anticipated [the insured's] business would give rise. That in turn involves at any rate a working understanding of the regulatory regime introduced by the Financial Services Act 1986, to which express reference is made in the relevant insuring clause.

He also took into account the fact that at the time the policy before him was underwritten, insurance market professionals would have seen the insured's principal exposure as being to mass retail or consumer claims.[74]

---

[69] Eg, in *Charterhouse Development (France) Ltd v Sharp* [1998] Lloyd's Rep IR 266, at 276, Longmore J held that insurers would know from a brochure attached to the proposal form that the insured might appoint a non-executive director to join the board of an investee company and so incur liability as a director.

[70] For the purposes of the pre-contractual duty of disclosure, insurers are taken to know the practices and customs of any trade or profession which they insure: see para 5.58.

[71] [1999] Lloyd's Rep IR 6.

[72] As to which, see paras 2.30–2.31.

[73] [2008] EWHC 222 (Comm); [2008] Lloyd's Rep IR 552 at [16].

[74] Ibid at [15]. See also *Countrywide Assured Group Plc v Marshall* [2002] EWHC 2082 (Comm); [2003] Lloyd's Rep IR 195 at 197, where Morison J held that, at the time the contract of professional indemnity insurance was made the parties must have contemplated that redress might have to be paid to third party claimants who had been mis-sold pensions.

7.35   In this regard, the decision of Cresswell J in *Encia Remediations Ltd v Canopius Managing Agents Ltd*[75] is instructive. The insured was a company engaged in the business of civil and environmental engineering. The insurance was 'Environmental Consultants Professional Indemnity'. Insurers relied upon exclusions which did not apply if and to the extent that the activity which gave rise to the claim against the insured was that stated in the schedule to the policy.[76] The schedule described the insured's business as 'civil and environmental engineering and as more fully declared in the proposal form(s) referred to below and any accompanying information submitted with the proposal form(s)'. Cresswell J held that 'civil and environmental engineering' encompassed a wide range of activities.[77] More specifically, the insured had, until recently, been part of a wider concern which had split into two companies. The risks of both companies had been presented to insurers together. Insurers knew that the two new companies were both parts of what had been a single entity which they had previously insured. In the circumstances, Cresswell J held that the relevant background to construing the contract before him included the information provided by the other company.[78] That material was fuller than that provided by the insured. Taking this material into account, the insured's business as stated in the schedule included the activities which gave rise to the claim against it.

7.36   So, insurers of solicitors could not complain that they were unaware of the potential liability of solicitors under undertakings, with summary enforcement by the courts[79] and, in due course, the ombudsman regime under the Legal Services Act 2007 will no doubt be part of the background material for the professional indemnity of lawyers, in the same way as the ombudsman regime under the Financial Services and Markets Act 2000 now is for professionals regulated under that Act.[80]

7.37   Another aspect of the insured's business or practice which may be relevant to questions of construction is the size of the insured firm. It may be relevant to questions of construction that the 'insured' is a large firm with many employees. As was said in *Fisher v Guardian Insurance Co of Canada*:[81]

---

[75] [2007] EWHC 916 (Comm); [2008] Lloyd's Rep IR 79.

[76] 'This Policy does not cover any liability whatsoever arising out of: (1) The manufacture, construction, alteration, repair, servicing, treatment of any goods or products sold, supplied or distributed by the Assured or from any business or occupation other than as stated in the Schedule, even though the same may be carried on by the Assured in conjunction with their Business as stated in the Schedule. (2) Any claim arising from the provision of advice design or specification where the Insured contracts to manufacture construct erect install or supply materials or equipment unless defined in the Business as stated in the Schedule.'

[77] [2007] EWHC 916 (Comm); [2008] Lloyd's Rep IR 79 at [180].

[78] Ibid at [183].

[79] As to which, see *Jackson & Powell on Professional Liability* (7th edn, Sweet & Maxwell, 2012), paras 11-070 to 11-079.

[80] Current policies of professional indemnity insurance for solicitors provide cover in respect of claims made against the insured to the Legal Services Ombudsman or any other regulatory body set up by statute.

[81] (1995) 123 DLR (4th) 336, at [55].

Modern law firms frequently comprise dozens, sometimes hundreds, of lawyers. Some are partners, some are employees. The members of the firm in both categories change from time to time, as partners and associates leave or retire, new partners are created, and new associates are employed. The only practical means of insuring against liability, in these circumstances, is for one application to be made by a responsible member of the firm, acting on behalf of all the others. If insurers could deny coverage to the hundreds of Canadian lawyers insured in this way, because of the misrepresentation of the individual who filled out the application on their behalf, the consequences to the public and to the profession would be enormous, quite unanticipated, and entirely inconsistent with the practical realities faced by the legal profession and the insurance industry.

This reasoning was applied by Rix J in the leading case of *Arab Bank Plc v Zurich Insurance Co*[82] when construing a clause by which insurers waived their right to avoid for non-disclosure, misrepresentation, or untrue statements in the proposal form.

Relevant background: the genesis of the policy

In *Investors Compensation Scheme Ltd v West Bromwich Building Society*,[83] Lord **7.38** Hoffmann explained that the relevant background included 'absolutely anything which would have affected the way in which the language of the document would have been understood by a reasonable man' as long as it was 'reasonably available' to the parties. But this was subject to one exception: 'the previous negotiations of the parties and their declarations of subjective intent'.[84] Lord Hoffmann observed that 'the boundaries of this exception are in some respects unclear. But this is not the occasion on which to explore them'.

Those boundaries had been explored in the earlier case of *New Hampshire Insurance* **7.39** *Co v MGN Ltd*, which concerned the liability of fidelity insurers of the Maxwell group of companies following the death of Robert Maxwell. The admissibility of evidence as to the 'genesis' of the policies in issue was considered by the Court of Appeal[85] and their judgment was applied by Potter J.[86] On the preliminary appeal, Staughton LJ held that he:[87]

> would be prepared to admit evidence of the factual information which was put by the brokers before the insurers as relevant to the making of a contract; not evidence of what they wanted, or anything like that, but evidence of the factual situation from which they were starting. For example, that there were a number of companies; that they had a number of employees; that they had or did not have different businesses, and matters like that. All that I would regard as the background and as

---

[82] [1999] 1 Lloyd's Rep 262. See paras 5.128–5.130.
[83] [1998] 1 WLR 896, at 912–13.
[84] As was decided by the House of Lords in *Prenn v Simmonds* [1971] 1 WLR 1381. See, in particular, the speech of Lord Wilberforce at 1384–5. See also *Chartbrook Ltd v Persimmon Homes Ltd* [2009] UKHL 35; [2009] 1 AC 1101.
[85] [1996] LILR 103.
[86] [1997] LILR 24.
[87] [1996] LILR 103, at 108.

tending to show, perhaps, the aim, the genesis of the transaction. Whether it will be of any use in any particular case is another matter altogether.

7.40   Millett LJ observed that evidence of the 'factual matrices':[88]

> does not extend to the negotiations or communications between the parties which led to the contract to be construed. Nor is such evidence admissible under guise of identifying the commercial aim or object of the contract. That, too, must be ascertained objectively by a consideration of the contract and the external circumstances and context in which it was entered into. The aim or object of the contract is usually undisputed. If it is disputed, the dispute will merely reflect the underlying dispute about the construction of the contract, for each party will naturally assert not only the contract means what he says it means, but that meaning accords with the aim or object of the transaction.

As to the presentation and broking of the risk, he went on:

> ... the Court is plainly entitled to be informed of the composition of the so-called Maxwell Group of companies, the names of the companies within the group; and their relationship with each other, in short the corporate structure of the group. It is entitled, for example, to be informed whether the company is formed of a single group with a single body of shareholders or two or more groups of companies ultimately owned by different shareholders. It may need to be put in possession of other information about the group or groups, such as the amount of their combined assets or turnover, if relevant to both parties. Evidence of the factual information which was provided by the brokers to the underwriters is admissible in order to refute a claim that such matters were not known to one party or the other, but that, in my opinion, is the only purpose to which such evidence is admissible.[89]

7.41   So evidence of factual material presented by the brokers when seeking to persuade insurers to accept the risk is admissible. However, evidence of statements by brokers as to the scope of cover or other terms which their clients are seeking is inadmissible. Both, of course, will have been communicated by the brokers, possibly as part of a single conversation.[90]

7.42   At the subsequent trial of preliminary issues Potter J derived no assistance from the admissible evidence on the relevant issue, namely whether there was a single group insurance of the 'Maxwell Group' or whether the insurance was composite insurance for each company within the group.

---

[88]   Ibid at 109.

[89]   The Court of Appeal also held that evidence was admissible to explain the different treatment of one company within the group.

[90]   As Lord Phillips MR warned in *'The Tychy'* (*No 2*) [2001] EWCA Civ 1198; [2001] 2 Lloyd's Rep 403, at [29]: 'When a formal contract is drawn up and signed, care must be taken to distinguish between admissible background evidence relating to the nature and object of the contractual venture and inadmissible evidence of the terms for which each party was contending in the course of negotiations.' See also *Ted Baker Plc v AXA Insurance UK Plc* [2012] EWHC 1406 (Comm); [2013] Lloyd's Rep IR 174, at [97]–[105] where Eder J grappled with evidence adduced to show that the policy he had to construe had been intended to replicate cover under an earlier policy by which a different insurer had provided cover to the insured. He concluded that the evidence was, in fact, of the parties' subjective intentions and so inadmissible.

In *Standard Life Assurance Ltd v Oak Dedicated Ltd*,[91] Tomlinson J was prepared to **7.43** admit evidence of earlier policies of which the one in issue was a renewal, following the judgment of Rix LJ, with whom the other members of the Court of Appeal agreed, in *HIH Casualty and General Reinsurance Ltd v New Hampshire Insurance Company*.[92] But Tomlinson J did not take into account evidence of the negotiations which led to the agreement of those policies.

In *Encia Remediations Ltd v Canopius Managing Agents Ltd*,[93] Cresswell J had also **7.44** received evidence as to earlier policies, the broking of the policy in issue and the placement at the same time of another risk by a company which had been part of the same undertaking as the insured.

Construing the policy against the relevant background

While it will always be necessary to bear the relevant background in mind when **7.45** determining the true meaning and effect of a contractual term, it is important to bear in mind that the words used by the parties are the core material.[94] Those words have to be analysed not only against the relevant background, but also with the assistance of established principles of construction. Care should be exercised in relation to decisions as to the meaning and effect of similar terms in other classes of insurance, which have their own contexts and backgrounds.[95]

Generally, the words used by the parties are to be given their usual and natural mean- **7.46** ing, reading the contract as a whole and in its full context.[96] In doing so, the courts

---

[91] [2008] EWHC 222 (Comm); [2008] Lloyd's Rep IR 552.

[92] [2001] EWCA Civ 735; [2001] 2 Lloyd's Rep 161, at [69]–[97]: Rix LJ considered in some detail when and to what extent earlier policies or the slip when followed by a policy could potentially assist in construing an insurance policy. Earlier policies were used as an aid to construction in *McConnell Dowell Sea Pty Ltd v Gerling Australia Insurance Pty Ltd* [2002] VSC 260. Rix LJ held that the slip was admissible 'as part of the matrix or surrounding circumstances of the later contract'. See also *Birla Nifty Pty Ltd v International Mining Industry Underwriters Ltd* [2014] WASCA 180; [2015] Lloyd's Rep IR 75, at [59] per McLure JA, with whom the other members of the Supreme Court of Western Australia Court of Appeal agreed.

[93] [2007] EWHC 916 (Comm); [2008] Lloyd's Rep IR 79.

[94] See, for example, *'The Tychy' (No 2)* [2001] EWCA Civ 1198; [2001] 2 Lloyd's Rep 403, per Lord Phillips MR at [29]: 'Before taking extrinsic evidence into account, it is important to consider precisely why it is said to assist in deciding the meaning of what was subsequently agreed and to consider whether its relevance is sufficiently cogent to the determination of the joint intention of the parties to have regard to it.'

And in *Roar Marine Ltd v Bimeh Iran Insurance Co* [1998] 1 Lloyd's Rep 423 Mance J said at 429: 'Courts will never construe words in a vacuum. To a greater or lesser degree, depending on the subject matter, they will wish to be informed of what may variously be described as the context, the background, the factual matrix or the mischief. Even if the most generous examination of surrounding circumstances is permitted, any decision on interpretation must pay due regard to the explicitness of particular wording and the nature and strength of any circumstances suggested as putting a different complexion upon it.'

[95] *Cox v Deeny* [1996] LRLR 288, at 295 per HH Judge Diamond QC sitting as a High Court Judge.

[96] See, for example, *Bank of Credit and Commerce International SA v Ali* [2001] UKHL 8; [2002] 1 AC 251, per Lord Bingham at [8], and *Hutton v Watling* [1948] Ch 398, per Lord Greene MR at 403: 'The true construction of a document means no more than that the court puts upon it ... the

have regard to a number of considerations and established canons of construction. An exhaustive statement of those considerations and canons is beyond the scope of this book,[97] but we address a number which have been the subject of decisions in the area of professional indemnity insurance or which bear particularly upon that area.

The contract should be read as a whole

7.47 When considering a particular provision in a contract, the other provisions form part of the context in which its meaning is to be ascertained. The interaction of the various terms can assist in ascertaining how a particular provision was intended to work. Moreover, while there is no presumption against surplusage in contracts of insurance,[98] if possible effect should be given to the entire contract, rather than finding that some clauses are redundant.

7.48 There is a presumption, but no more than that,[99] that the parties intended the same word to bear the same meaning whenever they used it. It is readily rebutted. For example, in *Haydon v Lo & Lo (a firm)*[100] the parties used the word 'claim' to refer both to claims by third parties against the insured and by the insured under the professional indemnity policy. Moreover, some professional indemnity policies contain definitions of 'claim' which address the question of aggregation of claims for the purposes of policy limits and which make little sense in insuring clauses which refer to 'claims made'.[101]

Commercial interpretation

7.49 The parties are assumed to have wanted their contract to work in a sensible way. In the context of commercial agreements, including contracts of professional indemnity insurance, that means in a commercial or businesslike way.[102] It follows that if a

---

meaning which the other party ... would put upon it as an ordinary intelligent person construing the words in a proper way in the light of the relevant circumstances.'

And in *MDIS Ltd v Swinbank* [1999] Lloyd's Rep IR 516 Clarke LJ said at [13]: '... the words used must be considered in the context of the particular clause as a whole and that the clause must in turn be considered in the context of the policy as a whole, which must in its turn be set in its surrounding circumstances or factual matrix.'

[97] For a full statement see Lewison, *The Interpretation of Contracts* (5th edn, Sweet & Maxwell, 2011).

[98] *Lancashire County Council v Municipal Mutual Insurance Ltd* [1997] QB 897, at 906 per Simon Brown LJ; *Tektrol Ltd v International Insurance Co of Hanover Ltd* [2005] EWCA Civ 845; [2005] 2 Lloyd's Rep 701.

[99] *In re Birks* [1900] 1 Ch 417; *Watson v Haggitt* [1928] AC 127.

[100] [1997] 1 WLR 198.

[101] See para 2.34.

[102] See, for example, *Mannai Investment Co Ltd v Eagle Star Life Assurance Co Ltd* [1997] AC 749, at 771, where Lord Steyn said: 'In determining the meaning of the language of a commercial contract ... the law ... generally favours a commercially sensible construction. The reason for this approach is that a commercial construction is more likely to give effect to the intention of the parties. Words are therefore interpreted in the way in which a reasonable commercial person would construe them. And the standard of the reasonable commercial person is hostile to technical interpretations and undue emphasis on niceties of language.'

strict grammatical or literal interpretation of the contract produces a commercially absurd result, then it is likely that the parties' use of words or grammar was imprecise or wrong and, if possible, a more sensible reading of the words should be found.[103]

Thus in *MDIS Ltd v Swinbank*[104] the 'operative clause' provided: **7.50**

> The underwriters will indemnify the Assured to the extent and in the manner detailed herein against any claim for which the Assured may become legally liable, first made against the Assured and notified to the Underwriters during the period of this Certificate arising out of professional conduct of the Assured's business as stated in the Schedule alleging:
> (a) Neglect Error or Omission
> any neglect error or omission including breach of contract occasioned by same.
> (b) Dishonesty of Employees
> any dishonest, fraudulent, criminal, malicious act(s) or omission(s) of any person employed at any time by the Assured.
> The Assured will not be indemnified against any claim or loss, resulting from the dishonest, fraudulent, criminal or malicious act(s) or omission(s) perpetrated after the Assured could reasonably have discovered or suspected the improper conduct of the employee(s).

The insured computer consultants had been sued by a former customer for misrepresentation. The claim had been settled at an early stage. Insurers refused to indemnify the insured, arguing that the insured had been guilty of fraud so as not to be entitled to an indemnity. The insured relied upon the word 'alleging' in the operative clause, pointing out that the only claim alleged against it by the third party was not for fraud.

Mance J found for insurers. The insured's construction would mean that if the **7.51** third party sued in fraud and the insured settled because it was undoubtedly liable in negligence, it would not be covered. He said:[105]

> Haphazard results are possible if the true construction of the policy involves them. But a court is entitled to ask whether they are really sensible or likely to have been intended when the word 'alleging' was deployed. The answer which I would give is that the use of that word is understandable in the context of wording establishing the claims made nature of the cover. But, ultimately, as between insured and insurers, it is established liability which this insurance pays, and it is upon the nature and causation of any liability established that I consider the insured's right to indemnification must depend.

Lord Steyn expanded upon this passage in his later speech in *Sirius International Insurance Co v FAI General Insurance Ltd* [2004] UKHL 54; [2004] 1 WLR 3251 at [19].

[103] *Antaios Compania Naviera SA v Salen Rederierna AB (The Antaios)* [1985] 1 AC 191, 201 per Lord Diplock, and *Chartbrook Ltd v Persimmon Homes Ltd* [2009] UKHL 35; [2009] 1 AC 1101, at [20] per Lord Hoffmann.

This was applied in *Blackburn Rovers Football & Athletic Club Ltd v Avon Insurance Plc* [2005] EWCA Civ 423; [2005] Lloyd's Rep IR 447 at [9].

[104] [1999] Lloyd's Rep IR 516, on appeal from *McDonnell Information Systems Ltd v Swinbank* [1999] Lloyd's Rep IR 98.

[105] [1999] Lloyd's Rep IR 98, at 103.

7.52 The Court of Appeal agreed. The construction for which the insured argued was not sensible in that, if right, the answer to the question whether the insured was entitled to an indemnity would depend upon how the third party chose to frame its claim rather than upon the true facts.[106]

7.53 Similar reasoning was applied by Christopher Clarke J in *Travelers Casualty and Surety Co of Canada v Sun Life Assurance Co of Canada (UK) Ltd*.[107] The insured had warranted that it had:

> no knowledge or information of any actual or alleged fact, circumstance, situation, act, error, omission, misrepresentation, neglect or breach of duty which could give rise to a Claim within the scope of the proposed coverage against the Insured.

The insured had also expressly acknowledged that 'if such fact etc exists, whether or not disclosed, any Claim arising therefrom is excluded from coverage under the Policy'. Insurers relied upon a literal interpretation of this acknowledgment, contending that there was a breach of warranty if there was an antecedent fact which could give rise to a claim. Christopher Clarke J disagreed:[108]

> This interpretation makes no sense in the context of a claims made policy expressly affording coverage for prior acts, ie acts that have taken place prior to the inception of the policy. By definition such claims will arise from facts in existence before the policy is written. To use the second sentence to deny coverage on the ground that facts that could lead to a claim existed before the inception of the policy is a contradiction in terms. Such a construction would also render any question of knowledge, or of the individuals who have to have it, otiose. Whilst grammatical purism might indicate that 'such' *prima facie* refers to its immediately preceding antecedent, the parties must have intended that the warranty would only be broken if an identified individual had or should have had (it is debatable which) some sort of appreciation of the significance of the facts which he or she knew. The second sentence of the warranty is an exposition of the consequence of the first; not a free standing exclusion.

For similar reasons, Christopher Clarke J rejected insurers' submission that there was a breach of warranty if an individual knew of facts which could give rise to a claim, but, reasonably, had no idea of their potential to do so.[109]

7.54 In the same way, a construction which has the effect of reducing the protection provided by a policy so as to render it minimal or illusory is unlikely to reflect the intention of the parties.

7.55 For example in *Rathbone Brothers Plc v Novae Corporate Underwriting Ltd*[110] a clause in the policy provided that 'insurance provided by this policy applies excess

---

[106] [1999] Lloyd's Rep IR 516, at [21]–[23] per Clarke LJ, with whom Judge LJ agreed.
[107] [2006] EWHC 2716 (Comm); [2007] Lloyd's Rep IR 619. Christopher Clarke J was applying the law of Ontario.
[108] Ibid at [34].
[109] Ibid at [35]. See also *Morley v United Friendly Insurance Plc* [1993] 1 Lloyd's Rep 490.
[110] [2014] EWCA Civ 1464; [2015] Lloyd's Rep IR 95.

over insurance and indemnification available from any other source'. One insured had provided an indemnity to another insured against whom a claim was made. Insurers argued that the indemnity had to be exhausted before the insured against whom a claim had been made was entitled to be indemnified under the policy. The argument failed. Elias LJ, with whom the other members of the Court of Appeal agreed, held:[111]

> It seems to me that if the insurers can take advantage of an indemnity given by one co-insured to another, this would significantly undermine the protection afforded by the policy. Employers frequently give indemnities to directors and employees for liabilities arising out of their negligent conduct. A major reason for taking out insurance is to protect against the risks of incurring liability as a consequence of such negligence. In my judgment, that would be obvious, both to the insurers and to the insured. It would frustrate the purpose of professional indemnity insurance to interpret the policy so as to exclude the insurers from liability in the very circumstances where that insurance is most likely to be needed. In my judgment, it would require very clear language to treat the indemnity granted by the insured company to be the primary source of cover ahead of the insurance for which the insured company has paid. The commercial understanding would be that the insurers receive the premium to meet precisely that kind of liability.

However, it is important to distinguish between a construction which produces **7.56** a bad result for one party in the sense that he has made a bad bargain, and a construction which, as between the parties, is uncommercial, particularly where the meaning of the words chosen by the parties is clear.[112] For example, in *Cooke and Arkwright v Haydon*[113] the insured was a firm of chartered surveyors. One partner was also a partner in a multidisciplinary firm of surveyors and engineers called Merak. Merak sub-contracted work to other firms, including the insured. Memorandum 1, which formed part of the policy, provided:

> It is hereby understood and agreed that insofar as concerns work carried out by the assured for and on behalf of the Merak Partnership this certificate is only to cover the liability as herein defined of the assured for claims first made against the assured during the period specified in the schedule by independent third party firms or individuals, subject always to certificate terms, conditions, limitations and exclusions.

A claim was made against Merak, which in turn claimed against the insured. **7.57** Insurers denied cover, relying upon Memorandum 1. The insured argued that it

---

[111] Ibid at [56]. See also *Trustees Executors Ltd v QBE Insurance (International) Ltd* [2010] NZCA 608; (2010) 16 ANZ Insurance Cases 61–874, a case concerning a policy insuring a company which provided personal and corporate trustee services, custodial investment administration services and mortgage lending and administration. Read literally, an exclusion of cover for 'any claim or claims arising from or contributed to by depreciation (or failure to appreciate) in value of any investments' excluded all cover for the insured's investment business. The New Zealand Court of Appeal did not consider that this could have been the parties' mutual intention.

[112] See paras 7.06–7.07.

[113] [1987] 2 Lloyd's Rep 579.

made no sense commercially to exclude claims made against it by Merak, passing on liability to third parties, but not to exclude claims against the insured directly by third parties where the insured had acted as Merak's sub-contractor. Hobhouse J, whose judgment was upheld on appeal, disagreed. He did because not only was the language of Memorandum 1 clear, but because:

> the alleged unbusinesslike effect of memorandum 1 assumes that the plaintiffs have an unbusinesslike arrangement with Merak. If the plaintiffs were to contract with Merak on terms which excluded any liability of the plaintiffs to Merak, or gave the plaintiffs some comparable protection (if wished, giving the plaintiffs the benefit of Merak's own insurances) then the scheme would not be unbusinesslike. There would be no risk of a liability of the plaintiffs on a claim by Merak, so why cover it in this policy? The defect, if any, in these policies is that the plaintiffs and their brokers agreed to the wording in memorandum 1 without, if such be the case, which I do not know, having adequate regard to the plaintiff's term of employment by Merak.

7.58 Moreover, for the court to depart from the literal meaning of the words used by the parties in order to achieve a commercial or businesslike result, there must be some alternative construction of those words which produces such a result. Where there is none, the court will be constrained to hold the parties to the uncommercial and unbusinesslike result which, in the absence of any plausible alternative, they must be presumed to have intended. This was the effect of the decision of Tomlinson J in *Standard Life Assurance Ltd v Oak Dedicated Ltd*.[114]

7.59 The insurance cover in that case was £75 million in excess of £25 million. The insured was a major provider of financial services, including advice as to endowment mortgages. This aspect of its business led to it paying out over £100 million to over 97,000 investors and the insured sought to recover its outlay from excess insurers.

7.60 The insured had an argument that each of the 97,000 claims should be treated as a single claim under the aggregation clause which permitted aggregation of claims arising from or in connection with or attributable to any one originating cause or source, arguing that all the claims were caused by its systemic failures in relation to the sale of endowment mortgages.[115] The problem was that the excess was £25 million 'each and every claim and/or claimant' and there was no aggregation clause for claimants. Understandably, insurers took the point.

7.61 Tomlinson J considered the factual background. It was, he held, 'virtually inconceivable' that a single claimant could have either a single claim for over £25 million or a series of related claims which together totalled more than £25 million. The insured's main, but not only, potential liability to claims was for mass mis-selling, and this was known to insurance market professionals at the time. The problem

---

[114] [2008] EWHC 222 (Comm); [2008] Lloyd's Rep IR 552.
[115] As to which see paras 10.38–10.41.

was that no one could think of any other plausible construction. Tomlinson J therefore concluded:[116]

> ... a commercial contract ought not to be construed in a manner repugnant to its purpose.... in the present context it does not greatly assist underwriters to point out, as they do, that their construction does not leave the contract devoid of all possible application. It is also right to point out that a deductible pitched at a level of £25 million does not wear the air of a per claimant deductible—no claim or even series of claims by a single claimant was realistically likely to reach this sort of level ...
>
> I am however left with the words used in the schedule and, as I think, more tellingly in the slip. No witness at trial could recall ever seeing this form of wording before, let alone in a financial institutions cover. No witness at trial could think of any plausible purpose for the inclusion of the words 'and/or claimant' in the excess provision in the slip other than the attempted achievement of a per claimant excess ...
>
> ... I conclude that the policy does not permit the aggregation of related claims made by separate claimants.

The parties had meant the words 'and/or claimant' to have some meaning. They had been included in this particular contract on purpose, albeit that it was not clear what that purpose was. There was only one plausible meaning of those words. **7.62**

Where the parties have chosen to include a standard term which is inappropriate to their contract, it may be impossible to construe that term so as to achieve an overall construction which makes commercial sense. For example, in *Royal & Sun Alliance Insurance Plc v Dornoch*[117] reinsurance of a directors and officers liability insurance included a claims control clause on the following terms: **7.63**

> Notwithstanding anything herein contained to the contrary, it is a condition precedent to any liability under this policy that:
> (a) The reinsured shall upon knowledge of any loss or losses which may give rise to claim under this policy, advise the Underwriters thereof by cable within 72 hours ...

This clause was appropriate for reinsurance of goods or other property against physical loss or damage, but not for liability insurance. In the case of insurance of goods and other property, loss is suffered when, for example, a fire damages the insured property. In such a case, reinsurers will wish to appoint loss adjusters promptly to investigate the cause of the fire while the evidence is still to hand. On the other hand, in the case of liability insurance of the directors and officers of a company, loss would only occur when the liability of those directors and officers was ascertained by a judgment or award against them or by settlement of a claim against them,[118] even though the reinsured would be expected to know of the

---

[116] [2008] EWHC 222 (Comm); [2008] Lloyd's Rep IR 552, at [98]–[100].
[117] [2005] EWCA Civ 238; [2005] Lloyd's Rep IR 544.
[118] See paras 9.106–9.132.

potential liability well before then. Any control of the claim would need to take place before the liability of the directors and officers was ascertained.

7.64 Reinsurers argued that it made no commercial sense for the notice requirement to arise only when the loss was ascertained and that the claims control clause should be read as requiring that notice be given of an alleged loss (ie when allegations were made against the directors and officers) rather than of an actual loss (eg when judgment was entered against the directors and officers). The difficulty with this argument was that, if accepted, it would mean that the reinsured had only 72 hours to give notice, failing which they would not be entitled to cover. This was also unbusinesslike, because there was no commercial need for notice to be given so quickly and no reason for such a severe penalty for failure to do so.

7.65 Finding against reinsurers, Longmore LJ, with whom the other members of the Court of Appeal agreed, said:[119]

> It does not, therefore, seem to me to be any part of the court's function to go out of its way to give a purposive or business common sense construction to one part of a clause in favour of one party and thus enable that party to seek to take advantage of another part of the clause which has draconian consequences for the other party. If the parties had decided to choose an appropriate form of clause suitable for the reinsurance of a reinsured's liability rather than his property, they might very well have chosen a clause with a longer notice period than 72 hours or at least a clause which did not make 72 hours' notice a condition precedent to any liability on reinsurers' part.[120]

Good faith

7.66 In *Cox v Bankside Members Agency Ltd*,[121] Phillips J said that a contract of insurance was one of the utmost good faith and that 'one must approach any question of construction of the policy on the premise that the parties will act in good faith'.[122] He then referred to the decision of the Court of Appeal in *Groom v Crocker*.[123]

---

[119] [2005] EWCA Civ 238; [2005] Lloyd's Rep IR 544, at [18].

[120] In *AIG Europe (Ireland) Ltd v Faraday* [2007] EWCA Civ 1208; [2008] Lloyd's Rep IR 454 the reinsurance of directors and officers liability cover included, as a condition precedent to the right to an indemnity, a requirement that the reinsured should, 'upon knowledge of any loss or losses which may give rise to a claim', give notice as soon as reasonably practicable and in any event within 30 days. It was held that a declaration that a company's accounts would be restated which was immediately followed by a significant drop in the value of the company's shares was a loss which might give rise to a claim which was known to the reinsured and should have been notified under the clause. This was the case, even though, as in *Royal & Sun Alliance Insurance Plc v Dornoch*, the parties had chosen to use a notification clause which was appropriate for the reinsurance of goods and other property rather than of liability to third parties. The notification clause was in terms which could be made to work.

[121] [1995] 2 Lloyd's Rep 437, at 451.

[122] See also *Goshawk Dedicated Ltd v Tyser & Co Ltd* [2006] EWCA Civ 54; [2006] 1 Lloyd's Rep 566, at [53].

[123] [1939] 1 KB 194.

The insurance policy in issue in *Groom v Crocker* was motor insurance, not profes- **7.67**
sional indemnity, but it provides helpful guidance as to how the mutual obligation
of good faith affects the construction of policy terms in liability insurance. In that
case, insurers had instructed solicitors to put in a defence to a claim against the
insured for a car accident admitting liability. This was not because the accident
was the insured's fault. It was not. It was because of an agreement with other insurers which compromised another claim as well. The insured objected and sued the
solicitors for negligence and libel.

Condition 2 of the policy was in these terms: **7.68**

> The Society shall if and so long as it so desires have absolute conduct and control of
> all or any proceedings against the insured … and shall be entitled to use the name
> of the insured to enforce for the benefit of the Society any order made for costs or
> otherwise or to make or defend any claim for indemnity or damage against third
> parties.

On its face this appeared to give insurers unfettered and complete control of
the claim.

However, the Court of Appeal held otherwise. The clause gave insurers the **7.69**
right to control the claim 'provided that they do so in what they bona fide consider to be the common interest of themselves and their assured'.[124] The claims
control clause was subject to an implied condition that the solicitor nominated
by insurers should act reasonably in the interests of both the insured and
insurers.[125]

Contra proferentem

If a contract is ambiguous, the ambiguity will be resolved against the party who **7.70**
put forward the term in question. This is usually described as the *contra proferentem* rule.[126] It has been said that the rule 'strongly applies' to contracts of
insurance.[127] It was summarized by Lord Mustill giving the Opinion of the Privy
Council in *Tam Wing Chuen v Bank of Credit and Commerce Hong Kong Ltd (in
liquidation)*:[128]

> … the basis of the *contra proferentem* principle is that a person who puts for-
> ward the wording of a proposed agreement may be assumed to have looked
> after his own interests, so that if the words leave room for doubt about whether
> he is intended to have a particular benefit there is reason to suppose that he
> is not.

---

[124] Ibid at 203 per Sir Wilfred Greene MR.
[125] Ibid at 226 per Mackinnon LJ. See further paras 12.52–12.55.
[126] Taken from the Latin maxim: *verba cartarum fortius accipiunter contra proferentem.*
[127] *Lancashire County Council v Municipal Mutual Insurance Ltd* [1987] QB 897 per Simon
Brown LJ at 905, citing *In re Etherington and Lancashire and Yorkshire Accident Insurance Co* [1909]
1 KB 591, at 596.
[128] [1996] 2 BCLC 69, at 77.

7.71 It is often the case that insurers have drafted their policy wordings and so any term on which they rely will be construed against them.[129] For example, in *Cox v Bankside Members Agency Ltd*[130] the notice provision in the policy was in these terms:

> The Assured shall give to the Underwriters immediate written notice of:
> (i)   any Claim made against the Assured,
> (ii)   any loss discovered by the Assured,
> (iii) the discovery by the Assured of reasonable cause for suspicion of dishonesty or fraud or negligence such as might give rise to a Claim under this Policy.
> If during the period of Insurance, the Assured shall first become aware of any circumstance which may subsequently give rise to a loss or a Claim against the Assured, they shall during the period of Insurance give written notice to the Underwriters of such circumstance and then any loss or Claim arising therefrom shall be deemed to be a loss first discovered, or Claim first made against the Assured during the period of Insurance.

7.72 Insurers argued that compliance with the notice provisions was a condition precedent to cover. Phillips J disagreed. They were not described as conditions precedent as would be expected if they were intended to have that status.[131] If insurers had intended it to be a condition precedent they could and should have said so expressly.[132]

7.73 When considering the meaning and effect of a warranty in policy of fire insurance in *Hussain v Brown*[133] Saville LJ said:[134]

> the breach of such a warranty produces an automatic cancellation of the cover, and the fact that a loss may have no connection at all with that breach is simply irrelevant. In my view, if underwriters want such protection, then it is up to them to stipulate for it in clear terms.[135]

7.74 However, professional indemnity policies are not always drafted by insurers, or by insurers alone. For example, in *Standard Life Assurance Ltd v Oak Dedicated Ltd*[136] Tomlinson J described how specialist brokers had developed policy wordings to provide professional indemnity cover to financial institutions, with the assistance of solicitors. Other forms of professional indemnity insurance are prescribed or

---

[129] So, in *Maxwell v Price (Halford, Third Party)* [1960] 2 Lloyd's Rep 155 the High Court of Australia applied the *contra proferentem* rule when considering the meaning and effect of the insuring clause in a policy of professional indemnity insurance insuring a firm of solicitors. It did not unambiguously provide that cover was only provided to the partners for their liabilities as partners in their current firm and so was not construed as being so limited. See para 9.03.

[130] [1995] 2 Lloyd's Rep 437.

[131] Ibid at 453. Cf *Stoneham v The Ocean, Railway and General Accident Insurance Company* (1887) 19 QBD 237.

[132] See further para 7.102.

[133] [1996] 1 Lloyd's Rep 627.

[134] Ibid at 630.

[135] In *Pratt v Aigaion Insurance Company SA* [2008] EWCA Civ 1314; [2009] 1 Lloyd's Rep 225 a warranty would have produced an absurd result if read literally, and was otherwise ambiguous. It was therefore construed against insurers.

[136] [2008] EWHC 222 (Comm); [2008] Lloyd's Rep IR 552, at [18].

negotiated by professional bodies.[137] In such cases, there is less scope for the application of the *contra proferentem* rule against insurers. So, in *HLB Kidsons v Lloyd's Underwriters*[138] the insurance policy in question was on similar terms to the current ICAEW Minimum Approved Policy Wording. When rejecting the insured's argument on construction, Rix LJ said:[139]

> If in such circumstances the ICA terms were nevertheless intended to operate as the appellants suggest they were, then they need to be revisited.

When considering the application of the *contra proferentem* rule it should also **7.75** be borne in mind that where a standard term is used, it does not matter which of the insured and insurers proposed it in the particular transaction: it should bear the same meaning whoever happened to have put it forward in the particular negotiations.[140]

Prevalence of terms

It is an established canon of construction that, where there is a conflict between **7.76** standard terms and terms specifically agreed between the parties, the latter are to prevail. This is because the parties will have paid greater attention to the specific terms which will have been tailored to suit their particular purpose.[141]

However, that is merely a presumption, and the parties can agree that the stand- **7.77** ard terms are to prevail. In the context of professional indemnity insurance, the SRA Minimum Terms and Conditions of Professional Indemnity Insurance require any policy of insurance for solicitors to which they apply to include a term providing that:

(a) The insurance is to be construed or rectified so as to comply with the requirements of these minimum terms and conditions; and
(b) any provision which is inconsistent with these minimum terms and conditions is to be severed or rectified to comply.

The effect of the inclusion of this term is that the parties demonstrate an overriding intention to have contracted on terms which are consistent with the SRA Minimum Terms and Conditions of Professional Indemnity Insurance. Any term which they have included in their contract which appears to be inconsistent with those terms does not reflect their true intention and should be construed so as

---

[137] See paras 1.12–1.31.

[138] [2008] EWCA Civ 1206; [2009] 1 Lloyd's Rep 8, at [121].

[139] Ibid at [119].

[140] *Gan Insurance Company Ltd v Tai Ping Insurance Company Ltd (Nos 2 and 3)* [2001] Lloyd's IR 667, at [21] per Mance LJ, referring to *Pioneer Shipping Ltd v BTP Tioxide Ltd (The 'Nema') (No 2)* [1982] AC 724, at 737F, per Lord Diplock; and *Miramar Maritime Corp v Holborn Oil Trading Ltd* [1984] AC 676, at 682, per Lord Diplock.

[141] See, for example, *Homburg Houtimport BV v Agrosin Private Ltd (The Starsin)* [2003] UKHL 12; [2004] 1 AC 715, per Lord Bingham at [11]. The prevalence of a special condition over a standard exclusion clause was one reason why Rix J found against insurers in *J Rothschild Assurance plc v Collyear* [1999] Lloyd's Rep IR 6: see para 5.98.

to comply with them. If it cannot be so construed, then the parties must have included it by error and did not intend to be bound by it.[142]

Implied terms

7.78 The approach to the implication of a term into a contract has been authoritatively stated by Lord Hoffmann in giving the Opinion of the Privy Council in *Attorney-General of Belize v Belize Telecom Ltd*.[143] As with the construction of the express terms of the contract, the focus is upon what the reasonable reader of those terms, with the benefit of the relevant background, would understand the parties to have intended.

7.79 So in *Kumar v AGF Insurance Ltd*,[144] had he not found against insurers on true construction of the express terms of the policy as to the exclusion of insurers' rights in the event of a breach of warranty based upon a dishonest declaration in the proposal form by a partner in the insured firm,[145] Thomas J would have implied a term that insurers should have no such rights on the following basis:[146]

> In my judgment it is clear that, on the assumption that the first paragraph of clause 5 did not, on its language, cover a situation where there had been a breach of warranty, the parties had been asked the question as to whether a term should be implied to similar effect, the answer would have been quite clear. Let me pose the question this way to the parties: if the signatory of the proposal form fraudulently concealed the circumstances, must the underwriter indemnify the innocent partner from liability to the client? The answer undoubtedly would have been 'of course.' That answer would have followed from the commercial background and the other reasons that I have set out in this judgment.[147]

7.80 However, the courts will not imply terms, however commercially sensible they may be, merely to change the effect of a contract when, by their choice of express terms, the parties have shown an intention to contract on a different basis.[148] Terms are

---

[142] If insurers of members of the Institute of Chartered Accountants in England and Wales produce their own version of the ICAEW Minimum Approved Policy Wording, they must include an endorsement to the effect that, in the event of any dispute, the Minimum Approved Policy Wording will override their own terms if the latter are less favourable to the insured.

[143] *Attorney-General of Belize v Belize Telecom Ltd* [2009] UKPC 10, [2009] 1 WLR 1988, at [21] per Lord Hoffmann, set out at para 7.02. See also *Mediterranean Salvage & Towage Ltd v Seamar Trading & Commerce Inc* [2009] EWCA Civ 531; [2009] 2 Lloyd's Rep 639, at [8] per Lord Clarke MR.

[144] [1999] 1 WLR 1747.

[145] As to which see paras 5.106 and 7.11.

[146] [1999] 1 WLR 1747, at 1756.

[147] In the same way, in *Shinedean Ltd v Alldown Demolition (London) Ltd (in liquidation)* [2006] EWCA Civ 939; [2006] 1 WLR 2696 it was a condition precedent to the insured's right to an indemnity that the insured should give insurers all information and assistance which insurers might require. No time was specified by which this should be done. It was held that there was an implied term that it be done within a reasonable time.

[148] See, for example, *Thornton Springer v NEM Mutual Insurance Co Ltd* [2000] 2 All ER 489, at [89]–[93] where Colman J declined to imply a term in to a policy of professional indemnity insurance that insurers would not withhold their consent unreasonably to the incurrence of defence costs. The positon was covered by express terms as to control of admissions and settlements and the QC clause.

not to be implied merely to save one party from the consequence of having entered a bad bargain. For example, in *QBE Insurance Ltd v Attorney-General*[149] the professional indemnity policies of a government department over a number of years had obliged the insured to give notice to insurers of knowledge of circumstances which could give rise to a claim against it. However, there was no term in those policies to the effect that, if any claim were subsequently made arising out of circumstances which had been notified, it would be deemed to have been made during the policy period during which the notification of circumstances had been made. Such a term was included in a later year, but so too was a clause excluding cover in respect of claims notified under previous policies. The insurance in each of the relevant years was with the same insurer.

7.81 When a claim was made which arose out of circumstances which had been notified under one of the earlier policies, insurers relied upon the exclusion clause. The insured contended that it was implicit in the requirement in the earlier policies that notice be given of circumstances which might give rise to a claim that the insured would be indemnified against any claims which arose from such circumstances under the policy during the currency of which he made a notification. The New Zealand Court of Appeal refused to imply any such term. The availability of express terms which had that effect was or should have been known to the insured and its brokers.[150] The parties, including the insured, had chosen a form of words which exposed the insured to the risk of a gap in cover. Such terms had been available for over a decade at the relevant time, but, the Court inferred, at an additional premium. The insured had made its choice.

7.82 It must also be possible to state with certainty what term should be implied. Thus in *Mabey and Johnson Ltd v Ecclesiastical Insurance Office Ltd*,[151] the professional indemnity policy insuring an engineering company did not include any aggregation or series clause to the effect that related claims would be treated as a single claim for the purposes of the limit of indemnity under the policy. Having found that no such term was expressly agreed, Morison J considered whether such a term could be implied. He held that it could not be. The contract worked without such a term:[152]

> On their face, the insured were insured against each and every claim up to a limit. In the absence of a series provision the contract was clear and certain, albeit commercially unwise for the insurers. The series provision changes the nature of the insurance which had been provided and cuts down the cover provided. Further, on the evidence there are a large number of clauses all of which are broadly designed to achieve the same result but which differ considerably in their detail.

---

[149] [2005] NZCA 193.
[150] See paras 3.37 and 7.30.
[151] [2001] Lloyd's Rep IR 369.
[152] Ibid at 15.

Nor was there any evidence of a market practice that such terms were invariably included, let alone that a particular term should be included.[153]

C. Particular Classes of Terms

Warranties

7.83 Warranties are written terms of the contract of insurance by which the insured warrants that specified matters of fact are accurate or that they are and will remain accurate. The insured may also warrant that he will perform some specified future obligation. The law in this respect will be changed significantly when the relevant provisions of the Insurance Act 2015 come into force. At the time of writing they are due to come into force on 12 August 2016. The consequent changes are considered below.

The current law

7.84 As things stand breach of any warranty discharges insurers from liability from the time of breach. There is no need for insurers to make any election or to take any action.[154] A breach of warranty need not be material or related to any loss under the policy.

7.85 The burden is on insurers to prove that any particular contractual term has the status of a warranty in that, objectively, the parties intended it to have that status. While there is no need for any specific wording, the most obvious way in which the parties can show this intention is by using the words 'warranty' or 'warranted'.[155] Where those words are not used, the approach to construction was helpfully summarized by Rix LJ in *HIH Casualty and General Insurance Ltd v New Hampshire Insurance Co*:[156]

> It is a question of construction, and the presence or absence of the word 'warranty' or 'warranted' is not conclusive. One test is whether it is a term which goes to the root of the transaction; a second, whether it is descriptive of or bears materially on the risk of loss; a third, whether damages would be an unsatisfactory or inadequate remedy.

7.86 In the area of professional indemnity insurance, most warranties will be made by the proposal form and other information provided to insurers when the contract is being negotiated. The declaration signed by the insured as part of the proposal form will often state that the information provided will form the basis of the contract of

---

[153] Ibid at 16.

[154] *Bank of Nova Scotia v Hellenic Mutual War Risks Association (Bermuda) Ltd (The Good Luck)* [1992] 1 AC 233.

[155] *Ellinger & Co v Mutual Life Insurance Company of New York* [1905] 1 KB 31, at 38 per Stirling LJ.

[156] [2001] EWCA Civ 735; [2001] 2 Lloyd's Rep 161, at [101].

insurance.[157] This has the effect of making the statements in it warranties, even if there is no term to that effect in the contract itself.[158]

For example, in *Arab Bank plc v Zurich Insurance Co*[159] the basis of contract clause **7.87** provided:

> I/We warrant that the above statements made by me/us or on my/our behalf are to the best of my/our knowledge true and complete and I/we agree that this proposal shall be the basis of the contract between me/us and the Insurer.

Basis of contract clauses may also appear in the policy wording. For example, in *Mabey & Johnson Limited v Ecclesiastical Insurance Office Plc (No. 2)*[160] the policy contained a basis of contract clause in the following terms:

> WHEREAS the 'Insured' has submitted a written proposal and declaration dated as shown in the Schedule attached to this Policy containing particulars and statements which (together with any other information which may have been supplied) shall be the basis of this Policy and are to be considered as incorporated herein and in consideration of the payment of the premium stated in the Schedule.[161]

Given the severe consequences for breach of warranty and the absence of any **7.88** requirement of materiality for there to be a breach, warranties are carefully construed.[162] So, in *Arab Bank plc v Zurich Insurance Co*[163] the declaration, set out in the preceding paragraph, was couched in terms of knowledge and belief. This was important because the policy in question, like most professional indemnity policies, was a composite policy.[164] In effect, each individual insured's rights were to be considered independently, with each insured separately for his own separate interest. The proposal form had been completed by Mr Browne, who was assumed to have acted fraudulently. There was no doubt that the statement of his own knowledge and belief was false and so a breach of warranty. But Rix J held that, on its true construction, the effect of the declaration was not that the other insured were in breach of warranty. He held that:[165]

> the warranty was not simply as to the statements' truth, but was qualified by the expression 'to the best of my/our knowledge'. Mr Browne of course knew that he had misstated his answers to the questions whether any director was aware of any circumstances which might give rise to a claim or otherwise affect the consideration

---

[157] The RIBA Architects Premier Policy Wording contains a provision to this effect, as does the ICAEW Minimum Approved Policy Wording.

[158] *Condogianis v Guardian Assurance Co Ltd* [1921] 2 AC 125. See also *Genesis Housing Association Ltd v Liberty Syndicate Management Ltd* [2013] EWCA Civ 1173; [2014] Lloyd's Rep IR 318.

[159] [1999] 1 Lloyd's Rep 262.

[160] (No. 2) [2003] EWHC 1523 (Comm); [2004] Lloyd's Rep IR 10.

[161] Similar wording appeared in the professional indemnity policy considered in *Newline Corporate Name Limited v Morgan Cole* [2007] EWHC 1628 (Comm); [2008] PNLR 2.

[162] See para 7.73 for the application of the *contra proferentem* rule to warranties.

[163] [1999] 1 Lloyd's Rep 262.

[164] See paras 1.32–1.45.

[165] [1999] 1 Lloyd's Rep 262, at 283.

of the proposal. On the assumed facts, however, none of the other directors, apart from Mr Pitts, was aware of the fraudulent valuations or that Mr Browne's warranty on their behalf was untrue or incomplete. It seems to me, therefore, that reliance on Mr Browne's warranty goes no further than reliance on his misrepresentations and non-disclosures. It would have been otherwise if the warranty had been purely as to the truth of the statements. Then ignorance would have been no defence, and I am prepared to assume that the terms of the proposal, incorporated into the policy by means of the 'basis of the contract' provision, would have taken precedence over the other provisions of the policy.

7.89 Some professional indemnity policies include terms which preclude insurers from relying on a breach of warranty made by an insured who has not acted dishonestly in relation to the breach.[166]

7.90 Because the effect of a breach of warranty is to discharge insurers from liability from the date of breach, insurers cannot lose the benefit of a defence of breach of warranty by affirmation, as they can in the case of a right to avoid for nondisclosure or breach of warranty.[167] However, they can lose the right to rely upon such a defence through the operation of estoppel. The same considerations apply to defences based upon non-compliance with conditions precedent. The requirements for an estoppel were set out by Rix LJ in *Kosmar Villa Holidays Plc v Trustees of Syndicate 1243*.[168] Insurers must make an unequivocal representation to the insured that they accept continuing liability under the contract (or, in the case of breach of condition precedent, that they do not rely upon that breach as providing them with a defence) and the insured must rely upon that representation to his detriment so that it would be inequitable to permit insurers to go back on it.[169]

The impact of the Insurance Act 2015

7.91 The provisions of the Insurance Act 2015 which reform the law of insurance in relation to warranties are due to come into force on 12 August 2016.[170]

7.92 Section 9 of the Insurance Act 2015 provides that, in the case of non-consumer insurance contracts (and so, in the case of contracts of professional indemnity insurance)[171] representations made in connection with the making or varying of such contracts cannot be turned into warranties by a term of the contract of insurance or of any other contract. It is specifically provided that this cannot be done by declaring such representations to form the basis of the contract of insurance. Any

---

[166] See paras 5.105–5.108.

[167] As to which, see para 5.72.

[168] [2008] EWCA Civ 147; [2008] Lloyd's Rep IR 489 at [70].

[169] See also *Argo Systems FZE v Liberty Insurance (PTE) (The 'Copa Casino')* [2012] EWCA Civ 1572; [2012] Lloyd's Rep IR 67, at [67] per Aikens LJ, with whom the other members of the Court of Appeal agreed.

[170] Section 23(2) of the Insurance Act 2015, 12 August 2016 being 18 months after the Act was passed.

[171] See para 5.02.

term which would put the insured in a worse position in relation to representations to which s 9 applies is of no effect.[172] The abolition of 'basis of contract' provisions represents a significant change in the law.[173] In the context of professional indemnity insurance this change is of particular significance because it is usually only by reason of 'basis of contract' clauses that the insured makes any warranties. It should be noted, however, that it remains open to insurers to seek to include express warranties in the contract of insurance which cover the same ground as representations in the proposal form. What is prohibited is provisions which convert those representations into warranties without more, not specific warranties which replicate pre-contractual representations.

Another significant change is made by s 10(1). This provides that the consequence **7.93** of a breach of warranty is no longer to be the automatic discharge of insurers' liability under the contract of insurance.[174]

The Insurance Act 2015 does not deny insurers any remedy for breach of warranty. **7.94** Section 10(2) provides that

> An insurer has no liability under a contract of insurance in respect of any loss occurring, or attributable to something happening, after a warranty (express or implied) in the contract has been breached but before the breach has been remedied.

This is subject to three exceptions.[175] The first is that, as a result of a change of circumstances, the warranty has ceased to be applicable to the circumstances of the contract. The second is that compliance with the warranty has been rendered unlawful by a subsequent law. The third is that insurers have waived the breach of warranty.

Some breaches of warranty are not capable of remedy. For example, a warranty as **7.95** to a state of affairs at the time the contract of insurance is made cannot be made good if it is broken. In the case of such breaches and of breaches which are capable of remedy but have not been remedied the effect of s 10(2) is to suspend the contract of insurance indefinitely. However, this is subject to the potential impact of s 11.

Section 11 of the Insurance Act 2015 applies to any term of a contract of insurance **7.96** (whether express or implied and whether a warranty or not) (i) which does not define the risk as a whole and (ii) which, if complied with, would tend to reduce the risk of loss of a particular kind or loss at a particular location or at a particular time. The sort of terms which fall within s 11 are terms by which the insured promises or is required to act in a particular way or to refrain from acting in particular way. A term by which the insured warranted that a state of affairs existed would not fall within s 11.

---

[172] Section 16(1) of the Insurance Act 2015.
[173] For the position before s 9 comes into force see paras 6.27–6.31 and 7.83–7.90.
[174] For the position before s 10(1) comes into force see para 7.84.
[175] Section 10(3) of the Insurance Act 2015.

7.97   An example of a term in a contract of professional indemnity insurance which defined the risk as a whole, but which might have otherwise fallen within the scope of s 11, appeared in the policy considered in *Body Corporate 326421 v Auckland Council*.[176] Cover was for any sum which the insured became legally liable to pay in respect of claims first made against the insured in the policy period where the insured's liability arose out of the carrying out of 'professional activities and duties'. These were defined as 'activities undertaken by or under the supervision of a) persons or personnel who are professionally qualified; or b) persons or personnel having not less than 5 years relevant experience in carrying out professional activities that would normally be undertaken by a professionally qualified person'. This term defined the risk insured. It would therefore fall outside the scope of s 11 of the Insurance Act 2015 even though the risk of claims against the insured tend to be reduced if all work were carried out by or under the supervision of individuals who fell within the definition of 'professional activities and duties'. The position would be different if the contract required the insured to have all work carried out by or under the supervision of such individuals.

7.98   Where the insured is in breach of a term which falls within the scope of s 11 and suffers a loss, s 11 provides that insurers may not rely upon the insured's breach to discharge their liability under the contract of insurance if the insured proves that 'the non-compliance with the term could not have increased the risk of the loss which actually occurred in the circumstances in which it occurred'.

7.99   The way in which ss 10 and 11 of the Insurance Act 2015 interact can be illustrated by the following example. The terms of a theoretical contract of professional indemnity insurance include a warranty by which the insured warrants that all work will be carried or supervised by a person who has been qualified for at least 5 years. This term would be both a warranty so as to fall within the scope of s 10 and a term which fell within the scope of s 11. Work is then carried out by employee A, who is neither qualified nor supervised so that the insured is in breach of warranty. The result is that insurers' liability under the contract of insurance is suspended pursuant to s 10(2), but this is subject to s 11. While the contract is suspended a loss occurs (ie the insured is held liable in damages to a third party claimant). The loss arises from work carried out by employee B, who has been qualified for 10 years, so that the insured can show that the breach of warranty could not have increased the risk of the claim which has been made. The insured can therefore rely upon s 11 and require insurers to meet the claim.

Conditions precedent

7.100   It is usual for policies of professional indemnity insurance to include terms requiring the insured to take certain action, particularly upon a claim being made against

---

[176]   [2015] NZHC 862 (discussed in para 9.85).

him or upon him becoming aware of matters with the potential to give rise to a claim. Compliance with such terms can be a condition precedent to the insured's right to an indemnity. Whether they have that effect or not depends upon their true construction in the light of the policy.[177]

If a term is a condition precedent, then failure to comply with it will provide insur- **7.101**
ers with a defence without any need to prove that they have suffered any detriment by reason of that non-compliance.[178]

As with warranties, the easiest way to make a term of an insurance policy a con- **7.102**
dition precedent is to state in terms that it is a condition precedent.[179] This can be done either by saying so in the particular clause or by a general provision that due observance of the conditions is a condition precedent to insurers' liability.[180] Where insurers put forward a term without specifying that it is a condition precedent and then contend that it is a condition precedent, they may well find that, having failed to avail themselves of the opportunity to make it clear that compliance was a condition precedent, the position is unclear so that, applying the *contra proferentem* rule, the issue is to be decided in favour of the insured.[181] It will usually be particularly difficult for insurers to establish that a term which is not specified to be a condition precedent is actually a condition precedent if it appears in a policy in which other terms are expressly identified as conditions precedent.[182] Insurers are taken to know the various options to them and have access to advice if they wish to make provisions more or less stringent.[183]

---

[177] The suggestion in *Alfred McAlpine Plc v BAI (Run-Off) Ltd* [2000] 1 Lloyd's Rep 437 that there was a category of 'innominate' terms, which, if the consequences of breach were sufficiently serious, would entitle insures to reject a particular claim, but not to repudiate the entire contract of insurance, was rejected by the Court of Appeal in *Friends Provident Life and Pensions Ltd v Sirius International Insurance Corporation* [2005] EWCA Civ 601; [2005] 2 Lloyd's Rep 517.

[178] *Pioneer Concrete (UK) Ltd v National Employers' Mutual General Insurance Association Ltd* [1985] 2 All ER 395. See also *Total Graphics Ltd v AGF Insurance Ltd* [1997] 1 Lloyd's Rep 599, at 608.

[179] In giving the Opinion of the Privy Council in *Diab v Regent Insurance Co Ltd* [2006] UKPC 29; [2007] 1 WLR 797, Lord Scott suggested that, even where a clause was stated to be a condition precedent, not every requirement in the clause would necessarily be a condition precedent. Time will tell whether this suggestion is developed by the English Courts.

[180] *Pilkington United Kingdom Ltd v CGU Insurance Plc* [2004] EWCA Civ 23; [2004] Lloyd's Rep IR 891, at [63]–[65] per Potter LJ, with whom the other members of the Court of Appeal agreed. This was followed in *AXA Insurance UK Plc v Thermonex Ltd* [2012] EWHC B10(Merc); [2013] Lloyd's Rep IR 323. See also *London Guarantie Company v Fearnley* (1880) 5 App Cas 911.

[181] See, for example, *Cox v Bankside Members Agency Ltd* [1995] 2 Lloyd's Rep 437, discussed in paras 7.71–7.72 and *MDIS Ltd v Swinbank* [1999] Lloyd's Rep IR 516, at [28] per Mance LJ.

[182] *Cox v Bankside Members Agency Ltd* [1995] 2 Lloyd's Rep 437, at 453 per Phillips J. See also (1) *Alfred McAlpine Plc v BAI (Run-Off) Ltd* [1998] 2 Lloyd's Rep 694, per Colman J at 700, citing *Stonehouse v Ocean Railway and General Accident Insurance Co* (1887) 19 QBD 237; and (2) *Tullow Uganda Ltd v Heritage Oil and Gas Ltd* [2014] EWCA Civ 1048; [2014] 2 CLC 61.

[183] *Friends Provident Life and Pensions Ltd v Sirius International Insurance Corporation* [2005] EWCA Civ 601; [2005] 2 Lloyd's Rep 517, at [28] per Mance LJ, with whom Sir William Aldous agreed.

7.103 However, as with warranties, it is possible for a term to be a condition precedent without it being expressly designated as such. This result was achieved in *HLB Kidsons (a firm) v Lloyd's Underwriters*.[184] The clause in question required the insured to give notice to insurers 'as soon as practicable' of circumstance of which it became aware during the policy period which might give rise to a claim. The clause continued:

> Such notice having been given any loss or claim to which that circumstance has given rise which is subsequently made after the expiration of the period specified in the Schedule shall be deemed for the purpose of this Insurance to have been made during the subsistence hereof.

7.104 Compliance with another provision in the policy as to giving notice was expressed to be a condition precedent to the insured's right to be indemnified. Despite the absence of similar words in the clause in question, the Court of Appeal held that the requirement that notice be given as soon as practicable was a condition precedent to the right to the extension of cover in respect of any claims made outside the policy period arising from the notified circumstances. If it were not a condition precedent, then there would be no limit to the time by which a notification could be made.[185] That would defeat the entire purpose of a 'claims made' policy from insurers' perspective, namely the avoidance of uncertainty as to their long-term exposure.[186]

7.105 The *HLB Kidsons* case shows how terms which define the cover under the policy are likely to be strictly applied. Such terms are not merely procedural: they go to the extent of cover. As was said in *Gulf Insurance Co v Dolon, Fertig and Curtis*:[187]

> If a court were to allow an extension of reporting time after the end of the policy period, such is tantamount to an extension of coverage to the insured gratis, something for which the insurer has not bargained. This extension of coverage, by the court, so very different from a mere condition of the policy, in effect rewrites the contract between the two parties. This we cannot and will not do.[188]

7.106 As with breach of warranty, insurers' right to rely on a defence of breach of a condition precedent can only be lost by estoppel.[189]

---

[184] [2008] EWCA Civ 1206; [2009] 1 Lloyd's Rep 8.

[185] The notification clause which was held not to be a condition precedent in *Cox v Bankside Members Agency Ltd* [1995] 2 Lloyd's Rep 437 required immediate notice (which was more suggestive of a condition precedent than 'as soon as practicable'), but also required notice to be given during the policy period. There was therefore no problem of enduring uncertainty in that case if compliance with the requirement to give immediate notice was not a condition precedent. It is likely that the requirement to give notice during the policy year was strict.

[186] See paras 2.03–2.04.

[187] (Fla 1983) 433 So.2d 512, at 512.

[188] See also *Pacific Employers Insurance Co v Superior Court* 221 Cal Rptr 779 (1990) and *Slater v Lawyers' Mutual Insurance Company* 278 Cal Rptr 479 (1991).

[189] *Kosmar Villa Holidays Plc v Trustees of Syndicate 1243* [2008] EWCA Civ 147; [2008] Lloyd's Rep IR 489. See further, para 7.90.

Exclusion clauses

Exclusion clauses in policies of professional indemnity insurance are not the same **7.107** as contractual provisions which exclude or limit a remedy in damages for breach of contract. They serve to define the cover provided. In some policies, very wide insuring provisions are then refined by a series of exclusion clauses which have the effect of limiting cover to liability to third parties for losses caused by breach of contract or other duty in the provision of professional services and advice. For example, liability for trading debts would usually be excluded.[190]

While any ambiguity in a clause excluding what would otherwise be a liability of **7.108** the party who put forward that clause should be resolved against that party and while it will not readily be assumed that the other party intended such clauses to be wider in scope than they expressly and unequivocally provide, there is less reason to adopt such an approach to clauses which serve to define cover. Moreover, the court does not start by looking for an ambiguity. Rather it seeks to construe the clause in the usual way and only if that process reveals a genuine ambiguity does give preference to the construction which favours the insured.[191]

Where the language in such clauses is clear, the courts will give effect to it accord- **7.109** ingly. For example, in *McCann v Switzerland Insurance Australia Ltd*[192] the High Court construed an exclusion of cover for liability 'brought about by the dishonest and fraudulent act or omission of the Assured', rejecting the insured's argument as to the effect of the words 'brought about', which would have deprived the clause of much of its effect.[193] In the same way, in *Baulderstone Hornibrook Engineering Pty*

---

[190] See further, paras 9.76–9.79, but see *Impact Funding Solutions Ltd v Barrington Support Services Ltd (Formerly Lawyers at Work Ltd)* [2015] EWCA Civ 31; [2015] Lloyd's Rep IR 371.

[191] *Direct Dial Insurance v McGeowan* [2003] EWCA Civ 1606; [2004] Lloyd's Rep IR 595, at [13] per Auld LJ, with whom the other members of the Court of Appeal agreed. See also *Trustees Executors Ltd v QBE Insurance (International) Ltd* [2010] NZCA 608; (2010) 16 ANZ Insurance Cases 61-874, at [38]–[40] and *Horwood v Land of Leather Ltd* [2010] EWHC 546 (Comm); [2010] Lloyd's Rep IR 453, at [55] per Teare J.

[192] [2000] HCA 6; (2000) 203 CLR 579.

[193] In *Macdonald v C E Heath Underwriting and Insurance (Australia) Ltd* [1997] NSWSC 185; (1997) 9 ANZIC 61.362, the relevant clause excluded an indemnity in respect of claims: '(b) by or on behalf of any person operated or controlled by the Assured or by any employees, nominees or trustees of the Assured and in which the Assured or any member of the Assured's family has a direct or indirect financial interest; (c) by any person advised or induced by the Assured or employees of the Assured to invest in or lend money to any person being a person referred to in the preceding subclause or to any person named as the Assured under this Policy …' The sole principal of the insured was the mother of a consultant employed by it. The consultant advised A to invest in a business which failed. That business had been started by the consultant and one of the insured's clients. It was held that the exclusion applied and the consultant was not entitled to an indemnity.

In *Smart v AAI Ltd* [2015] NSWSC 392 an exclusion clause was construed so as to ascertain its meaning and effect and was found to be of wide application. The exclusion clause in a policy of professional indemnity insurance for finance brokers excluded cover for claims 'arising directly or indirectly from or in respect of any liability which is assumed by the Insured outside the normal course of the Professional Services'. The insured had gone outside the normal course of business as a finance broker by borrowing sums from the third party claimants, purportedly so as to lend them on to the insured's clients. The clause was construed in accordance with the decision of the High Court

Ltd v Gordian Runoff Ltd[194] insurers under a professional indemnity policy insuring engineers relied upon an exclusion clause which provided that there should be no cover in respect of claims:

> arising out of construction work performed involving the means, methods, techniques, sequences, procedures and use of equipment, of any nature whatsoever which are employed by the Insured's contracting staff or others in executing any phase of any Project.

The New South Wales Court of Appeal held that the commercial purpose of the clause was clear and that it should be interpreted and applied accordingly.[195]

---

of Australia in *Darlington Futures Ltd v Delco Australia Pty Ltd* [1986] HCA 82; (19086) 161 CLR 500, at 510 ('the interpretation of an exclusion clause is to be determined by construing the clause according to its natural and ordinary meaning, read in the light of the contract as a whole, thereby giving due weight to the context in which the clause appears including the nature and object of the contract and, where appropriate, construing the clause *contra proferentem* in the case of ambiguity'). Beech-Jones J held that, so construed, the clause was widely drafted and encompassed the conduct of the insured which gave rise to the claim. That conduct involved the insured acting as lender rather than broker.

[194] [2008] NSWCA 243: see further, paras 9.83–9.84.

[195] Ibid at [259]. See also *Littlewood v Resource Underwriting Pty Ltd* [2006] NSWCA 62, where the professional indemnity insurance of an investment adviser excluded cover in respect of any claim: 'arising from investment, or any advice, inducement or recommendation to invest, or endorsement or opinion favouring investment, in any fund, scheme, arrangement, or entity in which there is or was at any relevant time a Related Interest unless shareholdings in public listed companies ...'

'Related Interest' was broadly defined and the New South Wales Court of Appeal held that the purpose of the exclusion was clear and that there was no reason not to give effect to it.

8

FRAUD AND DISHONESTY

A. Fraud, Dishonesty, and Professional Indemnity Insurance

8.01 It is not possible to obtain insurance against liability for one's own fraud or dishonesty. Apart from considerations of public policy,[1] it is implicit in the nature of insurance that loss caused by the deliberate dishonesty of the insured is not covered, just as there is no cover for any loss caused by the insured's wilful misconduct.[2] As Lord Atkin said in *Beresford v Royal Insurance Company Ltd*:[3]

> On ordinary principles of insurance law an assured cannot by his own deliberate act cause the event upon which the insurance money is payable. The insurers have not agreed to pay on that happening. The fire assured cannot recover if he intentionally burns down his house, nor the marine assured if he scuttles his ship, nor

---

[1] Cf *Haseldine v Hosken* [1933] 1 KB 822, where the Court of Appeal held that a solicitor could not recover under his professional indemnity insurance in respect of loss caused by having entered champertous agreements. See also *Goddard & Smith v Frew* [1939] 4 All ER 358, at 361–2 per Goddard LJ and *Lancashire County Council v Municipal Mutual Insurance Ltd* [1997] QB 897, at 907 per Simon Brown LJ and 911 per Staughton LJ.

[2] *Arab Bank plc v Zurich Insurance Co* [1999] 1 Lloyd's Rep 262, at 272. See also s 55(2)(c) of the Marine Insurance Act 1906.

[3] [1938] AC 586, at 595. As Blair J said in *Sea Glory Maritime Co v Al Sagr National Insurance Co (the Nancy)* [2013] EWHC 2116 (Comm); [2014] 1 Lloyd's Rep 14 at [298]: 'a claim under a contract of insurance will not be enforced where the effect of enforcing the claim would be to enable the assured to profit from his own crime and/or to be indemnified against the adverse consequences of his own wrongdoing'.

the life assured if he deliberately ends his own life. This is not the result of public policy, but of the correct construction of the contract.

However, there is no bar in principle to the provision of insurance against vicarious liability for fraud or dishonesty.[4]

8.02 The professional indemnity insurance policies considered in earlier authorities, including the leading case of *West Wake Price & Co v Ching*,[5] did not provide any cover for vicarious liability for fraud or dishonesty.[6] Such cover was available as part of a policy of fidelity insurance, which could be obtained separately from professional indemnity insurance. It was not part of the cover provided by professional indemnity insurance.[7] However, it is now common, but not universal, for professional indemnity policies to extend cover to vicarious liability for fraud and dishonesty, while continuing to exclude cover for those individuals who have acted fraudulently or dishonestly.

8.03 Where such cover is provided, issues arise as to insurers' obligations to those suspected or accused of fraud or dishonesty pending determination of their guilt[8] and, in determining their guilt or innocence, as to what has to be proved. Where such cover is excluded, it is necessary to know what must be shown to establish misconduct falling within the exclusion.

B. Fraud and Dishonesty

A jury question?

8.04 On one view the answer to the question whether a particular person has acted dishonestly in particular circumstances is a straightforward matter which does not require elaborate analysis of legal authority. As Etherton J said in *Mortgage Express Ltd v S Newman & Co (No 3)*:[9]

> In most situations there is little difficulty in identifying how an honest person would behave. Honest people do not intentionally deceive others to their detriment. Honest people do not knowingly take others' property. Unless there is a very good and compelling reason, an honest person does not participate in a transaction

---

[4] *Goddard & Smith v Frew* [1939] 4 All ER 358, at 361–2 per Goddard LJ. See also *Lancashire County Council v Municipal Mutual Insurance Ltd* [1997] QB 897, at 908 per Simon Brown LJ and *Stone & Rolls Ltd (in liquidation) v Moore Stephens (a firm)* [2009] UKHL 39; [2009] 1 AC 1391, at [27] per Lord Phillips.

[5] [1957] 1 WLR 45.

[6] See also *Davies v Hosken* [1937] 3 All ER 192 and *Goddard & Smith v Frew* [1939] 4 All ER 358.

[7] So, where the insured was sued both for vicarious liability for the fraud of his employee and for his own negligence in failing to supervise the employee adequately, he would only be covered under his professional indemnity insurance if his own negligence was the proximate cause of his liability: *West Wake Price & Co v Ching* [1957] 1 WLR 45. See further, paras 9.92–9.105.

[8] As to which see paras 12.07–12.15.

[9] [2001] Lloyd's Rep PN 669, at 673–4.

if he knows it involves a misapplication of trust assets to the detriment of the ben-eficiaries. Nor does an honest person in such a case deliberately close his eyes and ears, or deliberately not ask questions, lest he learn something he would rather not know, and then proceed regardless.[10]

It is important not to lose sight of this when considering the body of authority which has accumulated as to what constitutes dishonesty.

Nevertheless, as both the facts of *Mortgage Express Ltd v S Newman & Co* itself[11] and a series of decisions at the highest level show, deciding whether a person has acted dishonestly or not is not always a straightforward task. **8.05**

Dishonesty in criminal law

In criminal law, for a person to have been dishonest he must have acted in a way which is dishonest by the standards of ordinary and honest people. In other words, his conduct, viewed objectively, must have been dishonest. However, he must also have understood that he was acting contrary to those standards. As Lord Lane LC explained in *R v Ghosh*:[12] **8.06**

> In determining whether the prosecution has proved that the defendant was act-ing dishonestly, a jury must first of all decide whether according to the ordinary standards of reasonable and honest people what was done was dishonest. If it was not dishonest by those standards, that is the end of the matter and the prosecution fails. If it was dishonest by those standards, then the jury must consider whether the defendant himself must have realised that what he was doing was by those standards dishonest. In most cases, where the actions are obviously dishonest by ordinary standards, there will be no doubt about it. It will be obvious that the defendant himself knew that he was acting dishonestly.

It does not matter that he disagreed with those standards, but he must have under-stood that he was transgressing them.[13]

This test is also applied in disciplinary proceedings against professionals where the charge involves dishonesty.[14] The requirement that the person accused of dishon-esty should have appreciated that he was acting contrary to the ordinary standards of reasonable and honest people is not satisfied if the person should have appreci-ated this from facts known to him, but, without deliberately shutting his eyes to the obvious, he did not do so. Negligence, even to a high degree, is not dishonesty. So, for the purposes of disciplinary proceedings, a solicitor who should have appreci-ated that he was taking part in a number of dubious transactions, in that they had features which indicated that they were fraudulent, but who failed to do so, was not **8.07**

---

[10] See also *Mortgage Express Ltd v S Newman & Co (No 2)* [2000] Lloyd's Rep PN 745, per Aldous LJ at [40].

[11] See paras 8.23–8.26.

[12] *R v Ghosh* [1982] QB 1053, at 1064.

[13] Ibid.

[14] *Bryant v Law Society* [2007] EWHC 3043 (Admin); [2009] 1 WLR 163, at [153]–[154].

acting dishonestly when he participated in those transactions. He had honestly not appreciated that he was, or might well be, involved in a series of frauds.[15]

8.08 Although conveniently broken into objective and subjective elements, in practice the two elements are at least closely related and, possibly, overlap. For example, a person who took property which he honestly, but wrongly, believed was his, would not be acting contrary to the ordinary standards of reasonable and honest people. So his misunderstanding could be said to be relevant to the objective test in that it forms part of the conduct which is to be assessed against the standards of reasonably and honest people. And his misunderstanding is certainly relevant to the subjective test. The interaction between objective analysis of a person's acts against general standards of honest behaviour and that person's own understanding of the circumstances in which he performs those acts poses difficulties in the area of civil liability as well.

Dishonesty in civil law

Fraud: the tort of deceit

8.09 In order to establish liability for the tort of deceit it must be proved that a statement of fact was made with the intention of inducing the person to whom it was made to act in reliance on it and it must have been relied upon. The statement must be false and the person who made it must either have known that it was false or have been reckless as to whether it was true or not.[16] In this context, reckless means not caring whether the statement was true or false. As Bowen LJ explained in *Angus v Clifford*:[17]

> the old direction, time out of mind, was this, did he know that the statement was false, was he conscious when he made it that it was false, or if not, did he make it without knowing whether it was false, and without caring? Not caring, in that context, did not mean not taking care, it meant indifference to the truth, the moral obliquity which consists in a wilful disregard of the importance of truth ...

8.10 This does not require any finding that the maker of the statement realised that he was transgressing the ordinary standards of reasonable and honest people. However, in this context 'conscious knowledge of falsity must always amount to wickedness and dishonesty'.[18]

---

[15] Ibid.

[16] *Derry v Peek* (1889) 14 App Cas 337, at 374 per Lord Herschell.

[17] [1891] 2 Ch 449, at 471. See also *AIC Ltd v ITS Testing Services (UK) Ltd* ('*The Kriti Palm*') [2006] EWCA Civ 1601; [2007] 1 Lloyd's Rep 555, at [257] per Rix LJ and *Versloot Dredging BV v HDI Gerling Industrie Versicherung AG* [2013] EWHC 1666 (Comm); [2013] 2 Lloyd's Rep 131, at [155] per Popplewell J.

[18] *Armstrong v Strain* [1951] 1 TLR 856, at 871 per Devlin J. As to the relationship between fraud and dishonesty see (1) *Kensington International Ltd v Republic of Congo* [2007] EWCA Civ 1128; [2008] 1 WLR 1144 at [59] per Moore-Bick LJ, with whom the other members of the Court of Appeal agreed, and (2) in *Aviva Insurance Ltd v Brown* [2011] EWHC 362 (QB); [2012] Lloyd's Rep IR 211 at [61]–[73] per Eder J.

Dishonest assistance

The question of what is and is not dishonesty has arisen in a number of fairly recent **8.11** decisions concerning liability for assisting in a breach of trust. The first is the decision of the Privy Council in *Royal Brunei Airlines Sdn Bhd v Tan*.[19] Giving the Opinion of the Privy Council, Lord Nicholls explained that in this context dishonesty 'means simply not acting as an honest person would in the circumstances'.[20] Lord Nicholls explained that this is an objective standard, in that:[21]

> Honesty is not an optional scale, with higher or lower values according to the moral standards of each individual. If a person knowingly appropriates another's property, he will not escape a finding of dishonesty simply because he sees nothing wrong in such behaviour.[22]

However, Lord Nicholls also considered that there is a 'strong subjective element' in dishonesty, because the propriety of a person's conduct is to be judged on the actual knowledge of that person at the time, rather than upon the knowledge which a reasonable person would have had in the circumstances.[23]

Lord Nicholls explained that, while in many cases it will be obvious that a person **8.12** is acting dishonestly, other cases will be less clear. He gave the example of a solicitor who is instructed to facilitate a transaction which might constitute a breach of trust. The solicitor was expected 'to attain the standard which would be observed by an honest person placed in those circumstances'.[24] What that required in terms of action would depend upon the particular facts:[25]

> Ultimately, in most cases, an honest person should have little difficulty in knowing whether a proposed transaction, or his participation in it, would offend the normally accepted standards of honest conduct.

The test propounded by Lord Nicholls in the *Royal Brunei* case involved an object- **8.13** ive assessment of a person's acts, in the light of that person's subjective knowledge and understanding of the relevant circumstances.

The *Royal Brunei* case was considered by the House of Lords in *Twinsectra Ltd* **8.14** *v Yardley*.[26] In that case, the defendant solicitor (L) had been acting for a client (Y) who wished to purchase a property. The claimant company was prepared to

---

[19] [1995] 2 AC 378.
[20] Ibid at 389.
[21] Ibid at 389.
[22] See also *Walker v Stones* [2001] QB 902, at 939 per Sir Christopher Slade: 'A person may in some cases act dishonestly, according to the ordinary use of language, even though he genuinely believes that his action is morally justified. The penniless thief, for example, who picks the pocket of the multi-millionaire is dishonest even though he genuinely considers the theft is morally justified as a fair redistribution of wealth and that he is not therefore being dishonest.'
[23] [1995] 2 AC 378 at 389.
[24] Ibid at 390.
[25] Ibid at 391.
[26] [2002] UKHL 12; [2002] 2 AC 164.

lend money to the solicitor's client, but only upon terms that the loan was secured by a solicitor's undertaking in a form which L was unwilling to give. Another solicitor (S) was prepared to give the required undertaking and did so. S then transferred the money to L, who, ignoring the implications of S's undertaking, paid it away on the instructions of Y.

8.15 L knew of the terms of S's undertaking, but thought that once he had received the money, it was at the disposal of Y and that he should comply with Y's instructions. L considered that it was between S and Y whether Y applied the money in accordance with an assurance which Y had given S and whether Y's application of the money would mean that S was in breach of his undertaking. On the basis of this honest, if misguided, understanding, the House of Lords held by a majority that L should not have been found to have been dishonest.

8.16 The majority did so in terms which suggested that the subjective test in criminal law[27] was also required to establish dishonesty for the purposes of liability for assisting a breach of trust.[28] It should, however, be noted that in the *Twinsectra* case the trial judge, Carnwath J, had held that no trust had been established by S's undertaking. That finding had been reversed by the Court of Appeal, whose decision on this point was upheld by the House of Lords. Given that a Judge of the Chancery Division had held that, when received by L, the money was not subject to a trust, it would have been harsh to find that L had acted dishonestly for failing to appreciate that he was being asked to assist in a breach of trust.

8.17 Whatever its merits on the facts, the *Twinsectra* case was taken to have required 'consciousness that one is transgressing ordinary standards of honest behaviour'[29] for a person to be found to have acted dishonestly. The position has been clarified by the decision of the Privy Council in *Barlow Clowes International Ltd (in liquidation) v Eurotrust International Ltd*.[30] There, giving the Opinion of the Privy Council, Lord Hoffmann explained the decision of the majority in the *Twinsectra* case. What was required for a person to be found to have acted dishonestly was that:[31]

> his knowledge of the transaction had to be such as to render his participation contrary to normally acceptable standards of honest conduct. It did not require that he should have had reflections about what those normally acceptable standards were.

In the *Twinsectra* case, L had known all the facts, but his understanding of them was that, upon payment of the money to him by S, it was free from the undertaking which S had given to the lender and so L was obliged to pay it in accordance with

---

[27] See para 8.06.
[28] [2002] UKHL 12; [2002] 2 AC 164, at [20] per Lord Hoffmann and at [36] per Lord Hutton.
[29] Ibid at [20] per Lord Hoffmann.
[30] [2005] UKPC 37; [2006] 1 WLR 1476.
[31] Ibid at [15].

Y's instructions. On this understanding of the transaction, L had not transgressed against the normal standards of honesty.[32]

The distinction, which was obscured by some of the language used in the *Twinsectra* **8.18** case, is between a person's subjective knowledge and understanding of the facts and their significance on the one hand and a person's view as to whether, given his knowledge and understanding, he is transgressing the standard of reasonable and honest people. The former are the material which is to be considered objectively. The latter forms part of the criminal test, but not of the civil test.

The result is that the test of dishonesty is predominantly objective: 'Did the con- **8.19** duct of the defendant fall below the normally accepted standard?'[33] It does not matter whether the person accused of dishonesty himself realized or even considered whether he was falling below that standard. However, the objective test is to be applied to that person's conduct in the light of his actual knowledge, rather than on the basis that he had the knowledge which a reasonable person in his position would have had.[34] In this regard it is not necessary to know every detail. It is enough to know sufficient that an honest man would not have proceeded.[35] As Millett J said in *Agip (Africa) Ltd v Jackson*:[36]

> it is no answer for a man charged with having knowingly assisted in a fraudulent and dishonest scheme to say that he thought that it was 'only' a breach of exchange control or 'only' a case of tax evasion. It is not necessary that he should have been aware of the precise nature of the fraud or even of the identity of its victim. A man who consciously assists others by making arrangements which he knows are calculated to conceal what is happening from a third party, takes the risk that they are part of a fraud practised on that party.

So, while the test is predominantly objective, the actual understanding of the per- **8.20** son accused of dishonesty has to be considered: 'Carelessness is not dishonesty'.[37] While it is sufficient if the person accused of dishonesty 'knows of the elements of the transaction which make it dishonest',[38] that knowledge must extend to an

---

[32] Ibid at [17].

[33] *Abou-Rahmah v Abacha* [2006] EWCA Civ 1492; [2007] 1 Lloyd's Rep 115, at [66] per Arden LJ. It is for the Court to decide what that standard is and it is irrelevant that there may be 'a body of opinion which regards the ordinary standard of honest behaviour as being set too high': *Starglade Properties Ltd v Nash* [2010] EWCA Civ 1314; [2011] Lloyd's Rep FC 102, at [32] per Sir Andrew Morritt C with whom the other members of the Court of Appeal agreed.

[34] Ibid, referring to *Royal Brunei Airlines Sdn Bhd v Tan* [1995] 2 AC 378 at 389.

[35] *Barlow Clowes International Ltd (in liquidation) v Eurotrust International Ltd* [2005] UKPC 37; [2006] 1 WLR 1476, at [28].

[36] [1990] Ch 265, at 295. See also *Abou-Rahmah v Abacha* [2006] EWCA Civ 1492; [2007] 1 Lloyd's Rep 115, at [38]–[39] per Rix LJ. The Courts have not spoken with one voice on this point, but the view expressed by Millet J and Rix LJ represents the current law: *Al Khudairi v Abbey Brokers Ltd* [2010] EWHC 1486 (Ch); [2010] PNLR 32, at [139] per Newey J.

[37] *Royal Brunei Airlines Sdn Bhd v Tan* [1995] 2 AC 378, at 389 per Lord Nicholls. See also *Paragon Finance Plc v DB Thakerar & Co* [1999] 1 All ER 400, at 418.

[38] *Abou-Rahmah v Abacha* [2006] EWCA Civ 1492; [2007] 1 Lloyd's Rep 115, at [59] per Arden LJ. Arden LJ's approach was adopted by Newey J in *Al Khudairi v Abbey Brokers Ltd* [2010] EWHC 1486 (Ch); [2010] PNLR 32, at [134].

appreciation of the significance of those elements as well as to their existence. So, in *A-G of Zambia v Meer Care & Desai*,[39] when reversing a finding that a solicitor had dishonestly assisted a breach of trust, the Court of Appeal said:[40]

> It seems to us that the judge failed to give adequate consideration to the possibility that [the solicitor] was honest but not competent, and was not in truth knowledgeable or experienced in relation to the sort of transaction with which he was faced, and in particular did not really understand what was involved in money-laundering.

Fraud and dishonesty in the context of professional indemnity insurance

8.21 In the context of professional indemnity insurance, the test for dishonesty which emerges from the decisions on dishonest assistance in a breach of trust is usually the most appropriate. However, where there is a specific form of civil liability which involves fraud or dishonesty (eg the tort of deceit), the relevant test will be that for the particular form of liability.

Distinguishing fraud from incompetence

8.22 While, as in other areas of dishonesty, the application of this test to the facts of a particular case will be straightforward,[41] in others it may be difficult to decide whether a professional person is guilty of incompetence, even gross incompetence, or of dishonesty.

8.23 The litigation between the Solicitors Indemnity Fund ('SIF') and Miss Newman, a solicitor, provides a helpful illustration of the difficulties which can arise. SIF provided professional indemnity to Miss Newman, but subject to an exclusion 'in respect of any loss arising out of any claim … in respect of any dishonest or fraudulent act or omission'. Miss Newman had been instructed in respect of two property transactions which transpired to be mortgage frauds. Both transactions had a number of odd features, which, even before the issue of the Law Society's 'Green Card' listing warning signs of mortgage fraud, might have been thought to cause concern to an honest solicitor.

---

[39] [2008] EWCA Civ 1007; [2008] Lloyd's Rep FC 587.

[40] Ibid at [267].

[41] Eg *Abbey National Plc v Solicitors' Indemnity Fund Ltd* [1997] PNLR 306. The transaction as represented to the mortgagee was the acquisition of a lease of 125 years. The existing lease was only for 47 years and, although it had been intended to acquire an extension, that was never done. The solicitor did not inform the mortgagee of this and made several false representations to the effect that the transaction had been completed in accordance with his instructions. The balance of the mortgage advance was not accounted for. Steel J had no hesitation in finding that the solicitor had acted dishonestly.

Cheltenham & Gloucester Plc v Sun Alliance & London Insurance Plc, 21 May 2002, Outer House, Court of Session (Lord Clarke), *Goldsmith Williams (a firm) v Travelers Insurance Company Ltd* [2010] EWHC 26 (QB); [2010] Lloyd's Rep IR 309 and *Halliwells LLP v NES Solicitors* [2011] EWHC 947 (QB); [2011] PNLR 30 are other clear cases.

In relation to the first, the vendor's solicitor told her that he had received the deposit **8.24** directly from Miss Newman's client. Miss Newman received £196,000 from the lenders. She deducted her costs and disbursements from this sum and paid the balance to the vendor's solicitors. This left a shortfall on the purchase price of £2,189. Unusually, Miss Newman was told that the vendor would not push for that balance and was content with the money received. So Miss Newman's client paid no money towards the purchase through Miss Newman's client account and the vendor waived part of the agreed price. The only money which Miss Newman saw came from the mortgage lender.

In the second transaction, Miss Newman's client was buying by way of sub-sale. **8.25** Miss Newman's client was apparently paying £275,000, whereas her vendor was paying only £110,000. As with the other transaction, no money other than the mortgage advance passed through Miss Newman's client account. Miss Newman charged a noticeably large fee for her services, justified by the fact that she was going on holiday during the relevant period.

The issue of Miss Newman's honesty or dishonesty was tried twice, after the Court **8.26** of Appeal ordered a re-trial on appeal from the first trial.[42] Both trial judges acquitted Miss Newman of dishonesty. At the second trial,[43] Etherton J declined to find that Miss Newman had acted dishonestly by willfully shutting her eyes to what was going on or by failing to make the enquiries which an honest solicitor would have made in the circumstances. She had simply failed to identify and consider the various odd features.

In assessing the credibility of the insured's explanation of his conduct and under- **8.27** standing, regard should be had to the insured's 'personal attributes … such as his experience and intelligence, and the reason why he acted as he did'.[44] This may point to the conclusion that the insured must have had sufficient understanding to have acted dishonestly. For example, in *McCarthy v St Paul International Insurance Co Ltd*[45] the insured was a firm of solicitors which conducted a private mortgage lending business. This involved the firm soliciting funds from potential lenders. The business was managed for them by Mr Blackadder, who was not a solicitor, but who had banking experience. Mr Blackadder prepared an 'investment summary' for a particular lending opportunity which materially overstated the net worth of the intended borrower. It did so by including the full value of assets which were held by the borrower on trust for others or were owned jointly with his wife (who had a half share) or were in a trust controlled by the borrower's father. This was clear from information provided to Mr Blackadder. The trial judge held that, given his banking experience, Mr Blackadder must have known that these assets did not

---

[42] *Mortgage Express Ltd v S Newman & Co (No 2)* [2000] Lloyd's Rep PN 745.
[43] *Mortgage Express Ltd v S Newman & Co (No 3)* [2001] Lloyd's Rep PN 669.
[44] *Royal Brunei Airlines Sdn Bhd v Tan* [1995] 2 AC 378, at 391 per Lord Nicholls.
[45] [2007] FCAFC 28.

belong to the borrower: it could not have been an honest mistake. He therefore found that Mr Blackadder had acted dishonestly in taking them into account when preparing the 'investment summary'. This reasoning and conclusion were upheld on appeal.[46]

Deliberate breaches of duty and dishonesty

8.28   Where an insured has deliberately breached a duty owed to a client, he may well be found to have acted dishonestly. This will usually be the case where the motive for the deliberate breach was the insured's own interest. This was the basis upon which the insured solicitor in *Harle v Legal Practitioners Liability Committee*[47] was held not to have been merely incompetent and naive, but dishonest. He had acted for a client who had put money into a prime bank guarantee scheme. As is typical of such frauds, the scheme offered a return of 1000 per cent over 12 months, with the funds invested guaranteed by a 'prime bank'. The insured was to receive 10 per cent of the profits. It was, of course, too good to be true and the money was lost. Tellingly, the insured's own bank had refused to become involved, warning him that the proposed scheme was likely to be a 'scam'. The trial judge considered that while, through a combination of 'stupidity, gullibility, incompetence and cupidity, a solicitor might permit his clients to enter an investment proposal such as this one', to do so in the face of the bank's warning was only consistent with dishonesty. The Court of Appeal of the Supreme Court of Victoria agreed. The insured had deliberately chosen to put his own personal interest in a share of the promised profits ahead of his duty to his clients. He had hoped that the scheme would work, but had deliberately chosen not to warn his client of the clear risk that it would not, and so had acted dishonestly.[48]

8.29   The earlier decision of the High Court of Australia in *McCann v Switzerland Insurance Australia Ltd*[49] was to like effect, although there were different views as to the basis for the finding of dishonesty in that case. The insured were a firm of solicitors. One partner in the insured firm put his client's money into a fraudulent prime bank guarantee scheme, as part of which the partner took a secret profit, and which resulted in the loss of the money. The partner had hoped the scheme would work, but did not inform his client of the reasons for doubting that it would. By a majority of four to one the Court held that the partner had been dishonest. Gleeson CJ said:[50]

> [The partner] did not intend that [his client] should lose the $US8.55 million. But he paid it away, in breach of his fiduciary responsibilities, without proper (or any) security knowing there was a risk of its loss, and impelled by his own need for

---

[46]   Ibid at [49].
[47]   [2003] VSCA 133.
[48]   Ibid at [50]. See also *Schipp v Cameron* [1998] NSWSC 997 at [933].
[49]   [2000] HCA 65; (2000) 203 CLR 579.
[50]   Ibid at [17].

money. He preferred his personal interests to those of his client. He permitted his urgent need to make a secret commission to prevail over his duty to protect his client's funds. The Court of Appeal was right to find that his conduct in relation to the entire $US8.7 million was obviously dishonest and probably fraudulent.

Gaudron J held that the partner had been under a duty to inform his client of **8.30** certain information which pointed against proceeding with the transaction and that his failure to do so was deliberate, because the partner must have realized that it was his duty to do so. The only explanation for the deliberate failure to do so was that the partner had chosen to conceal the information from his client so he could make his secret profit. It followed that the omission was dishonest.[51] Kirby J agreed that the partner 'would not have imperilled the fund but for the dishonest self-interest which he was bent on pursuing', although he considered that the partner had provided false and dishonest information about the scheme to his client.[52] Hayne J considered that it was the partner's intention to make a secret profit, which meant that he was not only in breach of fiduciary duty, but dishonest.[53]

In other cases, the absence of apparent financial motive may weigh against a finding **8.31** of dishonesty. As Gaudron J said in the *McCann* case, the answer to the question whether a person has acted dishonestly will usually be answered by considering whether the act or omission in question was motivated by a desire to conceal the truth or obtain an advantage to which that person knew he was not entitled.[54]

The standard of proof

If insurers wish to rely upon any exclusion of cover in respect of fraud and dishon- **8.32** esty, they must prove that the insured was fraudulent or dishonest. The standard of proof is the civil standard, ie the balance of probabilities. As Lord Hoffmann said in *In re B (Children) (Care Proceedings: Standard of Proof) (CAFCASS intervening)*:[55]

> There is only one rule of law, namely that the occurrence of the fact in issue must be proved to have been more probable than not. Common sense, not law, requires that in deciding this question, regard should be had, to whatever extent appropriate, to inherent probabilities.

It is inherently less likely that a person acted dishonestly rather than negligently. So it will often be the case that the stronger the misconduct alleged, the less likely it will be that it occurred. To the extent that it is inherently improbable that a particular person was dishonest the evidence needed to rebut that inherent improbability

---

[51] Ibid at [61]–[62].
[52] Ibid at [87].
[53] Ibid at [138].
[54] Ibid at [56].
[55] [2008] UKHL 35; [2009] 1 AC 11, at [15]. See also *In re S-B (Children) Care Proceedings: Standard of Proof)* [2009] UKSC 17; [2010] 1 AC 678, followed in *Goldsmith Williams (a firm) v Travelers Insurance Company Ltd* [2010] EWHC 26 (QB); [2010] Lloyd's Rep IR 309 (Wyn Williams J).

on the balance of probabilities will have to be more cogent than would be needed to prove that he was negligent.[56]

C. Exclusion of Cover for Fraud and Dishonesty

Complete exclusion

8.33 Exclusion of cover in respect of fraud and dishonesty was implicit in the insuring clauses in older forms of professional indemnity policy. Typically, cover would be provided against loss:

> arising from any claim or claims … by reason of any neglect, omission or error … alleged to have been committed on the part of the firm or their predecessors or any person now or heretofore employed by the firm … in or about the conduct of any business conducted by or on behalf of the firm … in their professional capacity as solicitors …[57]

The cover provided by such clauses did not extend to liability for fraud, which involved a positive act rather than 'neglect, omission or error'.[58]

8.34 Nowadays it is far from unusual to find cover against vicarious liability for fraud and dishonesty in professional indemnity policies. So, where an insuring clause provides an indemnity against all sums which the insured shall become liable to pay 'in respect of any civil liability whatsoever', that may well be intended to include liability for fraud.[59] In practice, however, other provisions in the policy will usually indicate whether this was or was not intended.

8.35 Complete exclusions of cover for fraud and dishonesty are still found. For example, in the policy of solicitors' professional indemnity insurance in *McCarthy v St Paul International Insurance Co Ltd*[60] there was an express exclusion of cover in respect of liability:

> brought about by the dishonest or fraudulent act or omission of the Assured including any Partner or former Partner of the Assured or any person employed

---

[56] *Re H* [1996] AC 563, per Lord Nicholls at 586. See also *Hornal v Neuberger Products Ltd* [1957] 1 QB 247 and *In re Dellow's Will Trusts* [1964] 1 WLR 451, at 455 per Ungoed-Thomas J. See also *Neat Holdings Pty Ltd v Karajan Holdings Pty Ltd* [1992] HCA 66; (1992) 110 ALR 449.

[57] This was the wording considered in *Davies v Hosken* [1937] 3 All LR 192. The insuring clauses in *Haseldine v Hosken* [1933] 1 KB 822, *Goddard & Smith v Frew* [1939] 4 All ER 358, and *West Wake Price & Co v Ching* [1957] 1 WLR 45 were to like effect.

[58] *Davies v Hosken* [1937] 4 All ER 358.

[59] In *Hamptons Residential Ltd v Field* [1997] 1 Lloyd's Rep 302 at 308, Mance J expressed the view that such an insuring clause 'might not itself have been viewed as appropriate to cover dishonest, fraudulent, malicious or criminal acts or omissions'. However, there was a further insuring clause which provided comprehensive fidelity cover: see para 8.62. In *Arab Bank Plc v Zurich Insurance Co* [1999] 1 Lloyd's Rep 262, the insuring clause was in like terms. Reading the policy as a whole, Rix J concluded that the words 'any civil liability whatsoever' were prima facie wide enough to cover liability for dishonesty and that, read with other provisions in the policy, that was their effect.

[60] [2007] FCAFC 28.

in connection with the Practice (including any articled clerk and any solicitor or conveyancer who is a Consultant or Associate with the Firm) ...[61]

This cut down the otherwise wide effect of the insuring clause, which provided an indemnity:

against all loss to the Assured ... whensoever occurring arising from any claim or claims first made against the Assured ... in respect of any description of civil liability whatsoever incurred in connection with the Practice ...

The RIBA Architects Premier Policy contains an exclusion in wide terms. No **8.36** indemnity is provided in respect of:

Any claim directly or indirectly contributed to or caused by any dishonest, fraudulent, criminal or malicious act or omission of any partner director or principal of the Insured.

And liability for fraud and dishonesty, including vicarious liability, does not fall within the insuring clause.[62]

Limited exclusion of cover

Excluding cover for principals

Some professional indemnity policies provide cover against liability for fraud or **8.37** dishonesty of employees, but not of principals, whether directors or partners. For example, the policy insuring an insurance broking company in *Total Graphics Ltd v AGF Insurance Ltd*[63] indemnified the insured against losses from claims not only by reason of any negligent act, omission or error, but also:

By reason of any dishonest or fraudulent act or omission on the part of any person (other than a Partner or Director) at any time employed by the Insured.[64]

The effective cause of the insured's liability was the fraud of its sole director, so that insurers were entitled to rely on the exclusion in respect of the acts or omissions of a partner or director.

Excluding cover for those who commit or condone

Even in those policies which provide full cover against vicarious liability for fraud **8.38** and dishonesty, there will be terms regulating the cover provided and excluding cover for the individuals who were fraudulent or dishonest.

---

[61] The same wording appeared in the policy considered in *Murphy and Allen v Swinbank* [1999] NSWSC 1098 (upheld on appeal as *Guardian Trust Australia Ltd v Swinbank* [2000] NSWCA 345).
[62] See para 9.27.
[63] [1997] 1 Lloyd's Rep 599.
[64] The exclusion in *McCann v Switzerland Insurance Australia Ltd* [2000] HCA 65; (2000) 203 CLR 579 was to like effect. It provided that the insurance should not indemnify the insured in respect of any liability: 'brought about by the dishonest or fraudulent act or omission of the Assured including any Partner or former Partner of the Assured. Save that this exclusion shall not apply to liability arising out of any claim brought about by the dishonest or fraudulent act or omission of any person employed in connection with the Practice ...'

8.39   Cover is usually expressly excluded for those who commit or condone the fraudulent or dishonest acts which give rise to the liability.[65] So the ICAEW Minimum Approved Policy Wording provides that:

> in the event that the Insured incurs any liability Insured by this policy by reason of the dishonest or fraudulent act or omission of any former or present Partner, Director, Member, or employee, consultant, sub-contractor or Alternate of the Firm(s) no indemnity shall be afforded hereunder in respect of such Claim to any person committing or condoning any such dishonest or fraudulent act or omission.[66]

The SRA Minimum Terms and Conditions of Professional Indemnity Insurance permit an exclusion of liability of the insurer to indemnify any person to the extent that any civil liability or related defence costs arise from dishonesty or a fraudulent act or omission committed or condoned by that person.[67] Subject to the questions as to when the acts or omissions of a natural person are to be attributed to an insured body corporate[68] and determining whether the natural person was acting dishonestly or fraudulently,[69] there is no difficulty with the concept of what is involved in committing a dishonest or fraudulent act. However, the concept of 'condoning' merits some consideration.

8.40   The question as to what was required for an insured to condone the fraud or dishonesty of another was considered by Irwin J in *Zurich Professional Ltd v Karim*.[70] In that case, a firm of solicitors was run by a mother who was the dominant force, both in her family and in the firm. Her two children were notionally partners but

---

[65] Eg, in *Arab Bank plc v Zurich Insurance Co* [1999] 1 Lloyd's Rep 262, the definition of 'insured' was subject to the following proviso: 'PROVIDED that such definition of the term 'Insured' shall NOT be construed to mean that the Company shall indemnify any person knowingly committing, making or condoning any dishonest, fraudulent or malicious act or omission.'

[66] Clause C4.1. The words with capital letters are defined in the ICAEW Minimum Approved Policy Wording. Clause C.4.1 is subject to clause C5 which requires insurers to advance defence costs to an insured who is alleged to have committed or condoned a dishonest or fraudulent act or omission until either that insured admits to insurers the commission or condoning of the dishonest or fraudulent act or omission or a court of other judicial body finds the insured guilty of that dishonest or fraudulent act or omission.

[67] The RICS Policy Wording has a general exclusion of liability of insurers for any claim arising out of any dishonesty or fraud of any insured. This general exclusion is subject to an exception to the extent that a claim arises by reason of and is solely and directly caused by the dishonest and/or fraudulent act or acts (actual or alleged) of any past or present partner, director, member, consultant, or employee of the practice which cause any client of the insured loss. This exception is itself subject to a number of provisos, including the following:

> no indemnity shall be afforded in respect of any CLAIM arising out of such dishonesty or fraud on the part of any person after discovery by the INSURED, in relation to that person, of reasonable cause for suspicion of fraud or dishonesty

This proviso would encompass the individual who committed the dishonest and/or fraudulent act who would, of course, have reasonable cause for suspicion of his own fraud or dishonesty.

[68] As to which see paras 8.45–8.54.

[69] As to which see paras 8.04–8.32.

[70] [2006] EWHC 3355 (QB).

left everything to her. The son admitted that it was important to be a 'paper' partner so as to give clients and third parties confidence that the firm was not a sole practice. However, he was not even allowed to sign cheques.

The policy in question excluded liability for 'dishonesty or a fraudulent act or omis- **8.41** sion committed or condoned by the insured'. As a matter of construction, Irwin J held that this did not require proof that each insured knew of the particular act of fraud. It was sufficient that they condoned a persistent course of dishonesty. Were it otherwise, an insured who was aware of persistent dishonesty, but who took care not to know the details, would be entitled to cover. This was a result which was unlikely to have been intended by the parties.[71]

Irwin J found that the children had condoned their mother's dishonesty, not in **8.42** relation to specific fraudulent acts or omissions, but more generally. They knew that their mother was in sole charge, even though there were nominally partners. They knew that they were receiving money from the firm which could not legitimately come from the firm's income. Irwin J also found that it was dishonest for a solicitor to be a nominal partner so that another solicitor who would otherwise be a sole practitioner, could obtain work from mortgage lenders.[72]

Fraud or dishonesty can be condoned in other ways. For example, an insured who **8.43** provides assistance to another insured by making what are, in themselves, true statements to a third party in the knowledge that the other insured is acting dishonestly will be taken to have condoned that dishonesty.[73]

In all cases where an exclusion of cover in relation to fraud and dishonesty is to **8.44** apply there has to be a sufficient causal link between the fraud and dishonesty of the insured and the liability of the insured to the third party claimant. The degree of causal relationship will depend upon the wording of the exclusion clause. In *Goldsmith Williams (a firm) v Travelers Insurance Company Ltd*[74] one solicitor ('A') had submitted a dishonest and fraudulent mortgage application. Another solicitor ('B') had witnessed A's signature on the form and certified that the copy of A's passport was genuine. While both A's signature and passport were genuine, B knew that A had made false statements in the mortgage application so that she

---

[71] This approach was approved and adopted on slightly different wording by Wyn Williams J in *Goldsmith Williams (a firm) v Travelers Insurance Company Ltd* [2010] EWHC 26 (QB); [2010] Lloyd's Rep IR 309 at [97].

[72] In *Goldsmith Williams (a firm) v Travelers Insurance Company Ltd* [2010] EWHC 26 (QB); [2010] Lloyd's Rep IR 309 at [99] a solicitor who knew that a colleague had participated in earlier mortgage frauds was held to have condoned a mortgage fraud committed at a later date by the same colleague even though there was no evidence to show that she had participated in the later fraud or known of it. The solicitor knew that her colleague had made false representations on mortgage application forms and condoned that conduct. By doing so she permitted a state of affairs to arise in which her colleague was able to continue to steal from mortgage lenders.

[73] *Goldsmith Williams (a firm) v Travelers Insurance Company Ltd* [2010] EWHC 26 (QB); [2010] Lloyd's Rep IR 309 (Wyn Williams J), at [94].

[74] [2010] EWHC 26 (QB); [2010] Lloyd's Rep IR 309.

committed fraud herself. A stole the mortgage advance when it was paid to the firm. The relevant clause excluded liability in respect of any claim 'against any Insured arising from dishonesty or a fraudulent act or omission committed or condoned by such insured'. Wyn Williams J rejected an argument that the claim arose from the theft by A and not from the dishonest and fraudulent mortgage application, holding that the phrase 'arising' in the clause was 'apt to embrace both the mortgage application and the later theft'.[75]

Attribution of fraud and dishonesty: general principles

8.45 In the case of natural persons, it will be a question of fact whether they did or did not commit or condone the fraudulent or dishonest act or omission which has given rise to liability.

8.46 Where the insured are or include partners in a firm the position of partners who have neither committed nor condoned the dishonest or fraudulent act is straightforward: they fall outside the exclusion and are entitled to be indemnified for what is purely vicarious liability.

8.47 Where the insured include or is a body corporate, then the position is more complicated. In most cases it will be the body corporate which is liable to the third party claimant rather than individual directors, partners, employees, or other agents (other than the natural person who has acted fraudulently or dishonestly who may well be personally liable, but also uninsured). The question then arises whether the body corporate is to be taken as having committed or condoned the dishonest or fraudulent act in issue itself so that it is primarily liable or whether the body is merely vicariously liable for the dishonest or fraudulent act of its director, partner, employee, or other agent.[76] The nature of primary liability was explained by Lord Reid in *Tesco Supermarkets Ltd v Nattrass*:[77]

> A living person has a mind which can have knowledge or intention or be negligent and he has hands to carry out his intentions. A corporation has none of these: it must act through living persons, though not always one or the same person. Then the person who acts is not speaking or acting for the company. He is acting as the

---

[75] Ibid at [95]. See also *IAG New Zealand Ltd v Jackson* [2013] NZCA 302; [2014] Lloyd's Rep IR 907 where an insurance broker had first negligently failed to obtain the full insurance cover requested by his client and then dishonestly told them that he had obtained full cover. Before the clients discovered the truth they suffered a loss which should have been insured but was not. The insurance policy contained an exclusion which stated that the broker was 'not insured for civil liability in connection with any dishonest, fraudulent, criminal or malicious acts or omissions' committed by him. It was held that the liability to the clients was 'in connection with' his later lies to them rather than his earlier non-dishonest failure to obtain the requested insurance. Had he reported back accurately the clients would have obtained insurance before the loss occurred.

[76] Where the body corporate is primarily liable it may well often be difficult for the company not to be vicariously liable as well: *KR v Royal & Sun Alliance Plc* [2006] EWCA Civ 1454; [2007] Lloyd's Rep IR 368, at [51]. But a body corporate can be vicariously liable for an act or omission for which it is not primarily liable.

[77] [1972] AC 153, at 170E–F.

company and his mind which directs his acts is the mind of the company. There is no question of the company being vicariously liable. He is not acting as a servant, representative, agent or delegate. He is an embodiment of the company or, one could say, he hears and speaks through the persona of the company, within his appropriate sphere, and his mind is the mind of the company. If it is a guilty mind then that guilt is the guilt of the company. It must be a question of law whether, once the facts have been ascertained, a person in doing particular things is to be regarded as the company or merely as the company's servant or agent. In that case any liability of the company can only be a statutory or vicarious liability.

Attribution of fraud and dishonesty: professional indemnity insurance

There is no single test as to what is required for a natural person to be identified with **8.48** a body corporate so that his acts are its acts. In any particular case it is necessary to analyse the terms and policies of the law or other provision in question.[78] When considering an exclusion clause in a contract of professional indemnity insurance, the relevant provision is that clause in the context of the policy as a whole.[79]

So, in *KR v Royal & Sun Alliance Plc*[80] a clause in a policy insuring a limited liability **8.49** company against public liability for bodily injury which excluded cover for 'injury or damage which results from a deliberate act or omission or the insured' was held to exclude cover for injury or damage caused by the deliberate act or omission of the natural person who was to be regarded as the company, as opposed to those who were 'mere employees'. That construction gave effect to the exclusion in a way which was consistent with the principle that an insured cannot recover under an insurance policy for the intended consequences of his own deliberate act.[81]

In the specific context of professional indemnity insurance, where there is more than **8.50** one insured and the policy provides composite insurance so that each named insured is separately insured in his own interest[82] a clause which excludes cover for an insured for liability for his own fraudulent or dishonest acts or omissions has to be read in the context that the policy is intended to provide cover for other innocent insureds.[83] That intention would be defeated if the fraud or dishonesty of one insured were to be attributed to an insured body corporate simply because the dishonest insured had the management of the relevant matter on behalf of the body corporate.

---

[78] *Meridian Global Funds Management Asia Ltd v Securities Commission* [1995] 2 AC 500, at 507D–F and 511G–H per Lord Hoffmann giving the Opinion of the Privy Council. Lord Hoffmann explained that, while the 'directing mind and will' test is appropriate in some contexts (eg *Lennard's Carrying Co Ltd. v Asiatic Petroleum Co Ltd.* [1915] AC 705), it is not always apposite to fit the facts or a particular situation: ibid at 509B–511C.

[79] *KR v Royal & Sun Alliance Plc* [2006] EWCA Civ 1454; [2007] Lloyd's Rep IR 368, at [61] per Scott Baker LJ giving the judgment of the Court of Appeal. See also *Arab Bank Plc v Zurich Insurance Co* [1999] 1 Lloyd's Rep 262, at 278, column 2 per Rix J.

[80] [2006] EWCA Civ 1454; [2007] Lloyd's Rep IR 368.

[81] As to which see para 8.01.

[82] See paras 1.32–1.45.

[83] Cf *Gilmore v AMP General Insurance Co Ltd* (1996) 67 SASR 387 (Supreme Court of South Australia).

8.51 In *Arab Bank Plc v Zurich Insurance Co*[84], one of the issues was whether a limited liability company which was one of the insureds under a composite policy was to have attributed to it the assumed dishonesty of its managing director (one of ten directors and owner of about twenty per cent of the issued shares in the company) when providing recklessly inaccurate valuations. Rix J held it was not to be. He noted that where there was a composite policy of insurance it was implicit that one insured is not to be prejudiced by the dishonesty of another (the position being different under policies of joint insurance).[85] The policy before him went further: it was intended to provide cover to innocent insureds for the fraud or dishonesty of their close associates and agents. He concluded:[86]

> In the present case, where it follows from the definition of the 'insured' in the insuring clause in question that each separate 'person' is a separate insured, the question is similarly whether the fault, here the dishonesty, of one person is to be attributed to another person, a company, in circumstances where directors and their company are distinguished as separate insureds. In such circumstances, the logic of the policy's scheme is that even directors cannot by themselves be treated, at any rate ex officio, as the alter ego or directing mind and will of the company. It might be otherwise if one director held all or a majority of the shares in a company, as in the case of a 'one man company', or if the director's dishonesty had been committed or condoned as part of a scheme approved by the board of directors itself: in such a case the proviso would operate, and there would be no harm in describing the director's act as the act of the company.

8.52 While the wording of the policy in question will be decisive in any particular case, this reasoning is likely to apply to composite policies of professional indemnity insurance which provide cover to innocent insureds for their liability for the fraud and dishonesty of others. Policies of professional indemnity insurance often contain express terms which show that such cover is to be provided. For example, the SRA Minimum Terms and Conditions of Professional Indemnity Insurance provide that, while liability to indemnify a particular person who has himself committed or condoned dishonesty or a fraudulent act or omission may be excluded, the insurance must still cover all other insureds. The ICAEW Minimum Approved Policy wording contains a provision to like effect.[87] Such provisions make it clear that it is intended that innocent insureds are to be covered for their vicarious liability for the fraud or dishonesty of other insureds.

---

[84] [1999] 1 Lloyd's Rep 262.

[85] Ibid at 272, column 1. See paras 1.32–1.45.

[86] Ibid at 279, columns 1–2.

[87] Clause 4.2: ' … an indemnity shall be afforded hereunder to each and every person who has neither committed nor condoned any such dishonest or fraudulent act or omission'. The RICS Policy wording has a widely worded exclusion of liability of insurers for claims arising out of any dishonesty or fraud of any insured, but this is subject to an express exception which has the effect of providing cover to innocent insureds in relation to claims which cause clients loss.

However, as Rix J noted, the position is likely to be different in the case of a 'one-man' company[88] and dishonesty may be so pervasive in a larger company that the company will be taken to be dishonest itself.[89]   **8.53**

The SRA Minimum Terms and Conditions of Professional Indemnity Insurance   **8.54**
make specific provision in this regard. They provide that a body corporate will not have any dishonesty or fraudulent act or omission imputed to it, unless it was committed or condoned by all the directors in the case of a company or by all the members in the case of a limited liability partnership. This maximizes the protection for 'innocent' insured in that the body corporate through which they practise will be insured unless all its principals are complicit in the fraud or dishonesty. It also maximizes protection for clients of solicitors practising through bodies corporate who might find it hard to establish that they were owed any duty of care in tort by directors, members, or employees of bodies corporate with limited liability[90] and so have only an uninsured body corporate to sue in contract.

Reasonable grounds for suspicion

Another limitation which is sometimes found in relation to cover for vicarious   **8.55**
liability for fraud and dishonesty is that cover will not extend to any loss resulting from fraud or dishonesty carried out after the insured could reasonably have suspected or discovered the improper conduct of the dishonest individual. For example, in *MDIS Ltd v Swinbank*[91] the insuring clause provided cover against claims for which the insured became legally liable, alleging 'any dishonest, fraudulent, criminal, malicious act(s) or omission(s) of any person employed at any time by the Assured', but then provided:

> The Assured will not be indemnified against any claim or loss, resulting from the dishonest, fraudulent, criminal or malicious act(s) or omission(s) perpetrated after the Assured could reasonably have discovered or suspected the improper conduct of the employee(s).

The words 'could reasonably have discovered or suspected' are potentially wide. It is not necessary that the insured should have discovered or suspected the improper conduct; it is enough that he could reasonably have done so.

---

[88] *Moore Stephens (a firm) v Stone & Rolls Ltd (in liquidation)* [2009] UKHL 39; [2009] 1 AC 1391. See also *Royal Brunei Airlines Sdn Bhd v Tan* [1995] 2 AC 378, at 393. But see also the illuminating judgment in *Moulin Global Eyecare Trading Ltd v Inland Revenue Comr* [2014] HKFCA 22; (2014) 17 HKCFAR 218 and *Jetivia SA & Anor v Bilta (UK) Ltd* [2015] UKSC 23; [2015] 2 WLR 1168, which suggest that the decision of the Supreme Court in the *Moore Stephens* case is not of general application.

[89] *Malik v Bank of Credit and Commerce International SA (In Compulsory Liquidation)* [1998] AC 20, at 34 per Lord Nicholls.

[90] *Williams v Natural Life Health Foods Ltd* [1998] 1 WLR 830.

[91] [1999] Lloyd's Rep IR 516, on appeal from *McDonnell Information Systems Ltd v Swinbank* [1999] Lloyd's Rep IR 98.

8.56 The RICS Policy Wording excludes cover in respect of dishonest or fraudulent acts or omissions committed by a person after discovery by the insured of reasonable cause for suspicion of fraud or dishonesty.[92] It is unlikely that an insured is obliged by such terms to have in place procedures and safeguards to try to detect dishonesty among its principals and employees. The exclusions only apply once the insured has reasonable cause for suspicion. There is clearly some scope for differing views as to what does and does not constitute reasonable cause for suspicion. The burden of establishing that the insured had reasonable cause will be on insurers. It follows that the exclusion should not apply in any case where it was reasonable not to suspect an individual of fraud or dishonesty, even if others might have taken a different view.

Notification to insurers

8.57 Some professional indemnity policies which provide cover against vicarious liability for fraud and dishonesty contain provisions which require and entitle the insured to give notice of the discovery of reasonable grounds for suspicion of dishonesty or fraud on the part of any person for whose acts the insured may be vicariously liable. As with provisions requiring and entitling the insured to give notice of matters with the potential to give rise to a claim,[93] cover is usually extended to any claims to which such fraud or dishonesty gives rise outside the policy period will be deemed to have been made during it.[94] Notification clauses are considered in **Chapter 2**.

Recovery from the fraudulent or dishonest insured

8.58 Subject to any provision to the contrary, upon indemnifying those insured who are entitled to be indemnified, insurers will be subrogated to any rights those insured have against any other person against whom those insured have a right of recovery in respect of the loss against which they have been indemnified. Insurers will usually not have any such right against the individuals whose acts or omissions caused the insured to be liable because those individuals will themselves be among the insured. However, in the case of vicarious liability for fraud and dishonesty, the individuals who committed the fraudulent or dishonest acts or omissions will not be entitled to any indemnity. Provision is often made for recovery from them.[95]

---

[92] The RICS Policy Wording also requires that the insured's annual accounts must have been prepared and/or certified by an independent and properly qualified accountant or auditor in accordance with the RICS Rules of Conduct and that the insured's client accounts have been kept in accordance with those Rules.

[93] As to which see paras 2.50–2.51.

[94] The RICS Policy Wording contains a term to this effect. The dishonesty or fraud must have the potential to give rise to a claim against the insured. The ICAEW Minimum Approved Policy Wording requires notification whether the suspected fraud or dishonesty has given rise to a claim under the policy or not. There is no provision extending cover to any claims which later arise from the dishonesty which has been notified. The insured under the ICAEW Minimum Approved Policy Wording needs to give notice of dishonesty as a circumstance which might give rise to a claim in order to obtain an extension of cover.

[95] Eg the RICS Policy Wording grants insurers all rights of recovery against any parties from whom a recovery can be made upon notification of a claim or circumstances (ie before insurers have

The SRA Minimum Terms and Conditions of Professional Indemnity Insurance **8.59** permit policies to include provisions which require any insured who committed or condoned any dishonesty or any fraudulent act or omission to reimburse insurers 'to the extent that it is just and equitable having regard to the prejudice caused … by such … dishonesty, act or omission'. These words also apply to other breaches by the insured: in the context of fraud and dishonesty, justice and equity will almost invariably require that the dishonest or fraudulent insured should reimburse insurers in full. It should be noted that it is a right of reimbursement: insurers must have paid out money in order to have a right against the dishonest or fraudulent insured.

The ICAEW Minimum Approved Policy Wording adopts a different approach. **8.60** Any moneys which, but for the dishonest or fraudulent act or omission would be owing to the persons committing or condoning the dishonest or fraudulent act or omission and any moneys held by the insured for such persons are deducted from the indemnity under the policy.[96] The innocent insured are obliged, if requested by insurers and at insurers' expense, to take all reasonable steps to obtain such reimbursement. Insurers' rights of subrogation are also expressly preserved.

Fidelity insurance

Some professional indemnity policies also include fidelity insurance. This provides **8.61** cover not only against liability in respect of claims by third parties arising from the fraud or dishonesty of persons for whom the insured is vicariously liable, but also in respect of losses suffered by the insured itself as the result of fraud or dishonesty. For example, by the insuring clause in *J Rothschild Assurance plc v Collyear*[97] insurers undertook:

> To indemnify THE ASSURED against any loss or losses which, during the period specified in the First Schedule, they shall discover they have sustained by reason of any fraudulent act or omission of any past or present partner, director, principal or EMPLOYEE …[98]

---

indemnified the insured), but waives such right against any insured, save in respect of any insured whose dishonest, fraudulent, criminal, or malicious act or omission has caused the liability.

[96] Similar provisions in other policies of professional indemnity insurance require the insured to account to insurers for any asset or entitlement of any person who committed or condoned any dishonesty or fraudulent act or omission, provided that the insured is legally entitled to withhold such asset or entitlement from that person.

[97] [1999] Lloyd's Rep IR 6.

[98] In *Standard Life Assurance Ltd v Oak Dedicated Ltd* [2008] EWHC 552 (Comm); [2008] Lloyd's Rep IR 552 indemnity cover extended to liability arising by reason of 'any dishonest or fraudulent act or omission' alongside fidelity cover which provided indemnity against: 'FINANCIAL LOSSES directly incurred by the Assured by reason of any of the following insured events discovered within the Period of Insurance … Any dishonest, fraudulent or malicious act or omission by any past or present, officer, employee or agent of the Assured or of their agents or their predecessors in business, including but not limited to theft, abstraction or other improper appropriation of money or any Documents belonging to the Assured, or for which the Assured are legally liable'.

In such clauses the trigger for cover is the discovery of the loss.[99]

8.62 Such cover will usually contain exclusions in respect of those who commit or condone any fraud or dishonesty and in relation to losses suffered after the insured had reasonable grounds to suspect dishonesty. For example, the fidelity cover in *Hamptons Residential Ltd v Field*[100] provided that no indemnity would be provided:

(a) to any person committing or condoning such dishonest, or fraudulent, malicious or criminal act or omission and the sums payable under this Policy shall be only for the balance of Liability in excess of the amounts recovered from the dishonest or fraudulent person or persons or their estates or legal representatives.

(b) for claim(s) or loss(es) in respect of dishonest or fraudulent malicious or criminal acts or omissions committed by any person after discovery, in relation to that person, of reasonable cause for suspicion of fraud, malicious or criminal act or dishonesty.

Terms to this effect have been considered above in the context of professional indemnity insurance.[101]

---

[99] See paras 2.01–2.04.
[100] [1997] 1 Lloyd's Rep 302 and [1998] 2 Lloyd's Rep 248.
[101] See paras 8.37–8.56.

9

THE INDEMNITY

A. Who is Entitled to be Indemnified?

9.01 Professionals can practise alone, in partnership, or through limited liability companies or limited liability partnerships. They may leave one partnership and join another. They may cease to be partners and become employed consultants or members of a limited liability partnership or directors of a limited liability company. Because professional indemnity insurance is written on a 'claims made' rather than on an 'occurrence' basis,[1] professionals will wish to ensure that they remain insured for claims which might be made against them in former capacities, as well as in their current position.

9.02 Policies of professional indemnity insurance will define who is to be insured under them. Where more than one person is insured, the insurance will usually be composite, so that each insured is separately covered for his own interest.[2] This can result in one named insured being covered in respect of a liability incurred not in his current capacity, but in some former capacity.

---

[1] See paras 2.01–2.04.
[2] See paras 1.32–1.45.

9.03 That was the result in *Maxwell v Price (Halford, Third Party)*.[3] Mr Price, a solicitor, was found liable in negligence when acting for a client in having failed to set an action down for trial. At the relevant time, he was a sole practitioner. By the time the claim was made against him he was practising in partnership with another solicitor. By the insuring clause in his professional indemnity insurance when the claim was made against him insurers undertook to indemnify 'the firm', which was defined as:

> the person or persons named in the Schedule herein carrying on business under the firm and style stated in the said Schedule (hereinafter called 'the Firm' which expression shall include the aforesaid persons and any other person or persons who may at any time and from time to time during the subsistence of this Policy be a partner in the Firm or any one or more of them) ...

The words 'or any one ... of them' meant that the insuring clause should be read as providing insurance to Mr Price alone (as well as to his partner alone and to both of them together). So read, it indemnified Mr Price against the claim, which had been made against him during the policy period and otherwise fell within the terms of cover.

9.04 In the RIBA Architects Premier Policy the insured is defined as 'any person or Firm who is named in the Certificate' and 'any person who has been or during the Period of Insurance becomes a partner, member, director or principal of the Firm'. This is subject to a proviso: the liability has to arise 'directly out of Professional Business carried out by that person in the name of the Firm'. 'Firm' means the firm or body corporate described in the certificate of insurance. It would appear to follow that, unless that previous firm was named in the certificate, a partner or director of the current firm would not be insured against liabilities incurred while working for a previous firm. So, on this wording the decision in *Maxwell v Price (Halford, Third Party)*[4] would have gone the other way.[5]

9.05 It is usual to find wide definitions of 'the insured' in policies of professional indemnity insurance. They may include those named as partners, directors, or members, former partners, directors, or members of the firm (including consultants), current or former employees, those who are or who have been contracted to provide services to the firm, the estates and/or legal representatives of any such person, and any

---

[3] [1960] 2 Lloyd's Rep 155 (reported in Australia as *Price v Halford* [1960] HCA 38; (1960) 105 CLR 25).

[4] Ibid.

[5] The RICS Policy Wording has an extensive definition of 'insured'. Cover in respect of employees and former employees of the 'practice' (ie 'the practice or practices named in the schedule and their predecessors and any other practices which are disclosed ... in the proposal form') is limited to 'professional business' undertaken on behalf of the 'practice' and so does not extend to liability incurred while working elsewhere. There is no such limitation in relation to cover for other insureds, including partners, directors, or members of the 'practice'. The ICAEW Minimum Approved Policy Wording is to like effect.

named company or limited liability partnership or any service, administration, trustee, or nominee company owned by the insured entity.

Some professional indemnity policies limit cover to liability in respect of the firm **9.06** or business named in the schedule, either with or without its 'predecessors'. The insured and their insurance brokers need to be alert to the possibility that they will not be insured for claims made against them arising out of their practice before they joined their current firm. It is also prudent to ensure that there is certainty as to which practices are included within the definition of 'predecessors'.

Equal care is needed to ensure that the insurance covers all those individuals who **9.07** are currently working for or as part of the insured firm or company. In *Rathbone Brothers Plc v Novae Corporate Underwriting Ltd*[6] 'the insured' was defined in the policy as 'any insured company or any insured person' and 'insured person' was defined as

> an actual person who was, is or, during the policy period, becomes:—
> (i)   a director or officer, but not an external auditor or insolvency office-holder, of an insured company;
> (ii) an approved person;
> (iii) a paid employee (full time, part time or temporary) working under the direct control or supervision of an insured company;
> … insured person means exclusively those persons employed by an insured company in the performance of professional services. The term insured person does not mean any independent broker, independent financial advisor, external auditor or any similar agent or independent representative remunerated on a sales or commission basis, unless specifically agreed by the insurer and endorsed to this policy.

A claim was made by a third party against a natural person who was engaged by **9.08** the insured company as a consultant. Among other things insurers argued that this individual did not fall within any of the definitions of 'insured person'. The consultant accepted that he was not an 'employee for employment tribunal purposes'. However, he argued successfully that he was 'a paid employee (... part time or temporary)' on two grounds. The specific categories of 'insured' in the relevant clause were followed by broader words: 'those persons employed by an insured company in the performance of professional service'. This indicated how the specific categories were to be interpreted. This conclusion was supported by the applicable regulatory provisions. These categorized the consultant as 'a person employed, either under a contract of service or a contract for services, by the registered person', showing that 'a wide concept of employee is used for regulatory purposes and that this is a perfectly normal commercial use of the term'.[7] The second was that the wording of the exclusion in the last sentence of the definition of 'insured person' showed that

---

[6] [2014] EWCA (Civ) 1464; [2015] Lloyd's Rep IR 95.
[7] Ibid at [35] per Elias LJ with whom the other members of the Court of Appeal agreed on this issue.

the parties had intended the earlier words to have a broad meaning: otherwise there would be no need for the exclusion. That may well have been the parties' intention, but any doubt on the point could have been avoided by expressly including consultants in the definition of 'insured person'.

SRA Minimum Terms and Conditions of Professional Indemnity Insurance

9.09 The main insured under the SRA Minimum Terms and Conditions of Professional Indemnity Insurance is the 'insured firm', ie the firm which contracted with insurers for the insurance. The insured must also include any service, administration, trustee or nominee company owned by the firm as at the date of the occurrence of relevant circumstances, its principals[8] and employees, former principals and employees, and those who become principals or employees during the period of insurance, and the estates or legal personal representative of any insured who is a natural person.

9.10 The SRA Minimum Terms and Conditions of Professional Indemnity Insurance go to some lengths to provide for cover for earlier firms. They require that the insurance must indemnify each 'Insured' against civil liability to the extent that it arises from 'private legal practice'[9] in connection with a 'prior practice'.[10] For the purposes of this insurance, the 'Insured' must include the same insured for the 'prior practice' as are included in the 'insured' for the current 'insured firm', save that there will be no new principals or employees during the period of insurance.

9.11 Cover must be provided for each insured to the extent that his liability arises 'in connection with a prior Practice'. 'Prior practice' means:

> each practice to which the insured firm's practice is ultimately a successor practice by way of one or more mergers, acquisitions, absorptions or other transitions but does not include any such practice which has elected to be insured under run-off cover in accordance with clause 5.6(a) of the MTC

Detailed provision is made as to the circumstances in which a practice becomes a 'successor practice'.

9.12 The provisions set out a number of ways in which one 'practice'[11] (B) can be the successor to another practice (A). They concern the 'ownership' of each practice. 'Ownership' is not defined. A sole practitioner will own his practice and the equity

---

[8] See n 12 under para 9.12.

[9] See para 9.65.

[10] See paras 9.11–9.21.

[11] 'Practice' is defined as: 'the whole or such part of the private practice of a firm as is carried on from one or more offices in England and Wales'.

In relation to a firm which is licensed by the SRA under part 5 of the Legal Services Act 2007 'private practice': means any reserved legal activity, any other legal activity and any other activity in respect of which the firm is regulated pursuant to part 5 of the Legal Services Act 2007. 'Reserved legal activity' and 'any other legal activity' are defined in s 12 of the Legal Services Act 2007. In relation to all firms 'private practice' also 'includes without limitation all the professional services

partners will be the owners of the practice of an unincorporated partnership. A limited liability partnership will own its practice, as will a limited liability company.[12]

The provisions address the position after a 'transition', which is defined as 'merger, **9.13** acquisition, absorption or other transition which results in A no longer being carried on as a discrete legal practice'. If there is no such transition then practice B will not be a 'successor' to practice A.[13]

Practice B is the 'successor' to practice A for these purposes if, after a transition, **9.14** practice B holds itself out as being the successor of practice A. This can be done expressly or impliedly, for example by a stating on B's notepaper that it incorporates practice A. Only if there is no successor practice in this way or if the successor practice has failed to maintain insurance as required do the alternative ways in which there can be a successor practice arise. There are four other such ways.

The first is that practice B will be a successor practice to practice A if the principal[14] **9.15** of practice A was a sole practitioner and after the transition he becomes a principal of B's owner or, after 1 September 2000, a principal or employee of B's owner. If the former sole practitioner were subsequently to return to sole practice, practice B would still be the successor practice to his earlier sole practice.

The second applies where practice A's owner was either a 'recognised body'[15] or a **9.16** 'licensed body'[16] in respect of its 'regulated activities'[17] and after the transition that body is a principal of the owner of practice B. In those circumstances, B will be the successor practice of A.

---

provided by a firm including acting as a personal representative, trustee, attorney, notary, insolvency practitioner or in any other role in conjunction with a practice, and includes services provided pro bono publico'. These definitions of 'private' practice are subject to a number of exceptions.

'Private legal practice' is defined in the Minimum Terms: see para 9.65.

[12] This follows from the provision that owners can become 'principals' of the owner of Practice B. 'Principals' are defined in detail. They include sole practitioners, partners in an unincorporated partnership, directors of a limited liability company, and members of a limited liability partnership.

[13] In *Zurich Professional Ltd v Brown* [2010] EWHC 3300 (Ch); [2011] Lloyd's Rep IR 607 (Sir William Blackburne) an individual who had previously carried out work as an executor started sole practice as a solicitor under the name 'CS Law'. It was held that his work before practising as CS Law was not a prior practice to CS Law because there had been no transition.

[14] See n 11 under para 9.12.

[15] For this purpose a 'recognised body' is 'a body for the time being recognized by the Solicitors Regulation Authority under s 9 of the Administration of Justice Act 1985'. Under that provision 'recognition' means recognition by the Solicitors Regulation Authority of 'legal services bodies ... as being suitable bodies to undertake the provision of any solicitor services or other relevant services'. 'Legal services bodies' are the subject of detailed definition in s 9A of the Administration of Justice Act 1985.

[16] 'Licensed body' is defined as a body licensed by the Solicitors Regulation Authority under Part 5 of the Legal Service Act 2007.

[17] 'Regulated activities' are defined as any reserved legal activity, any other legal activity, and any other activity in respect of which the firm is regulated pursuant to part 5 of the Legal Services Act 2007. The definitions of 'reserved legal activity' and 'any other legal activity' in s 12 of the Legal Services Act 2007 are apt to apply to the same words in the definition of 'regulated activities' in the Minimum Terms.

9.17 The third applies where practice A's owner was an unincorporated partnership and, as a result of the transition, the majority of the partners in A became principals of B's owner. If those conditions are fulfilled, then B is the successor practice to practice A. It follows that the other partners in practice A will be insured by practice B (or any successor practice to practice B), even though they have not become principals of it.

9.18 The fourth way in which B can be a successor practice applies where practice A's owner was an unincorporated partnership and the majority of A's partners did not become principals in the same practice. In such a case, practice B will still be a successor practice to practice A if one or more of practice A's partners has become a principal of B and one of the following additional conditions is satisfied:

    (A) B is carried on under the same name as A or a name which substantially incorporates the name of A (or a substantial part of the name of A); and/or
    (B) B is carried on from the same premises as A; and/or
    (C) the owner of B acquired the goodwill and/or assets of A; and/or
    (D) the owner of B assumed the liabilities of A; and/or
    (E) the majority of staff employed by A's owner became employees of B's owner.

9.19 It is possible for the last provision to give rise to two or more 'successor practices'. Some provision is made for this in the SRA Minimum Terms and Conditions of Professional Indemnity Insurance, which permit provision for double insurance if the current insured firm ceases to practice during the period of insurance and, as a result, two or more insurers are on risk. In such circumstances, liability is apportioned between the insurers in accordance with the relative numbers of principals of the owners of the constituent practices immediately before the succession.

9.20 Where there is no successor practice, run-off cover must be provided.[18] Where there is a potential successor practice to a practice which has ceased, the practice which has ceased may, before it ceases to practise, elect to be insured under run-off cover or, if there is insurance cover complying with the SRA Minimum Terms and Conditions for Professional Indemnity Insurance, to be insured under that cover as a prior practice. If such an election is made, then there is no 'successor' practice.

9.21 The elaborate scheme for insuring 'prior' and 'successor' practices under the SRA Minimum Terms and Conditions for Professional Indemnity Insurance focuses upon practices rather than natural persons. A natural person who is an insured by reason of his position in the current practice (ie the 'insured firm'[19]) may not be an insured under the same policy for liabilities he incurred as a solicitor before he joined that practice. He will only be insured for such liability if that liability was incurred by a prior practice. In *Zurich Professional Ltd v Brown*[20] the insured firm

---

[18] See paras 9.22–9.24.
[19] See para 9.09.
[20] [2010] EWHC 3300 (Ch); [2011] Lloyd's Rep IR 607 (Sir William Blackburne).

was 'CS Law' (in fact a sole practitioner, Mr Brown). Before setting up CS Law Mr Brown had acted, among other things, as an executor. Mr Brown was an insured under CS Law's professional indemnity insurance, but only for liabilities in connection with the practice of CS Law. His practice before setting up CS Law was not a 'prior practice'[21] and so he was not insured against liabilities in respect of that practice under CS Law's policy.

Run-off cover

A professional who ceases practice may rely on his former colleagues to maintain **9.22** professional indemnity insurance on his behalf. He may not wish to do so or there may be no continuing practice to maintain professional indemnity insurance to cover him so that the retiring professional may wish to obtain insurance himself. The usual way in which this is done is by way of run-off cover. This is usually obtained by way of a single policy for a single premium providing cover against claims made during a period of six years. This provides a fair measure of security, but, while s 5 of the Limitation Act 1980 provides that the limitation period for claims for breaches of contracts which are not under seal is six years, professionals will remain at risk of claims for more than six years after they cease practice.[22]

Some policies of professional indemnity insurance provide such cover if the insured **9.23** ceases practice. For example, the following provision appeared in the policy of professional indemnity insurance for engineers considered in *Nettle v Mathieson Group Pty Ltd*:[23]

> Notwithstanding anything to the contrary contained herein, the Company hereby agrees to indemnify the Insured in respect of any claim or claims first made against the Insured after the expiration of the Period of Insurance in respect of any civil liability in the conduct of the Business or Practice by the Insured. Provided always that, such indemnity will:
> (a) only apply when the Insured has ceased carrying on the Business or Practice;
> (b) apply in accordance with the terms and conditions of the Policy, including the Excess and Limit of Indemnity, in force at the time the claim is first made against the Insured;
> (c) be provided for no additional premium;
> (d) remain in force for such period as the Company continues to underwrite the engineers Facility; and
> (e) only apply if the Insured is not entitled to indemnity in respect of such claim under any other professional indemnity insurance policy issued after the expiry of the Period of Insurance of this Policy.

---

[21] See n 13 under para 9.13.
[22] See *Jackson & Powell on Professional Liability* (7th edn, Sweet & Maxwell, 2012), paras 5-26–5-88.
[23] [2007] NSWCA 98.

9.24 The SRA Minimum Terms and Conditions of Professional Indemnity Insurance require run-off cover to be provided if the insured firm's practice ceases during or at the end of the period of insurance and the insured firm has not obtained succeeding insurance in compliance with the Minimum Terms. The run-off cover which must be provided in those circumstances must indemnify each insured, including those insured in respect of prior practices,[24] on the Minimum Terms but for an additional six years (ie six years from the date on which, but for the run-off cover, the period of insurance would have ended).

B. The Scope of the Indemnity

9.25 Professional indemnity policies will define the liabilities against which the insured is to be indemnified. This is usually done in one or more of three ways: first, by reference to the causes of action against which the insured is to be indemnified; second, by defining the nature of the activities which must give rise to the cause of action; and third, by excluding from cover certain types of liability.

Causes of action

Negligence and breach of a contractual duty of care

9.26 It will be a term of a professional's retainer that in acting for his client he will exercise the skill and care to be expected of a reasonably competent member of his profession in the circumstances. He will owe his client a concurrent duty of care in tort[25] and may owe a similar duty to non-clients.[26] Professional indemnity policies will provide cover against any liability for breach of this duty which gives rise to a loss.

9.27 Some current forms of professional indemnity policy continue to provide cover restricted to a limited range of potential liabilities, primarily for breach of the contractual and tortious duty of care. For example, the RIBA Architects Premier Policy indemnifies the insured against claims for breach of that duty of care (deemed to include a claim for breach of warranty of authority), together with defamation, slander of goods, injurious falsehood, loss and damage to documents, and unintentional breach of copyright.

Non-negligent breach of contract

9.28 While it is relatively rare for a term in the engagement of a professional to be construed as giving rise to a strict obligation (ie one that can be breached without negligence),[27] some terms have that effect.[28]

---

[24] See paras 9.11–9.21.

[25] *Henderson v Merrett Syndicates Ltd* [1995] 2 AC 145.

[26] *Hedley Byrne & Co Ltd v Heller & Partners Ltd* [1964] AC 465.

[27] See, for example, *Midland Bank Plc v Cox McQueen* [1999] PNLR 593; *Mercantile Credit Company Ltd v Fenwick* [1999] Lloyd's Rep PN 408; and *Barclays Bank Plc v Weeks Legg & Dean (a firm)* [1999] QB 309.

[28] Eg, *Platform Funding Ltd v Bank of Scotland Plc* [2008] EWCA Civ 930; [2009] QB 426.

Insuring clauses considered in earlier authorities on professional indemnity insur- **9.29**
ance indemnified the insured against claims against him due to 'neglect, omission or error',[29] 'any act, neglect, omission, mis-statement or error',[30] or 'any act of
neglect, default or error'.[31] While it was well-established that these wordings did
not provide cover against fraud or dishonesty,[32] their precise scope was uncertain.[33]

It was only in *Wimpey Construction UK Ltd v Poole*[34] that it was established that **9.30**
such wording extends beyond negligence and encompasses non-negligent breaches
of contract. Rejecting the argument that cover was limited to negligent breaches of
contract, Webster J said:[35]

> A professional indemnity policy does not necessarily cover only negligence. In my
> view I must give effect to the literal meaning of the primary insuring words and
> construe them so as to include any omission or error without negligence.

Webster J held that not every omission or error was included. Cover did not extend
to a deliberate error or omission. This is consistent with the general principle that it
is not possible to insure against liability for one's own deliberate act.[36] In this context, deliberate means a deliberate breach of contract, rather than a deliberate act,
the performer of which does not know will be a breach of contract.[37] The burden is
on the insured to show that his liability arose from a non-deliberate act or omission
in this sense. So, in *Total Graphics Ltd v AGF Insurance Ltd*[38] the insured, who had
acted with deliberate dishonesty in some respects when acting as insurance broker
for the third party claimant, was unable to show that his failure to arrange insurance
cover for his client with an agreed insurer was a 'negligent act, error or omission' so
as to fall within the insuring clause.

In *Lumberman's Mutual Casualty Co v Bovis Lend Lease Ltd*,[39] Colman J had to **9.31**
determine the scope of the following words:

> any neglect error or omission or breach of warranty of authority in the conduct
> of the insured or of any party presently or previously employed or engaged by the
> insured or for whom the insured is responsible …

---

[29] *Davies v Hosken* [1937] 3 All ER 192.
[30] *Goddard and Smith v Frew* [1939] 4 All ER 358.
[31] *West Wake Price & Co v Ching* [1957] 1 WLR 45.
[32] See para 8.33.
[33] *Wimpey Construction UK Ltd v Poole* [1984] 2 Lloyd's Rep 499, at 513–14.
[34] [1984] 2 Lloyd's Rep 499. The relevant words in the *Wimpey* case were 'omission, error or negligent act'. Another provision in the policy referred to 'any negligent act, error or omission'.
[35] Ibid at 514.
[36] See para 8.01.
[37] See also *McDonnell Information Systems v Swinbank* [1999] Lloyd's Rep IR 98, at 100, where
Mance J recorded that it was 'common ground between the parties that the words: "neglect error or
omission including breach of contract occasioned by same" extend beyond negligence alone, but do
not embrace deliberate neglect or error or deliberate omission to do that which the insured knows
he should do'.
[38] [1997] 1 Lloyd's Rep 599.
[39] [2004] EWHC 2197 (Comm); [2005] 1 Lloyd's Rep 494.

Insurers argued that the words connoted (i) negligence in general, (ii) negligent but non-deliberate error, and (iii) negligent, but non-deliberate omission. Colman J disagreed.[40] He observed that a breach of warranty of authority could be negligent or non-negligent and that the wording was designed to cover both. It was therefore hard to see why errors or omissions had to be negligent in order to fall within cover. He held that cover extended to non-negligent errors and omissions which gave rise to liability, for example under *Rylands v Fletcher*.[41]

Wider civil liability

9.32   Professional liability extends beyond liability in damages for breach of a contractual or tortious duty of care or even for breach of contract. Liability can arise for breach of fiduciary duty, breach of trust, breach of warranty of authority, breach of confidence, and so on. This is recognized in many current forms of professional indemnity insurance.

9.33   Some professional indemnity policies provide cover in respect of civil liability, whether that liability is to compensate the third party claimant or of some other nature (subject, of course, to specified exclusions of cover). Thus the ICAEW Minimum Approved Policy Wording defines claim not only as a demand for compensation or damages, but also as 'the assertion of a right' against the insured. The RICS Policy Wording is to similar effect.

9.34   Other policies contain definitions of 'claim' or insuring clause which are limited to claims for compensation (or civil compensation) and/or (civil) damages. For example, the SRA Minimum Terms and Conditions of Professional Indemnity Insurance require the insurance of solicitors to indemnify them against 'civil liability'. That is qualified by the definition of 'Claim', which, subject to particular provision about client money,[42] is as follows:

> a demand for, or an assertion of a right to, civil compensation or civil damages or an intimation of an intention to seek such compensation or damages ...

In relation to such policies the question can arise as to whether the third party claimant is seeking to recover (civil) compensation and/or (civil) damages from the insured.

Civil compensation and civil damages

9.35   'Civil compensation' and 'civil damages' are wide words, wide enough to include liability for fraud,[43] but they do limit cover to liability to compensate or otherwise pay damages. They require the third party claimant to be seeking to recover against

---

[40]   Ibid at [69]–[70].
[41]   (1868) LR 3 HL 330.
[42]   As to which see para 9.48.
[43]   See para 8.34.

the insured for a loss for which the insured was responsible. This is established by two decisions of the Court of Appeal.

In the first, *Charterhouse Development (France) Ltd v Sharp*,[44] cover was provided **9.36** for 'compensatory damages'. Longmore J held[45] that the phrase:

> 'compensatory damages' must be given a broad meaning, viz that the damages, if they are to be recoverable, must be claimed by or on behalf of a person in respect of loss which that person has suffered, rather than a sum claimed by an entity, such as the State, … which has suffered no personal loss.[46]

The same approach was adopted by the Court of Appeal in the second of the deci-   **9.37** sions, *Bedfordshire Police Authority v Constable*.[47] There the issue before the Court was whether 'compensation' payable out of the police fund pursuant to s 2 of the Riot (Damages) Act 1886 fell within the scope of an insuring clause by which insurers agreed to indemnify the claimant police authority in respect of all sums which it 'may become legally liable to pay as damages'. Longmore LJ, with whom the other members of the Court of Appeal agreed, held that the answer depended upon the nature of the liability of the police authority. He referred to the earlier decision of the Court of Appeal in *Hall Brothers Steamship Co Ltd v Young*.[48] In that case it had been held that sums payable under a provision in French law by a shipowner for damage suffered by a pilot boat without any fault on the part of the shipowner fell outside an indemnity in respect of damages. Longmore LJ identified the key concept as responsibility. Whereas in the *Hall Brothers* case the shipowner had had no responsibility for the operation of the pilot vessel, in the *Bedfordshire Police Authority* case the police were responsible for maintaining law and order. So, while the sum payable to the owners of the pilot vessel was not damages, the compensation payable by the police authority for damage to property during a riot was.[49]

A different answer was reached on the facts in *Kantfield Pty Ltd v Lockwood*.[50] The   **9.38** insured accountant was appointed receiver of a company and, in that capacity,

---

[44] [1998] Lloyd's Rep IR 266.

[45] Ibid at 279.

[46] See also *Lancashire County Council v Municipal Mutual Insurance Ltd* [1997] QB 897. In that case, the Court of Appeal considered whether an award of exemplary damages for false imprisonment fell within cover against 'all sums which the insured shall become legally liable to pay as compensation'. The insurance in that case expressly included liability for wrongful arrest, malicious prosecution, and false imprisonment, where awards of damages would be expected to include exemplary damages, so that care is needed in applying the reasoning of the Court of Appeal to policies of professional indemnity insurance.

[47] [2009] EWCA Civ 64; [2009] Lloyd's IR 607.

[48] [1939] 1 KB 748.

[49] [2009] EWCA Civ 64; [2009] Lloyd's IR 607, at [20]–[27]. At [28] Longmore LJ explained how the earlier decisions in *Yorkshire Water Services Ltd v Sun Alliance and London Insurance plc* [1997] 2 Lloyd's Rep 21 and *Bartoline Ltd v Royal & Sun Alliance Insurance plc* [2006] EWHC 3598 (QB); [2007] Lloyd's Rep IR 423 were consistent with his reasoning.

[50] [2003] VSC 420.

incurred personal liability for goods purchased as the company's agent. He sought to recover under his firm's professional indemnity policy. Apart from the fact that there was a specific exclusion for trading debts,[51] the claim against insurers failed because it was not for 'compensation or damages' as required by the insuring clause. Byrne J held:[52]

> the expression in the definition of claim, 'compensation or damages', shows that what is there intended is a claim for pecuniary redress for some actionable wrong. An obligation in contract or otherwise to pay a sum in a certain event is not properly to be seen as an obligation to compensate; it is an obligation to perform the contract.

9.39 The decision in the *Kantfield* case was approved in *Kyriackou v ACE Insurance Ltd*.[53] There the insured financial adviser had been subject to a claim by the Australian Securities and Investments Commission ('ASIC'), a statutory regulator. The claim had been for an injunction. The insured argued that, although not pleaded, the injunction was sought in support of a future claim for damages and so fell within his professional indemnity insurance because it was a claim for 'civil compensation or civil damages'. The claim failed on the simple basis that ASIC was not making a claim for civil liability of any kind. In dismissing the claim, Harper JA, with whom Tate JA agreed, referred to the *Kantfield* case and said that the decision of Byrne J was:

> authority for the proposition, with which I respectfully agree, that a claim for civil damages or civil compensation does not include a claim in debt. Like reasoning points equally strongly to the conclusion that nor does such a claim encompass a claim for restitution, or for a civil penalty. Still less does it include a claim for any of the relief sought by ASIC.
>
> Aggrieved persons may have claims of various kinds—for example, in restitution, or debt, or damages—or some combination of these ... But a claim for damages requires a breach of a duty or obligation and would therefore exclude claims for restitution or debt ... [54]

9.40 In the same way, a defence to a claim under a guarantee raising grounds for relief in equity is not a claim or counterclaim for 'compensation or damages'.[55] And a claim against a local authority for return of overpaid taxes is not a claim for damages.[56] But when a former client raises a defence of set-off to a claim by the insured firm for its fees alleging that the firm acted in breach of contract and negligently, this will

---

[51] As to which see para 9.76.

[52] [2003] VSC 420, at [12].

[53] [2013] VSCA 150.

[54] Ibid at [51]–[52]. Kyrou AJA, the third member of the Court, found against the insured on the basis that ASIC had not made a claim for civil compensation or civil damages and did not express any view as to whether claims for debt or restitution did or did not fall within the scope of the insuring clause.

[55] *Amlin Corporate Member Ltd v Austcorp Project No 20 Pty Ltd* [2014] FCAFC 78, at [47]–[63] per Gleeson J, with whom Allsop P and Middleton J agreed.

[56] *Moore (Township) v Guarantee Co of North America* (1995) 26 OR (3d) 73.

be a claim for damages: it could have been raised as an independent claim against the insured.[57]

It is open to debate whether some causes of action are for compensation or not. For example, a claim against a fiduciary for exploiting for his own benefit information or an opportunity of which he learned in his capacity as a fiduciary cannot readily be described as compensatory, not least, if, as may be the case, the beneficiary would not himself have exploited the information or opportunity.[58]   **9.41**

Assistance can be derived from the decision of the Court of Appeal in *City Index Ltd v Gawler*,[59] which concerned the Civil Liability (Contribution) Act 1978. Under that Act, one person who is liable in respect of the same damage as another can recover a contribution from that person to the extent that it is just and equitable that he should do so. The cause of action relied upon in the *City Index* case was knowing receipt of trust funds, the usual remedy for which is an order requiring repayment of the funds, not an award of damages. However, the trust funds will have been depleted (and so loss suffered) to the extent that funds have been wrongly paid away. In that sense, there is a loss for which compensation is being sought against the knowing recipient.   **9.42**

The alleged knowing recipient had joined a number of others who were potentially liable in damages to the claimant. They argued that the alleged knowing recipient could not claim against them under the Civil Liability (Contribution) Act 1978 because it was not liable in respect of damage, but to return the money it had received. All three members of the Court of Appeal disagreed. Carnwath and Mummery LJJ concluded that a contribution claim could be made by adopting a 'wide view' of the Act.   **9.43**

Arden LJ agreed with the result, but on the different ground that there was a distinction between 'restitution for benefit gained on the one hand and a claim for loss suffered on the other, that is, between a claim for an account of profits and a claim for damages for loss'.[60] This is a helpful distinction when considering whether a third party claimant is seeking to recover compensation from the insured or not. Whether the claim is framed as one for damages or for some other remedy such as an account, it will be for compensation if the third party claimant is seeking to make good a loss, but not if he is merely seeking to strip the insured of unauthorized profits.[61]   **9.44**

---

[57] *Amlin Corporate Member Ltd v Austcorp Project No 20 Pty Ltd* [2014] FCAFC 78, at [53], referring to *Myers v Simcoe Erie Group* (1994) 115 DLR (4th) 607, a decision of the Ontario Court of Appeal.

[58] As in *Boardman v Phipps* [1967] 2 AC 46 and *Regal (Hastings) Ltd v Gulliver* [1967] 2 AC 134 (note).

[59] [2007] EWCA Civ 1382; [2008] Ch 313.

[60] Ibid at [67].

[61] In *Peninsular and Oriental Steam Navigation Co v Youell* [1997] 2 Lloyd's Rep 136, the insured had settled the claims of holidaymakers by refunding what they had paid for their holidays. Liability

SRA Minimum Terms and Conditions of Professional Indemnity Insurance

9.45 The SRA Minimum Terms and Conditions of Professional Indemnity Insurance have a definition of 'claim' which falls into two parts. The first provides that 'claim' means:

> a demand for, or an assertion of a right to, civil compensation or civil damages or an intimation of an intention to seek such compensation or damages.

The meaning of 'civil compensation or civil damages' falls to be considered in the light of the authorities on similar wordings considered above.[62]

9.46 The actual words were considered in the context of an earlier version of the SRA Minimum Terms and Conditions of Professional Indemnity Insurance in *Sutherland Professional Funding Ltd v Bakewells (a firm)*.[63] The insured solicitors had entered a contract with the claimant under which, among other things, they gave a guarantee in respect of loans to be made by the claimant to clients of the solicitors to fund disbursements incurred when making claims for personal injuries. The solicitors sought a declaration that their professional indemnity insurers were liable to indemnify them against this liability. Dismissing the claim, HH Judge Hegarty QC expressed the view that he could not see 'any obvious reason why the word "damages", as used in the definition of "Claim" in the Minimum Terms and Conditions should be given any wider meaning than it normally bears in an insurance context so as to extend to a liquidated liability in the nature of the debt'. However, it was not limited to damages for negligence or breach of a contractual duty of care.[64]

9.47 HH Judge Hegarty QC then considered 'civil compensation'. He noted that the words 'civil compensation' appeared to be something different to 'civil damages'. He observed that it seemed to him that 'that, in this context, the expression "civil compensation" may well bear a different and somewhat wider meaning than "civil damages"'. That said, the concept involved a payment the purpose of which was to make amends to the recipient for something. This was different from a contractual obligation to pay a debt. However, the judge was not prepared to rule out the possibility that 'civil compensation' might extend to an obligation to pay a liquidated sum.[65]

9.48 The second part of the definition of 'claim' in the SRA Minimum Terms and Conditions of Professional Indemnity Insurance makes particular provision for liability to account for client money:

---

insurers suggested that this was restitution rather than compensation. It was held that the holiday-makers could have recovered the cost of their holidays as damages.

[62] Paras 9.35–9.44.
[63] [2011] EWHC 2658 (QB); [2013] Lloyd's Rep IR 93, HH Judge Hegarty QC, sitting as a High Court Judge, at [117]–[121].
[64] Ibid at [117].
[65] Ibid at [118]–[121].

For these purposes, an obligation on an insured firm and/or any insured to remedy a breach of the Solicitors' Accounts Rules 1998 (as amended from time to time), or any rules (including, without limitation, the SRA Accounts Rules) which replace the Solicitors' Accounts Rules 1998 in whole or in part, shall be treated as a civil liability for the purpose of clause 1 of the MTC, whether or not any person makes a demand for, or an assertion of a right to, civil compensation or civil damages or an intimation of an intention to seek such compensation or damages as a result of such breach, except where any such obligation may arise as a result of the insolvency of a bank (as defined in section 87 of the SA) or a building society which holds client money in a client account of the insured firm or the failure of such bank or building society generally to repay monies on demand.[66]

This makes it clear that, where one solicitor has stolen clients' money, his innocent **9.49** partners will be entitled to an indemnity insofar as they have to make good his defalcations. The obligation to account to a client for his money is not usually put as a claim for civil compensation or civil damages. However, the innocent partners will suffer a loss in honouring their obligation to account to the client. The qualification in respect of the insolvency of a bank or building society makes it clear that insurers are not prepared to underwrite the solvency of the banking system.[67]

The nature of the activities

Policy wordings

Professional indemnity insurance is intended to protect professionals (and their **9.50** clients) from losses caused by breaches of duty in the provision of professional services. It may also provide wider cover, but it is usual to find some term restricting cover to the claims which assert a cause of action within the insuring clause and which arise out of the provision of professional services. For example, the insuring clause in the SRA Minimum Terms and Conditions of Professional Indemnity Insurance provides an indemnity against civil liability 'to the extent that it arises from private legal practice in connection with the insured firm's practice'.[68]

The ICAEW Minimum Approved Policy Wording provides 'arising out of and/ **9.51** or in connection with the conduct of any Professional Business'. 'Professional

---

[66] 'The SRA Accounts Rules' are defined as the SRA Accounts Rules 2011. 'The MTC' are the SRA Minimum Terms and Conditions of Professional Indemnity Insurance. 'The SA' is the Solicitors Act 1974. And 'building society' is defined as 'a building society within the meaning of the Building Societies Act 1986'.

[67] For a discussion of the trigger of cover in relation to this aspect of the definition of 'claim' in the SRA Minimum Terms and Conditions of Professional Indemnity Insurance see para 2.123.

[68] See further paras 9.65–9.72. There is a detailed definition of 'private legal practice' in the SRA Handbook Glossary 2012, which contains the definitions of words in italics in the SRA Minimum Terms and Conditions of Professional Indemnity Insurance.

Business' is defined very widely, no doubt in order to reflect the very wide range of services provided by firms of accountants: 'Professional Business' means:

> advice given or services provided of whatsoever nature by or on behalf of the Insured to a third party, wherever or by whomsoever given or provided irrespective of whether or not a fee is charged, but provided that if a fee is charged in respect of such advice or service then that fee is taken into account in ascertaining the income of the Firm(s).

This extends to any insured whilst holding any individual personal appointment, including trustee or personal representative.[69]

9.52 The RICS Policy Wording adopts a mixed approach. Cover is provided for civil liability 'which arises in consequence of the conduct of PROFESSIONAL BUSINESS by the INSURED'. Professional business is defined so as to include both 'those services (including the giving of advice) which are undertaken by members of the Royal Institution of Chartered Surveyors' and services which have 'otherwise been declared' to insurers.

9.53 The RIBA Architects Premier Policy Wording limits the scope of cover through a combination of the definition of 'Insured' in the Policy Wording and the certificate of insurance. Individuals and firms are only 'Insured' in respect of liability which arises directly out of Professional Business carried on by that person in the name of the Firm. Professional Business means the business described in the certificate.

The proposal form, certificate of insurance, and schedule

9.54 The nature of the activities to be covered can be defined by reference to the particular profession or activities set out in the proposal form, the certificate of insurance or schedule. For example, in *Charterhouse Development (France) Ltd v Sharp*[70] claims had to 'arise out of the ordinary course of the provision by the Assured of the financial and associated services described in the proposal form'. The insured had attached to the proposal form a brochure describing its services in some detail, enabling Longmore J to find that the activities which gave rise to the claim satisfied that requirement.[71]

In the conduct of professional business

9.55 It is not uncommon to find that cover under contracts of professional indemnity insurance is in respect of claims which arise from the conduct of 'professional business'. As noted above, the ICAEW Minimum Approved Policy Wording requires the claims to be in connection with 'the conduct of any Professional Business

---

[69] Specific, detailed provision is made as to the extent of cover provided to insured who are acting as company secretaries, registrars, or directors.

[70] [1998] Lloyd's Rep IR 266. See also *Encia Remediations Ltd v Canopius Managing Agents Ltd* [2007] EWHC 916 (Comm); [2007] Lloyd's Rep IR 79.

[71] In *MDIS Ltd v Swinbank* [1999] Lloyd's Rep IR 516, the claims had to arise 'out of the professional conduct of the Assured's business as stated in the Schedule'.

carried on by, or on behalf of, the Insured', with a very wide definition of what constitutes 'Professional Business'.[72]

Given the range of work undertaken by modern accountancy practices, there is **9.56** obvious sense in this wide definition. In *Drayton v Martin*,[73] the insured was both an accountant and an investment adviser. The two roles were interlinked: advice as to reducing liability for tax merged into advice as to what investments to make. In the circumstances, the Federal Court of Australia held that the advice given by the insured had been given 'in connection with' his practice as an accountant so that he was entitled to an indemnity under his accountants' professional liability policy. This decision was upheld on appeal.[74]

A requirement that liability arise from the conduct of a professional business does **9.57** not mean that, to be covered, the claim against the insured must be for a failure of expert professional judgment or skill. It need merely arise from the carrying on of the professional business. This is illustrated by the decision in *Suncorp Metway Insurance Ltd v Landridge Pty Ltd*.[75] There the insured was an estate agent, which was insured against claims 'for breach of a professional duty by reason of any act, error or omission committed or alleged to have been committed by the Insured in the conduct of the Business'. As part of that business the insured managed certain premises. The tenant of those premises complained about the state of the premises, but the insured's receptionist failed to pass on the complaint. The insured's property manager had failed to spot the problem, which required little skill to identify: it was a hole in the floor. The tenant suffered personal injuries as a result of the failure to deal with her complaint. Insurers argued that the insured had not been in breach of any professional duty: no professional training or competence had been engaged in the failure to deal with the tenant's complaint.

The Supreme Court of Victoria, Court of Appeal, disagreed. As Nettle JA explained: **9.58**

> The fact is that there may be little in the way of intellectual activity or skill in many of the activities that constitute part of the practice of a profession. But negligence in their performance would undoubtedly constitute a breach of professional duty. To take but one example, of which this court may be expected to know something, it takes very little skill or cerebral activity to file a return in the time required by statute or to serve a pleading within the time limited by the rules of court. Yet it cannot be supposed that the negligent failure of a solicitor to file or serve in time would not be covered by a policy of the kind described.

However, where the insured carries out both professional and non-professional **9.59** activities, the need for some special skill and knowledge in order to undertake a task

---

[72] See para 9.51.
[73] [1996] FCA 1504; (1996) 137 ALR 145. The relevant provisions of the policy were similar, but not identical, to those in the ICAEW Minimum Policy Wording set out in para 9.51.
[74] *HIH Casualty and General Insurance Ltd v FAI General Insurance Co Ltd* [1997] FCA 272.
[75] [2005] VSCA 223; (2005) 13 ANZIC 61.660.

may be required to bring the activity within cover for professional indemnity. For this purpose, it will not matter that the insured is not acting subject to a professional engagement: it will be the nature of the activity which will determine whether it falls within cover or not.[76] The response by a local authority to a request for details of its records concerning a piece of land is not advice of a professional nature and so the local authority is not entitled to an indemnity when inaccurate information is given, giving rise to a claim against it.[77] In the context of such mixed activities, what is required to fall within the scope of professional indemnity insurance is 'advice and services of a skilful character according to an established discipline'.[78]

Specific definitions in the policy: examples

9.60 Where the sphere of professional activity which is insured is defined in the policy, whether by a standard clause or by the proposal form, certificate of insurance or schedule, an insured who trespasses out of that area will risk being uninsured should a claim be made against him. So in *JCS Cost Management Ltd v Johnston*[79] cover was in respect of liability 'in connection with the Insured's Professional Business Practice'. This was defined in an endorsement to the policy as 'quantity surveyor and project manager'. The insured was sued for alleged negligent advice as to the condition of a house. This was not the sort of advice which a quantity surveyor or project manager gives and so the insured's claim for an indemnity failed.[80]

9.61 However, if the third party claim is sufficiently linked to the professional activity definition in the policy, the insured will be entitled to an indemnity. For example, in *Smart v AAI Ltd*[81] cover was provided in respect of claims 'resulting from the conduct of the Professional Services' which were defined as 'the professional business described in the Schedule, and no other'. The schedule defined the insured's professional business as 'mortgage broker/finance broker/mortgage originator/mortgage manager and debt reduction'. The insured persuaded the third party claimants to lend him money, representing that he would lend it on to clients of his mortgage broking business. While insurers were entitled to refuse cover for this claim because of an exclusion in respect of liability 'assumed outside the normal course of the Professional Services',[82] the third party's claim did result from the provision of 'Professional Services' as defined because of the relatively

---

[76] *Attorney-General v Aon New Zealand Ltd* [2008] NZHC 479, at [130].
[77] *Government Insurance Office of New South Wales v Council of the City of Perth* [1999] NSWCA 42; (1999) 134 ALR 605.
[78] *GIO General Ltd v Newcastle City Council* (1996) 38 NSWLR 558, at 568 per Kirby J.
[79] [2014] NZHC 2718.
[80] See also *Yanaky v Arch Insurance (Canada)* 2014 ONSC 4719. In that case a financial planner had professional indemnity insurance on terms which included a detailed definition of 'professional services'. These included advising or servicing specific types of investment. The claim against the insured concerned an investment which did not fall within any of those types and so the insured was not covered in respect of his liability.
[81] [2015] NSWSC 392.
[82] See n 193 under para 7.109.

low threshold of causation and because the chain of events which led to the claims being made started in circumstances which were 'consistent with the professional business of broking loans'.[83]

Specific definition in the policy: construction contractors and professionals

By way of contrast to solicitors, accountants, and surveyors, in the case of some **9.62** insured, professional indemnity insurance will only be intended to provide an indemnity in respect of a part of the insured's usual activities. For example, design and build contractors will incur not only potential liability for professional services such as the design of the building, but also potential liabilities as building contractors which would not usually fall within the scope of professional indemnity insurance. It is therefore not surprising to find that professional indemnity policies for design and build contractors define with some care the nature of the activities which are to be insured.

So, in *Kajima UK Engineering Ltd v The Underwriting Company Ltd*[84] the insured **9.63** design and build contractor was covered against civil liability 'arising out of the Professional Activities undertaken by or on behalf of Insured'. 'Professional Activities' were defined as:

> design or specification; supervision of construction/installation; feasibility study; technical information calculation; surveying undertaken only by or under the direction and direct control of properly qualified architect or engineer or surveyor or quantity surveyor.

The definition also provided that 'Professional Activities' did not include 'the supervision by the Insured of its own or its sub-contractor's work where such supervision is undertaken in its capacity as Building or Engineering Contractor'.

In the same way in *Body Corporate 326421 v Auckland Council*[85] building contrac- **9.64** tors were insured against liability in relation to the carrying out of 'Professional Activities and Duties'. These were defined in the policy as:

> ... those activities and duties undertaken by or under the supervision[86] of:
> a) persons or personnel who are professionally qualified; or
> b) persons or personnel having not less than 5 years relevant experience
> in carrying out professional activities that would normally be undertaken by a professionally qualified person

> For the avoidance of doubt Professional Activities and Duties includes the duty to warn of defects in the professional activities and duties of others, but does not include:
> (i) The day to day supervision of manual operatives, labour or construction work usually undertaken by building, engineering or business support service providers.

---

[83] [2015] NSWSC 392, at [201] per Beech-Jones J.
[84] [2008] EWHC 83 (TCC); [2008] Lloyd's Rep IR 391.
[85] [2015] NZHC 862.
[86] For what is entailed in supervision see para 9.82.

This definition was buttressed by an exclusion which is considered below.[87] As in the *Kajima UK Engineering* case, the aim is clear: to limit cover to professional liability, rather than to the wider contractual liability to which building contractors will be liable under construction contracts.

Solicitors: private legal practice

9.65 To be covered under the SRA Minimum Terms and Conditions of Professional Indemnity Insurance claims must arise from 'private legal practice', which is defined as 'the provision of services in private practice as a solicitor or REL'.[88] That is a wide definition. As Taylor LJ said of the role of solicitors in *Balabel v Air India*,[89] when considering the scope of legal professional privilege:[90]

> Their role then would have been confined for the most part to that of lawyer and would not have extended to business adviser or man of affairs. To speak therefore of matters 'within the ordinary business of a solicitor' would in practice usually have meant the giving of advice and assistance of a specifically legal nature. But the range of assistance given by solicitors to their clients and of activities carried out on their behalf has greatly broadened in recent times and is still developing.

9.66 There are, however, limits beyond which a solicitor will not be providing services in private practice as a solicitor. In *Haseldine v Hosken*,[91] a solicitor was sued by a third party claimant for champerty and maintenance, having entered champertous agreements with a client in respect of proceedings against the third party claimant. He sought unsuccessfully to claim on his professional indemnity policy. Holding that he was not entitled to succeed, Greer LJ said:[92]

> The acts intended to be covered were those he was doing not to secure a benefit for himself, but those he was doing on behalf of his client. Read in that way this policy does not indemnify Mr Haseldine in respect of the consequences of his making the two agreements by which he was to secure an interest in the result of the litigation— agreements which, in view of the law of this country, he ought not to have made. The damage that arose did not arise owing to any neglect, omission or error of Mr Haseldine in his professional capacity as a solicitor, and therefore was not covered by the policy sued on.

9.67 This decision was followed in *Sutherland Professional Funding Ltd v Bakewells (a firm)*.[93] The liability of the insured solicitors as guarantor of loans taken out by their clients to fund disbursements incurred in the conduct of litigation did not 'arise from private legal practice'. Holding that the words 'arise from' imported a

---

[87] See para 9.85.
[88] 'REL' means 'registered European lawyer'. This definition is expanded by a number of instances of what is included within 'the provision of services in private practice as a solicitor or registered European lawyer' and a number of instances of what is not.
[89] [1988] Ch 317.
[90] Ibid at 331–2.
[91] [1933] 1 KB 822.
[92] Ibid at 837–8. See also the judgment of Slesser LJ at 839.
[93] [2011] EWHC 2658 (QB); [2013] Lloyd's Rep IR 93. For the relevant facts see para 9.46.

test of proximate causation,[94] HH Judge Hegarty QC, sitting as High Court Judge, held that, while it might be the case that had the insured solicitors conducted the claims without negligence, the loans would have been repaid, this was not sufficiently linked to their liability as guarantors. He concluded that the liability which the insured solicitors undertook 'was intended to secure a benefit for themselves and that Sutherland's claim does not arise from any neglect, omission or error of [the partner who had had conduct of the claims] in his professional capacity as a solicitor'.[95]

A number of Australian decisions adopt the distinction between practice as a solicitor (recognizing the wide range of advice and other services which are provided in that way) and entrepreneurial activity outside that practice.[96] For example, in *Solicitors' Liability Committee v Gray*[97] the insured solicitors became involved in property syndication. One such scheme, for a syndicate of barristers, went wrong and the insured were sued. It was held that the insured were not acting in the private practice of a solicitor, but were engaged in the syndication of loans. Under the scheme, the insured were to be paid an acquisition fee rather than on the usual terms for solicitors, the conveyancing was done by another firm, and the insured gave no tax or other technical or legal advice. The insured were acting as businessmen or entrepreneurs, not as solicitors.[98]   **9.68**

To fall within the definition of 'private legal practice' the solicitor must be providing   **9.69**
some service as a solicitor, taking full account of the wide range of services provided by solicitors. Use of a solicitor's client account simply as a vehicle for receipt and distribution of money without the solicitor being engaged to provide any service as a solicitor will not involve the solicitor acting in private legal practice.[99]

---

[94] Ibid at [94]. See paras 9.92–9.93 for a discussion of proximate cause.

[95] Ibid at [95]–[99]. A different result was reached in *Impact Funding Solutions Ltd v Barrington Support Services Ltd* [2013] EWHC 4005 (QB), another case involving a claim against solicitors by a lender which had made loans to the solicitors' clients. The claim in the *Impact Funding Solutions* case was for breach of a term in the contract between the lender and the solicitors by which the solicitors warranted, among other things, that they would conduct the underlying claims with reasonable skill and care. HH Judge Waksman QC, sitting as High Court Judge, had found that the solicitors had failed to do so. In a claim by the lenders against the solicitors' professional indemnity insurance pursuant to the Third Parties (Rights Against Insurers) Act 1930, he held that the proximate cause of the solicitors' liability to the lender was their negligent conduct of the claims so that the liability arose from private legal practice.

[96] The distinction was well made in *Leary v Federal Commissioner of Taxation* (1980) 32 ALR 221, at 240 by Brennan J. See also *Schipp v Cameron* [1998] NSWSC 997, at [907] per Einstein J.

[97] [1997] FCA 652; (1997) 77 FCR 1.

[98] See also *Carr v Swart* [2007] NSWCA 337: solicitor assembled syndicate to invest in prime bank guarantee scheme (which transpired to be a scam); no conventional retainer; fee based on the anticipated profits rather than any conventional basis; solicitor's role expressed to be limited to 'custodial and account providing capacity'; these together with other factors showed that the insured was not undertaking 'the business of practising as a solicitor' so that he was not entitled to be indemnified against liability to the investors.

[99] *Cassells Brock & Blackwell LLP v LawPro* (2006) 80 OR (3d) 570 (Ontario Superior Court of Justice), affirmed by the Court of Appeal for Ontario at 2007 ONCA 122; (2007) 85 OR (3d) 318.

9.70 It is also possible for a person who is qualified as a solicitor to provide services which a solicitor might provide, but not do so as a solicitor in private practice. So in *Zurich Professional Ltd v Brown*[100] an individual who was qualified to act as a solicitor acted as an executor and charged a fee for his work. However, he used notepaper which was not of the kind which a solicitor is obliged to use, did not appear to believe that he was acting as a solicitor, did not maintain professional indemnity insurance as required if he was practising as a solicitor and said in terms in several letters that he was not practising as a solicitor. These factors outweighed the few occasions on which he had suggested that he was and Sir William Blackburne held on these facts that he had not been acting as a solicitor.

9.71 A solicitor who is acting dishonestly can still be acting in private practice as a solicitor for the purposes of the insurance coverage of any innocent insured who are vicariously liable to third parties as a result of his dishonesty. And the partners of a dishonest solicitor will be vicariously liable as long as he was acting in the ordinary course of the firm's business.[101]

9.72 Where a solicitor is also a director or officer of a body corporate (other than a body corporate which falls within the definition of the Insured)[102] he will not be deemed to be acting in private practice as a solicitor insofar as he incurs liability in that capacity. This follows from the fact that the SRA Minimum Terms and Conditions of Professional Indemnity Insurance permit insurers to exclude cover for such liability, which could be the subject of separate directors and officers insurance. They must, however, provide cover for any liability for legal work performed by the director or officer and indemnify the other insured against any vicarious liability.

Exclusions

9.73 The scope of the liability for which insurers agree to indemnify the insured will usually be defined in part by a number of exclusions.

9.74 For example, the SRA Minimum Terms and Conditions of Professional Indemnity Insurance permit policies of professional indemnity insurance for solicitors to exclude cover for liability for death and bodily injury, property damage, partnership disputes, liability as an employer, debts and trading liabilities, and fines and penalties.

9.75 This is a typical list, but the actual exclusions vary from policy to policy. Other typical exclusions include co-insurance, liability caused by ionizing radiations or contamination by radioactivity, work carried out in the USA or Canada, terrorism, pollution, and such like.

---

[100] [2010] EWHC 3300 (Ch); [2011] Lloyd's Rep IR 607.

[101] *Dubai Aluminium Co Ltd v Salaam and Others* [2002] UKHL 48; [2003] 2 AC 366, and s 10 of the Partnership Act 1890.

[102] As to which see para 9.09.

Trade Debts

Even in policies of professional indemnity insurance which only provide an indem- **9.76**
nity in relation to claims by third parties for compensation or damages (and so not
for claims in debt),[103] it is usual to find a term excluding cover for trade debts.[104]
The exclusion of liability for debts and trading liabilities in the ICAEW Minimum
Approved Policy Wording does not apply to claims made against the insured for
negligence in the normal course of the conduct of a receivership or procedures
under the Insolvency Act 1986 or equivalent legislation in Northern Ireland or the
Republic of Ireland. This would not entitle an accountant who incurred personal
liability as a receiver other than in negligence to be indemnified. So if, like the
accountant in *Kantfield Pty Ltd v Lockwood*,[105] a receiver incurred personal liability
for the debts of the company, he would not be covered.

The SRA Minimum Terms and Conditions of Professional Indemnity Insurance **9.77**
contain an extensive exclusion clause headed 'Debts and trading liabilities'. It provides that the contract of insurance may exclude or limit insurers' liability to the
extent that any claim or related defence costs arise from any:

(a) trading or personal debt of any insured; or
(b) legal liability assumed or accepted by an insured or an insured firm under any
    contract or agreement for the supply to, or use by, the insured or insured firm
    of goods or services in the course of the insured firm's practice[106] ... or
(c) guarantee, indemnity or undertaking by any particular insured in connection
    with the provision of finance, property, assistance or other benefit or advantage
    directly or indirectly to that insured.

This clause appears to be widely worded. However, in *Impact Funding Solutions* **9.78**
Ltd v Barrington Support Services Ltd[107] the Court of Appeal applied a purposive
construction to it, holding that:[108]

the essential purpose of the exclusion is to prevent insurers from being liable for
what one might call liabilities of a solicitor in respect of those aspects of his practice
which affect him or her personally as opposed to liabilities arising from his professional obligations to his or her clients. Thus if a solicitor incurs liability to the sup-
plier of, for example, a photocopier, insurers do not cover that liability nor would
they cover obligations to a company providing cleaning services for the solicitor's
offices. If the office premises are leased by the partnership or held subject to a mortgage to a bank, the obligations under such lease or mortgage (or any guarantee of

---

[103] See paras 9.35–9.47.
[104] The RIBA Architects Premier Policy Wording excludes cover for 'any claim arising out of or in connection with any trading loss or trading liability incurred by any business managed by or carried on by or on behalf of the Insured'. The RICS Policy Wording has an exclusion for 'any CLAIM arising out of any trading loss or trading liabilities incurred by the INSURED including loss of any business or custom'.
[105] [2003] VSC 420: see para 9.38.
[106] There is an exception to this sub-clause in relation to legal liability arising in the course of an insured firm's practice in connection with or its use of the HM Land Registry network.
[107] [2015] EWCA Civ 31; [2015] Lloyd's Rep IR 12.
[108] Ibid at [19] per Longmore LJ, with whom the other members of the Court of Appeal agreed.

such lease or mortgage) would not be covered either. It is these sorts of personal obligations (which may nevertheless be part of a solicitor's practice as a solicitor) which are not intended to be covered. These obligations are to be distinguished from the obligations which are incurred in connection with the solicitor's duty to his clients which are intended to be covered.

9.79 It followed that liabilities arising from obligations assumed by a solicitor under a contract with a commercial lender which made loans to the solicitor's client to fund disbursements were not excluded from cover by this exclusion. Such obligations are 'essentially part and parcel of the obligations assumed by a solicitor in respect of his professional duties to his client rather than obligations personal to the solicitor'. They are professional obligations which are not intended to fall within the exclusion clause.[109]

Supervision

9.80 Clauses requiring activities to be carried out by individuals with professional qualifications and/or experience or subject to a required degree of supervision are frequently found in policies of professional indemnity insurance for surveyors and construction professionals either as part of the definition of the insured activities[110] or as an exclusion clause. Such terms appear in the general conditions in the RIBA Architects Premier Policy Wording (in respect of surveys and valuations) and as an exclusion in the RICS Policy Wording (in respect of surveys and valuations).

9.81 Guidance as to what is required for there to be adequate supervision can be derived from the decision of the Court of Appeal in *Summers v Congreve Horner & Company*.[111] The clause in that case was an exclusion clause which provided that the policy would not indemnify the insured against any claim or loss:

> Arising from survey/inspection and/or valuation reports of real property unless such surveys/inspections and/or valuations shall have been made:
> (a) by a Fellow or Professional Associate of the Royal Institution of Chartered Surveyors; or by a Fellow or Associate of the Incorporated Society of Valuers and Auctioneers; or by a Fellow or Associate of Faculty of Architects and Surveyors; or by a Fellow or Associate of Royal Institute of British Architects; or by a Fellow or Associate of Royal Institute of Architects of Scotland; or
> (b) by anyone who has not less than five years experience of such work or such other person nominated by the Assured to execute such work subject always to supervision of such work by a person qualified in accordance with (a) above.

9.82 Staughton LJ, with whom Woolf LJ, agreed, held that this clause did not mean that the person being supervised had to be constantly watched. But it did require that

---

[109] Ibid at [21]–[22]. A different approach was adopted and a different conclusion was reached in *Sutherland Professional Funding Ltd v Bakewells (a firm)* [2011] EWHC 2658 (QB); [2013] Lloyd's Rep IR 93, at [142]–[165]. At the time of writing the decision of the Court of Appeal in the *Impact Funding Solutions* case is subject to appeal to the Supreme Court.

[110] See para 9.64.

[111] [1992] 40 EG 144.

he be watched over for at least some of the time. The degree of supervision required was that which 'good practice in the profession of surveying would regard as necessary, in the light of the stage in training and experience reached by the unqualified person'.

Construction contractors and professionals

9.83 Professional indemnity insurance of construction professionals can go to great lengths to define precisely what activities are to be insured and which are not.[112] For example, in *Baulderstone Hornibrook Engineering Pty Ltd v Gordian Runoff Ltd*[113] the insured were engineers. The activities which were insured were 'engineering, project management, surveying, designing, geotechnical, environmental monitoring, construction management, certification and as defined in the policy wording'. There were also a large number of exclusions, including the following:

> (p) arising out of construction work performed involving the means, methods, techniques, sequences, procedures and use of equipment, of any nature whatsoever which are employed by the Insured's contracting staff or others in executing any phase of any Project.

9.84 The New South Wales Court of Appeal held that the evident purpose of exclusion (p) was 'to remove from the scope of indemnity claims that arise out of the performance of construction work'. The insured had incurred liability because of the use of a defective method for backfilling and compaction in one area of the site. The method used had not been specified as part of the design but left to be established on site by the contractor. It was therefore part of the construction work and the insured was not entitled to an indemnity.

9.85 In the same way in *Body Corporate 326421 v Auckland Council*,[114] not only did the definition of insured activities seek to restrict cover to what might broadly be called claims for professional negligence arising from the provision of professional services,[115] but the policy included an exclusion in the following terms:

> The Insurer shall not be liable under the Policy to indemnify the Insured in respect of any Claim … arising out of defective workmanship by or on behalf of the Insured, defective materials, manual labour operations, or any defective materials, workmanship or production techniques used in the actual manufacture of any product.

> This Exclusion shall not apply where such liability is otherwise indemnifiable hereunder and arises from:
> a. an act of neglect or error or omission with respect to the design or specification of materials

---

[112] See paras 9.62–9.64 for a discussion of how this is done through the description of insured activities.

[113] [2008] NSWCA 243; (2008) 15 ANZ Insurance Cases 61–780.

[114] [2015] NZHC 862.

[115] See para 9.64.

b. an act of neglect or error or omission with respect to advice given in connection with the selection of materials undertaken by professionally qualified persons or personnel as per item a) of Definition of Professional Activities and Duties ...

On the facts at least one proximate cause of the insured's liability was defective workmanship,[116] so that insurers were entitled to deny cover relying on this exclusion.

9.86 A further way in which cover can be limited or excluded in contracts of professional indemnity insurance for contractors or construction professionals is in relation to the nature of the liability insured. Unlike professionals, building contractors in particular will often undertake strict liability for breach of contract.[117] And they and construction professionals can give warranties to the intended owners or occupiers of buildings or cutting across a chain of contracts. Policies of professional indemnity insurance often seek to exclude or reduce cover for strict liabilities.

9.87 The insuring clause in the RIBA Architects Premier Policy Wording provides an indemnity in respect of civil liability in consequence of 'any breach of the professional duty of care owed by the Insured to the claimant which term is deemed to include a breach of warranty of authority'. This is bolstered by an exclusion headed 'Warranties, Penalties and Collateral Warranties', which provides that there is no cover in respect of:

> Any claim arising out of any performance warranty (including but not limited to fitness for purpose warranties) guarantee, penalty clause or liquidated damages clause unless the liability of the Insured to the claimant would have existed in the absence of such warranty, guarantee or clauses.

9.88 The RICS Policy Wording contains a detailed and lengthy exclusion clause in relation to contractual liability.

9.89 The scope of an exclusion clause in a contract of professional indemnity insurance for architects in relation to 'warranties, penalties and collateral warranties' was considered in *Oakapple Homes (Glossop) Ltd v DTR (2009) Ltd (In Liquidation)*.[118] The relevant part of the exclusion clause (clause 5.9) excluded cover for:

> Any claim arising out of any performance warranty (including but not limited to fitness for purpose warranties) guarantee, penalty clause or liquidated damages clause unless the liability of the Assured to the claimant would have existed in the absence of such warranty, guarantee or clauses.

> Except that, notwithstanding anything stated immediately above, the indemnity provided to the Assured under this Policy will apply to a claim arising from the performance by the Assured of obligations agreed to be performed by them under a Collateral Warranty, Duty of Care Agreement or similar Agreement, provided that:

---

[116] As to the position where there are two proximate causes see paras 9.94–9.95.
[117] As to which see para 9.28.
[118] [2013] EWHC 2394 (TCC); [2014] Lloyd's Rep IR 103.

(a) the benefit of such Warranty or Agreement is no greater or longer lasting than that in the original contract to which it relates

(b) no Indemnity will be given for:

  (i) any guarantee or warrant of fitness for purpose, satisfaction of performance specification or period of project works, or

  (ii) any financial penalty or liquidated damages.

The insured architects were in liquidation. The claimant sought an order requiring **9.90** the insured to execute a number of collateral warranties. The liquidator was concerned to ensure that any liability under the warranties would be covered by the architects' professional indemnity insurance and, in particular, that cover would not be excluded by the exclusion clause. The insured had acted as architects on the conversion of a former cotton mill into flats. The warranties were to be in favour of the first owners and occupiers of the flats and to anyone providing finance to the first owners and occupiers.

Insurers argued that the benefit of the warranties would be greater than that in **9.91** the original contract because the insured would not be able to rely upon the contributory negligence of the party to the original contract to reduce liability to the beneficiaries of the collateral warranties and that the measure of damages payable under them might be greater than that payable under the original contract. Ramsey J rejected their argument. He held that the 'benefit' of the collateral benefit referred to the scope of the obligations, not to the remedy for breach of them. He explained:[119]

> the reference to 'the benefit of the warranty' in exclusion 5.9 is not a reference to the damages claimable under the warranty. The benefit of the warranty is the benefit in providing contractual liability by [the insured] to the beneficiaries. It cannot be a reference to the quantum of damages. The purpose of the clause in the policy is to give insurance cover where there is an obligation on an architect under a collateral warranty or duty of care agreement by reference to obligations under the architect's original contract.

The obligations of the insured architects under their retainer were the same as those which were the subject of the collateral warranties.

C. Cause of the Insured's Loss

Proximate cause

An insured will only be entitled to recover an indemnity against insurers in respect **9.92** of his liability to a third party if the proximate cause of that liability falls within the scope of cover. The need for the insured's loss to have been proximately caused by an insured peril is a basic rule of insurance law. 'Proximate' does not mean the

---

[119] Ibid at [54].

nearest in time, or the first. It means the dominant, real, operative, efficient, or effective cause. As Lord Shaw of Dunfermline said in *Leyland Shipping Co Ltd v Norwich Union Fire Insurance Society Ltd*:[120]

> What does 'proximate' here mean? To treat proximate as if it was the cause which is proximate in point of time is, ... out of the question. The cause which is truly proximate is that which is proximate in efficiency. That efficiency may have been preserved although other causes may in the meantime have sprung up which have yet not destroyed it, or truly impaired it, and it may culminate in a result of which it still remains the real efficient cause to which the event can he ascribed.

9.93 So, for example, where a ship is scuttled, the proximate cause of the sinking is not the ingress of water, but the scuttling of the ship[121] and where a faulty impeller leads to an explosion which damages a boiler house, it is the faulty impeller which is the proximate cause of the damage to the boiler house.[122] In this area 'judicial analysis of causation tends to coincide with common sense'.[123]

More than one proximate cause

9.94 It is not infrequent for there to be two proximate causes of a loss and this possibility has long been recognized in English law.[124] For example, in *Midland Mainline Ltd v Eagle Star Insurance Co Ltd*[125] the insured claimed under a business interruption policy for losses caused by the imposition of speed restrictions following a railway crash. The crash was caused by wear and tear to a rail. Steel J held that the cause of the losses was the imposition of the speed restrictions. The Court of Appeal disagreed. There were two proximate causes: the wear and tear to the rail, which had led to the imposition of the speed restrictions, and then the speed restrictions themselves.

9.95 Where there are two proximate causes of a loss and one is insured and the other is not, then the insured will be entitled to an indemnity.[126] However, if there are two proximate causes and one is insured but the other is expressly excluded, then the exclusion applies and the insured is not entitled to recover from insurers.[127]

---

[120] [1918] AC 350, at 369.

[121] *P Samuel and Company Ltd v Dumas* [1924] AC 431.

[122] *Commonwealth Smelting Ltd v Guardian Royal Exchange Assurance Ltd* [1986] 1 Lloyd's Rep 121.

[123] *The Board of Trustees of the Tate Gallery v Duffy Construction Ltd* [2007] EWHC 361 (TCC); [2007] Lloyd's Rep IR 758, at [43] per Jackson J. See also *Gray v Barr* [1971] 2 QB 554, at 567 per Lord Denning MR.

[124] *Reischer v Borwick* [1894] 2 QB 548; *Leyland Shipping Co Ltd v Norwich Union Fire Insurance Society Ltd* [1918] AC 350; *J J Lloyd Instruments Ltd v Northern Star Insurance Co Ltd (The 'Miss Jay Jay')* [1987] 1 Lloyd's Rep 32.

[125] [2004] EWCA Civ 1042; [2004] 2 Lloyd's Rep 604.

[126] *ACE European Group v Standard Life Assurance Ltd* [2012] EWCA Civ 1713; [2013] Lloyd's Rep IR 41, at [23] per Tomlinson LJ, with whom the other members of the Court of Appeal agreed.

[127] *P Samuel and Company Ltd v Dumas* [1924] AC 431, at 467–8 per Lord Sumner; *Wayne Tank and Pump Co Ltd v Employers Liability Assurance Corporation Ltd* [1974] 1 QB 57; *Total Graphics Ltd v AGF Insurance Ltd* [1977] 1 Lloyd's Rep 599; and *Midland Mainline Ltd v Eagle Star Insurance Co*

Application to professional indemnity insurance

There is no doubt that in order to recover under a policy of professional indemnity **9.96** insurance the insured must show that the proximate cause of his loss was a risk against which he was insured. So, in *Goddard and Smith v Frew*[128] the insured were a firm of estate agents. A rent collector employed by them had stolen some money collected from tenants of one of the insured's clients. The insured paid their client and sought to recover their loss from their professional indemnity insurers. The Court of Appeal held that the real loss to the insured was the rent collector's embezzlement. That was the true, proximate cause of the loss and it was not covered by their professional indemnity policy. In other words, the cause of the insured's loss was not the failure to hand over the money to their client, but their employee's theft.

West Wake Price & Co v Ching[129] was another case in which the insured's employee **9.97** stole client money. The insured were sued for negligence or breach of duty as accountants, for money had and received and for moneys converted by the insured to their own use. Notwithstanding the form in which it was pleaded, Devlin J had no doubt that the claim was primarily based on the fraud of the employee.[130] If the proximate cause test had to be applied, then the choice was between the fraud of the employee and the negligence of the insured in supervising him[131] and the answer was that the fraud of the employee was the proximate cause.[132]

In *Total Graphics Ltd v AGF Insurance Ltd*,[133] the insured was an insurance broker. **9.98** He had been instructed by his client to accept a quotation from one insurer. He did not do so. Indeed, he did not even approach that insurer at any stage. Instead he placed the insurance with other insurers, whom he deliberately misled. Those other insurers avoided cover and the client suffered a large, uninsured loss for which he sought damages from the insured. Mance J held that the 'dominant, real or effective cause' of the lack of insurance was the insured's 'flagrant misconduct in the placing of the insurance with the insurers who he did approach'. Even if some other basis of liability in negligence might have been established, this would not have entitled the insured to recover against his professional indemnity insurers.[134]

Ltd [2004] EWCA Civ 1042; [2004] 2 Lloyd's Rep 604. See also *Handelsbanken Norwegian Branch of Svenska Handelsbanken AB (PUBL) v Dandridge ('The Aliza Glacial')* [2002] 2 Lloyd's Rep 421, at 431 per Potter LJ and *KR v Royal & Sun Alliance Plc* [2006] EWCA Civ 1454; [2007] Lloyd's Rep IR 368, at [36] per Scott Baker LJ.

[128] [1939] 4 All ER 358.
[129] [1957] 1 WLR 45.
[130] Ibid at 48.
[131] Ibid at 49.
[132] Ibid at 58.
[133] [1997] 1 Lloyd's Rep 599.
[134] Ibid at 605–6.

9.99 In *MDIS Ltd v Swinbank*,[135] the insured had been sued for negligent mis-statement and had settled the claim. Insurers contended that the statement in issue had been made fraudulently rather than negligently. The insured's answer was that, on the true construction of the insuring clause, cover was determined by the way in which the third party claimant put forward his claim against the insured. The insuring clause was in these terms:

> The underwriters will indemnify the Assured to the extent and in the manner detailed herein against any claim for which the Assured may become legally liable, first made against the Assured and notified to the Underwriters during the period of this Certificate arising out of professional conduct of the Assured's business as stated in the Schedule alleging:
>
> (a) Neglect Error or Omission
>
> any neglect error or omission including breach of contract occasioned by same ...'

The insured relied upon the word 'alleging'. Mance J disagreed,[136] and his decision was upheld on appeal. Dismissing the insured's appeal, Clarke LJ said that the effect of the clause was clear. It was that insurers would only be liable if the proximate cause of the insured's loss was one of the specified perils.[137]

9.100 In the case of professional indemnity insurance, however, the cause of the insured's loss is his liability to the third party claimant. That liability will have both a basis in fact and a basis in law, in that the relevant facts will have entitled the third party claimant to recover against the insured by way of one or more causes of action. In cases such as *Goddard and Smith v Frew*,[138] *West Wake Price & Co v Ching*,[139] and *Total Graphics Ltd v AGF Insurance Ltd*,[140] the issue was the effective factual cause of the insured's liability. Thus in the *West Wake* case the choice was between the employee's theft and the employer's negligent supervision of the employee.

9.101 Sometimes, however, the factual basis of the insured's liability to the third party claimant will be clear, but there will be more than one cause of action by which the third party claimant could recover his loss from the insured. For example, in *Sturge v Hackett*[141] the insured was the tenant of a flat in a manor house. While trying to burn out a bird's nest in a cornice under the eaves outside his flat, the insured negligently caused a fire which destroyed most of the manor house and its contents. The insured had cover against all sums for which he was held legally liable as occupier of the flat. At trial his claim against insurers failed because it

---

135 [1999] Lloyd's Rep IR 516.
136 *McDonnell Information Systems Ltd v Swinbank* [1999] Lloyd's Rep IR 98.
137 [1999] Lloyd's Rep IR 516, at [20].
138 [1939] 4 All ER 358.
139 [1957] 1 WLR 45.
140 [1997] 1 Lloyd's Rep 599.
141 [1962] 1 WLR 1257.

was held that the fire had not started from the part of the premises of which he was occupier so that he had only been liable in the common law tort of negligence (which did not require him to have been the occupier of the flat) and not as an occupier who allowed a fire to escape from his premises. The Court of Appeal allowed the insured's appeal on the ground that the cornice where the fire started was part of his premises. In doing so, Diplock LJ, who gave the judgment of the Court of Appeal, said:[142]

> It is rightly conceded by the respondent insurers that this question turns upon whether upon the facts an action against the defendant by those who suffered damage as a result of the fire could be framed in a form in which it would be a necessary averment that the defendant was the occupier of the flat; and that if an action could successfully be brought against him in that form it is irrelevant that a different cause of action, for example based on his personal negligence, could also be successfully alleged against him.

It follows that if the proximate cause of the insured's loss is an act or omission **9.102** which can be pleaded against the insured in a number of ways and if he is insured against liability in one of those ways, then, upon his liability being ascertained, the insured will be entitled to an indemnity from insurers. So in *Capel-Cure Myers Capital Management Ltd v McCarthy*[143] the insured had professional indemnity cover against liability under the Financial Services Act 1986. Under the policy, insurers were obliged to pay the costs of defending a claim. The insured had not obtained cover for liability for breach of contract, negligence, or breach of fiduciary duty. The insured was sued in a single set of proceedings for delivering securities which it held for a client pension fund to two banks without authority. The insured was sued for breach of contract, negligence, breach of fiduciary duty, and under the Financial Services Act 1986. Insurers declined to fund the defence of the claim.

Finding against insurers, Potter J held that it was necessary to distinguish **9.103** between a loss caused by a combination of causes and a loss resulting from a single cause which could be properly described as amounting to more than one peril or as giving rise to more than one cause of action. Here, the claim against the insured:[144]

> is properly framed in a form in which it would be a necessary averment that the plaintiffs are by virtue of their status and/or activities under various statutory duties to the plaintiffs which on the facts they have breached, and if an action could successfully be brought against them in that form, it is irrelevant that a different cause of action (such as breach of contract or fiduciary duty) could also be successfully alleged against them on the same facts.[145]

---

[142] Ibid at 1261.
[143] [1995] LRLR 498.
[144] Ibid at 503.
[145] See paras 9.150–9.151 for the position where costs are incurred in defence of a claim by a third party which includes elements which are insured and elements which are not insured.

9.104 The reference to 'properly framed' is important. As Mustill J explained in *Rigby v Sun Alliance & London Insurance Ltd*,[146] if the claim is or can be framed in more than one way, then 'the primary or natural cause of action must lie within the cover and must be the real root of the insured's liability, and ... if this requirement is satisfied the existence of a secondary cause of action is immaterial'. So, if the insured had no cover for dishonesty and the true quality of his acts was that they were dishonest rather than careless, it would not avail him against insurers if he had been sued and held liable in negligence.

9.105 In *Sturge v Hackett*[147] and *Capel-Cure Myers Capital Management Ltd v McCarthy*,[148] it could be said that the insured was equally liable to the third party claimant in respect of the cause of action which was insured and that or those which were not insured. However, had cover been expressly excluded for one or more of those other causes of action, then the insured would not have been entitled to an indemnity.[149]

D. Ascertainment of Liability

The principle

9.106 Professional indemnity insurance is, in the main, against loss caused by liability to third party claimants.[150] Although insurers may be obliged to fund the defence of a third party claim, their primary obligation is to indemnify or hold harmless the insured against his liability to third party claimants. It follows that insurers can only be liable to indemnify the insured when his liability to the third party is determined, both as to liability and quantum. Until that has been done, there is nothing against which insurers can be called upon to indemnify the insured (although insurers may, of course, choose to take over the defence of the claim and negotiate and fund a settlement of it).

9.107 The need for the insured's liability to have been ascertained was established by decisions in the context of the Third Parties (Rights Against Insurers) Act 1930.[151] The insured only acquires the right to sue insurers for money when his own liability to the third party has been ascertained by the judgment of a court, the award of an arbitrator, or settlement.[152]

---

[146] [1980] 1 Lloyd's Rep 359, at 364 per Mustill J.

[147] [1962] 1 WLR 1257.

[148] [1995] LRLR 498.

[149] See para 9.95.

[150] But see paras 9.133–9.151 for circumstances in which insurers may be liable to provide an indemnity under a contract of professional indemnity insurance in the absence of ascertainment.

[151] See paras 13.48–13.49.

[152] *Post Office v Norwich Union* [1967] 2 QB 363, per Lord Denning MR at 373–4; see also the judgment of Salmon LJ at 378. Their reasoning was described as 'unassailably correct' by Lord Bridge in *Bradley v Eagle Star Insurance Co Ltd* [1989] AC 957, at 966.

The ascertainment may also be by way of an order for interim payment[153] and, **9.108**
where professional indemnity insurance is provided to cover them, by awards of
ombudsmen[154] and by adjudications under the Housing Grants, Construction
and Regeneration Act 1996. The insured's liability may also be ascertained by the
admission of the third party's claim in the insured's bankruptcy or insolvency.[155]
However, a voluntary payment into an escrow account to fund remedial works as
and when the costs of those works need to be paid for is not an ascertainment. In
such a case there is only an ascertainment as and when each payment is made out
of the escrow account.[156]

It is important to understand the significance of ascertainment. If the insured's **9.109**
liability to the third party has not been ascertained, then he cannot sue insurers to
recovery an indemnity. There is nothing against which he can be indemnified.[157]
It does not follow that the ascertainment is binding as between the insured and
insurers as to either the existence of the insured's liability to the third party claimant or as to the true basis of that liability, or as to the amount in which he is liable.[158]
Ascertainment is therefore a necessary condition of insurers' liability to indemnify
the insured, but it does not follow that it is a sufficient condition.[159] As Devlin J
explained in *West Wake Price & Co v Ching*:[160]

> The essence of the main indemnity clause—as indeed of any indemnity clause—is
> that the assured must prove a loss. The assured cannot recover anything under the
> main indemnity clause or make any claim until they have been found liable and
> so sustained a loss. If judgment were given against them for the sum claimed, they
> would undoubtedly have sustained a loss and the question would then arise what
> was the cause of the loss. If the proximate cause ... of the loss was the dishonesty of
> their servant, they could not recover under the policy; if on the other hand it was
> their own neglect, they could recover.

---

[153] *Cox v Bankside Members Agency Ltd* [1995] 2 Lloyd's Rep 437, at 452–3 per Phillips J. See also
Teal Assurance Co Ltd v W R Berkley Insurance (Europe) Ltd (No 2) [2015] EWHC 1000 (Comm), at
[37]–[38] per Eder J.

[154] See, for example, para 2.32 and *London Borough of Redbridge v Municipal Mutual Insurance
Ltd* [2001] Lloyd's Rep IR 545.

[155] *Law Society v Shah* [2007] EWHC 2841 (Ch); [2009] Ch 223. See also *Financial Services
Compensation Scheme Ltd v Larnell* [2005] EWCA Civ 1408; [2006] QB 808. If the insured is
bankrupt or insolvent, then his right to claim against insurers will have been assigned to the
third party claimant pursuant to the Third Parties (Rights Against Insurers) Act 1930: see paras
13.40–13.43.

[156] *Teal Assurance Co Ltd v W R Berkley Insurance (Europe) Ltd (No 2)* [2015] EWHC 1000
(Comm).

[157] *Enterprise Oil Ltd v Strand Insurance Co Ltd* [2006] EWHC 58 (Comm); [2006] 1 Lloyd's
Rep 500 at [165]. See also *William McIlroy (Swindon) Ltd v Quinn Insurance Ltd* [2011] EWCA Civ
825; [2011] Lloyd's Rep IR 697.

[158] See, for example, the judgment of the Lord President, Lord Rodger, in *Cheltenham &
Gloucester Plc v Sun Alliance and London Insurance Plc* 2001 SC 965; 2001 SLT 1151, at [17].

[159] *Lumberman's Mutual Casualty Co v Bovis Lend Lease Ltd* [2004] EWHC 2197 (Comm);
[2005] 1 Lloyd's Rep 494, at [39].

[160] [1957] 1 WLR 45 at 49.

9.110   The relevant principles have been stated authoritatively by Christopher Clarke J in *Omega Proteins Ltd v Aspen Insurance UK Ltd*,[161] a case concerning product liability insurance. Having reviewed the authorities Christopher Clarke J summarized their effect as follows:[162]

(1)   The insured must establish that it has suffered a loss which is covered by one of the perils insured against: *West, Wake; Post Office v Norwich Union Fire Insurance Society Ltd* [1967] 1 Lloyd's Rep 216; *Bradley v Eagle Star Insurance Co Ltd* [1989] AC 957; *Horbury Building Systems Ltd v Hampden Insurance NV* [2007] Lloyd's Rep IR 237, page 245.

(2)   That may be done by showing a judgment or an arbitration award against the insured or an agreement to pay.

(3)   The loss must be within the scope of the cover provided by the policy.

(4)   As a matter of practicality, the judgment, award, or agreement may settle the question as to whether the loss is covered by the policy because the insurers will accept it as showing a basis of liability which is within the scope of the cover.

(5)   But neither the judgment nor the agreement are determinative of whether or not the loss is covered by the policy (assuming that the insurer is not a party to either and that there is no agreement by the insurer to be bound).

(6)   It is, therefore, open to the insurers to dispute that the insured was in fact liable, or that it was liable on the basis specified in the judgment; or to show that the true basis of his liability fell within an exception.

(7)   Thus, an insured against whom a claim is made in negligence, which is the subject of a judgment, may find that his insurer seeks to show that in reality the claim was for fraud or for something else which was not covered, or excluded by, the policy: *MDIS Ltd v Swinbank*.[163]

(8)   Similarly, an insured who is held liable in fraud (which the policy does not cover) may be able to establish, in a dispute with his insurers, that, whatever the judge found, he was not in fact fraudulent, but only negligent and that he was entitled to cover under the policy on that account.

9.111   In *Lumberman's Mutual Casualty Co v Bovis Lend Lease Ltd*,[164] Colman J held that it was an implied term of a contract of liability insurance that:

it is an essential element of the assured's cause of action that his loss has been specifically ascertained by means of a judgment, arbitration award or settlement agreement.

The decision of Colman J has been doubted.[165] There is, with respect, no reason to elevate the principle that the insured must have suffered an insured loss in order to claim an indemnity from insurers into a term of the contract of insurance and no other decision has suggested that this should be done. Colman J adopted

---

[161] [2010] EWHC 2280 (Comm); [2011] Lloyd's Rep IR 183.

[162] Ibid at [49]. This summary was adopted and followed by HH Judge Waksman QC, sitting as a High Court Judge in *Impact Funding Solutions Ltd v Barrington Support Services Ltd* [2013] EWHC 4005 (QB).

[163] [1999] Lloyd's Rep IR 516.

[164] [2004] EWHC 2197 (Comm); [2005] 1 Lloyd's Rep 494, at [42].

[165] See paras 9.128–9.132.

the approach of Potter LJ in *Commercial Union Assurance Co Plc v NRG Victory Reinsurance Ltd.*[166] There, Potter LJ held that it was an implied term in a reinsurance contract that reinsurers would treat the decision of a foreign court of competent jurisdiction as binding save in certain limited circumstances.[167] That is rather different from the implied term found by Colman J.[168]

Judgments and awards

Not binding on insurers

The judgment of a court or award by an arbitrator or arbitrators will be sufficient to ascertain the insured's liability to a third party claimant. It does not follow that a judgment or award will be binding on insurers, who may go behind it, not only in order to show that the true basis of the insured's liability was other than that found in the judgment, but also to show that the insured was not in fact liable, contrary to the judgment against him.[169]   **9.112**

It may appear surprising that insurers can seek to go behind a judgment and seek to show that the insured was not in fact liable as found. But, as Flaux J explained in *Astrazeneca Insurance Co Ltd v XL Insurance (Bermuda) Ltd,*[170] a case concerning reinsurance: **9.113**

> I consider that the better view is that, absent some agreement to be bound, it will be open to a liability insurer or a reinsurer to challenge findings of liability in an underlying judgment in proceedings to which it was not a party in order to question whether in fact the insured is under a liability. In other words, whilst the judgment may ascertain or establish the loss, it will not necessarily establish the legal liability of the insured or reinsured, although it may be compelling evidence of such liability, depending on the circumstances in which it was obtained.[171]

---

[166] [1998] 2 Lloyd's Rep 600.

[167] As to which see para 9.113.

[168] See further *Enterprise Oil Ltd v Strand Insurance Co Ltd* [2006] EWHC 58 (Comm); [2006] 1 Lloyd's Rep 500, at [163], where Aikens J warned against the danger of drawing analogies from authorities on reinsurance when considering issues concerning liability insurance.

[169] Insurers may be bound by a judgment if they were parties to the proceedings: *Astrazeneca Insurance Co Ltd v XL Insurance (Bermuda) Ltd* [2013] EWCA Civ 1660; [2014] Lloyd's Rep IR 509, at [19] per Christopher Clarke LJ, with whom the other members of the Court of Appeal agreed.

[170] [2013] EWHC 349 (Comm); [2013] Lloyd's Rep IR 290, at [65]. The judgment of Flaux J was upheld on appeal: [2013] EWCA Civ 1660; [2014] Lloyd's Rep IR 509 (see, in particular, the judgment of Christopher Clarke LJ, with whom the other members of the Court of Appeal agreed, at [17]). See also (1) *Cheltenham & Gloucester Plc v Sun Alliance and London Insurance Plc* 2001 SC 965; 2001 SLT 1151, at [4] per the Lord President, Lord Rodger; (2) *Enterprise Oil Ltd v Strand Insurance Co Ltd* [206] EWHC 58 (Comm); [2006] 1 Lloyd's Rep 500, at [167] per Aikens J; and (3) *Omega Proteins Ltd v Aspen Insurance UK Ltd* [2010] EWHC 2280 (Comm); [2011] Lloyd's Rep IR 183, at [49(5) and (6)] per Christopher Clarke J.

[171] Flaux J thereby declined to follow the obiter observations of the Court of Appeal in *Commercial Union Assurance Co Plc v NRG Victory Reinsurance Ltd* [1998] 2 Lloyd's Rep 600, at 610–11 to the effect that the judgment of a foreign court could be binding on reinsurers subject to certain conditions. That view had been subject to criticism as Flaux J explained at [64].

9.114 However, the judgment of a court of competent jurisdiction after a contested trial is not to be lightly ignored. In the context of professional indemnity insurance, in *McDonnell Information Systems v Swinbank*[172] Mance J, referring to a passage in the judgment of Devlin J in *West Wake Price & Co v Ching*[173] said:[174]

> ultimately, as between insured and insurers, it is established liability which this insurance pays, and it is upon the nature and causation of any liability established that I consider the insured's right to indemnification must depend. In a case which goes to judgment, the judgment will, as Devlin J said, 'in all probability settle the facts in the light of which the question could be answered'.[175]

In practice insurers will need good reason to seek to show and to succeed in showing that a judgment after a contested trial was incorrect. However, if insurers do not accept the findings in a judgment between the insured and the third party claimant, it will be for the insured to prove that he was in fact liable on the balance of probabilities.[176]

Alternative bases of liability

9.115 The passage from the judgment of Mance J set out in the preceding paragraph was applied by Tomlinson J in *London Borough of Redbridge v Municipal Mutual Insurance Ltd*.[177] The issue before him was whether the liability insurers of a local authority could rely upon an exclusion of liability in respect of loss or damage directly or indirectly caused by or arising from fraud, dishonesty, or criminal offence on the part of certain named employees when refusing to indemnify the insured against awards made by the Pensions Ombudsman. In those awards, the Pensions Ombudsman had made no finding that any of the named employees were guilty of fraud, dishonesty, or criminal offence (not least because he had no jurisdiction to determine such issues), but insurers maintained that the conduct of one of the named employees amounted to a criminal offence so as to entitle them to rely on the exclusion clause.

9.116 Tomlinson J disagreed. He held that it was neither permissible nor possible to look beyond the determination by the Pensions Ombudsman of the basis of the

---

[172] [1999] Lloyd's Rep IR 98.

[173] [1957] 1 WLR 45.

[174] [1999] Lloyd's Rep IR 98 at 103. This passage in the judgment of Mance J was expressly approved by Clarke LJ when the case went on appeal: *MDIS Ltd v Swinbank* [1999] Lloyd's Rep IR 516, at [24].

[175] See also *Astrazeneca Insurance Co Ltd v XL Insurance (Bermuda) Ltd* [2013] EWCA Civ 1660; [2014] Lloyd's Rep IR 509, at [17] per Christopher Clarke LJ, with whom the other members of the Court of Appeal agreed:

'It is not, therefore, necessarily sufficient for the insured to show that he has been held liable to a claimant by some court or tribunal or that he has agreed to settle with him. In practice the fact that this has occurred may cause or persuade the insurer to pay, but, if it does not, the insured must prove that he was actually liable.'

[176] *Astrazeneca Insurance Co Ltd v XL Insurance (Bermuda) Ltd* [2013] EWCA Civ 1660; [2014] Lloyd's Rep IR 509, at [17] per Christopher Clarke LJ, with whom the other members of the Court of Appeal agreed.

[177] [2001] Lloyd's Rep IR 545.

insured's liability. It was impermissible because one court could not say that the basis of liability was other than as found by an earlier court. It was impossible, because if the earlier court had found liability on one basis, it was not logically possible to find that the insured's liability arose from different facts and matters.[178] He concluded:[179]

> It may of course be possible to say that liability should not have been found in the light of the facts relied upon, or even that the finding of liability could have been justified on different or additional grounds. Neither of those possibilities however detracts to my mind from the proposition that in liability insurance one is concerned, as between insured and insurers, with established liability and thus with the basis on which liability was in fact established. Just as it does not avail an insurer in a case where liability has been established by judgment to say that liability ought not to have been established so also, in my view, it does not avail an insurer to say that liability might have been established on a different basis, or that the cause of the liability arising should be regarded as different from that stated.

It would appear to follow that if the insured were successfully sued by the third party claimant in negligence, it would not be open to insurers to refuse to indemnify the insured on the basis that the insured had in fact acted dishonestly. In the first edition of this book it was suggested that this cannot be correct. Insurers should be entitled to argue that the proximate cause, or a proximate cause of the insured's liability, was excluded from cover so that they are not liable to indemnify him.[180] It may be that this was what Tomlinson J had in mind when he referred to the possibility that 'the finding of liability could have been justified on different or additional grounds'. **9.117**

It was suggested that the correct approach is set out in the following passage from the judgment of Clarke LJ in *MDIS Ltd v Swinbank*:[181] **9.118**

> Claimants may have many reasons of their own why they choose to put their case in a particular way, regardless of what would be held to be the true proximate cause of the insured's liability. One common example ... was a claim against say a solicitor or accountant which could be put as a claim for fraud or a claim for negligence. In such a case it would ordinarily be sufficient (and much easier) for the claimant to put its case only in negligence. Thus the claim might be put in negligence or it might be put in negligence and fraud and in either case it might be settled. It is common ground that in both cases underwriters would not be liable if the proximate cause of the loss was the fraud of the insured and that in the second case they would not be liable if they could establish that the proximate cause of the loss fell within the exception to clause 2(b) because of the principle in *Wayne Tank and Pump Co Ltd v Employers Liability Assurance Corp Ltd* [1974] 1 QB 57 ...

---

[178] Ibid at [12].
[179] Ibid.
[180] See paras 9.92–9.105.
[181] [1999] Lloyd's Rep IR 516, at [22]. See also the passage from the judgment of Devlin J in *West Wake Price & Co v Ching* [1957] 1 WLR 45 at 49 set out in para 9.109 and *Enterprise Oil Ltd v Strand Insurance Co Ltd* [2006] EWHC 58 (Comm); [2006] 1 Lloyd's Rep 500, at [167] per Aikens J.

underwriters' liability depends upon the true facts and not simply upon the way in which the claimant chooses to put its case.

Clarke LJ was considering whether the insured or insurers were entitled to try to show that the insured would have been liable on some basis other than that alleged by a third party whose claim the insured had settled, but it is clear that Clarke LJ considered that, where a third party claimant chose only to claim in negligence, insurers should be entitled to show that the true basis of liability was fraud, whether the claim in negligence had gone to trial or been settled.

9.119 The views expressed in the preceding two paragraphs are now supported by the judgment of Christopher Clarke J in *Omega Proteins Ltd v Aspen Insurance UK Ltd*.[182] The case concerned liability of insurers under a policy of product liability insurance. The insured had been sued and found liable for breach of contract. The contract of insurance included an exclusion which provided:

> The Company will not indemnify the Insured against any liability arising ... under any contract or agreement unless such liability would have attached in the absence of such contract or agreement.

9.120 Insurers argued that the insured had been found liable for breach of contract and not on any other basis. It followed, they submitted, that the insured's sole liability was in contract so that the exclusion applied. Rejecting insurers' arguments, Christopher Clarke J held that it was open to the insured to prove that it would also have been liable in the absence of any contract and that the insured had proved that it would have been so liable in tort.

9.121 Christopher Clarke J explained that he could not agree with the reasoning or the conclusion of Tomlinson J in the *London Borough of Redbridge* case. His reasons for disagreeing included an analysis of the authorities considered above. It is submitted that the decision of Christopher Clarke J is to be preferred. This view is supported by the judgment of Christopher Clarke LJ, with whom the other members of the Court of Appeal agreed, in *Astrazeneca Insurance Co Ltd v XL Insurance (Bermuda) Ltd*,[183] where he explained that:[184]

> Under English law the ultimate arbiter of whether someone is liable, if insured and insurer cannot agree, is the tribunal which has to resolve their disputes (or any relevant appeal body). It may hold that there was in fact no actual liability and that an insured who thought, or another tribunal which decided, that there was, liability was in error either on the facts or the law or both.

If it is open to insurers to establish that another tribunal was in error in finding the insured liable it must also be open to them to show that there was an alternative basis on which the insured was liable.

---

[182] [2010] EWHC 2280 (Comm); [2011] Lloyd's Rep IR 183.
[183] [2013] EWCA Civ 1660; [2014] Lloyd's Rep IR 509.
[184] Ibid at [17].

Ascertainment and settlements

Where the insured has reached a settlement with the third party claimant, there is **9.122** no question of insurers being bound by any findings as to the basis on which the insured was liable or as to the amount of his liability, because no such findings will have been made. While the insured will be contractually bound to comply with the terms of any agreement to settle a claim against him, that agreement may reflect uncertainty as to whether the insured was in fact liable to the third party claimant and as to the amount, if any, which the third party would have recovered by way of trial or arbitration. The insured may well have acted reasonably in reaching that agreement, but he will not have established that he was in fact liable to the third party claimant at all or, necessarily, up to the amount he agreed to pay by way of settlement.

Where an insured has reached a settlement with a third party claimant and seeks to **9.123** recover his outlay from insurers, he will need to establish that he was in fact liable to the third party claimant, that the proximate cause of his liability fell within the cover under the policy, and that the settlement of his liability was reasonable.[185] So, where insurers can show that the insured had an arguable defence, the insured will be unable to obtain summary judgment against insurers: the issue which gives rise to the arguable defence will have to be resolved. [186]

In *Structural Polymer Systems Ltd v Brown*,[187] the insured established that it would **9.124** have been liable to the third party claimants. Insurers maintained that the settlement was unreasonable. Moore-Bick J disagreed:[188]

> In my judgment this argument proceeds on a false basis. Since the plaintiffs must show that they were liable to the claimants in order to bring themselves within the policy at all, no question arises as to whether the settlement was reasonable in the sense of fairly reflecting the overall merits of the action, only whether it was reasonable in terms of the amount paid compared with the true extent of the claimants' recoverable loss. As [counsel for insurers] accepted, under a settlement of this kind involving several parties, the precise amount paid to each recipient may reflect other than strictly legal considerations. Ultimately he accepted, therefore, that provided the plaintiffs can show that they were liable to one or other of the claimants in an amount at least equal to the total sum paid under the Settlement Agreement, the amount of the settlement cannot be regarded as unreasonable.

---

[185] *Structural Polymer Systems Ltd v Brown* [2000] Lloyd's Rep IR 64, where the insured accepted that he had to satisfy these requirements. However, at 68 Moore-Bick J said, after referring to authority: 'It follows that in the present case the plaintiffs must show that one or other of them, or for that matter the two of them together, were actually liable in an amount not less than that paid under the Settlement Agreement.' See also (1) *Lumberman's Mutual Casualty Co v Bovis Lend Lease Ltd* [2004] EWHC 2197 (Comm); [2005] 1 Lloyd's Rep 494, at [44] and (2) *Astrazeneca Insurance Co Ltd v XL Insurance (Bermuda) Ltd* [2013] EWHC 349 (Comm); [2013] Lloyd's Rep IR 290 (Flaux J) and [2013] EWCA Civ 1660; [2014] Lloyd's Rep IR 509.
[186] *Commercial Union Assurance Co Plc v NRG Victory Reinsurance Ltd* [1998] 2 Lloyd's Rep 600.
[187] [2000] Lloyd's Rep IR 64.
[188] Ibid at 72.

9.125 The form of the settlement between the insured and the third party claimant is not determinative of the insured's right to be indemnified. So, in *Peninsular and Oriental Steam Navigation Co v Youell*[189] the insured operated luxury cruise ships. A number of cruises had to be aborted and the insured settled with the disappointed passengers on terms which involved making refunds, issuing travel credits, and incurring the cost of alternative accommodation and travel arrangements. It then sought to recover its outlay against its liability insurers. Finding for the insured, Potter LJ, with whom the other members of the Court of Appeal agreed, said:[190]

> all that it was necessary for [the insured] to demonstrate was a liability in damages to the passengers compensated. If such liability existed, the form and nature of the compromise designed to avoid and/or satisfy claims in respect of such liability should not be determinative of the question whether or not there was a claim under the policy.

9.126 Nor is the way in which the third party chose to advance his claim against the insured irrebuttably deemed to be the basis upon which the insured would have been liable. Thus, in *MDIS Ltd v Swinbank*[191] the insured computer consultants had settled a claim by a third party who alleged misrepresentation. Insurers denied that they were liable to indemnify the insured, relying on an exclusion of indemnity in respect of claims resulting from 'the dishonest, fraudulent, criminal or malicious act(s) or omission(s) perpetrated after the assured could reasonably have discovered or suspected the improper conduct of the employee(s)'. The Court of Appeal held that it was open to insurers to do so. The insured had established a loss, but still had to establish that the proximate cause of the loss was negligence.[192]

9.127 As well as needing to show that he was liable to the third party on a basis which fell to be covered under the insurance, the insured must prove the amount of his loss. Usually this will be the amount he agreed to pay and, if he is entitled to be indemnified against the cost of defending a claim, the costs of the defence. In *Structural Polymer Systems Ltd v Brown*,[193] some of the third party claims were outside the scope of cover under the insurance policy. Moore-Bick J held that the insured was only entitled to recover the costs of the claims in respect of which they were entitled to be indemnified (claims for giving incorrect advice) and ordered insurers to pay 'such part of the costs of defending the proceedings ... as is referable to claims based on the giving of erroneous advice.'[194]

---

[189] [1997] 2 Lloyd's Rep 136.
[190] Ibid at 141.
[191] [1999] Lloyd's Rep IR 516, at [22].
[192] Ibid at [25]. See also *McCann v Switzerland Insurance Australia Ltd* [2000] HCA 65; (2000) 203 CLR 579 at [126]–[127] per Hayne J.
[193] [2000] Lloyd's Rep IR 64.
[194] Ibid at 75–6. As to defence costs see paras 9.150–9.151.

In the later case of *Lumberman's Mutual Casualty Co v Bovis Lend Lease Ltd*,[195] **9.128**
it was not part of the total costs which fell outside the scope of cover, but part
of the total sum paid in settlement of various claims against the insured, some
of which fell within the scope of cover, but others of which did not. Colman
J held that such a global settlement did not provide the required ascertainment and that it was not possible to try to establish what part of the global
sum was attributable to the insured claims by calling evidence. He held that
the 'primary function' of ascertainment is that it 'specifically identifies and
thereby represents the assured's loss attributable to the relevant liability'.[196]
Establishing a right to ascertainment under a policy of liability insurance
was different from proving the quantum of damages for breach of contract.
Colman J explained:[197]

> In the context of liability insurance the process of ascertainment is not merely the
> process of evidencing loss but represents that stage in the assured's relationship
> with the third party by which he sustains those compensatory liabilities to the
> third party specifically identified by the judgment, award or settlement agreement
> which, by the terms of the policy, is an essential element in the cause of action
> against insurers.

In *Enterprise Oil Ltd v Strand Insurance Co Ltd*,[198] Aikens J expressed his dis- **9.129**
agreement with Colman J's conclusion, although the point did not arise for decision. He drew attention to the fact that the decisions in *Post Office v Norwich
Union*[199] and *Bradley v Eagle Star Insurance Co Ltd*[200] did not support the proposition that it was a precondition for recovery under a liability policy that the
specific amount of the insured's loss be ascertained by virtue of the wording of
the judgment, award, or settlement. Nor did Aikens J agree that that this was
correct. Ascertainment did not bind insurers and he found no support in other
authorities for Colman J's view as to its significance. Moreover, if right, Colman
J's approach would lead to great commercial inconvenience and would be likely
to discourage settlements.

Aikens J's reasoning was approved, again obiter, by Morison J in *AIG Europe* **9.130**
(Ireland) Ltd v Faraday Capital Ltd:[201]

> In my judgment, Aikens J has correctly identified the flaw in Colman J's reason-
> ing which led him to what is an instinctively surprising conclusion. He rejected
> the idea that extrinsic evidence could be called to explain the losses and to make
> the attribution to insured and uninsured items. I do not understand why this is
> so. I simply say at this stage that I agree with Aikens J's analysis, which produces

---

195 [2004] EWHC 2197 (Comm); [2005] 1 Lloyd's Rep 494.
196 Ibid at [46]–[47].
197 Ibid at [56].
198 [2006] EWHC 58 (Comm); [2006] 1 Lloyd's Rep 500, at [163]–[173].
199 [1967] 2 QB 363.
200 [1989] AC 957.
201 [2006] EWHC 2707 (Comm); [2007] Lloyd's Rep IR 267, at [69]–[71].

a commercially sensible conclusion. I would, therefore, not have followed the *Lumberman's* case, had I been forced to choose ...

In every case it is simply a matter of evidence to establish what the insured losses were; and the court should receive such evidence as the parties wish to advance on the question, without any preconceived notions of admissibility.

9.131 Not only have two Commercial Court Judges expressed their disagreement with the decision of Colman J in the *Lumberman's* case, but it is hard to reconcile that decision with that of Moore-Bick J in the earlier case of *Structural Polymer Systems Ltd v Brown*.[202] Some of the claims against the insured by the third party claimant had been outside the scope of cover. Insurers argued that they should be entitled to investigate the insured's liability in respect of these uninsured claims and that this was a reason why summary judgment should not be entered against them. Moore-Bick J rejected this argument, not only because the evidence showed that there was no substance to the uninsured claims, but also because:[203]

the fact that a variety of different claims were compromised is not sufficient to justify giving leave to defend in the absence of a triable issue as to whether the plaintiffs, or one or other of them, were liable in an amount not less that the sum paid under the Settlement Agreement in respect of claims made against them arising out of the giving of negligent advice.

Moore-Bick J does not appear to have considered that the fact that the settlement included uninsured claims was a bar to recovery by the insured.

9.132 In the circumstances, the decision of Colman J in the *Lumberman's* case is unlikely to be followed. It should be open to both the insured and insurers to adduce evidence to show that a settlement or, in the case of a global settlement which encompassed both insured and uninsured claims, what part of that settlement did or did not fall within the scope of the insuring clause in the contract of liability insurance between the insured and insurers.[204]

E. Indemnity without Ascertainment of Liability

9.133 In *Astrazeneca Insurance Co Ltd v XL Insurance (Bermuda) Ltd*,[205] Christopher Clarke LJ observed that the need for the insured to prove that he was liable to the third party claimant was 'potentially very inconvenient for insureds'.[206] An insured who acts reasonably in settling a claim might fail to establish that, had the

---

[202] [2000] Lloyd's Rep IR 64.
[203] Ibid at 73.
[204] Different considerations would arise if the parties had agreed that the extent of the obligation of one to indemnify the other should be established by a particular mechanism and the party claiming an indemnity fails to use that mechanism: see *Cia Banca de Panama SA v George Wimpey & Co Ltd* [1980] 1 Lloyd's Rep 598.
[205] [2013] EWCA Civ 1660; [2014] Lloyd's Rep IR 509.
[206] Ibid at [18].

claim been tried, he would have been found liable. And even if he is found liable in proceedings brought by the third party, he might fail to prove that he was liable in subsequent proceedings against his insurers. That is, however, the effect of a straightforward policy of liability insurance in English law. But, as Christopher Clarke LJ explained, it does not have to be that way:[207]

> There are ways of obviating or reducing these difficulties. The policy does not have to be a liability policy. The insured can seek (no doubt at a price) cover which insures him against claims made, or judgments given, or against occurrences. The policy may contain a follow the settlements clause whereby the insurer is bound to follow the settlements of the insured, in which case the reinsurer will be bound if the insured has made a settlement in a reasonable and businesslike manner. The policy may contain a QC clause or a clause similar thereto. The policy may contain provisions whereby actual liability is, as between the insurer and the insured, taken to have been established if certain conditions are met.

In the field of professional indemnity insurance there are three ways in which the difficulties which can arise are or may be mitigated. The first is that the policy may provide cover for the cost of taking steps to mitigate loss and to avoid claims being made against the insured. The second is the use of a QC clause to require the settlement of a claim against the insured for which the insured is not or may not be liable. The third is the provision of an indemnity for the costs of defending claims by third parties, irrespective of the merits of those claims. Each will be considered in turn. **9.134**

Mitigation costs

When a claim from a third party is made or anticipated it may make commercial sense for the insured and insurers to take steps to mitigate their potential exposure. This can result in the payment of a smaller amount than would have been paid by way of damages, third party claimant's costs, and the costs of defence. This will result in insurers indemnifying the insured without ascertainment or proof of liability. But there is nothing odd about that in practice. Insurers frequently settle claims by third parties against their insured using their right to control the defence and settlement of such claims.[208] They do so when there has been no prior ascertainment and often when there is less than a fifty per cent chance that the insured would be held liable to the third party.[209] **9.135**

Some policies of professional indemnity insurance contain specific provision for the payment by insurers of mitigation costs. For example, the policy insuring a **9.136**

---

[207] Ibid at [19].
[208] As to which see paras 12.07–12.15.
[209] There is no implied term in liability insurance that the insured will make reasonable efforts to prevent or minimize loss which would fall within cover: *Yorkshire Water Services Ltd v Sun Alliance & London Insurance Plc* [1997] 2 Lloyd's Rep 21, a case concerning public liability insurance.

firm of architects and engineers considered in *Teal Assurance Co Ltd v WR Berkley Insurance (Europe) Ltd*[210]had an extension to cover in the following terms:

> In addition to the coverage granted under this Policy, but subject to the same Self-Insured Retention and limits of liability, we agree to indemnify the Named Insured for the Named Insured's Actual and Necessary Costs and Expenses incurred in rectifying a Design Defect in any part of the construction works or engineering works for any project upon which you are providing design/build services provided:
> (A) the Insured reports the Claim for such Actual and Necessary Costs and Expenses as soon as practicable after discovery of such Design Defect but in no event after any certificate of substantial completion has been issued;
> (B) the Insured proves to us that its Claim for Actual and Necessary Costs and Expenses arises out of the Insured's rendering of professional services which resulted in a Design Defect for which a third party could otherwise make Claim against the Insured ... [211]

9.137 This provision enabled the insured to recover under the policy without any claim having been made by a third party, and without there having been any conventional ascertainment by way of judgment, award, or settlement. Indeed, the indemnity was not in respect of sums payable or paid by the insured to a third party claimant. Under this clause ascertainment occurs when sums are expended on rectifying a 'Design Defect' which arises out of the rendering of professional services by the insured and for which a third party could make a claim against the insured.[212]

9.138 A similar clause was in the policy of professional indemnity insurance for financial advisers considered by the Court of Appeal in *ACE European Group v Standard Life Assurance Ltd*.[213] Cover was provided for 'Mitigation Costs', which were defined as:

> any payment of loss, costs or expenses reasonably and necessarily incurred by the Assured in taking action to avoid a third-party claim or to reduce a third-party claim (or to avoid or reduce a third-party claim which may arise from a fact, circumstance or event) of a type which would have been covered under this Policy (notwithstanding any Deductible amount).

9.139 This was subject to the following condition:

> The Assured must seek the consent of the Underwriters as soon as practicable if any proposed payment of Mitigation Costs exceeds the Deductible stated in the schedule. The Underwriters' consent to such payment shall not be unreasonably withheld or delayed. Pending consent, the Assured may proceed to incur Mitigation Costs but, the indemnity in relation to the amount of Mitigation Costs payable under this Policy will be reduced in amount to the extent that it has been incurred unreasonably.

---

[210] [2013] UKSC 57; [2013] 4 All ER 643.
[211] The term is set out in the judgment of Andrew Smith J at first instance: [2011] EWHC 91 (Comm); [2011] Lloyd's Rep IR 285, at [9].
[212] *Teal Assurance Co Ltd v WR Berkley Insurance Europe Ltd (No 2)* [2015] EWHC 1000 (Comm).
[213] [2012] EWCA Civ 1713; [2013] Lloyd's Rep IR 415.

The insured did not need to prove that it was or would be liable to third party **9.140** claimants in order to recover an indemnity under this extension of cover. It had to show that it had incurred costs 'reasonably' in order to avoid or reduce third party claims. The words 'of a type which would have been covered under this Policy' refer to the way in which third party claims would have been framed, not to third party claims in respect of which the insured was legally liable.

On the facts the insured had identified a large number of potential claims by third **9.141** parties arising from mis-selling of a particular investment fund. Mitigation costs were incurred by topping up the fund so that investors in the fund (the potential third party claimants) would have no ground for complaint.

QC clauses

Many contracts of professional indemnity insurance contain clauses which pro- **9.142** vide that a third party claim will not be taken to trial if a Queen's Counsel advises in particular terms, whether as to the merits of the third party claim or taking the wider interests of the insured and insurers into account.[214]

Such clauses can operate so as to require insurers to indemnify the insured in **9.143** circumstances in which there has been no ascertainment of liability by way of judgment, award, or settlement (other than a settlement following advice from a Queen's Counsel) and in circumstances in which the insured has not proved that he is liable to the third party claimant.

Clauses which provide that the insured is not required to contest a third party **9.144** claim unless a Queen's Counsel advises that the defence is likely to succeed[215] have the effect of making the Queen's Counsel the tribunal which is to resolve any dispute between the insured and insurers as to whether the insured is legally liable to the third party claimant. For example, if the test to be applied is the chances of a successful defence and the Queen's Counsel advises that there is less than a fifty per cent chance of the defence succeeding, the insured is not obliged to go to trial and so can settle the claim.

Clauses which involve the Queen's Counsel applying criteria beyond the merits of **9.145** the defence to the claim by the third party involve a greater departure from conventional ascertainment and proof by the insured of his liability to the third party claimant. For example, the QC clause in the ICAEW Minimum Approved Policy Wording provides:

> Neither the Insured nor Insurers shall be required to contest any legal proceed-
> ings unless a Queen's Counsel or in the Republic of Ireland a Senior Counsel (to

---

[214] These clauses provide a helpful means of resolving conflicts between the insured and insurers: see paras 12.65–12.76.
[215] Eg the clause in the RIBA Architects Premier Policy Wording set out in para 12.73.

be mutually agreed upon by the Insured and Insurers or failing agreement to be appointed by the President of the Institute of Chartered Accountants in England and Wales/of Scotland/in Ireland as applicable) shall advise that, taking due account of the interests of both Insurers and Insured, such proceedings should be contested.[216]

9.146 The factors to be taken into account under this clause would include potential reputational damage to the insured if the claim went to trial and the possibility of achieving a settlement so as to avoid the risk of losing at trial, even if the Queen's Counsel's assessment is that the chances of doing so are less than fifty per cent. So such clauses can work so as to require insurers to provide an indemnity in circumstances in which the insured has not proved and cannot prove that he is liable to the third party claimant.

Defence costs

9.147 In liability insurance other than marine insurance there is no right on the part of the insured to recover costs incurred in the successful defence of a claim by a third party in the absence of a provision in the contract of insurance beyond a conventional indemnity in respect of sums which the insured is legally obliged to pay as damages to a specified class of claims by third parties.[217]

9.148 Most, but not all, contracts of professional indemnity provide an additional indemnity in respect of the costs of defending claims brought against the insured by third parties. For example, in *Thornton Springer v NEM Insurance Co Ltd*[218] a policy of professional indemnity insurance for accountants provided:

> Underwriters shall in addition indemnify the Assured in respect of all costs and expenses incurred with their written consent in the defence or settlement of any claim made against the Assured which falls to be dealt with under this Certificate provided that if a payment in excess of the amount of indemnity available under this Certificate has to be made to dispose of any claim or claims against the Assured, Underwriters' liability for such costs and expenses shall be such proportion thereof as the amount of indemnity available under this Certificate bears to the amount required to dispose of such claim or claims.

9.149 Cover under this term extended to costs incurred in the successful defence of claims by third parties.[219] In so finding Colman J considered it significant that the clause referred to the settlement of claims as well as to the defence of them. If

---

[216] The RICS Policy Wording has a QC clause to similar effect.
[217] *Thornton Springer v NEM Insurance Co Ltd* [2000] 2 All ER 489, at [33]–[44] per Colman J; *Astrazeneca Insurance Co Ltd v XL Insurance (Bermuda) Ltd* [2013] EWHC 349 (Comm), at [137] per Flaux J; [2013] Lloyd's Rep IR 290; [2013] EWCA Civ 1660; *Astrazeneca Insurance Co Ltd v XL Insurance (Bermuda) Ltd* [2014] Lloyd's Rep IR 509, at [72] per Christopher Clarke LJ, with whom the other members of the Court of Appeal agreed.
[218] [2000] 2 All ER 489.
[219] Ibid at [48] per Colman J.

insurers consented to a settlement and so were obliged to indemnify the insured against sums payable to the third party claimant pursuant to the settlement, it would make no sense that they could deny liability for the costs of defending the claim until it was settled.

Where the claim by a third party falls partly within the terms of cover and partly **9.150** without, the same principles as to two proximate causes apply as those which apply to the main insuring clause against liability to the third party.[220] As long as a proximate cause of the incurrence of defence costs fell within the cover provided, it does not matter that there was some other proximate cause unless there is an exclusion clause in respect of that cause.

The approach to allocation of costs between insured and uninsured claims or par- **9.151** ties is to be found in *New Zealand Forest Products Ltd v New Zealand Insurance Co Ltd*.[221] In that case the insured was one of a number of defendants to legal proceedings. All the defendants shared the same lawyers. Insurers sought to restrict their liability to indemnify the insured in relation to his costs. Giving the Opinion of the Privy Council, Lord Clyde held that the insured was entitled to recover from insurers not only costs which were incurred exclusively in his defence, but also any costs which reasonably related to the defence of the claim against him, even though they were also incurred in relation to the defence of others parties who were not insured.[222] As Lord Mance JSC explained in *Zurich Insurance Plc UK Branch v International Energy Group*:[223]

> Once it is shown that an insured has on a conventional basis incurred defence costs which are covered on the face of the policy wording, there is, as the *New Zealand Forest* case shows, no reason to construe the wording as requiring some diminution in the insured's recovery, merely because the defence costs so incurred also benefitted some other uninsured defendant.[224]

---

[220] See paras 9.94–9.95.
[221] [1997] 1 WLR 1237.
[222] Ibid at 1246D–F.
[223] [2015] UKSC 33; [2015] 2 WLR 1471, at [38]. See also [176] per Lord Sumption JSC.
[224] See also (1) *Thornton Springer v NEM Insurance Co Ltd* [2000] 2 All ER 489, at [121] per Colman J; and (2) *John Wyeth & Brothers v Cigna Insurance Company of Europe SA NV* [2001] EWCA Civ 175; [2001] Lloyd's Rep IR 420, at [56] per Waller LJ, with whom the other members of the Court of Appeal agreed.

10

THE AMOUNT OF THE INDEMNITY
The Excess, Policy Limits, and Aggregation of Claims

A. The Basic Policy Limits

Limits on the amount of the indemnity

The amount of the indemnity provided under a policy of professional indemnity insur- **10.01**
ance will be within specified limits. A primary policy may provide that the insured
should himself bear a deductible or excess. It will specify the maximum amount payable by insurers in respect of a single claim (or a number of claims which are treated
as a single claim).[1] It may also specify the maximum payable in total by insurers, ie in
the aggregate.[2] A primary policy may also provide for one or more reinstatements.[3]

---

[1] See paras 10.18–10.84.

[2] The SRA Minimum Terms and Conditions of Professional Indemnity Insurance provide that
there should be no aggregate limit. It follows that insurers will be liable to indemnify up to the limit
per claim for whatever number of claims are made (or deemed to be made) during the policy period for
which liability is ascertained. The RICS Policy Wording has a number of aggregate limits for elements
of cover such as liability for asbestos and pollution, but no aggregate limit for the more usual forms of
civil liability. The ICAEW Minimum Approved Policy Wording does provide for an aggregate limit
for claims other than claims arising from either 'authorised work' as defined in the ICAEW's Probate
Regulations or from 'insurance mediation work' as defined in the ICAEW's Designated Professional
Body Handbook. In relation to those two classes of claims the policy limit is per claim with no aggregate limit. The RIBA Architects Premier Policy does not have an aggregate limit.

[3] See paras 10.09–10.12.

10.02   An excess policy will provide an indemnity above the lower layer or layers of cover up to a specified amount. It will usually provide that insurers will not be liable unless and until insurers of the underlying policy or policies have paid the full amount of their liability or have admitted liability for the full amount or been held liable to pay the full amount.[4]

Defence and third party costs

10.03   The fixed amount of the indemnity available under a particular policy will also depend upon whether the policy limit is inclusive or exclusive of one or more of the costs of defending third party claims and the costs payable to third party claimants. It will be a matter of construction of the relevant provisions in any particular policy as to whether the limit of indemnity includes either. This can have a material impact of the amount of insurance cover available to meet any liability to a third party claimant.

10.04   So, in *Citibank NA v Excess Insurance Company Ltd*[5] the operative clause of the policy provided that insurers:

> will indemnify the Insured … against
> 1. all sums which the Insured shall become legally liable to pay as damages and claimants costs and expenses in respect of any accident which arises in connection with the Business or Professional Activities and Duties.
> 2. all costs and expenses incurred with the written consent of [insurers] in respect of any claim against the insured which may be the subject of indemnity under this Policy.

The indemnity was subject to the following limit:

> The liability of [insurers] for all damages costs and expenses payable by the Insured under this Section in respect of any one claim or series of claims arising out of any one original cause shall not exceed the amount specified in the Schedule in respect of this Section.

It was clear that the limit applied to both sums payable to third parties by way of damages and in costs. Insurers maintained that it also applied to sums incurred by way of defence costs. Thomas J disagreed.[6]

10.05   The operative clause distinguished between sums payable to third party claimants on the one hand and costs and expenses incurred with the consent of insurers on the other. The word 'payable' in the clause limiting liability referred back to paragraph 1 of the operative clause, which referred to sums 'payable' by the insured, but not to paragraph 2, which did not use the word 'payable'. Moreover, on the facts

---

[4] See, for example, the excess policies considered in *Cox v Deeny* [1996] LRLR 288 and *Friends Provident Life and Pensions Ltd v Sirius International Insurance Corporation* [2004] EWHC 1799 (Comm); [2005] Lloyd's Rep IR 135; [2005] EWCA Civ 601; [2005] 2 Lloyd's Rep 517.
[5] [1999] Lloyd's Rep IR 122.
[6] Ibid at 128.

defence costs were not 'payable' by the insured in that, save for the VAT element of the bill, the solicitors' costs were paid by insurers.[7]

The position as to defence costs was clear on the terms of the policy in *Gloucestershire* **10.06**
Health Authority v M A Torphy and Partners Ltd (t/a Torphy and Partners),[8] where the policy stated:

> Further it is understood and agreed that the insurers will pay in addition to the limit of indemnity as stated in the schedule the costs and expenses incurred with the insurer's written consent in the defence and/or settlement of any claim.

The third party claimant contended that this also applied to its own costs of bringing the claim. The argument was rejected,[9] in accordance with the usual position which is that, absent specific provision, the insured's liability in respect of the costs of a third party claimant's claim against him falls within the basic insuring clause under which he is entitled to be indemnified against any sums which he may become legally liable to pay arising from any claim made against him during the policy period.[10] The obligation to indemnity in relation to the costs of a third party claimant is part of the indemnity against civil liability.[11]

The SRA Minimum Terms and Conditions of Professional Indemnity Insurance **10.07**
require that, as well as providing an indemnity up to the relevant limit, the insurance must indemnify the insured against defence costs. The same is true of the ICAEW Minimum Approved Policy Wording and the RICS Policy Wording and the RIBA Architects Premier Policy Wording.

All provide that defence costs are payable by insurers in addition to the basic indemnity. **10.08**
No limit is prescribed for the sum payable for defence costs, but where the amount payable in respect of a claim, whether by settlement or otherwise, exceeds the limit of indemnity, insurers are only required to pay the same proportion of the total defence costs as the amount of the indemnity payable by them bears to the amount payable in respect of the claim.

Reinstatement

Where policies have an aggregate limit, they may also provide for cover to be rein- **10.09**
stated. Reinstatement clauses have the effect of reinstating cover once it has been

---

[7] The insured would be liable for the solicitors' costs if not paid by insurers: see paras 12.16–12.19.
[8] [1999] Lloyd's Rep IR 203.
[9] Ibid at 205.
[10] Some professional indemnity policies do include defence costs within the single limit of indemnity. See, for example, the primary policies considered in *Cox v Deeny* [1996] LRLR 288, set out in para 10.10.
[11] *Cox v Bankside Members Agency Ltd* [1995] 2 Lloyd's Rep 437, at 462 per Sir Thomas Bingham MR: 'Once a claim is made on one of the policy grounds, interest and costs which result from a bona fide decision by the insurers to resist it must in my view by regarded as arising from the claim and it is artificial to treat the chain of causation as broken by the insurers' decision.'
See also *Forney v Dominion Insurance Co Ltd* [1969] 1 WLR 928 at 934–5 and *Aluminium Wire and Cable Co Ltd v Allstate Insurance Co Ltd* [1985] 2 Lloyd's Rep 280, at 287–8.

exhausted. Policies can provide for one or more reinstatements with or without the payment of additional premiums. The working of such clauses where professional indemnify insurance has been obtained by a primary policy and a number of excess policies was considered by HH Judge Diamond QC, sitting as a High Court Judge, in *Cox v Deeny*.[12]

10.10   The clause under consideration was in these terms:

AUTOMATIC REINSTATEMENT

It is agreed that the amount of any Claim hereunder (which amount shall include costs and expenses incurred with the written consent of the Insurers in defence or settlement of such claim), shall be automatically reinstated from the date of notice of claim but it is agreed that Insurers' total liability under this Policy in respect of all claims made during the period specified (including costs or expenses incurred with the written consent of the Insurers in defence or settlement of such claim) in the Schedule shall in no event exceed the sum stated in Item 3(b) of the Schedule.

Notwithstanding anything contained in the foregoing paragraph it is agreed that the Insurers' total liability under this Policy in respect of any claim or claims arising from one originating cause shall in no event exceed the sum stated in Item 3(a) of the Schedule.

It is further agreed that such reinstatement of cover shall only apply when the insurers of any policy or policies of insurance providing cover in excess of this Policy have paid, or have agreed to pay or have been held liable to pay to the extent of the indemnity provided in such policy or policies.[13]

The amount specified in item 3(b) of the Schedule was £2 million. The amount specified in Item 3(a) was £1 million. There were two excess layers above the primary layer, each providing cover limited to £1 million, but with a reinstatement 'as per Primary Policy'. Both excess policies had a total limit of indemnity of £1 million 'in respect of any claim or claims arising from one originating cause'.

10.11   HH Judge Diamond QC explained how this clause works in practice.[14] The effect of the clause is to 'reinstate the amount of any claim' under the policy, not to reinstate the policy itself, which remains in force. The insured is provided with additional cover equivalent to the amount paid in respect of a claim or claims. This is done retrospectively, because the amount paid will not be known at the time when notice is first given of the claim or claims. However, the reinstatement does not apply so as to provide cover for later claims which arise from the same originating cause as those which have been paid: in such cases, the limit is provided by Item 3(a).

---

12   [1996] LRLR 288.
13   A slight variant of this clause appeared in the policies considered in *Cox v Bankside Members Agency Ltd* [1995] 2 Lloyd's Rep 437. Another example of a reinstatement clause can be found in the report of *Hamptons Residential Ltd v Field* [1997] 1 Lloyd's Rep 302, at 305.
14   [1996] LRLR 288, at 295.

Because there were two excess layers, reinstatement in *Cox v Deeny*[15] only took **10.12** effect once the excess layers have been exhausted. This gave rise to the issues before the Court. The main issue was whether the same claim could be the subject of indemnity under both the original and the reinstated cover.[16] HH Judge Diamond QC held that it could be, holding that:

> there are no express provisions of the clause which provide that the same claim cannot be pressed both against original and reinstated cover. Nor can any such limitation be applied. Any such construction in my view would be wholly inconsistent with the provision that reinstatement is to apply 'from the date of notice of claim'.[17]

Erosion of policy limits

The limit of indemnity under a policy of professional indemnity insurance may **10.13** be eroded in a number of ways. First, and most simply, the insured's liability to a third party in respect of a single claim may exceed the policy limit. Second, a single insured may be liable to several third parties, each of whom has his own claim, but all of whose claims are deemed by an aggregation clause in the contract of insurance to be a single claim for the purposes of the limit of indemnity. The total liability to those third parties may exceed the policy limit. Third, there may be several insured, each of whom is liable to a different third party. The total liability of the various insured may exceed an applicable limit on cover in the policy. Fourth (and potentially overlapping with the others), there may be several claims against one or more insured which fall to be insured under a policy with an aggregate limit which is lower than the total liability of the insured to the third parties. In all save the first case the question arises as to how the available indemnity is to be allocated between the various liabilities.

It fell to be decided in the context of the Lloyd's litigation[18] and in the particular **10.14** context of a case management plan adopted by the Commercial Court, to cope with and regulate the volume of large claims which formed the Lloyd's litigation. Under the case management plan, some claims were to be tried before others. It was

---

[15] [1996] LRLR 288.

[16] This possibility would arise where, for example, £500,000 had been paid out under the primary layer in relation to one claim and then the insured was held liable for £3.5 million in respect of another claim, which did not arise from the same originating cause as the first. There would be cover of £500,000 available under the primary policy and cover of £2 million under the excess policies. The question was whether primary insurers, having paid out £500,000 before reinstatement, would be further liable in respect of £500,000 by way of reinstatement. (They could not be liable for more, because of the limit of £1 million in respect of any claim or claims arising from one originating cause.)

[17] HH Judge Diamond QC also held that, where a layer did not indemnify up to its full limit of £1 million because of the operation of the single originating clause provision, so that there was a 'gap' in cover for Claim A, the higher layers did not come on risk because of that 'gap'. However, the 'gap' could be filled by later claims, in which case the higher layers would be liable to indemnify the insured, first of all in respect of Claim A: [1996] LRLR 288, at 296–7.

[18] See chapter 19 of *Jackson & Powell on Professional Liability* (7th edn, Sweet & Maxwell, 2011), particularly at para 19-016.

anticipated that, if the claims succeeded, the defendants would have inadequate professional indemnity insurance. Were the insured to share the total available proceeds rateably (ie in proportion to their relative liabilities to third party claimants) or was it a case of first come, first served? In *Cox v Bankside Members Agency Ltd*,[19] Phillips J and the Court of Appeal held that there was no basis for imposing a rateable scheme upon the various insureds.

10.15 Rejecting the argument in terms which apply beyond the specific context of the Lloyd's litigation, Phillips J said:[20]

> A group cover against E & O liability of the kind I have to consider is not a joint policy. It is a policy which provides cover to each of the assured severally. In contradistinction to the position of co-insurers, the co-assured are not exposed in relation to the same interest and the same perils. Rights to claim under the cover will almost inevitably arise sequentially. I can see no basis for implying agreement between the co-assured that if E & O liabilities are established one by one which result in the limit of cover being exceeded, those who have recovered under the policy will be obliged to share their recoveries pro rata with those whose liability is established only after the cover has been exhausted.

> When co-assured enter into a contract of insurance that gives them several rights, subject to an overall limit, it seems to me that each simply takes the risk that cover may become exhausted, leaving all thereafter exposed to third party claims.

10.16 While 'first come, first served' will result in a very different degree of recovery between claimants where the insured has neither excess insurance nor the means to satisfy judgments beyond the limit of cover,[21] it is now established as the correct approach. This is clear from the decision of the Supreme Court in *Teal Assurance Co Ltd v WR Berkley Insurance (Europe) Ltd*.[22] That case concerned a multi-layered programme of professional indemnity insurance for a firm of architects and engineers. The insured faced a number of claims and it was in the insured's interests for them to erode the primary and lower excess layers in a particular order so that claims which were excluded from cover on the higher levels were indemnified by the lower layers where the policies did not exclude cover for them.

10.17 The Supreme Court held that the insured was not entitled to manipulate the order in which claims were to be indemnified under the programme of insurance. Insurers' liability to indemnify arose as and when each third party claim was ascertained by way of judgment, arbitration award, or settlement.[23] Lord Mance JCS, with whom the other members of the Supreme Court agreed, stated:[24]

---

[19] [1995] 2 Lloyd's Rep 437.
[20] Ibid at 443. See also 466 per Saville LJ.
[21] As was pointed out by Lord Denning MR in his dissenting judgment in *Harker v Caledonian Insurance* [1979] 2 Lloyd's Rep 193, at 197, a case concerning motor insurance.
[22] [2013] UKSC 57; [2013] 4 All ER 643.
[23] See further paras 9.106–9.132.
[24] [2013] UKSC 57; [2013] 4 All ER 643, at [17].

Where an insurance has a limit, it makes no sense to speak of the insured having causes of action or recoverable claims which together would exceed that limit. If the limit is US$10m and the insured incurs ascertained third party liability of US$10m in respect of each of two successive third party claims, it makes no sense to speak of the insured having two causes of action or two recoverable claims against its insurer totalling US$20m. Likewise, if its liability is ascertained at US$7.5m each claim, the insured will have two causes of action or claims against its insurer, but the second will only be for US$2.5m. The ascertainment, by agreement, judgment or award, of the insured's liability gives rise to the claim under the insurance, which exhausts the insurance either entirely or *pro tanto*.[25]

B. Aggregation Clauses

It is usual for there to be a provision in a contract of professional indemnity insurance treating related claims as a single claim for the purposes of the limits of cover under the policy. The purpose of an aggregation clause is: **10.18**

> to enable two or more separate losses covered by the policy to be treated as a single loss for deductible or other purposes when they are linked by a unifying factor of some kind.[26]

There is no single standard form of provision and a policy without such a provision would be workable, albeit commercially imprudent for insurers.[27]

Depending upon the facts, such clauses can work in favour of the insured, of primary layer insurers, excess layer insurers, or reinsurers.[28] They should therefore be constructed 'in a balanced fashion giving effect to the words used'.[29] Different wordings can produce very different results. It should not be assumed that the parties were indifferent to the meaning of the words they chose[30] and the language used 'can be expected to be the subject of careful negotiation'.[31] So, as Lord Hobhouse explained in *Lloyds TSB General Insurance Holdings Ltd v Lloyds Bank Group Insurance Co Ltd*:[32] **10.19**

> there are often well established alternatives open to the parties in the drafting of their agreement. The choice made from among these alternatives represents part of

---

[25] See also *Ram v Motor and General Insurance Company Ltd* [2015] UKPC 22, at [17].

[26] *Lloyds TSB General Insurance Holdings Ltd v Lloyds Bank Group Insurance Co Ltd* [2001] Lloyd's Rep IR 237, at 245 per Moore-Bick J, approved by Lord Hoffmann in *Lloyds TSB General Insurance Holdings Ltd v Lloyds Bank Group Insurance Co Ltd* [2003] UKHL 48; [2003] 4 All ER 43 at [15].

[27] *Mabey and Johnson Ltd v Ecclesiastical Insurance Office Plc* [2000] Lloyd's Rep IR 369.

[28] *Lloyds TSB General Insurance Holdings Ltd v Lloyds Bank Group Insurance Co Ltd* [2003] UKHL 48; [2003] 4 All ER 43, per Lord Hobhouse at [30].

[29] Ibid.

[30] *Axa Reinsurance (UK) Plc v Field* [1996] 1 WLR 1026 at 1035 per Lord Mustill.

[31] *Lloyds TSB General Insurance Holdings Ltd v Lloyds Bank Group Insurance Co Ltd* [2003] UKHL 48; [2003] 4 All ER 43 at [17] per Lord Hoffmann.

[32] [2003] UKHL 48; [2003] 4 All ER 43, at [31].

the bargain struck by the parties and must be respected by anyone (judge or arbitrator) adjudicating upon a dispute arising under the document.

A single claim?

10.20 Before addressing various provisions which have the effect of deeming two or more losses or claims to be a single claim for the purposes of the limits of cover, it is appropriate to consider what will constitute a single claim for such purposes before the application of any deeming provision.

10.21 The issue here is not whether a claim has been made or what is encompassed within a claim when made.[33] It is how many claims a third party claimant is making against the insured for the purposes of the limits of cover. The third party claimant may have a number of grounds for claiming against the insured. They may be so closely related as to constitute a single claim, but they may be entirely independent of each other. The decision of the Privy Council in *Haydon v Lo & Lo (A Firm)*[34] provides a useful example of the issues which can arise.

10.22 In *Haydon v Lo & Lo (A Firm)*, a rogue clerk in the insured solicitors' probate department stole on 51 occasions, 43 times from one estate, and 8 times from another. Excess insurers argued that each theft was a separate claim so that the entire loss would fall on primary insurers. They argued that each theft gave rise to a new cause of action on the date it was committed. In relation to the thefts from the second estate, the insured was not sued directly by the estate, which claimed against others implicated in the fraud in 14 separate actions. The insured was then joined as third party by a number of defendants to those 14 actions. Excess insurers argued that, even if their argument that each theft gave rise to a separate claim were rejected, each third party proceeding was a separate claim.

10.23 The Privy Council disagreed with both arguments. 'Claim' does not mean 'cause of action'.[35] While not determinative, the way in which the person claiming against the insured formulates his complaint provides a useful starting point.[36] That will often give a good indication as to whether he is making one claim or more than one claim for policy purposes. There was nothing to displace the impression which arose from the way that the first estate had claimed against the insured: there was

---

[33] As to which, see paras 2.19–2.46.

[34] [1997] 1 WLR 198.

[35] You can pay a claim, but you cannot pay a cause of action: see *West Wake Price & Co v Ching* [1957] 1 WLR 45, at 57 per Devlin J.

[36] [1997] 1 WLR 198, at 205. See also *Australia & New Zealand Bank Ltd v Colonial & Eagle Wharves Ltd: Boag (Third Party)* [1960] 2 Lloyd's Rep 241. In *Haydon v Lo & Lo (A Firm)*, while distinguishing this decision on the facts, not least because it was concerned with liability under an 'all risks' policy, the Privy Council agreed with the judgment of McNair J insofar as he held that the way in which the third party claimant put forward his case against the insured could not determine how it was to be treated as between the insured and insurers. Hoffmann J expressed the same view in *Alliance & Leicester Building Society v Edgestop Ltd* [1999] Lloyd's Rep PN 868, at 872.

a single claim for restitution, even though the loss was caused by a number of separate thefts.[37] As for the second estate, it too had only one claim and it did not become more than one claim because it was only made through a number of third party proceedings against the insured.[38]

In deciding whether the third party is advancing one claim or a number of claims, **10.24** it is necessary to consider the underlying facts and to ask whether the third party is claiming only one object or a number of different objects.[39] In *Haydon v Lo & Lo (A Firm)*,[40] the Privy Council applied the following passage from the judgment of Devlin J in *West Wake Price & Co v Ching*:[41]

> I think that the primary meaning of the word 'claim'—whether used in a popular sense or in a strict legal sense—is such as to attach it to the object that is claimed; and is not the same thing as the cause of action by which the claim may be supported or as the grounds on which it may be based.

> If you say of a claim against a defendant that it is for £100, you have said all that is necessary to identify it as a claim; but if you say of it that it is for fraud or negligence, you have not distinguished it from a charge or allegation. In particular, if you identify a claim as something that has to be paid … it must be something that is capable of separate payment: you cannot pay a cause of action. It follows, I think, that if there is only one object claimed by one person, then there is only one claim, however many may be the grounds or the causes of action which can be raised in support of it: …

This reasoning was applied by Thomas J in *Citibank NA v Excess Insurance Company* **10.25** *Ltd.*[42] The insured had been found to have been negligent in 1983 in the way in which they had laid some cables, in 1989 for fitting the wrong fuses to a switchboard, and again in 1991 for failing to discover their earlier error in fitting the wrong fuses. As a result of these breaches a fire had broken out, causing damage which cost over £2 million to rectify. The insured had cover of £2 million 'in respect of any one claim or series of claims arising out of any one original cause'. The third party argued that there were two 'original causes' of the loss: the incorrectly laid cable and the incorrect fuses.

Thomas J disagreed. Even if there were two originating causes, there was only one **10.26** claim. The clause only applied where there was more than one claim. He held:[43]

> To suggest as [the third party claimant] has done that each separate cause of action which was the cause of a single claim gives rise to separate additional limits of liability for that claim stands the clause on its head; it is a contention contrary to its plain commercial purpose.

---

[37] Ibid at 205–6.
[38] Ibid at 207.
[39] Ibid at 205–6.
[40] [1997] 1 WLR 198.
[41] [1957] 1 WLR 45, at 55 and 57.
[42] [1999] Lloyd's Rep IR 122.
[43] Ibid at 127.

10.27 The third party claimant had another argument. The trial judge had held the insured solely liable for the cost of repairing the cabling which was damaged or destroyed in the fire. He had apportioned the balance of the cost of making good the damage between the insured and two other defendants. The third party claimant argued that the damage to the cabling was a different claim to that for the rest of the damage. Again, Thomas J rejected the argument. Applying the approach set out in *Haydon v Lo & Lo (A Firm)*[44] he held:

> In my view, looking at the demand in the letter before action, the formulation of the statement of claim and the annexed schedule of damages (where one single sum was claimed) and the reality of the position, I have no doubt but that there was one claim by [the third party claimant] for the damage caused by the fire. The division made by [the trial judge] was solely for the purpose of distinguishing between the sole liability of [the insured] for the damage to the cabling and the other damages for which all of the three defendants in that action were liable.

10.28 There were multiple claims in *Mabey & Johnson Ltd v Ecclesiastical Insurance Office Ltd (No 2)*.[45] The insured were a firm of engineers. They had entered two contracts to design and supply bridges in Ghana. The design of all the bridges was flawed. The later designs had adopted the earlier, flawed work. Insurers argued that there was only one claim in respect of the badly-designed bridges. Morison J disagreed. There were two separate contracts. Each required the insured to provide a reasonably competent design. There were different breaches of different contracts leading to different insured losses. The fact that the second negligent design adopted the earlier design without checking it did not mean that there was a single claim.[46]

10.29 In general, where separate breaches of duty give rise to claims by a third party claimant for different objects, rather than for the same, single object, there will be more than one claim.[47] However, it will always be a question of considering the underlying facts against the policy wording. For example, if a claim were brought against an

---

[44] [1997] 1 WLR 198.

[45] [2003] EWHC 1523 (Comm); [2004] Lloyd's Rep IR 10.

[46] See also *Alliance & Leicester Building Society v Edgestop Ltd* [1999] Lloyd's Rep PN 868. In that case the claimant building society alleged in one action that the defendant solicitors had been in breach of duty in relation to four loans made on the security of four different hotels. The solicitors' insurers argued that there was only a single claim for the purposes of the limit of cover. Hoffmann J regarded this as untenable, stating at 871:

> The solicitors were engaged to act for the Society in respect of each of the ... hotels under separate retainers and gave separate undertakings to act in accordance with the Society's instructions. They were four wholly separate transactions. The only things which they have in common is the identity of the plaintiff and the *modus operandi*—features which they share with the other two actions—and the fact that they happen to have been brought in one action rather than four separate ones.

[47] As in *Wright Engineers Ltd v United States Fire Insurance Company* (1983) 48 BCLR 37 (Supreme Court of British Columbia); (1986) 19 CCLI 74 (British Columbia Court of Appeal) and *Elstrom, Smith & Co v Kansa General Insurance Co* (1988) 29 BCLR (2d) 41 (Supreme Court of British Columbia), discussed in n 77 under para 2.46. But for the position under the RIBA Architects Premier Policy Wording see paras 10.79–10.84.

architect for negligently failing to observe and have remedied a number of instances of defective workmanship, it would not follow from the fact that a specific sum was claimed for each unobserved defect that each defect was the subject of a separate claim. On the other hand, if the architect were sued for negligent design of one part of a building and also for negligently failing to spot defective workmanship in another part of the building, that might well give rise to two claims, even if the third party claimant brought only one set of proceedings against the architect.[48]

Aggregation clauses to be read as a whole

Like any other term in a contract, aggregation clauses have to be read as a whole **10.30** and in the context of the other relevant terms of the contract of insurance and the relevant background.[49] Particular care is needed when considering the construction placed upon words and phrases used in aggregation clauses in existing authorities. This is because the overall effect of an aggregation clause is the result of the interaction of a number of elements. First, there is the unifying factor, usually expressed in terms of either one or both happenings (or, in the case of omissions, non-happenings) and causes (or originating causes). Second there is the degree of causal relationship between unifying factor or factors. Third, at least in some cases, there is the particular nature of what has to be causally linked to the unifying factor.[50]

So, for example, a finding as to the meaning of 'event' will require consideration of **10.31** what causal relationship the parties have specified that event must have to claims or losses under the particular policy. It does not follow that 'event' would bear the identical meaning in the context of a different causal relationship. Evans LJ expressed the position in these terms in *Caudle v Sharp*, when considering whether an insured's 'blind spot' could be a relevant event for the purposes of the aggregation clause before the Court:[51]

> In my judgment, the three requirements of a relevant event are that there was a common factor which can properly be described as an event, which satisfied the test of causation and which was not too remote for the purposes of the clause.

The answers to those questions were interrelated.

Events, occurrences, and causes

While there is a wide range of aggregation clauses, all need to identify the unifying **10.32** factor, the presence of which will deem a number of claims to be a single claim.

---

[48] In this regard, the examples considered by Sir John Donaldson MR in *Thorman v New Hampshire Insurance Co (UK) Ltd* [1988] 1 Lloyd's Rep 7 are helpful: see paras 2.42–2.46.

[49] See paras 7.01–7.07.

[50] For example, in *Lloyds TSB General Insurance Holdings Ltd v Lloyds Bank Group Insurance Co Ltd* [2003] UKHL 48; [2003] 4 All ER 43, discussed in paras 10.38–10.40, the nature of the third party claims to which the unifying factor had to be causally related was defined with some specificity (see para 10.38).

[51] [1995] LRLR 433, at 438. See further paras 10.50–10.51.

That unifying factor tends to be one or more of an event, occurrence, act, omission, or cause (or originating cause) or, sometimes, a series of related events or occurrences. An 'event' or an 'occurrence' is not the same as a 'cause'. As Lord Mustill explained in *Axa Reinsurance (UK) Plc v Field*:[52]

> In ordinary speech, an event is something which happens at a particular time, at a particular place, in a particular way....A cause is to my mind something altogether less constricted. It can be a continuing state of affairs; it can be the absence of something happening.

10.33 The difference between events and occurrences on the one side and causes on the other is not limited to the fact that the former have to have happened. As Morison J explained in *Countrywide Assured Group Plc v Marshall*:[53]

> Whilst an event, occurrence or claim is 'something which happens at a particular time, at a particular place in a particular way' a 'cause' is not just 'something altogether less constricted' it is a word which is fulfilling a different function. The word event, occurrence or claim describes what has happened; the word 'cause' describes why something has happened.

10.34 The difference is illustrated by a comparison between the application of the different aggregation clauses in *Axa Reinsurance (UK) Plc v Field*[54] and *Cox v Bankside Members Agency Ltd*.[55] Both cases concerned the same underlying facts, which were the subject matter of the decision in *Deeny v Gooda Walker Ltd*,[56] where Phillips J had found that three Lloyd's underwriters had been negligent in relation to underwriting in certain specific respects.

10.35 In *Cox v Bankside Members Agency Ltd*,[57] the issue was the application of the following aggregation clause in the professional indemnity insurance of the members' and managing agents at Lloyd's who had been held liable for the underwriters' negligence:

> Insurers' total liability under this Policy in respect of any Claim or Claims arising from one originating cause, or series of events or occurrences attributable to one originating cause or related causes, shall in no event exceed the sum stated in Item 3(a) of the Schedule.

Phillips J held that there were three 'originating causes', namely the approach to underwriting of each of the negligent underwriters. He rejected the argument that there was only one originating cause, namely a common error. Each underwriter's errors had been of a different and distinct nature. Moreover:[58]

---

52 [1996] 1 WLR 1026 at 1035.
53 [2002] EWHC 2082 (Comm); [2003] Lloyd's Rep IR 195 at 201.
54 [1996] 1 WLR 1026.
55 [1995] 2 Lloyd's Rep 437.
56 [1996] LRLR 183.
57 [1995] 2 Lloyd's Rep 437.
58 Ibid at 455.

A culpable misappreciation by an individual which leads him to commit a number of negligent acts can arguably be said to constitute a single event or originating cause responsible for all the negligent acts and their consequences. The same is not true when a number of individuals each act under an individual misappreciation, even if the nature of that misappreciation is the same.[59]

The issue in *Axa Reinsurance (UK) Plc v Field*[60] was whether this reasoning applied   **10.36**
equally to the application of the following provision in the excess of loss reinsurance of the insurers in *Cox v Bankside Members Agency Ltd*:

> For the purpose of this reinsurance the term 'each and every loss' shall be understood to mean each and every loss and/or occurrence and/or catastrophe and/or disaster and/or calamity and/or series of losses and/or occurrences and/or disasters and/or calamities arising out of one event.

The House of Lords held that it did not: a misappreciation could be a cause, but it was not an event.[61]

The same distinction between unifying factors which are expressed in terms of   **10.37**
events (or acts or omissions) on the one hand and causes or sources on the other can be seen in two decisions concerning aggregation of claims for mis-selling of pensions.

The first is the decision of the House of Lords in *Lloyds TSB General Insurance*   **10.38**
Holdings Ltd v Lloyds Bank Group Insurance Co Ltd.[62] The insured had faced some 22,000 claims, mainly ranging between £15,000 and £35,000. The total paid to third party claimants was some £125 million. The insured sought to recover some of its outlay under its liability indemnity insurance, which formed part of its bankers' composite insurance policy. There was a deductible of £1 million for each and every claim, but the insured argued that the claims should be aggregated under the following clause:

> If a series of third party claims shall result from any single act or omission (or related series of acts or omissions) then, irrespective of the total number of claims, all such third party claims shall be considered to be a single third party claim for the purpose of the application of the deductible.

The insurance required that, to be covered, a third party claim had to:

> be for financial loss caused by a breach on the part of the assured or an officer or employee of the assured of the provisions of the Financial Services Act 1986 (including without limitation any rules or Regulations made by any regulatory authority or any self regulatory organisation pursuant to the provisions of the Act) … in respect of which civil liability arises on the part of the assured.

---

[59] When Phillips J gave his judgment, the judgment of Clarke J in *Caudle v Sharp* [1995] LRLRL 80 had yet to be overturned by the Court of Appeal: see [1995] LRLR 433. Hence the reference by Phillips J to 'event'.
[60] [1996] 1 WLR 1026.
[61] See also *Caudle v Sharp* [1995] LRLR 433.
[62] [2003] UKHL 48; [2003] 4 All ER 43.

10.39 The insured argued that its own failure to train and monitor its representatives was a single act or omission for the purposes of the aggregation clause. This argument failed: any such failure was not the cause, or proximate cause, of the third party claimants' financial loss. The relevant acts or omissions were the giving of bad advice to individual third party claimants by individual representatives leading to individual losses.[63]

10.40 The insured also argued that the third party claims resulted from 'a related series of acts and omissions', in that the various breaches of duty by its representatives were related by reason of their common cause: lack of adequate training and monitoring. Again, the argument failed. The relevant acts or omissions were those of the various representatives. The aggregation clause did not permit the identification of some common cause for those acts or omissions. Such a result might be achieved if the clause had deemed all claims arising from the same originating cause to be a single claim, but that was not what the clause in question said or meant.[64]

10.41 By way of contrast, in *Countrywide Assured Group Plc v Marshall*[65] the aggregation clause provided that 'one claim' or 'one loss' meant:

> one occurrence or all occurrences of a series consequent upon or attributable to one source or original cause.

The background was the mis-selling of pensions and the unifying factor relied upon by the primary insurers was the failure to provide adequate training to the insured's representatives. Noting that the words 'one source or original cause' were wide, Morison J held:[66]

> In my view, the lack of proper training of the selling agents and selling employees was behind the whole problem. It was this which, on the assumed facts, was a consistent and necessary factor which allowed the mis-selling to occur. Maybe, the activities of individual salesmen were also causative but the clause entitles one to move back and find a single source or original cause; and in this case, there is one.

10.42 In order to decide whether two or more claims or losses arise from a single event or occurrence the conventional test, particularly in reinsurance, is to apply the four 'unities' of 'cause, locality, time and, if initiated by human action, the circumstances and purposes of the persons responsible'.[67] While a single occurrence can give rise to numerous claims or losses, for example, an earthquake, in the context

---

[63] Ibid at [22] per Lord Hoffmann and at [43]–[45] per Lord Hobhouse.

[64] Ibid at [25] per Lord Hoffmann and at [47]–[52] per Lord Hobhouse.

[65] [2002] EWHC 2082 (Comm); [2003] Lloyd's Rep IR 195.

[66] [2002] EWHC 2082 (Comm); [2003] Lloyd's Rep IR 195, at 201.

[67] A test formulated by Mr Michael Kerr QC in his award as arbitrator in the *Dawson's Field* arbitration, which concerned whether the destruction of three aircraft by hijackers was a single occurrence. The test involves considering the position from the point of view of an informed observer standing in the insured's shoes. This test has been developed and applied in number of authorities: *Kuwait Airways Corporation v Kuwait Insurance Co SAK* [1996] 1 Lloyd's Rep 664; *Mann v Lexington Insurance Co* [2001] 1 Lloyd's Rep 1; *Scott v Copenhagen Reinsurance Co (UK) Ltd* [2003]

of professional indemnity insurance aggregation clauses with a single occurrence as a unifying factor will tend to be relatively narrow in scope.[68]

In general, a unifying factor which is a 'cause' or 'source' will be wider in scope. And **10.43** the scope of a unifying factor can be widened by the addition of further words. For example, the addition of 'originating' to 'cause' allows 'the widest possible search for a unifying factor in the history of the losses which it is sought to aggregate'.[69] And the use of the words 'originating cause or source' stress an intention that the unifying factor is not limited to the proximate cause of the claim or loss, but allows losses to be traced back to 'wherever a common origin can reasonably be found'.[70]

Series of events or occurrences

Some aggregation clauses deem that claims or losses arising from a series of related **10.44** events are to be treated as a single claim. Guidance as to what is meant by 'a related series of acts or omissions' was given by the House of Lords in *Lloyds TSB General Insurance Holdings Ltd v Lloyds Bank Group Insurance Co Ltd*.[71]

In rejecting the insured's arguments,[72] Lord Hoffmann and Lord Hobhouse gave **10.45** examples of what would or might constitute a related series of acts and omissions in the particular context of the policy before them. Lord Hobhouse's example was of a representative who prepared a document which misrepresented the benefits of a particular pension scheme and then showed that document to a number of investors who were persuaded by it to switch to that scheme. While the provision of the document to each person would be a distinct act, together those acts could form a 'related series of acts' from which a 'series of third party claims' resulted.[73] Lord Hoffmann reserved his position as to whether this example was correct: claims were not related merely because they were very similar, although he could see that the production and distribution of a document could be an act or series of acts which were causally relevant to the claims.[74] Lord Hoffmann gave his own example:[75]

[2003] EWCA Civ 688; Lloyd's Rep IR 696; and *Aioi Nissay Dowa Insurance Co Ltd v Heraldglen Ltd* [2013] EWHC 154 (Comm); [2013] Lloyd's Rep IR 281.

[68] For an example of how several claims can arise from a single occurrence for the purposes of a contract of professional indemnity insurance see *Forney v Dominion Insurance Co Ltd* [1969] 1 WLR 928 discussed in paras 10.59–10.60.

[69] *Axa Reinsurance (UK) Ltd v Field* [1996] 1 WLR 1026, at 1035H per Lord Mustill.

[70] *Standard Life Assurance Ltd v ACE European Group* [2012] EWHC 104 (Comm); [2012] Lloyd's Rep IR 655, at [259] per Eder J. See also *Municipal Mutual Insurance Ltd v Sea Insurance Co Limited & Others* [1998] Lloyd's Rep IR 421, at 434 per Hobhouse LJ.

[71] [2003] UKHL 48; [2003] 4 All ER 43. See also *AIG Europe Ltd v OC320301 LLP (formerly the International Law Partnership LLP)* [2015] EWHC 2398 (Comm), at [35]–[42] per Teare J, discussed in paras 10.69–10.75.

[72] See paras 10.38–10.40.

[73] [2003] UKHL 48; [2003] 4 All ER 43, at [46]. At [45] Lord Hobhouse gave an example of how a single act (a presentation to a room full of people) could give rise to a 'series of third party claims'.

[74] Ibid at [28].

[75] Ibid at [29].

the distribution of a misleading document in identical terms by someone who was not himself negligent but ought to have been corrected by someone else who was. The two acts or omissions would be a series which together caused each of the losses.

10.46   What these examples and the decision in the *Lloyds TSB* case show is that phrases such as 'related series of acts and omissions' are not to be read in isolation, but in the wider context of the aggregation clause and other related provisions. In the *Lloyds TSB* case, the wider context showed the need for the acts and omissions to be the proximate cause of the third party claims. In other contexts, that might not be the case.

10.47   For example, the aggregation clause in *Hamptons Residential Ltd v Field*[76] was as follows:

> all claims or losses ... arising out of or attributable to or consequent upon
> (a) the same or similar or related occurrences circumstances events acts errors or omissions of the Assured including an act or acts of dishonesty or
> (b) any series or multiplicity of similar or related occurrences circumstances events acts errors or omissions of the Assured including a series or multiplicity of acts of dishonesty
> and whether involving or committed or omitted by any person or persons or companies acting together or jointly or in concert or separately or independently shall constitute a single claim and only one excess shall apply to and be available for the total of those claims or losses.

This clause is much wider in scope than that in the *Lloyds TSB* case, not only because it provides for the aggregation of claims and losses arising from similar as well as related 'occurrences circumstances events acts errors or omissions', but also because the causal link need not be so great: it is sufficient if the claims and losses are attributable to or consequent upon such matters.

10.48   Some aggregation clauses require that a 'series of occurrences' should arise from the specified unifying factor or factors. In this context, it has been held that what is required is that there should be a number of occurrences which share 'some connecting factor'[77] or 'a number of events of a sufficiently similar kind following one another in temporal succession'.[78] So, in *Caudle v Sharp*[79] the negligent underwriting of thirty-two similar reinsurance treaties by the same underwriter constituted a 'series of occurrences' for the purposes of the aggregation clause.[80] Where the aggregation

---

[76] [1997] 1 Lloyd's Rep 302; [1998] 2 Lloyd's Rep 248.

[77] *Countrywide Assured Group Plc v Marshall* [2002] EWHC 2082 (Comm); [2003] Lloyd's Rep IR 195, at 200 per Morison J.

[78] *Distillers Co Bio-Chemicals (Australia) Pty Ltd v Ajax Insurance Co Ltd* [1974] HCA 3; (1974) 130 CLR 1, at 21 per Stephen J, with whom Gibbs J agreed.

[79] [1995] LRLR 433.

[80] Ibid at 439. The clause is set out in para 10.50.

clause required that a 'series of third party claims' should result from the unifying factor, this clearly carried with it the possibility of claims by a number of different third parties, each claiming for his own loss, but did not import any more.[81]

Causation

As well as identifying the unifying factor or factors, an aggregation clause has to provide for a causal relationship between the factor or factors on the one hand and the losses or claims on the other. Phrases such as 'arise from', 'result from', 'attributable to', and 'consequent upon' are used. The need for there to be some causal relationship between the unifying factor and the claims also informs the meaning of the unifying factor.   **10.49**

So, in *Caudle v Sharp*[82] the 'event' relied upon for the purposes of the aggregation clause was a failure by Mr Outhwaite, a Lloyd's underwriter, to undertake the necessary research before underwriting 32 reinsurance contracts, which had resulted in vast losses.[83] In the excess of loss reinsurance treaties before the Court of Appeal, cover was provided for losses in excess of £1.25 million 'each and every loss'. 'Each and every loss' was defined as: **10.50**

> each and every loss and/or occurrence and/or catastrophe and/or disaster and/or calamity and/or series of losses and/or occurrences and/or catastrophes and/or disasters and/or calamities arising out of one event.

Rejecting the reinsured's argument, Evans LJ observed that Mr Outhwaite's disastrous underwriting was 'an event in the history of Lloyd's', but it was not an event for the purposes of the aggregation clause. He explained:[84]

> The losses or series of losses envisaged by the clause must have 'arisen out of' one event, which in this context straightaway implies some causative element and some degree of remoteness, or lack of remoteness, which must be established in the circumstances of the particular case.[85]

Evans LJ went on to consider what degree of causative potency was required by the words 'arisen out of' in the context of the excess of loss reinsurance treaty at issue. In that context, the words did not require that the event was the proximate cause of the losses or claims, but, while the test was wider than that, there was still some restriction.[86]   **10.51**

---

[81] *Lloyds TSB General Insurance Holdings Ltd v Lloyds Bank Group Insurance Co Ltd* [2003] UKHL 48; [2003] 4 All ER 43, per Lord Hobhouse at [45].

[82] [1995] LRLR 433.

[83] An individual's misappreciation or misunderstanding is unlikely to be an 'event', although it may be a 'cause' or 'originating cause': see paras 10.32–10.43.

[84] [1995] LRLR 433, at 438.

[85] As Nourse LJ put it in the same case at 443: 'An event must be something out of which a loss or series of losses arises. Here neither Mr Outhwaite's state of mind nor his failure to instruct himself can be said in any real sense to have been something out of which the losses arose.'

[86] [1995] LRLR 433, at 439.

10.52 The aggregation clause in *Lloyds TSB General Insurance Holdings Ltd v Lloyds Bank Group Insurance Co Ltd*[87] had a stricter requirement for causation: the relevant acts or omission had to be the proximate cause[88] of the liability to the third party claimants.[89] The liability of the insured to third party claimants did not result from its failure to have a proper training and monitoring system, but from the bad advice given to each third party claimant by various of the insured's representatives.[90] As Lord Hoffmann explained:[91]

> The language of the aggregation clause, read with the definition of 'act or omission', shows that the insurers were not willing to accept as a unifying factor a common cause more remote than the act or omission which actually constituted the cause of action. An act or omission could qualify as a unifying factor in respect of more than one loss only if it gave rise to civil liability in respect of both losses.

10.53 By way of contrast the aggregation clause in *Standard Life Assurance Ltd v ACE European Group*[92] had a very low requirement for causation. The causal link informed the approach to the unifying factor, but this time so as to widen the scope of the clause. In the *Standard Life* case the aggregation clause for the purposes of the self-insuring deductible of £10 million in a policy of professional indemnity insurance provided:

> All claims or series of claims (whether by one or more than one claimant) arising from or in connection with or attributable to any one act, error, omission or originating cause or source, or the dishonesty of any one person or group of persons acting together, shall be considered to be a single third-party claim for the purposes of the application of the Deductible.

Having observed that the use of the words 'originating cause or error' indicated that a wide search for a unifying factor was appropriate,[93] Eder J explained that the causal link required ('arising from or in connection with or attributable to') was weaker than those in the cases which he had considered. In particular:[94]

> The phrase 'in connection with' is extremely broad and indicates that it is not even necessary to show a direct causal relationship between the claims and the state of affairs identified as their 'originating cause or source', and that some form of connection between the claims and the unifying factor is all that is required.

Against that background Eder J held that all claims against the insured arising from mis-selling of a particular fund fell to be treated as a single claim, notwithstanding that the mis-selling occurred over a number of years to many thousands

---

[87] [2003] UKHL 48; [2003] 4 All ER 43. For the facts see para 10.38.
[88] As to which see paras 9.92–9.93.
[89] [2003] UKHL 48; [2003] 4 All ER 43, at [43] per Lord Hobhouse.
[90] Ibid at [22] per Lord Hoffmann.
[91] Ibid at [23].
[92] [2012] EWHC 104 (Comm); [2012] Lloyd's Rep IR 655.
[93] See para 10.43.
[94] [2012] EWHC 104 (Comm); [2012] Lloyd's Rep IR 655, at [262].

of customers in many different ways. The claims were all fundamentally based on the same mis-description of the fund.

C. Particular Aggregation Clauses

SRA Minimum Terms and Conditions of Professional Indemnity Insurance

The SRA Minimum Terms and Conditions of Professional Indemnity Insurance **10.54** permit an aggregation clause to be included in the following terms:

(a) all Claims against any one or more Insured arising from:
   (i) one act or omission;
   (ii) one series of related acts or omissions;
   (iii) the same act or omission in a series of related matters or transactions;
   (iv) similar acts or omissions in a series of related matters or transactions and
(b) all Claims against one or more Insured arising from one matter or transaction
   will be regarded as one Claim.

This wording has been expanded in recent years.[95] It should be noted that the various **10.55** unifying factors do not include any cause or originating cause.[96] To be aggregated, the claims must arise from acts or omissions or from one matter or transaction.

It is likely that the various sub-clauses will overlap in many circumstances. All the **10.56** various unifying factors are subject to the words 'arising from' and what has to arise from them is a claim, the basic definition of which is 'a demand for, or an assertion of a right to, civil compensation or civil damages or an intimation of an intention to seek such compensation or damages'.

In the context of sub-clause (a), the claims have to 'arise from' one of the unifying **10.57** factors set out in (i), (ii), (iii), or (iv), all of which refer to acts or omissions. The focus is therefore on the acts or omissions which give rise to the demands for, or assertions of the right to, civil compensation or civil damages or intimations of the intention to seek such compensation or damages. Those are likely to be the acts or omissions which form the subject matter of the claim and it is in this sense that the claims must 'arise from' the relevant acts or omissions.

In the context of sub-clause (b), the unifying factor is not an act or omission or **10.58** any number of acts or omissions, but a single 'matter or transaction'. The causal

---

[95] In the first set of Minimum Terms and Conditions of Professional Indemnity Insurance for Solicitors, namely those for 2000, the aggregation was simply for: 'all Claims against one or more Insured arising from the same act or omission or from one series of related acts or omissions will be regarded as one Claim …' The wording changed from 2005 onwards. It should be noted that no aggregate limit is permitted in the SRA Minimum Terms and Conditions of Professional Indemnity Insurance so that aggregation is the primary insurers' main protection against multiple claims against honest insured.

[96] See paras 10.32–10.43.

relationship between a 'matter or transaction' and a claim will be different from that between a claim and the act or omission from which it arises. In the latter case, the claim will be for 'civil compensation or civil damages' suffered as a result of an act or omission. In the former, the claim will concern the matter or transaction and, in that sense, 'arise from' it. But the basis upon which 'civil compensation or civil damages' are claimed will be some act or omission in the insured's conduct of that matter or transaction.

One act or omission

10.59 It will usually be straightforward to determine whether a number of claims arise from a single act or omission or from a number of acts and omissions. So, in *Forney v Dominion Insurance Co Ltd*[97] the total cover in the aggregate was £15,000, but there was a limit of £3,000 'in respect of any one claim or number of claims arising out of the same occurrence'. The insured solicitor was acting for the relatives of a deceased man who had died in a car accident caused by his own negligence. His mother-in-law, widow, and son had all been injured in the same accident and so had claims against the deceased's estate. The solicitor gave notice to the deceased's insurers of the family's claims against the estate. He also obtained for the widow a grant of letters of administration to the estate. He failed to advise that someone other than the widow should be appointed (because the widow could not sue herself) or to issue effective proceedings on behalf of the widow, mother-in-law, or son within the required time. The mother-in-law, widow, and son all sued the solicitor, recovering more than £3,000 in total.

10.60 The insured argued that he had breached separate duties owed to each third party claimant and that each breach was a separate occurrence for the purpose of the limit on indemnity. Donaldson J disagreed. He accepted that, from the point of view of each third party claimant, it was the breach of the duty owed to that claimant which gave rise to the claim. However, the wording clearly contemplated that more than one clam could arise from a single occurrence so that the occurrence had to be looked at from the point of view of the insured.[98] From that point of view, there were two occurrences. The first was the appointment of the widow as administratrix of the deceased's estate and the subsequent failure to have her appointment revoked. This meant that the widow could not issue effective proceedings because she would be the nominal defendant. The second was the failure to issue proceedings in time on behalf of the mother-in-law and son. The two occurrences were 'different both in nature and chronology'.[99]

---

[97] [1969] 1 WLR 928.
[98] Ibid at 934. Donaldson J distinguished *South Staffordshire Tramways Co Ltd v Sickness and Accident Assurance Association* [1891] 1 QB 402. In that case, about 40 passengers were injured when a vehicle overturned and it was held that 'accident' in the insurance policy meant 'accident to a passenger', so there were about 40 'accidents'.
[99] Ibid.

One series of related acts or omissions

The question as to what will constitute a 'series of related acts or omissions' will fall **10.61**
to be considered against the decision of the House of Lords in *Lloyds TSB General
Insurance Holdings Ltd v Lloyds Bank Group Insurance Co Ltd*[100] insofar as it concerned
the words 'related series of acts or omissions'. However, this is subject to one caveat.
In reaching his decision in the *Lloyds TSB* case, Lord Hoffmann attached some significance to the fact that in the aggregation clause in question the words 'or related
series of acts or omissions' appeared in brackets after 'any single act or omission'.[101] In
the aggregation clause in the SRA Minimum Terms and Conditions of Professional
Indemnity Insurance, the similar words are a free-standing unifying factor.

'Series' will normally mean 'sequence',[102] although it would be odd if the parties **10.62**
had intended aggregation to occur if two related acts or omissions occurred sequen-
tially but not if they occurred simultaneously. It is therefore possible that 'series'
means no more than 'a number', there being no further unifying factor implicit in
the word 'series', given that the series must be of 'related acts or omissions'.

Whether they need to be sequential or not, the acts or omissions must be related in **10.63**
some way. It seems likely that they must be related in that they all gave rise to the
claim or claims which are to be treated as a single claim, as in the example given by
Lord Hoffmann in the *Lloyds TSB* case.[103]

It might be thought that the acts or omissions could be related if they all arose from **10.64**
some common, anterior cause, for example a failure to train and monitor staff.
However, given that this can be readily achieved by the choice of 'originating cause'
as a unifying factor,[104] it is unlikely that a Court would hold that the parties had
intended to achieve this result by the words 'related acts or omissions'. Moreover,
if acts or omissions were treated as 'related' because of some broad, underlying
cause, for example, a solicitor's failure to understand the basic rules of conveyancing, leading to a catalogue of different errors when acting for different clients on
different property transactions, the clients of that solicitor might find themselves
deprived of compensation for losses suffered as a result. That would be contrary
to the primary purpose for which solicitors are obliged to obtain insurance under
the Minimum Terms and Conditions of Professional Indemnity Insurance for
Solicitors,[105] and it is unlikely that such a result was intended.

---

[100] [2003] UKHL 48; [2003] 4 All ER 43: see paras 10.38–10.40 and 10.44–10.45.
[101] Ibid at [25] per Lord Hoffmann.
[102] See para 10.48.
[103] See para 10.45. If the clause were read so that the acts and omissions had to be related to
each other, rather than so that each act or omission had to be related to each claim, it would have a
wider scope. The former approach has been adopted in a number of Canadian authorities helpfully
summarized and applied by the Court of Appeal of Ontario in *Simpson Wigle Law LLP v Lawyers'
Professional Indemnity Company* 2014 ONCA 492.
[104] See paras 10.32–10.43.
[105] See paras 1.05–1.06.

The same act or omission in a series of related matters or transactions

10.65 The words 'the same act or omission' do not refer to a single act or omission: that has already been covered by sub-clause (a)(i). Rather, they refer to two or more acts or omissions which are 'the same'. Given that there is a free-standing unifying factor for 'similar acts or omissions', 'same' must mean 'identical'.

10.66 As well as being identical, the act or omission must be in a 'series of related matters or transactions'. The same considerations apply to 'series' here as arise in relation to 'a series of related acts or omissions'.[106] They are considered below in the context of 'similar acts or omissions in a series of related matters or transactions'.[107]

10.67 The question whether two or more matters or transactions are related should be addressed from the point of view of the insured solicitor.[108]

Similar acts or omissions in a series of related matters or transactions

10.68 This unifying factor largely replicates the preceding one, the difference being that the acts and omissions can be similar, rather than the same. Similarity is clearly a question of fact and degree. What is required is 'a real or substantial degree of similarity as opposed to a fanciful or insubstantial degree of similarity'.[109] This is a fairly low threshold.

10.69 So in *AIG Europe Ltd v OC320301 LLP*[110] the insured solicitors had acted for numerous individuals who wanted to buy or invest in two developments in Turkey and Morocco. The clients advanced money which was to be held on trust (a different trust for each development) and their money was only supposed to be released when certain criteria had been fulfilled. It was assumed for the purposes of determining the issue of aggregation under the solicitors' professional indemnity insurance that the clients' moneys had in each case been paid out in circumstances in which there was inadequate security, mainly because the development companies had not acquired title to the land on which the developments were intended to be constructed. While there were differences as to detail as to how this came about, Teare J accepted insurers' submission that the acts and omissions from which all the claims arose were similar. In all cases the developer could not pay the vendor of the land (both in Turkey and Morocco) and the insured solicitors had failed to ensure that the criteria for paying out each client's money were satisfied so that each client's funds were at risk.

10.70 It is not enough that two or more claims arise from similar acts or omissions. The acts or omissions must be 'in a related series of related matters or transactions'.

---

[106] See para 10.48.
[107] See paras 10.70–10.75.
[108] *Forney v Dominion Insurance Co Ltd* [1969] 1 WLR 928: see para 10.60.
[109] *AIG Europe Ltd v OC320301 LLP* [2015] EWHC 2398 (Comm), at [30] per Teare J.
[110] [2015] EWHC 2398 (Comm).

Here 'related' could apply in a number of ways. For example, if a solicitor acts for a **10.71** client who is selling one property and buying another, the 'matters and transactions' could be said to be the discharge of the mortgage of the property to be sold, the sale of that property, the purchase of the new property, the execution of the mortgage, and all necessary registration. Those various matters or transactions could be said to be 'related' in the sense that they are connected to and dependent upon each other.

However, the words 'similar acts or omissions' suggest repetition. For example, a **10.72** solicitor who is on a panel instructed by a mortgage lender might make the same error or omission when advising a number of mortgagor borrowers about the mortgage lender's standard terms and conditions in relation to a particular type of loan. The various mortgage transactions could be said to be 'related' in that they concerned the same mortgagee and the same terms and conditions, even though each was, in a sense, an independent transaction.

Following the decision of Teare J in *AIG Europe Ltd v OC320301 LLP*[111] the **10.73** narrower construction is to be preferred. The facts in that case have been set out above.[112] Teare J identified three different ways in which a number of 'matters and transactions' could be 'related' in the context of the facts of the case before him. The first was a series of matters which were related in that they were dependent on each other. The second was that matters were related in that they concerned the same development. The third was that the matters were independent, but of a similar nature. Teare J held that the first meaning was the correct one.[113]

He rejected the third possible construction because it would result in a clause which **10.74** was both very wide (not least given his finding as to what was required for acts or omissions to be 'similar'[114]) and uncertain in scope.[115] Both the first and second possible constructions would result in a sufficient degree of certainty, but the first was to be preferred:[116]

> In the present case there is common ground on the pleadings that the individual transactions were not conditional or dependent on each other. In addition, the natural meaning, or at any rate the most natural meaning of the phrase 'a series of related matters or transactions' in the context of a solicitors' insurance policy is, in my judgment, a series of matters or transactions that are in some way dependent on each other. It is difficult to talk of transactions being related unless their terms are in some way inter-connected. Finally, the first possible meaning can reasonably be said to be appropriate in the context of an aggregation clause because there is sense in aggregating such claims where they arise out of similar acts or omissions in transactions that are dependent on each other.

---

[111] [2015] EWHC 2398 (Comm).
[112] Para 10.69.
[113] [2015] EWHC 2398 (Comm) at [37]–[42].
[114] See para 10.69.
[115] [2015] EWHC 2398 (Comm), at [38].
[116] Ibid at [40].

10.75 While it may be that the third possible construction would result in this limb of the aggregation clause having a very wide and uncertain application, the first construction means that the scope of this term is very narrow. And it is hard to see why the parties would think it appropriate for two or more claims in a series of dependent matters or transactions to be aggregated if they arise from similar acts and omissions, but not if they arise from acts or omissions which are not similar. In this regard it should be noted that specific provision is made in the aggregation clause in the SRA Minimum Terms and Conditions of Professional Indemnity Insurance that all claims arising from one matter or transaction are to be treated as a single claim. At the time of writing insurers have permission to appeal to the Court of Appeal.

All claims arising from one matter or transaction

10.76 It will usually be straightforward to identify all the claims against any insured which arise from one matter or transaction. However, there may be scope for dispute as to what constitutes a single 'matter' or 'transaction'.[117]

The RICS Policy Wording

10.77 The RICS Policy Wording provides that the maximum indemnity available to the insured in respect of each claim or 'SERIES OF CLAIMS' will not exceed the 'INDEMNITY LIMIT FOR CLAIMS'. 'SERIES OF CLAIMS' is defined as follows:

> a number of CLAIMS (whether made against or involving one or more persons or entities comprising the INSURED and whether made by the same or different claimants and whether falling under one or more insuring clauses of this policy) that arise directly or indirectly from the same originating cause.

10.78 These are wide words. The unifying factor is 'originating cause' and the requirement for causation is low: the link between the 'originating cause' and the various claims may be direct or indirect. This will permit the aggregation of claims which can be traced back to a common causative factor.[118] The clause is similar in effect to that considered in *Municipal Mutual Insurance Ltd v Sea Insurance Co Ltd*,[119] which was in these terms:

> all occurrences of a series consequent on or attributable to one source or original cause …

In *Lloyds TSB General Insurance Holdings Ltd v Lloyds Bank Group Insurance Co Ltd*,[120] Lord Hoffmann said of this clause:[121]

---

[117] Cf *Canadian Lawyers' Insurance Association v Young* (1997) 147 DLR (4th) 31, where it was held that claims by seven former clients of a solicitor whose funds had been placed in the same investment which the solicitor had mismanaged were not 'in relation to the same professional service'.

[118] See paras 10.32–10.43.

[119] [1998] Lloyd's Rep IR 421.

[120] [2003] UKHL 48; [2003] 4 All ER 43.

[121] Ibid at [16].

This meant that as long as one could find any act, event or state of affairs which could properly be described as a cause of more than one loss, they formed part of a series for the purposes of the aggregation clause.

The RIBA Architects Premier Policy Wording

The aggregation clause in the RIBA Architects Premier Policy Wording falls into two parts. **10.79**

The first part provides that insurers' liability under the main insuring clauses will not exceed the limit of indemnity[122] 'in respect of each and every claim (or series of claims arising from the same originating source)'. As has been explained, the words 'originating source' permit a wide search for some common cause.[123] The requirement for causation is less wide than that in the RICS Policy Wording. **10.80**

The second part is as follows: **10.81**

> Where any claim, circumstance or event is notified to Insurers which is the same as or arises out of or is connected with any claim, circumstance or event notified at the same time or previously such claim, circumstance or event shall be deemed to be the same claim, circumstance or event for the purposes of assessing the Limit of Liability available to the Insured, and no additional Limit of Indemnity shall apply.

To an extent this provision merely makes clear what would otherwise be the case. First, if a claim has already been made, a further notification of what is, in substance, still the same claim would not be a separate claim so that a single limit of indemnity would apply. Second, if a circumstance has already been notified during the period of insurance, then any claim to which that circumstance gives rise will be deemed to have been made during the period of insurance.[124] **10.82**

But the provision goes further than that. The words 'arises out of or is connected with' appear to allow a weaker link between the subjects of two or more notifications. Two claims could be connected with each other if, for example, they concerned the same project, even though they did not have the same originating source so as to fall within the first part of the clause. The first might concern allegedly negligent design by an architect employed by the insured and the second allegedly negligent contract administration by another employee. They would not have the same originating source, but they would be connected in that they concerned the same project.[125] **10.83**

---

[122] The limit of indemnity is a matter for agreement in each contract. There is no prescribed minimum level of cover for architects, although the Architects Registration Board recommends and expects that architects will maintain professional indemnity cover of at least £250,000 per claim.

[123] See para 10.43.

[124] See paras 2.50–2.51 and 2.150.

[125] So that the result in *Citibank NA v Excess Insurance Company Ltd* [1999] Lloyd's Rep IR 122 as discussed in paras 10.25–10.27 would be different.

10.84 A possible explanation of the second part of the clause may be the requirement in the RIBA Architects Premier Policy Wording that the insured give notice in writing 'of any claim or of the receipt of notice from any person of an intention to make a claim and regardless of any previous notice, give notice in writing of any Claim Form, Particulars of Claim, Arbitration Notice or any other formal document commencing legal proceedings of any kind'. The second part of the clause clearly ensures that the provision of successive notifications by an insured will not amount to separate claims. However the wording used appears to go beyond what would be needed to achieve that end.

11

THE OBLIGATIONS OF THE INSURED IN RELATION TO CLAIMS BY THIRD PARTIES

A. Notification of Claims

The insured will usually be required to give notice to insurers of the making of **11.01** any claim against him by a third party.[1] In a 'claims made and notified policy', the giving of such notice within the period prescribed by the policy will be an essential trigger of cover.[2] In 'claims made' policies, the giving of notice will not be part of the trigger of cover. However, insurers will want to receive prompt notice of any claim made against the insured so that they can decide what steps to take to reduce or manage their exposure.[3]

Insurers' interest in prompt notification of claims should not be overstated. In **11.02** many, indeed probably the vast majority of cases, it will be of little, if any, practical consequence to insurers whether they receive notice within hours of the claim

---

[1] As to what is required for a claim to have been made, see paras 2.19–2.38.
[2] See paras 2.47–2.49.
[3] See n 96 under para 2.51.

first being made against the insured or only after a few weeks or even months. As Phillips J said when considering the notification requirements under a policy insuring Lloyd's managing and members' agents in *Cox v Bankside Members Agency Ltd*:[4]

> While I can appreciate why underwriters would wish to receive immediate notice of claims, it does not seem to me that this is an essential requirement from their viewpoint. Indeed in the majority of cases I would not expect that a limited delay in notifying underwriters of a claim would have any adverse effect on underwriters.

The position may be different if the subject matter of the insurance or claim is such that real prejudice will or may well be suffered if insurers are not able to investigate the cause of the loss promptly, for example if a fire has occurred or goods are rotting on a quayside. In such cases, it would be appropriate for there to be a term requiring that, if the insured is to be indemnified, notice must be given within a very short time. However, in cases of insurance against legal liability for financial loss such as professional indemnity insurance, such a term would not usually be necessary to protect insurers' interests.[5] One clear exception to this is adjudications under the Housing Grants, Construction and Regeneration Act 1996 which are considered below.[6]

Requirements as to timing

11.03 It is usual for the obligation to give notice of a claim to include a requirement as to the time by which notice should be given. In many cases, notice will be given through the insured's broker and, in the absence of any provision identifying a particular person to whom notice is to be given, notice must be given to all insurers. When considering what is intended by stipulations as to time where notice must be given to the following market, the expert evidence given in *HLB Kidsons v Lloyd's Underwriters*[7] should be borne in mind. It was summarized by Gloster J as follows:[8]

> It is recognised in the market that it takes time for notification of a claim or circumstance to be made to following insurers, with the result that there may be a delay between the time of first notification of the matter by the assured to his broker and notification by the broker to the following market. The kind of delay that is acceptable would normally be measured in weeks or at most 'some months'. More than this would not be acceptable, especially since the market recognises the importance of insurers receiving information about claims and circumstances promptly.

However, this needs to be put in context. Gloster J was receiving evidence as to the position in relation to a following market: the position may well be different if there

---

[4] [1995] 2 Lloyd's Rep 437, at 454.
[5] *Royal & Sun Alliance Insurance Plc v Dornoch* [2005] EWCA Civ 238; [2005] Lloyd's Rep IR 544, at [16] per Longmore LJ, with whom Mance and Brooke LJJ agreed.
[6] Paras 11.12–11.15.
[7] [2007] EWHC 1951 (Comm); [2008] Lloyd's Rep IR 237.
[8] Ibid at [174(xxvi)].

is a single insurer or if the policy provides that notice should be given to a specified person on behalf of all insurers.

Immediately

It is not unusual for policies of professional indemnity insurance to require the **11.04**
insured to give insurers 'immediate' notice of the making of a claim against the insured. For example, in *Guinness Peat Properties Ltd v The Fitzroy Robinson Partnership (a firm)*[9] a firm of architects was insured by a policy which included the following term:

> The insured shall as a condition precedent to their right to be indemnified under sections 1 and 2 of this policy, give to the company immediate notice in writing: (a) of any claim made against them (b) of the receipt of notice from any person of an intention to make a claim against them.

On its natural meaning 'immediate' gives 'minimal scope for delay'.[10] In *Farrell v* **11.05**
Federated Employers Assurance Association Ltd,[11] the Court of Appeal rejected a submission that a condition that the insured give notice of every writ served on it 'immediately on receipt' had been complied with by giving notice to insurers nearly two months after it had been served. It was argued that 'immediately' should be construed as suggested by Fletcher Moulton LJ in *In re Coleman's Depositories Ltd and the Life and Health Assurance Association*,[12] namely 'as meaning with all reasonable speed considering the circumstances of the case'. Lord Denning MR held that this required notice to be given within about four weeks at the latest, rather than two months.[13] Megaw LJ held that it was impossible to say that notice had been given as required.[14] Sellers LJ agreed with both judgments.[15] It is suggested that the period indicated by Lord Denning MR was as favourable to the insured as possible in the circumstances.[16]

Even where the insured is required to give immediate notice, some interval must be **11.06**
allowed between receipt of a claim and notification. Where the insured is a large firm with a number of offices in different places, it may be that the parties will be taken to have intended that a requirement that notice be given immediately should be construed as allowing for internal reporting of a claim within the firm before it

---

[9] [1987] 1 WLR 1027.
[10] *Cox v Bankside Members Agency Ltd* [1995] 2 Lloyd's Rep 437, at 454 per Phillips J. See also *R v Berkshire Justices* (1878) 4 QBD 469, at 471 per Cockburn CJ, a case concerning the meaning of 'immediately' in the context of the Licensing Act 1872.
[11] [1970] 1 WLR 1400.
[12] [1907] 2 KB 798, at 807.
[13] [1970] 1 WLR 1400, at 1406.
[14] Ibid at 1409.
[15] Ibid.
[16] In *Aspen Insurance UK Ltd v Pectel Ltd* [2008] EWHC 2804 (Comm); [2009] Lloyd's Rep IR 440, Teare J, applying the construction of 'immediate' given by Fletcher Moulton LJ in *In re Coleman's Depositories Ltd and the Life and Health Assurance Association* [1907] 2 KB 798, held that the insured should have given insurers notice of a potential claim in relation to a fire which had occurred on 29 March 2004 by 'early April' of that year.

reaches the individual responsible for giving notice to insurers. Express provision to this effect was made in the policy considered in *Standard Life Assurance Ltd v Oak Dedicated Ltd*.[17] The insured was a substantial financial institution. Cover was subject to a very large excess. The policy required the insured's corporate risk department to give immediate notice of any claim against the insured where the sum claimed was 'clearly stated to be in excess of sixty per cent of the applicable excess or is likely to exceed that figure in the experience of the Corporate Risk Department of the Assured'. The notification clause contained the following provision:

> 'Immediate' in this context shall be deemed to mean as soon as Standard Life Assurance Company Corporate Risk Department become aware of any situation.[18]

11.07 In the same way, where some assessment of a claim is or may be needed before notice of it is given, a requirement of 'immediate' notice should be construed as allowing time for such an assessment. So, in *Friends Provident Life and Pensions Ltd v Sirius International Insurance Corporation*[19] it was a condition of the excess policy insuring financial advisers that:

> Any claim(s) made against the assured ... shall, if it appears likely that such claim(s) ... may exceed the indemnity available under the policy/ies of the primary and under-lying excess insurers, be notified immediately by the assured in writing to the underwriters hereon.

The insured might need some time to form a view as to whether a claim was likely to exceed the indemnity under the lower layer or layers of cover. That may have been provided for by the words 'if it appears'.[20]

As soon as practicable

11.08 Other policies require the insured to give notice of the making of a claim 'as soon as practicable' or 'as soon as reasonably practicable'. Terms to that effect are found in the ICAEW Minimum Approved Policy Wording and in the RICS Policy Wording.[21] Such a requirement is less stringent than one requiring immediate notification, although it still imports a degree of urgency.[22]

---

[17] [2008] EWHC 222 (Comm); [2008] Lloyd's Rep IR 552.

[18] See also the reporting and notice provision considered by Christopher Clarke J in *Travelers Casualty and Surety Co of Canada v Sun Life Assurance Co of Canada (UK) Ltd* [2006] EWHC 2716 (Comm); [2007] Lloyd's Rep IR 619, which was only triggered once a claim was 'known or discovered by the Assistant Vice President, Insurance and Risk Management'.

[19] [2005] EWCA Civ 601; [2005] 2 Lloyd's Rep 517.

[20] See also the wording in *Standard Life Assurance Ltd v Oak Dedicated Ltd* [2008] EWHC 552 (Comm), [2008] Lloyd's Rep IR 522, set out in the preceding paragraph.

[21] The ICAEW Minimum Approved Policy Wording also provides that notice must be given not later than 7 days after the end of the period of insurance. RICS Policy Wording provides that notice must be given within 10 working days after the expiry of the policy period.

[22] The RIBA Architects Premier Policy Wording requires notice to be given 'as soon as possible'. In *Kier Construction Ltd v Royal Insurance (UK) Ltd* (1992) 30 Con LR 45, at 85 HH Judge Bowsher QC, having referred to *Verelst's Administratrix v Motor Union Insurance Co* [1925] 2 KB 137 and *King's Old Country Ltd v Liquid Carbonic Canadian Corp Ltd* [1942] 2 WWR 603 as to what as

The question of whether the insured had given notice 'as soon as practicable' arose **11.09**
in *Travelers Casualty and Surety Co of Canada v Sun Life Assurance Co of Canada
(UK) Ltd.*[23] The insured was a major financial institution which provided financial
and investment advice. Notice of a claim or potential loss had to be given 'as soon as
practicable' once it was known by the insured's 'Assistant Vice President, Insurance
and Risk Management'. The primary cover was for US$50 million in excess of
US$25 million and notice only had to be given of claims or potential losses which
exceeded US$12.5 million. The relevant individual knew that the insured faced a
potential loss of more than that sum by October 2001, but no notice was given. On
17 March 2002 the individual was informed that on 'the worst case scenario' the
insured could be obliged to pay US$125 million by way of redress. The individual
sent an e-mail to the insured's brokers on 22 March 2002 for onward transmission
to insurers. It expressly was not a notification of a claim. The brokers did not forward this e-mail until 12 April 2002. It was only on 16 April 2002 that the brokers
gave a valid notice of the claim to insurers.

Christopher Clarke J held that the relevant individual had the knowledge neces- **11.10**
sary to trigger the obligation to give notice in October 2001. It was obviously
practicable to have given notice before 16 April 2002, so that the insured was in
breach of the obligation.[24] However, if the individual had only acquired sufficient
knowledge when informed of the possible worst case on 17 March 2002, then he
would not have regarded the delay between then and 16 April 2002 as such as to
constitute a breach of the requirement to give notice as soon as practicable.[25]

The decision of Christopher Clarke J in *Travelers Casualty and Surety Co of Canada* **11.11**
v Sun Life Assurance Co of Canada (UK) Ltd[26] is consistent with that of Gloster J
in *HLB Kidsons v Lloyd's Underwriters.*[27] In that case, the insured firm of accountants was required to give notice 'as soon as practicable'. A number of presentations
were made to insurers over a period of time concerning potential claims against the
insured for alleged negligence in relation to tax avoidance products. The obligation to give notice was held to have been triggered by advice received from leading
counsel on 26 March 2002. The insured sent a letter to its brokers on 28 March
2002 and this, together with some other documentation, was presented to the leading underwriter at Lloyd's on 19 April 2002 and to the companies' market between
18 April and 21 May 2002. Gloster J held that these notifications complied with

---

required by 'as soon as possible' held that: It is difficult to conceive of circumstances where a delay
of four weeks between the acquisition of knowledge of an occurrence and the giving of notice in a
commercial situation should be regarded as being within time even under the less stringent words
"as soon as possible"'.

[23] [2006] EWHC 2716 (Comm); [2007] Lloyd's Rep IR 619.
[24] Ibid at [360].
[25] Ibid.
[26] [2006] EWHC 2716 (Comm); [2007] Lloyd's Rep IR 619.
[27] [2007] EWHC 1951 (Comm); [2008] Lloyd's Rep IR 237.

the requirement that notice be given as soon as practicable. However, the following Lloyd's market was only notified in July 2002 and this was too late.[28] In making these findings, Gloster J took account of expert evidence that 'some latitude would be allowed'.[29]

Adjudications

11.12 Part II of the Housing Grants, Construction and Regeneration Act 1996 introduced a form of dispute resolution for the construction industry with effect from 1 May 1998. A party to a 'construction contract' is entitled to refer any dispute arising under that contract to adjudication.[30] The decision of an adjudicator will be final and binding if the contract so provides, but otherwise is binding (and enforceable) only until the dispute is finally determined by a judgment, arbitrator's award, or settlement.[31] Adjudication is intended to provide quick resolution of disputes and, to that end, a tight timetable is prescribed. The adjudicator is to be appointed and the dispute must be referred to him within seven days of the notice of adjudication and the adjudicator must reach his decision within twenty-eight days (subject to agreement by the parties or, up to a maximum of fourteen days, by order of the adjudicator).[32] An adjudication can be initiated at any stage of a construction project and without prior notice, as long as a dispute has arisen.

11.13 'Construction contract' is defined in s 104 of the Housing Grants, Construction and Regeneration Act 1996. The definition is wide and encompasses agreements to undertake architectural, design, or surveying work or to provide advice on building, engineering, interior or exterior decoration, or on the laying-out of landscape.[33] So, the contractual engagements of architects, engineers, quantity surveyors, project managers, and other professionals engaged in the construction industry are likely to fall within the definition. To fall within the adjudication scheme, a contract must also be in writing.[34]

11.14 Given the enforceability of awards in adjudications, the insured will want to be indemnified in respect of them. Given the extremely tight timetable, insurers will need extremely prompt notice of an adjudication if they are not to be prejudiced. It is therefore not surprising to find that professional indemnity policies of construction professionals contain stringent requirements as to notification of adjudications.

---

[28] Ibid at [212], [217], and [221]. The finding that the last notification was not made in time was the only finding as to whether notice had been given as soon as practicable, which was the subject of appeal. The appeal was on this point was dismissed: [2008] EWCA Civ 1206; [2009] 1 Lloyd's Rep 8.

[29] Ibid at [217]. For the expert evidence, see para 11.03.

[30] Section 108(1) of the Housing Grants, Construction and Regeneration Act 1996.

[31] Ibid, s 108(3).

[32] Ibid, s 108(2).

[33] Ibid, s 104(2).

[34] Ibid, s 107.

For example, the RICS Policy Wording requires the insured to give notice of the **11.15** receipt of any notice of intention to adjudicate within two working days of its receipt by the insured. The RIBA Architects Premier Policy Wording requires notice to be given immediately to a specified person, therefore avoiding the need to notify each insurer. Given the context, 'immediately' is likely to be given a more strict interpretation than might be the case for notice of other claims. Another policy wording in current use for construction professionals contains a specific regime for adjudications under which the insured is required to give notice to named solicitors within two working days of the receipt of any notice of intention to adjudicate. It also requires the insured not to agree to any more onerous timetable than that provided in s 108(2) of the Housing Grants, Construction and Regeneration Act 1996. Another policy in current use requires direct notification to insurers by fax or e-mail within two working days: this avoids the delay which would arise from involving brokers. Compliance with these provisions is expressly stated to be a condition precedent to the insured's right to an indemnity.

Form and scope of notice

If the contract requires notice to be given in writing, then, unless insurers waive **11.16** that requirement, it must be complied with. Otherwise, oral notice is sufficient. Unless otherwise provided, each insurer must be notified, and, where a particular person is nominated to receive notice, that person must be notified.[35]

While there is sometimes scope for disagreement as to the scope and effectiveness **11.17** of a notification of circumstances,[36] giving notice of a claim which has actually been made against the insured should be relatively straightforward. The insured's obligation is to give notice to insurers of the claim made against him by a third party claimant. The scope of that claim does not depend upon the insured's interpretation or understanding, but upon how it was formulated by the third party claimant.[37]

Status of notice

When giving notice to insurers of a claim (or of circumstances with the potential **11.18** to give rise to a claim) the insured may give an explanation of the relevant facts, which includes some assessment of his own potential liability and of the quantum of any possible award against him. Disclosure of such matters to the third party claimant might not assist in the defence or settlement of the claim. The insured's purpose in informing his insurers is to protect his right to an indemnity under his professional indemnity insurance. That would not be sufficient for a claim of privilege so as to avoid producing the notification on disclosure in any subsequent

---

[35] *Brook v Trafalgar Insurance Company Ltd* (1946) 79 Ll L R 365.
[36] See paras 2.91–2.120.
[37] See paras 2.39–2.46.

proceedings. However, in this context the intention of insurers in requiring the giving of notice is of greater significance. Their purpose will usually be to obtain information about which they can seek legal advice as to whether the third party claim should be defended or settled. If that is their dominant purpose[38] then the documents by which the insured gave notice will be subject to privilege.[39] This is so even though no solicitors have been appointed at the time that the notice is given.[40]

Consequences of non-compliance

11.19 Where the giving of notice of a claim is part of the trigger of cover, failure to comply with the obligation as to time will be fatal to the insured's right to an indemnity. The same is true if the notice requirement is a condition precedent.[41] Where notice is not given in time so that the insured is in breach of a condition precedent insurers can rely upon that breach to defeat a claim for indemnity under the policy even though they have suffered no prejudice.[42] Insurers' potential remedies for breach of a term which is not a condition precedent are considered below.

B. Co-operation with Insurers

Usual terms

11.20 It is usual to find terms in contracts of professional indemnity insurance requiring the insured to provide information about a third party claim to insurers and to co-operate in the defence of such claims. The co-operation of the insured is of great importance to insurers, who will usually need to be informed of the relevant facts and circumstances and to be provided with relevant documents (both in order to assess the merits of the third party claim and to comply with the obligation to provide disclosure). If a claim is to be contested, insurers will usually need the relevant insured to provide witness statements and to attend to give evidence if required.

11.21 Examples of clauses requiring the insured to provide information as part of the obligation to notify insurers are set out in para 2.104. Some professional indemnity policies contain further provisions requiring the insured to continue to provide information and assistance to insurers in the conduct of the defence of third party claims, if, as is usually the case, the conduct of the defence of such claims has been taken over by insurers in the name of the insured.

---

[38] *Waugh v British Railways Board* [1980] AC 521.
[39] *Guinness Peat Properties Ltd v The Fitzroy Robinson Partnership (a firm)* [1987] 1 WLR 1027.
[40] Ibid. See also *In re Highgrade Traders Ltd* [1984] BCLC 151.
[41] As to which, see paras 7.100–7.106.
[42] *Pioneer Concrete (UK) Ltd v National Employers Mutual General Insurance Association Ltd* [1985] 2 All ER 395.

For example, the RICS Policy Wording requires the insured to give insurers all **11.22** information and assistance as insurers reasonably require and the insured is able to provide.[43] The insured is also required to co-operate with insurers and their appointed representatives in the conduct of the defence of third party claims or of any claims brought by insurers by way of subrogation against third parties. The respects in which the insured is to co-operate are set out in some detail.[44]

More typically, the ICAEW Minimum Approved Policy Wording simply provides **11.23** that insurers are entitled to the insured's 'full co-operation' if they choose to take over the defence of a claim or to investigate a notified circumstance. The insured is also obliged to provide all information and documentation which is reasonably requested by insurers. Where no time is specified for the provision of assistance or advice, it will usually be implicit that they be provided within a reasonable time.[45]

The insured was in breach of such a term in *K/S Merc-Scandia XXXII v Certain* **11.24** *Lloyd's Underwriters (The 'Mercandian Continent')*.[46] The insured ship repairers had liability insurance. A third party made a claim against them and an issue arose as to jurisdiction. The insured produced a forged letter to support an argument that the appropriate jurisdiction was Trinidad, rather than England and Wales. The forgery was soon discovered and had no effect on the outcome of the third party claim. It was, nevertheless, a breach of the obligation to keep insurers 'fully advised'.[47]

Adjudications

The adjudication regime introduced by the Housing Grants, Construction and **11.25** Regeneration Act 1996 has been explained above.[48] Unless the parties to a construction contract have agreed otherwise, the award of an adjudicator is binding only unless and until it is set aside by a judgment, arbitrator's award, or settlement.

---

[43] In *Total Graphics Ltd v AGF Insurance Ltd* [1997] 1 Lloyd's Rep 599, the insured was subject to a continuing obligation to give insurers 'such information and assistance as the Insurers may reasonably require'. A similar term was found in the policy considered in *MDIS Ltd v Swinbank* [1999] Lloyd's Rep IR 516.

[44] Under the RIBA Architects Premier Policy Wording the insured has no general duty to co-operate or provide information beyond the obligation to give notice of claims and circumstances, including full details. There is a specific duty to give all such assistance as insurers reasonably require in relation to proceedings to challenge, appeal or set aside the decision of an adjudicator under the Housing Grants, Construction and Regeneration Act 1996 (as to which see paras 11.12–11.15 and 11.25–11.27).

[45] As was held in *Shinedean Ltd v Alldown Demolition (London) Ltd (in liquidation)* [2006] EWCA Civ 939; [2006] 1 WLR 2696.

[46] [2001] EWCA Civ 1275; [2001] 2 Lloyd's Rep 563.

[47] See also *Ted Baker Plc v AXA Insurance UK Plc (No 2)* [2014] EWHC 3548 (Comm); [2015] Lloyd's Rep IR 325, a case concerning business interruption insurance. Eder J held that the insured had failed to give particulars of its claim under the policy for one year (but not for others) and was in breach of its obligation to 'deliver to [insurers] such books of account and other business books vouchers invoices balance sheets and other documents proofs information explanation and other evidence as may be reasonably required by [insurers] for the purpose of investigating or verifying the claim'.

[48] See paras 11.12–11.15.

11.26 There are two ways in which insurers can and do seek additional protection in relation to awards by adjudicators. The first is to exclude cover in respect of adjudications if the insured has agreed that the adjudicator's decision will be final, unless insurers agree otherwise. A provision to that effect is found in the RIBA Architects Premier Policy Wording. The RICS Policy Wording adopts a slightly different approach: the insured agrees not to accept the decision of any adjudicator as finally determining a dispute without the prior written consent of insurers (who are not entitled to delay or withhold their consent unreasonably).

11.27 The second way in which insurers can and do protect their interests is to include a provision requiring the insured to allow insurers to bring proceedings in the insured's name to challenge, appeal, or vary any award or other decision of an adjudicator and to provide reasonable assistance in relation to any such proceedings. Such a provision is found in the RICS Policy Wording and in the RIBA Architects Premier Policy Wording. It is necessary because, if an adjudicator has found against an insured and in favour of a third party claimant, there will or may be no extant claim against the insured. Insurers' rights of subrogation will or may not extend to the bringing of a legal action or arbitration to seek to recover sums paid in compliance with an adjudicator's award.

C. Prohibition of Admissions of Liability and Settlements

11.28 It is usual to find a term in a contract of professional indemnity insurance prohibiting the insured from making any admission of liability to a third party claimant. For example, the RICS Minimum Policy Wording stipulates that:

> In the event of a CLAIM or the discovery of CIRCUMSTANCE(S), the INSURED shall not admit liability, incur any costs or make any offers of settlement in connection therewith or otherwise prejudice the conduct or the defence or settlement of such CLAIM or CIRCUMSTANCE(S) without INSURERS' prior written consent (such consent not to be unreasonably withheld or unreasonably delayed), regardless of the provisions of any complaints handling procedure or whether the amount in dispute is less than the EXCESS.

11.29 The ICAEW Minimum Policy Wording provides that the insured shall:

> As a condition precedent to their right to be indemnified hereunder not admit liability for, or settle any claim without the written consent of the insurers ...

11.30 The RIBA Architects Premier Policy Wording prohibits the insured from admitting

> Liability and no admission, arrangement, offer, promise or payment shall be made by the Insured without Insurers' written consent.

11.31 The courts will give effect to such clauses, even if an admission of liability was justified on the facts. For example, in *Total Graphics v AGF Insurance Ltd*[49] the relevant

---

49 [1997] 1 Lloyd's Rep 599.

term, which was expressed to be a condition precedent to the insured's right to recovery, provided:

> The insured shall not admit liability for any claim or incur any costs or expenses in connection therewith without the written consent of the insurers, who shall be entitled at any time to take over and conduct in the name of the insured the defence or settlement of any claim …

By the time the third party claimant brought its claim the insured was in liquidation. The liquidator admitted liability. There was little doubt but that the insured had been in breach of duty. The third party claimant then sought to obtain an indemnity in respect of the judgment it had obtained from insurers under the Third Parties (Rights Against Insurers) Act 1930.[50] The claim failed for a number of reasons, one of which was breach of this condition, which was a condition precedent, so that no prejudice needed to be shown. However, had prejudice been needed, it arose from the liquidator's failure to contest the issues of liability and quantum with the result that those issues had been determined without argument.[51]

Guidance as to what is required for there to be a settlement or an admission of **11.32** liability can be found in cases concerning reinsurance. In *Beazley Underwriting Ltd v Al Ahleia Insurance Co*[52] the contract of reinsurance provided that:

> No settlement and/or compromise shall be made and no liability admitted without the prior approval of Reinsurers.

Reinsurers argued that the reinsured had both entered a settlement or compromise and made admissions of liability without their consent. In rejecting their arguments Eder J considered what was required to constitute both a settlement or compromise and an admission of liability.

He accepted reinsurers' argument that a settlement made 'without prejudice to **11.33** liability' would still be a settlement falling within the clause. What the clause prohibited was a legally binding agreement in any form or the actual transfer of some kind of consideration, including the making of an *ex gratia* payment without any admission of liability.[53]

When it came to admissions of liability, Eder J agreed with what Andrew Smith J **11.34** had said in *Gan Insurance Company Ltd v Tai Ping Insurance Company Ltd (Nos 2 and 3)*:[54]

> The word 'admitted' imports the acceptance of the validity of a previous liability.

---

[50] As to which, see paras 13.39–13.58.
[51] [1997] 1 Lloyd's Rep 599, at 608.
[52] [2013] EWHC 667 (Comm); [2013] Lloyd's Rep IR 561.
[53] Ibid at [90].
[54] [2001] Lloyd's Rep IR 667, at [33].

He also held that an admission of liability has to be communicated in clear and unequivocal terms. It does not have to be admission of liability in respect of the whole claim. An offer to pay a sum of money is not, of itself, an admission of liability.[55]

11.35   In contracts of insurance where 'claim' is not defined as a claim against the insured, a clause prohibiting the insured from compromising or settling claims may have wider application. So, in *Horwood v Land of Leather Ltd*,[56] a case concerning product liability insurance, the insured was held to have breached a term requiring it not to 'take any steps to compromise or settle any claim or admit liability without specific instructions in writing from the Insurer' by settling a claim against a third party to which the insurer would have been subrogated upon indemnifying the insured. Teare J held that this was the effect of the clause in question, but would have been prepared, had it been necessary, to imply a term that the insured would act reasonably and in good faith with due regard to insurers' interests and rights of subrogation under the policy.

11.36   Difficulty can arise if the insured is required by his statutory regulator or professional body to act in breach of such terms. The point arose in the context of the review of pensions mis-selling in the 1990s. Under the Financial Services Act 1986 many regulatory powers were vested in the Securities and Investments Board ('SIB'). Firms were regulated as members of self-regulatory organizations ('SROs') or of recognized professional bodies ('RPBs'). SIB gave guidance by way of a statement to SROs and RPBs as to the conduct of a review of the possible mis-selling of pensions by their members. The validity of this statement was challenged by way of judicial review on a number of grounds.[57]

11.37   One ground relied upon was that the effect of SIB's statement was or might be to require firms to admit liability in breach of the terms of their professional indemnity insurance. In drafting the statement, SIB had sought to avoid this problem, but it was possible that it had not entirely succeeded in doing so. While not giving any definitive ruling as to whether the statement as issued had avoided the problem, the Divisional Court held that, in failing to state that firms were not required to take any step which would invalidate their insurance cover without their insurers' consent, the statement was irrational. The Court suggested that SIB should issue a declaration amending its statement to that effect.[58]

11.38   A lawyer who believes he has been negligent may be under a professional obligation to advise his client to seek independent legal advice elsewhere. This may

---

[55]   [2013] EWHC 667 (Comm); [2013] Lloyd's Rep IR 561, at [92]–[93].
[56]   [2010] EWHC 546 (Comm); [2010] Lloyd's Rep IR 453.
[57]   *R v Securities and Investments Board, ex parte Independent Financial Advisers Association* [1995] 2 BCLC 76.
[58]   Ibid at 90.

require the lawyer to tell the client the reason why he should seek independent legal advice.[59] This may be why the SRA Minimum Terms and Conditions of Professional Indemnity Insurance do not contain a term prohibiting the insured from making any admission of liability. It is unlikely that a term would be implied into a professional's contract of engagement requiring him to advise his client of his own breach of duty.[60]

D. Insurers' Contractual Remedies for Breach

Classes of terms

Where compliance with a term of the contract is a condition precedent to the **11.39** insured's right to an indemnity, breach will provide insurers with a defence. So, where it is a condition precedent to insurers' liability that the insured shall provide 'all such proofs and information relating to the claim as may be reasonably required' and the insured fails to do so within a reasonable time, insurers are entitled to repudiate cover, even though they might not have in fact suffered any prejudice.[61]

If the relevant term is not a condition precedent, then it will fall into one of the **11.40** following three classes of terms. The first is terms of which any breach entitles the innocent party to bring the contract to an end and to treat himself as discharged from all future liability under it. The guilty party will still be liable in damages and both parties will retain their accrued rights up to the time the contract was brought to an end. The second is terms of which any breach, no matter how serious, only sounds in damages. The third category is terms which will only entitle the innocent party to bring the contract to an end and to treat himself as discharged from all future liability under it if the breach is sufficiently serious. Breaches of this category of term also sound in damages. Somewhat confusingly in the context of insurance, in the wider law of contract, terms falling within the first class of term are usually described as 'conditions' and terms falling within the second class of term are usually described as 'warranties'. The third class of term is usually described as 'innominate'.[62]

---

[59] Outcome O(1.16) in the SRA Handbook requires solicitors to inform current clients if they discover any act or omission which could give rise to a claim by their current clients against them.

[60] *Chesham Properties Ltd v Bucknall Austin Project Management Services Ltd* (1996) 82 BLR 92, at 115–26.

[61] *Shinedean Ltd v Alldown Demolition (London) Ltd (in liquidation)* [2006] EWCA Civ 939; [2006] 1 WLR 2696.

[62] For a helpful summary of these basic principles, see *K/S Merc-Scandia XXXII v Certain Lloyd's Underwriters (The 'Mercandian Continent')* [2001] EWCA Civ 1275; [2001] 2 Lloyd's Rep 563 at [13] per Longmore LJ. In *Alfred McAlpine plc v BAI (Run-Off) Ltd* [2000] 1 Lloyd's Rep 437, the possibility of a further class of innominate term was raised, namely a term which, if the breach was sufficiently serious, would entitle insurers to deny cover for a particular claim, but not to bring the entire contract to an end. However, this was disapproved in *Friends Provident Life and Pensions Ltd v Sirius International Insurance Corporation* [2005] EWCA Civ 601; [2005] 2 Lloyd's Rep 517.

11.41 Where a breach of contract entitles the insured to bring the contract to an end, the effect is different from avoidance of the contract for non-disclosure or misrepresentation. Such avoidance undoes the contract from the beginning, whereas bringing the contract to an end merely discharges both parties from future performance of their obligations under it, leaving their accrued rights in place and the party in breach liable in damages.[63] In the context of liability insurance, including professional indemnity insurance, the insured will not have an accrued right to an indemnity until his liability has been ascertained.[64]

11.42 If compliance by the insured with a term is not expressed to be a condition precedent to the insured's right to an indemnity, then it is unlikely to fall within the first class of terms so as to entitle insurers to bring the contract to an end for any breach, no matter how trivial. This is because, if the parties did not intend compliance with a term to be a condition precedent to entitlement to an indemnity, they are unlikely to have intended that insurers should have the greater right to bring the entire contract to an end in the event of the slightest breach of that term.

Damages

11.43 Where a breach of contract by the insured does not entitle insurers to bring the contract to an end, insurers' remedy will be in damages. For example, late notification by the insured may cause insurers loss because of their failure to notify their reinsurers as a result of the insured's delay. In other cases, it may be harder to establish what, if any, loss has flowed from, for example, a failure to provide information promptly. In *Friends Provident Life and Pensions Ltd v Sirius International Insurance Corporation*[65] Mance LJ considered the possible heads of damage an insurer might recover for late notification. He observed:[66]

> If they can prove serious consequences, then these will often be capable of quantification, in one way or another, even if only as losses of a chance or opportunity, and can be set off against the claim.
>
> Of course, there are cases, like the *Bankers Insurance*[67] case decided by Buckley J, where it may be said that the consequences are too intangible to measure in precise

---

[63] *Manifest Shipping Co Ltd v Uni-Polaris Shipping Co Ltd, The Star Sea* [2001] UKHL 1; [2003] 1 AC 469; *K/S Merc-Scandia XXXII v Certain Lloyd's Underwriters (The 'Mercandian Continent')* [2001] EWCA Civ 1275; [2001] 2 Lloyd's Rep 563.

[64] *K/S Merc-Scandia XXXII v Certain Lloyd's Underwriters (The 'Mercandian Continent')* [2001] EWCA Civ 1275; [2001] 2 Lloyd's Rep 563, at [13] per Longmore LJ. For ascertainment, see paras 9.106–9.132.

[65] [2005] EWCA Civ 601; [2005] 2 Lloyd's Rep 517.

[66] Ibid at [32]–[33].

[67] *Bankers Insurance Co Ltd v South* [2003] EWHC 380 (QB); [2004] Lloyd's Rep IR 1, a case concerning travel insurance. Insurers lost about 3½ years as a result of late notice of an accident. Buckley J was prepared to infer that some significant further fading of memories would have occurred and that some of the witnesses would probably be more difficult to trace and some would probably be unwilling to assist given the passage of time.

financial terms, although, where an insured's breach has caused this difficulty, courts should incline to a quantification favourable to insurers.

The latter approach was adopted by Edwards-Stuart J in *Milton Keynes Borough* **11.44**
Council v Nulty.[68] The case concerned late notification by an insured of a fire. Insurers lost the chance of an early investigation into the causes of the fire, which were not clear. While he did not accept some of the insurers' evidence as to what they would have done had the insured given them notice as required by the policy, Edwards-Stuart J accepted that insurers had suffered material prejudice. Openly acknowledging that the assessment of damages was a matter of impression rather than logic in the circumstances, he held that the insurers had lost a fifteen per cent chance of showing that the insured was not liable for the fire and that they could set off that sum against their liability under the policy.

Some professional indemnity policies give insurers the right to determine what **11.45**
loss has flowed from such breaches. So, the ICAEW Minimum Approved Policy Wording provides that where the insured's breach of or non-compliance with any condition has caused prejudice to insurers in the handling or settlement of any claim against the insured in the amount of loss sustained or in obtaining reimbursement from any dishonest or fraudulent person,[69] the amount of indemnity to be provided (including the costs of third party claimants) shall be reduced to 'such sum as in the Insurers' reasonable opinion would have been payable by them in the absence of such prejudice'. The RICS Policy Wording contains a similar term, as does the RIBA Architects Premier Policy Wording.

Such terms confer upon insurers the power to determine the consequences of a **11.46**
breach of contract by the insured. If their effect were to oust the jurisdiction of the court entirely, they would be contrary to public policy and void.[70] However, the better view is that a decision by insurers under such clauses is subject to challenge in the courts on the grounds that it was not reasonable or that insurers applied an incorrect view of the law.[71] It should also be noted that insurers' right to determine the amount of any reduction in the indemnity only arises if they have in fact been caused prejudice and that too is a matter which the insured could challenge. However, notwithstanding the potential to overturn a decision by insurers, under these and similar provisions insurers will be able to reach valid decisions which might not have been made by a court.

---

[68] [2011] EWHC 2847 (TCC); [2012] Lloyd's Rep IR 453.
[69] As to which, see paras 8.58–8.60.
[70] *Czarnikow v Roth Schmit & Co* [1922] 2 KB 478; *Lee v The Showmen's Guild of Great Britain* [1952] 2 QB 329; *West of England Shipowners Mutual Insurance Association (Luxembourg) v Cristal Ltd (The 'Glacier Bay')* [1996] 1 Lloyd's Rep 370; *Brown v GIO Insurance Ltd* [1998] Lloyd's Rep IR 201.
[71] For a full discussion of the ways in which decisions by insurers can be challenged see paras 5.89–5.91.

The position when insurers have denied cover

11.47 If insurers have received notice of a claim and denied cover to the insured, the insured will not usually be able to comply with obligations which require him to obtain insurers' consent before doing something (eg settling the claim). If it transpires that insurers were not entitled to deny cover, they may not be able to rely upon the insured's failure to obtain their consent during the period when they were wrongly denying cover. In *William McIlroy (Swindon) Ltd v Quinn Insurance Ltd* Edwards-Stuart J said:[72]

> Under general principles of English contract law I consider that where an insurer has notified the insured that it will not be granting indemnity in respect of a claim notified by the insured, the insurer cannot insist on compliance by the insured with his obligations under the policy in relation to that claim such as, for example, the obligation not to negotiate a settlement or admit liability. The insurer, having refused to perform his primary obligations under the contract in respect of that claim cannot at the same time insist on the insured complying with his primary obligations in respect of that claim. The conduct of the insurer means that the insured is effectively uninsured and must therefore take such steps as he reasonably can to protect his own interests. Such steps may well include attempting to negotiate a reasonable settlement of the claim against him.

11.48 However, general principles of English contract law do not entitle one party to a contract not to perform his obligations merely because the other party is in breach of that contract. Where insurers are in repudiatory breach of contract, it will be open to the insured to accept that breach as bringing the contract to an end and to sue for damages. If the insured does so, he will be relieved from performance of future obligations under the contract of insurance. But, if he does not, then in the absence of some waiver or disabling act on the part of insurers, he will continue to be bound by the terms of the contract. So, in *Diab v Regent Insurance Co Ltd*,[73] a case concerning property insurance, insurers made it clear to the insured that if he made a claim under the policy for losses caused by a fire it would be rejected. This was, potentially, a repudiatory breach of contract, but the insured had not accepted it. Rather he had pursued a claim under the policy. It followed that he was not relieved from the obligation to comply with a condition precedent which required him to provide full particulars of his losses within fifteen days of the fire.[74]

11.49 Whether compliance with an obligation by the insured is possible or not will depend upon the position adopted by insurers. An insurer 'who denies liability and thereafter refuses to have anything to do with the claim on that account precludes

---

[72] [2010] EWHC 2448 (TCC); [2011] Lloyd's Rep IR 407, at [70] (the decision was overturned on appeal on other grounds: see [2011] EWCA Civ 825; [2011] Lloyd's Rep IR 697).

[73] [2006] UKPC 29; [2007] 1 WLR 797.

[74] See also *Super Chem Products Ltd v American Life & General Insurance Co Ltd* [2004] UKPC 2; [2004] 2 All ER 358.

co-operation by his very refusal'.[75] But if insurers deny liability but offer to co-operate in handling the underlying claim without prejudice to their denial, the insured will remain obliged to co-operate unless he has accepted insurers' repudiatory breach.[76]

An insured who settles a claim after insurers have denied cover without obtaining **11.50** their consent as required by the contract of insurance runs the risk that he will not be able to prove that he was in fact liable so as to be entitled to an indemnity.[77] If the insured has accepted a repudiatory breach he may be able to recover any sum paid in settlement of the third party's claim on the ground that he has acted reasonably in mitigation of his loss. But if he has not accepted the breach, he will need to show that he was liable in respect of the claim which he has settled even if insurers have lost the right to allege that he was in breach of contract in settling without having obtained their consent.

It follows that an insured, when faced with a denial of cover by insurers, needs **11.51** to decide whether to accept that denial as a repudiatory breach of the contract of insurance. If he does not do so, he needs to continue to offer to provide information and co-operation and to seek insurers' consent as required by the contract. If insurers reject the insured's overtures, they cannot complain. But if they accept them, then the insured will remain bound by the relevant terms of the contract of insurance.

Insurers who have denied cover are also usually well advised to offer to continue **11.52** to investigate and co-operate without prejudice to their denial. This may lead to an acceptable resolution of the underlying claim and so of the insured's claim under the policy. It may also provide insurers with further defences if the insured neither accepts the denial of cover as a repudiatory breach nor complies with his continuing obligations in relation to the provision of information, co-operation, admissions of liability, and settlements. But if insurers take the stance that they will have nothing more to do with the claim, they will not be entitled to rely upon the insured's failure to provide information, co-operate, or seek their consent.

E. Solicitors

The SRA Minimum Terms and Conditions of Professional Indemnity Insurance **11.53** do not contain terms of the kind which have been considered earlier. They leave it to the parties to a particular contract to agree whatever general conditions they wish, as long as the contract provides that the special conditions which the Minimum

---

[75] *Lexington Insurance Company v Multinacional de Seguros SA* [2008] EWHC 1170 (Comm); [2009] Lloyd's Rep IR 1, at [71] per Christopher Clarke J.

[76] Ibid at [69]–[74].

[77] Ibid at [73]. For the need for the insured to be liable see paras 9.122–9.132.

Terms and Conditions require prevail. It is therefore open to insurers to seek to include terms as to the giving of notice of claims, as to co-operation in the conduct of defence of claims, and the provision of information and assistance, and so on.

11.54 However, the special conditions in the SRA Minimum Terms and Conditions of Professional Indemnity Insurance restrict insurers' remedies for any breach of such general conditions as may be agreed. They provide that insurers are to have no right to avoid or repudiate the insurance. Nor are insurers to be entitled to reduce or deny liability on any grounds whatsoever, including any breach of any term or condition of the insurance, save insofar as permitted by the exclusions set out in the SRA Minimum Terms and Conditions of Professional Indemnity Insurance. Finally, the policy must provide that any amount payable by insurers by way of indemnity will be paid to the third party claimant or at the direction of the third party claimant, without any set-off against that indemnity in respect of any payment due to insurers from the insured, including unpaid premium or other reimbursement of insurers.

11.55 It follows that insurers cannot make compliance with any term as to notification of claims or circumstances a condition precedent to the insured's right to an indemnity. Nor can insurers reduce the amount of indemnity in the way envisaged in the ICAEW Minimum Approved Policy Wording, the RICS Policy Wording, and the RIBA Architects Premier Policy Wording.[78] They could, however, maintain a claim for damages, but not set off such damages against their own liability to indemnify the insured.

F. The Continuing Duty of Good Faith and Fraudulent Claims

The continuing duty of good faith

11.56 Like all contracts of insurance, contracts of professional indemnity insurance are contracts of the utmost good faith. Both the insured and insurers are required to exercise the utmost good faith to each other when making and performing the contract of insurance. The pre-contractual duty of disclosure, which, until the relevant provisions of the Insurance Act 2015 come into force, is an incident of the duty of good faith, is considered in **Chapter 5**. That duty ceases once the contract of insurance is made, although it will arise in relation to any variation or renewal of the contract.[79]

11.57 The duty of good faith continues after the contract is made.[80] However, it no longer arises by operation of law, independently of the intention of the parties, but from

---

[78] As to which, see para 11.45.

[79] See paras 5.65–5.68.

[80] *Manifest Shipping Co Ltd v Uni-Polaris Shipping Co Ltd, The Star Sea* [2001] UKHL 1; [2003] 1 AC 469, in particular per Lord Hobhouse at [48].

an implied (or, where appropriate, express) term of the contract.[81] The duty is not the same as the pre-contractual duty. In relation to the insured, it arises where he is expressly obliged to provide information to insurers[82] or, perhaps, when he makes a claim.[83] The duty ends when the parties become engaged in litigation.[84]

Fraudulent claims

In relation to the making of a claim, it is well established that, if the insured makes a fraudulent claim, not only are insurers not obliged to satisfy that claim, but they are also relieved of any liability to satisfy any honest claim (for example, in a lesser amount) which the insured may have.[85] In the context of professional indemnity insurance, a claim is made when the insured claims an indemnity in respect of his established liability to a third party claimant, not when he gives notice that a claim has been made against him.[86]   **11.58**

The use of fraudulent devices to support a claim under an insurance policy will provide insurers with a complete defence to the claim.[87] Fraudulent devices are used to bolster potentially weak claims or to put insurers off lines of inquiry or investigation which might prevent or delay payment of a claim.[88] Again, there is a requirement of materiality. The fraudulent device must be directly related to the claim, it must have been intended by the insured to promote his prospects of success and it must have tended to yield a not insignificant improvement or significant or even substantial improvement in the insured's prospects to any final determination of the parties' rights.[89]   **11.59**

It is in relation to the provision of information that the post-contractual duty of good faith is more likely to be of relevance in the context of professional indemnity   **11.60**

---

[81] Ibid at [49]–[52]. In Australia, such a term is implied by s 13 of the Insurance Contracts Act 1984 (Cth).

[82] Where insurers seek information without any express obligation on the insured to provide it, the insured's only duty is to be honest.

[83] *K/S Merc-Scandia XXXII v Certain Lloyd's Underwriters (The 'Mercandian Continent')* [2001] EWCA Civ 1275; [2001] 2 Lloyd's Rep 563.

[84] *Manifest Shipping Co Ltd v Uni-Polaris Shipping Co Ltd, The Star Sea* [2001] UKHL 1; [2003] 1 AC 469.

[85] Ibid, in particular per Lord Hobhouse at [62]–[68].

[86] *K/S Merc-Scandia XXXII v Certain Lloyd's Underwriters (The 'Mercandian Continent')* [2001] EWCA Civ 1275; [2001] 2 Lloyd's Rep 563 at [22(1)] per Longmore LJ in the context of a contract of insurance of shiprepairers' liability.

[87] *Versloot Dredging BV v HDI-Gerling Industrie Verisicherung AG (The 'DC Merwstone')* [2014] EWCA Civ 1349; [2015] QB 608. See also *Agapitos v Agnew (No 1) (The 'Aegeon')* [2002] EWCA Civ 247; [2003] QB 556.

[88] Ibid at [112] per Christopher Clarke LJ, with whom the other members of the Court of Appeal agreed.

[89] Ibid at [165] per Christopher Clarke LJ, approving the test of materiality propounded by Mance LJ in *Agapitos v Agnew (No 1) (The 'Aegeon')* [2002] EWCA Civ 247; [2003] QB 556, save that Christopher Clarke LJ indicated a preference for a positive formulation of the third element ('significant or even substantial improvement') rather than the negative wording suggested by Mance LJ ('not insignificant').

insurance. The duty of good faith requires the insured to provide material information. Breach of an express contractual requirement to provide information will sound in damages, if any are suffered. The potential relevance of the continuing duty of good faith is that it might entitle insurers to avoid the insurance contract entirely. However, the severity of the remedy limits the circumstances in which it can be successfully raised.

11.61 At the post-contract stage, insurers will have the usual remedies for breach of contract, including, where appropriate, the right to bring the contract to an end. The remedy of avoidance *ab initio* is 'more extreme' and so should only be available where there is 'at least the same quality of conduct as would justify the insurer in accepting the insured's conduct as a repudiation of the contract'.[90] This brings the consequences of a breach of the post-contractual duty of good faith into line with the position of a pre-contractual breach, where the information which is not disclosed must both be objectively material to the risk to be underwritten and the non-disclosure must in fact have induced insurers to accept the risk on the terms which they did.[91] It follows that:[92]

> It is ... only appropriate to invoke the remedy of avoidance in a post-contractual context in situations analogous to situations where the insurer has a right to terminate for breach. For this purpose (A) the fraud must be material in the sense that the fraud would have an effect on underwriters' ultimate liability ... and (B) the gravity of the fraud or its consequences must be such as would enable the underwriters, if they wished to do so, to terminate for breach of contract. Often these considerations will amount to the same thing; a materially fraudulent breach of good faith, once the contract has been made, will usually entitle the insurers to terminate the contract. Conversely, fraudulent conduct entitling insurers to bring the contract to an end could only be material fraud. It is in this way that the law of post-contract good faith can be aligned with the insurers' contractual remedies. The right to avoid the contract with retrospective effect is, therefore, only exercisable in circumstances where the innocent party would, in any event, be entitled to terminate the contract for breach.

11.62 So, on the current law, insurers' rights in the event of a fraudulent claim or the use of fraudulent devices depend upon the materiality of the fraud. Thus, in *K/S Merc-Scandia XXXII v Certain Lloyd's Underwriters (The 'Mercandian Continent')*[93] the insured was guilty of fraud in relation to the provision of information to insurers in that a forged letter was produced in support of an argument as to jurisdiction. However, that fraud was not material to insurers' liability under the policy of insurance. The forgery had quickly been detected and the question of whether the

---

[90] *K/ S Merc- Scandia XXXII v Certain Lloyd's Underwriters (The 'Mercandian Continent')* [2001] EWCA Civ 1275; [2001] 2 Lloyd's Rep 563, at [26] per Longmore LJ.

[91] See paras 5.23–5.34.

[92] *K/S Merc-Scandia XXXII v Certain Lloyd's Underwriters (The 'Mercandian Continent')* [2001] EWCA Civ 1275; [2001] 2 Lloyd's Rep 563, at [35] per Longmore LJ.

[93] Ibid.

claim should be tried in Trinidad or in England and Wales did not affect insurers' ultimate liability. It followed that the insurers were not entitled to avoid the policy.

The Insurance Act 2015

When it comes into force,[94] section 12 of the Insurance Act 2015 will change and **11.63** clarify the law in relation to insurers' remedies in the event of fraudulent claims. It provides:

(1) If the insured makes a fraudulent claim under a contract of insurance—
    (a) the insurer is not liable to pay the claim,
    (b) the insurer may recover from the insured any sums paid by the insurer to the insured in respect of the claim, and
    (c) in addition, the insurer may by notice to the insured treat the contract as having been terminated with effect from the time of the fraudulent act.
(2) If the insurer does treat the contract as having been terminated—
    (a) it may refuse all liability to the insured under the contract in respect of a relevant event occurring after the time of the fraudulent act, and
    (b) it need not return any of the premiums paid under the contract.
(3) Treating a contract as having been terminated under this section does not affect the rights and obligations of the parties to the contract with respect to a relevant event occurring before the time of the fraudulent act.
(4) In subsections (2)(a) and (3), *'relevant event'* refers to whatever gives rise to the insurer's liability under the contract (and includes, for example, the occurrence of a loss, the making of a claim, or the notification of a potential claim, depending on how the contract is written).

Insurers will therefore no longer be able to avoid the contract *ab initio* for a post- **11.64** contractual breach of the duty of good faith where the insured makes a fraudulent claim or deploys a fraudulent device in pursuit of a claim.

---

[94] At the time of writing s 12 is due to come into force on 12 August 2016.

12

THE DEFENCE OF CLAIMS BY
THIRD PARTIES

A. Introduction

In the event of a claim, the insured should notify insurers, usually through his **12.01** broker. After notification, the insured and insurers will owe each other a number of duties in the course of the investigation and defence of the claim. Insurers will almost invariably have the right to take conduct of and defend the claim and they will usually avail themselves of that right. If insurers instruct lawyers to act in the conduct, settlement or defence of the claim, those lawyers will owe both the insured and insurers duties in acting on a joint retainer, a fact that may give rise to a number of conflicts of interest. Conflicts arise in two main areas: first, in relation to coverage issues, and second, in relation to the way in which the defence of the claim is to be handled. The legal principles applying to those conflict situations and the contractual mechanisms by which they might be resolved are considered below.

B. The Role of the Broker

12.02   An insurance broker is, for most purposes in relation to the placing of the insurance,[1] the agent of the insured.[2] On occasion, the broker may act for insurer and insured at the same time. In the event that a claim is made in relation to the risk placed by the placing broker, his duty is to act for the insured as the conduit for the giving of notice and provision of any other information in accordance with the insured's contractual obligations. Where there is an issue as to coverage the insurance broker may seek to persuade insurers to accept that they are on risk. He may also become involved in the management of the claim by the third party against his client, the insured.

12.03   The insurance broker must not put himself in a position of conflict by accepting instructions from insurers without first obtaining the consent of the insured. This is no more than an application of the more general rule that fiduciaries should not put themselves in a position of conflict as between two separate principals. So in *Fullwood v Hurley*[3] Scrutton LJ said:

> No agent who has accepted an employment from one principal can in law accept an engagement inconsistent with his duty to the first principal … unless he makes the fullest disclosure to each principal of his interest, and obtains the consent of each principal to the double employment.

12.04   Applying this principle to placing brokers acting for the insured seeking to make a claim on the policy, Megaw LJ in *Anglo-African Merchants Ltd v Bayley & Others*,[4] said, obiter:[5]

> If an insurance broker, before he accepts instructions to place an insurance, discloses to his client that he wishes to [act in some respect for insurers] … and if the would-be assured, fully informed as to the broker's intention to accept such instructions from the insurers and as to the possible implications of such collaboration between his agent and the opposite party, is prepared to agree that the broker may so act, good and well. In the absence of such express and fully informed consent, in my opinion it would be a breach of duty on the part of the insurance broker so to act.[6]

12.05   An obvious danger of failing to obtain such consent is the risk that the insurance broker learns of information relevant to the claim in his capacity as agent of

---

[1]   As to the role of the broker in placing insurance, see **Chapter 3**.

[2]   The broker may act for insurers, at the same time as the insured, to bind temporary cover: *Stockton v Mason* [1978] 2 Lloyd's Rep 430, and see further, para 3.07.

[3]   [1928] 1 KB 498, at 502.

[4]   [1970] 1 QB 311.

[5]   Ibid at 323.

[6]   Although obiter, the principle was confirmed on very similar facts by Donaldson J in *North and South Trust Co v Berkeley* [1971] 1 WLR 470.

insurers, which information insurers may (quite properly) prohibit the insurance broker from passing on to the insured.[7] If the insurance broker seeks the insured's consent in advance and the insured does not give his consent, insurers can simply instruct other agents for those purposes.

The fact that an insurance broker is acting pursuant to a limited authority to bind **12.06** cover on behalf of insurers does not render those brokers agents of the insurers where they have placed cover on behalf of the insured. They are agents of the insurer for the purpose of binding cover. However, in relation to placing the risk and receiving and forwarding payment of claims, the insurance broker remains the agent of the insured.[8] As David Steel J pointed out in so finding:[9]

> The basis of the criticism [which arises where the broker acts for the insurer in obtaining an assessor's report without seeking the insured's consent first] is not to the effect that the brokers thereby have to be treated as agents of the insurers but in accepting such instructions, the brokers are in breach of their retainer by the insured given the conflict of interest that thus arises.

C. Insurers' Right to Conduct the Defence

The usual position

It is usual for contracts of professional indemnity insurance in England and Wales **12.07** to contain 'Conduct of Defence' clauses. These clauses will give insurers the right but not a duty to take over the defence of any claims falling within the scope of the insuring clause made against the insured. For example, under the RIBA Architects Premier Policy Wording insurers:

> shall be entitled, if they do desire, to take over and conduct in the name of the Insured the investigation representation defence or settlement of any claim, circumstance or event and shall have full discretion in the conduct of the same.[10]

---

[7] On the facts in *Anglo-African Merchants Ltd v Bayley & Others* [1970] 1 QB 311, the insurance broker accepted an instruction from insurers, without the insured's consent, to obtain an assessor's report, the contents of which insurers were not prepared to permit the broker to disclose to the insured. Megaw J found it surprising to hear it suggested that this was a practice in the Lloyd's and company markets, but suggested he would not have upheld the practice, resulting as it did in the broker serving two masters without consent. The practice was considered again and held to be unreasonable by Donaldson J in *North and South Trust Co v Berkeley* [1971] 1 WLR 470. However, he held that in the event that the broker does act in breach of duty by obtaining an assessor's report on behalf of insurers without the consent of the insured, that breach does not entitle the insured to have access to the report: despite the breach, the broker acted as agent of the insurer in obtaining an assessor's report which remains the property of insurers.

[8] *Callaghan and Hedges v BJ Thompson* [2000] Lloyd's Rep IR 125.

[9] Ibid at 132, referring to *Anglo-African Merchants Ltd v Bayley* [1970] 1 QB 311 and to *North and South Trust Co v Berkeley* [1971] 1 WLR 470.

[10] Terms to similar effect are to be found in the ICAEW Minimum Approved Policy Wording and in the RICS Policy Wording. A term to that effect can be agreed between solicitors and their insurers: it is not prohibited by the SRA Minimum Terms and Conditions of Professional Indemnity Insurance.

Insurers almost invariably exercise this right, even when there is an issue as to coverage. It will usually be the case that, as part of the cover provided under the contract of professional indemnity insurance, insurers are obliged to indemnify the insured against the costs of defending claims by third parties, whether they exercise their right to take over conduct of the defence of those claims or not.[11]

12.08 Clauses giving insurers the right to take over the conduct of the defence of claims by third parties usually have the effect that insurers can settle or fight the claims. Where there is a QC clause, however, insurers may be frustrated in their wish to contest a claim against the insured to trial.[12]

SRA Minimum Terms and Conditions of Professional Indemnity Insurance

12.09 Although most professional indemnity policies do not impose a duty on insurers to defend, the SRA Minimum Terms and Conditions of Professional Indemnity Insurance contain a potential duty to defend on the part of insurers. Clause 4.10 of the SRA Minimum Terms and Conditions provides as follows:

> Conduct of a claim pending dispute resolution
>
> The insurance must provide that, pending resolution of any coverage dispute and without prejudice to any issue in dispute, the insurer will, if so directed by the [Law Society of England and Wales], conduct any claim, advance defence costs and, if appropriate, compromise and pay the claim. If the Society is satisfied that:
> (a) the party requesting the direction has taken all reasonable steps to resolve the dispute with the other party/ies; and
> (b) there is a reasonable prospect that the coverage dispute will be resolved or determined in the insured's favour; and
> (c) it is fair and equitable in all the circumstances for such direction to be given; it may in its absolute discretion make such a direction.

12.10 This provision does not impose an absolute duty to defend on insurers. First, the obligation to defend only arises upon the direction of the Law Society, which direction will be made as a matter of its discretion, if it is satisfied of each of the matters listed in the three sub-clauses. In relation to the exercise of its discretion, if the Law Society is satisfied of the third, namely that it is fair and equitable in all the circumstances for a direction to be given, it is hard to imagine circumstances in which the Law Society would not exercise its discretion to make an appropriate direction. So, where the insured is co-operating in the resolution of the coverage dispute and has a reasonable prospect of succeeding, insurers may be obliged to continue to fund the defence of the claim against the insured by the third party claimant.

---

[11] See paras 9.147–9.151.
[12] See paras 9.142–9.146 and 12.65–12.76.

Second, the clause is only available to the insured once a coverage dispute has arisen. **12.11**
A reservation of rights is not itself a dispute and would be insufficient to trigger
the clause (although insurers who have reserved their rights would be obliged to
continue to meet defence costs). Rather, insurers must have declined cover and the
insured sought to challenge declinature before the matter can be referred to the Law
Society for a direction.

Third, the duty under clause 4.10 is limited in time. The obligation to conduct **12.12**
the defence lapses upon the resolution of the coverage dispute. If that dispute is
resolved in favour of the insured, clause 4.8 of the Minimum Terms and Conditions
provides that insurers must continue to pay defence costs 'as and when they are
incurred' but there is no continuing obligation on insurers to maintain the conduct of the defence (although as a matter of practice, it is likely that insurers would
continue to do so). If the coverage dispute is resolved in favour of insurers, then that
will end their involvement in the claim in any event.

One potential consequence of clause 4.10 is that, where the insured is alleged by **12.13**
the third party claimant to have been negligent, but insurers deny liability on the
ground that the insured was in fact guilty of fraud or dishonesty, the Law Society
can direct insurers to conduct the defence of the third party's claim if the insured
has a reasonable prospect of defeating insurers on the issue of fraud or dishonesty
and the other conditions are satisfied. Moreover, insurers can be directed to compromise and even pay the claim if that is appropriate, before the question of the
insured's fraud or dishonesty is determined, leaving insurers to look to their right
to recover from the dishonest insured should the insured subsequently be found
to have been fraudulent or dishonest. This could arise where the insured's conduct
involved a clear breach of contract and negligence so that the third party was able
to apply for and obtain summary judgment well before the resolution of the issue
of dishonesty and fraud as between the insured and insurers.

Where the claim against an individual insured is solely for that individual's fraud **12.14**
or dishonesty, insurers might take the position that they are not obliged to fund the
defence of the claim because the insured is not entitled to an indemnity in respect
of his own dishonesty. However, in that situation the insured is protected by clause
4.8 of the Minimum Terms and Conditions which provides:

> Advancement of defence costs
> The insurance must provide that the insurer will meet defence costs as and when
> they are incurred, including defence costs incurred on behalf of an insured who is
> alleged to have committed or condoned dishonesty or a fraudulent act or omission,
> provided that the insurer is not liable for defence costs incurred on behalf of that
> insured after the earlier of:
> (a) that insured admitting to the insurer the commission or condoning of such
>   dishonesty, act or omission; or
> (b) a court or other judicial body finding that that insured was in fact guilty of
>   such dishonesty, act or omission.

12.15 The combined effect of these clauses is that an allegedly dishonest insured may be able to obtain a direction from the Law Society that insurers are obliged to conduct the defence of the claim against him pending the resolution of the coverage dispute. Even without such a direction, the insured is still entitled to advancement of defence costs up until the point where he admits dishonesty or is found to have been dishonest. At that point, insurers will be entitled to be reimbursed all of those defence costs,[13] but by then it may be too late.

D. Conflicts of Interest (1): Instructing Solicitors to Conduct the Defence

Who is the client?

12.16 Professional indemnity insurers will almost invariably reserve the right to instruct solicitors to investigate into and conduct the defence of a claim made against the insured.[14]

12.17 Where insurers exercise their contractual right to instruct a solicitor to conduct the defence of a claim by a third party against the insured, they thereby create the relationship of solicitor and client between the solicitor and the insured.[15] However, the solicitor thereby instructed will normally act on a joint retainer with the insured and insurer both being clients.[16] The normal consequence of this is that the insured becomes liable to pay the solicitor's costs, even if insurers are also liable for those costs.[17] Those costs are properly deemed to be incurred by the insured, even if they are funded by insurers.[18]

---

[13] See clause 7.2 of the SRA Minimum Terms and Conditions of Professional Indemnity Insurance.

[14] The insurer cannot compel the insured to accept the services of insurers' choice of solicitor without an express clause in the policy to this effect: *Barrett Bros (Taxis) Ltd v Davies* [1966] 1 WLR 1334.

[15] *Groom v Crocker* [1939] 1 KB 194, at 202–3; *Cox v Bankside Members Agency Ltd* [1995] 2 Lloyd's Rep 437, at 451; *Nicholson v Icepack Coolstores Ltd* [1999] 3 NZLR 475; *Nishimatsu-Costain-China Harbour Joint Venture v IP Kwan & Co (A Firm)* [2000] HKCA 372; [2001] HKLRD 84, at [31]–[32].

[16] In *K/S Merc-Scandia v Certain Lloyd's Underwriters, The Mercandian Continent* [2001] 2 Lloyd's Rep 563, insurers took conduct of the defence and appointed solicitors. Longmore LJ suggested that the solicitors, 'although appointed by underwriters, were solicitors on the record on behalf of the assured and, on the principles set out in *Groom v Crocker* [1938] K.B. 194 owed the assured all the duties that a solicitor owes to his client. Thus the assured, not the underwriters, were the clients of [the solicitors] but for the purposes of the policy they began incurring costs with the consent of the underwriters.' It is suggested that insurers must have been a client of the solicitors also. The insurers had retained them, and were giving them instructions in relation to the conduct of the defence.

[17] *Adams v London Improved Motor Coach Builders Ltd* [1921] 1 KB 495 at 501 and 504; *Cox v Bankside Members Agency Ltd* [1995] 2 Lloyd's Rep 437, at 451; and *Ghadami v Lyon Cole Insurance Group Ltd* [2010] EWCA Civ 767; [2010] 6 Costs LR 903.

[18] *Davies v Taylor (No 2)* [1974] AC 225 at 230; *Lewis v Avery (No 2)* [1973] 1 WLR 510, at 513.

In practice, appointed legal representatives will usually be paid by insurers,[19] will   **12.18**
take their instructions from insurers, and will regard insurers as their primary
client. As HH Judge Bowsher QC observed in *Gloucestershire Health Authority v
M A Torphy and Partners Ltd (t/a Torphy and Partners)*:[20]

> The defendant's insurers took over the conduct of the action. They appointed solici-
> tors. Those solicitors plainly recognised that they had a dual duty, firstly to the insurers
> and, secondly, to the defendants. I think it is fair to say firstly and secondly in that
> way because that probably was the way in which they saw it. It is difficult for anyone
> to serve two masters and that difficulty is recognised by solicitors who do this work ...

In the United States, the prevailing view appears to be that when insurers appoint   **12.19**
lawyers to conduct the defence of the insured, the retainer brought into being exists
between the insured and the solicitor alone.[21] In Australia, the prevailing view is
that the solicitor has two clients, insured and insurer.[22]

Conflicts of interest and the SRA Code of Conduct

In light of the fact the solicitor so appointed will act for two separate parties in relation   **12.20**
to the same dispute with overlapping but different interests, there is clearly potential
for conflicts to arise. The SRA Code of Conduct 2011 sets out ten mandatory principles, the fourth of which requires solicitors to 'act in the best interests of each client'.

Conflicts of interest are dealt with in chapter 3 of the SRA Code of Conduct 2011.   **12.21**
A distinction is drawn between a conflict of interest between a firm and its client
(an 'own interest conflict') and a conflict between two or more clients (a 'client
conflict'). Solicitors are never allowed to act where there is a conflict or significant
risk of a conflict between their interests and those of their clients.

Where there is a conflict or significant risk of conflict between the interests of two   **12.22**
or more clients (ie of a client conflict) a solicitor can only act for both or all of them
in limited circumstances. Those circumstances are set out in Outcomes O3.6, and
O3.7. Of these only O3.6 is of potential relevance in the context of solicitors acting
for the insured and insurers in the conduct of a defence of a claim by a third party.
It provides as follows:

> O(3.6) where there is a client conflict and the clients have a substantially common
> interest in relation to a matter or a particular aspect of it, you only act if:
> (a) you have explained the relevant issues and risks to the clients and you have a
>   reasonable belief that they understand those issues and risks;

---

[19] Although the insured is usually obliged to pay the VAT portion.
[20] [1999] Lloyd's Rep IR 203.
[21] See, for example, *Pine Island Farmers Coop et al v Erstad & Riemer PA et al* 636 NW 2d 604
(2001) Minn App (Court of Appeals).
[22] See, for example, *State Government Insurance Commission (SA) v Paneros* (1988) 48 SASR 349
and *Mercantile Mutual Insurance (NSW Workers Compensation) Ltd v Murray* [2004] NSWCA 151;
(2004) 13 ANZ Insurance Cases 61–612. For the position in New Zealand, see *Nicholson v Icepack
Coolstores Ltd* [1999] 3 NZLR 475.

    (b) all the clients have given informed consent in writing to you acting;

    (c) you are satisfied that it is reasonable for you to act for all the clients and that it is in their best interests; and

    (d) you are satisfied that the benefits to the clients of you doing so outweigh the risks.

The Code of Conduct provides that when 'deciding whether to act in these limited circumstances, the overriding consideration will be the best interests of each of the clients concerned and, in particular, whether the benefits to the clients of [the solicitors] acting for all or both of the clients outweigh the risks'.

12.23 There are two points at which these rules of conduct can become engaged. The first is where there is either an own interest conflict or a client conflict or a significant risk of either.[23] The fact that the insured and insurers have potentially conflicting interests in theory should not give rise to a client conflict or to a significant risk of a client conflict. Nor should the fact that the solicitor will often receive a significant amount of work from insurers compared to the insured give rise to an own interest conflict or a significant risk of an own interest conflict. Were it otherwise, solicitors could never act on the instructions of both the insured and insurers in the defence of a claim by a third party against the insured. Something more is needed.

12.24 If that 'something more' arises so as to give rise to an own risk conflict or to a significant risk of an own risk conflict, the solicitor cannot continue to act. If that 'something more' arises so as to give rise to a client conflict or to a significant risk of a client conflict, the Code of Conduct is again engaged: the solicitor has to decide whether it is appropriate to seek to bring himself within outcome O3.6 and, if he considers that it is appropriate, to do so. Only in those circumstances can he continue to act for both or all clients.

12.25 In the context of professional indemnity insurance and of outcome O3.6 it will usually be the case that the insured and insurers have a substantial common interest in relation to the defence of a claim by a third party claimant. The insured and insurers will share a common interest in defeating the claim or resolving it on the most favourable terms possible. When a client conflict or significant risk of a client conflict has arisen, it will depend upon the particular circumstances whether a solicitor can properly seek to bring himself within outcome O3.6 or whether the conflict is such that he should cease to act for both the insured and insurers.

---

[23] Solicitors are required by Outcomes O3.1, O3.2, and O3.3 to have effective systems and controls in place to identify own interest conflicts and client conflict, appropriate to the size and complexity of the firm and the nature of the work undertaken. The SRA Code of Conduct lists a number of 'indicative behaviours' which 'tend to show' compliance with the Outcomes. None is directed to solicitors who are acting for the insured and insurers in the defence of a claim against the insured.

If an issue as to coverage arises, insurers may instruct one firm of solicitors to advise **12.26** on coverage issues, and a second firm to conduct the defence on a joint retainer. In those circumstances, a solicitor will usually be able to act for both insured and insurer on a joint retainer without breaching the requirements of the SRA Code of Conduct. However there may be circumstances where a solicitor can only act for the insured, with his costs being paid by insurers. That in turn may give rise to the problem of insurers' contractual right to take over the conduct of the defence in the insured's name.

Joint retainer, conflicts of interest, and general principles of law

In *Bristol & West Building Society v Mothew*,[24] Millett LJ set out in general terms **12.27** the position of the solicitor acting for two clients (there, a lender and borrower). He said:[25]

> The principal is entitled to the single-minded loyalty of his fiduciary. This core liability has several facets. A fiduciary must act in good faith; he must not make a profit out of his trust; he must not place himself in a position where his duty and his interest may conflict; he may not act for his own benefit or for the benefit of a third person without the informed consent of his principal.

'The double employment rule'

Where a solicitor is appointed to conduct the defence on behalf of the insured **12.28** but largely takes his instructions from insurers, 'the double employment rule'[26] requires a solicitor, where there is a potential conflict between the interests of two of his clients, not to act for both unless he obtains the informed consent of each client. This is reflected in chapter 3 of the SRA Code of Conduct. Where such consent is obtained, the solicitor may act for both.[27]

Express or implied consent of the insured

Where there is no actual conflict or significant risk of conflict such consent is **12.29** likely to be found to have been given by the insured in the process of subscribing for insurance. In professional indemnity policies in which insurers expressly reserve the right to appoint their own legal representatives, it is likely that the insured will be taken to have consented to the same by entering the contract on those terms. Obtaining further written consent from the insured by way of an appropriately worded client care letter would put the question of consent beyond doubt.

---

[24] [1998] Ch 1. See too *Ultraframe (UK) Ltd v Fielding* [2005] EWHC 1638 (Ch).
[25] Ibid at 18.
[26] As Millett LJ referred to it, ibid at 18–20.
[27] *Clark Boyce v Mouat* [1994] 1 AC 428, at 435G per Lord Jauncey giving the Opinion of the Privy Council.

The actual conflict rule

12.30   Even if the insured can be taken to have given his consent (whether on an express or implied basis) to the solicitor acting both for himself and insurers, plainly the solicitor could not continue to act for both in the event of an actual conflict of interest arising. In *Bristol & West Building Society v Mothew*,[28] Millett LJ described the rule as follows:[29]

> ... the fiduciary must take care not to find himself in a position where there is an actual conflict of duty so that he cannot fulfil his obligations to one principal without failing in his obligations to the other ... If he does, he may have no alternative but to cease to act for at least one and preferably both. The fact that he cannot fulfil his obligations to one principal without being in breach of his obligations to the other will not absolve him from liability. I shall call this the 'actual conflict rule'.[30]

The consequences of an actual conflict between insured and insurers are discussed later in this chapter.

12.31   When a solicitor realizes that a conflict of interest has arisen, whether as to the conduct of the defence to the claim by the third party claimant or because he has learnt of information from the insured which suggests grounds upon which insurers might deny cover, he should tell his clients.[31] If they give their informed consent to him continuing to act, he may do so. For example, by obtaining the insured's informed consent to the solicitor continuing to act both for him and for insurers in circumstances in which the solicitor will be under a duty to pass on information relevant to coverage to insurers, the solicitor will no longer be in breach of duty to the insured when he does so.[32]

12.32   Where informed consent is not given, the solicitor cannot continue to act for both the insured and insurers. So in *Nishimatsu-Costain-China Harbour Joint Venture v IP Kwan & Co (A Firm)*[33] a firm of solicitors had been instructed by insurers to act for them in an arbitration between insurers and the insured as to coverage. Insurers then appointed the same firm to conduct the defence of a third party claim against the insured which potentially fell within the policy. The insured did not consent and the High Court of Hong Kong Special Administrative Region Court of Appeal granted an injunction restraining the solicitors from acting in both disputes.

---

[28] [1998] Ch 1.

[29] Ibid at 19.

[30] For a discussion of a solicitor's actual conflict of interest, see *Hilton v Barker, Booth & Eastwood* [2005] UKHL 8; [2005] 1 WLR 567.

[31] *Groom v Crocker* [1939] 1 KB 194, at 227 per McKinnon LJ.

[32] *Nishimatsu-Costain-China Harbour Joint Venture v IP Kwan & Co (A Firm)* [2000] HKCA 372; [2001] HKLRD 84, at [64] per HA Rogers JA, with whom Leong JA agreed. The insured gave such consent in *Campbell v The Members of Lloyd's Syndicate QBE Casualty 386* [2014] VSC 655; he did so by signing a letter in unequivocal terms.

[33] [2000] HKCA 372; [2001] HKLRD 84.

E. Conflicts of Interest (2):
Confidentiality, Privilege, and Coverage Disputes

The duty of confidentiality: SRA Code of Conduct

The SRA Code of Conduct 2011 sets out a solicitor's professional duty of confiden- **12.33**
tiality in Chapter 4. It provides, in part:

> The duty of confidentiality to all clients must be reconciled with the duty of disclos-
> ure to clients. This duty of disclosure is limited to information of which you are
> aware which is material to your client's matter. Where you cannot reconcile these
> two duties, then the protection of confidential information is paramount. You should
> not continue to act for a client for whom you cannot disclose material information,
> except in very limited circumstances, where safeguards are in place. Such situations
> often also give rise to a conflict of interests which is discussed in Chapter 3.[34]

This is reinforced by outcomes O4.1, O4.2, and O4.3:

> O(4.1) you keep the affairs of clients confidential unless disclosure is required or
> permitted by law or the client consents;
>
> O(4.2) any individual who is advising a client makes that client aware of all infor-
> mation material to that retainer of which the individual has personal knowledge;
>
> O(4.3) you ensure that where your duty of confidentiality to one client comes into
> conflict with your duty of disclosure to another client, your duty of confidentiality
> takes precedence …

The tension that arises between the duty of confidentiality and the duty to inform **12.34**
when a solicitor learns of information from the insured which, if passed to insurers,
will indicate potential grounds for denying cover is obvious.

Conflicts arising in relation to coverage disputes

Confidentiality and privilege

Legal professional privilege and confidentiality are closely related. Privilege can **12.35**
only apply to documents that are otherwise confidential. The duty of confidentiality is a duty not to misuse that information, where misuse for these purposes means
unauthorized disclosure of that information to a third party.[35] Where confidential
information is obtained by the solicitor pursuant to a joint retainer, then any disclosure of that information must be with the consent of all the clients. Conversely,
where the solicitor obtains information pursuant to a joint retainer, he or she must
disclose it to all of the clients.[36] It follows that in the course of the joint retainer,

---

[34] Chapter 3 of the SRA Code of Conduct is discussed in paras 12.20–12.26.
[35] *Bolkiah v KPMG* [1999] 2 AC 222; *Coco v AN Clark (Engineers) Ltd* [1969] RPC 41.
[36] *Hellenic Mutual War Risks Association (Bermuda) Ltd v Harrison (The Sagheera)* [1997] 1
Lloyd's Rep 160, at 165 per Rix J.

privilege in relation to such information cannot be asserted by one client against the other, absent agreement to the contrary.

Express waiver of privilege

12.36 While there remains a common interest between the insured and insurers, then there will usually be no issue as to waiver of privilege in relation to information provided by the insured to the solicitors. It is when information is provided to solicitors which might impact on coverage that difficulties arise. The question as to whether the insured had given his consent to the disclosure to insurers of information imparted by the insured to the solicitors arose in *Brown v Guardian Royal Exchange Assurance Plc*.[37] The insured was a solicitor. He had professional indemnity insurance with the defendant insurers. A claim was brought against the insured by a third party claimant which was duly notified to insurers. Insurers appointed solicitors to conduct the defence. The solicitors were acting on behalf of both the insured and insurers.

12.37 During the course of preparation of the defence to the third party claim, a conference took place between the solicitors, the insured, and counsel. Following that conference and in the light of what had occurred at it, the solicitors informed the insured that insurers were reserving their rights under the fraud and dishonesty exclusion. At this point there was at least a real prospect of a conflict of interest between the insured and insurers, and probably an actual conflict of interest. On any view, an actual conflict arose shortly afterwards when insurers repudiated liability shortly after reserving their rights. Quite properly, the solicitors ceased to act for the insured solicitor at this point.

12.38 Arbitration proceedings were commenced under the policy. Insurers sought to rely on an exclusion in respect of dishonesty and fraud as the basis for their denial of cover. Insurers then sought discovery of the solicitor's files for the period in which they were acting for both parties, including communications between the solicitor and the insured, together with instructions to counsel. At first instance it was held that the documents were privileged. Insurers appealed. Insurers accepted that the relevant documents were privileged against everyone but themselves. They relied on clause 8(c) of the policy as entitling them to disclosure, the material part of which provided:

> Where solicitors or other expert advisers are so employed their fees and expenses will be for the account of the Insurers who may require the solicitors' reports to be submitted directly to them.[38]

12.39 On appeal, Hoffmann LJ, with whom Waite and Neill LJJ agreed, noted that problems that may arise when an investigation of the claim is made also raises questions

---

[37] [1994] 2 Lloyd's Rep 325.
[38] This was the old Solicitors' Master Policy, which preceded the Solicitors Indemnity Fund as the primary insurance cover for solicitors.

relevant to whether the insurers are liable. In this case, the claim for negligence against the insured required an investigation of exactly what he knew or did not know at the time of the transaction. Insurers could not decide whether or not to defend the claim without full information on these matters. But lurking within those matters was an issue on which the insured and the insurers had conflicting interests, namely the possibility that the investigation might reveal that the insured had been dishonest.[39]

Hoffmann LJ then held that although there was authority for the propositions that **12.40** no privilege could exist between parties: (i) who instruct a solicitor in a matter as to which they have a joint or common interest;[40] or (ii) who jointly instruct a solicitor in a matter in which they have different interests and communicate with him in his joint capacity,[41] he could conclude that the insured was not entitled to assert privilege as against insurers as a result of the clear wording of clause 8(c). He held:[42]

> The answer in my view depends entirely upon the construction of cl. 8. It says that the insurers are entitled to reports. Two questions arise. First, reports as to what? In my judgment, reports as to everything which the solicitors have learned about the claim. There is nothing in the language of the clause which would justify restricting the scope of the reports in the way for which [Counsel for the insured] contends.

> Furthermore, I think that his principle would in practice be very difficult to apply in the present case, I do not see how [the solicitor] could have given the insurers an intelligible report on the prospects of the claim succeeding without at the same time expressing a view on whether [the insured] had been fraudulent, negligent or neither. In my view the effect of the policy was that anything which [the insured] said to [the solicitor] was to be treated as having been said to the insurers and [the insured] must be taken to have known this.[43]

It is therefore not surprising to find that policies of liability insurance include terms **12.41** similar to that considered in *Brown v Guardian Royal Exchange Assurance plc*. For example (from a solicitors' insurance policy):

> The Insured agree that any solicitor appointed by the Insurer shall disclose to the Insurer any information, evidence or documents which the Insured has provided to that solicitor whether privileged or not.

And, again from a solicitors' insurance policy:

> Appointed Solicitors shall act at the sole direction of the INSURERS and shall disclose to the INSURERS as required any evidence, document or information given to or which becomes known to Appointed Solicitors in the course of so acting.

---

[39] [1994] 2 Lloyd's Rep 325 at 328.
[40] Insurers had relied upon the dictum of Bridge LJ in *Cia Barca de Panama SA v George Wimpey & Co Ltd* [1980] 1 Lloyd's Rep 598 at 615: 'If A and B have a common interest in litigation against C and if at that point there is no dispute between A and B, then if subsequently A and B fall out and litigate between themselves and the litigation against C is relevant to the disputes between A and B, then in the litigation between A and B neither A nor B can claim legal professional privilege for documents which came into existence in relation to the earlier litigation against it.'
[41] [1994] 2 Lloyd's Rep 325 at 327.
[42] Ibid at 329.
[43] See also *State Government Insurance Commission (SA) v Paneros* (1988) 48 SASR 349.

However, to be effective, such clauses must be clear and unambiguous.[44]

Implied waiver of privilege

12.42 Where professional indemnity policies do not contain clauses which expressly provide that insurers will be entitled to receive information imparted by the insured to jointly retained solicitors, insurers will be left to rely on general principles to obtain access to information imparted or disclosure of documents created while there was a joint retainer by them and the insured of a firm of solicitors. The courts will normally find that implied consent was given between insured and insurers while there was no conflict of interest, although a finding that information was imparted to the solicitors by the insured on the basis that it would be kept confidential as against insurers will militate against implied consent.[45] The position is more difficult when insurers have reserved their rights, so that there is at least a real possibility of a conflict of interest. This potential conflict may turn into an actual conflict. If and when it does so, any implied consent on the part of the insured will end.

12.43 The need for solicitors and counsel to be alert to the possibility that an actual conflict of interest has arisen is illustrated by the decision of the Court of Appeal in *TSB Bank Plc v Robert Irving & Burns.*[46] In that case, the insured was a firm of surveyors against whom proceedings had been brought by a bank for allegedly negligent overvaluation. The insured had properly notified insurers, who appointed solicitors to conduct the defence of the third party claim. The policy contained an exclusion of liability for valuations carried out by a particular valuer in the firm. The solicitors' investigation had suggested that some of the valuations relied upon by the bank might in fact have been undertaken by the excluded valuer. Counsel then interviewed a non-excluded valuer as to the extent to which he relied upon the valuations of the excluded valuer. Following this interview, insurers repudiated liability and the insured brought part 20 proceedings against it seeking an indemnity. Insurers defended in part on the basis of what was learned from the non-excluded valuer in conference with counsel. The insured then applied to strike out those elements of the defence which relied on that information, alleging that it was privileged. The insured succeeded at first instance and insurers' appeal was dismissed.

12.44 The Court of Appeal held that where there was a joint retainer of solicitors by insured and insurer there was an implied waiver of privilege between them. The

---

[44] *Nicholson v Icepack Coolstores Ltd* [1999] 3 NZLR 475. See also *Marshall v Adamson* [1936] 4 DLR 383 and *Mercantile Mutual Insurance (NSW Workers Compensation) Ltd v Murray* [2004] NSWCA 151 at [57].

[45] *Marshall v Adamson* [1936] 4 DLR 383; *Nicholson v Icepack Coolstores Ltd* [1999] 3 NZLR 475.

[46] [2000] 2 All ER 826. At first instance the judge held that there were in fact two retainers: first a joint retainer by the insured and insurers and, second, a separate retainer of the solicitor by insurers to advise them as to their rights under the policy. The latter was held to be immaterial by the Court of Appeal.

implied waiver of privilege included any communications made when a potential conflict of interest existed between the insured and the insurer, but was limited so as to exclude any communications made after an actual conflict of interest had arisen.[47] In reaching this conclusion, the Court of Appeal relied upon the decision in *Groom v Crocker*.[48] There MacKinnon LJ had held that:[49]

> ... the solicitor, nominated by the society, is the solicitor for the assured, who is his client. But he is also appointed by the society to protect its interests. If in regard to any question of tactics in conducting the litigation the solicitor has reason to discern a conflict, or possible conflict, of interest between the society and the assured, it is the duty of the solicitor to inform the assured of the matter. If the assured then insists on a course that the society disapproves, it can refuse to conduct or control the proceedings any longer, and leave the assured to do so at his own cost, and at the risk, if the society are right in their view, of not being able to recover that cost under his policy. If people act reasonably, it is obvious that the business method contemplated by the policy can be carried out with perfect smoothness.

Morritt LJ held that it would be inconsistent with the observations of **12.45** MacKinnon LJ:[50]

> if the common solicitor were permitted not to point out an actual conflict of interest to the insured thereby enabling the insurer to obtain from the insured the material necessary to repudiate liability under the policy. Though Mackinnon LJ refers to 'a conflict, or possible conflict' I do not think that a possible conflict would suffice to entitle an insured to maintain privilege against his insurer. It is of the essence of the original joint retainer and the basis for the implied waiver that there is such a possible conflict of interest.[51]

However, if the insured chose to continue to retain the same solicitor after he **12.46** had been informed that the conflict had arisen and had had a reasonable opportunity to consider instructing other solicitors, then a further waiver of privilege would be implied.[52] On the facts, the actual conflict of interest had arisen before the conference with counsel. The insured had not been informed. They were therefore entitled to claim privilege in respect of the information provided at the conference.

---

[47] Ibid at 394.
[48] [1939] 1 KB 194 and see paras 12.52–12.55.
[49] Ibid at 227–8.
[50] [2000] 2 All ER 826, at 833–4.
[51] See also Tuckey LJ at 835–6: 'the waiver of privilege implicit in the joint retainer extends to communications made by the insured to the solicitors where there is merely a possible conflict of interest. Without such a waiver I can see that it would be very difficult for a solicitor ever to accept a joint retainer in a case such as this. Many solicitors do and it is in the interests of both insurers and insureds that they should continue to be able to do so. It is only where, as here, there is an actual conflict of interest that the waiver comes to an end and even then it will continue if, after notification of the conflict, the insured decides not to instruct separate solicitors. For these reasons I do not think that this clarification of the law will cause real difficulty in practice.'
[52] [2000] 2 All ER 826, at 834.

12.47 The Court of Appeal was clearly influenced by the sense that the insured had had no warning that frank answers to the questions might lead to the loss of cover. But a number of points can be made:

(1) Had there been an express provision to the effect that 'any solicitor appointed by the Insurer shall disclose to the Insurer any information, evidence or documents which the Insured has provided to that solicitor whether privileged or not', then either the consent would have survived the advent of an actual conflict of interest or the express term would have needed to be construed in a very strained way.

(2) The line of questions at the conference was relevant to the issue of liability to the third party claimant.[53] If it was the case that the valuer who had purported to carry out the valuation in question had in fact relied entirely on the work of the excluded valuer, that was highly damaging to the defence to the claim. It would appear that, had the purpose of the conference simply been to explore the facts and the question of cover had not been on the agenda, then if the insured had provided information suggesting that the valuation in question was in fact the work of the excluded valuer, insurers would have been entitled to use that information against the insured.[54]

12.48 Putting *Brown v Guardian Royal Exchange Assurance Plc* and *TSB Bank v Robert Irving & Burns* together, one gets this result:

(1) A joint retainer under which the insured is presumed to consent to the provision to insurers of all information he gives to the lawyers is permissible unless there is an actual, as opposed to a potential, conflict of interest.

(2) As long as there is no actual conflict of interest, the lawyers may investigate the merits of the claim, even though in doing so they may obtain information which would entitle insurers to avoid cover.[55]

(3) However, once the lawyers appreciate (or should appreciate) that an actual conflict of interest has arisen, they should notify the insured, who should make an informed decision as to whether to continue with the joint retainer.[56]

---

[53] Morritt LJ held that a principal purpose of the questioning was to elicit answers which might found a repudiation of policy cover. The other principal purpose appears to have been to elicit information relevant to the assessment of the merits of the claim by the third party.

[54] Which was what happened in *Brown v Guardian Royal Exchange Assurance Plc* [1994] 2 Lloyd's Rep 325.

[55] In *San Diego Navy Federal Credit Union v Cumis Insurance Society Inc* Cal.Rep. 494 (1984), the Californian Court of Appeal said that jointly 'retained counsel is bound to learn about coverage issues as he prepares the ... suit'.

[56] If the insured does not continue with the joint retainer, questions arise as to whether the solicitor should step aside, leaving insurers to appoint one solicitor to deal with the coverage dispute and another to act on a joint retainer to protect the conduct of the claim, or whether the solicitor can continue to act for insurers, at least on the coverage issues.

An issue that arises from the approach set out in the decisions in *Brown v Guardian* **12.49**
Royal Exchange Assurance Plc and *TSB Bank v Robert Irving & Burns* is the point at
which an actual conflict arises so as to bring to an end the implied waiver of privilege. It is suggested that an actual conflict arises when there are sufficient grounds
to suspect that insurers may be entitled to repudiate liability. In *San Diego Navy
Federal Credit Union v Cumis Insurance Society Inc*,[57] it was held, following earlier
American authority, that 'a serious conflict of interest occurs when insurer's counsel [also acting for the insured] obtains information bearing directly on the issue
of coverage during the course of preparation of the third party suit'. At this point,
the conflict of interest is not just potential. Lawyers acting for both insured and
insurers should always be alert to the possibility that an actual conflict of interest
has arisen. At that point, the insured needs to be advised accordingly.

F. Conflicts of Interest (3): Conduct of Defence

If insurers take over conduct of the defence, there is further potential for conflicts **12.50**
to arise between them and the insured in how the defence is to be conducted.
While both insurers and the insured might usually be thought to have a common
interest in defeating the third party claim or resolving it as cheaply as possible,
in practice their interests can diverge. The insured may have his own potential
exposure by way of one or both of a deductible or an uninsured excess above the
level of his cover. He may also be concerned as to his professional reputation and
as to the impact of any judgment or settlement on future premiums. Insurers may
wish to settle at a level which requires the insured to pay a deductible but reduces
their own exposure or not to settle at or near to the limit of cover when there is
a prospect of achieving a more favourable result. If insurers' obligation to meet
defence costs is separate from the limit of cover under the insuring clause, it may
be in their interests to settle quickly rather than continue to defend the third party
claim. Insurers may also have wider interests in the outcome of a particular claim,
for example where an adverse finding might have implications for their exposure
on other claims against other insureds.

Situations of conflict in the conduct of the defence

The following examples illustrate the range of disputes that can arise between **12.51**
insured and insurer in the conduct of a claim:

(1) An insurer may wish to compromise a dispute for a sum falling within
the insured's excess, while the insured may be unwilling to do so—eg, if a
claimant claims £500,000 but offers to settle a claim for £100,000 when the

---

[57] Cal. Rep. 494 (1984).

insured's excess is £100,000, the insurer will wish to accept the offer (as it will pay nothing), but the insured may wish to continue to defend (to try to avoid paying anything).

(2) An insured may wish to compromise a dispute for a sum falling within the insured's cover, while the insurer may be unwilling to do so—eg, if a third party claimant claims £2m when the limit of indemnity is only £1m, and the third party claimant offers to settle for £1m, the insured may want to accept the offer (as it will all be covered by insurance and he will avoid any uninsured claim), but the insurer may wish to continue to defend (to try to avoid paying anything).

(3) The insured may have its own specific reasons (eg, concern for his reputation) for supporting or opposing a settlement—eg, a solicitor's negligence case where the solicitor is likely to lose on the question of breach of duty but where there is a good causation defence. By compromising the claim, the solicitor would avoid having his name in the law reports.

(4) An insurer may have its own reasons for supporting or opposing a settlement. For example, the result in the particular case, if it proceeds to judgment, might adversely impact upon attempts to negotiate or litigate a number of similar claims.

(5) When acting for an insured claimant in recovery proceedings, where there is a claim for both insured and uninsured losses, there may be a dispute as to what settlement to accept from the defendant and how any settlement sum is to be divided up.

Insurers' duties in conducting the defence

12.52 Policies of professional indemnity insurance will usually give insurers a wide discretion as to how to conduct the defence of a third party claim against the insured. They are, however, constrained by the post-contractual duty of good faith which applies to insurers when they decide to take conduct of their insured's defence.[58] In this context, the duty of good faith requires insurers to consider the interests of the insured when taking decisions and requires them not to act irrationally in relation to those interests. The impact of the duty of good faith on insurers' right and power to conduct the defence of a third party claim were considered by the Court of Appeal in *Groom v Crocker*.[59] In that case, condition 2 of a policy of motor insurance provided:

> The Society shall if and so long as it so desires have absolute conduct and control of all or any proceedings against the insured … and shall be entitled to use the name of the insured to enforce for the benefit of the Society any order made for costs or otherwise or to make or defend any claim for indemnity or damage against third parties.

[58] For the insured's continuing duty of good faith, see paras 11.56–11.57.
[59] [1939] 1 KB 194.

On its face this provision gave insurers unfettered powers to conduct the defence **12.53** of a third party claim. However, the Court of Appeal held that insurers had to exercise those powers in accordance with their obligation to act in good faith. As Sir Wilfrid Greene MR explained:[60]

> The right given to insurers is to have control of proceedings in which they and the assured have a common interest—the assured because he is the defendant and the insurers because they are contractually bound to indemnify him. Each is interested in seeing that any judgment to be recovered against the assured shall be for as small a sum as possible. It is the assured upon whom the burden of the judgment will fall if insurers are insolvent. The effect of the provisions in question is, I think, to give to the insurers the right to decide upon the proper tactics to pursue in the conduct of the action, provided that they do so in what they bona fide consider to be the common interest of themselves and their assured. But the insurers are in my opinion clearly not entitled to allow their judgment as to the best tactics to pursue to be influenced by the desire to obtain for themselves some advantage altogether outside the litigation in question with which the assured has no concern.

Scott LJ held that condition 2 gave the insurers an absolute right to control their **12.54** insured's defence, but that the scope of this right was subject to certain implied boundaries and limitations. It was not a right which insurers would be entitled to exercise arbitrarily. They were bound to exercise a real discretion upon each question as it arose in the conduct of the defence, making each decision after due consideration of the circumstances of the particular case. He also held that the insurers were not obliged to consult the insured to find out his wishes. However, insurers should take their decisions with their minds on the facts of the particular allegations made against the insured, whilst not forgetting their own rights arising from the bargain expressed in the policy—namely, that in return for his indemnity, the insured gave insurers the freedom to deal with the pecuniary risk to which they were exposed as economically as possible. However, that did not mean that insurers could take into account considerations wholly extraneous to the subject matter of the insurance.[61]

These rights vested in insurers will in turn impact on the duty of the jointly retained **12.55** solicitor. Sir Wilfrid Green MR set out the position:[62]

> The duty of a solicitor so nominated to the assured for whom he is to act cannot of course be the same as that which arises in the ordinary case of solicitor and client, where the client is entitled to require the solicitor to act according to his own instructions. The whole object and usefulness of these provisions would be defeated if the assured were to be entitled to interfere with the conduct of the proceedings in that way. The assured in my opinion is not entitled to complain of anything done by the solicitor upon his instructions, express or implied, of the insurers, provided it falls within the class of things which the insurers are, as

---

[60] Ibid at 203.
[61] Ibid at 223.
[62] Ibid at 202–3.

between themselves and the assured, entitled to do under the terms of the policy when properly construed. A solicitor who, acting on the instructions express or implied from the insurer, does something to which the insurers, as between themselves and the assured, are not entitled to require the assured to submit, would in my view be acting beyond his competence, and, if what he does is something which in the ordinary way would be breach of duty to his client, he will be liable accordingly.

Conflicts arising in relation to the limit of indemnity and duties of the jointly retained solicitor

12.56 The interests of insured and insurers should broadly remain aligned, while the potential quantum of the third party claim remains well within the limit of cover. However, those interests may diverge in the event of a claim with the potential to result in a judgment against the insured in excess of the level of indemnity. Courts in the United States have recognized the potential conflict in the event of a judgment in excess of policy limits in the following terms:

> The insured's interest will almost always favour settlement, even up to the policy limits, since the insured has nothing to gain and much to lose by litigating rather than settling. Conversely ... the insurer will be inclined to go to trial, since doing so will not expose it to liability greater than the cost to settle the case. The 'equal consideration' requirement prohibits the insurer from taking a gamble that only its insured stands to lose. In order to avoid such a result, an insurer that breaches its duty to consider settlement offers in good faith may be held liable for the entire judgment obtained against the insured regardless of policy limitations.[63]

Duty on solicitor to advise of the limit of indemnity

12.57 In *Citibank NA v Excess Insurance Company Ltd*,[64] contrary to the expectation of the solicitor conducting the defence, there was a real risk—which in due course was realized—that the insured would be held liable for more than the amount of insurance cover. As a result, the solicitor failed to make the enquiries which it was held that he should have done, namely as to the effect on the insured of having to satisfy a judgment above the amount insured. In fact, the insured had no funds to satisfy the judgment so it had a strong interest to settle within the policy limit if possible. Having criticized the jointly retained solicitor on these grounds, Thomas J said:[65]

> I have little doubt that had the position been appreciated and the position been explained to [the third party claimant] and the other parties, then a settlement within the policy limit would have been achievable; in my experience, in such

---

[63] *Magnum Foods v Continental Casualty Co* 36F 3d, 1491, at 1504 (10th Circuit, 1994). For a similar issue arising in relation to a professional indemnity policy, see *St Paul Fire & Marine Insurance Co v Roch Bros Co* 639 F Supp 134, at 139.
[64] [1999] Lloyd's Rep IR 122.
[65] Ibid at 134.

circumstances the prospect of the individual defendant's insolvency with an exhausted policy limit invariably induces settlement. None of this took place.

This issue was also considered by Auld LJ in *Cormack and Cormack v Express Insurance* **12.58** *Ltd*,[66] where solicitors instructed by the lead insurer warned the insured before trial that there was a risk of under-insurance. The insured initially said he would rather settle. However, a payment into court by insurers was not accepted and the insured seemed content to prepare for trial. The claim eventually succeeded, with damages and costs exceeding the limit of cover. There was a shortfall in the claimant's costs, which they sought to recover from insurers pursuant to s 51 of the Senior Courts Act 1981.[67] Auld LJ said:[68]

> If and when a significant conflict arises, say when there is a realisation that if the matter proceeds the cover limit may be exceeded, the insurer should have regard both to its own interest and to the separate interest and exposure of the insured. This may, depending on the circumstances, require the insurer to pay greater attention to the insured's expressed concerns or to involve him more in the making of decisions, as Thomas J suggested in *Citibank* at p. 132. These may include, for example, whether and when to seek settlement and for how much rather than to continue the proceedings. The manner and extent of such greater involvement of the insured are clearly matters of judgment and balance depending on the facts of each case.

The same potential for conflict exists where the total exposure to the third party **12.59** claimant may exceed the primary level of cover and there is an excess layer. The pragmatic solution to such conflicts is to obtain advice as to whether an offer to settle the third party claim should be made and, if so, at what level without regard to the varying interests of the insured, primary insurers, and excess insurers. One way in which this can be done is by including and invoking a QC clause.[69] Another way is for each of the insured and insurers (or primary and excess insurers) to obtain their own independent advice.

Further duties of the jointly retained solicitor

Solicitor's duty to provide information

While privilege continues to be waived, the solicitor should keep the insured **12.60** informed to the extent reasonably necessary.[70] He should plainly warn the insured of any conflict of interest when it arises.[71] Further, the solicitor should provide to the insured any documents relating to the claim if requested to do so.[72]

---

[66] [2002] Lloyd's Rep IR 398.
[67] See paras 13.03–13.38 for further discussion of the costs awards that may be made pursuant to s 51(1) Senior Courts Act 1981.
[68] [2002] Lloyd's Rep IR 398, at 405–6.
[69] As to which, see paras 12.65–12.76.
[70] *Groom v Crocker* [1939] 1 KB 194, at 203, and see paras 12.52–12.55.
[71] Ibid at 227 per Mackinnon LJ (quoted at para 12.45).
[72] *Re Crocker* [1936] Ch 696.

*Solicitors cannot act on instructions of insurers beyond insurers' rights
under the policy*

12.61 The limits on insurers' ability to conduct the defence of a third party claim
impact upon the obligation of solicitors to comply with their instructions. This
was made clear by Sir Wilfrid Greene MR in *Groom v Crocker*.[73] In that case,
the insured was driving a car with his brother as passenger. The car collided
with a lorry, the driver of which was entirely to blame. The insured's brother
sued both the insured and the employers of the driver of the lorry. The insured's
of the insured and the insurers of the lorry-driver's employer entered an agreement involving the claim involving the insured and another claim with which
the insured had nothing to do. In accordance with that agreement, solicitors
instructed by the insured's insurers put in a defence to his brother's claim admitting liability.

12.62 In finding that taking wholly extraneous concerns into account went beyond the
discretion afforded to the insurer pursuant to its rights to conduct the defence,
Sir Wilfrid Greene MR applied the test of whether insurers' instructions to the
solicitor went beyond the rights insurers had as against their insured. If they
had no right to act in a particular way as against the insured, they could not
achieve the same result by instructing the jointly retained solicitor to do that
very same thing.

12.63 On that basis, as insurers were not entitled to require the insured to admit liability, solicitors acting on their joint behalf were not entitled to act on instructions to draft a defence admitting liability in circumstances in which the insured
had not only not consented to the same, but where the solicitors knew that the
insured did not agree that liability was to be admitted. Agreeing, Scott LJ added
that the solicitors had acted in breach of the contractual duty they owed to the
insured as their client. In acting in accordance with instructions which insurers
had no right to give and with which the solicitors knew their client, the insured,
did not agree, the solicitors had in fact repudiated the relationship of solicitor
and client.[74]

Solicitor's duty in the event of a conflict

12.64 Again if the solicitor to the insured and insurer finds himself in an actual conflict
as to the conduct of the defence, he must advise that there is a conflict and inform
the parties of any available mechanisms by which the dispute as to how the case
should be managed might be resolved.

---

[73] [1939] 1 KB 194.
[74] Ibid at 224.

G. Conflicts of Interest (4): Mechanisms to Resolve Conflicts

Apart from pragmatic agreement between the insured and insurers (usually with **12.65** each having at least the option of taking independent legal advice), there are two main ways in which it is possible to resolve conflicts of interest, whether as a result of coverage issues or as a result of the way in which insurers seek to defend the claim. These are (i) the general principles of law and the standards of professional conduct which dictate how parties involved in the conflict must respond to those conflicts;[75] and (ii) mechanisms provided in the contract itself. There are four main mechanisms which can be included within a contract of professional indemnity insurance: first, a delivery-up clause of the sort that appeared in *Brown v Guardian Royal Exchange Assurance Plc*;[76] second, an arbitration clause; third, an insurer settlement clause;[77] and fourth, the 'QC' clause. This section of this chapter focuses on the last.

The QC clause

Both the insured and insurers may wish that a particular third party claim is **12.66** fought or settled. The insured's interests will include the potential damage to his reputation if the claim is fought and lost, his own potential financial exposure by way of deductible, exposure above the limit of his insurance cover, and the level of premium he may be required to pay for professional indemnity insurance in future. Insurers may wish to limit their potential exposure by reaching a commercial settlement or to reject an offer in the hope that the third party claim can be resolved at a lower cost to themselves. As has been explained, even where insurers are given wide powers to decide how the defence to a third party claim is to be conducted and whether it is to be settled, insurers have to exercise those powers in accordance with their obligation of good faith.[78]

Purpose of a QC clause

As well as potentially extending cover under a contract of professional indem- **12.67** nity insurance,[79] QC clauses are designed to provide a means of resolving a conflict of views between the insured and insurers as to whether a third party claim should be contested to trial or settled. In particular, they can enable

---

[75] See paras 12.16–12.64.
[76] Designed to resolve privilege issues in the context of coverage disputes.
[77] Clauses empowering the insurer to settle the claim whether the insured agrees or not have been upheld: *Beacon v Langdale* (1939) 65 Ll L Rep 57. But see paras 12.52–12.55.
[78] See paras 12.52–12.55.
[79] See paras 9.142–9.146.

regard to be had to concerns which the insured may have as to his professional reputation and standing.[80] In *West Wake Price v Ching*,[81] Devlin J noted that it was obvious that 'one of the main objects of the Q.C. clause is to give the assured additional cover, not only against the costs of litigation but also as a protection against unwelcome publicity'.[82] An insured may take the view that the adverse publicity entailed by fighting what may well be a successful defence to trial is less attractive than a settlement on confidential terms. Professionals might very reasonably take the view that the public scrutiny of their conduct by way of cross-examination at trial may lead the public, however unfairly, to conclude that even in the event of 'acquittal', there is 'no smoke without fire'. This clearly what Devlin J was referring to when he said:[83]

> It does not have to be read twice to see that its main object is to protect the assured from having to face litigation which, whether successful or not, might be damaging to his reputation.

The structure and operation of QC clauses which are tied to insuring clauses

12.68 There is no standard form of QC clause. In *West Wake Price v Ching*,[84] the QC clause in an accountant's professional indemnity policy provided as follows:

> We further agree to pay any such claim or claims which may arise without requiring the assured to dispute any claim, unless a Queen's Counsel (to be mutually agreed upon by the underwriters and assured) advise that the same could be successfully contested by the assured, and the assured consents to such claim being contested, but such consent not to be unreasonably withheld.

12.69 Devlin J explained that this clause contained three promises by insurers. Together, they constituted an unusual clause, but, when broken down and analysed individually, they were familiar promises within the law of insurance. The three promises were: (1) that insurers would pay the costs of legal proceedings;[85] (2) that insurers would pay a claim against the insured without proof of actual loss, if it were more likely than not that there would be a loss, the question of likelihood being determined by the Queen's Counsel; and (3) that insurers would pay a claim without proof of loss, even if it were unlikely that the claim would cause a loss, if the insured reasonably objected to contesting it.[86]

---

[80] *Citibank NA v Excess Insurance Company Ltd* [1999] Lloyd's Rep IR 122, at 134 per Thomas J.
[81] [1957] 1 WLR 45.
[82] Ibid at 49.
[83] Ibid at 53.
[84] [1957] 1 WLR 45.
[85] This was, Devlin J explained, an engagement 'supplementary to the contract of insurance' in the way that a suing and labouring clause is supplementary to a contract of marine insurance (as to which, see *Johnson v Salvage Association* (1887) 19 QBD 458).
[86] [1957] 1 WLR 45, at 50.

The promise to indemnify absent proof of loss

The first promise poses no difficulty. The second promise comes into operation if a **12.70** claim is made and if the Queen's Counsel advises that it is likely to succeed. Devlin J observed that behind the promise to pay without proof of (that is to say, ascertained) loss lies the practical reality that there are circumstances in which the insured does not want to have to wait until he can prove that a loss has actually occurred before being entitled to an indemnity for the same. This is entirely sensible.

The promise to indemnify despite it being more likely than not that
the claim would fail

The third promise requires insurers to pay the claim, whether or not it can be suc- **12.71** cessfully contested, if the insured has reasonable grounds for refusing to contest it. As to this promise, Devlin J remarked as follows:[87]

> This is not, I think, an indemnity insurance at all. The underwriters undertake to pay on the happening of an event, namely, the making of a claim within the categories defined in the policy, even though it may be beyond question a bad claim and therefore one which cannot legally involve the assured in any loss; the assured need prove neither that the loss has occurred nor that there is any likelihood of a loss occurring. It is, in short, what is called contingency insurance.

This gives an extra layer of protection (or veto) to the insured in the event that the Queen's Counsel does advise that the claim might be successfully resisted. If there are good reasons why, despite the fact that the claim's prospect of success are poor, the insured wishes to settle rather than to fight, then insurers are obliged to pay the claim. The reasons would have to be good in the context of the assessment by the Queen's Counsel of the prospects of successfully defending the third party claim.

Examples of QC clauses

The QC clause discussed in the *West Wake* case is not in a form usually found in **12.72** contracts of professional indemnity insurance today. The QC clause in the ICAEW Minimum Approved Policy Wording provides:

> Neither the Insured nor Insurers shall be required to contest any legal proceedings unless a Queen's Counsel or in the Republic of Ireland a Senior Counsel (to be mutually agreed upon by the Insured and Insurers or failing agreement to be appointed by the President of the Institute of Chartered Accountants in England and Wales/of Scotland/in Ireland as applicable) shall advise that, taking due account of the interests of both Insurers and Insured, such proceedings should be contested.

The QC clause in the RICS Policy Wording is to similar effect.

---

[87] Ibid at 51.

12.73   The RIBA Architects Premier Policy Wording has a materially different provision:

> The Insured shall not be required to contest any legal proceedings unless a Queen's Counsel (or by mutual agreement between the Insured and the Insurers a similar authority) shall advise that such proceedings could be contested with the probability of success.

The test under this clause is the prospects of defending the claim by the third party claimant successfully, rather than a balancing exercise between the interests of the insured and insurers as under the ICAEW Minimum Approved Policy Wording and the RICS Policy Wording. The relevant considerations under those Wordings would include, but would not be limited to, the prospects of a successful defence.

12.74   In *Forney v Dominion Insurance Co Ltd*,[88] a case decided in 1969, the QC clause provided:

> the insured shall not be required to contest any legal proceedings unless a Queen's Counsel ... shall advise that on the actual facts of the case concerned such claim could be contested by the insured with a reasonable prospect of success and the insured consents thereto, such consent not to be unreasonably withheld.

Donaldson J described such a wording as 'the usual QC clause' at the time of those proceedings. It included a provision similar to that in the *West Wake* case, allowing the insured to withhold his consent to legal proceedings being contested if there were reasonable grounds for doing so. This wording is rarely, if ever, found today. But QC clauses which require the Queen's Counsel to consider the respective interests of the insured and insurer preserve considerations such as reputational issues, while leaving them to be taken into account by the Queen's Counsel rather than the insured.

When is the clause triggered/invoked?

12.75   In *West Wake Price v Ching*,[89] the QC clause formed part of the insuring clause. In that case, Devlin J considered that the making of a claim was the event which brought the QC clause into operation, requiring insurers to fulfill one or other of the three obligations in the clause.[90]

12.76   However, most QC clauses are not tied to an indemnity clause and therefore the trigger cannot be the making of a claim covered by the terms of the policy. Rather, it will be for the insured to invoke the clause. As insurers usually have ultimate discretion as to how to conduct the defence of the third party claim, they will usually have no need to invoke the clause: they simply take a view on whether to settle or defend. The clause will be triggered as a result of the insured disagreeing with insurers' decision.

---

[88] [1969] 1 WLR 928.
[89] [1957] 1 WLR 45.
[90] Ibid at 51.

13

THIRD PARTY RIGHTS
AGAINST INSURERS

A. Introduction

Contracts of professional indemnity insurance give each party, insurers and **13.01** insured, rights against the other. While a major purpose of statutory and professional requirements to obtain professional indemnity insurance is to ensure that the clients of professionals and others who have claims against them are able to recover any losses caused by any breach of a legal duty owed to them by their professional advisers,[1] third party claimants have no general right to claim directly against insurers. There are, however, three ways in which third parties might do so.

First, insurers may be ordered to pay all or part of a third party's costs where they **13.02** have sought unsuccessfully to defend a claim brought against an insured. Second, if the insured becomes insolvent, whether before or after the claim is made, the third party is the statutory assignee of the insured's right to be indemnified under the Third Parties (Rights Against Insurers) Act 1930. Third, it is in theory possible for a professional indemnity policy expressly to confer a benefit on a category of third party claimants, thereby directly affording the benefit of that insurance to those third parties. Each is considered in turn.

---

[1] See paras 1.05–1.06.

B. Insurers' Personal Liability to a Third Party Claimant in Costs

General principles

13.03 A third party who sues a professional insured may now be able to apply for and obtain a costs award directly against the insured's indemnity insurers. The jurisdiction to make a costs order against a non-party (which a professional indemnity insurer will be in a claim by a third party against a professional insured) is derived from s 51 of the Senior Courts Act 1981, which provides:

> Costs in civil division of Court of Appeal, High Court and county courts.
> (1) Subject to the provisions of this or any other enactment and to rules of court, the costs of and incidental to all proceedings in—
>   (a) the civil division of the Court of Appeal;
>   (b) the High Court; and
>   (c) any county court,
>   shall be in the discretion of the court.

Until the decision of the House of Lords in *Aiden Shipping Co Ltd v Interbulk Ltd*[2] in 1986, it had not been appreciated that this section and its predecessors could be used as a basis upon which a costs order could be made against a non-party.[3] The one exception was the jurisdiction to make a 'wasted costs' order against the solicitors who were acting for a party, but were not themselves a party.

13.04 In deciding whether to make an order for costs against a non-party, the court is exercising its discretion. It does so by applying settled principles to the particular facts of the case. Given the range of civil litigation, the circumstances in which the court has to consider whether to make such an order will be of almost limitless variety. General guidance as to the approach to be adopted was provided by Balcombe LJ in the leading case of *Symphony Group Plc v Hodgson*,[4] where he identified the following factors which should be taken into account:[5]

(1) An order against a non-party will always be exceptional.[6]
(2) Such an order will be even more exceptional if the party seeking the order could have joined the non-party.

---

[2] [1986] AC 965.

[3] Until the decision of the House of Lords in the *Aiden Shipping* case, it had been consistently held that s 51(1) and its predecessors could not be used against a non-party: *Forbes-Smith v Forbes-Smith* [1901] P 258; *John Fairfax & Sons Pty Ltd v E C de Witt & Co (Australia) Pty Ltd* [1958] 1 QB 323, and the *Aiden* case itself in the Court of Appeal, [1985] 1 WLR 1222.

[4] [1994] QB 179. The application in this case was not made against insurers.

[5] Ibid at 192–4.

[6] This should not be seen as a pre-condition or as a requirement set out in s 51 of the Senior Courts Act 1981. It merely reflects the fact that in most ordinary cases there will be no warrant for even considering an order for costs against a non-party: see *Globe Equities Ltd v Globe Legal Services Ltd* [1999] BLR 232 at [21] per Morritt LJ, with whom Butler-Sloss and Sedley LJJ agreed.

(3) If the applicant could have done so, and did not, he should have warned the non-party as soon as possible of the possibility that he might seek a costs order against him.

(4) The application should normally be determined by the trial judge.

(5) The fact that the judge expressed opinions in his judgment does not constitute bias or the appearance of bias.

(6) It is a summary procedure.[7] Findings already made in the proceedings can only be admissible against the non-party if his connection with the proceedings was so close that he will suffer no injustice as a result of admitting them.

(7) The fact that an employee or director of a company gives evidence in an action does not mean that the company is necessarily taking part in the action.[8]

(8) Judges should be alert to applications made because of the applicant's frustration at the inability to recover costs from a legally aided party.

These can be no more than guidelines. They may not be exhaustive in that the facts **13.05** of a particular application may require further factors to be taken into account and, in any particular case, the court has to have regard to the facts before it.[9] However, the proper judicial exercise of discretion requires the court to take into account all relevant factors and then to weigh them appropriately. While there will not always be a single 'right' result, in that different judges could reasonably reach different conclusions, adherence to guidelines enables the parties and their advisers to be able to predict with some degree of certainty what the likely outcome will be and ensures a degree of consistency appropriate to a system of civil justice.

Balcombe LJ's guidelines were not written in stone. They have been and will **13.06** continue to be the subject of elucidation and development in later decisions. Of particular significance in this regard are the decisions of the Court of Appeal in *Murphy v Young & Co's Brewery*[10] and *TGA Chapman Ltd v Christopher*.[11] Both concerned applications for costs against insurers.

---

[7] While the Court can permit cross-examination of witnesses (as was ordered in *Grecoair Inc v Tilling* [2009] EWHC 115 (QB)), an application for costs against a non-party will not be treated like a full trial, with pleadings, disclosure, and cross-examination: applications under s 51 of the Senior Courts Act 1981 'are to be kept within proper bounds, and the court is to do the best justice it can without in every case having the full procedures pre-trial and at the trial' (*Centrehigh Ltd v Amen* [2013] EWHC 625 (Ch); [2013] 4 Costs LO 556, per Morgan J at [42]).

[8] The usual rule of witness immunity from civil liability recognized in decisions such as *Marrinan v Vibart* [1963] 1 QB 234 does not preclude the evidence of a witness who is not a party from being relied upon in support of a later application for an order for costs against him: *Equitas Ltd, Additional Underwriting Agencies (No. 9) Ltd v Horace Holman & Company Ltd* [2008] EWHC 2287 (Comm); [2009] 1 BCLC 66 at [82]–[84] per Andrew Smith J (see also *Deutsche Bank AG v Sebastian Holdings Inc* [2014] EWHC 2073 (Comm); [2014] 4 Costs LR 711, at [32] per Cooke J).

[9] As Laws LJ said in *Petromec Inc v Petroleo Brasileiro SA Petrobras* [2006] EWCA Civ 1038; [2007] 2 Costs LR 212 at [19]: 'Section 51 [of the Senior Courts Act 1981] confers a discretion not confined by specific limitations. While the learning is, with respect, important in indicating the kind of considerations upon which the court will focus, it must not be treated as a rule-book.'

[10] [1997] 1 WLR 1591.

[11] [1998] 1 WLR 12.

13.07   The insurers in *Murphy v Young & Co's Brewery*[12] were legal expenses insurers. Their insured had required them to fund an unsuccessful claim for unfair dismissal. Cover was limited to £25,000. The insurers had no interest in the outcome of the claim save insofar as it affected their liability to pay costs. The insurers did not initiate the litigation: they were contractually bound to support it. Moreover, counsel had advised the insured that their case was a strong one. The insurers exercised no control over the litigation, nor had they intermeddled wantonly and officiously. It followed that there were no exceptional circumstances to justify the making of an order for costs against a non-party.

13.08   Phillips LJ, with whom the other members of the Court of Appeal agreed, took the opportunity to summarize the effect of decisions since *Symphony Group Plc v Hodgson*[13] and, in the light of those decisions, to propound some further principles relevant to the exercise of the discretion under s 51(1) of the Senior Courts Act 1981:[14]

(1) Where a non-party has intermeddled wantonly and officiously in a dispute concerning others and an application for costs is made against him, the Court is likely to be receptive to such an application.
(2) Where a non-party has supported an unsuccessful party on terms that place the non-party under a clear contractual obligation to indemnify the unsuccessful party against his liability to pay the costs of the successful party, it may well be appropriate to make an order under s 51 that the non-party pay those costs directly to the successful party. Such an order may, for instance, save time and costs in short-circuiting the Third Parties (Rights against Insurers) Act 1930.
(3) Where a party has been funded by his trade union, that will be relevant to a decision whether to make an order against the union. To this must be added the facts that the union is likely to have been under an implied obligation to do so, to have had an interest in the litigation, to have had the conduct of the litigation, and to be subject to an expectation based upon convention that it will bear the costs of the successful party should its member lose. These factors will all tend to make it likely that it will be appropriate to make an order for costs against the trade union.[15]

---

12 [1997] 1 WLR 1591.
13 [1994] QB 179.
14 [1997] 1 WLR 1591, at 1601–2.
15 Cf *Hill v Archbold* [1968] 1 QB 686, where the issue was whether a trade union had power to pay the costs incurred by its general secretary and another official in an unsuccessful libel action. Holding that this was not illegal maintenance, Lord Denning MR, with whom Danckwerts and Winn LJJ agreed, said at 695: 'Comparatively few litigants bring suits, or defend them, at their own expense. Most claims by workmen against their employers are paid for by a trade union. Most defences of motorists are paid for by insurance companies. This is perfectly justifiable and is accepted by everyone as lawful, provided always that the one who supports the litigation, if it fails, pays the costs of the other side. It is the universal experience in this court that if a trade union or an insurance company supports a case and fails, it pays the costs of the other side.'

(4) Where an unsuccessful defendant's costs are funded by insurers who have provided cover against liability, which is not subject to any relevant limit, the same considerations set out under (3) are likely to apply.

(5) The position is more complex where a defendant's costs have been funded by insurers at risk under a policy under which their liability is limited to a sum which is insufficient to cover both liability and costs.

As to the last point, Phillips LJ said that he was:[16]   **13.09**

> not persuaded that it will always be appropriate to order liability insurers to pay the plaintiffs' costs where they have unsuccessfully defended a claim made against their insured if the result of such an order will be to render them liable beyond their contractual limit of cover. It seems to me that the appropriate order may well turn on the facts of the particular case.[17]

The position of underinsurance was considered in *TGA Chapman Ltd v Christopher.*[18]   **13.10** In that case, the defendant insured had negligently burnt down the plaintiffs' warehouse. The plaintiffs sued, claiming over £1 million. The insured had no assets, but had liability insurance with a limit of £1 million for one loss, inclusive of claimants' costs. The plaintiffs obtained judgment for over £1 million. The main defence, contributory negligence, failed completely. The plaintiffs settled for £1 million but sought costs against liability insurers. The policy had given insurers the right to 'take over and conduct in the name of the policyholder or insured with complete and exclusive control the defence or settlement of any claim' and 'to start legal action in the name of the policyholder or insured (but at its expense and for its own benefit) to recover from others compensation in respect of anything covered by the policy'.

Phillips LJ, with whom the other members of the Court of Appeal agreed, said that   **13.11** the basis upon which the plaintiffs sought a costs order against insurers was that, in reality, it was insurers rather than the insured who were the defendants. He identified the following relevant features:

(1) insurers determined that the claim would be fought;
(2) insurers funded the defence of the action;
(3) insurers had the conduct of the litigation;
(4) insurers fought the claim exclusively in their own interests (where the insured was without means); and
(5) the defence failed in its entirety.[19]

While Balcombe LJ had indicated in *Symphony Group Plc v Hodgson*[20] that an order against a non-party will always be exceptional and, in the context of liability

---

[16] [1997] 1 WLR 1591, at 1602.
[17] Cf the decision of the same Court of Appeal at the same time in *Tharros Shipping Co Ltd v Bias Shipping Ltd (No 3)* [1997] 1 Lloyd's Rep 246.
[18] [1998] 1 WLR 12.
[19] Ibid at 20.
[20] [1994] QB 179.

insurance and litigation, there was nothing extraordinary in the features he had identified, Phillips LJ explained they were exceptional in the context of civil litigation as a whole, and it was against that range that they had to be considered.[21] And in *Dymocks Franchise Systems (NSW) Pty Ltd v Todd & Others, Associated Industrial Finance Pty. Ltd (Third Party)*[22] Lord Simon Brown, giving the opinion of the Privy Council, explained that in this context 'exceptional' means outside the ordinary run of cases where it is the parties to an action who pursue or defend claims for their own benefit and at their own expense.

13.12 Insurers countered that their interest in the litigation arose from the existence of an insurance policy without which the third party claimant would have recovered nothing. Their liability under that policy was limited and they had acted in good faith and reasonably in defending the claim. The Court of Appeal accepted that these features were also present, but held that insurers should nevertheless be ordered to pay the third party claimant's costs, finding it was a 'paradigm case' for such an order.[23]

Applications against liability insurers

13.13 The decision of the Court of Appeal in *TGA Chapman Ltd v Christopher*[24] shows how liability insurers who conduct the defence of a claim against their insured reasonably and in good faith may be ordered to pay the third party claimant's costs when that defence fails entirely, not least when the defence was conducted solely for the benefit of insurers. The crucial features identified in that case will be found in some claims in respect of which the defendant has the benefit of professional indemnity insurance. Where they are present, an order for costs will usually be made.[25] As HH Judge Jack QC said in *Pendennis Shipyard Ltd v Magrathea (Pendennis) Ltd*:[26]

> the decisive factor here is that [insurers] took over the defence of the action and conducted it themselves for their own benefit. If an insurer does that, the insurer may ordinarily expect to pay the costs of the plaintiff if the defence is unsuccessful.

However, while some cases will be clear cut, it is far from inevitable that professional indemnity insurers will be subject to an order that they pay the third party's costs directly if the defence to the third party's claim fails.

---

[21] [1998] 1 WLR 12, at 20. See also *Citibank NA v Excess Insurance Company Ltd* [1999] Lloyd's Rep IR 122, at 131, where Thomas J added the observation that much liability insurance was unlimited (eg, motor insurance and employers' liability) and that in practice it is only where there is liability insurance with a financial limit (as in the case of professional indemnity insurance) that applications under s 51 of the Senior Courts Act 1981 are likely to be made against insurers.

[22] [2004] UKPC 39; [2004] 1 WLR 2807.

[23] [1998] 1 WLR 12, at 22.

[24] [1998] 1 WLR 12: see paras 13.10–13.12.

[25] See, for example, *Plymouth & South West Co-Operative Society Ltd v Architecture, Structure & Management Ltd* [2006] EWHC 3252 (TCC); [2007] Lloyd's Rep IR 596, where HH Judge Thornton QC was clear that it was appropriate to make an order against insurers.

[26] [1998] 1 Lloyd's Rep 315, at 320. The insurers were a P&I Club.

While it would be wrong to elevate them into rigid rules,[27] it is helpful to consider **13.14** the various features identified by Phillips LJ in *TGA Chapman Ltd v Christopher*[28] in turn, to explore how and when professional indemnity insurers are likely to be subject to an order under s 51(1) of the Senior Courts Act 1981. In *Citibank NA v Excess Insurance Company Ltd*,[29] Thomas J said of the five features identified by Phillips LJ:

> The reason why those features are determinative is because, if they are established, it is clear that the costs in defending the litigation were incurred in consequence of the conduct of the insurers and for the insurers' real benefit. In other words, the real defendants were the insurers and, where they defended to protect their own interests, they should be responsible for costs if they failed …
>
> The decision in *Chapman* has laid down clear principles that a court can apply. If the circumstances are such that the application for a costs order falls within those principles, then it should follow that there should be a costs order under section 51; if they do not, they should not.

Decision to fight the claim

Professional indemnity policies will usually give insurers the right to take over **13.15** the defence of a claim in respect of which, if successful, they would be obliged to indemnify the insured. Such clauses may give insurers the right to control the litigation, albeit subject to an implied obligation to act reasonably in the interests of both themselves and the insured.[30] Some professional indemnity policies contain 'QC clauses' under which neither insurers nor insured can be required to contest a claim by a third party unless a Queen's Counsel advises that it should be, taking account of the interests of both parties.[31] Insurers will not have an entirely unfettered right to require that a claim be contested, but it will usually be their decision.

In many cases, the insured take a keen interest in the conduct of the defence of the **13.16** claim against them and, in particular, in a decision to fight a claim. Settlement will often involve the payment of the excess or deductible by the insured[32] and will usually have implications for the level of premium payable in future. There may also be issues of professional reputation at stake. Finally, the insured may be adamant that he was not at fault.

For example, in *Citibank NA v Excess Insurance Company Ltd*[33] the insured **13.17** expressed the clear view at the outset that he considered there was a full defence to the claim. Had insurers insisted on settling at that stage, the insured would have

---

[27] See para 13.05.
[28] [1998] 1 WLR 12. The features are set out in para 13.11.
[29] [1999] Lloyd's Rep IR 122, at 131.
[30] *Groom v Crocker* [1939] 1 KB 194. See further, paras 12.52–12.55.
[31] See paras 12.68–12.76.
[32] See paras 12.50–12.51.
[33] [1999] Lloyd's Rep IR 122.

objected. The insured had an interest in preserving his reputation at this stage. Thomas J concluded that, while the primary decision to defend was taken by insurers, the insured would not have been content for insurers to settle the claim for any significant amount at that stage.

Funding the defence of the claim

13.18 It will almost inevitably be the case that insurers have funded the defence of the claim.

Conduct of the defence

13.19 There are two essentially separate aspects to the conduct of the defence to a claim by a third party. The first is the obtaining of information and documents so that a defence can be put forward, the obtaining of further documents for the purposes of disclosure, the making of witness statements, and so on. The insured will usually be involved in this aspect of the defence to a greater extent than insurers. The second aspect involves seeking and considering advice and taking decisions as to whether to continue to defend, make an offer, and similar strategic and tactical matters. It is the second aspect which is of particular relevance to an application for costs.[34]

13.20 So, while the insured may attend conferences with counsel at which counsel advises on the merits, if any decisions as to the conduct of the defence in the light of that advice are taken by insurers, they will be held to have the conduct of the defence, notwithstanding the presence of the insured.[35]

13.21 In the same way, in *Monkton Court Ltd v Perry Prowse (Insurance Services) Ltd*[36] it was insurers who had the general conduct of the litigation in terms of decision-making. Although the insured was party to decisions to make a payment into Court of its excess and to a decision not to contest liability, insurers had the conduct of the litigation with the 'predominant' or 'almost exclusive' aim of defending their own interests.[37]

Defence solely in insurers' interests?

13.22 The fact that the defence is conducted solely in insurers' interests will often prove critical, not least because insurers will almost inevitably have funded the defence and it will have failed.[38] However, it may be sufficient, together with other features,

---

[34] *Citibank NA v Excess Insurance Company Ltd* [1999] Lloyd's Rep IR 122, at 133, followed in *Monkton Court Ltd v Perry Prowse (Insurance Services) Ltd* [2002] Lloyd's Rep IR 408, at 410. See also *Plymouth & South West Co-Operative Society Ltd v Architecture, Structure & Management Ltd* [2006] EWHC 3252 (TCC); [2007] Lloyd's Rep IR 596, at [24].

[35] *Citibank NA v Excess Insurance Company Ltd* [1999] Lloyd's Rep IR 122, at 133.

[36] [2002] Lloyd's Rep IR 408.

[37] Ibid at 411.

[38] *Cormack and Cormack v Excess Insurance Ltd* [2002] Lloyd's Rep IR 398, at 406 per Auld LJ.

if the defence was conducted predominantly in insurers' interests.[39] In this context, it is necessary to have regard:[40]

> to the reasonableness and good faith of the insurer in its involvement of the insured and its responsiveness to his interests and concerns. Contrary to [counsel for the third party claimant's] submission, the latter are not irrelevant matters, since they go to the question whether the insurer, when its insured was approaching or at risk of exceeding the limit of his indemnity cover, behaved solely in its own interest as if it were the Defendant.

So, where an insured with a continuing interest in the defence was kept informed **13.23** of the offers being made and of insurers' decision to offer no more and was content to fight to trial, despite the risk of underinsurance, insurers had not been conducting the defence exclusively or so predominantly in their own interests so as to justify an order for costs against them.[41]

In the same way, in *Gloucestershire Health Authority v M A Torphy and Partners Ltd* **13.24** *(t/a Torphy and Partners)*[42] insurers appointed solicitors to conduct the defence, but those solicitors recognized that they owed a duty to the insured as well as to insurers. There was nothing to suggest that the solicitors or insurers had acted in any way improperly or without proper regard to the interests of the insured. The insured had co-operated fully in the defence of the claim. They had been properly warned of their potential uninsured liability and to take their own advice. Declining to make an order for costs against insurers, HH Judge Bowsher QC said:[43]

> The insurers plainly have their own interests to protect but I do accept the evidence which has been given on behalf of the insurers that quite apart from any philanthropy on their part, they would simply go out of business if they did not act fairly and reasonably towards their clients in dealing with claims against the insured. It seems to me that that is what they have done.

It is relevant that an insured who is maintaining an interest in the defence of a **13.25** claim does not seek to invoke any QC clause or to urge insurers to make an offer to settle the claim.[44] On the other hand, if the insured has been wound up or ceased trading, then it is hard to see what interest it could have in defending the action.[45]

---

[39] In *Monkton Court Ltd v Perry Prowse (Insurance Services) Ltd* [2002] Lloyd's Rep IR 408, at 411, it was held to be sufficient that the defence was being conducted 'almost exclusively' in the interests of insurers.

[40] [2002] Lloyd's Rep IR 398, at 406.

[41] Ibid at 405–6.

[42] [1999] Lloyd's Rep IR 203.

[43] Ibid at 206.

[44] *Gloucestershire Health Authority v M A Torphy and Partners Ltd (t/a Torphy and Partners)* [1999] Lloyd's Rep IR 203, at 207.

[45] *Monkton Court Ltd v Perry Prowse (Insurance Services) Ltd* [2002] Lloyd's Rep IR 408 (insured wound up) and *Plymouth & South West Co-Operative Society Ltd v Architecture, Structure & Management Ltd* [2006] EWHC 3252 (TCC); [2007] Lloyd's Rep IR 596 (insured had ceased trading). The same applies where an insured would be underinsured and insolvent if found liable and the third party makes an offer to settle within the limit of cover. In such circumstances the insured

13.26 Even if the prospects of underinsurance appear slight, the insured may well still have an interest in the outcome of the litigation. Apart from any excess or deductible and the implications for the level of premium payable in future years, the insured may have his professional reputation to protect. So, where the insured maintains that he is not liable, the protection of his professional reputation may be a material part of the reason for the continued defence of the action, at least until any adverse judgment on liability.[46] On the other hand, where there is little or no prospect of avoiding a finding that the insured was negligent, arguments that the defence was maintained in order to protect the insured's professional reputation will rarely succeed, not least in the absence of evidence that the insured was himself concerned to do so.[47]

Failure of the defence

13.27 Unless the defence has failed, there will usually be no question of any order for costs against the professional indemnity insurers of the defendant. In *TGA Chapman Ltd v Christopher*,[48] the defence had failed 'in its entirety'. Some defences do. But others fail in part, for example, losing on liability and causation, but reducing the amount of damages claimed either by successfully challenging the evidential or legal basis on which they are claimed, or through a reduction for contributory negligence. It might be thought that in such circumstances the defence had not failed entirely.

13.28 However, if the result is still an award in excess of the limit of the insured's cover and resources, the success on quantum will have served no practical purpose save to increase the costs of the trial. So, in *Plymouth & South West Co-Operative Society Ltd v Architecture, Structure & Management Ltd*[49] the defence succeeded in reducing damages by about one-third at trial. This did not preclude a finding that the defence had failed in its entirety, because the third party had won the argument as to the basis of assessment of damages, but had been unable to prove its precise loss because of a failure by the insured to maintain proper records at the time.[50]

Delay in deciding to withdraw cover

13.29 Coverage issues can and do arise between insurers and insured, not least when third party claims are made against the insured. Resolution of those issues can occur during the course of litigation between the third party claimant and the insured, with insurers meeting the costs of defending those proceedings either subject to a

---

has no commercial interest in rejecting the offer in the hope of obtaining a more favourable result and insurers who reject the offer will be at risk of a finding that they were conducting the litigation exclusively or at least predominantly in their own interests: *Palmer v Palmer* [2008] EWCA Civ 46; [2008] Lloyd's Rep IR 535.

[46] *Citibank NA v Excess Insurance Company Ltd* [1999] Lloyd's Rep IR 122, at 134.
[47] *Monkton Court Ltd v Perry Prowse (Insurance Services) Ltd* [2002] Lloyd's Rep IR 408, at 411.
[48] [1998] 1 WLR 12.
[49] [2006] EWHC 3252 (TCC); [2007] Lloyd's Rep IR 596.
[50] Ibid at [32].

reservation of rights or to a contractual obligation to maintain funding pending resolution of the issue.[51] If coverage issues are resolved against the insured, then the third party will find himself suing someone who is uninsured and, in many cases, not able to satisfy any judgment. He may consider an application against insurers under s 51 of the Senior Courts Act 1981.

An application in those circumstances was made in *Bristol & West Building Society* **13.30** *v Bhadresa*.[52] The insured defendant was a solicitor whose professional indemnity cover was provided by the Solicitors' Indemnity Fund Ltd ('SIF'). Under the Solicitors' Indemnity Rules, SIF was required to fund the defence to a claim unless and until it had determined that the solicitor had acted dishonestly, when it was obliged not to fund his defence. A number of claims had been brought by the same third party claimant against two solicitors. SIF had funded and controlled the defence of those claims for nearly two years before determining that both solicitors had been dishonest and withdrawing cover. In the case of one solicitor, this was only a few weeks before trial. Substantial judgments were obtained against both solicitors. One was only able to pay a fraction of the sum and the other did not have the means to satisfy the judgment against him.

The third party claimant applied for an order that SIF should pay the costs of **13.31** the claims against both solicitors for the periods during which it had funded the defence of those claims. It argued that it had only brought the claims on the basis that the solicitors would be entitled to an indemnity from SIF. It alleged that SIF had represented that this would be the case by appointing and continuing to instruct solicitors from its panel to conduct the defence. This argument failed on the facts: it was clear that the third party claimant was well aware of the possibility that the solicitors were dishonest, of SIF's duty to consider this, and of the consequences if SIF determined that the solicitors had been dishonest.[53]

Having rejected that argument, Lightman J turned to the exercise of discretion **13.32** under s 51(1) of the Senior Courts Act 1981. He declined to make an order against SIF for a number of reasons. He explained that he did not consider that:[54]

> (at any rate in any ordinary case such as the present) delay by a party's insurer in its decision-making whether it is entitled or bound to refuse cover is an exceptional circumstance that can justify an order under section 51. The timeliness of the decision-making processes by [SIF] as to whether the Solicitors were dishonest is not a matter in respect of which [the third party claimant] has any legitimate interest or right of inquiry. [SIF] at all times owed duties to act responsibly and fairly towards the Solicitors as solicitors insured under the Scheme: it owed no (potentially conflicting) duty of care or of expedition to [the third party claimant] as the plaintiff in actions against the insured.

---

[51] See paras 12.07–12.15.
[52] [1999] Lloyd's Rep IR 138.
[53] Ibid at 144.
[54] Ibid at 145.

Lightman J was also concerned that determination as to whether SIF was guilty of culpable delay would require SIF to waive privilege. It would not be right to require a respondent to an application to waive privilege.[55]

13.33 While Lightman J's decision was influenced by the fact that SIF was established under s 37 of the Solicitors' Act 1974 and so was part of a statutory scheme to provide indemnity to solicitors and, through them, their clients, his reasoning applies to professional indemnity insurance more widely, not least because such insurance fulfils the same purpose as the scheme of which SIF was a part.[56] While SIF had an obligation under the Solicitors Indemnity Rules to act responsibly towards solicitors when seeking to determine whether they were guilty of dishonesty, professional indemnity insurers have to approach similar issues in the context of the overriding obligation of utmost good faith.[57]

The extent of an award of costs

13.34 The court can make an order that insurers pay the costs of a third party claimant for the whole action or for part of it. For example, in *Citibank NA v Excess Insurance Company Ltd*,[58] having decided that the conduct of the defence until a finding of liability against the insured had been in the joint interests of insurers and the insured, but that thereafter it was solely in the interests of insurers, Thomas J ordered insurers to pay the costs of the third party claimant after the judgment on liability.

13.35 The causative effect of insurers' conduct will also be relevant. So, in *Cormack and Cormack v Excess Insurance Ltd*[59] it was held that it was necessary to show that insurers' conduct had caused the third party claimant to incur additional costs. In cases where the claim would not have been contested, this will be fairly straightforward.

13.36 Causation was shown in *Pendennis Shipyard Ltd v Magrathea (Pendennis) Ltd*,[60] where HH Judge Jack QC made an order that a P&I club should pay the entire costs of the claim by the third party. The P&I Club argued that some of the early costs would have been incurred whether it had supported the defence or not. It was held that there was no reason to distinguish between the costs which the insured would have had to pay and those which its insurers, the P&I Club, should pay. Those costs were likely to have been substantially less, even at the early stages, had the P&I Club not taken over the defence. At a later stage, the P&I Club had withdrawn its instructions from the solicitors who had conduct of the defence. It argued

---

[55] Ibid. On waiver of privilege, see paras 13.37–13.38.
[56] See paras 1.05–1.06.
[57] See paras 12.52–12.55.
[58] [1999] Lloyd's Rep IR 122.
[59] [2002] Lloyd's Rep IR 398, at 406–7, approving a dictum of Lightman J in *Bristol & West Building Society v Bhadresa* [1999] Lloyd's Rep IR 138 at 146. See also *Gloucestershire Health Authority v M A Torphy and Partners Ltd (t/a Torphy and Partners)* [1999] Lloyd's Rep IR 203, at 207.
[60] [1998] 1 Lloyd's Rep 315.

that it should not have to pay the costs after that point. Again, the argument was rejected: the third party still had to deal with the issues raised in the defence which had been served on the instructions of the P&I Club.

Privilege

As indicated by the review of the cases above, in deciding whether to make an order **13.37** for costs against insurers, the courts have had occasion to consider the conduct of the defence and the respective roles of the insured and insurers, often in some detail. Such matters are subject to litigation privilege and insurers might complain that, if they are to resist an application against them for costs, they would be forced to waive privilege.[61] In the context of applications for wasted costs against lawyers, problems can and do arise where the lawyers are unable to put material before the court because their clients or former clients have not waived privilege.[62]

The position is different in applications for costs against insurers, because insurers **13.38** will, at least with the agreement of the insured, be able to waive privilege themselves if they wish to put material before the court. It is, however, not possible to compel insurers and the insured to waive privilege. The cases show a range of approaches from full disclosure to none. In general, if privileged material will assist insurers, for example by showing that the defence of the claim was conducted in the joint interests of themselves and the insured, they may be well advised to waive privilege and deploy that material.

C. Third Parties (Rights Against Insurers Act) 1930

The statutory assignment

The problem

The purpose of the Third Parties (Rights Against Insurers) Act 1930 is to ensure **13.39** that, where an insured is bankrupt or insolvent, a third party claimant will be able to recover directly from insurers the money which the insured would have been entitled to receive in respect of the insured's liability to the third party. Before the passing of the Act, the money from insurers would form part of the assets of the bankrupt individual or insolvent company and be distributed among creditors according to the applicable rules and priorities. The third party claimant would not be a secured creditor or have any proprietary right to or interest in the insurance money. The result would be some benefit to other creditors (who would receive a

---

[61] See *The Owners and/or Demise Charterers of the Dredger 'Kamal XXVI' and the Barge 'Makal XXIV' v The Owners of the Ship 'Ariela'* [2010] EWHC 2531 (Comm); [2011] 1 Lloyd's Rep 291, where it was held that the making of a fraudulent claim by the insured had the effect that the fraud exception applied to communications between non-fraudulent insurers and solicitors instructed by them to defeat claims for legal advice and litigation privilege.
[62] See, for example, *Medcalf v Mardell* [2002] UKHL 27; [2003] 1 AC 120.

share of the insurance money, or, potentially, if secured, the entire amount), but injustice to the third party claimant.[63]

The solution

13.40 Faced with this injustice, Parliament enacted the Third Parties (Rights Against Insurers) Act 1930.[64] The solution adopted is a statutory assignment to the third party claimant of the insured's rights under the policy. Section 1(1) of the Act provides:

> Where under any contract of insurance a person (hereinafter referred to as the insured) is insured against liabilities to third parties which he may incur, then—
> (a) in the event of the insured becoming bankrupt or making a composition or arrangement with his creditors; or
> (b) in the event of the insured being a company, in the event of a winding up order being made, or a resolution for a voluntary winding-up being passed, with respect to the company or of the company entering administration or of a receiver or manager of the company's business or undertaking being duly appointed, or of possession being taken, or any property comprised in or subject to the charge or of a voluntary arrangement proposed for the purposes of Part I of the Insolvency Act 1986 being approved under that Part;
> if, either before or after that event, any such liability as aforesaid is incurred by the insured, his rights against the insurer under the contract in respect of the liability shall, notwithstanding anything in any Act or rule of law to the contrary, be transferred to and vest in the third party to whom the liability was so incurred.[65]

No contracting out

13.41 Section 1(3) of the Act provides that any provision in a contract of insurance falling within s 1(1), which purports to alter the rights of the parties to the contract if one or more of the events set out in (a) or (b) occurs, will be of no effect. This is the case whether the terms purports to do so directly or indirectly. This provision will not strike down a term requiring the insured to have paid the third party before being entitled to recover from insurers.[66] Such terms are rarely found in professional indemnity policies, although excess layer policies may require the primary

---

[63] The decisions which led to the passing of the Act were *Harrington Motor Co. Ltd, Ex parte Chaplin* [1928] 1 Ch 105 and *Hood's Trustees v Southern Union General Insurance Co of Australasia Ltd* [1928] 1 Ch 793. The background to and purposes of the Act are explained in *Post Office v Norwich Union Fire Insurance Limited* [1967] 2 QB 363, at 373, *Bradley v Eagle Star Insurance Co Ltd* [1989] 1 AC 957, at 967–8, and *Cox v Bankside Members Agency Ltd* [1995] 2 Lloyd's Rep 437, at 457.

[64] The Law Commission produced proposals for reform of the Act: Law Com No 272, Cm 5217, July 2001. This led to the passing of the Third Parties (Rights Against Insurers) Act 2010 discussed in paras 13.59–13.76.

[65] 'The legislative intention was, I think, that ... the provisions of the 1930 Act should apply upon an insured losing the effective power to enforce its own rights and dispose of its own assets.' (*The Fanti and The Padre Island* [1989] 1 Lloyd's Rep 239, at 247 per Bingham LJ, approved by Lord Goff at [1991] 2 AC 1, at 38.)

[66] *Firma C-Trade SA v Newcastle Protection and Indemnity Association ('The Fanti')* [1991] 2 AC 1.

and other lower layer insurers to have either paid or admitted liability to pay in full before liability attaches under them. Such a condition would not itself require actual payment in full, as long as the primary or lower layer admitted liability in full.[67]

Scope of s 1(1)

Section 1(1) applies to liability insurance and so to professional indemnity insur- **13.42** ance.[68] The words 'liabilities to third parties which he may incur' are 'perfectly general' and are not limited to liabilities in tort or to liabilities in tort and contractual liabilities akin to liabilities in tort.[69] The Act, including s 1(1), applies to limited liability partnerships as it does to companies.[70]

Conditions to be satisfied

Two conditions must be met in order for the statutory assignment to take place. **13.43** The first is that the insured's liability to the third party is 'incurred'. The liability is that against which he is insured. That is a different liability from the liability of insurers to indemnify the insured, which liability only arises when the insured's liability to the third party is ascertained.[71] On the ordinary meaning of the language in s 1(1), the insured's liability to the third party is incurred when the third party has a cause of action which he can bring against the insured. The second condition is that one of the events set out in (a) and (b) must occur. Once both conditions are satisfied, the statutory assignment will take effect.[72] While, as explained below,[73] it will still be necessary for the insured's liability to the third party to have been ascertained before the third party will be able to recover from insurers, the third party may have rights and obligations as statutory assignee before such ascertainment. For example, he may be able to sue for a declaration that insurers are not

---

[67] Cf the excess policies considered in *Cox v Deeny* [1996] LR LR 288 and *Friends Provident Life and Pensions Ltd v Sirius International Insurance Corporation* [2004] EWHC 1799 (Comm); [2005] Lloyd's Rep IR 135; [2005] EWCA Civ 601; [2005] 2 Lloyd's Rep 517, which required the underlying insurers to have paid or admitted liability to pay or have been held liable to pay in full.

[68] There is some debate as to whether s 1(1) applies to insurance such as legal expenses insurance and health insurance: see *Tarbuck v Avon Insurance Plc* [2002] QB 571, followed in *T&N Ltd (In Administration) v Royal & Sun Alliance Plc* [2003] EWHC 1016 (Ch); [2004] Lloyd's Rep IR 106, but doubted in *Re OT Computers Ltd (In Administration)* [2004] EWCA Civ 653; [2004] Ch 317. For the position under the Third Parties (Rights Against Insurers) Act 1930 see para 13.60.

[69] *Re OT Computers Ltd (In Administration)* [2004] EWCA Civ 653; [2004] Ch 317, at [14]–[23] per Longmore LJ, with whom the other members of the Court of Appeal agreed.

[70] Section 3A of the Third Parties (Rights Against Insurers) Act 1930.

[71] For ascertainment between the insured and insurers, see paras 9.106–9.132.

[72] *Re OT Computers Ltd (In Administration)* [2004] EWCA Civ 653; [2004] Ch 317. The third party's right may be 'contingent and inchoate' until the existence and amount of the insured's liability to the third party is established: ibid at [28] per Longmore LJ. See also *Cox v Bankside Members Agency Ltd* [1995] 2 Lloyd's Rep 437, at 443 per Phillips J, and at 467 per Saville LJ; *Centre Reinsurance International Co v Freakley* [2005] EWCA Civ 115; [2005] Lloyd's Rep IR 303; and *Financial Services Compensation Scheme Ltd v Larnell* [2005] EWCA Civ 1408; [2006] QB 808.

[73] See paras 13.48–13.49.

entitled to deny cover[74] or be obliged to comply with policy terms as giving notice of service of proceedings upon the insured.[75] He will also have a statutory right to obtain information about the insured's insurance cover.[76]

Third party claimant's position before the statutory assignment

13.44   Until the statutory assignment has taken effect, the third party has no legal interest in or legally enforceable rights in respect of the contract of insurance between insurers and the insured. So, while s 3 of the Act provides that, once the insured is subject to one of the matters set out in s 1(1)(a) or (b), no agreement or other transaction between insurers and the insured will be effective so as to defeat or affect the rights transferred to the third party under the Act;[77] the third party cannot prevent an insured and his insurers from entering an agreement which compromises the insured's rights if that insured is not yet subject to one of those matters.

13.45   So, in *Normid Housing Association Ltd v Ralphs and Assicurazioni Generali SpA*[78] the third party was suing the insured architect for damages in respect of damage to a large number of properties which allegedly had damp or defective roofs. The total claimed was £57 million. As between the insured and his insurers, there were issues as to whether the third party's claims should be treated as a single claim (in which case the limit of indemnity would be £250,000) or as a number of separate claims for each property. Insurers offered to settle their potential liability to the insured for £250,000 and the insured was minded to accept the offer. The third party sought an injunction to restrain him from doing so. It succeeded at first instance, but the Court of Appeal set the order aside.

13.46   Giving the judgment of the Court of Appeal, Slade LJ said:[79]

> Prima facie, if, before the commencement of the bankruptcy or winding up, the insured accepts a sum from insurers in full satisfaction of all his claims under the policy, the provisions of the Act can be of no avail to the third party because, by the time when the bankruptcy or winding up supervenes, the insured will no longer be left with any existing rights which are capable of being the subject of the statutory transfer provided by section 1. Correspondingly, the statutory rights of the third party will never arise.

Insofar as the third party's claim was based upon an allegation that the proposed agreement would deprive it of its rights under the Act, the third party did not yet

---

[74]   *Post Office v Norwich Union Fire Insurance Society Ltd* [1967] 2 QB 363, at 374 per Lord Denning MR.

[75]   As in *Farrell v Federated Employers Insurance Association Ltd* [1970] 1 WLR 1400: see further paras 13.52–13.53.

[76]   See para 13.55.

[77]   See para 13.58.

[78]   [1989] 1 Lloyd's Rep 265.

[79]   Ibid at 270.

have any such rights.[80] There was therefore no basis for preventing the insured from accepting insurers' offer.[81]

In the *Normid* case, there was no allegation that the insured and insurers were **13.47** acting in bad faith or collusively with the intention of damaging the third party's interests. Nor was it alleged that the insured was under any contractual or professional obligation to obtain professional indemnity insurance (although it is often a term of the engagement of architects and other construction professionals that they provide evidence of professional indemnity insurance to a stated level). In *Cox v Bankside Members Agency Ltd*,[82] Sir Thomas Bingham MR said he would be willing to accept that if a third party claimant was able to show that an insured was proposing to surrender or repudiate his professional indemnity cover to which he was prima facie entitled and to show that he was liable to suffer loss as a result, then it might well be open to the court to restrain the insured by injunction from doing so.

Principles governing the operation of the 1930 Act

Insured's liability to the third party must be ascertained

In order to recover against insurers, the third party must have established that **13.48** the insured is liable to him and the amount of that liability. This must be done by judgment, arbitration award, or settlement.[83] An insured who proceeds directly against insurers without having done so will not recover from them. In *Post Office v Norwich Union Fire Insurance Society Ltd*, Lord Denning MR said:[84]

> It seems to me that the insured only acquires a right to sue for the money when his liability to the injured person has been established so as to give rise to a right of indemnity. His liability to the injured person must be ascertained and determined to exist, either by judgment of the claim or by an award in arbitration or by agreement. Until that is done, the right to an indemnity does not arise.

In the *Post Office* case, the third party had brought proceedings directly against insurers, without having established the fact and amount of the insured's liability

---

[80] Ibid at 272.

[81] The Court of Appeal raised the possibility of obtaining a freezing order to restrain the insured from disposing of his assets, without saying anything about the merits of such an application. The third party applied for a freezing order, but this too was set aside by the Court of Appeal, because what was sought to be restrained was entry into a normal business transaction: *Normid Housing Association Ltd v Ralphs & Mansell and Assicurazioni Generali SpA (No 2)* [1989] 1 Lloyd's Rep 274.

[82] [1995] 2 Lloyd's Rep 437, at 458.

[83] Admission of a claim in bankruptcy will suffice: *Law Society v Shah* [2007] EWHC 2841 (Ch); [2009] Ch 223. See also *Financial Services Compensation Scheme Ltd v Larnell* [2005] EWCA Civ 1408; [2006] QB 808.

[84] [1967] 2 QB 363, at 373–4. See also Harman LJ at 376 and Salmon LJ at 378.

and the claim against insurers failed. The reasoning of Lord Denning MR and of Salmon LJ in that case was approved by Lord Brandon in *Bradley v Eagle Star Insurance Co Ltd* as being 'unassailably correct'.[85]

13.49 The correct procedure is to bring proceedings against the insured. Where leave of the court is needed to bring proceedings, that should be given automatically.[86]

Third party in no better position than the insured

13.50 The requirement of ascertainment is part of a wider principle: as against insurers, the third party is not to be in any better position than the insured. Given that the insured would only have a right to an indemnity once his liability to the third party was ascertained, the third party must also have that liability ascertained if he is to claim against insurers as statutory assignee of the insured's rights.

13.51 So, if insurers have the right to avoid the policy or to accept a repudiatory breach committed by the insured, the third party claimant will not recover.[87] In the same way, where the policy provides that it is a condition precedent to insurers' liability that the insured will not admit liability and the insured breaches that term, insurers will be able to rely upon that breach as against the third party claimant.[88] To the extent that cover is subject to a deductible or excess to be paid by the insured, the third party claimant will not be able to claim against insurers.[89] And insurers can rely upon any applicable exclusion clause in the policy.[90] Finally, if insurers would not be bound by the ascertainment, in that they could maintain that it overstated the insured's legal liability to the third party claimant, they can do so when the third party claims directly against them relying upon that ascertainment.[91]

13.52 Where, as will usually be the case, the insurance contract requires notice of the claim to be given to insurers, the third party will need to comply with that requirement. So, in *Farrell v Federated Employers Insurance Association Ltd*[92] the employers'

---

[85] [1989] 1 AC 957, at 966. Lords Keith, Oliver, and Jauncey agreed with Lord Brandon's speech. See also *Ram v Motor and General Insurance Company Ltd* [2015] UKPC 22, at [17] per Lord Hodge giving the Opinion of the Privy Council.

[86] *Post Office v Norwich Union Fire Insurance Society Ltd* [1967] 2 QB 363, at 375, 376–7, and 378. Alternatively, the claim may be resolved within the bankruptcy or insolvency.

[87] *McCormick v National Motor & Accident Insurance Union Ltd* (1934) 39 LILR 361.

[88] *Total Graphics Ltd v AGF Insurance Ltd* [1997] 1 Lloyd's Rep 599.

[89] *Re OT Computers Ltd (In Administration)* [2004] EWCA Civ 653; [2004] Ch 317; *Centre Reinsurance International Co v Freakley* [2005] EWCA Civ 115; [2005] Lloyd's Rep IR 303.

[90] So, in *Goldsmith Williams v Travelers Insurance Co Ltd* [2010] EWHC 26 (QB); [2010] Lloyd's Rep IR 309 (discussed in paras 8.43 and 8.44) insurers defeated a claim under the Third Parties (Rights Against Insurers) Act 1930 by relying on an exclusion in respect of fraud and dishonesty committed or condoned by the insured.

[91] See paras 9.106–9.132 and *Cheltenham & Gloucester Plc v Sun Alliance and London Insurance Plc* 2001 SC 965; 2001 SLT 1151, at [17] per the Lord President, Lord Rodger.

[92] [1970] 1 WLR 1400.

liability policy contained a condition precedent requiring the insured to give immediate notice of the service of a writ upon it. The insured company was in receivership so that the conditions for the statutory assignment were met. Unaware of the receivership, the third party, an injured ex-employee, issued proceedings and tried to serve them on the insured. The receivers were served, but returned the writ. The third party obtained judgment in default against the insured and sought to recover against insurers, who first learnt of the proceedings after judgment had been entered.

Insurers relied upon the failure to give notice of the service of proceedings as a **13.53** breach of the condition precedent as providing them with a defence. The Court of Appeal agreed. Lord Denning MR said:[93]

> The injured person is here claiming the benefit of a policy which is issued to the employers. He must take it as he finds it. He cannot claim the advantages and reject the disadvantages. He cannot claim the benefit and reject the conditions of it; see *Austin v Zurich General Accident and Liability Insurance Co Ltd* [1945] 1 KB 250.

The later decision in *Pioneer Concrete (UK) Ltd v National Employers Mutual General Insurance Association Ltd*[94] is to like effect and makes it clear that there is no need for insurers to show that they have been prejudiced by breach of such a condition precedent.[95]

Third party claimants will also be bound by an arbitration clause, even if they lack **13.54** the means to proceed by way of arbitration.[96] However, there is a limit to the extent to which the third party claimant assumes the insured's obligations. He only does so insofar as they go to the particular liability. So, where the insured had failed to pay the premium, it has been held that insurers could not set that outstanding debt off against their liability to indemnify.[97] Moreover, the third party claimant will not be subject to a defence based upon public policy which would have prevented the insured from recovering an indemnity because of his fraudulent conduct. Such defences affect the specific individual.[98]

---

[93] Ibid at 1406.

[94] [1985] 2 All ER 395.

[95] If on its true construction the policy only permits notice to be given by the insured or his duly authorized agent (as was held in *CVG Siderurgicia del Orinoco SA v London Steamship Owners' Mutual Insurance Association Ltd ('the Vainqueur José')* [1979] 1 Lloyd's Rep 557) then the third party may be unable to give a valid notice.

[96] *Smith v Pearl Assurance Co Ltd* [1939] 1 All ER 95; *Socony Mobil Oil Co Inc v The West of England Ship Mutual Ins Ass (London) Ltd ('The Padre Island')* [1984] 2 Lloyd's Rep 408.

[97] *Murray v Legal and General Insurance Society Ltd* [1970] 2 QB 495. This decision has been doubted: see *MacGillivray on Insurance Law* (12th edn, Sweet & Maxwell, 2014), para 29-020, where it is noted that in *Cox v Bankside Members Agency Ltd* [1995] 2 Lloyd's Rep 437, at 451, Phillips J declined to follow the decision.

[98] *Total Graphics Ltd v AGF Insurance Ltd* [1997] 1 Lloyd's Rep 599, at 606 per Mance J. Given that insurers had other defences, this part of his judgment was obiter.

Provision of information as to insurance

13.55 In order to avail himself of the rights conferred by the statutory assignment, the third party claimant will need to know what insurance the insured had. Section 2 of the Act provides him with a means of doing so. Section 2(1) provides:

> Duty to give necessary information to third parties
>
> In the event of any person becoming bankrupt or making a composition or arrangement with his creditors, or in the event of the estate of any person falling to be administered in accordance with an order under section 421 of the Insolvency Act 1986, or in the event of a winding-up order being made, or a resolution for a voluntary winding-up being passed, with respect to any company or of the company entering administration or of a receiver or manager of the company's business or undertaking being duly appointed or of possession being taken by or on behalf of the holders of any debentures secured by a floating charge of any property comprised in or subject to the charge it shall be the duty of the bankrupt, debtor, personal representative of the deceased debtor or company, and, as the case may be, of the trustee in bankruptcy, trustee, liquidator, administrator, receiver, or manager, or person in possession of the property to give at the request of any person claiming that the bankrupt, debtor, deceased debtor, or company is under a liability to him such information as may reasonably be required by him for the purpose of ascertaining whether any rights have been transferred to and vested in him by this Act and for the purpose of enforcing such rights, if any, and any contract of insurance, in so far as it purports, whether directly or indirectly, to avoid the contract or to alter the rights of the parties thereunder upon the giving of any such information in the events aforesaid or otherwise to prohibit or prevent the giving thereof in the said events shall be of no effect.

13.56 There is no need for the third party claimant to have established that the insured is liable to him in order to obtain information under s 2. It is sufficient that the third party claimant is alleging that the insured is liable to him. Any provision in a contract of insurance which would have the effect of avoiding the contract or otherwise affecting the rights of the parties to it if such information is provided is of no effect.

13.57 If the information provided under s 2(1) provides material ground for supposing that the rights against a particular insurer have been assigned, then that insurer comes under the same duty to provide information.[99] There is no need for the insured's liability to the third party claimant to have been ascertained for this obligation to arise.[100]

Compromises between the insured and insurers

13.58 Upon the happening of any of the events set out in s 1(a) and (b) of the Act, the insured loses the ability to compromise his rights under the liability insurance so as

---

[99] Section 2(2) of the Act.
[100] *Re OT Computers Ltd (In Administration)* [2004] EWCA Civ 653; [2004] Ch 317.

to defeat or reduce the statutory assignment. Section 3 of the Third Parties (Rights Against Insurers) Act 1930 provides:

> Where the insured has become bankrupt or where in the case of the insured being a company, a winding-up order or an administration order has been made or a resolution for a voluntary winding-up has been passed, with respect to the company, no agreement made between the insurer and the insured after liability has been incurred to a third party and after the commencement of the bankruptcy or winding-up or the day of the making of the administration order, as the case may be, nor any waiver, assignment, or other disposition made by, or payment made to the insured after the commencement or day aforesaid shall be effective to defeat or affect the rights transferred to the third party under this Act, but those rights shall be the same as if no such agreement, waiver, assignment, disposition or payment had been made.

Third Parties (Rights Against Insurers) Act 2010

On 25 March 2010 the Third Parties (Rights Against Insurers) Act 2010 was **13.59** enacted following recommendations for reform from the Law Commission.[101] However, it is not yet in force: at the time of writing it is anticipated that, following amendments made pursuant to the Insurance Act 2015, it will be brought into force during the autumn of 2015. The main changes effected by this Act ('the 2010 Act') are set out in case it is brought into force during the currency of this edition. It is possible that the 2010 Act will be amended before it is brought into force.

The statutory assignment

Section 1(1) of the 2010 Act provides that the rights of a 'relevant person' under **13.60** a contract of insurance which provides insurance against a liability[102] which that person has incurred transfer to and vest in the person to whom the liability is or was incurred.[103] So, as with the 1930 Act there are two conditions to be satisfied: (i) liability has to be incurred to a third party and (ii) the insured has to be a 'relevant person'. The first condition is the same as that under the 1930 Act: it is the liability of the insured to the third party claimant rather than of insurers to indemnify the insured which has to be 'incurred'. As is the case under the 1930 Act, such liability is incurred when the third party claimant has a cause of action

---

[101] Law Com No 272, Cm 5217, July 2001.

[102] This does not include liability under a contract of reinsurance (s 15 of the 2010 Act) but does extend to insurance of liabilities which are incurred voluntarily (eg under a contract) so that the doubt as to whether the 1930 Act applies to such liabilities referred to in para 13.42 does not arise under the 2010 Act (s 16 of the 2010 Act).

[103] The rights transferred are no greater than the liability of the insured to the third party claimant, even if insurers' liability to the insured is greater (eg insurers are liable to pay the insured's costs of defending a claim brought by the third party against the insured): s 8 of the 2010 Act. Any provision in a contract of insurance which purports, whether directly or indirectly, to avoid or terminate the contract or alter the rights of the parties under it in the event of the insured becoming a 'relevant person' is of no effect: s 17 of the 2010 Act.

which he could bring against the insured.[104] The 2010 Act makes new and detailed provision as to the second condition.

13.61 In relation to natural persons s 4(1) sets out a wider range of circumstances in which an insured will be a 'relevant person' for the purposes of the statutory assignment. If (i) a deed or arrangement registered in accordance with the Deeds of Arrangement Act 1914, (ii) an administration order made under Part 6 of the County Courts Act 1984, (iii) an enforcement restriction order made under Part 6A of the County Courts Act 1984, (iv) a debt relief order made under Part 7A of the Insolvency Act 1986, (v) a voluntary arrangement approved in accordance with Part 8 of the Insolvency Act 1986, or (vi) a bankruptcy order made under Part 9 of the Insolvency Act 1986 is in force in respect of a natural person, then that person is a 'relevant person'. In the case of a debt relief order made under Part 7A of the Insolvency Act, a natural person is only a 'relevant person' if the debt relief order is made after the liability to the third party has been incurred.[105] Natural persons who die insolvent are also relevant persons only if they die after the liability to the third party has been incurred.[106] In the other cases it does not matter whether the liability is incurred before or after the relevant order or arrangement comes into force. S 4(1) provides a wider definition of 'relevant person' to the equivalent provision in the 1930 Act.[107]

13.62 The position of bodies corporate and unincorporated bodies is covered by s 6 of the 2010 Act. A body corporate is a 'relevant person' if a compromise or arrangement between the body and its creditors (or a class of them) is in force and that compromise or arrangement has been sanctioned in accordance with s 899 of the Companies Act 2006.[108] A body corporate is also a relevant person if it has been dissolved under ss 1000, 1001, or 1003 of the Companies Act 2006 and has neither been restored to the register pursuant to s 1025 of the Companies Act 2006 nor been ordered to be restored to the register pursuant to s 1031 of the same Act.[109] Together with the creation of the right of a third party claimant to sue insurers directly to establish the liability of the insured to the third party claimant,[110] this removes the need to apply to restore a company which has been dissolved under ss 1000, 1001, or 1003 of the Companies Act 2006 in order to proceed against the company's insurers.

13.63 Whether a body is a body corporate or an unincorporated body it is a 'relevant person' in any of the following circumstances: (i) a voluntary arrangement approved

---

[104] See para 13.43.
[105] Section 4(4) of the 2010 Act.
[106] Section 5 of the 2010 Act.
[107] Section 1(1)(a) of the 1930 Act: see para 13.40.
[108] Section 6(1)(a) of the 2010 Act. This is subject to further, detailed provisions in s 6(5) and (6) of the 2010 Act.
[109] Section 6(1)(b) of the 2010 Act.
[110] See para 13.66.

in accordance with Part 1 of the Insolvency Act 1986 is in force in respect of it; (ii) the body is in administration under Part 1B of the Insolvency Act 1986; (iii) a person appointed in accordance with Part 3 of the Insolvency Act 1986[111] is acting as receiver or manager of the body's property; (iv) the body has been or is being wound up voluntarily in accordance with Chapter 2 of Part 4 of the Insolvency Act 1986; (v) a person appointed under s 135 of the Insolvency Act 1986 is acting as provisional liquidator of the body; or (iv) the body has been or is being wound up by the court following the making of a winding-up order under Chapter 6 of Part 4 of the Insolvency Act 1985 or Part 5 of the same Act.[112]

Once rights have been transferred to the third party claimant, then, subject to a **13.64** number of exceptions,[113] those rights can be enforced by the third party claimant against the insured only if and to the extent that the liability of the insured exceeds the amount recoverable from insurers by reason of the transfer.[114]

The third party claimant's rights against insurers and ascertainment

Under the 1930 Act the liability of the insured to the third party claimant has to **13.65** be ascertained before the third party claimant can recover any sum from insurers.[115] The third party claimant will usually need to bring proceedings against the insured or establish the insured's liability in bankruptcy or insolvency procedures or proceedings. If the potential liability of insurers to indemnify is uncertain or in issue this may be an unattractive course of action for a third party claimant who may need to incur significant costs in proceeding against an insolvent insured with no guarantee that insurers will provide an indemnity if and when liability is ascertained. While it may be possible for a third party claimant to seek a declaration as to insurers' potential liability,[116] the position is not clear under the 1930 Act.

The 2010 Act provides that a third party claimant who claims to have acquired **13.66** rights under a contract of insurance by operation of the statutory assignment and who has not yet established the liability of the insured which is insured under that contract may, at his option, bring proceedings against insurers both for a declaration of the insured's liability to him and/or for a declaration as to insurers' potential liability to him.[117] The third party claimant may make the insured a

---

[111] This includes a person appointed under section 101 of the Law of Property Act 1925: s 6(9)(a) of the 2010 Act.
[112] Section 6(2) of the 2010 Act.
[113] Section 14(2) of the 2010 Act.
[114] Section 14(1) of the 2010 Act. Sections 14(6) and (7) make provision for the position where insurers are insolvent and where the third party can make a claim in respect of insurers' liability to the Financial Services Compensation Scheme under Part 15 of the Financial Services and Markets Act 2000.
[115] See para 13.48.
[116] *Post Office v Norwich Union Fire Insurance Society Ltd* [1967] 2 QB 363, at 374 per Lord Denning MR.
[117] Section 2(1) and (2) of the 2010 Act.

party to proceedings for a declaration as to the insured's liability to him.[118] While the making of a declaration is usually an equitable remedy and so a matter for the discretion of the Court, s 2(3) of the 2010 Act provides that a third party claimant who proves the liability of the insured or of insurers is entitled to a declaration to that effect. If the contract of insurance contained an arbitration clause, that clause remains effective: the third party claimant is able to seek a declaration as to the insured's liability to him in the same arbitration.[119]

13.67 The ability of insurers to rely upon any defence which they would have had, had the claim been brought by the insured, is preserved.[120] This is subject to one exception: where the third party claimant has already brought proceedings in time against the insured and those proceedings have not been concluded by a judgment or decree, then insurers cannot raise any defence of limitation which the insured was unable to rely upon in the earlier proceedings.[121]

13.68 Insofar as the terms of the policy of insurance require the insured to do anything (eg to give notice),[122] s 9(2) of the 2010 Act provides that anything done by the third party claimant which, if done by the insured would have amounted to or contributed to fulfilment of any condition, is to be treated as done by the insured.[123] The transferred rights under the policy are not subject to any condition requiring the insured to provide information or assistance to insurers if that condition cannot be fulfilled because the insured is either a natural person who has died or a body corporate which has been dissolved.[124] Nor are the transferred rights subject to any condition requiring the insured to have discharged its liability to the third party claimant before insurers are liable to indemnify the insured.[125]

---

[118] Section 2(9) of the 2010 Act. This would be sensible if there were a prospect of recovering at least a proportion of any excess or if there were underinsurance. And the insured could be ordered to provide disclosure. The insured is only bound by a declaration as to his liability to the third party claimant if the insured is a party to the proceedings: s 2(10).

[119] Section 2(7) of the 2010 Act.

[120] Section 2(4) of the 2010 Act; see paras 13.51–13.54. This includes any defence of set off: s 10 of the 2010 Act, reversing the decision in *Murray v Legal and General Insurance Society Ltd* [1970] 2 QB 495 discussed in para 13.54.

[121] Sections 2(5) and 12(1) and (2) of the 2010 Act. The proceedings against the insured are concluded if there is a judgment or decree, even if there is a pending appeal or right of appeal: s 12(3) of the 2010 Act.

[122] As in *Farrell v Federated Employers Insurance Association Ltd* [1970] 1 WLR 1400, discussed in para 13.52.

[123] So, where on its true construction, a term requiring the giving of notice requires that a valid notice can only be given by the insured (as in *CVG Siderurgicia del Orinoco SA v London Steamship Owners' Mutual Insurance Association Ltd ('the Vainqueur José')* [1979] 1 Lloyd's Rep 557), the giving of notice by the third party claimant will suffice under the 2010 Act.

[124] Section 9(3) of the 2010 Act.

[125] Section 9(5) of the 2010 Act. This reverses the decision of the House of Lords in *Firma C-Trade SA v Newcastle Protection and Indemnity Association ('the Fanti')* [1990] 2 AC 1. However, there is an exception to s 9(5) of the 2010 Act in respect of contracts of marine insurance other than insurance against liability for death or personal injury.

Provision of information as to insurance

Section 11 and Schedule 1 of the 2010 Act significantly increase the ability of a **13.69** third party to obtain information about potential insurance coverage.[126]

They provide that a person falling within one of two definitions is entitled to serve **13.70** a notice requesting the provision of information as to whether there is a contract of insurance which covers the potential liability of another person to the person who serves the notice. The notice may also request the provision of information about such a contract if it exists and, in particular, the identity of the insurer, the terms of the contract, whether the insured has been informed that insurers have claimed not to be liable, whether there have been any proceedings between insurers and the insured about insurers' liability (and, if so, 'relevant details of those proceedings'[127]), where there is a limit on the fund available to meet claims, how much has already been paid out and whether there is any fixed charge to which any sums paid out under the contract in respect of the liability would be subject.[128] This is more specific than the provision as to what information can be obtained in the 1930 Act.[129]

The first category of person who can serve a notice is a person who reasonably **13.71** believes that another person has incurred a liability to him and that that person is a 'relevant person'.[130] In this category the person on whom the notice is served is the person whom is believed to have incurred the liability.

The second category is a person who reasonably believes that a liability has been **13.72** incurred to him, that the person who incurred the liability is insured against it under a contract of insurance, that the rights of that person have been transferred to him under s 1 of the 2010 Act, and that there is some other person who is able to provide the specified information.[131] In this category the notice can be sent to anyone whom the person serving it reasonably believes is able to provide the information. This is a far wider class than under the 1930 Act.[132] It would include insurance brokers who had arranged the insurance and insurers themselves.[133]

In each category the notice requesting provision of information must include par- **13.73** ticulars of the facts relied upon in support of the request.[134] Special provision is

---

[126] For the position under the 1930 Act see paras 13.55–13.57.
[127] 'Relevant details of proceedings' are set out in para 1(4) of Schedule 1 to the 2010 Act. They include the contents of all documents served in the proceedings in accordance with rules of court or orders made in the proceedings and the contents of any such orders (or equivalent documents in arbitrations).
[128] Paragraph 1(3) of Schedule 1 to the 2010 Act.
[129] See para 13.55.
[130] Paragraph 1(1) of Schedule 1 to the 2010 Act. For 'relevant person' see paras 13.61–13.63.
[131] Paragraph 1(2) of Schedule 1 to the 2010 Act.
[132] Section 2(1) of the 1930 Act: see para 13.55.
[133] For the positon of insurers under the 1930 Act see s 2(2) of that Act and para 13.57.
[134] Paragraph 1(6) of Schedule 1 to the 2010 Act. There is no express provision enabling the recipient of a notice to challenge the accuracy or adequacy of the particulars given.

made for the situation where the person who is said to have incurred the liability is a defunct body corporate.[135] In such a case the notice can be served either on anyone who was an officer or employee of the body corporate immediately before the statutory transfer or on anyone who was acting as an insolvency practitioner or official receiver of the body corporate immediately before it became defunct.[136]

13.74 The duties of disclosure of a person who receives a notice and the rights of inspection of a person who gives a notice are the same as those under the Civil Procedure Rules in relation to parties to court proceedings in which standard disclosure has been ordered.[137] A person who receives a notice must serve a list of documents within twenty-eight days of receipt of the notice.[138] The duty to provide information is not limited to disclosure of documents: it extends to information which a person can obtain without due difficulty from a document in his control or, in the case of natural persons, information within their knowledge.[139]

13.75 As under the 1930 Act, any provision in a contract of insurance which either directly or indirectly avoids or terminates the contract or alters the rights under it in the event of information being provided or otherwise seeks to prevent or limit the provision of disclosure in response to a notice is of no effect.[140]

Transitional provisions

13.76 Even though it will be repealed when the 2010 Act comes into force, the 1930 Act will continue to apply to cases in which both the event referred to in s 1(1) of the 1930 Act[141] and the incurring of the liability to the third party claimant occur before the day on which the 2010 Act comes into force.[142] Otherwise the 2010 Act will apply.

D. Contracts (Rights of Third Parties) Act 1999

13.77 The third way in which third party claimants could claim directly against insurers is under the Contracts (Right of Third Parties) Act 1999. Section 1 of this Act enables a third party who is not a party to a contract to enforce a term of a contract.

---

[135] Ie a body corporate which has been dissolved under Chapter 9 of Part 4 of the Insolvency Act 1986 or under ss 1000, 1001, or 1003 of the Companies Act 2006 (and has not been restored to the register by virtue of ss 1025 or 1031 of the Companies Act 2006): paras 3(4) and (5) of Schedule 1 to the 2010 Act.

[136] Paragraph 3(1) and (2) of Schedule 1 to the 2010 Act.

[137] Paragraph 4(1) of Schedule 1 to the 2010 Act.

[138] Paragraph 4(3) of Schedule 1 to the 2010 Act. The recipient of the notice is not under a duty of disclosure in relation to documents which he did not have when the list was served: para 4(4) of Schedule 1 to the 2010 Act.

[139] Paragraph 7 of Schedule 1 to the 2010 Act.

[140] Paragraph 5 of Schedule 1 to the 2010 Act.

[141] See para 13.40.

[142] Paragraph 3 of Schedule 3 to the 2010 Act.

However, to do so, the contract must either provide in terms that he may do so or purport to confer a benefit on him. A term will not confer a benefit on a third party if, on the proper construction of the contract, the parties did not intend the term to be enforceable by the third party. The third party may be named specifically or be a member of a class or answer to a particular description.

It is unlikely that this Act would apply to contracts of professional indemnity **13.78** insurance. While one of the purposes of statutory and professional requirements that professional indemnity insurance be obtained is the protection of the clients of professionals, there will not usually be any term in the policy to that effect. Nor, on their true construction, will policies of professional indemnity insurance indicate an intention that third party claimants could enforce any such term. Moreover, it is not at all unusual to find an express term in professional indemnity policies expressly providing that it is not intended that third parties should be able to enforce its terms.[143]

---

[143] Eg the ICAEW Minimum Approved Policy Wording provides: 'A person who is not a party to this certificate has no rights under the Contracts (Rights of Third Parties) Act 1999 ...'

INDEX

All indexing is to paragraph number; references to footnotes will be by paragraph number followed by 'n' and number of the note.